THE PRINCIPLES OF GERMAN CIVIL LAW

德国民法原理

［英］欧内斯特·J. 舒斯特（Ernest J. Schuster）　著

戴永盛　校勘

中国政法大学出版社

2019·北京

图书在版编目（ＣＩＰ）数据

德国民法原理/(英) 欧内斯特·J. 舒斯特著；戴永盛校勘. —北京:中国政法大学出版
社,2019.12
　ISBN 978-7-5620-7955-2

　Ⅰ.①德… Ⅱ.①欧… ②戴… Ⅲ.①民法－研究－德国 Ⅳ.①D951.63

中国版本图书馆CIP数据核字(2017)第331894号

出 版 者　中国政法大学出版社

地　　址　北京市海淀区西土城路 25 号

邮寄地址　北京 100088 信箱 8034 分箱　邮编 100088

网　　址　http://www.cuplpress.com (网络实名：中国政法大学出版社)

电　　话　010-58908437(编辑室)　58908334(邮购部)

承　　印　北京九州迅驰传媒文化有限公司

开　　本　710mm×1000mm　1/16

印　　张　48.25

字　　数　880 千字

版　　次　2019 年 12 月第 1 版

印　　次　2019 年 12 月第 1 次印刷

定　　价　218.00 元

THE PRINCIPLES OF
GERMAN CIVIL LAW

BY

ERNEST J. SCHUSTER

LL. D. (MUNICH)
OF LINCOLN'S INN, BARRISTER-AT-LAW

OXFORD
AT THE CLARENDON PRESS
LONDON AND NEW YORK: HENRY FROWDE
ALSO SOLD BY
STEVENS & SONS, LIMITED, 119 & 120 CHANCERY LANE, LONDON
1907

LONDON

HENRY FROWDE, M. A.
PUBLISHER TO THE UNIVERSITY OF OXFORD
AND
STEVENS & SONS, LIMITED

PREFACE

THIS book is intended (1) to assist the study of English law from a comparative point of view; (2) to give an insight into the latest and most perfect attempt to systematize the whole of the private law of a country; (3) to give some practical help to the increasing number of practitioners who in the course of their daily work have to deal with questions of foreign and private international law. The following few words of explanation on each of these three points will, I hope, further elucidate my aims and objects.

1. The time-honoured sarcasm about the jurist who knows every system of law except his own is not quite without justification. There are no doubt in every country some men who, partly by desultory reading and partly on hearsay, have acquired some vague notions about foreign law, and who have studied their own law by the same methods and with the same results. Such men have as little in common with the true representatives of the science of comparative law as the silver-tongued orators who discourse on Plato to fashionable audiences have in common with the genuine students of philosophy. But they have—in this country more than elsewhere—succeeded in creating an amount of prejudice on the subject which it is difficult to remove, notwithstanding the fact that some of the most eminent writers on English law and some of the most successful practical lawyers are known to have a deep and comprehensive knowledge of Roman law or of modern continental law or of both. There are, however, many indications of the fact that the narrow conceptions about the objects and methods of legal education which have to a certain extent helped to maintain the prejudice referred to above are gradually disappearing. Even those who look upon the study of law exclusively as a help to professional success have begun to see that the grasp of legal principles is of greater value than mere knowledge of cases and of isolated rules. Such a grasp of principles is, however, unobtainable, unless law is looked upon as an organic whole of which every part is correlated to the other, and unless the origin and growth of each individual institution is examined with the same care as the evolution of a particular species of the fauna or flora of a country is examined by the biologist. Both as regards the examination of the

manner in which the various parts of the system are correlated, and as regards the study of the evolution of the particular species, the comparative method is as indispensable to the scientific lawyer as it is to the biologist.   A preface is not the place for dwelling on the many suggestive facts which illustrate this proposition.   I may, however, give one example which is of direct practical interest.   An English lawyer has often to advise on acts to be done on behalf of persons who by reason of age, mental or physical disease, sex, or change of status, are incapable of incurring legal responsibility, or of receiving, or of disposing of, money or other property.   In any such case it is frequently very difficult to ascertain who can incur responsibility or give a valid discharge, or make an effectual disposition in the place of the incapable person.   The reason of this is that the majority of textbook writers have not realized that agency created by rules of law—as distinguished from agency created by act of the parties—is a subject which requires independent treatment as a special legal institution.   A comparison with foreign law will show this want immediately, and will at the same time prove that the difficulties which beset the subject in English law are to a great extent accidental and removable.   The obscurity which seems to prevail in many minds as to the responsibility of corporate bodies and unincorporated societies for the acts of their agents would similarly have tended to disappear if the investigation of the subject from a comparative point of view had been pursued more widely.   As to this and many other matters comparison teaches us that things which, looked upon by themselves, appear as part of the natural order of things, are found to be peculiarities of the system to which they belong.   The mere fact that they are recognized as peculiarities makes them better known and better understood.

2.   The reason why the systematization of law has been brought to its highest perfection in Germany is found in the fact that the law of Justinian, in its modern developments, which was the nucleus of the German common law, has, ever since the establishment of the Bologna law school, been a favourite subject of inquiry for the lawyers of all nations, and that the scientific expositions of that law were thus based on the work of many generations of eminent men in Germany and elsewhere [1].   By the new Codes which came into force on January 1, 1900, the German people—to use the words of the late Professor Maitland (see *Independent Review*, 1906, p. 219)—'have brought that law up to date and are facing modern times with modern ideas, modern machinery, modern weapons'.   The

---

[1]   On this point see Sohm's *Institutes* translated by Ledlie, 2nd ed. , on p. 11.

new Codes adapt the fruits of the learning of many centuries to the needs of the
present time.   As a complete and scientific exposition of actual law they therefore
occupy a unique position.

3. The steady expansion of international commercial dealings, the greater
frequency of marriages between members of different nationalities, and the
constantly growing number of causes facilitating and inducing changes of domicil
on the part of persons engaged in mercantile, industrial, or scientific pursuits
have largely increased the number of the occasions on which English lawyers have
to deal with foreign law.   The usual course on any such occasion is to consult an
advocate practising in the country of which the law has to be applied, and in
ordinary commercial cases that course no doubt has many advantages.   But in
cases where questions arise as to matters on which the conceptions of English law
differ materially from those of continental law (e. g. as to the validity of marriages,
the effect of marriage on property, as to settlements and trusts, as to the nature
and effects of testamentary dispositions, as to powers of appointment and similar
topics) the communication between English and foreign lawyers, as experience
shows, frequently leads to difficulties and misunderstandings.   For this reason a   vi
knowledge of the main principles of foreign law is of direct practical advantage to
any practitioner who is likely to have to deal with international questions.   The
main conceptions of continental law are based on identical principles; any lawyer
who has mastered these principles as applied in any particular system, and
specially in a system composed of such varied component parts as that of modern
German law, has mastered the difficulties which intervene in the communications
with foreign lawyers.   He will understand the answers to his questions because
he will put his questions in a way which the foreign lawyer will understand.

I have tried to carry out the three objects thus indicated: (1) by comparing
German with English law whenever such a comparison seemed to be useful in
clearing up the conceptions of English law; (2) by constantly keeping in view
the connexion of the individual rules with the whole system; (3) by dwelling with
special fullness on those comparisons between English and German law as to
which practical questions are likely to arise.

I had originally intended to devote a separate portion of the book to the rules
of German law as to the matters generally described under the head of 'private
international law', but I found that a complete survey of the law on this subject
would occupy too much space.   I have, however, stated the rules as to conflict
of laws in connexion with all the matters comprised in Family Law and the Law of

Inheritance and some other subjects with reference to which questions as to the choice of law are most likely to arise.   In this respect also I have taken some pains to call attention to the points as to which the German rules differ from those applicable in this country.

One of the chief hindrances which obstruct the path of the exponent of any system of foreign law consists in the difficulty of finding apt expressions for the reproduction of technical terms.   Where an English equivalent expression was available such expression has of course been used; and, correspondingly, English technical expressions have in most cases been avoided where the German expression intended to be reproduced did not convey exactly the same meaning. In certain exceptional cases I have, however, ' for reasons of convenience amounting almost to necessity', deviated from the last-mentioned maxim.   The most conspicuous transgression of this sort occurs with reference to the use of the word ' lease' as an equivalent of the German ' *Mietvertrag* ', and the corresponding use of the expression ' lessee' as an equivalent of the German ' *Mieter* ' (see p. 221).   I have also applied the expression ' public act' (see pp. 81–82) in a somewhat narrower sense than the corresponding German expression (*öffentliche Urkunde*).   The substitution of more correct terms would in these cases have necessitated a mode of expression so complicated and cumbrous, that the infringement of the rule appeared to be the smaller evil.   In some cases I have coined forms of expression which at first will appear unfamiliar, but to which I trust the reader will soon get accustomed; in others I had to use Latin terms as I was unable to find convenient English words.

I have, on principle, used the modern German spelling, but in some cases I have unwittingly relapsed into the old form and only discovered my error when it was too late to correct it.   In the glossary of German words at the end of the book these inconsistencies have been avoided.

A word of explanation is necessary as to the motives which induced me to write a treatise on the present German law, instead of giving a translation of the Codes and the principal Statutes.   A translation without notes would have been unintelligible, and a translation with notes would have been unwieldy.   The language of the Codes is so highly technical and the various parts of each Code and the several Codes and Statutes respectively are so inextricably interdependent, that it requires a most elaborate system of explanations and cross-references to show the exact meaning of any particular enactment.   The admirable annotated French translation, which is being prepared with government assistance by Professor

Saleilles and other eminent authorities, and which is addressed to readers familiar with continental legal conceptions, has so far only dealt with about one half of the Civil Code, and already covers over 1, 500 very large pages.   Apart from this   viii reason, which would alone be more than sufficient, a systematic exposition of the law is much more fruitful for students than a mere exegetic treatment, and the arrangement which I have adopted has been mapped out with special reference to the wants of English readers.   The English garb in which the exposition of the German Law appears may also be of use to German readers wishing to familiarize themselves with English terminology, and wishing to compare their law with English law.

I have intentionally refrained from giving any bibliographical material, as such material may easily be obtained from any of the fuller German textbooks. The number of comprehensive systematic treatises dealing with the whole of the law or with special branches of the same, the number of the annotated editions of Codes and Statutes is indeed legion, and monographs abound on every conceivable point.   As a matter of personal gratitude I only wish to mention the great assistance I have received from the lucid and fascinating pages of Dernburg's *Bürgerliches Recht*, from the admirable summaries and copious and illuminating notes in Planck's edition of the Civil Code and Introductory Statute, and in Staub's edition of the Commercial Code, and from the masterly arrangement and wealth of material by which Neumann's excellent *Handausgabe* of the Civil Code and Introductory Statute (containing also the text of the most important other statutes affecting German private law) is distinguished.

My warmest thanks are also due to my friends Mr. J. C. Ledlie, Mr. John D. Rogers, and Mr. E. A. Whittuck, who have read through the proofs and to whom I am indebted for many valuable criticisms and suggestions, and to my son Mr. George E. Schuster, from whom I have received much useful assistance.

E. J. S.

LINCOLN'S INN :
November, 1906.

TABLE OF CONTENTS

INTRODUCTION

FIRST BOOK
GENERAL RULES OF LAW

FIRST DIVISION
PERSONS, THINGS, AND RIGHTS

CHAPTER I: PERSONS

A. General Rules

CHAPTER II: THINGS

CHAPTER III: RIGHTS

A. Substantive Rights

SECOND DIVISION
THE CREATION, TRANSFER, AND EXTINCTION OF RIGHTS

CHAPTER I

CHAPTER II: ACTS-IN-THE-LAW

CHAPTER III: PRESCRIPTION

SECOND BOOK
LAW OF OBLIGATIONS

FIRST DIVISION
GENERAL RULES

CHAPTER I: NATURE OF OBLIGATORY RIGHTS AND DUTIES

CHAPTER II: CREATION OF OBLIGATIONS

SECOND DIVISION

RULES RELATING TO PARTICULAR KINDS OF OBLIGATIONS

FIRST SUB-DIVISION

OBLIGATIONS CREATED BY ACT-IN-THE-LAW

CHAPTER I: AGREEMENTS RELATING
TO THE TRANSFER OF PROPERTY

CHAPTER II: AGREEMENTS RELATING TO THE TEMPORARY USE OF PROPERTY

CHAPTER III: OWNERSHIP

CHAPTER V: REAL RIGHTS GRANTED BY WAY OF SECURITY

A. Charges on Immovables

FOURTH BOOK
FAMILY LAW

CHAPTER I: HUSBAND AND WIFE

CHAPTER III: GUARDIAN AND WARD

FIFTH BOOK
LAW OF INHERITANCE

CHAPTER I: GENERAL SURVEY

CHAPTER II: STATUTORY RIGHT OF INHERITANCE

CHAPTER IV: CONTRACTUAL RIGHT OF INHERITANCE

CHAPTER V: COMPULSORY RIGHT OF INHERITANCE (*LEGITIM*)

CROSS-REFERENCES AND ABBREVIATIONS

Where a figure stands by itself the section of this book indicated by such figure is referred to. The decisions of the German Imperial Court (*Reichsgericht*) in civil matters are referred to by the letters RGZ and an indication as to the volume and the page on which they appear. The other abbreviations are explained in the following table.

TABLE OF GERMAN CODES AND STATUTES REFERRED TO

(The date is the date of the promulgation of the Code or Statute; where the original Statute has been amended by a subsequent Statute and an amended text has been promulgated the date of such promulgation of the amended text is given in brackets.)

Date.	German Title.	Short English Translation of Title.	Abbreviation used in References.	Pages on which Code or Statute is referred to.[2]
18 Aug. 1896	Bürgerliches Gesetzbuch.	Civil Code.	BGB	[See detailed list below]
18 Aug. 1896	Einführungsgesetz zum BGB.	Imperial Statute introducing the Civil Code.	EG	[See detailed list below]
20 Sept. 1899	Preussisches Ausführungsgesetz zum BGB.	Prussian Statute introducing the Civil Code.	Prussian AG[1]	226, 234, 431, 447.
10 May 1897	Handelsgesetzbuch.	Commercial Code.	HGB	[See detailed list below]
10 May 1897	Einführungsgesetz zum HGB.	Imperial Statute introducing the Commercial Code.	EG (HGB)	4
	Allgemeine deutsche Wechselordnung.	Bills of Exchange Code.	WO	166, 197-199, 327-329, 353.
	Strafgesetzbuch für das Deutsche Reich.	Criminal Code.	StGB	69, 191, 551.
21 June 1869 (26 July 1900)	Gewerbeordnung für das Deutsche Reich.	Trade Regulation Statute.	GO	260, 262-267, 386.

---

[1] The other State laws introducing the Code are referred to in a corresponding manner, e.g. Bavarian AG, Baden AG. Several of these State laws are referred to on pages 361, 400, 427.

[2] 此列数字指书中边码 (即原书页码)。 ——校勘者注

Continued

Date.	German Title.	Short English Translation of Title.	Abbreviation used in References.	Pages on which Code or Statute is referred to.
1 June 1870	Gesetz über die Erwerbung und den Verlust der Bundes- und Staatsange- hörigkeit.	Statute as to the acquisition and loss of Federal and State Nationality.	Nationality Statute.	27.
7 June 1871	Gesetz betreffend die Verbindlichkeit zum Schadenersatz für die bei dem Betriebe von Eisenbahnen, Bergwer- ken u.s.w. vorkommenden Tötungen und Verletzungen.	Statute regulating the liability for deaths and injuries caused in the working of Railways, &c.	Haftpflichtgesetz.	159, 344.
2 May 1874	Reichsmilitärgesetz.	Imperial Military Law.		602.
17 May 1874 (1901)	Strandungsordnung.	Statute relating to stranded ships and wreckage.		405.
6 Feb. 1875	Gesetz über die Beurkundung des Perso- nenstands und die Eheschliessung.	Statute relating to the authentication of personal status and the celebration of marriage.	Personal Status Act.	29, 481.
9 Jan. 1876	Gesetz betreffend das Urheberrecht an Werken der bildenden Künste.	Artistic Copyright Act.		72.
10 Jan. 1876	Gesetz betreffend den Schutz der Pho- tographien gegen unbefugte Nachbil- dung.	Photograph Copyright Act.		72.
11 Jan. 1876	Gesetz betreffend das Urheberrecht an Mustern und Modellen.	Artistic Models Copyright Act.		72.
30 Jan. 1877 (20 May 1898)	Civilprozessordnung.	Civil Procedure Act.	CPO	[See detailed list below]

Continued

Date.	German Title.	Short English Translation of Title.	Abbreviation used in References.	Pages on which Code or Statute is referred to.
10 Feb. 1877 (20 May 1898)	Konkursordnung.	Bankruptcy Act.	KO	23, 100, 182, 234, 652-654.
21 July 1879 (20 May 1898)	Gesetz betreffend die Anfechtung von Rechtshandlungen eines Schuldners ausserhalb des Konkursverfahrens.	Statute relating to the avoidance of acts done by a debtor for the purpose of defrauding his creditors.	Anfechtungsgesetz.	234.
1 May 1889	Gesetz betreffend die Erwerbsund Wirtschaftsgenossenschaften.	Co-operative Societies Act.	CSA	47, 48.
7 April 1891	Patentgesetz.	Patent Act.		72, 73, 191.
1 June 1891	Gesetz betreffend den Schutz von Gebrauchsmustern.	Useful Models Act.		72-74, 191.
20 April 1892 (20 May 1898)	Gesetz betreffend die Gesellschaften mit beschränkter Haftung.	Limited Partnership Act.	LPA	45-47.
12 May 1894	Gesetz zum Schutze der Warenbezeichnungen.	Trade Marks Act.		70, 71.
15 June 1895 (20 May 1898)	Gesetz betreffend die privatrechtlichen Verhältnisse der Binnenschiffahrt.	Inland Navigation Act.		361.
27 May 1896	Gesetz zur Bekämpfung des unlauteren Wettbewerbs.	Unfair Competition Act.		70, 342, 343.
5 July 1896	Gesetz betreffend die Pflichten der Kaufleute bei der Aufbewahrung fremder Wertpapiere.	Statute relating to the custody of negotiable instruments.		300, 301.
24 March 1897 (20 May 1898)	Grundbuchordnung.	Land Registration Act.	GBO	378-380, 398, 441, 442, 637, 659.

Continued

Date.	German Title.	Short English Translation of Title.	Abbreviation used in References.	Pages on which Code or Statute is referred to.
17 May 1898	Gesetz über die Angelegenheiten der freiwilligen Gerichtsbarkeit.	Non-contentious Jurisdiction Act.	FGG	91, 579.
20 May 1898	Gesetz über die Zwangsversteigerung und Zwangsverwaltung.	Compulsory Sale Act.	ZVG	254, 456.
13 July 1899	Hypothekenbankgesetz.	Mortgage Bank Act.		42.
21 Sept. 1899	Preussisches Gesetz über die freiwillige Gerichtsbarkeit.	Prussian Non-contentious Jurisdiction Act.	Prussian FGG	90, 91.
19 June 1901	Gesetz betreffend das Urheberrecht an Werken der Literatur und Tonkunst.	Literary and Musical Copyright Act.		71.
19 June 1901	Gesetz betreffend das Verlagsrecht.	Statute as to Publishing Agreements.	GVR	291-297.
12 May 1901	Gesetz über die Privaten Versicherungs-unternehmungen.	Private Insurance Act.	PIA	36, 42, 48-49, 116, 313.[1]

MODE OF CITATION

German Codes and Statutes are divided into paragraphs (§§) or articles; in the case of the several *Ausführungsgesetze* the division is into articles, and the articles are often subdivided into §§.   In the other Statutes and in the codes the articles or §§ are generally divided into subsections, which are not numbered, but which in the text-books are referred to as 'Absatz 1', 'Absatz 2', &c.   In this treaties the indications '§' or 'art.' are generally omited, and the subsections are indicated by figures in brackets (*e.g.* BGB § 179, Abs. 3 in the German books); where figures appear by themselves they indicate the sections of this book.

---

1 表中本栏内容，原书无。著者在书中个别地方将 Gesetz über die Privaten Versicherungsunternehmungen 译作 Private Insurance Statute，现统一修改为 Private Insurance Act。——校勘者注

DETAILED LIST OF REFERENCES
BGB

	PAGES [1]		PAGES		PAGES
1	18	104	20	163	115
2	20, 107	105	84	164	119, 122
3-5	20	106	20	165	115
6	21	107	85	166	122, 123
7-11	28	108, 109	86	167	116, 117
12	69	110	85	168	124
13-17	30	111	86	169-173	126
18	31	112, 113	85	174	120
19	32	114	21, 22, 85, 86	175, 176	126
20	31	115	86	177	119, 120
21, 22	38	116-118	93	178	120
23	39	119	95, 96, 596	179	121, 187
26	36, 39	120	95	180	120
27-30	39	121	96	181	124
31	39, 157	122	93, 97, 187, 362	182	127
32-40	39	123	109, 110	183	127, 128
41-43	40	124	110	184, 185	127
45, 46	40	125	89	186	106
47-53	41	126-129	91	187	106, 107
54	50	130, 131	87	188	107, 108
55	39	132	88	189-193	108
56	38	133	104	194	67
57	10, 38	134	99, 100, 101	195	131
58, 59	38	135	101	196, 197	132
60-63	39	136	100, 101	198, 199	130
64	36, 39	137	100	200, 201	131
65-68	39	138	99, 103, 611	202-204	134
70	36, 39	139-141	82	205	133
71-73	40	142	83	206, 207	132
74	41	143, 144	82	208-217	133
75	40	145-148	97	218, 219	131
76	41	149, 150	98	220	131, 133
80, 81	41	151	88	221	130
85, 86	41	152	91	222	130, 138
87, 88	42	153	87	223	130, 438, 462
90	9, 58	154, 155	99	224	130
91, 92	9, 61	156	98	225	10, 130
93	62	157	104	226	68, 244
94-98	63	158, 159	112	227	75
99-100	64	160, 161	113	228-231	76
101-103	65	162	114	232-240	77

1 指书中边码（即原书页码）。——校勘者注

continued

continued

continued

continued

	PAGES		PAGES		PAGES
926	393	1031	423	1110	432
927, 928	395	1032, 1033	417	1111	432, 433
929–931	396	1034, 1035	423	1112	432
932	397, 398	1036	424, 426	1113	9, 436
933, 934	397	1037, 1038	426	1114	447
935	398	1039, 1040	425	1115	443
936	397, 398	1041–1044	426	1116	441, 442
937	400	1045–1047	425	1117, 1118	443
938–944	394, 400	1048	424	1119	443, 444
945, 946	400	1049	427	1120–1131	446
947	400, 401, 402	1050	426	1132	447
948	400	1051–1057	427	1133–1135	456
949	401	1058	424	1136	435
950	400, 401, 402	1059	416	1137	439, 457
951	401	1060	426	1138	438, 439
952	66	1061	422, 429	1139	439
953–955	403	1062–1064	429	1140	442
956	403, 404	1065	422	1141	438
957	403	1066	423	1142	449, 451
958–964	404	1067	423, 424	1143	450, 451
965–983	363	1068	422, 425, 429	1144, 1145	453
984	9, 405	1069	417, 422	1146	449
985	406	1071	425	1147	456
986	193, 406	1072	429	1148	457
987, 988	377, 407	1073	425	1149	435
989	408	1074, 1075	424	1150	449, 450, 451
990	407, 408	1076, 1077	425	1151	444
991, 992	408	1078	425, 426	1152	441
993	377, 407	1079, 1080	425	1153	196, 450, 457
994	408, 409	1081, 1082	424	1154, 1155	458
995	408	1083	426	1156	439, 458
996–999	409	1084	424	1157	439, 457
1004, 1005	410	1085	423, 428	1158, 1159	458
1006	377	1086–1088	428	1160	448, 456
1007	198, 376	1089	423, 428	1162	442
1008–1011	388	1090	428, 429	1163	443, 445, 449,
1012	412	1091	428		450, 453
1013–1017	413	1092	416	1164	450, 451
1018	418	1093	428	1165	454
1019–1022	419	1094–1098	228	1167, 1168	453
1023–1026	420	1099–1101	229	1169	454
1027	421	1104	229	1170, 1171	455
1028	421, 429	1105	431, 432	1172	451, 452
1029	421	1106, 1107	432	1173, 1174	451
1030	422, 425	1108, 1109	432, 433	1175	454, 455

continued

continued

	PAGES		PAGES		PAGES
1395–1398	501	1508	509, 517	1613–1615	542
1399–1404	502	1509, 1510	517	1616	544
1405, 1406	503	1511	518	1617–1619	545
1407	502	1512–1514	521	1620–1625	546
1408, 1409	501, 503	1515	520	1626–1628	548
1410	505	1516, 1517	521	1630	550
1411, 1412	504, 505	1518	510	1631, 1632	551
1413–1417	505	1519	392, 521	1633, 1634	548
1418–1420	506	1520–1524	521	1635, 1636	528
1421–1424	507	1525	513, 514, 521	1637	529
1425–1431	508	1526–1528	521	1638	548
1432	509	1529	522	1639	552
1433	510	1530	522, 539	1640–1642	553
1434	509	1531–1533	522	1643	552, 553
1435	498	1534	522, 539	1644	85, 553
1436	508, 510	1535–1544	522	1645, 1646	553
1437	509	1545	508, 522	1647	554
1438	392, 511	1546–1548	522	1648	549
1439	512, 513, 514	1549	392, 508, 523,	1649, 1650	555
1440	512		539	1651	547, 555
1441	513, 514	1550–1557	523	1652–1663	555
1442	511	1558–1563	498	1664	549
1443–1445	512	1564	515, 527	1665	548, 555
1446	512, 513	1565, 1566	526	1666	551, 554, 555
1447	512	1567	492, 526	1667, 1668	554
1449–1455	513	1568–1573	526	1669	553
1456	512	1574	527	1670–1672	554
1457, 1458	513	1575, 1576	529	1673	551, 554
1459	514, 539	1577	528	1674, 1675	547
1460–1462	514	1578	527, 528	1676–1678	548
1463–1467	515	1579, 1580	527	1679	549
1468, 1469	516	1581–1583	528	1680	548
1470	508, 517	1584, 1585	529	1681	554
1471, 1472	517	1586, 1587	515, 529	1682, 1683	556
1478	516, 517	1588	482	1684, 1685	549
1474	517	1589, 1590	530	1686–1695	550
1475	516, 517	1591, 1592	531	1696, 1697	549
1476–1478	517	1593–1599	532	1698	548
1479–1481	516	1600	531	1699	483, 543
1482	515, 517	1601	540	1703	543
1483	515, 517, 518	1602	541	1705	545
1484	517	1603	540	1706	544
1485–1490	519	1604, 1605	539	1707	550
1491–1505	520	1606–1608	540	1708–1716	543
1506	521	1610–1612	541	1717, 1718	532

continued

	PAGES		PAGES		PAGES
1719–1722	533	1844	565	1950	638
1723–1740	534	1845	569	1951	639
1741–1752	536	1848	558	1952	638
1753	537	1849–1851	559	1953	586, 587, 598,
1754	536, 537	1852	558		638, 639
1755	536	1853	565	1954–1959	640
1757–1763	537	1854	569	1960–1966	635
1764–1766	538	1855–1881	558	1967–1969	649
1767	537	1882	549, 570	1971, 1972	654
1768–1772	538	1883	569	1973, 1974	655
1773	548, 557	1884	569, 570	1975	650, 652, 653
1774	565	1885	570	1976	650, 652
1775	563	1886–1893	571	1977	652
1776, 1777	561, 562	1894, 1895	570, 571	1978–1981	653
1778	561	1896	557	1982	650, 652
1779	562	1897	558, 559, 561,	1983, 1984	652
1780–1788	564		562, 564–571	1985–1987	653
1789	565	1898, 1899	562	1988	650, 652
1791	565	1900	562, 564	1989	654
1792	558, 563, 564,	1901	567	1990, 1991	650, 654
	565	1902	568	1992	650
1793	565, 567	1903–1905	558	1993, 1994	651
1794	565	1906–1908	559	1995–1997	650, 651
1795, 1796	566	1909	548, 560	1998, 1999	651
1797, 1798	563	1910–1914	560	2000	651, 654
1799	565	1915	563, 565–569,	2003, 2004	651
1800, 1801	567		571	2005	651, 652
1802	568	1916, 1917	563	2006	652
1803	552, 565, 567	1918–1921	570	2008	651
1804	568	1922	392, 586	2009	650
1805, 1806	567	1923	586, 597, 598	2013	650, 652–654
1809	568	1924–1930	588	2014–2017	656
1810	567	1931, 1932	588, 589	2018–2024	645
1812–1820	568	1933	588	2025	374, 645
1821	567, 568	1935	591	2026	645
1822, 1823	568	1936	587, 588	2027	374, 645
1824	85, 568	1937	587, 593	2028, 2029	645
1825	552, 568	1938	587	2030	644
1826, 1827	568	1939	611	2031	646
1828–1831	552, 568	1940	619	2033	210, 646
1832	568	1941	593	2034	646
1833–1836	566	1942	392, 586, 638	2035	228, 646
1837	558	1943–1947	638	2036	646, 655
1838	567	1948	639	2037, 2038	646
1839–1843	569	1949	640	2039	646, 647

continued

continued

	PAGES		PAGES		PAGES
2298, 2299	622	2324	633	2358–2360	637
2300	636	2325–2330	631	2361–2367	638
2301	623	2333–2338	632	2368	637, 638
2302	622	2339–2343	592	2369, 2370	638
2303	627, 628	2344	587, 592	2371	210, 598, 662
2305–2308	628	2345	612	2372–2374	662
2309	627	2346	587, 592	2375, 2376	663
2310–2314	629	2347–2351	592	2377	598, 663
2315, 2316	630	2352	597, 612	2378–2381	663
2317	627	2353	638	2382	655, 663
2318–2320	633	2354–2356	637	2383, 2384	663
2321, 2322	634	2357	637, 638	2385	663, 664

EG

	PAGES		PAGES		PAGES
2	6	58	5, 24, 368, 533, 578	111	368, 385
7	83			112	368
8	560	59	5, 368, 412, 533, 578	113	368, 431
11	481, 509, 583			114	368
13	480, 490	60, 61	5, 368	115	368, 418, 431
14	495	62	5, 368, 431	116	368
15	497, 499	63	5, 368, 412	117	368, 435
16	499	64	5, 368, 579, 580	118	368, 431
17	525			119	368
19, 20	542, 544	65	5, 368, 412	120	368, 433
21	544	66	5, 368	121	368
22	535, 538	67	5, 226, 368, 387, 413, 414	122	368, 388
23	560			123	368, 389
24	583	68	5, 368, 414	124	368, 388, 390
25	584	69	5, 368, 412	125	368, 386
26	585	70–72	5	126	368
27	499, 525, 584	73, 74	5, 368	127, 128	368, 378
28	499, 583	75, 76	5	129	368, 395
29	26	81	5	130, 131	368
32	342	82	38	134, 135	551
34	483	83, 84	37	147	579
40	480	85	40	165, 166	37
41	27	86	35, 234	182	413
42	159, 344	87	19	184	418
44	602	88	5, 19, 368	186	377
46	482	91	442	187	416
47	103	94	225, 461	189	378
52–54	5	95	259, 263, 265	200	497
55	4, 5, 6	96	431	218	497
56	5	109	226, 368		
57	5, 24, 368, 579	110	368		

HGB

	PAGES		PAGES		PAGES
1-3	25	114	54, 304	233	36
4	25, 51, 52, 117	115	54, 303, 304	234	36, 44
15	44, 51, 54	116	54, 117, 303	235	36, 45
18-21	70	117, 118	54, 304	236-242	45
22	70, 424	119	54, 303	243-247	44
23, 24	70	120	54, 306, 307	248	44, 45
25	70, 203	121	54, 306	249-264	45
26	203	122	54, 307	265	45, 47
29-31	70	124	51, 53, 205	266-311	45
37	70	125	51, 54, 118	320	45, 117
38	52	126	54	321-334	45
39	52, 306	128	54, 206	339-341	56
40-47	52	131	55, 308	343, 344	25
48	117, 118	132, 133	55	345	145, 150
49, 50	51, 118	135	55	346	105
54	118	136	305	347	151
55, 56	119	137	308	348	9, 190
59	260, 264	138	55, 308, 309	349	319
60, 61	265	139	55, 308	350	317, 323
62	262, 263	140	55, 310	351	190, 317, 319,
63	262	141	55, 308, 310		323
64	260	142	308, 309, 310	352	145, 160
66-69	266	143	54	353	145
70	266, 268	145-158	55	354	257
71	266	161	55, 56, 117	355	3, 104, 331
72	262, 266	162, 163	56	356, 357	331
73	264	164	56, 304	358	150
74	101	165, 166	56	359	108, 150
75	101, 190	167-169	56, 307	360	144
76	101, 190, 263,	170-174	56	361	145
	264	175	56	362	88
80-82	264	176, 177	56	363	199, 286, 325,
84	119, 269	179	200		326
85-87	119	180	44	364, 365	197, 198, 199,
88, 89	280	182	43, 44		325
90	270, 280	183	44, 200	366, 367	398
91, 92	280	184-186	44	368	472
93-96	278	188, 189	43	369-371	193
98	278	195	43, 44	373, 374	222
99	278, 279	200	43	375	145
100-104	278	202	152	376	175, 187
105	51, 53	210	43	377	89, 165, 219
106, 107	54	211	44	378	165, 219
109	54, 302	222	199	380	214
110, 111	54, 305	231	36, 44	381	209, 273
112, 113	54, 306	232	36, 117, 118	382	213

continued

	PAGES		PAGES		PAGES
383	280	438, 439	284, 289	611	188
384	269, 281	440	284, 289, 290	613	188
385–387	269	441, 442	284	614	286
388	281, 282	443	284, 291	619	289
389	281	444–446	284, 285, 286	621	289
390–393	282	447–449	284, 286	642	285
394, 395	281	450	284, 286, 373	643	284
397–399	282	451–454	284	644, 645	284, 286
400–405	283	455	284, 285	646	284
406	280	456	158, 284, 287	647	284, 373
407–411	283	457	188, 284	648–650	284
412–414	284	458	158, 284, 287	651	284, 286
415	283	459–462	284, 287	652–658	284
416–418	298	463	284	659	284, 286
419	300	464, 465	284, 289	660, 661	284
420	298, 299	466	188, 287	662	284, 288
421–423	299	467, 468	287	663–678	284
424	373	469	288	679	460, 461, 462
425	284	470	289	680–699	462
426	284, 285	471	288	700–733	361
427	284, 289	472, 473	284	734–739	345
428	284, 286	474	396	740	358
429	158, 188, 284, 287	485	158, 287	741	359
		486	159	742–749	358
430	188, 284	489–509	361	750–753	359
431	158, 284, 287	511, 512	159	778–784	313
432	284, 288	556–566	284	785–803	314
433	284, 285	567	290	806–819	314
434	284	568–605	284	820–893	315
435	142, 284, 286	606	158, 287	894–897	314
436	284, 286	607	287	898–905	315
437	284, 290	608, 609	289		

CPO

	PAGES		PAGES		PAGES
27	584	606	483	863	632
29	149	632	484	866, 867	442
50	50	693	163	869	456
52	132, 502	695	163	883–887	185
203–206	88	697	163	888	185, 492
253	163	735	50	889–892	185
256	406	736	53	946–971	30
263	163	804	460	977–981	394
281	163	850	195		

TABLE OF ENGLISH STATUTES REFERRED TO

---

1 指书中边码（即原书页码）。——校勘者注

TABLE OF ENGLISH CASES REFERRED TO

1　指书中边码（即原书页码）。——校勘者注

INTRODUCTION

1. HISTORICAL SKETCH

a. German Law before 1900.

1. THE Holy Roman Empire of the German Nation came to a formal end in 1806, but long before that date it had ceased to have any authority over the numerous states and territories comprised therein.   In 1815 the German Confederation was formed without powers of legislation, and continued until 1866, the date of the formation of the North German Federation.   No machinery was therefore in existence prior to 1866 for the creation of a general German law. The German Bills of Exchange Code was enacted as State law in the several German States in 1848–1850, and in a similar way the German Commercial Code was introduced in 1861–1866, but they represented uniform state law, and did not emanate from any legislature common to all the States.   The remaining body of law was full of diversities in all directions, which were complicated by the fact that the areas of the several legal systems were not as a general rule conterminous with the State areas.   The so-called German common law was a modified form of Roman law as embodied in Justinian's compilation which was finally received in Germany in 1495, but subject to numerous varieties of local customs, and was in many German regions supplemented or displaced by local codes.   These local codes were the following: the *Bavarian Codex Maximilianus* (1756) [1]; the Prussian *Landrecht* (1794); the Code Napoléon (1804) (which was in force in several provinces), and its slightly altered German reproduction, the *Badisches Landrecht* (1809); the Austrian Civil Code (1811); and the Saxon Civil Code (1863).   The common law and the law of the local codes was of course subject to modifications by the state law of the places in which they prevailed.

2. In 1866 the North German Federation was formed with powers to legislate   2

---

1   原文如此，该法典的完整名称为 Codex Maximilianeus Bavaricus Civilis。——校勘者注

on certain specified matters for the whole federal territory.   On its formation the Commercial Code and the Bills of Exchange Code were re-enacted as federal law, and federal legislation began.   The establishment of a federal Supreme Commercial Court (1869) also helped in the promotion of uniformity, but the period between 1866 and 1871 was mainly a time of transition from the impotence of the old Confederation of 1815, which was merely a Federation of States, to the youthful vigour of the German Empire, which was formed in 1871, and constituted a true federal State. [1] All the laws of the North German Federation were re-enacted as Imperial laws by the Imperial Legislature, and numerous new Imperial statutes followed, dealing partly with public and partly with private law.   Among these the Judicature Acts of 1877 which came into force in 1879 were particularly important, as they established uniformity in the organization and procedure of the Courts, and created the Supreme Imperial Court at Leipzig, which gave unity to the interpretation of the several systems of local law and of the existing Imperial law.

b.   The preparation and enactment of the Civil Code.

3. The work of preparing the draft of a Civil Code embodying the main parts of German private law was started in 1874 by the appointment of a commission composed of eleven members, who finished the work now known as the first draft of the Code in 1887, which was then published and submitted to the criticism of experts and others; in 1890 a second commission was appointed with instructions to revise the first draft in the light of the criticisms which had appeared in the periodical press and in separate books and pamphlets.   The second draft was finished in 1895, and after the introduction of numerous modifications on the part of the Federal Council and the Imperial Parliament the final product became law on the 18th of August, 1896, and came into force on the 1st of January, 1900. The Code was accompanied by a statute for its introduction (*Einführungsgesetz*), containing transitory provisions as to the relation of State law to Imperial law, and rules as to the conflict of laws, which latter had been contained in the second

---

[1]   The German Empire consists of the Kingdoms of Prussia, Bavaria, Saxony, and Wurttemberg, the Grand Duchies of Baden, Hesse, Mecklenburg-Schwerin, Mecklenburg-Strelitz, Saxe-Weimar, and Oldenburg, the Duchies of Brunswick, Saxe-Meiningen, Saxe-Altenburg, and Saxe-Coburg-Gotha, the Principalities of Anhalt, Schwarzburg-Rudolstadt, Schwarzburg-Sondershausen, Waldeck, Reuss (Senior Line), Reuss (Junior Line), Schaumburg-Lippe, and Lippe, the Free Cities of Hamburg, Bremen, and Lübeck, and the Imperial Province of Alsace-Lorraine.

draft but were transferred to the EG by the Federal Council.

4. Entirely transformed editions of the Commercial Code and the Code of Civil Procedure, supplemented in each case by introductory statutes, and several other Imperial statutes intended to carry out in detail some of the principles laid down in the Code, were also enacted before the coming into force of the Civil Code. Thus a voluminous body of revised or new law came into force on the 1st of January, 1900, by the side of the Civil Code.

2. COMPONENT PARTS OF GERMAN PRIVATE IMPERIAL LAW

5. The term private law as distinguished from public law is not defined by German statute law. Justinian's definition (i. 1, 4) ' *publicum ius est quod ad statum rei Romanae spectat, privatum quod ad singulorum utilitatem pertinet* ' , still indicates the line of cleavage; but it should be remembered that there are cases where public bodies exercise private rights as property owners or as employers of labour, and that such rights, though exercised for the public benefit, are regulated by private law. The German Civil Code and the other enactments referred to in this treatise deal with private law only, but there are matters on the border line to which attention will be called in their several proper places.

6. The most important part of German private law is contained in the Civil Code and the Commercial Code, and these Codes supplement each other in such a way that it is impossible to ascertain the law on a question relating to any transaction of a commercial nature without referring to both Codes. A disregard of this rule may lead to most serious mistakes, as the following example may show. A reader of BGB 248 will be led to assume that an agreement for payment of compound interest not coming under one of the exceptions specified in that section must inevitably be void, but a reference to HGB 355 shows that as regards a large number of transactions occurring in daily life the assumption is erroneous. The HGB does not merely deal with mercantile institutions such as trading partnerships and companies, the law as to firm names, mercantile agency, &c. , but it also establishes a separate set of rules applicable to transactions governed by mercantile law. The question whether mercantile law is applicable to any particular transaction, or whether the transaction is governed by the ordinary law, does not necessarily depend on the nature of the transaction, but on other circumstances to which reference will be made below (36). Thus a sale of chattels, a loan, or

an agreement for services, may, according to the nature of the particular case, be governed by mercantile law or by general law; in the first-mentioned event the provisions of the BGB are applicable in so far only as the HGB or the EG (HGB) does not provide otherwise. —EG (HGB) 2.

7. The Civil Code and the Commercial Code do not comprise the whole of the law on the subjects with which they purport to deal. Thus, for instance, the law of partnership and companies contained in the two Codes is supplemented by the statutes relating to partnerships with limited liability (1892, revised 1898), to co-operative associations (1889, revised 1898), and to mortgage banks (1899); the law as to property deposited for safe custody is supplemented by the statute relating to the safe custody of negotiable instruments (1896); the law as to contracts of sale by the statute relating to the hire and purchase system (1894); the law as to unlawful acts by the statute relating to unfair competition (1896). Moreover the whole of the legislation relating to copyright, patents, trademarks, and similar matters remains untouched by the two Codes.

3.   RELATION OF IMPERIAL LAW TO STATE LAW

8. By EG 55 all rules of State law referring to matters within the domain of private law are repealed, except in so far as the EG itself, or the BGB, contains any provisions to the contrary. The provisions of the EG and the BGB upholding State law may be divided into four groups:

(1) Provisions on subjects on which Imperial legislation was purposely postponed, and which in the meantime were to remain under the existing rules of State law, such as publishers' contracts and insurance contracts [1]. —EG 75, 76.

(2) Provisions on subjects having some indirect connexion with the public law of the individual states; (the assignment of salaries and pensions receivable by public officials (EG 81); the acquisition of land by aliens (EG 88); and the privileges of the members of reigning houses and certain other houses of quasi-princely rank (35) may be classed under this head).

(3) Provisions retained in order to maintain local customs in matters in which the feelings of the population would have been unduly roused by sudden changes brought about by the Imperial authorities (e. g. entails, local customs as

---

[1]   The law as to publishers' contracts has in the meantime been the subject of Imperial legislation— see post (242–251); a draft statute relating to insurance contracts is now (March, 1906) before the *Reichstag*.

to the tenure and inheritance of land, and as to the working of mines. —EG 52–74).

(4) Provisions on subjects on which the general rules are laid down by the BGB, the details being referred to State legislation (*e. g.* BGB 919 entitles the owner of land to require the owner of adjoining land to concur in erecting boundary marks in accordance with rules to be determined by State law).

9. In order to facilitate the transition between the old and the new law, and at the same time to regulate the matters left to State law, a statute providing for the introduction of the new law (*Ausführungsgesetz*) was passed in each of the twenty-five German States and in Alsace-Lorraine, containing transitory provisions and determining matters left to State law, in so far as it was not intended to maintain the previously existing State law on such matters.

4. RELATION OF CODES AND STATUTES TO CUSTOMARY LAW

10. In the first draft of the BGB it was provided (s. 2) that customary law was to remain in force in so far only as it was expressly reserved by the Code or any statute, but this provision was struck out by the second commission on the ground that it was not intended to abolish customary law. It is now the prevalent opinion that Imperial customary law may exist, or come into existence, for the purpose of supplementing Imperial law, and that in the same way local customary law may supplement State law as to such matters as under the rules stated above (8) are left to State law. As regards matters which are withdrawn from the operation of State law, local customs are without effect (see EG 55 and the definition of ' *Gesetz* ' in EG 2).

5. RECAPITULATION OF THE SOURCES OF GERMAN PRIVATE LAW

11. It will be seen from the rules stated above that, in order to find out the law on any given point, it is not sufficient to refer to the provisions of the BGB and HGB, or of any other Imperial statute that may be applicable to the matter in hand, but that in each case it must be ascertained:

(1) whether the subject of the inquiry is one on which the State law, including the AG of the particular State, contains any supplementary provisions;

(2) whether any Imperial customary law affects the particular subject;

(3) whether, in the event of the subject being one which may be affected by State law, any local customary law relating thereto is in existence.   These circumstances alone make it clear that the BGB did not, either in intention or in effect, reduce the whole of German law into one compact mass.

6.   ARRANGEMENT OF THE CODES

12. The arrangement of the BGB is, to a great extent, based on the arrangement of the *Pandektenlehrbücher*, *i. e.* the systematic books on modernized Roman law which was the ' Common Law ' of Germany before the introduction of the Civil Code; in these books a detailed account of that law was given for the use of students and practitioners.   The Code is divided into five books, of which the first contains general rules, while the second, third, fourth, and fifth books respectively deal with the ' law of obligations ', ' the law of things ', ' family law ', and ' the law of inheritance '.   This arrangement is not, strictly speaking, logical, inasmuch as the second book deals with a special class of rights, while the third deals with rights referring to a special class of property, and the fourth and fifth with the results of a special class of events and the rights created under special classes of relationships.   It would be more consistent to make either the nature of the property or the nature of the rights the main basis of division, but the five heads are so familiar to German lawyers that it was never proposed to abandon them.   In England the most familiar division is the separation of the rules relating to real and those relating to personal property, and the distinction between the two methods of classification serves to illustrate a vital difference between Germanic law generally—including English law—on the one side, and Roman law on the other.   The rights relating to land were, in countries inhabited by Germanic populations, treated as rights *sui generis*; feudal tenure, entails, recoveries, leases and releases, and other similar institutions, have no reason of existence except in relation to land.   Alienation, marriage, birth and death (more especially under the older law), affect land in a manner entirely different from the manner in which they affect other property.   Under Roman law no such distinction existed.   The word *res* comprised all movable and immovable objects; property in land was not in its nature different from property in slaves or in pieces of furniture.   The distinction between several classes of rights and several classes of events affecting rights was, therefore, a more natural basis of the scheme of classification than the distinction between land and other property.   The Civil

Code, as mentioned before, has retained the classifications introduced by the books on Roman law; but, owing to the fact that it has to a large extent allowed Germanic institutions to modify the Roman system on which it is mainly constructed, the distinction between immovables and movables has assumed a much larger importance than it had in the old textbooks.

13. The general part of the BGB deals mainly with the persons, natural or artificial, in whom rights may vest; with the nature and classification of the particular objects called things (the rights relating to which are, as mentioned above, discussed in the second book); with acts-in-the-law (being the principal factors by which rights are created, transferred, and extinguished); with the influence of time as creating and extinguishing rights (prescription), and some other matters of minor importance. The book relating to obligations abandons the old division between contractual obligations and obligations *ex delicto*. It contains (*a*) general rules relating to obligations (dealing with contractual agreements separately in so far as this is necessary); (*b*) special rules as to particular kinds of obligations which are enumerated promiscuously without any systematic order. The book relating to things brings out the development which, as mentioned above (12), has led to a more marked distinction between the law as to land and the law as to movables; a separate division deals with rights relating to immovables; the rules as to the acquisition and loss of property are given separately in respect of immovables and in respect of movables, and the rules as to charges and pledges are dealt with similarly in a manner separating the two classes of property. The book on family law deals with the law of husband and wife, of parent and child, and of guardian and ward; the book on the law of inheritance with testamentary and intestate succession, the law of compulsory portions (*portio legitima*), the law as to the administration of the estates of deceased persons, and the legal position of heirs and legatees.

14. The HGB is divided into three parts, dealing respectively with: (1) mercantile trade as a whole (definition of 'mercantile traders', rules as to mercantile register, trade name, mercantile book-keeping, general powers of agency, mercantile assistants and apprentices, mercantile agents and brokers); (2) mercantile partnerships (private partnerships, commandite partnerships and companies); and (3) mercantile transactions.

7. General Characteristics of the New Codes

a. As to Substance of Provisions.

15. The law of the BGB is built up on foundations borrowed from Roman law with additions contributed from Germanic sources, but some of the provisions are of an entirely modern and original character.   The rules relating to contracts for services; the rule enabling debtors to repay debts, bearing a rate of interest exceeding six per cent. per annum, notwithstanding any contractual stipulation to the contrary; the provision empowering the Court to give relief against penalties; the rules as to the relations between husbands and wives, are only a few examples of numerous and important innovations.   The new Code was not intended to construct an ideal system on the basis of natural law; its object was to maintain (as far as this was compatible with the necessities of unification) the connexion of the present with the past, but without neglecting the change in the conditions of life brought about by modern social and economical developments.   The innovations contained in the HGB are mostly due to the necessity of harmonizing its contents with the contents of the BGB.   Many rules which formerly existed for commercial law only, but which now have been embodied in the general law, were removed from the HGB and introduced into the BGB; on the other hand, it became necessary to exclude the operation of such general rules contained in the BGB as were not to be applied to transactions governed by commercial law (see, for instance, HGB 348, referred to below).

b. As to Methods of Expression.

16. The casuistic method of the Prussian *Landrecht*, the rules of which were to fit every conceivable state of facts, was deliberately and decisively abandoned by the authors of the BGB.   Their aim was to introduce detailed rules only for specific purposes, and to be generally content with the establishment of broad principles, leaving it to legal science (19) and to the decisions of the Courts to fill in the details gradually.   Provisions like the following— ' The debtor is bound to perform his obligation in the manner required by good faith having regard to ordinary usage. ' —BGB 242.   ' The contract for services may be rescinded without notice by either party, in the event of there being any cogent ground for such a course. ' —BGB 626.   ' A wife is not bound to conform to her husband's ruling, if such ruling is due to an abuse of his rights. ' —BGB

1354 (2)—leave considerable freedom to those who have to administer the law and give it an amount of elasticity, which ordinary statute law does not give.

Some of the sections merely contain definitions (*e. g.* BGB 90–92, 516 (1), 741, 868, 872), and sometimes a section merely sums up the contents of immediately following sections (*e. g.* BGB 1323, 1330).

Sometimes a right is defined and the expression by which this right is afterwards called is added in brackets. —BGB 273, 984, 1113, 1204.

Words and forms of speech are frequently used in a technical meaning not defined by the Code, but so obvious from their mode of application that such technical meaning must be deemed to be implied by the Code itself.   Thus the   10 words 'cannot' and 'may not' respectively have distinct technical meanings; when the BGB says that an act *cannot* be done, this means that an act attempted to be done, notwithstanding the prohibition, is void, but when the BGB declares that an act *may not* be done, an act violating the prohibition is not on that ground void, but gives a right to damages to any person in whose favour the prohibition was made (compare *e. g.* BGB 225, which declares that the operation of prescription cannot be excluded by agreement, and means that any such agreement is of no effect, with BGB 627 (2), which provides that notice to determine certain kinds of contract for services *may not* be given except on certain grounds, and means that any notice given, notwithstanding the prohibition, is effective, but entitles the party injured by the determination of the contract to damages).   The word 'shall' implies that the omission to do the prescribed act gives an aggrieved party a claim for damages, the word 'must', that the omission renders the whole transaction ineffective (see *e. g.* BGB 57, which provides (1) that the rules of a non-trading corporation *must* contain certain particulars, and (2) that the name of any such corporation *shall* be distinguishable from the name of any other corporation registered in the same place; the non-compliance with the first-mentioned requirement has the effect of annulling the incorporation, whilst non-compliance with the second requirement leaves the incorporation untouched).

The authors of the BGB have taken great pains to show, when establishing any rule, how the burden of proof respecting compliance with the rule is to be apportioned between the parties, and they have adopted peculiar modes of expression intended to give a guidance as to their meaning.   The rules are too complicated and subtle to be reproduced in this place, and it is not certain whether they will always be followed, more particularly as they have not been carried out with complete consistency.

8. Methods of Interpretation

17. The Codes themselves do not lay down any general rules of interpretation in respect of their own provisions—(as to the methods of interpretation applicable to declarations of intention in connexion with acts-in-the-law, see 107)—but the methods of expression and definition to which attention has been called above (16) furnish a valuable clue in many cases. A somewhat dangerous method of interpretation derived from Roman law, and not unfrequently carried out by the German Courts, is the interpretation by analogy. Where a gap has been left by any statutory rule it is filled up, according to this method, by reference to another rule contained in the same statute, in connexion with which a point corresponding to the point left open in the first-mentioned rule is expressly provided for, and the *ratio iuris* of the last-mentioned expression is taken to be a general rule of law applicable to all cases. This method which assumes that the omission in the first case was accidental, while it may have been deliberate, and also that a judge may fill in a gap left by the legislator's want of care, is not in accordance with English methods of interpretation.

18. Another kind of assistance in respect of the interpretation of the BGB is provided by the historical evidence as to the mode of its production comprised in the publication issued under the title of *Material for the BGB*. These materials include: (1) the several drafts of the Code (*viz.* those of the first and second commissions and the one submitted to the *Reichstag* by the Federal Council); (2) the Minutes of the Proceedings of the second commission; (3) the 'Motives' published with the first draft; (4) the Memorandum issued by the federal council accompanying the draft submitted to the *Reichstag*; (5) the Report of the select committee of the *Reichstag*; (6) the shorthand notes of the debates in the *Reichstag*. These materials cannot be used as direct evidence for the meaning of any part of the Code, inasmuch as in Germany as well as in England the rule is paramount that the legislator's expressions and not his intentions are conclusive, but this rule does not detract from the cogency of another rule of equally universal application, according to which the history of any legal provision is an indispensable guide to the *ratio legis*, and the 'Materials' offer the most valuable guidance to the history of the enactments embodied in the Code. Where any rule is taken from the Common law, or from one of the old Codes, or from any local system of Customary law, the application formerly given is of necessity an almost conclusive guide as to its present application (see, for instance, the rules as to transactions *contra bonos mores* below, 105), and it is only in respect of new or modified law that important new questions can arise. For the purpose of finding whether, and to what extent, any provision of the Code is derived from old sources the 'Materials' are undoubtedly the most convenient and most authoritative work of reference.

19. The authority of textbook writers both as regards the old and the new law is of great importance in Germany. Certain works are by common consent picked out as the most worthy of attention, and such works are quoted in the written pleadings (which, according to German practice, frequently embody nearly everything which in England would be used in the addresses of counsel), and in the judgments of the Courts in the same way as some of the older works are quoted in English Courts.

20. Lastly, there is the guide to interpretation which in practice is the most important of all, *viz.* the rules established by the practice of the Courts. Theoretically the rule of English law, according to which the judgment of any Court establishing any rule of law is conclusive for all co-ordinate and subordinate Courts, is not accepted in Germany, and any young 'assessor' fresh from his final examination may overrule the judgment of the Imperial Supreme Court, but in practice the ruling of any superior Court is of the greatest weight and authority, and the Imperial Supreme Court as well as the Prussian Chamber Court publish regular official reports of their more important judgments, not to speak of the numerous reports of decided cases published privately. It is forbidden by statute for any Division of the Imperial Supreme Court to deliver a judgment dissenting from the previous ruling of any other Division. If it is thought that the previous ruling was mistaken, a meeting of all the Civil or all the Criminal Divisions (as the case may be) must be summoned, and the full Court can then overrule the judgment of the Divisional Court (statute relating to the Organization of the Courts of Justice 1877, revised 1898, s. 137). A perusal of any of the German reports will show that previous rulings of other Courts are constantly referred to in the reported judgments. While they are not absolutely binding, it would not occur   13 to any serious judge to overrule a principle laid down in any superior Court, without giving very substantial reasons for his dissent.

21. The methods of expression and interpretation to which attention has been called (16–20) admit of a constant adaptation of the law to the successive variations of the surrounding conditions. No doubt the wide margin left to judicial discretion will gradually disappear. After a time certain rules consistently adopted by the

Courts will be treated as rules of customary law; these rules however will not be applied literally, but only as indicating the principles which ought to be followed, and will not therefore in any event be less elastic than the rules established by case law in England.   It is not proposed to discuss the advantage of codified over uncodified law, but it is necessary to insist on the fact which cannot be disputed by any one familiar with the working of continental Codes, that the persons who in discussing the merits or demerits of codification oppose codified law to case law, entirely miss the point at issue.   A Code like the Code Napoléon or the BGB does not replace or hinder the development of case law.   It replaces a number of heterogeneous statutes, and the new laws take the shape of amended sections instead of appearing as separate enactments.   Moreover its methods of expression favour a recognition of general principles in the place of the casuistic irregularity which is fostered by the absence of any authoritative systematization of law.

FIRST BOOK

GENERAL RULES OF LAW

FIRST DIVISION
PERSONS, THINGS, AND RIGHTS

CHAPTER I
PERSONS

A. GENERAL RULES

1. NATURAL PERSONS AND CORPORATE BODIES

22. THE expression person is in German Law applied to any individual entity capable of rights, that is to say, capable of being the owner of, or of exercising rights over property, and of having and enforcing claims against others.   Entities capable of rights are divided into two classes, which, in continental language, are respectively called natural and juristic persons.   According to modern ideas every human being is capable of rights, but there is no characteristic sign, the possession of which marks any combination of human beings or any other artificial entity as a 'person' in the legal sense.   Corporate rights must always be expressly conferred, either by virtue of a general enactment, making their attainment dependent on compliance with certain prescribed conditions, or by a special act of the competent authorities of the state within which the right of personality is to be enjoyed.

2. ASSOCIATIONS OF PERSONS NOT FORMING
CORPORATE BODIES IN THE STRICT SENSE

23. The distinction between natural persons (*singuli*) and juristic persons (*universitates* [1]) is derived from Roman law.   Germanic law and the law merchant, which is now part and parcel of German law, recognizes various forms of

---

1   原文如此，似应为 *universitas*。——校勘者注

associations, which form an intermediate stage between the two classes.   In England trading companies have gone through a gradual process of evolution,
18   which only at a late stage of their existence gave them the character of corporate bodies in the full sense of the word, and there are still unincorporated companies or societies which occupy an intermediate position between associations of natural persons and juristic persons or corporations. [1]   In the same way some of the forms of association recognized by German law, though not corporations in the strict sense, partake of so many qualities belonging to juristic persons that it is necessary to refer to them in connexion with the subject of personality.

B.   NATURAL PERSONS

1.   BEGINNING OF PERSONALITY

24. The question at what moment a human being begins to be capable of rights is of great importance, as the following example will show.   If an only child is born after the death of his father, and dies after having been capable of rights for one moment only, any property to which such child was entitled under his father's will or intestacy becomes vested in him during that moment, and under the German law of intestacy passes to his mother as his next-of-kin; if, on the other hand, the child never became capable of rights, the person who, under the father's will or intestacy, would have taken the property in the event of the child not having been born becomes entitled to it.   The capacity for rights, according to BGB 1, begins with the completion of birth.   Complete severance from the mother is not required; the completion of the act of birth in the medical sense, coupled with the survival of the child for one moment at least after such completion, is all that is necessary.   The entry in the Register of Births (which must state the exact hour as well as the date of the birth) is *prima facie* evidence of the time of a birth.   Still-born children are registered in the register of deaths only, and the non-registration of the birth of a child whose death is registered is *prima facie* evidence of the fact that the child's birth was not completed.   A *nasciturus*, is not capable of rights in the strict sense of the word, but may have inchoate rights

---

[1]   Thus, for instance, an English trade union has the capacity to own property and to act by agents without, however, being deemed to be a corporation (Taff Vale Railway *v.* Amalgamated Society of Railway Servants (1901), A. C. 426).

which the BGB protects (see 454, 472).

2.   EFFECT OF STATUS ON CAPACITY FOR RIGHTS, DISPOSING CAPACITY, AND OWNERSHIP OF PROPERTY

a.   Capacity for Rights (*Rechtsfähigkeit*).

25. As stated above (22), every natural person is in all modern systems   19
of law deemed capable of rights, but this capacity is not always unrestricted.
Certain classes of persons are, according to some systems of law, deprived of the
enjoyment of certain classes of rights.   Thus, in England before 1870, an alien
was incapable of owning real property, and an alien is still incapable of being the
owner or part owner of a British ship. [1]   According to Austrian law, a member of
a monastic order, having made vows of poverty, is incapable of acquiring
property of any kind, though he is capable of retaining the property owned by him
at the time of joining the Order (see statutes quoted in Stubenrauch's edition of
the Austrian Code, I. 459).   According to the present German law, it is left to
State legislation to decide whether, and to what extent, an alien is capable of
acquiring immovable property (EG 88), and whether testamentary or other gifts
in favour of members of religious orders are effective (EG 87), but no other
restriction as to the capacity for rights of natural persons exists.

b.   Disposing Capacity (*Geschäftsfähigkeit*).

aa.   *Generally.*

26. Capacity for *rights* must be distinguished from disposing capacity, by
which is meant the power of disposing of property and of incurring obligations by
acts-in-the-law.   Under the law of all countries, deficiency of age and mental
disorder have the effect of removing or restricting the capacity to dispose of rights,
and in all countries there are various degrees of incapacity.   Thus, for instance,
the contracts of infants may, under English law, be voidable or valid, according
to the circumstances of each case, and the same rule applies as to the contracts of
lunatics.   According to German law, a distinction is drawn between the total
absence of capacity for acts-in-the-law and *restricted* capacity.   A person fully

---

[1]   A distinction between subjects of the country concerned and aliens also exists in several countries
as regards patents, trade-marks, &c.

20 capable is called *geschäftsfähig*; a person wholly incapable, *geschäftsunfähig*; a person of restricted disposing capacity is called *in der Geschäftsfähigkeit beschränkt*. The effect of these distinctions, and the distinction between capacity for acts-in-the-law and capacity in respect of the commission of unlawful acts, will be explained below (92). Incapacity or restricted capacity either exists naturally (as in the case of infants or persons of unsound mind not officially placed under guardianship) or it is declared by a Court of law (as in the case of lunatics, prodigals, and dipsomaniacs, placed under guardianship by judicial order). The expression 'capacity' will, in the further course of this treatise, be applied to indicate capacity for acts-in-the-law, and a corresponding use will be made of the expressions 'incapacity' and 'restricted capacity'.

bb. Infants (Minderjährige).

27. Generally speaking, all persons not having attained the age of 21 years are infants according to German law—BGB 2—but a person having attained the age of 18 years may be declared by a competent Court to be of full age if the following requirements are complied with:

(1) the person concerned must consent;

(2) the person exercising parental power (441) must give his consent;

(3) the Court must be of opinion that the order will be advantageous to the person concerned. —BGB 3–5.

An infant under the age of 7 is under complete incapacity; an infant having attained the age of 7 is of restricted capacity. —BGB 104, 106.

cc. Unsoundness of mind (Geisteskrankheit).

28. There is in England a distinction between persons of unsound mind not so found, and persons found lunatics after an inquisition by the Court in Lunacy, but this distinction has not the same effect as the corresponding distinction in German law. A lunatic so found according to English law is not, by reason of that fact alone, incapable for all purposes. On the other hand, a person placed under guardianship by a German Court on the ground of mental disease is under complete incapacity. —BGB 104.

21 Persons of unsound mind not placed under guardianship on the ground of mental disease are under complete incapacity if their unsoundness of mind is of a nature to prevent the free exercise of their power of volition and is not merely of a temporary character.

dd.   Mental infirmity (Geistesschwäche).

29. The English Lunacy Act 1890, s. 116 (*d*) , takes notice of a class of persons who ' through mental infirmity arising from disease or age are incapable of managing their affairs ' , and enables the Court in Lunacy to make orders as to the management of the property of such persons, without, however, imposing any restriction on their disposing capacity.   According to BGB 6, 114, persons belonging to this class may be placed under guardianship on the ground of mental infirmity, and the effect of such an order is to restrict the capacity of the person concerned.

ee.   Prodigality (Verschwendung).

30. The restrictions as to the disposing powers of a person placed under guardianship on the ground of extravagance are derived from the ideas of Roman law, which attribute to the natural heirs of a person owning property an inchoate right to such property entitling them to take steps to prevent its wasteful consumption by the actual owner.   English law takes the opposite view, and entirely discards the notion of incapacity arising on the ground of prodigality (*Re Selot's Trusts* (1902) , 1 Ch. 488).   According to BGB 6, 114, an order placing the *prodigus* under guardianship may be made on the application of any one out of a certain specified class of persons who can prove that the person in question, by extravagant living, exposes himself or his family to the risk of poverty.   Such an order imposes ' restricted capacity ' on the *prodigus* and completely changes his status; its effect goes much further than the effect of a similar order made under French law (Code Civil, s. 513).

ff.   Dipsomania (Trunksucht).

31. An entirely novel ground for placing a person under guardianship was introduced by BGB 6, which enacts that this proceeding may be applied to ' any person who by reason of dipsomania is incapable of managing his affairs, or exposes himself or his family to the risk of poverty, or endangers the safety of others ' .   The effect of an order obtained in such a case is the same as in the case of mental infirmity or prodigality. —BGB 114.

22

gg.   Effect of punishment for criminal offences.

32. According to English law, a convict loses his disposing capacity (see Forfeiture Act 1870, s. 8).   No similar provision exists in German law.

c.   Forfeiture or compulsory
transfer of property consequent upon criminal punishment,
bankruptcy, and marriage.

(1) *Under English Law.*

33. Certain changes of status have in certain systems of law the effect of bringing about the forfeiture of property or the compulsory transfer of property, or of its possession or management.

In England forfeiture by reason of felony has been abolished, but forfeiture by reason of outlawry still exists theoretically, and the property of a convict (whose disposing power is suspended, as mentioned above) is transferred to an administrator (Forfeiture Act 1870, ss. 9 and 10).

In a similar way the property of a bankrupt (with some unimportant exceptions) becomes vested in a trustee in bankruptcy upon trust for realization and division among the creditors (Bankruptcy Act 1883, ss. 20 (1), 44).

Before the coming into force of the Married Women's Property Act, 1882, marriage had the effect at Common Law of vesting parts of the wife's property in the husband and restricting her disposing powers as to other parts, but under the present English law marriage no longer deprives the wife of any part of her property.

(2) *Modern German Law.*

In modern German law forfeiture as a criminal punishment does not exist.

23   The bankruptcy of a person does not cause his property to be vested in a trustee as it does in England, but it has the effect of transferring its possession and management (except as to certain exceptional kinds of property) to an administrator who has to apply the proceeds for the benefit of creditors in the same way as an English trustee in bankruptcy (KO 1–6, 7).

The marriage of a woman, in the absence of a marriage contract, has the effect of transferring the management of her property, and to a great extent also the disposing power over it, to her husband, and a marriage contract may have still more far reaching effects (414, 417).

3. EFFECT OF SOCIAL RANK, NATIONALITY, AND DOMICIL ON THE APPLICATION OF LAW

a. Generally.

34. In the older Roman law the modes of acquiring and exercising rights were largely dependent on the nationality and social rank of the person concerned. A Roman citizen was governed by a law differing from the law applicable to persons not having the privilege of citizenship, and great differences existed also between the rights of freedmen and those of free citizens, while slaves were incapable of rights.   Distinctions of this kind, which were considerably reduced in the later development of Roman law, asserted themselves in a very marked manner in the Germanic systems.   Some of the distinctions due to class privileges have in several German districts continued to exist till quite recent times, as for instance in many parts of the two Mecklenburgs, where prior to 1900 the rules as to the effect of marriage on property and as to the devolution of property on death applied in the case of a nobleman were entirely different from those applied in the case of a citizen of lower degree.

The mediaeval law merchant created a special system of law for mercantile traders which to a certain extent survived in the HGB, but subject to this exception and to an exception in favour of certain families of princely rank, social status, profession, and occupation have ceased to have any effect on the application of law.   Nationality and domicil, however, still affect the legal positions of the persons concerned.   The effect of princely rank, the status of mercantile traders, and the effect of nationality and domicile under German law are discussed in the following paragraphs.

b. Effect of Princely Rank.

35. Members of the reigning houses are only affected by the provisions of the BGB, in so far as the state laws or the family statute affecting any member of any such house contain no conflicting provisions. —EG 57.   By virtue of this exceptional enactment the general rules of German law as to the attainment of majority, the celebration and dissolution of marriage, the effect of marriage on property, parental power and guardianship, the law as to the devolution of property on death, and the mode of transferring or mortgaging property included in family settlements, [1] are in most cases not applied to the members of reigning houses, and for this purpose the members of the princely branch of the Hohenzollern family and of the houses of Hanover, Hesse-Cassel, and Nassau are placed in the same position as the members of reigning houses. —EG 57.   Some of these privileges are also retained by the members of houses who at the Congress of Vienna were deprived of their sovereign rights and by the nobility of the Holy Roman Empire; as regards the attainment of majority and the celebration or dissolution of marriage the latter are placed under the general law. —EG 58.

c.   Mercantile Traders and Mercantile Transactions.

36. The transactions of a person coming under the definition of a *Kaufmann* (which expression in the course of this treatise is reproduced by ' mercantile trader') are in many respects subject to special rules of law.   The definition of a ' mercantile trader' includes persons belonging to one of the following classes:

(*a*) persons permanently engaged for profit in one out of a number of specified kinds of businesses (*e. g.* the business of banker, carrier, or publisher, the sale or purchase of goods, insurance and agency business, &c.) ;

(*b*) persons permanently engaged for profit in any other business or trade (not being the business of farming or forestry) , if such business is carried on in a manner and on a scale usual in the case of one of the more important mercantile businesses or trades, and if the trade name of such business is entered in the mercantile register. —HGB 1–3.

A person engaged in one of the more important kinds of mercantile businesses is called a *Vollkaufmann* (true mercantile trader in the full sense of the word) ; an artisan or a person engaged in a smaller trade (if coming within the definition of a mercantile trader) is called *Minder-Kaufmann* (lesser mercantile trader). — HGB 4.

The HGB uses the term ' mercantile transaction' (*Handelsgeschäft*) to denote any transaction entered upon by a mercantile trader in the course of his business, and for this purpose it is immaterial whether the person concerned is a full trader or a lesser trader.   Any transaction coming within the scope of the businesses, referred to above, sub (*a*) , is deemed a mercantile transaction even

---

[1]   In some states the privilege extends to other matters, *e. g.* in Prussia no action can be brought to recover money lent to any member of the Prussian Royal family (Prussian Code, First Part, Title 11, s. 676, the section remains in force by virtue of Prussian AG 89).

if it does not come within the scope of the ordinary business of the persons entering upon the same.   Moreover any transaction entered upon by a mercantile trader and any written document signed by a mercantile trader and creating an obligation binding upon him, is deemed to be entered upon or signed in the course of his business unless the contrary can be proved. —HGB 343, 344.   If both parties to a transaction are mercantile traders, the transaction is called a bilateral mercantile transaction; if only one party is a mercantile trader, it is called a unilateral mercantile transaction.   As a general rule the special provisions applicable to mercantile transactions affect both parties even if one of them is not a mercantile trader; the exceptional cases in which this rule is departed from will be pointed out in their proper places. (For examples of special provisions relating to mercantile transactions, see 96, 97, 107, 144 sub (2) (3) (4), 147 sub (4) (5), 148, 171, 175, 192 sub (3), 193, 231, 273, 333, 404.)

d.   Nationality and Domicil.

aa.   General statement.

37. The question as to what law is to be applied for the determination of any particular issue frequently depends upon the so-called 'personal statute' of one   26 of the parties, by which is meant the system of law to which he is personally subject, as distinguished from the system of law to which the particular transaction may be otherwise subject (*e. g. lex situs*, *lex contractus*, *lex loci solutionis*).   The 'personal statute' according to English law is determined by the domicil of the person concerned without regard to his nationality.   According to German law as now established, the nationality as a general rule determines the personal statute, but domicil cannot be entirely disregarded (as for instance when the law of the nationality is not uniform but varies from place to place, as in the case of the British Empire).   Domicil is also of importance, in many cases, for the purpose of establishing the jurisdiction of the particular Court before which an action is brought.   It is therefore necessary to inquire into the German conception of domicil as well as that of nationality.   The personal statute of a person who does not belong to any State is determined by the law of the State to which he belonged immediately before his last expatriation; if he never belonged to any State it is determined by the law of his domicil, and, in the absence of a domicil, by the law of the place at which he was resident at the decisive moment. —EG 29.

bb.   Nationality (Staatsangehörigkeit).

38. Every subject or citizen of a German state is deemed to be of German nationality, and the expression 'a German', as used in German Codes and Statutes, means the subject or citizen of one of the German States.   The status of a subject of any German State is acquired by one of the following methods:

(1) by descent; (a legitimate child becomes a subject of the State of which the father, an illegitimate child becomes a subject of the State of which the mother, is a subject);

(2) by legitimation; (if the father is the subject of a German State at the date of legitimation, the child becomes a subject of the same State);

(3) by marriage; (if the husband is the subject of a German State at the date of the marriage, the wife becomes a subject of the same State);

(4) by admission or naturalization; (any German on complying with certain unimportant requirements, provided that he is domiciled in the State of which he desires to become a subject, can transfer his allegiance from State to State; a non-German may, if he complies with certain prescribed conditions, be *naturalized* in any German State; the admission or naturalization of any male person includes the wife and such of the infant children as are under his parental power (444); an appointment in the German Government or municipal service has the effect of naturalization unless the contrary is expressly stated).—Nationality Statute 6– 11; EG 41.

39. A German loses his nationality:

(1) by order of dismissal made on his application to the central authority of the State of which he is a subject; the application cannot be refused on any ground other than noncompliance with the applicant's duties as to military service—see Nationality Statute 14–19; EG 41;

(2) by order made *ex officio* by the central authority of the State of which he is a subject (which order may be made: (a) if he resides abroad and in the case of war does not comply with a notice to return to Germany; (b) if he enters into the government service of any foreign State and does not comply with a notice to renounce such service—Nationality Statute 20, 22);

(3) by ten years' continuous residence outside the German Empire without registration in the proper consular register; (the period may by international agreement be reduced to five years in the event of naturalization in a foreign state).

The loss of nationality affects the members of the family of a German losing his nationality in the same way as naturalization affects the members of the family of a naturalized German. —Nationality Statute 21; EG 41.

If the wife of a man who loses his German nationality by reason of ten years' absence has justifiably retained her German domicil, she retains her German nationality (see 42).

cc. Domicil (Wohnsitz).

(1) Distinction between German and English Law.

40. The distinction of English law between the domicil of origin (being the place in which the father of the person concerned was domiciled at the time of his birth) and the domicil of choice (being the place selected as a domicil after the abandonment of the domicil of origin) does not exist in Germany.   According to English law the domicil of origin always revives on the abandonment of the domicil of choice, before the acquirement of a fresh domicil of choice; it is therefore impossible according to the English doctrine to be without a domicil, but according to German law a person may be without a domicil.   According to English law a person cannot have more than one domicil at the same time, but according to German law a person may be domiciled in several places at the same time. —BGB 7 (2).

(2) German conception of Domicil.

41. Subject to the differences created by the two divergences referred to above, the conception of the German law as to domicil is similar to the conception of English law.   A person of full age and capacity not being a married woman is according to German law domiciled in the place in which he has a permanent abode, that is to say an abode being permanent in intention as well as in fact (BGB 7 (1) (3)).

(3) Domicil of dependent persons and of persons in the Government service.

42. A person under incapacity or of restricted capacity cannot establish or remove his domicil, without the consent of his statutory agent (116). —BGB 8. A professional member of the armed forces (being of full age) is deemed to be domiciled in the place of his garrison, and if the military or naval unit to which he belongs is not garrisoned within the German Empire, he is deemed to be domiciled in the place in which such unit had its last permanent quarters, before leaving the German Empire.   Persons doing compulsory military service come under the same rules as civilians. —BGB 9.   A married woman shares her husband's domicil, as long as the husband does not establish his domicil in a place outside the German Empire, which is at the same time a place to which she cannot be compelled to follow him (412), and to which in fact she does not follow him. A married woman not sharing her husband's domicil under the last-mentioned rule, and also the wife of a husband having no domicil, may establish a domicil of her own according to the general rules—BGB 10. The father's domicil is shared by a legitimate, the mother's by an illegitimate infant child; the adoptor's domicil by an adopted infant child. The legitimation or adoption of a child having attained majority is without influence on his domicil—BGB 11.

4. TERMINATION OF PERSONALITY (DEATH)

a. Effect of Death.

29   **43.** The capacity for rights ceases with death. Some of the rights acquired and some of the duties undertaken by a person during his lifetime, are transferred to the person or persons who are said to represent his estate, but a right to which the deceased was not entitled at his death cannot accrue to his estate under any circumstances. It is therefore frequently important to ascertain whether a person to whom a right would have accrued if he had been living at a particular moment, did actually live at that moment, and for such a purpose it is necessary to know at what precise moment his life came to an end.

b. Proof of Death of Untraceable Persons.

44. In the case of a person dying within the German Empire the entry in the register of deaths, which according to the prescribed rules must contain particulars as to the exact hour at which death took place, is *prima facie* evidence as to the time of death (Personal Status Act 15, 59). In the case of a person dying within any state outside the German Empire the entry on the register kept according to the law of such state is generally accepted as *prima facie* evidence on the point in question. In the case of a death in a country in which no register is kept, other evidence must be produced. A difficulty arises, however, in the case of persons who have left their homes and have not been beard of for some time. Such persons, who in the technical language of German law are called *Verschollene* (and who in the course of this treatise will be referred to as 'untraceable persons'), may be made the subjects of a judicial 'declaration of death' (*Todeserklärung*), the nature and effects of which are discussed in the following paragraphs.

c.   Judicial Declaration of Death.

45. Under the rules of Roman law an untraceable person was not deemed to be dead before the lapse of a specified period from the time of his birth, which the glossators fixed at one hundred years, but which in German practice was reduced to the Psalmist's limit of seventy.   The presumption of death was not 30 properly established before a declaration of the competent Court as to the absence of news was obtained.   Under English law the question whether the Court may authorize a presumption of death does not depend upon the age of the party concerned, but upon the length of the period during which no news has been received (seven years).   The new German law adopts a combination of the two systems.   A person who, if living, would be under the age of seventy, may be declared to be dead if no news has been received for ten years reckoned from the end of the calendar year during which the last news was received.   In the case of a person who, if living, would have attained the age of seventy years, the period is reduced to five years.   No person can in any event be declared to be dead before the end of the calendar year during which he would, if living, have attained the age of thirty-one years.

Shorter periods are sufficient in the case: (1) of any member of the armed forces engaged in war found to be missing during such war; (2) of any person who was on board a vessel lost or presumed to be lost at sea; (3) of any person known to have been exposed to any mortal danger (*e. g.* to a fire causing loss of life in such manner that the bodies of the persons burnt to death cannot be identified). —BGB 13–17.

The procedure to be observed on applications for declarations of death, and the rules as to the selection of the Court competent for the purpose are laid down by CPO 946–971. [1]

d.   Presumption as to Time of Death.

46. The order declaring a person to be dead must contain a statement as to

---

[1]   The effect of a declaration of death goes further than that of a mere presumption of death.   If the spouse of a person declared to be dead, but actually living, re-marries, such re-marriage dissolves the first marriage (p. 451 note 4).

the time at which he is presumed to have died.   The time in the absence of any contrary evidence has to be fixed according to the following rules:

(*a*) in an ordinary case the time of the death is presumed to be the earliest moment at which the declaration of death would have been admissible;

31   (*b*) in the case of a person missing during a war, the date of the conclusion of peace (and in the absence of a formal conclusion of peace the end of the calendar year during which the war was determined) is presumed to be the date of the death;

(*c*) in the case of a shipwrecked person, the date of the loss or presumed loss of the vessel is presumed to be the date of the death;

(*d*) in the case of a person who was exposed to any mortal danger, the time of the event causing such danger is presumed to be the time of the death.

Where the time according to one of the above-mentioned rules is fixed by the date only, the end of the day is presumed to be the exact moment of death—BGB 18.

The Roman law had certain rules as to the order in which several persons becoming victims to the same fatal accident were presumed to have died; (*e. g.* if a father died in the same shipwreck with his infant child, the father was presumed to have survived such child, whereas, on the other hand, an adult child dying with his father in a similar way, was presumed to have survived the father) ; BGB 20, on the other hand, establishes a presumption to the effect that persons who have succumbed to a common danger have died at the same moment.   The effect of this is that neither person can become entitled to any right in the estate of the other as his survivor.

5.   PRESUMED DURATION OF LIFE

47. The presumption established by the declaration of death operates in two directions: it does not merely mean that in the absence of proof to the contrary the death has the effect which it would have had if it had actually taken place at the time in question; it also means that the person declared to be dead is deemed to have lived up to the moment in which he is presumed to have died.   The presumption as to the time of death contained in the declaration of death, is therefore, at the same time, a presumption as to the duration of the life of the person concerned.   If in the case of an untraceable person no declaration of death has been obtained, he is presumed to have lived up to the time to which he

would have been presumed to have lived if a declaration of death had been   32
obtained. —BGB 19.

C.   JURISTIC PERSONS (CORPORATE BODIES)

1.   GENERAL RULES

a.   Definition.

48. As mentioned above (23) the line of demarcation between corporate
bodies in the strict sense and unincorporated associations of persons, is not very
sharply defined in modern law, and there is no definition of the term ' juristic
person ' which is universally accepted, or which entirely excludes certain
associations of persons, who according to the general opinion are not to be deemed
corporate bodies.   The expression itself, though familiar to continental lawyers,
was not, prior to the enactment of the BGB and the new HGB, used in any
statute.   The new Codes have now given it official recognition without, however,
attempting to define it.   The best course for practical purposes is to deal, in the
first instance, with corporate bodies recognized as such by express provision of
law, or by common consent, and to deal separately with the associations of
persons not generally considered to partake of the character of corporate bodies.
A corporate body recognized as such may be defined as an entity capable of
rights, and consequently capable of owning property, and of possessing and
enforcing claims against others, and subject to corresponding duties.   The persons
by whose contributions the property of the corporate body is originally constituted,
or for whose benefit the corporate body is created, are not, in any sense of the
word, owners of the property of the corporation, or entitled to any rights, or
subject to any duties, to which the corporation is entitled or subject.

b.   Purposes for which Corporations are created.

49. Corporations according to their purposes may be divided into four
classes: (1) Public corporations; (2) Charitable foundations; (3) Trading
corporations; (4) Incorporated associations formed for purposes other than profit.

In England public corporations exist for the purpose of carrying out the
administrative functions of counties, districts or boroughs under more or less   33
ancient charters, or under the Municipal Corporation Acts, or the Local Government

Acts 1888 and 1894; whilst other public bodies with corporate rights have been created for special purposes (*e. g.* the Mersey Dock and Harbour Board). On the Continent the most important juristic person of a public nature is the State itself (*Fiskus*), which in England is not a corporate body.

The expedient of vesting property in trustees for charitable, educational, or religious purposes is not as a rule resorted to in continental countries, and it is therefore customary to establish corporate bodies as owners of funds devoted to any such object. For this purpose the charitable, educational, or religious foundation itself is formed into a corporate body.

Trading corporations formed for the benefit of the persons whose contributions constitute the corporate funds are the most modern and at the present time the most frequently occurring examples of corporate bodies. The most usual form in which they occur, both in England and Germany, is that of companies with a capital divided into shares.

Incorporated associations formed for purposes other than profit (*e. g.* mutual assistance, social, political, educational, or philanthropic objects) exist in England either under Acts relating to particular forms of association (*e. g.* Friendly Societies, &c.) or are formed under the Companies Acts (see Companies Act 1867, s. 23). In Germany a special form of incorporation has been provided for such associations by the BGB.

c. Distinction between Corporations Aggregate and Corporations Sole.

50. The distinction of English law between corporations aggregate and corporations sole is unknown in continental law. It owes its origin to the fact that the notion of a juristic or artificial person established itself in this country by very slow steps. The ' corporation aggregate ' originally partook much more of the character of a Germanic association of persons (*Genossenschaft*) than of a Roman '*universitas*' . The ' corporation sole ' under these circumstances filled up a gap left over by reason of the fact that certain property, more particularly property used for religious purposes, was not in fact held by any natural person or by any association of natural persons. The donor of Church land originally solved the difficulty by endowing a particular saint; sometimes the fabric of the Church was personified, but ultimately the fiction of endowing the rector or other ecclesiastical officer came into regular use. The rector was not the particular rector who held the office when the gift was made, but a fictitious person

34

represented by the successive holders of the office. [1]   The corporation sole is therefore in its very inception an artificial person coming much nearer to the Roman ' *universitas* ' than the original corporation aggregate, but the popular notion that property must be owned by some natural person or association of natural persons still retained its influence in the name of the Corporate Body.   In course of time the corporation aggregate came to be looked upon as an artificial entity like the corporation sole.   In the same way as ' The Rector of the Parish of ... ' as owner of the Church and glebe land is an artificial person, ' The Mayor, Aldermen, and Burgesses of ... ' or ' The Master, Fellows, and Scholars of ... ' as owners of the corporate property constitute a purely artificial entity, but the name by which that entity is described in either case indicates an historical development, which in some respects still influences the English conception of a corporate body.   In the countries in which the ideas of Roman law have had a more direct influence, the distinction between a corporation sole and a corporation aggregate can have no meaning, as Roman law looks upon a corporation as an entity independent of the individuals who contribute or manage its funds, or appropriate its income and profits.   The name of a corporation is therefore always an impersonal name according to the continental conception; the parish, the city, the university owns property; the incumbent, the citizens, the members are merely managers or beneficiaries.   The corporation is always one person, never an aggregate of persons.

d.   Capacity for Rights of Corporate Bodies.

51. The very existence of a corporate body implies that it is capable of rights, and the acquisition or loss of corporate rights is in the German technical language described as the acquisition or loss of *Rechtsfähigkeit*, but, as corporations are the creatures of law, it also follows that the capacity for rights may be restricted either generally or by the statute or charter by which, or under which, any particular corporate body is formed.   The most important general restriction which in some form or other has probably existed in all civilized countries is generally embodied in laws summed up under the title of laws against the ' dead hand' or Mortmain Acts.   The object of all statutes described by this title is to prevent the accumulation of land on the part of owners not being natural

35

---

[1]   For details of the whole development, see Pollock & Maitland, *History of English Law*, 2nd ed. , vol. i, pp. 499‑511.

persons, and this is generally done by prohibiting, regulating, or restricting the acquisition of land on the part of corporate bodies.   In England this policy was carried out by a number of statutes beginning with the statute ' *de viris religiosis* ' of Edward I, [1] which have all now been consolidated by the Mortmain and Charitable Uses Act 1888; certain classes of corporations are however allowed to acquire and hold land (*e. g.* companies incorporated under the Companies Acts, see Comp. Act 1862, ss. 18, 191).

In Germany it is left to State legislation to restrict the acquisition by corporate bodies of land the value of which exceeds 5, 000 marks. —EG 86. [2]

The restrictions as to the capacity for rights imposed by the charter or statute from which a corporation derives its existence are of course independent of any general rules.

Certain rights which can be exercised by a natural person cannot, by reason of their particular nature, be exercised by a corporation.   Thus the rules regulating the relations of husband and wife, or parent or child, cannot of course affect corporate bodies.   It is not so obvious, however, that the functions of a guardian or executor cannot be performed by a corporation.   In England a corporation may be appointed executor and trustee; in Germany a guardian must be a natural person, but a corporation may be appointed executor.

36

e.   Capacity for Acts-in-the-law.

52. A corporation without capacity for acts-in-the-law is as inconceivable as a corporation without any capacity for rights, but like the capacity for rights the disposing capacity may be restricted by the constitution of the corporation.   A natural person may act either in person or through an agent.   A corporation, on the other hand, must of necessity act through one or more persons appointed as its primary agents; these primary agents must be distinguished from agents appointed by the primary agents, whose powers may be as varied as the powers of the agents of natural persons, but the primary agents must always have certain express or

---

1   关于英国爱德华一世《宗教人士法》（Statute' De Viris Religiosis）的简要介绍，参见张秋实："爱德华一世时期的土地立法"，载《南京大学法律评论》2012 年第 1 期。——校勘者注

2   In Prussia land of a value exceeding the limit of 5, 000 marks may not be acquired by a corporate body without the permission of a public authority. —Prussian AG 7.   In Bavaria the limit is 10, 000 marks, and the restriction is confined to religious corporations. —Bavarian AG 8.   In Wurtemberg the limit is 5, 000 marks, and the restriction is confined to religious, charitable, and educational corporations.   The acquisition of land for the purpose of erecting a church does not require permission. —Würtemberg AG 140.

implied powers of acting on behalf of the corporation whom they represent.   In English law such powers are not as a rule defined by any general rules, but vary according to the constitution of the particular corporation; in Germany, on the other hand, certain fixed rules are laid down as to the powers of the primary agents of each class of corporations regulated by general law.   Thus it frequently happens in the case of companies formed under the British Companies Acts that the powers of the directors do not go as far as the powers of the company, and that acts, though *intra vires* of the company, are invalid on the ground that they are *ultra vires* of the directors, and ought therefore to have been confirmed by a general meeting.   In the case of trading corporations formed under German Imperial law this would be impossible, as the law confers general powers on the directors of such undertakings to act on behalf of the company, and it is impossible to restrict such general powers in any way so as to affect third parties. —HGB 231–235; Limited Partnership Act (1892, revised 1898), ss. 35–37; Act relating to Co-operative Societies (1889, revised 1898), ss. 24, 27; Private Insurance Act (1901), s. 34.   In the case of societies incorporated under the provisions of the BGB restrictions affecting third parties may be imposed upon the powers of directors subject to compliance with the prescribed rules as to registration, but in the absence of such registered restrictions the directors of a society of the nature described are entitled to exercise all the powers of the society. —BGB 26, 64, 70.

f.   Classifications of Corporations formed under German Law.

53. A classification of corporations according to the purposes for which they   37
are constituted has been given above (49); it is now proposed to classify German corporations with reference to the several Codes and statutes under which they are formed, excluding, however, corporations formed for purposes of public law.

The BGB deals with incorporated societies (55) and incorporated foundations (57), the HGB with share companies (59) and ' commandite companies' (60), the Limited Partnership Act with limited partnerships (61). Among the separate statutes by which special classes of corporations were created those relating to Colonial Societies (1888, revised 1899), Co-operative Societies, and friendly societies (1876, 1884) are the most important; the corporations formed for the purposes of compulsory insurance against accidents (consolidated 1900), sickness (1882 – 1900), and old age (consolidated 1899), and the mutualinsurance societies (1901) also deserve special mention. The rules as to the incorporation and regulation of forestry associations are left to State legislation. — EG 83. [1]

The practice followed in England, according to which certain classes of trading corporations (railway companies, canal companies, &c.) are always constituted by special Act does not exist in Germany. Railways and similar undertakings (if carried on by private enterprise) are always owned by share companies formed in accordance with the provisions of the HGB. [2]

2. RULES RELATING TO PARTICULAR CLASSES OF CORPORATIONS

a. Incorporated Societies.

aa. *Mode of Incorporation.*

54. The BGB refers to two classes of incorporated societies: those established for economic purposes, and those established for other purposes. The expression 'economic purpose' does not necessarily imply that the object must include the acquisition of pecuniary profits. Any society having for its object the production or purchase, or storage, or sale of goods or produce of any sort, or the lending or borrowing of money, is deemed to have an 'economic purpose' though no profits are earned and the business is only carried on for the convenience of the members.

A society established for any economic purpose not coming under the provisions of the HGB or of one of the numerous other statutes quoted above (53) is incorporated by charter granted by the State in the territory of which its principal office (seat) is situated. —BGB 22. The conditions upon which such a charter may be granted depend upon State law, but the constitution of a society incorporated by charter is, in the absence of any express enactment of State law to the contrary, regulated by the provisions of the BGB. —EG 82.

A society formed for non-economic purposes, if consisting of not less than seven members, may be incorporated by registration in the prescribed manner. The application for registration must be accompanied by a copy of the articles (which must state the objects of the society, and the regulations as to the

---

1   As to societies in Bavaria and Saxony existing on the 1st of January, 1900, see EG 165, 166.

2   State legislation may provide that an ecclesiastical or religious association cannot be incorporated except by special Act. —EG 84.

admission and registration of members, as to members' contributions, if any, as to the constitution of the directorate, and as to general meetings) and by copies of the documents relating to the appointment of the directors. —BGB 21, 56–59. It must be addressed to the competent Local Court [1], which is bound to allow the registration of the society if the prescribed requirements are complied with, unless an objection is raised by the administration authorities on the ground of the society belonging to a prohibited class of associations, or having been formed for any political, social-political, or religious purpose.   The final decision on the validity of any such objection is left to the Administrative Courts [2].   After registration the words 'registered society' (*eingetragener Verein*) are added to the name of society.   The entry in the register must specify the name and principal place of business of the society, the date of the articles, the names of the directors, and any restrictions that may be imposed on their powers, and must be published in the local official gazette. —BGB 55, 60–66.

A society not having its principal place of business within the German Empire may, in the absence of any Imperial enactment giving other directions as to the particular class of societies to which it belongs, be incorporated by a resolution of the Federal Council. —BGB 23.

bb.   *Constitution of Incorporated Societies.*

55. Incorporated societies, whether registered or incorporated by charter, must have a directorate (*Vorstand*) consisting of one or more persons who, in the absence of any express restriction, have power to act on behalf of the society in all judicial proceedings and in all other affairs. [3]   These powers may be restricted by the articles so as to affect third parties, but in the case of a registered society a third party is not deemed to have notice of any such restriction, unless an entry relating thereto is made upon the register, and unless he is, or by the application of proper care would have been, cognizant of such entry. —BGB 26, 70.   In the

---

[1]   The Local Courts are courts of first instance in minor matters and also act in all matters relating to the commercial registers and land registers and as Guardianship Courts (451) , and generally as Probate Courts (468).

[2]   The Administrative Courts are entirely distinct from the other Courts, and there is a considerable variety as to their constitution in the different States.

[3]   An incorporated society is responsible for all damage inflicted upon any person by a director or any other properly constituted agent through any act done in the execution of his official duties, if the act is one which in itself gives rise to a claim for compensation. —BGB 31.   As to the passing of resolutions where there are several directors, and as to the appointment of substitutes and special agents, see BGB 28–30.

absence of any provision in the articles to the contrary, the appointment of a director may at any time be revoked, and the revocation is effective notwithstanding a contractual stipulation excluding the right; the disregard of such a stipulation would make the society liable to damages. The articles may make the dismissal of a director dependent on the existence of a cogent reason (*e. g.* gross neglect of duty or incompetence). —BGB 27, 40.

In the case of a registered society any change in the constitution of the directorate must be notified by entry on the register. —BGB 67, 68.

Certain rules, partly imperative and partly capable of modification by the articles, are laid down as to alterations in the articles, members' rights, general meetings, &c. —BGB 32–40. In the case of registered societies alterations in the articles are without effect until they are recorded on the register. —BGB 71.

40

The directors of a registered society are bound to deliver a list of members to the registering authority whenever required to do so. —BGB 72.

cc. *Dissolution of Incorporated Societies.*

56. The corporate rights of an incorporated society may come to an end either by reason of the society's bankruptcy (BGB 42, 75), or by virtue of an order of the competent Court, made in any of the following events:

(*a*) In the event of the public welfare being endangered through an unlawful resolution of a general meeting, or through unlawful conduct on the part of the directors;

(*b*) in the event of a society formed for a non-economic object beginning to pursue any economic object;

(*c*) in the event of a society formed for any object unconnected with politics, social politics, or religion beginning to pursue any political, social political, or religious object;

(*d*) in the event of any society incorporated by charter pursuing any object not authorized by the articles sanctioned by such charter;

(*e*) in the event of the number of the members of a registered society being reduced below three. —BGB 43, 73.

The dissolution of a registered society may also be resolved upon by at least three-fourths of the members present at a general meeting, or by such other majority as the articles may provide in that behalf. —BGB 41.

On the dissolution of a society formed exclusively for the benefit of its members, its property is, in the absence of any other direction in the articles, divided among the members for the time being in equal shares; on the dissolution of any society not formed exclusively for the benefit of its members the property is, in the absence of any other direction in the articles, taken over by the treasury authorities of the State in which such society has its principal establishment, who as far as practicable must apply it in a manner corresponding to the objects for which the society was formed. —BGB 45, 46. [1]

In any case in which the corporate property does not go to the treasury   41 authorities the liquidation is carried on in accordance with rules laid down by BGB 47–53, 74, 76, which include the necessary safeguards as to publicity and creditors' rights.

b.   Incorporated Foundations.

57. A person wishing to devote a fund to the furtherance of any particular purpose, may, of course, form a society consisting of seven or more members for the purpose of administering such fund, and such society, if the purpose is a lawful one, and no objection is raised on the ground of its political, social-political, or religious tendency, can be incorporated by registration under the provisions described above (54).   The BGB, however, provides another expedient, by means of which the same object can be carried out in a manner which in some cases may appear more convenient.   Corporate rights may be obtained for the fund itself, subject to the approval of the act of foundation by the public authorities of the State in which the principal place of business is to be situate; if the principal place of business is to be outside of the German Empire the act of foundation must be sanctioned by the Federal Council. —BGB 80.   The foundation (*Stiftung*) may be constituted by a written act of foundation during the founder's lifetime or by testamentary disposition. —BGB 81.   The constitution of an incorporated foundation, in so far as it is not regulated by State law or Imperial law, depends on the terms of the act of foundation (BGB 85), but in any case there must be a directorate with powers of agency.   Such powers may, however, be restricted by the act of foundation in the same way as the powers of the directors of an incorporated society may be restricted by the articles.   The corporate rights of an incorporated foundation cease in the event of the bankruptcy of the foundation. — BGB 86.   If it has become impossible to carry out the original objects of the

---

[1]   State law may provide for another destination. —EG 85.

foundation, or if the pursuance of any such object endangers the public welfare, the competent authority appointed in that behalf by State legislation may, after hearing the directors, alter the constitution of the foundation, or order its

42 dissolution.   In the case of the objects of the foundation being modified, the founder's intention must as far as practicable be taken into consideration. —BGB 87.   In the event of the dissolution of the foundation the corporate property becomes vested in the persons named in the act of foundation, and the winding-up is, as far as practicable, carried out in accordance with the rules prescribed for the liquidation of incorporated societies. —BGB 88.

c.   Trading Corporations governed by the HGB and other Statutes.

aa.   General Observations.

58. According to British law every association consisting of more than ten persons formed for the purpose of carrying on the business of banking, and every association consisting of more than twenty persons formed for the purpose of carrying on any other business having for its object the acquisition of gain, not formed by charter, or special act, or under any general act, must be registered as a corporate body under the Companies Acts (Comp. Act 1862, s. 4).   No similar general rule exists in German law.   The only enactments which prescribe a fixed form of association for the purpose of carrying on a particular trade are: (1) The Private Insurance Act of 1901, by virtue of which certain kinds of insurance business must be carried on by share companies registered under the HGB, or by mutual assurance societies incorporated by order of the supervising insurance authority created by that statute; (2) the Mortgage Bank Act of 1899, which provides that only such share companies, or commandite companies registered under the HGB, as are authorized by the Federal Council may carry on the business of a mortgage bank, and that such business cannot be carried on by any other partnership, company or society, or by any single trader.   Subject to these exceptions, every kind of business can be carried on by single individuals, or by any number of individuals associated together as a private partnership, or as an unincorporated society (64), or in any other form of association.   The more important commercial undertakings, if not in the hands of public authorities, are,

43 as a general rule, carried on by trading corporations, among which share companies, commandite companies, and limited partnerships are the most important.

The doctrine known in England as the doctrine of *ultra vires* has no application in the case of any German trading corporation.   According to British law any transaction entered into by an incorporated company, for any object not included in the objects mentioned in the memorandum of association, is void on the ground of being *ultra vires* of the corporation.   In Germany no transaction entered upon by one of the primary agents of a trading corporation formed under the HGB (59, 60), or the Limited Partnership Act (61), is invalid on the ground that it is outside of the scope of the corporation's usual business, or of the objects for which the corporation was created.   If an English company, established for the purpose of trading in colonial produce, undertook the construction of a bridge, or of a flying machine, the contract would be invalid, but a similar contract entered upon on behalf of a similar German company by one of its primary agents would be binding on the company if otherwise in order.

bb. Share Companies.

59. A share company (*Aktiengesellschaft*) is incorporated by registration in the mercantile register (HGB 200, 210) on a written application signed by the promoters and the members of the directorate and supervising board.   The following conditions must have been complied with:

(1) There must be at least five shareholders. —HGB 182;

(2) the whole of the authorized capital must have been subscribed for, and 25 per cent. of the nominal amount of the shares issued for payment in cash must have been paid. —HGB 188 (1), 189 (1), 195 (3);

(3) a memorandum of association must have been executed giving particulars as to the trade name and principal place of business of the company, as to its objects, as to the amount of the capital and of each share, as to the composition and mode of appointment of the directorate, and as to the mode of convening general meetings and issuing public notices.   In the event of any individual shareholders being entitled to any special advantages, and in the event of shares being issued for any consideration other than cash payment, particulars as to these subjects must be added to the memorandum, which must also contain   44 details as to the promotion expenses if any such expenses have been incurred. —HGB 182–186.

The application for registration must be accompanied by certain documents proving that the above-mentioned requirements have been complied with, and giving information on certain other matters connected with the promotion of the company. —HGB 195 (2).

The nominal amount of any individual share may not, as a rule, be less than 1, 000 marks; but shares registered in the names of shareholders and not transferable without the consent of the company may be of smaller amount, 200 marks being the minimum. In the case of undertakings intended to assist certain specified kinds of public objects, the Federal Council may give its consent to the issue of shares of any amount not being less than 200 marks. —HGB 180.

The liability of a shareholder is limited to the nominal amount of his shares and any premium payable on their issue. —HGB 211. A directorate (*Vorstand*) consisting of one or more directors, who either severally or jointly have power to act on behalf of the company (any restriction on such powers not being operative as between them and third parties), must be appointed. The provisions as to the dismissal of directors, and the effect of changes in the directorate as regards third parties, are similar to those mentioned with reference to the directors of registered incorporated societies (55). —HGB 231, 234, 15.

In addition to the directorate a share company must have a ' board of supervision' (*Aufsichtsrat*), consisting of at least three members who control the directorate, but are not empowered to act on behalf of the company except in connexion with transactions or legal proceedings between the company and the directors. —HGB 243–248.

Rules are laid down as to the holding of general meetings; the modification of the memorandum of association; the keeping and auditing of accounts; the responsibility of the directors and the members of the board of supervision; the events in which liquidation or bankruptcy proceedings must be resorted to, and the mode of liquidation.

45 The more important facts relating to a company's affairs have to be registered from time to time in the mercantile register and advertised in certain public journals, the names of which must be mentioned in the first entry on the register. —HGB 235–242, 248–311.

cc. Commandite Companies.

60. A share company *en commandite* (*Kommanditgesellschaft auf Aktien*) is an association between shareholders liable for the amount of their shares in the ordinary way and partners personally liable to an unlimited extent for the debts of the company, like the partners of an ordinary mercantile partnership (68). The partners who are personally liable (*Persönlich haftender Gesellschafter*) have powers similar to the powers of the directors of an ordinary share company (59).

Subject to the slight modifications necessary by the introduction of partners with personal liability, the rules as to the registration, constitution, and liquidation of a share company *en commandite* are the same as those relating to an ordinary share company. —HGB 320–334.

Commandite companies of this kind are not very frequent in Germany; in the U. K. the provisions of the Companies Act 1867, ss. 4–8, which were intended to give facilities for the creation of similar companies, have never been utilized.

dd.   Limited Partnerships.

61. The elaborate provisions regulating the formation and registration of German share companies are too cumbrous and circumstantial to suit the particular objects of associations which have only a small number of shareholders selected from a limited circle.   Such associations are in this country called ' private companies', and may easily be brought within the elastic framework of the Companies Acts.   The gap left open by German law was filled by the Limited Partnership Act 1892 (of which the amended text, enacted in 1898, is now in force), by which two or more persons were enabled to form a partnership with limited liability, and endowed with corporate rights without being required to comply with the complicated formalities prescribed in the case of public share companies. —LPA. 1–4.

In order to avoid the utilization of these facilities for the object of evading the rules as to the formation of share companies, the Act contains provisions which prevent its application to purposes other than those for which it was intended. The capital of the partnership is not divided into shares of a fixed amount, but each partner's contribution, whatever it may be, forms his share, which cannot be subdivided without the consent of the partnership.   It may, however, be provided by the articles that the consent of the partnership shall not be required for the sale of part of a share by one partner to another, or for the subdivision of a share among a partner's 'heirs' (468). —LPA 17.

A partner's share cannot be transferred except by public act (97)—LPA 15 (3)—and the transferor remains liable for a period of five years from the date of the transfer for the amount remaining unpaid on the share transferred by him. — LPA 15.   These and other similar provisions hampering the dealing in shares are sufficient to prevent the use of this form of partnership in the case of any undertaking intended to have a large and fluctuating body of shareholders.

The capital of a limited partnership must amount to at least 20,000 marks—

LPA 5 (1)—and one-fourth part of so much of the capital, as is to be contributed by cash payment, must be paid up before the partnership is registered. —LPA 7 (2). One or more managers (*Geschäftsführer*)—LPA 6—whose powers cannot be restricted so as to affect third parties, must be appointed before registration. — LPA 35, 36. The application for registration must be accompanied by: (1) a copy of the articles which must be signed by all the partners in person or by attorney; (2) all documents appointing the manager or managers; (3) a list of the partners with the amounts of their respective contributions; (4) in the event of the undertaking being one of a nature requiring government permission, the document by which permission is granted must be produced. The applicants must state that the required payment in cash, and the transfer of property contributed in lieu of cash, have been duly effected. —LPA 7 (1), 8, 9, 10. By the effect of the registration the limited partnership becomes a corporate body. — LPA 11. The articles may provide that the partnership may make calls beyond the amount of the capital originally fixed. —LPA 26. If the amount of such calls is not limited by the articles, a partner after having paid the full amount of his original contribution, may clear himself of further liability by placing his share at the disposal of the partnership in full discharge and satisfaction of all further calls. —LPA 27. Repayments of capital during the continuance of the partnership are forbidden. —LPA 30 (1).

A limited partnership may have a board of supervision like a share company, but this is not imperative, and the provisions of the HGB relating to the board of supervision of a public company are applicable in so far only as the articles do not provide otherwise. —LPA 52.

The annual publication of the balance sheet and profit and loss account required in the case of share company—HGB 265—is unnecessary in the case of a limited partnership not carrying on banking business; a limited partnership carrying on banking business, though required to publish yearly balance sheets, is not required to publish any profit and loss account. —LPA 41 (3).

The provisions about partners' meetings, alteration of the articles, liquidation, and other internal matters—LPA 45–51, 53–84—do not call for any more detailed examination.

ee.   Co-operative Societies.

62. A co-operative society (*Erwerbs- und Wirtschaftsgenossenschaft*) may be formed by not less than seven members under the Co-operative Societies Act of 1889 (as amended by the Acts of 1896 and 1898) for one or more of the following purposes: (1) loans and advances to members; (2) combined purchases of raw materials; (3) combined selling of agricultural produce or manufactured goods; (4) combined production and sale of goods; (5) combined purchase of articles of consumption; (6) combined acquisition of agricultural machinery for the purpose of being used by the members on account of the association; (7) the erection and purchase of cheap dwellings.   A society of this nature by complying with certain prescribed regulations as to registration and otherwise may acquire corporate rights.   The liability of the members may be limited to a fixed amount or may be unlimited. —CSA 2, 4.   A directorate must be appointed composed of at least   48 two members whose power to act on behalf of the society cannot be restricted so as to affect third parties—CSA 24-28; the appointment of a board of supervision consisting of at least three members, with powers similar to the powers of the corresponding board of a share company, is also required. —CSA 36-41.   One-tenth part of the nominal amount of a member's share must be paid up by instalments, of which the dates must be fixed before the registration of the society; the amounts due to a member in respect of his share of profits are, in the absence of a provision to the contrary, credited to such member as they accrue, in part satisfaction of his liability on his shares until the nominal amount is made up.   A member withdrawing from the society, or excluded from it on one of the grounds justifying his exclusion, is entitled to the payment of the amount credited on his share—CSA 7, 17, 73—but the dissolution of the society within six months from the date of the withdrawal or exclusion prevents the operation of such withdrawal or exclusion. —CSA 75.   Subject to compliance with certain conditions and such restrictions as may be laid down by the articles, the share of a member may be transferred to another person, but in the event of the society being dissolved within six months from the date of the transfer and of such dissolution resulting in bankruptcy proceedings, the transferor remains liable as surety for the transferee. —CSA 76.   The death of a member has the same effect as his withdrawal. —CSA 77.

A co-operative society is not authorized to deal with any person not being a member of the society except in so far as such dealings are authorized by the articles; the loans of loan societies and the sales of co-operative consumers' societies must in any case be confined to members. —CSA 8.

The constitution of a German co-operative society in some respects resembles the constitution of a building society formed under the English Building Societies

Act of 1874.

ff. Mutual Insurance Societies.

63. The concession enabling a mutual insurance society (*Versicherungsverein auf Gegenseitigkeit*) to carry on business has the effect of incorporating such society. —PIA 15. The articles must provide for the creation of a ' foundation fund ' (*Gründungsfonds*) which, after payment thereout of the preliminary expenses, serves as a guarantee fund for the benefit of the insured and for the provision of the working expenses. The supervising insurance authority (58) may, if satisfied that sufficient security is provided in other ways, grant dispensation from this requirement. —PIA 22–27.

A directorate and a board of supervision with powers and duties similar to those of the directorate and board of supervision of a share company (59) must be appointed.

A mutual insurance society, which does not carry on business within narrow local or personal limits, must be registered in the Commercial Register, and publish certain details as to its formation and the contents of its articles. —PIA 16, 30–33, 53. A person who is not insured by the society cannot become a member, and, in the absence of a contrary provision in the articles, a member who ceases to be insured by the society forfeits his membership. The articles of a society may authorize it to insure persons other than members in consideration of the payment of fixed premiums. —PIA 20, 21. The functions which, in the case of a share company, are exercised by the general meeting of shareholders may be wholly or partly delegated to a members' committee, constituted in such manner as the articles may provide. —PIA 29, 36. In the event of bankruptcy the claims of the parties entitled to the repayment of the foundation fund rank after the claims arising under insurance contracts, and the claims of the persons who then are, or during the year preceding the date of bankruptcy were, members of the society rank after the claims of outsiders. —PIA 51.

D.   UNINCORPORATED SOCIETIES AND PARTNERSHIPS

a.   Unincorporated Societies.

64. There is no general prohibition against the formation of unincorporated societies, however large, for trading or other purposes, and such societies are expressly recognized by the BGB and the CPO.

Any person purporting to act on behalf of an unincorporated society (not   50
being a partnership) is personally liable as between himself and the party with
whom the business is transacted; several persons purporting to act together on
behalf of any such association are liable jointly and severally. —BGB 54.   This
liability runs concurrently with the liability of the society, or of its members, if
the particular act was authorized.

An unincorporated society cannot sue, but it can be sued in the same manner
as an incorporated society—CPO 50—and a judgment obtained in an action
against an unincorporated society may be enforced against the property of such
society. —CPO 735.   In all other respects an unincorporated society (*nicht
rechtsfähiger Verein*) is governed by the same rules as a non-mercantile partnership.
—BGB 54.

The distinction between an unincorporated society and a partnership consists
in the fact that as regards its internal organization an unincorporated society like
an incorporated society has a large and fluctuating body of members, and is
represented in all outward acts by a small representative body (committee,
council, managing board, &c.), while a partnership is, as a general rule,
formed by a small number of persons acting together for a common purpose, one
or more or each of the partners having power to act for the partnership.   Where it
appears from the articles of association that an association has the former
characteristics, it is treated as an unincorporated society; where this is not shown
by the articles, or where no articles exist, it is treated as a partnership.

b.   Partnerships.

aa.   *Classification.*

65. A partnership may be: (1) a non-mercantile partnership; (2) a mercantile
partnership with unlimited liability for all the partners (*offene Handelsgesellschaft*);
(3) a commandite partnership (*Kommanditgesellschaft*) , with limited liability for
one or more of the partners, and unlimited liability for the other partner or
partners.   The rules relating to non-mercantile partnerships are laid down by the
BGB; mercantile partnerships and commandite partnerships are governed by the
same rules except in so far as the HGB contains any special provisions relating to
them. —HGB 105 (2).

bb.   Non-mercantile Partnership.

(1)   *How distinguished from Mercantile Partnership.*

51   **66.** In England no distinction is drawn between mercantile and non-mercantile partnerships, but a partnership in the legal sense presupposes a ' business ' carried on ' with a view to profit ' (Partnership Act 1890, s. 1 (1)).   An English partnership may exist without a firm name, and be established for a merely temporary purpose.   In Germany a *mercantile* partnership is characterized by the following facts: the partnership must be formed for the purpose of carrying on ' mercantile trade ' (36) under a firm name; in the case of a non-mercantile partnership the common purpose which the partners agree to further by their joint efforts is not required to be in the nature of a ' business ' or entered upon ' with a view to profit ' , and may be of a merely temporary character and the use of a firm name is not permitted. —HGB 105; BGB 705.

Non-mercantile partnerships may thus belong to one of the following three classes: (1) associations of artisans and small traders not being ' mercantile traders ' (36); (2) associations of persons combining funds for a single joint transaction with a view to profit (*Gelegenheitsgesellschaft*, ' joint adventure ' in Scots law); such associations are generally called ' syndicates '; (3) associations of persons combining funds for a common enterprise, but not with a view to profit.   Classes (1) and (2) would be, but class (3) would not be, termed partnerships under British law (see Partnership Act 1890, s. 1 (1)).

A non-mercantile partnership has the following special characteristics: (1) it has no right to have a firm name—HGB 4; (2) the property contributed by the partners is not—as in the case of a mercantile partnership—deemed to belong to the partnership as such, but is vested in the partners as co-owners in the stricter sense (*Gesamthänder*) (304).   —HGB 124; BGB 718; (3) in a non-mercantile partnership a partner as such has not—as in the case of a mercantile partnership— an implied authority to act on behalf of the partnership. —BGB 705, 715; HGB 125, 15; (4) a non-mercantile partnership is not entitled to grant powers of procuration to a manager or clerk in the manner in which this may be done by a 52   mercantile partnership. —HGB 4, 49, 50, 118; (5) a non-mercantile partnership is not bound to keep books of account in the manner required in the case of mercantile traders and mercantile partnerships. —HGB 4, 38–47.

(2)   *Other characteristics.*

67. A non-mercantile partnership is formed by an agreement between the parties (not required to be in writing or in any other prescribed form), by which they mutually undertake to further the attainment of a common object, in the manner determined by such agreement, and more particularly to furnish the agreed contributions to the common fund. —BGB 705.

The partners can agree that the business of the partnership is to be carried on by one or more of them, and the partner or partners so authorized are, in the absence of evidence to the contrary, assumed to have power to act for the other partner or partners in all matters relating to the partnership. —BGB 709, 714. As mentioned above (66) the partnership property is held by the partners as co-owners in the stricter sense (*Gesamthänder*), with the effect that no partner can alienate his share or demand a partition before the dissolution of the partnership. —BGB 718, 719.   As to the liability of the partners for the partnership debts, see 182.

Any judgment creditor of a partner may demand the dissolution of the partnership, which is also brought about by the bankruptcy of a partner. —BGB 725, 728.   The partnership is also dissolved:

(a) by effluxion of the partnership term;

(b) where no time has been fixed for the duration of the partnership, or where the partnership term has been fixed for the life of a partner, by notice communicated by one partner to the other partners. —BGB 723, 724;

(c) by notice given before the effluxion of the partnership term to a partner on the ground that he has by a wilful or grossly negligent act or omission committed a breach of the duties imposed upon him by the partnership agreement, or that he has become incapable of performing such duties, or on any other similar cogent ground. —BGB 723;

(d) by the attainment of the special object for which the partnership was 53 formed, or by the fact that such attainment has become impossible. —BGB 726;

(e) by the death of a partner (unless the agreement provides other wise). — BGB 727 (1).

Bankruptcy proceedings cannot be taken against a non-mercantile partnership.

In the case of dissolution, the partnership property must, in the first instance, be applied for the payment of the partnership debts, and any surplus or deficiency is divided among the partners *pro rata* of their shares.   In the event of the insolvency of any partner the other partners have to make up the deficiencies. —BGB 733–735.   The partnership cannot be sued as such, and in order to enforce any judgment against the partnership property, a judgment must be obtained against all the partners jointly. —CPO 736.

cc. *Mercantile Partnerships.*

(1) *General characteristics.*

68. A partnership having for its object the carrying on of a mercantile trade (36) under a firm name is a mercantile partnership (*offene Handelsgesellschaft*), if the liability of every partner is unrestricted. —HGB 105.

(2) *Quasi-corporate character of a mercantile partnership.*

A mercantile partnership is not under German law deemed to be a corporate body, but it has some of the characteristics of a corporation; it may be registered as owner or incumbrancer of any immovable in the firm name and may sue and be sued in that name. [1]—HGB 124.

(3) *Partners' implied power of agency.*

The implied power of agency of a partner in a mercantile firm referred to above (66) which enables him to act on behalf of the firm in any judicial proceedings and in any other transactions (whether within or without the scope of the partnership business) may be excluded by the partnership agreement or made exercisable subject to the concurrence of any clerk holding powers of procuration; it may also be withdrawn by order of a competent Court on the ground of gross breach of duty, incompleteness, or some other cogent reason, but any such restriction does not affect third parties, unless it is duly registered in accordance with the requirements as to publicity mentioned below, sub (5). —HGB 114, 117, 125, 126.

(4) *Personal liability of partners.*

The creditors of the partnership, besides having a claim against the partnership property, are also entitled to proceed against the partners or any of them, all the partners being jointly and severally liable for the partnership debts. —HGB 128.

According to English law the liability of partners is only a joint liability, but after the death of a partner his estate is severally liable, while in Scotland the law is the same as in Germany—see Partnership Act 1890, s. 9.

---

1 Under Scotch law a partnership firm is deemed a ' legal person ' —Partnership Act 1890, s. 4 (2).

(5) *Publicity as to constitution of mercantile partnership.*

The utmost publicity as to the constitution of a mercantile partnership is secured in Germany by the provisions as to the registration in the Commercial Register of the district in which the partnership business is carried on: (1) of the names of the partners on the formation of the partnership; (2) of the name of any new partner on his admission; (3) of the withdrawal or death of a partner and of the dissolution of the partnership; (4) of any restriction affecting the power of agency of any partner. —HGB 106, 107, 125, 143.   The observance of these rules is secured by the provision that a person who ought to have registered a fact cannot, as between himself and another person excusably ignorant of such fact, avail himself of such fact, unless the appropriate entry relating thereto was made on the register. —HGB 15.

(6) *Relations of partners inter se.*

The statutory rules regulating the relations of the partners *inter se* may be modified by the partnership articles. —HGB 109, 110-122.   See also *post*, 256–64.

(7) *Dissolution of partnership and bankruptcy.*

The rules as to the grounds for the dissolution of the partnership are mainly 55
the same as those mentioned above in the case of non-mercantile partnerships, [1] but there are certain differences; thus the attainment of the object of the partnership cannot be a ground of dissolution, because in the case of a mercantile partnership the object must of necessity be of a continuous nature; again, the right of a partner to determine the partnership by notice on the ground of the misconduct of another partner, or some other similar ground, is not recognized in the case of a mercantile partnership; an order of the Court to dissolve the partnership may however be obtained on any ground which entitle a partner in a non-mercantile partnership to determine the partnership by notice.   A mercantile partnership is dissolved by the bankruptcy of the firm. —HGB 131-133.   In some of the events specified as grounds of dissolution the partnership may (subject to compliance with certain specified requirements as to the payment out of the share of the partner concerned) be continued by the remaining partners. —HGB 138-141.   The

---

[1]   The right of a private creditor of a partner to bring about the dissolution of the partnership is subject to the special requirements mentioned in HGB 135.

rules as to the administration of the partnership property in the case of the dissolution are the same as in the case of a non-mercantile partnership.   As to the manner in which the liquidation is carried out, see HGB 145–158.

dd.   Commandite Partnership.

69. A partnership having for its object the carrying on of mercantile trade under a firm name is a commandite partnership if the liability of one or more of the partners, as between such partner or partners and the partnership creditors, is limited to the amount of a fixed contribution, whilst the liability of the other partners or partner is unlimited. —HGB 161.   A partner liable for a fixed amount only is called *Kommanditist* and a partner liable to an unlimited extent is called *persönlich haftender Gesellschafter*.   A commandite partner must be entered as such on the register together with the amount of his contribution; such a partner is not authorized to act on behalf of the partnership.   He is liable to the partnership creditors to the extent of the uncalled part of his registered contribution.   A reduction of the commandite contribution does not affect parties without notice, unless it has been duly registered; on the other hand a creditor of the partnership cannot avail himself of any agreed increase, unless such increase has been registered or unless a properly authenticated notification relating to such increase has been communicated to him.   The death of a commandite partner does not cause the partnership to be dissolved. —HGB 161–177.

ee.   Dormant Partnership.

70. A commandite partnership must be distinguished from the so-called 'dormant partnership' (*stille Gesellschaft*) subsisting between a mercantile trader or a mercantile partnership and a person who makes a contribution to the capital of such trader or partnership in return for a share in the profits, without being a partner in the proper sense of the word.   A dormant partner is not required to be registered in the mercantile register, and in the event of the bankruptcy of the person or partnership to whose capital he has made a contribution is entitled to prove for the amount of such contribution, subject of course to the deduction of his share (if any) in the losses. —HGB 341.   If the capital of the dormant partner was partly or wholly withdrawn during the year preceding the bankruptcy, or if during such time it was agreed that the whole or any part of his share in any realized loss should not be debited to him, the trustee in bankruptcy is entitled to ask for restitution, unless the bankruptcy arose in consequence of any event which happened after such withdrawal or agreement.   The relation which exists

56

between a dormant partner and a mercantile trader or mercantile partnership is not dissolved by the death of the former. —HGB 339 (2).

The dormant partnership of German law has some resemblance to the relation existing, according to British law, between a person advancing money to a trader and receiving a share in the profits in lieu of interest (see Partnership Act 1890, s. 2 (*d*)).   There are, however, two differences which deserve notice: (1) according to British law the person advancing money in the manner referred to is considered a full partner unless there is a contract *in writing* showing the true relation between the parties, while, according to German law, the contract between the dormant partner and the person or persons carrying on business is not required to be in writing; (2) according to British law the person occupying the position of the 'dormant partner' is postponed to other creditors in the event of the bankruptcy of the person or persons to whom money has been advanced (*ibid.* s. 3), while this is not the case according to German law.

57

CHAPTER II
THINGS

1. DEFINITION

58   **71.** IN the first chapter we have dealt with persons who are, according to German terminology, the subjects of rights. The objects to which rights relate may either be things (*Sachen*) or may themselves be in the nature of rights. The legal definition of a 'thing' must start from the popular conception, and disregard the refinements of metaphysics as well as those of physical science. The senses do not perceive things, but only experience certain sensations associated together, and assumed to be caused by a unit existing independently of the consciousness of the person whose senses are affected, which unit is called a 'thing'. The popular conception as to what deserves this name is consistent enough to be made the basis of legal rules. In English law a difficulty arises, not so much from a dissociation of legal rules from popular conceptions, as from the fact that the expression 'thing' has received an extended use by a fiction of law, which causes it to include not only the 'things' of popular usage which are called 'chattels', or 'things in possession', but also certain rights called 'things in action'.

The definition contained in BGB 90 which declares that only *corporal* objects are things avoids the peculiar difficulty of English law; but the term '*corporal* objects' —even leaving aside the metaphysical questions to which reference has been made is in itself ambiguous. Some German writers declare that only such things are *corporal* objects as are tangible and occupy space, whilst others are of opinion that anything which can be perceived by its physical effects and can form the object of rights is a *corporal* object. This would include energy of all sorts, such as water power, electricity, heat, &c. Having regard to the necessity of taking the popular conceptions as a basis the first-mentioned view appears more satisfactory.

59   The next difficulty arises as to the limitation of the unit described as a thing.

Here again the scientific conception of each so-called unit as an agglomeration of other units (atoms, ions, vortices, &c.) must be disregarded, and the popular conception resorted to.   Any object which loses its essential qualities by sub-division may be looked upon as a thing.   In the case of animals, whether living or dead, this is clear at first sight.   A building is another example.   The question is not so simple, however, when liquids, or gases, or very loosely aggregated solids (such as sand, wheat, and other grain, tea, pounded sugar, tobacco, &c.) are considered.   In such cases the aggregate for the time being enclosed in one receptacle (bottle, barrel, bag, &c.) is considered a thing. Aggregates composed of distinct units (such as flocks of sheep, art collections, &c.) are not considered things according to German terminology, there being a special technical term, ' aggregate of things ' (*Sacheninbegriff*), used in their case. Sometimes it is difficult to say whether a given object is to be looked at as an aggregate or as a unit, and an object may be an aggregate for one purpose and a unit for another; thus, for instance, a pack of cards loses its essential qualities by sub-division, and is therefore a thing as a collective whole, but each individual card can also be looked upon as a thing.   In some cases the delimitation of a unit, considered as a thing in the eye of the law, depends upon purely arbitrary considerations.   Thus, in Germany, a parcel of land, being a unit for registration purposes, is looked upon as an individual thing, but such a unit may be sub-divided in the registry, in which case each part becomes a thing, or it may be added to another unit, in which case the two united parcels form one thing.

In Roman law certain things were described as *res extra commercium*, being things which could not be the objects of private rights.   In modern law no such things exist.   There are material substances which cannot be the objects of rights, but they are not things within the meaning which has been explained.   The atmospheric air in which we live cannot be the subject of rights, but a bottle of atmospheric air, like a bottle of carbonic acid, or any other gas, can be the object of rights.   The fact that the sale or purchase of certain things is prohibited or restricted does not, according to modern notions, place them *extra commercium*. The sale of a church or a human corpse is, as a general rule prohibited, but both may be objects of rights, and are therefore ' things ' .   A living human being is a ' thing ' in countries where slavery is a legal institution, but in Christian countries human beings have ceased to be the objects of rights, and therefore have ceased to be things.   A parent or guardian may have the right to the custody of a child, but this does not mean that the child is an object of rights, but rather that the parent or guardian may exercise some of the rights of which the child is the *subject*.

For purposes of convenient description things are classified according to several modes of classification; of these a list will be given.   The mode of describing the component parts of things, and the objects derived from things also requires separate statement.   It will also be necessary to refer to certain classes of things which derive their principal importance from the fact that their holder as such is entitled to certain rights which they represent (*e. g.* negotiable instruments).

2.   CLASSIFICATION OF THINGS

a.   Movable and Immovable Things.

72. This distinction, owing to the influence of Germanic ideas, has assumed much greater importance in the BGB than it had in Roman law (12, 13).   It corresponds in a certain measure to the English division between real and personal property, but, according to English law, certain movable objects are classed with real property, and, on the other hand, immovables held for a term of years, however long, are classed with personal property.   The term ' chattel real' used in respect of such immovables, like the term 'thing in action', is a metaphorical expression used in English law which has no counterpart in Continental law.

A thing is called immovable if it cannot be moved without being divided into several units.   In this connexion it must be noticed that, if a house is called a thing, the expression house includes the plot of land on which the house stands; therefore, even if the whole house is bodily removed without being taken to pieces, there is a severance between the building and the land.   It must also be noted that certain things which are in some respects treated like immovables are in reality movables; ships are the most conspicuous instance of this fact.

b.   Things Fungible and Things not Fungible.

73. The *res fungibiles* of Roman law are in German called *vertretbare Sachen*, and are described by the BGB as 'movable things which in ordinary dealings are usually determined by number, measurement, or weight' . —BGB 91 (see Dig. 12. 1. 2, *res quae pondere numero mensura constant*).   The fact that a thing usually determined and dealt with by number, measurement, or weight, is sometimes determined and dealt with specifically, or that a thing usually dealt with specifically is sometimes dealt with by number, measurement, or weight, does not alter its character.   Money is a fungible thing, though a particular coin may be bought, lent, pawned, deposited, or given away.   A literary manuscript is not a fungible thing, though a prolific but unsuccessful author may, as a last resource, sell his manuscript by weight.

c.   Consumable and Non-consumable Things.

74. 'Consumable things' —*verbrauchbare Sachen* (*res quae usu consumuntur*) are defined by the BGB as 'movable things intended to be used or enjoyed by means of being consumed or alienated'. —BGB 92 (1).   The most conspicuous instances of things intended to be used or enjoyed by means of being *consumed* are eatables, fuel, &c. ; the principal instance of things intended to be used by means of being *alienated* are money, bank-notes, dividend warrants, cheques, &c. The essence of the distinction between consumable and non-consumable things is that the consumption or alienation must be the intention of ordinary usage.   Most things are, of course, slowly consumed by use (*consumitur annulus usu*), but things called non-consumable things are intended to be preserved, notwithstanding their use.   Movable things forming part of a stock-in-trade, or other aggregates of things intended to be used by successive alienation of the individual things forming part of it are deemed consumable things. —BGB 92 (2).   For a practical application of the distinction, see 414, sub 3.

3.   COMPONENT PARTS AND ACCESSORIES

a.   Essential and Non-essential Component Parts.

75. Any part of a thing which, on being severed from the other parts, is   62 destroyed or essentially modified or causes the destruction or essential modification of such other parts is called an *essential* component part (*wesentlicher Bestandteil*) of such thing; a component part which can be severed from the thing of which it forms part without producing the consequences which occur on the severance of an essential component part is called a non-essential component part (*unwesentlicher Bestandteil*) of such thing.   The question whether a particular component part is essential or non-essential is not always easy to solve, and frequently depends on varying circumstances.   Thus the component parts of a watch produced in a factory, while it remains in such factory, are not essential parts of the watch, inasmuch as each part can be replaced by another corresponding part, and each part can be used for another corresponding watch, but as soon as the watch is in the hands of a purchaser the watch is useless if one small wheel is taken out, and the small wheel is useless when severed from the watch. Under the first-mentioned circumstances it is a non-essential, under the last-mentioned circumstances an essential part of the watch.

An essential component part of a thing cannot be the object of separate rights. —BGB 93. The consequences of this rule are of a twofold nature: (1) the owner of a thing cannot create a separate real right (308) as to an essential component part of such thing; (2) all separate real rights relating to a thing originally independent are lost as soon as such thing becomes an essential component part of another thing. Any component part, whether essential or not, may, however, be made the object of an obligatory right (79). The owner of a house may let a room belonging to it, but not so as to give the tenant a right available against third parties. The tenant, according to English phraseology, would not acquire an estate in his room, but merely be entitled to damages in the event of his tenancy being interfered with. According to English law an estate in part of a house may be granted.

63

The BGB supplements the definition given above in the following ways:

(1) it enumerates a number of objects which are to be deemed essential component parts, whether otherwise coming within the definition or not (*e. g.* things affixed to the soil). —BGB 94;

(2) rights attached to the ownership of land such as servitudes (352) are deemed component parts of such land though not coming within the definition. — BGB 96;

(3) things attached to land for a temporary purpose are not deemed component parts of the land though otherwise coming within the definition. —BGB 95.

b. Accessories (*Zubehör*).

76. Certain things, without being component parts of another thing, are so closely connected therewith that acts affecting the principal thing (*Hauptsache*) also affect them. Things standing in such a relation to the principal thing are known as *Zubehör* (accessories). A thing does not come within the statutory definition of accessories unless it complies with the following requirements mentioned by BGB 97 (1):

(*a*) it must not be a component part of the principal thing;

(*b*) it must be intended to serve the economic purposes of the principal thing in a permanent manner (*perpetui usus causa*) ;

(*c*) it must be placed in a local position corresponding to such intention;

(*d*) it must be movable (in Roman law immovables might be accessories, in English law the term ' appurtenance ' , which corresponds to ' accessory ' , is applied to immovables exclusively) ;

(*e*) it must be a thing which, in accordance with common usage, is apt to be looked upon as an accessory; the fact that an ' accessory ' is temporarily severed from the principal thing does not alter its quality. —BGB 97 (2).

BGB 98, by way of illustration, gives some instances of things intended to serve the economic purposes of the principal thing in a permanent manner, but such instances are not intended to be exhaustive.   They are: (*a*) in the case of a building serving industrial purposes, the machinery and tools used for such 64 purpose; (*b*) in the case of a farm, the cattle and farm implements and the agricultural products, in so far as they are necessary for the purpose of carrying on farming operations, as well as the whole stock of manure produced on the farm.

In some respects, and for certain purposes, accessories are deemed to be annexed to the principal thing (see, for instance, as to the transfer of ownership, 327; as to charges, 378).

4. FRUITS AND PROFITS

77. The definition of the terms ' fruits ' and ' profits ' is of importance for the purpose of determining questions between a person entitled to the temporary enjoyment of property and the ultimate owner of such property (*e. g.* usufructuary and owner (358) ; husband and wife in a case in which the husband is entitled to the income of the wife's property (414) ; parent and child during the child's minority (447)).

The fruits of a thing consist of the natural products of such thing and such other benefits as are derived from using it in accordance with the purpose for which it is intended; the fruits of a right consist in the income derived from the proper exercise of the right.

The benefits derived from any thing or right by virtue of any contractual or other legal relation to the person entitled to the use of such thing, or to the exercise of such right, are also deemed fruits of such thing. —BGB 99.

The expression ' profits ' includes ' fruits ' , as well as the personal advantage derived from the use of a thing or the exercise of a right. —BGB 100.

The most obvious examples of the fruits of a thing are crops derived from land owned by the cultivator of the land; if the crops are derived from land leased to the cultivator they are the fruits of a right, the lessee, according to German law, having a mere obligatory right, and no estate in the land.   As to minerals obtained by the owner of the land, the question whether they are to be deemed part of the corpus or fruits of the land depends upon the destination of the land; as to minerals obtained by virtue of a right, it is expressly enacted by BGB 99 (2) that component parts of the soil obtained pursuant to a right to obtain such component parts are deemed 'fruits' of such right.   If, therefore, land is owned or leased for mining purposes, or as a quarry, the minerals are the fruits of the land or of the right, being obtained in conformity with the purposes of the ownership or of the lease.   If, on the other hand, the land is owned or leased for agricultural purposes, the minerals taken away from the land are deemed to have been part of the corpus.   In the case of investments in stocks or shares the dividends or interest received at stated intervals are the fruits of rights.   The most obvious instance of benefits derived from a thing by virtue of a contractual relation to a person exercising a right over such thing are the payments of rent received by a landlord from his tenant.

Where fruits consist in periodical money payments, they are, as between persons successively entitled, considered as accruing from day to day, and apportioned in the same way as rent is apportioned in England under the Apportionment Act, 1870.   In all other cases fruits derived from a thing belong to the person entitled to the use of such thing at the time of the severance; whereas income derived from a right belongs to the person exercising such right at the time when it falls due—BGB 101.

There is no rule corresponding to the English rule about emblements.

A person who is under obligation to surrender the fruits received by him while in temporary possession of a thing (e. g. the purchaser of a thing who after being let into possession cancels the sale in consequence of a breach of warranty on the vendor's part (192) ; or a possessor ejected by the true owner (343)) may recover the expense properly incurred in the production of the fruits, in so far as such expense does not exceed the value of the fruits—BGB 102. [1]

5. Things Representing Rights (Negotiable Instruments)

78. Certain things are characterized by the fact that they are mainly intended to be used as physical embodiments of rights; a lawful holder of a thing belonging   66
to this class is, as such, entitled to the right which it embodies, and no other person except such lawful holder is entitled to exercise the right.

The most obvious example of a thing embodying a right is a bank-note, but cheques and bills of exchange, debentures payable to bearer or passing by endorsement, interest coupons payable to bearer, and all other classes of documents coming under the definition of negotiable instruments, belong to the same class.

Most of the documents in question represent obligatory rights (79), but the right to the possession or ownership of the thing which represents the obligation is a real right (308), and is governed by the law of things.   Among the exceptional classes of negotiable instruments which embody real rights, certificates of charge issued to bearer (374) form the most conspicuous instances; the holder of such a certificate is entitled to the rights of an ordinary mortgagee, and may at any time be registered as such if he thinks fit.

A thing originally intended for no other purpose than the embodiment of a right may, by a combination of circumstances, cease to represent such right and become useful for another purpose.   A postage stamp no longer current, though ceasing to represent a right, may yet continue to be the object of legal transactions by reason of its value for collectors.   Even the worthless bearer bonds of defaulting States may be used as wall papers or for other decorative purposes.

Things representing rights must be distinguished from things serving as evidence of the existence of rights, *e. g.* certificates of indebtedness, not being in the nature of negotiable instruments.   The ownership of a thing serving as evidence of a right, like the ownership of a thing representing a right, is vested in the person entitled to the right—BGB 952.

The subject of things representing rights will be further dealt with in connexion with the law of obligations (177).

---

[1]   Periodical outgoings are apportioned in the same way as payments received periodically; outgoings not being of a periodical kind must be paid by the person chargeable with the outgoings at the time when they are payable—BGB 103.

CHAPTER III
RIGHTS

A. SUBSTANTIVE RIGHTS

1. CLASSIFICATION OF RIGHTS

79. ALL systems of law distinguish between a right available against the whole world and a right available against a particular person only.

Rights of the former class are called *jura in rem* by English authors; German jurists call them 'absolute rights' .   An absolute right is either a right relating directly to the person entitled thereto (*Persönlichkeitsrecht*) , *e. g.* the right to good repute, liberty of the person, and freedom from violence—or a right relating to some outside objet—*e. g.* the right to the exclusive occupation of a plot of land. If the object to which an absolute right relates is a tangible object within the German definition of a 'thing' (71) the right is called a 'real right' (*dingliches Recht*) , see 308, but no generally recognized term exists with reference to absolute rights relating to intangible objects—*e. g.* copyright, patent right, &c. — a class of objects unknown to Roman and Germanic law, but steadily growing in importance in all modern systems; the expression 'rights relating to immaterial objects' is used by some writers, and will in the course of this treatise designate the rights in question.

A right *in personam* is, according to the terminology of the BGB, described by the term 'claim' (*Anspruch*)—BGB 194; in legal literature the expression 'obligatory right' (*obligatorisches Recht*) is used in respect of all rights *in personam* not having the distinctive character referred to below.   The relation between the person entitled to an obligatory right and the person against whom such right is available, which was formerly called 'obligation' , is now described as 'obligatory relation' (*Schuldverhältniss*).

The rights arising under family law and under the law of inheritance are partly absolute rights and partly rights *in personam*; some of them are ordinary rights, real or obligatory, and distinguished from other rights merely by the events which create them (*e. g.* birth, legitimation, adoption, marriage, death), or by the peculiar relation between the parties whom they affect (*e. g.* parent and child, guardian and ward, husband and wife); other rights belonging to this category have an entirely distinctive character.   Thus a father's or husband's right of usufruct over an infant child's or a wife's property does not differ from any other right of usufruct, nor does the transfer of ownership brought about by death differ in its effect from the transfer of ownership brought about by act *inter vivos*; but, on the other hand, the personal rights arising as between husband and wife (412), and the rights exercisable over a child's or ward's person by virtue of the parental power (445) or the law of guardianship (462), are rights *sui generis*, which do not exist in other relations.

A distinction, which though familiar to English jurists, is neglected by German writers is that between antecedent and remedial rights.   A remedial right arises in every case in which a recognized antecedent right is violated; the antecedent right, *viz.* the right originally existing, may be either an absolute right or a right *in personam*, but the remedial right must necessarily be a right *in personam*, as it is available only against the particular person by whom the antecedent right was infringed.   The right of a servant to receive his wages is an antecedent right, the right to compensation for non-payment of wages is a remedial right; when we speak of a right arising by virtue of an act-in-the-law we always mean an antecedent right, but when we speak of a right arising in consequence of an unlawful act we mean a remedial right.   A remedial right must be distinguished from the remedy which the law provides for its enforcement.   The rules relating to such remedies belong to the branch of law which, according to English terminology, is called 'adjective law', so as to distinguish it from 'substantive law'.   In the present treatise only such remedies will be discussed as are available without the assistance of the Courts and are specially dealt with by the BGB.

The following restriction is by German law imposed on the exercise of any right to whatever class it may belong: 'The exercise of a right which can have no purpose except the infliction of injury on another is unlawful. ' —BGB 226. This rule is known as the 'prohibition of chicanery' (*Schikaneverbot*), and has been found to be of considerable practical importance.

The classes of rights dealt with by the special parts of the BGB will be discussed in the special parts of this treatise; the following sections refer to such classes of rights only as are dealt with in the general part of the BGB, and to some cognate classes of rights which are dealt with by separate statutes.

2.   Right to Name and Firm Name

a.   General Rule.

80.   According to English law a person may describe himself by any name he thinks fit, both in private life and in business, and may use different names for different purposes, as long as by doing so he does not deceive any other person, or violate any right to which any other is entitled.   German law, on the other hand, does not allow a person to describe himself by any name other than the name acquired by birth—440, sub 1—or in some other lawful manner (order of a competent authority, adoption—428, sub 3—marriage—412—divorce—422, sub 4, &c.)—StGB 360 (8).   The right to a name thus acquired can be asserted in several ways.

b.   Right to Family Name.

A person may assert the right to use his family name

(1) if any other person disputes such right;

(2) if any other person makes an unauthorized use of the name.

In either event an injunction may be obtained restraining the act complained of as well as any repetition of the offence—BGB 12; if the unauthorized use of a name was wilful or due to negligence damages may also be obtained under the general rules as to unlawful acts.

c.   Right to Firm Name.

The name under which business is carried on by a single trader or by a partnership or company must be chosen in accordance with definite rules laid down by HGB 18–25, 29–31 [1] ; a person using an unauthorized firm name may be punished by fine and restrained from the continuance of such unauthorized use

70

---

1   A single trader who starts a new business must use his own family name and at least one Christian name fully written out, and he must not use any indication making it appear that he is trading in partnership with any other person; the firm name of a mercantile partnership must contain the name of at least one of the partners with an indication of the fact that there are other partners, or the names of such partners.   Persons acquiring an existing business may, with the consent of the former owners, continue the use of the old firm name.

on the application of any person aggrieved thereby.   The grievance need not necessarily be founded on the fact that the aggrieved person is himself a trader or a member of a partnership having a firm name identical with or similar to the unauthorized firm name.   The mere fact that the name of a private person is used in violation of the rules in respect of the choice of firm names may give a right of action to such person.   Damages may be recovered on the same grounds as in the case of the unauthorized use of a private name—HGB 37 (2) ; see also German Trade Marks Act 14; Unfair Competition Act 8. [1]

3.   RIGHT TO TRADE-MARKS

81. German law protects two distinct methods by which a trader distinguishes his goods: (1) the *Ausstattung*, by which is meant the particular way in which goods are packed or made up; (2) the *Warenzeichen*, being the trade-mark in the strict sense of the word.   Both methods of distinguishing goods are protected without registration if they are known to the trade as methods appropriated by a particular trader, but a trade-mark in the stricter sense of the word is also protected without being so known, if it has been registered.   The registration is preceded by an official inquiry as to whether the trade-mark in respect of which the application is made is not one in general use (*Freizeichen*) , and also as to the possibility of distinguishing it sufficiently from previously registered trade-marks.   Words descriptive of the goods (in the same way as under English law) and marks consisting exclusively of letters and figures are not admissible as trade-marks.   The use of any public armorial bearings, or of any indecent or obviously deceptive trade-mark is also prohibited—German Trade Marks Act 4–6.   The registration of a trade-mark lapses after ten years unless renewed for another period of ten years by payment of a renewal fee, and fresh renewals may be effected from time to time—*Ibid.* 8.

The infringement of a trade-mark or of a make-up entitled to protection entitles the person aggrieved thereby to an injunction, and if such infringement is due to any wilful or grossly negligent act damages may also be recovered—*Ibid.* 12, 14, 15. [2]

71

---

[1]   As to the international protection of trade names, see Art. 8 of the Paris Convention for the protection of industrial property.

[2]   The international protection of Trade Marks is regulated by the Paris Convention, of which the German Empire is a member since 1903, and by several treaties between the German Empire and other States.

4. RIGHTS RELATING TO IMMATERIAL OBJECTS

a. General Characteristics.

82. The recognition of the rights of an author or inventor is of comparatively modern origin, and has the following characteristics which distinguish it from the recognition of other rights: (*a*) rights as to material objects are recognized in modern law without reference to the nature of the object to which they refer, whereas rights relating to immaterial objects are not recognized unless the objects conform to certain specified conditions (originality, usefulness, &c.); (*b*) rights as to immaterial objects are always recognized for a limited time only.

b. Author's Right (Copyright).

83. The expression 'author's right' (*Urheberrecht*) is more expressive than copyright because it includes the author's or composer's exclusive right to the publication (which expression includes public reading, recitation, and performance) of an unpublished work (common law copyright) as well as the exclusive right to the reproduction of a published work (copyright in the ordinary sense of the word). Author's right in Germany is dealt with as regards literary and musical copyright by the Statute of June 19, 1901; as regards artistic copyright by the Statute of January 9, 1876; as regards photographs by the Statute of January 10, 1876; and as regards artistic models and designs by the Statute of January 11, 1876. The last-mentioned statutes will shortly be replaced by new enactments, of which the drafts are now before the *Reichstag*.

The protection of literary and musical author's rights extends for a period of thirty years beyond the author's life; if, at the expiration of thirty years from the author's death, ten years have not elapsed from the date of first publication of any of his works, or if, at such time any of his works still remain unpublished, the period of protection for such work is ten years from the date of publication. The protection against the reproduction of a work belonging to one of the 'formative arts' (*Bildende Künste*), including paintings, drawings, engravings, etchings, sculpture, &c. , but excluding works of architecture and photographs, extends for a period of thirty years beyond the artist's life; the protection against the reproduction of photographs extends for a period of five years reckoned from the end of the year of first publication. The protection against the reproduction of artistic models and designs extends for a period of one year, which by payment of additional fees may be extended for further periods not exceeding in the aggregate a period of fourteen years.

The owner of the author's right under any of the above-mentioned statutes is, in case of an infringement of his right, entitled to an order restraining the infringement, and in the event of the infringement being of wilful or negligent nature, is also entitled to damages.   The right to an injunction is not given by the statutes themselves, but results from general rules (as to damages, see ss. 36 and 37 of the Copyright Act of 1901; s. 16 of the Artistic Copyright Act of 1876; s. 14 of the Artistic Models Copyright Act of 1876; and s. 9 of the Photograph Copyright Act of 1876). [1]

c.   Inventor's Right.

84. Inventor's rights are safeguarded in Germany by the German Patent Act of 1891 and the Useful Models Act 1891.   The grant of a patent, in the same way as in England under the Act of 1902, is dependent on a previous inquiry as   73 to the patentable nature of the invention.

An invention within the meaning of the patent law may refer to a new product or to a new process for producing a known product.   The German law in all cases requires novelty and the possibility of making an industrial use of the invention. An invention of which the application would be *contra bonos mores* is not patentable and no patent is granted in respect of any article of food or enjoyment (*e. g.* cigars, perfumes, &c.) or of any medical article, but the invention of any process by which any such article is produced is patentable—German Patent Act 1–3.   By the patent the patentee acquires the exclusive right to produce or sell in his trade the patented article, or any article produced by means of the patented process—*Ibid.* 4.

The duration of the patent right is limited to fifteen years subject to forfeiture on non-payment of the prescribed fees—*Ibid.* 7–9.

An abuse of the patentee's monopoly is prevented by a provision enabling the Patent Office authorities to revoke a patent after a lapse of three years from the date of its publication, if it appears that the patentee has omitted to work it on an appropriate scale within the German Empire, or if he has unreasonably refused to

---

[1]   International Copyright is regulated by the Berne Convention and by several separate treaties between the German Empire and other States.

grant a licence in any case where it appears desirable in the public interest that a licence should be granted—*Ibid.* 11.   (The provision of the English Patent Act 1902, s. 3, which enables the Judicial Committee of the Privy Council either to compel the granting of a licence or to revoke the patent is intended to serve the same purpose.)

A patentee whose right has been infringed is entitled to an injunction restraining further infringements, and if the person infringing his right has been acting wilfully, or with gross negligence, the patentee may claim damages or a penalty—*Ibid.* 35, 37.

The Useful Models Act differs from the Patent Act both as regards the nature of the inventions protected under it and as to the mode of obtaining protection.

The protection is given to ' models of articles destined for work or use, in so far as such models are intended to serve the purpose of the work or use by means of some novelty in their shape or arrangement, or by any appliance of a novel kind'.   Inventions of useful models would frequently also be capable of the protection of patent law, but in many cases inventions not sufficiently original to make them patentable are capable of receiving protection as useful models.

The distinction, as to the mode of obtaining protection, consists in the fact that, whilst in the case of an application for a patent, a preliminary investigation has to be made in the above-mentioned manner as to the patentable nature of the invention, a useful model becomes protected by the mere fact of registration, but subject to the right of any person, whether aggrieved or not, to obtain the removal of the model from the register, on proving that it does not comply with the requirement as to novelty and the other requirements involved by the definition given above—Useful Model Act 6.

Protection is only granted for three years, subject to the right of renewal for a further period of three years on payment of the prescribed fee—*Ibid.* 8.   The registered inventor of a useful model is otherwise entitled to rights similar to those of a patentee. [1]

---

[1]   The international protection of Inventors' Rights is regulated by the Paris Convention and by several separate treaties between the German Empire and other States.

B.   ADJECTIVE RIGHTS

1.   GENERAL SURVEY

85. The adjective rights requiring discussion in this place are those which entitle a party to protect or enforce his rights without the assistance of the courts. German law recognizes a general right to protect a threatened interest, where judicial proceedings would be unable to prevent the apprehended mischief.   The acts which are allowed for such purposes come under the head of ' self-defence' (*Selbstverteidigung*), which includes the defence of property, and ' self-help' (*Selbsthülfe*).

Self-defence within certain limits is also authorized by English law; self-help is allowed in a number of isolated instances (retaking of goods taken out of the custody of the lawful possessor, abatement of a nuisance, expulsion of a trespasser, distress of cattle damage feasant, distress for rent, &c.), but there is no general   75 rule corresponding to the German provisions on the subject.   In addition to the rights of self-help and self-defence German law recognizes certain adjective rights which may be conveniently referred to in this place.   They are rights which have no independent existence but only serve for the purpose of protecting a substantive right.   A person entitled to a substantive right may in certain events compel the person under liability or the possessor of a thing or document to which the right refers to furnish security or to produce the thing or document for inspection (87). Under English law rights of such a nature could not be asserted before action brought but under German law they exist independently of any litigation on the subject-matter.

2.   SELF-DEFENCE AND SELF-HELP

a.   Self-defence. [1]

86. The following rules are applied on this subject:

(*a*) An act required to be done by a person for the purpose of warding off an

---

[1]   The word ' self-defence' is used as the equivalent of the German *Selbstverteidigung*, though in its literal sense it has a somewhat narrower meaning.   The German term *Notwer* is applied in a case coming under rule (*a*); the term *Notstand* is applied in a case coming under rule (*b*).

unlawful attack directed against himself [1] or against some other person is not unlawful—BGB 227;

(*b*) a person who injures or destroys a thing belonging to another, with the intention of avoiding any danger threatened to be inflicted by such thing, is not acting unlawfully, if the infliction of such injury or such destruction was required for the purpose of averting the danger and if the damage inflicted by the act of self-defence is not out of all proportion to the danger averted thereby [2] ; if the danger averted by the alleged act of self-defence was caused by the default of the person acting in self-defence (*e. g.* by the insufficient fencing of an enclosure) he is liable for the damage caused by his act—BGB 228.

76

b.   Self-help (*Selbsthülfe*).

A case for self-help arises if the enforcement of a right is in danger of being frustrated or materially hindered by the omission of immediate measures for its protection, and if it is impossible to obtain the assistance of the public authorities with sufficient speed.   In any such case it is not unlawful:

(1) to take away, injure, or destroy a thing interfering with the enforcement of the right; (2) to restrain the liberty of the person against whom the right is available, in so far as there is reasonable ground for suspecting that he intends to abscond; (3) to use force for the purpose of preventing any person from resisting an act which he is bound to permit [3] ; provided: (*a*) that the act of self-help does not go further than is necessary for averting the threatened injury or loss; (*b*) that the necessary steps for obtaining the judicial assistance available under the circumstances of the case be taken forthwith.

A person who erroneously assumes that an act of self-help is justified in any

---

[1]   An attack against the property of the person concerned is for this purpose deemed an attack directed against him.

[2]   Illustration: A person who kills a ferocious dog attacking his own dog acts in lawful self-defence; but a person who kills a valuable hunter which has strayed from a neighbouring paddock into his garden to the danger of his flower-beds is not acting in lawful self-defence, as the loss inflicted on the horse's owner is quite out of proportion to the loss which would have been incurred by the destruction of the flower-beds.

[3]   Illustrations: If a vendor refuses to deliver a specific thing purchased from him the purchaser may take such thing away by force; if a debtor is on the point of leaving the country he may be detained by force; if a person forcibly resists a lessee who wishes to take possession of the tenement let to him such resistance may be overcome by force.   For special instances in which the right of self-help is separately recognized, see 211, 313.

case in which it is not justified and acts on such assumption is liable for any damage caused thereby, even if the mistake was not caused by negligence—BGB 229–231.

3. RIGHT TO SECURITY; RIGHT TO INSPECT THINGS AND DOCUMENTS

a. Right to Security.

87. The right to claim security for the performances of a duty or for the safety of property, while in the possession of another person, is accorded by the BGB in a great variety of cases (see for instance 362, 414, 446 sub 4, 541). The general rules on the subject only regulate the manner in which security must be given in any case in which the right is exercised. A person required to give security may do so: (1) by lodging money or negotiable instruments with a bank or public authority in accordance with the requirements of State law; (2) by pledging government stock or movable things, or by mortgaging immovable things situate in Germany in favour of the person demanding security; (3) by obtaining the guarantee of a solvent surety. The last-mentioned mode of giving security is only permissible in the event of the other modes being impracticable. Certain specified requirements as to the quantum and quality of the security to be given in each case have to be complied with. If the value of the security becomes diminished without any default on the part of the person for whose benefit it is given, sufficient supplementary security must be supplied—BGB 232–240.

b. Right to Inspection of Things and Documents.

Any person, having an existing or possible right over a thing available against the possessor of such thing, is entitled to the production of such thing, or to permission to inspect it, if such inspection is of advantage to him.

A person upon whom the inspection of a document confers an advantage recognized by law is entitled to claim its production for the purpose of inspection in the following cases: (1) if the document was intended for his benefit; (2) if it refers to any obligatory relation which affects him; (3) if it refers to any negotiations to which he was a party.

The thing or document of which inspection is sought must, in the absence of any cogent ground necessitating another arrangement, be produced at the place where it is kept.

The risk and cost of the production must be borne by the party asking for inspection; production may be refused until a sufficient advance is made for costs and security is given in respect of the risk—BGB 809–811.

SECOND DIVISION
THE CREATION, TRANSFER, AND EXTINCTION OF RIGHTS

CHAPTER I
GENERAL STATEMENT

88. THE creation, extinction, or transfer of a right may be effected by a purely physical fact, or by a manifestation of the human will.   The birth or death of a human being, the growth of a plant, the retirement or the advancement of the sea, an earthquake and a fire, are conspicuous instances of physical facts by reason of which rights are created, transferred, or extinguished; the lapse of time may also be referred to as a physical fact with similar consequences.

A manifestation of the human will may be intended to create, transfer, or extinguish a right (*e. g.* a gift, a sale, a promise, a disclaimer, a release, &c.), or it may create a right without intending to do so (*e. g.* the utterance of a slanderous statement or the infliction of a bodily injury).   A manifestation of the human will intended to create, transfer, or extinguish a right recognized by law, is called a *Rechtsgeschäft* by the BGB, and will in the course of this treatise be referred to as an act-in-the-law.

The physical facts, other than the lapse of time, by which rights are created, transferred, or extinguished are more fitly referred to in connexion with each separate class of rights on which such facts exercise an influence.

The rules as to the extinction of rights by lapse of time, *praescriptio extinctiva*, will be discussed in a general manner (131-137) , while, on the other hand, the rules as to the acquisition of rights by lapse of time (*usucapio*) , which are applied exclusively in connexion with the acquisition of the ownership of things, will be separately referred to under that head (329, 330, 334).

The special rules affecting particular classes of acts-in-the-law will be separately referred to in the separate parts of this treatise, but the rules which are equally applicable to all classes of acts require a general statement, which is contained in the second chapter of this division.   Manifestations of the human will which are not in the nature of acts-in-the-law are not dealt with in the general part of the BGB.

CHAPTER II
ACTS-IN-THE-LAW

1. INTRODUCTORY OBSERVATIONS

89. AN act-in-the-law, as mentioned above (88), is a manifestation of the human will intended to create an effect recognized by law. Such a manifestation may consist in the use of written or spoken words, or in any other outward act (*e. g.* the delivery of a thing, the occupation of land, &c.) ; it may also be of an entirely passive nature (silence, deliberate acquiescence), but it must in every case furnish evidence of a clear intention on the part of the person from whom it proceeds. The active or passive manifestation furnishing such evidence is called 'declaration of intention' (*Willenserklärung*).

An act-in-the-law constituted by the declaration of intention of one person only (*e. g.* a notice to determine a lease, a testamentary disposition) is called 'unilateral' (*einseitig*), whilst an act-in-the-law requiring concurrent declarations of intention on the part of several persons is called 'an agreement' (*Vertrag*). The declaration by which an unilateral act is constituted may either be one which is not effective unless communicated to another party (*e. g.* a notice), or it may be effective without communication (*e. g.* a will). In the first case it is called 'a declaration of intention requiring communication'(*empfangsbedürftige Willenserklärung*).

An act-in-the-law which is inoperative from the beginning is called 'void' (*nichtig*); an act-in-the-law which remains operative, unless impugned within a specified time, is called 'voidable' (*anfechtbar*). The grounds which cause the nullity or voidability of an act-in-the-law belong to one of the following three classes:

(1) Want of capacity in one of the parties;

(2) defects in the declaration of intention (*e. g.* non-observance of the prescribed form, discrepancy between real and apparent intention, unlawful character of the proposed transaction);

(3) extraneous circumstances (*e. g.* fraud or unlawful threats).

81   The want of capacity of one of the parties may be remedied by the concurrence or ratification of a third party, as to which concurrence and ratification special rules are laid down by the BGB—See below, 94, 129, 130.

A declaration of intention may be made by a party in person, or by a person acting as agent on his behalf.   The rules on this subject are given in the BGB under the head of *Vertretung* (agency). —See below, 115–128.

The operativeness of an act-in-the-law may be made dependent either upon the performance of a condition (111) or upon the expiration of a period of time (114).   In the first case the act is called an ' act subject to a condition ' (*bedingtes Rechtsgeschäft*).   In the second case an ' act subject to a stipulation as to time ' (*befristetes Rechtsgeschäft*).

It will be necessary to discuss in greater detail the following subjects: (*a*) void and voidable acts-in-the-law; (*b*) capacity; (*c*) modes of declaring intention and deficiencies in declarations of intention; (*d*) effect of fraud and unlawful threats; (*e*) acts-in-the-law subject to conditions or stipulations as to time; (*f*) agency; (*g*) authorization and ratification (assent).

2.   NULLITY OF ACTS-IN-THE-LAW

a.   Acts Void *ab initio.*

90. The expression ' nullity ' , as used in continental Codes and textbooks, is somewhat misleading.

In English law a transaction called ' void ' is inoperative for all purposes *ab initio.*   In French law, on the other hand, there are only very few instances of nullity in which the transaction is absolutely inoperative *ab initio.*   In most cases the nullity must be established by the order of a Court made in an action brought specially in that behalf (action *en nullité*) , and unless such action is brought within the time limited for the particular purpose the transaction is looked upon as valid (see, for instance, Code Civil Art. 1304, as to void agreements).   The German expression here rendered by ' void ' has in German law the same meaning as the corresponding English expression, except when it is used with reference to a marriage (409).

The following rules refer to acts which are void under German law:

82   (*a*) if any part of an act is void, the whole act is void, unless it may be

assumed under the circumstances of the case that the parties intended the valid part of the contract to be severable from the invalid part—BGB 139;

(*b*) if the transaction intended by an act-in-the-law is void, but the requirements for the validity of another transaction which has the same effect are complied with, such other transaction will be allowed to take the place of the intended transaction if it can be assumed that the substituted transaction would have been intended by the parties, had they known of the nullity of the intended transaction: (*e. g.* a contractual promise made by an infant as to the disposal of his estate after his death, made without the concurrence of his statutory agent, is void as a promise, but if the infant has attained the age of sixteen, and the promise is made in the form prescribed for a testamentary disposition, the transaction would be upheld on the infant's death as a testamentary disposition)—BGB 140;

(*c*) an act originally void but subsequently confirmed in a valid manner by the parties is deemed to have been done at the time of the confirmation. The obligations of the parties to an agreement confirmed in this manner, in the absence of an arrangement to the contrary, are deemed to have been binding on them as from the original date—BGB 141.

b.   Voidable Acts.

91. A voidable act is impugned by an act of avoidance, which must be effected by a declaration addressed to the party entitled to notice of the act of avoidance, whom the BGB calls *Anfechtungsgegner* (party subject to avoidance)—BGB 143.

The right to avoid a voidable act-in-the-law is accorded to specified classes of persons, and available within specified periods of time, in accordance with rules laid down separately as to each case of voidability (see, for instance, as to the effect of mistake, *post* 99).

The following rules are applicable to voidable acts generally:

(1) The confirmation of a voidable act by a party entitled to avoid it puts an end to the voidability, and such confirmation may be made informally even where the act to which it refers was one which, to be effective, was required to be done in a prescribed form—BGB 144;

(2) if a voidable act is successfully impugned it is deemed to have been void *ab initio*; a third party acquiring a right created by a voidable act is, in many cases, protected by special rules (see *e. g.* 33), but these rules are applied in so far only as the party concerned is excusably ignorant of the voidability of 83 such act—BGB 142 (2).

3. Capacity

a. General Statement. [1]

92. As mentioned above (26), the term *Geschäftsfähigkeit* is used by the BGB to denote capacity for acts-in-the-law.   This term is not identical in meaning with the term *Handlungsfähigkeit*, which was formerly used in German Codes (see, for instance, Saxon Code, s. 81), and which included capacity for incurring liability in respect of unlawful acts (as to which, see 285) as well as capacity for acts-in-the-law.

Continental law deals with the disabilities caused by infancy and other causes in a manner which in two respects materially differs from the manner in which they are treated by English law:

(1) According to continental law each class, which is subject to any such disability, comes under certain fixed rules; according to English law the rules depend upon the particular character of the transaction.   Thus, under German law, an infant under the age of seven is wholly incapable, while an infant over that age has a restricted capacity; under English law, on the other hand, some acts done by an infant (*e. g.* contracts for necessaries) are not rendered invalid by reason of his infancy, while in other cases it depends upon the circumstances whether such an act is void or voidable.   Similarly, a person placed under guardianship on the ground of insanity is under German law incapable throughout, whilst under English law the act of a lunatic so found by inquisition is valid if done during a lucid interval.

84   (2) Under German law every person under incapacity or restricted capacity has a ' statutory agent ' (*gesetzlicher Vertreter*), being either one of his parents (441, 444) or his guardian or curator (460, 461), who, except in certain cases of a special nature, has power to act on his behalf or to sanction or ratify his acts; under English law the management of the affairs of a person under disability (*e. g.* an infant or a person of unsound mind) is frequently very difficult owing to

---

[1]   The capacity of a person is determined by the law of his nationality, but a foreigner doing any act in Germany which does not affect foreign land or matters connected with family law or the law of inheritance, is deemed capable for such act, if he would be capable for it under German law—EG 7 (1), (3).

the absence of an authorized agent whose acts are binding on such a person.

b.   Incapacity.

93. A declaration of intention made by a person under incapacity is void—BGB 105 (1)—but, as mentioned above, the statutory agent of any such person has, as a general rule, power to act on his behalf.   The cases of a special nature in which this power cannot be exercised, or is subject to restrictions, may be summed up as follows:

(1) certain kinds of acts cannot, under any circumstances, be done by an agent (*e. g.* the declaration required on the solemnization of a marriage (408); the execution of a marriage contract providing for general community of goods (417); the execution of a testamentary instrument, or the declaration taking its place (486));

(2) the alienation of certain classes of objects belonging to a person under incapacity cannot be effected by his statutory agent without the leave of the Guardianship Court or the assent of a supervising guardian (441, 446, 461, 463).

A declaration of intention made by any person during a state of unconsciousness, or during a temporary disturbance of the mental faculties, is void in the same way as if the person making the declaration were permanently incapable—BGB 105 (2).

c.   Restricted Capacity.

94. As a general rule a person of restricted capacity can do valid acts with the assent (129) of his statutory agent, and any act done without such assent is invalid, but this rule is subject to the qualifications and modifications shown by the following statement, which also deals with other matters connected with the same subject:

(1) *Acts which can be done without statutory agent's assent.*

The following classes of acts can be done by a person of restricted capacity   85 without the statutory agent's assent: (1) any act by which he obtains a benefit without giving a *quid pro quo*; (2) any act done by him in the exercise of a trade carried on with the assent of the statutory agent and the leave of the Guardianship Court (provided that it is not an act which in itself requires the leave of the Guardianship Court); (3) any act done by him in pursuance of a general authority given by the statutory agent to enter into agreements for personal services (221),

provided that the particular agreement is not one of a kind requiring the leave of
the Guardianship Court; (4) any testamentary disposition made by him after
having attained the age of sixteen years by means of an oral declaration before a
notary or judicial officer (487, sub 2), unless he is under guardianship on any
ground other than infancy [1]—BGB 107, 112, 113, 114, 2229, 2238 (2), 2247.

(2) *Acts as to which statutory agent's assent is insufficient.*

The alienation of the classes of objects referred to above (93) rule (2),
cannot be validly effected by a person of restricted capacity, though assented to
by the statutory agent, without the leave of the Guardianship Court, or the assent
of a supervising guardian—BGB 1644, 1824.

(3) *Mode of giving assent.*

The assent may be given by authorization or by ratification, in accordance
with the general rules on the subject (129, 130). If the statutory agent of a
person of restricted capacity allows the object required for the performance of a
promise on the part of such person to come into his possession, this is deemed
equivalent to ratification, unless the object is one which cannot be alienated
without the leave of the Guardianship Court or the assent of a supervising
guardian—see above, sub (2)—BGB 110, 1644, 1824.

(4) *Rules for the protection of third parties.*

86   The following rules serve for the protection of third parties dealing with persons
of restricted capacity:

(1) a party whose interests are intended to be affected by a unilateral act
done by a person of restricted capacity (*e. g.* by a notice to determine a lease)
may decline to be bound by such act, unless the statutory agent's written authority
is produced to him, or unless he has received notice from the statutory agent that
he has authorized the act—BGB 111, 114;

(2) a party to an agreement with a person of restricted capacity, entered
upon by the latter without his statutory agent's authorization, may require the
statutory agent to ratify the agreement within fourteen days; if the ratification is
not declared within that period it is deemed to have been refused; if the
restriction as to the capacity of the person concerned is removed before the
expiration of the period his ratification takes the place of the statutory agent's

---

[1]   As to the renunciation of a right of inheritance, see 479.

ratification—BGB 108, 114;

(3) if the restricted capacity of a contracting party was unknown to the other party, or if it was falsely represented to such other party that the required authorization had been given, the party misled by such ignorance or such misrepresentation may, at his option, withdraw from the agreement [1]—BGB 109, 114.

4.   NATURE AND EFFECT OF DECLARATIONS OF INTENTION

a.   Communication of Declaration of Intention.

aa.   General principles.

95. The question as to what constitutes the communication of a declaration of intention presents no difficulty when the parties are in the presence of each other, but where the declarant is at a distance from the addressee two doctrines directly opposed to one another are possible; according to one, communication is made as soon as the message containing the declaration is dispatched; according to the other, it remains incomplete until the message is received by the addressee. The former is called the *Äusserungstheorie* (doctrine of utterance), while the latter is called the *Empfangstheorie* (doctrine of receipt).   There is also a third   87 doctrine called the *Vernehmungstheorie* (doctrine of perception), according to which the receipt of the message is insufficient unless its contents have actually come to the knowledge of the addressee.

The rules of English law relating to the communication of an offer and an acceptance on the formation of an agreement, apply the 'doctrine of perception' in respect of the offer, and the 'doctrine of utterance' in respect of the acceptance. An offer (unless made under seal) produces no effect whatsoever until it becomes known to the offeree; if it is revoked, or if the offeror becomes incapable or dies before that time, it can no longer be accepted.   On the other hand, an acceptance forwarded by the acceptor in a manner authorized by the offeror, is deemed to be duly communicated to the latter, though it never reaches him.

The present German law, on principle, adopts the 'doctrine of receipt', but, as will be seen from the statement given below (96), this principle is not carried out with complete consistency (see particularly rules (4)–(7)).

---

[1]   As to the retrospective effect of an order by which the guardianship over an adult is removed, see BGB 115.

bb.   Rules as to communication.

96. (1) A declaration of intention required to be communicated to another person becomes effective at the moment in which it reaches such other person— BGB 130 (1) ;

(2) a communication required to be made to a person under incapacity or of restricted capacity, does not as a general rule become effective until it reaches the statutory agent of such person, but a declaration required to be made to a person of restricted capacity, and intended exclusively for his benefit, or made with reference to an act authorized by the statutory agent, becomes effective as soon as it reaches the person of restricted capacity—BGB 131 ;

(3) the effect of a declaration is not impaired by the fact that the declarant dies or becomes incapable before its receipt on the part of the addressee [1] —BGB 130 (2) ;

88   (4) a written declaration of intention, delivered through the agency of the official process-server, in the manner allowed for the service of any judicial process, is deemed to have been received, though not actually received by the addressee ; if the declarant is ignorant of the identity or whereabouts of the addressee the declaration may be communicated in a manner corresponding to the service of judicial process by public citation, *i. e.* by notice on the notice-board of a competent Court, and by advertisement in a public journal—BGB 132 ; CPO 203–206 ;

(5) an agreement may be concluded without the communication of the acceptance to the offeror if tacit acceptance is usual as regards that particular class of agreements, or if the offeror has waived the communication of the acceptance ; the length of the period during which the offer in such a case remains binding depends upon the offeror's expressed or implied intention—BGB 151 ;

(6) a mercantile trader (36) under the circumstances mentioned below is deemed to have accepted a proposal to undertake a particular transaction for account of another (231) unless he declines it immediately on receipt of the offer ; the rule is applied : (*a*) if it is part of the trader's regular business to undertake transactions of the kind to which the proposal relates, and if the offeror is in regular business connexion with him ; (*b*) if the trader has specially offered his services for the particular kind of business to the person entrusting him with

---

1   In the case of an offer intended to lead up to an agreement this rule is not applied, if it appears from the special circumstances of the case that its application was not intended by the party making such offer—BGB 153.

the mandate [1] —HGB 362.

Illustration: A stockbroker who receives an order to buy shares or stocks from a regular client is deemed to have undertaken the execution of the order, unless he declines it immediately on receipt.   On the other hand, if the order had come from a person who was not a regular client, or if the order had been to buy coffee or cotton, there would be no contract of agency between him and the person who gave the order unless he accepted the offer of the agency in the ordinary way, or unless he had specially offered his services for the particular kind of business to the person giving the order.

89

(7) In the case of a bilateral mercantile sale of goods the notice to be given by a purchaser who wishes to exercise his right of cancellation in respect of any defects of quality (192) is deemed duly communicated as soon as it is forwarded to the vendor's address—HGB 377 (3).

b.   Form of Declaration of Intention.

(1) *General statement.*

97. Under German, as under English law, an act-in-the-law is not required to be done in any particular form, unless it belongs to a special class of transactions for which a particular form is prescribed by rule of law, or by agreement between the parties.   Where no such special form is prescribed, a declaration constituting or forming part of an act-in-the-law may be made by spoken or written words, or by means of any other act from which the declarant's intention may be inferred, subject of course to the above-mentioned rules as to communication (95, 96). Where, however, a rule of law or a contractual stipulation requires a special form to be observed, an act not complying with such requirement is void, unless (in the case of any contractual requirement) the contrary has been agreed upon—BGB 125.

Under English law three kinds of formalities may be prescribed: (*a*) writing under hand (Sale of Goods Act, s. 4; Statute of Frauds, s. 4; Bills of Exchange Act, ss. 3, 17 (2)); (*b*) writing under hand in the presence of two witnesses (Wills Act, s. 9); (*c*) the delivery of a writing under seal called a deed (the

---

[1]   In the case of a person who is not a mercantile trader but is publicly appointed for a particular class of agency business (*e. g.* an auctioneer, a surveyor, a solicitor) or who has publicly offered his services for such class of business, default in the execution of instructions not immediately declined gives rise to a claim for damages, but no contract of agency is formed in such a case—BGB 663; *Rechtsanwaltsordnung* 30.

last-mentioned form being required for all contracts not supported by valuable consideration, and also for certain classes of transactions supported by valuable consideration—see, for instance, Real Property Amendment Act 1845, s. 3).

Under German law there are two principal kinds of formalities, one of a more, and the other of a less solemn kind.   Certain classes of acts must be authenticated before a judge or public notary in the manner described by the German statutes as *gerichtliche oder notarielle Beurkundung*, and more particularly referred to below sub (2), (which kind of authentication will in the further course of this treatise be described as ' authentication by public act '); certain other classes of acts must be embodied in one or more written documents which must satisfy the requirements mentioned below sub (3).   The more stringent form is required in the case of transactions creating real rights or affecting family relations, or rights of inheritance (see, for instance, 310, 416, 428 sub (2), 479, 487, 506), the less stringent form is required for certain kinds of transactions by which obligatory rights are created or transferred (208, 269, 390), while certain other classes of transactions, which may be entirely informal if they are of a mercantile nature, must be evidenced by written documents if they are not of a mercantile nature (271, 278).   It will be understood that any classes of acts-in-the-law referred to in the further course of this treatise can be done informally, unless the formal requirements are expressly mentioned.

(2) *Authentication by public act.*

A public act consists of one or more declarations made before a judge or public notary, in the presence of certain prescribed additional witnesses, stating by word of mouth the terms of the transaction requiring authentication, or confirming terms set out in a written document delivered to the officiating judge or notary.   The act is evidenced by the minutes taken down by the officiating judge or notary, who together with the parties and the additional witnesses must sign the same.   If the declarations confirm the terms of a written document, such document must be attached to the minutes.   As a general rule State law requires the minutes and all documents annexed thereto to be kept with the official records of the judge or notary before whom the act is authenticated, the parties being entitled to receive certified copies. [1]   Where an agreement is required to be

---

1   According to Prussian law a party who can prove that the original minutes are required for use in any proceeding outside the German Empire may demand their delivery—Prussian FGG 44.

authenticated by public act the offer and the acceptance may, as a general rule, each be effected by separate proceedings, but in some special cases the contemporaneous presence of all the parties before the same judge or notary is required (see, for instance, 327, 416)—BGB, 128, 152; FGG 174–177; Prussian FGG 42, 43, 49.

91

(3) *Rules as to declarations required to be made in writing.*

The following rules are applicable to cases in which writing is prescribed by rule of law: (1) a party whose declaration is required to be in writing [1] must sign the document containing the declaration; the affixing of a mark in the presence of a judge or notary is deemed equivalent to the affixing of the declarant's signature; (2) where in the case of an agreement the declaration of each of the parties is required to be in writing all the parties must affix their signatures to one document setting out the terms of the agreement, except in a case in which such a document is made out in a set of several copies; in the last-mentioned case it is sufficient for each party to sign the parts of the set intended to be kept by the other parties.

Where a declaration is required to be in writing by virtue of any agreement between the parties these rules are somewhat relaxed; a telegraphic declaration of intention and an agreement effected by an exchange of letters is in such a case deemed to comply with the requirement of a written form, unless a contrary intention is shown.

In some cases in which a declaration is required to be in writing, the writing is required to be ' publicly attested' (*öffentlich beglaubigt*).   In such a case the signature of the declarant must be attested by a public authority or official competent for the purpose under State law or by a public notary.

A declaration required to be in writing is deemed duly made if made by a public act in the manner referred to sub (2) ; such public act also sufficiently replaces any required public attestation—BGB 126, 127, 129.

c.   Discrepancy between Real and Apparent Intention.

aa.   General statement.

98. German lawyers have for a long time been divided between two conflicting

---

[1]   In the case of a lease for a period exceeding a year writing is required on the part of lessor and lessee (208).   In all other cases in which writing is prescribed by rule of law the requirement refers to the declaration of one of the parties only (*e. g.* the surety (271) ; the party granting the annuity (269)).

92   doctrines, the doctrine of 'real intention' (*Willenstheorie*) and the doctrine of
'declared intention' (*Erklärungstheorie*).   The supporters of the former of these
maintain that a person cannot be really bound by any expression of intention
which does not rightly give effect to the intention which was in his mind, while
the adherents of the latter uphold the rule which is universally accepted in
England 'that where one by his words or conduct causes another to believe the
existence of a certain state of things and induces him to act on that belief so as to
alter his own previous position, the former is concluded from averring against the
latter a different state of things as existing at the same time' (Pickard *v.* Sears
(1837) 6 Ad. & E. 469, 474).   Neither view has in practice been carried out
with complete consistency; even the adherents of the theory of 'real intention'
have always made ample concessions to the requirements of ordinary intercourse
(*Verkehrsbedürfniss*), while on the other hand the advocates of the opposite
doctrine have been compelled to admit that there are cases in which the real
intention of a party ought in justice to prevail over his apparent intention.   This
occasional deviation from the doctrine of 'declared intention' also exists under the
rules of English law and equity.   The present German law starts from the doctrine
of real intention, but makes it subject to so many exceptions, and to so many rules
for the protection of innocent parties, that in the result the difference between
English and German law on this subject is not of much practical importance.

A discrepancy between real and apparent intention occurs: (*a*) where the
expression of intention is not seriously meant; (*b*) where the tenor of the
declaration does not express what is really intended to be declared.   The latter
class of cases is generally dealt with under the head of 'mistake' and will be
discussed separately (99).

The rules as to the former class of cases are necessary under a system
starting from the doctrine of 'real intention', but in a system like that of English
law, in which the opposite doctrine prevails, the special rules stated below follow
as a direct result of the general doctrine, and consequently seem superfluous.   The
BGB deals with (1) mental reservation; (2) fictitious transactions; (3) declarations
not intended to be taken seriously, in the manner shown by the following rules:

93   (1) A declaration of intention is not void on the ground that the declarant in
the recesses of his mind does not intend to be bound by his expressed intention,
unless this hidden intention was known to the other party—BGB 116.

(2) A declaration of intention, which has to be communicated to another,
and which, with the knowledge of such other, is purely fictitious, is void for all

purposes.   If the fictitious transaction is intended to effect a real transaction which it conceals the rules relating to the real transaction are applied.

Illustration: If a debt intended to be assigned by way of mortgage as security for a loan is in fact assigned absolutely, the transaction as between the assignor and the assignee, is treated as a mortgage [1]—BGB 117.

(3) A declaration of intention which is not intended to be taken seriously, and is made in the expectation that the absence of serious intention will be detected, is void; if the declaration was one requiring to be communicated to another party such other party, if not guilty of negligence, is entitled to be compensated for any loss suffered by his reliance on the validity of the declaration; if the declaration was not required to be communicated any person relying on it, if not guilty of negligence is entitled to compensation—BGB 118, 122.

Under English law rule (1) would be taken for granted; while rule (2) is applicable on the ground that the intention of the parties not to be bound by the apparent agreement is in reality the result of a supplemental agreement of which evidence may be given, even where the apparent agreement is in writing (see, for instance, Bowes v. Foster 2 H. & N. 779); rule (3) is not applied under English law.

bb.   Mistake.

(1) General statement.

99. The rules of German law as to the effect of mistake differ from the corresponding English rules, both as regards the extent of the sphere within which mistake is admitted as a ground of relief, and as regards its effect when so admitted.   The sphere is much larger under German law; on the other hand the effect does not go as far as it does under English law in the cases in which it is a ground of relief.

There are two classes of cases of so-called 'mistake' which must be kept strictly apart.   In the one class of cases relief is sought on the ground that the declared intention does not express the real intention of the declarant or declarants; in the other class of cases the relief is sought on the ground that the

94

---

[1]   The BGB contains a number of provisions which protect innocent parties against the consequences of the nullity of a fictitious transaction; see, for instance 176 sub (3), 333 and BGB 405.   An innocent party suffering any loss by relying on the genuineness of a fictitious transaction would generally be entitled to compensation under the rules as to unlawful acts (287).

declarant when making the declaration was under a mistaken assumption as to certain facts, and that he would not have made such declaration had he known the true facts.   In the one class of cases the mistake refers to the expression of the intention, in the other to the *formation* of the intention.

In many English textbooks a distinction is drawn between 'unilateral mistake' and 'common mistake', but the cases which are referred to as instances of 'common mistake' are all cases in which the true intention of the parties, though not completely shown by the written document purporting to embody the agreement between them, may be discovered from other written documents or from other sources of which evidence under the particular circumstances is held to be admissible (see, for instance, *re* Boulter 4 Ch. D. 241). [1]

The principles applied in such cases would, under German law, be considered under the head of the interpretation of acts-in-the-law (107); common mistake, as such, is not a ground of relief.

The recovery of money paid under a mistake of fact, which English writers discuss as part of the subject of 'mistake', is under German law dealt with in connexion with the rules as to unjustified benefits (298, 299).

(2) *Mistake as to expression of intention.*

95   The rules of the BGB on this subject are as follows:

(*a*) 'Any person, who, when declaring his intention, was under a mistake as to the tenor of his declaration, and did not intend to make a declaration of such tenor, may avoid such declaration if it may be assumed that he would not have made it if he had known the true facts and given reasonable consideration to the matter' —BGB 119 (1);

(*b*) A declaration of intention, which has been incorrectly transmitted by the person or institution employed in its transmission, may be avoided under the same circumstances as a declaration which is voidable under rule (*a*)—BGB 120.

A mistake of the nature provided for by rule (*a*) is apt to arise in cases in which a person accepts an offer or signs a document of which he fails to understand or misunderstands the effect; or if he himself uses words which have

---

[1]   The case of Couturier *v.* Hastie, which is frequently referred to as an illustration as to the effect of common mistake, turns entirely on the construction of the written document in which the agreement was embodied; see the observations of Pollock C. B. 22 L. J. (Ex.) 97, 101, and the judgment of the H. L. 25 L. J. (Ex.) 253, 254.

an import not known to him when uttering them.   English law grants relief in such cases if the mistake arises through the fraud of a third party [1] (Foster *v.* Mackinnon L. R. 4 C. P. 704; Lewis *v.* Clay 67 L. J. (Q. B.) 224).

As regards wrongly transmitted messages English law in effect arrives at the same result as the German rule (*b*), but the English rule is based on more logical reasoning than the German rule.   According to the English rule, a wrongly transmitted message is not a declaration of intention of the original sender, and the acceptance of an offer contained in such wrongly transmitted message cannot therefore produce an agreement between the sender and the addressee (Henkel *v.* Pape L. R. 6 Ex. 7).

(3) *Mistake as to formation of intention.*

The BGB enacts that an error as to such characteristics of the other party, or of the subject-matter of a transaction, as are deemed essential in ordinary intercourse, is to have the same effect as an error in the tenor of the declaration—BGB 119 (2).   96

This rule enables a vendor to rescind a sale if he finds that the other party is less solvent that he imagined, and it enables the purchaser to rescind if he finds that he had over-estimated the productiveness of the purchased object. [2]   But for the safeguards mentioned below sub (4), such a provision would produce great hardship.

Under English law a mistake made by one of the parties as to the qualities of the other party or of the subject-matter of an agreement, apart from questions of misrepresentation, or expressed or implied special conditions, is not a ground of relief.

(4) *Effect of mistake.*

As shown by the comparison of the rules, the sphere within which mistake is a ground of relief is much larger in German than in English law; on the other hand, the relief available under German law on the ground of mistake is of a less far-reaching kind than the relief available under English law.   According to English law mistake, where operative, avoids the transaction in which it occurs.   Under

---

[1]   If the mistake arises through the fraud of a party to the same transaction the relief is granted on the ground of fraud and not on the ground of mistake.   The case of Raffles *v.* Wichelhaus 2 H. & C. 906, which is frequently referred to as illustrating the effect of mistake, comes under a different head; it was a case in which an ambiguous expression was used, to which each party gave a different sense, so that no real agreement was concluded between the parties.

[2]   Mistake is a ground of relief apart from any question as to warranty or condition as to qualities.

German law the party misled by the mistake has a right of avoidance, which is restricted in the following manner: (*a*) as mentioned above sub (2), it cannot be exercised unless the facts of the case warrant the conclusion that the party intending to avoid the act would, if he had known the true facts and given a reasonable consideration to the matter, 'not have made the declaration which he did make'; (*b*) the avoidance must be made without culpable delay as soon as the party claiming relief becomes aware of the mistake; in any case the right cannot be exercised after the lapse of thirty years from the date of the declaration; where the party subject to avoidance (91) is absent, the act of avoidance is deemed to be effected by the forwarding of a written notice to his address—BGB 121; (*c*) if the declaration avoided by the declarant was made to a party to whom it had to be communicated such other party, if excusably ignorant of the ground of avoidance, is entitled to compensation for the loss suffered by him by reason of his having acted on the faith of the validity of the declaration. In the case of a declaration which does not require to be communicated to another person, any third party suffering loss by acting on the faith of the validity of the transaction, and excusably ignorant of the existence of the ground of avoidance, is entitled to the corresponding relief—BGB 122.

97

d.   Formation of Agreements.

aa.   Legal effect of offer.

100. Under English law an offer, unless made under seal, is not binding on the offeror, and can therefore be withdrawn at any time before it is accepted; under German law an offeror, who does not expressly declare that his offer is not to be binding upon him, is bound by such offer if it is accepted within the period of time shown by the rules stated below; after the expiration of such period the offer is deemed to be revoked in the same way as, under English law, an offer is deemed to be revoked after the lapse of a reasonable time (Ramsgate Hotel Company *v.* Montefiore L. R. 1 Ex. 109)—BGB 145, 146.   The time within which an offer must be accepted is regulated by the following rules:

(1) if the offeror has fixed a period of time the offer may be accepted within such period—BGB 148;

(2) if the offeror has fixed no time an offer *inter praesentes* [1] must be accepted

---

[1]   An offer made by telephone is deemed to be made *inter praesentes*—BGB 147 (1).

at once, and an offer *inter absentes* must be accepted[1] within the period within which the offeror would, under ordinary circumstances, expect an answer—BGB 147.

Illustration: A letter containing an offer is forwarded on Monday from Berlin to London; as an offer made by post may in the usual course of business be accepted by post, and as the transmission of a letter between Berlin and London takes two days, the offeror is bound until Friday.   A telegram accepting the offer on Thursday evening would therefore be sufficient, if duly received by the offeror, and he would be bound by the agreement in accordance with the offer even if he withdrew the offer by a letter which reached the offeree before he sent his telegram. According to English law there would be no contract under such circumstances.

(3) If in any case the acceptance—through delay in transmission occurring in a manner which ought to be perceived by the offeror—reaches the latter after the expiration of the period fixed by rules (1) and (2) he remains bound notwithstanding such delay, unless, either before or immediately after the receipt of the acceptance he informs the offeree of the fact that it was not received within the required period—BGB 149.

98

Illustration: If in the case referred to in the illustration of rule (2), the offer is accepted by a letter posted in London on Wednesday, which does not reach the offeror till Saturday, the offeror is bound, unless he writes at once that the acceptance arrived too late.

(4) An acceptance which reaches the offeror after the expiration of the period fixed by rules (1) and (2) is deemed a new offer by the offeree—BGB 150 (1).

(5) An offer made by any person who bids at a sale by auction ceases to be binding as soon as a higher bid is made, or as soon as the lot to which the bid refers is withdrawn from the auction—BGB 156.

Under English law an offer may be made by public announcement to the world in general; an agreement then arises as soon, as any ascertained person accepts such offer.   Under German law, on the other hand, an offer as such must always be made to an ascertained person.   The public promise of a reward for a specified act (*Auslobung*) is not looked upon as an offer, but as a binding unilateral promise, which must be performed even in a case in which the party claiming the reward at the time of doing the specified act was ignorant of the promise (283).

---

[1]   As to what constitutes communication of the acceptance, see 96.

bb.   What constitutes acceptance.

101. The following rules relate to acceptance:

(1) an agreement is not formed unless the offer is accepted without modification or restriction; an acceptance by which the terms of the offer are extended, restricted, or otherwise modified, is deemed to be a refusal of the original offer coupled with a new offer—BGB 150 (2);

(2) the parties must be *ad idem* as to all points which, according to the declaration of intention of one or both of the parties, are to be dealt with by the agreement; an agreement as to any isolated points, though embodied in a separate memorandum, is merely a preliminary negotiation, and, in the absence of any arrangement to the contrary, is not binding on the parties—BGB 154 (1) [1];

(3) an agreement intended to be embodied in a formal document is, in the absence of an arrangement to the contrary, not binding on the parties before the execution of such formal document—BGB 154 (2);

(4) an agreement believed by the parties to be complete on all points, but which is subsequently found to be incomplete as to one particular point, is inoperative unless it is shown that, under the circumstances of the case, the parties would have been willing to be bound even if they had been aware of the incompleteness—BGB 155.

e.   Effect of Illegality and Immorality.

aa.   General statement.

102. An act-in-the-law is void, as a general rule, if the intention declared thereby infringes a legal prohibition, or is *contra bonos mores* (*gegen die guten Sitten*)—BGB 134, 138.   Acts violating a legal prohibition may conveniently be referred to as illegal acts, but the expression *contra bonos mores* is not correctly rendered by ' immoral '.   Grossly immoral acts would no doubt fall under the description, but many acts infringing the strict laws of morality are upheld by the Courts, whilst on the other hand many acts, which under the particular circumstances of the case may not be immoral at all, are repudiated as violating *bonos mores*.   The

---

1   Illustration: A manufacturer *A* offers his agency for the sale of his goods to *B*; *B* writes that he is willing to accept the agency, if satisfactory terms can be arranged as to commission, allowance for expenses, supply of patterns, and some other points; *A* states his terms as to some of the points which *B* accepts.   No agreement exists between *A* and *B*, until all the points mentioned by *B* have been agreed upon.

expression, like the English expression ' acts against public policy ' , is applied to such classes of acts as could not be enforced by the Courts without giving offence to public feeling (*quae facta laedunt pietatem*, *existimationem*, *verecundiam nostram et*, *ut generaliter dixerim*, *contra bonos mores fiunt*—Dig. 28. 7. 15, Papinian).

bb.   Illegal acts.

(1)   Generally.

103. Any act-in-the-law, expressly prohibited or penalized by law, is void on   100 the ground of illegality, unless the enactment containing the prohibition provides otherwise—BGB 134.

It is immaterial whether the prohibition arises under Imperial law or State law. Among prohibited acts which do not come within the range of criminal law the following may be mentioned: (1) any agreement for compound interest which does not belong to one of the excepted classes (106); (2) any gaming transaction (265); (3) any agreement protecting a person against liability for his own wilful default (148); (4) any agreement not belonging to one of the excepted classes, dealing with a right expected to arise on the death of a living person—BGB 312; (5) any agreement for the transfer of the whole of a person's after-acquired property or of an aliquot part thereof to another person. —BGB 310; see also BGB 311.

(2)   Statutory or judicial restraints on alienation.

104. Among acts prohibited by law the alienation of objects which the law declares inalienable [1] is dealt with in an exceptional manner; where a restraint on alienation is imposed in the public interest, a disposition disregarding such restraint is inoperative, but where the restraint is imposed exclusively for the protection of any particular parties, [2] an act disregarding the restraint is inoperative

---

1   A restraint on alienation imposed by an act of the parties, like the restraint on anticipation of a married woman's income commonly inserted in English marriage settlements, has no direct operation under German law.   A disposition disregarding the restraint is valid, but the party disregarding it is liable in damages to any person prejudiced thereby—BGB 137.

2   Among the statutory restraints on alienation the prohibition of the sale or mortgage of any rights which are incapable of attachment by a judgment creditor (*e. g.* a workman's rights to wages, an official's rights to salaries and pensions) and the restrictions imposed upon bankrupts—BGB 400, 1274 (2); KO 6, 7—are the most important.   These restraints, as well as the restraints imposed by judicial order—which by virtue of BGB 136 are deemed equivalent to restraints imposed by law—are imposed for the protection of particular persons only.   The principal example of a restraint imposed in the public interest is the restraint imposed in certain events upon the alienation of the property of a person accused of crime after the exercise of

only as between the party subject to the restraint and the parties for whose protection the restraint is imposed; a third party dealing with the person subject to the restraint is in the same position as a purchaser buying a movable thing from a vendor with a defective title (333)—BGB 134–136, KO 13.

cc. Acts ' contra bonos mores '.

105. The expression *contra bonos mores* (*gegen die guten Sitten*) is not defined by the BGB.   Some of the acts which formerly were held void, as being *contra bonos mores*, are now expressly prohibited, but as regards acts not expressly prohibited the rules established by the decisions under the old law will probably be maintained.

The following classes of acts will probably continue to be held void on the ground that they are *contra bonos mores*:

(1) any act by which a right of custody or control or cohabitation arising under family law is waived (*e. g.* an agreement for perpetual separation between husband and wife—*Seuffert's Archiv* vol. 24 p. 373; an agreement by which a father binds himself to allow his child to be educated by another person—RGZ 10, 114);

(2) any act by which a permanent restraint is imposed on marriage (see Prussian Code I. 4, s. 10);

(3) any act permanently restricting the disposing capacity of the person concerned (*e. g.* a voluntary settlement by which the settlor deprives himself of the control of his whole fortune—RGZ 4, 162);

(4) any act by which the earning capacity of any person is unduly hampered [1];

---

the powers of seizure exercisable by the State authorities.

1   The rules as to agreements in restraint of trade laid down by the German Courts are similar to those upheld by the English Courts.   An agreement not to compete in the trade of another must be limited either as to time or as to space, but the question as to the extent of the limits is one which depends upon the circumstances of the particular case, the leading principle being that the limits must not exceed what is reasonably necessary for the protection of the covenantee (as to English law, see Nordenfelt *v.* Maxim, &c. Co. (1894) A. C. 535—as to German law RGZ 31, 97; 47, 238).   Special rules are laid down by HGB 74–76 as to agreements in restraint of trade between mercantile clerks and apprentices and their employers.   Such an agreement is void if made during the infancy of the clerk or apprentice notwithstanding the assent of the statutory agent; it may not extend over a time exceeding three years from the date at which the clerk or apprentice leaves the employer's service, and must otherwise be reasonably limited as to time, space, and the kinds of business which are forbidden.   An agreement transgressing such limits is not void altogether but valid *pro tanto* within the authorized limits.   See also p. 175 note 1.

(5) any act aiming at the promotion of sexual immorality by direct or indirect   102
means (*e. g.* the letting of a house for immoral purposes). [1]

It will be seen that on the whole the prohibitions of German law are similar
to those of English law.   Separation agreements and voluntary settlements of the
whole of a person's property (subject to the restrictions imposed by the Statute of
Elizabeth and the Bankruptcy Act) are valid under English law, but invalid under
German law.   On the other hand, the rules as to champerty and maintenance are
unknown to German law.

dd.   *Usurious Transactions and Undue Influence.*

(1) *General statement.*

106. Among acts-in-the-law which are void on the ground of being *contra
bonos mores*, the BGB specially singles out some which may be described as
'usurious', taking the word in a somewhat extended sense, and other transactions
which in England are dealt with as acts done under undue influence.

Under the old German usury law no claim for interest exceeding a certain
rate was enforceable.   In the countries subject to the Roman law certain particular
evasions of the usury laws were voidable on the ground of *laesio enormis*; moreover
the *Lex Anastasiana*, which was directed against the purchase of money claims
below their real value, and corresponded in a certain measure to the English
equitable rule as to the purchase of reversionary interests at an undervalue,
protected improvident persons against those who wished to take advantage of their
necessitous condition.

The reaction of opinion, which in England led to the repeal of the usury
laws, and to the enactment of the statute dealing with sales of reversionary
interests (31 & 32 Vict. c. 4), led to corresponding results in Germany.   The
maximum rate of interest was in the first instance abolished in respect of loans
made to mercantile traders (old HGB art. 292), and the abolition was made
general by a statute of the North German Federation passed in 1867, and   103
subsequently extended to the whole Empire.   Soon afterwards the pendulum
began to swing in the opposite direction.   In England the reaction only led to the
Moneylenders Act of 1900, which enables the Courts in the case of loans made by

---

1   The German law does not go as far in this respect as English law.   The sale of ornaments intended
to be given to a prostitute by a jeweller aware of the destination of the ornaments is not a transaction *contra
bones mores* (*Seuffert's Archiv* vol. 49, Nr. 238—compare Pearce *v.* Brooks L. R. 1 Ex. 213).

moneylenders to reduce excessive rates of interest; but German modern law has gone much further.   The amendments of the German Criminal Code, introduced in 1880 and 1893, impose criminal punishments on a certain class of transactions of a usurious nature, and render such transactions void.   The section as to the civil effects of usurious transactions is now repealed by EG 47, and the whole matter is regulated by BGB 138 (2).   This sub-section provides for the nullity of ' any act-in-the-law by which a person, by taking advantage of the necessitous condition, improvidence, or inexperience of another person, obtains from such other person in his own favour, or in favour of a third person, pecuniary advantages, the value of which exceeds the value of the consideration for which they are given or promised, to such an extent that they are, under the special circumstances of the case, conspicuously out of proportion to such consideration'. It will be seen that this covers all the cases to which the English Moneylenders Act is applicable, as well as many of the cases coming under the rules as to undue influence.

As regards transactions which are usurious in the narrower sense of the word, the prohibition of excessive advantages applies to every person, whether a professional moneylender or otherwise, and the relief, to which the moneylender's victim is entitled, is not merely the rectification of the terms of the bargain, but a judicial declaration of the complete nullity of the transaction.   This does not, however, mean that the borrower may retain the amount of a loan actually received, as the operation of the rules as to ' unjustified benefits' (298) would obviate such a result.

The nullity of acts done under undue influence is dependent on the presence of an objective and of a subjective element.   The objective element is the excessive undervalue of the consideration, which, as under modern English law, is not in itself a ground of nullity.   The subjective element is under German law 104   presumed from the necessitous condition, or the improvidence, or the inexperience of the person acting under undue influence, whilst under English law inexperience alone, or the fact that the parties stand in confidential relation to each other, is taken into consideration.   Undue influence, without the objective ingredient of undervalue, is not a ground of nullity under German law; whilst under English law cases may occur in which a transaction is set aside on the ground of undue influence, even where no excessive advantages have been derived thereunder by the other party.

(2) *Rules as to Interest.*

The following special rules as to interest require to be mentioned:

(*a*) an agreement for the payment of compound interest is invalid except that: (*aa*) a savings bank or other bank may agree to pay interest on interest not withdrawn by a depositor; (*bb*) where any person keeps a continuous debtor and creditor account with a mercantile trader, a balance being struck at regular intervals, interest is payable on such balance, whether including interest or otherwise—BGB 248; HGB 355 (1) ;

(*b*) where money is lent at a rate of interest exceeding 6 per cent. per annum, otherwise than on the security of a debenture payable to bearer, the debtor may at any time, notwithstanding any stipulation to the contrary, repay the sum owing to him, provided that he has six months previously given notice to the creditor of his intention in that behalf—BGB 247.

5. INTERPRETATION OF ACTS-IN-THE-LAW

a.   General Rules.

107. The BGB contains the following express general rules as to the interpretation of acts-in-the-law: (*a*) 'where a declaration of intention has to be interpreted, the real meaning of the act of volition must be inquired into, without attaching undue importance to the literal meaning of the expression of intention' —BGB 133; (*b*) agreements must be interpreted in accordance with the requirements of good faith, having regard to business usage—BGB 157.   The second rule is, in the case of dealings between mercantile traders, supplemented by the provision of HGB 346, to the effect that as between such persons all acts   105 and omissions must be interpreted with reference to mercantile usage.

With reference to the first rule, it should be borne in mind that the words 'real meaning' do not in this case refer to the 'real' as opposed to the 'apparent' intention, but to such real intention as may, by means of a reasonable interpretation of the declaration, be gathered from the latter.   Where there is a discrepancy between the real and apparent intention, a party may be entitled to avoid the act, on the ground of mistake (see 99); but the rule now under discussion is applicable where the act is to be upheld in accordance with the proper interpretation of the declaration relating to it, having regard to the context or to the surrounding circumstances.   If a contractor on the 31st December, 1904, starts the building of a large warehouse, which he agrees to complete on the 31st December, 1905, and the 31st January, 1905, is inserted into the agreement through a copying mistake, no question arises as to avoiding the agreement on the ground of mistake.   The literal interpretation of the written agreement in such a case is not in accordance with the evident intention of the parties, both of whom must of course have known that the date inserted by the copyist could not possibly be the date agreed upon, and therefore the intention of the parties must be ascertained from other sources.   In England the rule of interpretation under discussion is applied by Courts of Equity on applications for the rectification of deeds (see Bonhote *v.* Henderson (1895) 1 Ch. 742, 2 Ch. 202), and generally in the cases classed under the head of 'mistake common to both parties'.

The second rule carries out the same principle as the first rule, with particular reference to agreements.   The appeal to good faith shows that, in the cases to which the rule is to be applied, the parties are assumed to be well aware of the fact that a literal interpretation of the words used by them would not carry out the bargain which they had in view when entering upon the agreement.

The reference to custom is only a particular application of the general principle.   Where special modes of expression have, in a particular trade or among a particular class of people, a meaning different from the ordinary meaning, it would clearly be against good faith, in the case of an agreement between persons accustomed to use such special meaning, to assert that the ordinary meaning was intended.

The general rules as to the interpretation of acts-in-the-law are supplemented by the rules referred to below—144 to 147—as to the manner in which obligatory duties have to be carried out, in the absence of express agreement on any particular point.

The special rules as to the computation of time stated in the next following paragraph, are also in the nature of rules of interpretation.

German law has not as yet availed itself of the device, which has with great advantage been introduced in England, of giving a statutory meaning to certain expressions commonly used in legal documents (see for instance Conveyancing Act 1881, ss. 7-9), except in so far as certain expressions applied to certain kinds of matrimonial contractual arrangements (such as 'general community of goods', 'community of income and profits', and 'community of movables') have the meaning given to them respectively by BGB 1437-1518, 1519-1548

(416) and 1549–1557.

b.   Rules as to Computation of Time.

108. The BGB contains a series of rules on this subject, which, in the absence of express provisions to the contrary, are to be applied to the interpretation of all Imperial and local statutes, judicial orders, and acts-in-the-law. —BGB 186.   They provide as follows:

aa.   As to the beginning of a period.

(1) If a period begins on the happening of any event, or the doing of any act, then, subject to the exceptions stated sub (2), the day on which the event happens, or on which the act is done, is not included in the computation of the period—BGB 187 (1).

Illustration: A contract for services is terminable fourteen days after notice. The notice is given on the 10th April; the fourteen days run from the 11th April; a promise to pay three months after date, means three months after the act of promise; therefore the date on which the promise is made is not included in the computation.

(2) If a period is to commence on a given day, such day is included in the 107 computation—BGB 187 (2).

Illustration: A courier is engaged for three months from the 1st January—the 1st January is included in the period.   The same rule is also applicable to the calculation of a person's age; that is to say, the day of birth is included in the computation; a person born on the 1st January completes each year of his life on the 31st December.

bb.   As to the end of a period.

(1) A period described by a number of days ends with the end of the last day—BGB 188 (1).

Illustration: In the illustration given to rule *aa.* (1) the period of service ends at the end of the 24th April, but under the effect of rule *aa.* (2) a person born on the 10th April completes his fourteenth day at the end of the 23rd April.

(2) A period described by weeks, months, years, or parts of a year, in a case coming under rule *aa.* (1), ends at the last moment of the week-day or monthly date on which the event or act from which the period runs, happened, or was

done; in a case coming under rule *aa.* (2) it ends at the last moment of the week-day or monthly date preceding the week-day or monthly date at which the period began to run—BGB 188 (2).

Illustration: Under BGB 2 a person comes of age on the completion of his twenty-first year; therefore a person born on the 30th July, 1883, comes of age at the last moment of the 29th July, 1904.   Under English law the rule as to the attainment of majority is the same as in German law, but as rights are always deemed to exist from the first moment of the day on which they accrue, the person in question would, if he came under English law, be deemed to have attained his majority at the *first* moment of the 29th July.

(3) Where a period is described by months, and where the day of the month at which, according to the computation directed by rule (2), the period would end, is non-existent in the particular month, the period comes to an end at the last moment of the last day of such month (*e. g.* if a house is let for two months from the 1st January, the tenancy comes to an end on the 28th February in an ordinary year, and on the 29th February in a leap-year)—BGB 188 (3).

The authors of the BGB seem to have overlooked the possibility of a period described by years ending on a non-existing monthly date (*e. g.* a yearly notice given on the 29th February, 1904).

cc.   Extension of a period.

Where a period is extended by the addition of a new period, the new period begins to run from the moment at which the original period ends—BGB 190.

dd.   Date falling on a holiday.

If the day on which an act has to be done is a Sunday or public holiday, the business day next succeeding such Sunday or holiday takes its place—BGB 193. (Under English law the next preceding business day generally takes the place of the day originally fixed; but see Bills of Exchange Act 1882, s. 14 (1).)

ee.   Mode of reckoning portions of years, months, &c.

A half-yearly period is taken as equal to six calendar months, a quarterly period as equal to three months, a half-monthly period as equal to fifteen days; the half-monthly period, if it has to be reckoned in combination with a period of one or several months, is taken as coming at the end of such period—BGB 189. If a period described by months or years is not continuous, the month is reckoned at thirty days and the year at 365 days (*e. g.* if a person having a right to be away from his work for a maximum period of two months in the year, takes the whole of January for the first part of his holiday, and takes the remainder of his holiday in July, he is not entitled to take more than twenty-nine days in July)—BGB 191. The expression 'beginning of the month' means the first, 'middle' the fifteenth, and 'end' the last day of the month—BGB 192.

In the case of any mercantile transaction (36) the expression 'eight days' means what it says—HGB 359 (2); but in all other cases the expression, according to the meaning given to it in ordinary German language, means seven days only.

6. MISREPRESENTATION, FRAUD, AND UNLAWFUL THREATS

a. Misrepresentation and Fraud.

109. In English law a transaction, induced by innocent misrepresentation, may be set aside under the rules on the subject established by the Courts of Equity. No corresponding right exists in German law. A person is not entitled to relief against an act induced by misrepresentation, unless the misrepresentation was intended to deceive (*arglistige Täuschung*). Fraudulent misrepresentation may in some cases consist in the non-disclosure of material facts. German law does not, like English law, single out special transactions as acts *uberrimae fidei*, but determines, according to the circumstances of each particular case, whether non-disclosure is fraudulent or not.

An act-in-the-law which is induced by a misrepresentation intended to deceive, is voidable at the option of the party deceived—BGB 123 (1).

The fraudulent misrepresentation of a third party does not entitle the party deceived by it to avoid the act induced by it, except in a case where the declaration of intention constituting such act is required to be communicated to another. In such a case the act is voidable altogether if the party to whom the declaration has to be communicated is aware, or by the application of proper care would have become aware, of the misrepresentation; otherwise it is only voidable as against any person deriving a right under the act with knowledge, or imputed knowledge, of the misrepresentation—BGB 123.

Illustration: *A*, who is falsely told by *D* that *B* has a valid patent for an

109

invention, makes an agreement with *B* for the purchase of this patent (*B* not assuming any responsibility for its validity), and for the employment of *C* as manager of a business to work the patent (see 141).   If *B* is aware, or by the application of proper care would have become aware, of the invalidity of the patent, the agreement is voidable altogether; if *B* excusably believes that the patent is valid, but *C* is aware of the invalidity, the right derived by *B* under the agreement is not forfeited on that ground, but the agreement may be avoided in so far as *C* derives any right thereunder.   *B*'s right may, however, be defeasible on the ground of mistake (99).

110   The right to avoid an act-in-the-law, voidable by reason of fraudulent misrepresentation, is barred by the lapse of one year from the date of the discovery of the misrepresentation, and cannot in any case be exercised after the lapse of thirty years from the date of the act—BGB 124.

Under English law an agreement induced by the fraud of a third party is not voidable or void on the ground of misrepresentation, but such an agreement will generally be held void on the ground of mistake (99) ; if any party benefiting by the agreement is aware of the fraud he would, as a general rule, be held to be a participator in the fraud.

b.   Unlawful Threats.

110. An act-in-the-law induced by unlawful threats is voidable at the option of the party induced by such threats, whether proceeding from a party to the act or from a third party—BGB 123 (1).

It will be seen that this rule goes much further than the English rule as to duress under which relief is not obtainable except in a case of actual or threatened physical violence, committed by a party to the transaction; an act done under the influence of actual violence would, under German law, not be looked upon as a manifestation of the will of the party compelled thereby, and would on that ground alone be inoperative. The expression *unlawful* threat includes any threat prohibited by law (*e. g.* a threat of criminal proceedings).

The right of avoidance is barred after the lapse of a year from the time at which the influence of the threat has ceased to be effective, and cannot in any case be exercised after the lapse of thirty years from the date of the act—BGB 124.

7. Acts-in-the-law subject to Conditions or Stipulations as to Time

a. Conditions.

aa.   Generally.

111. The effect of an act-in-the-law may be made subject to the happening of an uncertain future event, which is called a condition (*Bedingung*).   The event must be objectively uncertain.   Mere subjective uncertainty is insufficient.

Illustration: *A* receives a cablegram from a distant colony to the effect that he has a grandchild, without any indication as to its sex.   He executes a settlement to be operative in the event of the grandchild being a male; this is not a 'condition' within the meaning of the BGB, as *A*'s uncertainty as to the sex of the child is purely subjective.

Under English law the word 'condition' has a wider meaning; a promise being deemed to be a conditional promise if it is made dependent on the existence of any fact present or future, certain or uncertain.   Thus under the Sale of Goods Act 1893, s. 11, a stipulation as to the quality of existing goods may be a condition of the validity of a contract for sale, though such quality is a present fact and objectively certain.

If an act is to be inoperative, unless a specified event happens, the condition is called a condition precedent (*aufschiebende Bedingung*); if, on the other hand, the operativeness of an act is to come to an end on the happening of a specified event, the condition is called a condition subsequent (*auflösende Bedingung*).   In the case of a condition precedent, a new state of things is created by the fulfilment of the condition; in the case of a condition subsequent, its fulfilment restores the former state of things.

Illustration: A promise to pay £1,000 to *B*, if he shall at any time be called to the Bar, is a promise subject to a condition precedent; a promise to pay a yearly sum to *B*, which yearly sum shall cease to be payable in the event of his being called to the Bar, is a promise subject to a condition subsequent.

Certain kinds of conditions are called unreal conditions (*uneigentliche Bedingungen*), because they are conditions in appearance only, and do not correspond to the definition given above.   This is the case whenever it is either absolutely certain that the specified event must happen or absolutely certain that it cannot happen.   The effect of an unreal condition of the first-mentioned kind— illogically called a necessary condition (*notwendige Bedingung*)—is the same as if there had been a real condition, and as if the event had happened; the effect of an unreal condition of the kind secondly mentioned—equally illogically called an impossible condition (*unmögliche Bedingung*)—is the same as if there had been a real condition and the event had not happened. [1]

112   A condition the performance of which is dependent on the choice of the person on whom a right is conferred conditionally is called a potestative condition (*Potestativbedingung*).   Potestative conditions must be distinguished from burdens imposed upon gifts *inter vivos*, or testamentary gifts (204, 501).   In the case of a potestative condition precedent the whole transaction remains in suspense until the performance of the condition; in the case of a gift subject to a burden the gift is operative subject to the right of the donor or of his heirs to enforce the obligation imposed by the burden or (in certain events) to demand restitution.

bb.   Period of suspense.

112. The expression 'period of suspense' is used to indicate the period of time during which it is uncertain whether a condition will be fulfilled or not.   The rights and duties of the intended parties during such period of suspense are governed by the following rules:

(1) In the absence of any stipulation to the contrary the effects of the fulfilment of a condition only operate as from the date of fulfilment—BGB 158.

Illustrations:

1. A person entitled to the ownership of an estate, on condition of his attaining the age of twenty-one, is not entitled to the rents or profits received or chargeable with the outgoings paid during the period of suspense.

2. A person who forfeits an estate in the event of his re-marriage may retain the rents and profits and is chargeable with the outgoings during the period of suspense.

(2) If the condition was imposed with a stipulation providing that on its

---

[1]   Under Roman law an 'impossible condition" contained in a testamentary disposition was looked upon as non-existent, but the BGB does not admit this exception to the general rule.   If under Roman law a legacy was made payable in the event of the sun not rising on any particular day the legatee became entitled on the testator's death; under modern German law the legacy is not payable.

fulfilment the effects of such fulfilment shall operate as from a prior date the intended parties must, as far as possible, place each other in the position which they would have mutually occupied if the condition had been fulfilled at such prior date—BGB 159.

Illustration: A person entitled to the ownership of an estate, on condition of his attaining the age of twenty-one, under a testamentary disposition providing that, in the event of his attaining that age, he is to be entitled to such ownership as from the date of the testator's death, is entitled to claim the fruits and profits obtained during the period of suspense by the person, who under the will or under the statutory rules (473) was in possession during such period; on the other hand such person is entitled to the re-imbursement of his outlay for outgoings.

113

(3) Where any object has been sold or mortgaged subject to a condition precedent, any subsequent disposition [1] relating to such object made during the period of suspense is, in the event of the condition being fulfilled, inoperative, in so far as it would frustrate or restrict the effects of the conditional disposition; but a third party deriving title under any such subsequent disposition may acquire an indefeasible right under the rules protecting a person who in good faith acquires a right from another whose title is defective (333).   The same rule is applied—*mutatis mutandis*—to any disposition relating to an object held subject to a condition subsequent—BGB 161.

Illustration: *A* sells a horse to *B*, on condition of its winning the Derby, retaining possession of the horse; he subsequently sells and delivers the same horse to *C* during the period of suspense.   If the horse does not win the Derby the sale to *C* is valid in any event; if it wins the Derby *C* retains the ownership of the horse unless he knew of the previous conditional sale, or unless his ignorance was due to gross negligence.

(4) A person entitled to any right on the fulfilment of a condition precedent, or whose right is restored by the fulfilment of a condition subsequent, is in the event of the fulfilment of the condition entitled to claim compensation from the party whose right is terminated by the fulfilment of the condition, if such party by his wilful or negligent default during the period of suspense has caused the frustration or restriction of the right—BGB 160.

---

1   A disposition made by a judgment-creditor, or by a trustee in bankruptcy of the person by whom the conditional disposition was made, is deemed a disposition made by such person—BGB 161 (1).

Illustration: If an object sold subject to a condition precedent is during the period of suspense sold and delivered to another purchaser who acquires a good title under rule (3), the first purchaser is, on the fulfilment of the condition, entitled to compensation from the person by whom the second sale was effected.

cc. Effect of unlawful interference.

114   **113.** A party who, in violation of the requirements of good faith, promotes or frustrates the fulfilment of a condition, is not allowed to benefit by the effect of such unlawful interference.   If the fulfilment is brought about in such manner, the result is the same as if the condition had not been fulfilled; if the fulfilment is frustrated in such manner, the result is the same as if the condition had been fulfilled—BGB 162.

In the case of a 'potestative condition' (111), the promotion or hindrance of its fulfilment is not of course against good faith, if proceeding from the party on whose volition the fulfilment of the condition is made dependent, but it may be an act of bad faith if proceeding from the other party.

Illustration: A party who is to receive a certain payment, on condition of completing a certain work by a certain time, may of course work as hard as he likes for the purpose of completing the work within the stipulated time, but if the completion of the work is prevented by the interference of the party who has undertaken the payment, the above-mentioned rule takes effect, and the condition is deemed to have been fulfilled.

b.   Stipulations as to Time.

114. It may be stipulated by an act-in-the-law that its effects are to begin or to come to an end after the effluxion of a certain period of time.   If it is uncertain whether the end of such period will ever be reached (*dies incertus an, certus quando*; *dies incertus an, incertus quando*), the stipulation as to time is really in the nature of a condition.

A stipulation as to time (*Zeitbestimmung*), in the technical sense of the word, only exists in cases in which it is certain that the act will become operative, or cease to be operative, at the end of the stipulated period of time; on the other hand, the length of the period of time may either be ascertainable beforehand or otherwise.   Whether *A* promises to pay *B* or his estate, a yearly sum for a period of five years from the date of the promise (*dies certus an, certus quando*), or whether the death of *C* be stipulated for as the end of the period of payment (*dies certus an*, *incertus quando*) , the stipulation as to time comes within the definition.

The rules as to dealings with the property during the intermediate period are the same—*mutatis mutandis*—as the rules as to dealings with property during the period of suspense pending the fulfilment of a condition—BGB 163.   115

8.   AGENCY

a.   Definition of the Term.

115. An act of agency (*Vertretung*) , within the meaning of the German term, is a manifestation of the agent's volition intended to operate, as if it were a manifestation of the principal's volition.   A mere act of transmission is not an act of agency within the meaning of the German law; a person transmitting a declaration of intention is called a messenger (*Bote*) , and is not within the definition of an agent.

An agent must also be distinguished from a person acting in his own name, though employed on behalf of another person.   Thus a ' commission merchant ' (239) employed to buy goods, but dealing with the vendor of the goods in his own name, is not an agent within the meaning of the German definition.

In the usual English terminology the expression ' agent ' is frequently applied to designate any person employed by another, whether as a messenger, as an independent contractor, or as an agent within the meaning defined above, but in the course of this treatise it will be used in the narrower sense only.

An act of agency is ' active ' where the agent makes a declaration of intention on his principal's behalf; it is ' passive ' where he receives a declaration of intention addressed to the principal through his agency.   As, according to the definition, the act of agency must be a manifestation of the agent's own volition, active or passive acts of agency on the part of a person under *incapacity* are inoperative, but by virtue of an express enactment contained in BGB 165, the effectiveness of an active or passive act of agency is not impaired by the fact that the agent is of *restricted capacity*.

b.   Modes of establishing Agency.

aa.   *Agency created by Legal Rules.*

116. Powers of agency are frequently conferred by legal rules on persons

standing in certain relations to others.   The powers of the statutory agent who
116   acts on behalf of any person under incapacity, or in concurrence with any person
of restricted capacity (92) , and of the ' primary agents ' who act on behalf of the
corporate bodies referred to above (52) , as well as those exercisable by a partner
in a mercantile partnership on behalf of such partnership (68) , or by a wife on
her husband's behalf (412) sub (5) , are all powers conferred by legal rules.

In each of these cases, the law either defines the powers conclusively or
establishes a presumption in favour of certain defined powers; where a mere
presumption is established, the effect of restrictions on third parties is made
subject to certain conditions as to publicity. [1]

bb.   *Agency created by Act of Principal.*

(1) *Generally.*

117. The authority of an agent to act on behalf of his principal, where not
given by legal rules, is created by an act of the principal.   The agent's power
derived under such an act is termed *Vollmacht* in German law, and is here
translated by the term ' power of agency '.   The English term ' power of
attorney '   —by which an ordinary translator renders *Vollmacht*—is inappropriate,
as it suggests the idea of a formal document, whereas the German power of agency
can be conferred informally and even by implication.   The rule of English law,
according to which an authority to execute a contract under seal must be given by
deed under seal, has no counterpart in German law, it being expressly enacted
that the declaration of intention, by which a power of agency is conferred, need
not be made in the form required for the act which it authorizes—BGB 167 (2).

The declaration of intention conferring the power of agency must be
communicated to the agent who receives authority to act thereunder, or to the
party with whom the agent is authorized to transact business on the principal's
117   behalf—BGB 167 (1) ; it is in the nature of a unilateral act, and the rules as to
the communication of unilateral acts required to be communicated to other parties
(96) are applicable to it.

---

[1]   A foreign life insurance company, with an establishment in Germany, must appoint an agent with
unrestricted powers to enter into life insurance and annuity contracts (German Private Insurance Act of
1901 , s. 86) ; but as the appointment must always be made by a written document, the power, though
prescribed by law, is one created by the principal's act.

(2) *Powers of Agency conferred on Mercantile Employees.*

(a) *Powers of Procuration (Prokura).*

118. The HGB contains special rules on this subject, and distinguishes between *Prokura* (power of procuration) and *Handlungsvollmacht* (mercantile power of agency); the power of procuration differs from the ordinary power of agency, both in the mode of its creation and in the fact that the scope of the authority of an agent with powers of procuration is defined by law; managers and confidential clerks are thus enabled to act on behalf of their principals, without giving rise to doubts as to the scope of their authority.   In England it is customary to confer similar powers, but their scope depends upon the special circumstances of each case, and is generally unknown to the third parties dealing with the person who signs the name of his employer's firm with the prefix ' p. p. ' and the addition of his own name. [1]

A power of procuration within the meaning of the BGB can only be conferred: (1) by a person who is a mercantile trader in the full sense of the word (*Vollkaufmann*) (36); (2) by a mercantile partnership, or commandite partnership (68, 69); (3) by a share company (59); (4) by a limited partnership (61)—HGB 4, 116, 161, 232, 320; LPA 46.

The declaration of intention, by which a power of procuration is conferred, must be made by express words, and must be communicated to the person on whom the power is conferred, or to a third party, or must be made by public announcement, or by registration in the Commercial Register—HGB 48 (1).

The power of procuration enables the person on whom it confers authority to bind his principal or principals by all transactions (except sales or mortgages of immovables) which come within the scope of mercantile trade, even if they are entirely outside the range of the particular class of business transacted by the principal or principals—HGB 49.

The powers may be restricted, as between the principal and the agent, but except in cases of fraud, such a restriction does not operate against third parties, even where they are affected with notice of the restriction—HGB 50 (1, 2).

Where the principal or principals carry on several business establishments, the powers may be restricted to transactions entered upon on behalf of one of such

118

---

[1]   The English Bills of Exchange Act 1882, s. 25 gives a meaning to a signature per procuration which is entirely opposed to commercial usage.

establishments, but such a restriction is operative only in so far as each establishment carries on business under a distinctive firm name—HGB 50 (3).

A power of procuration may be conferred on several employees collectively, or on an employee jointly with a partner in a firm (where such partner himself has not full powers of agency); in the case of a share company it may be conferred on an employee jointly with a member of the directorate—HGB 48 (2), 125 (3), 232 (2).

(b) Ordinary Mercantile Power of Agency (Handlungsvollmacht).

119. An ordinary mercantile power of agency is conferred in the same way as any other power of agency. If the authority extends to the whole conduct of a mercantile business, it is deemed to include the power to enter into all kinds of transactions usual in any branch of the particular kind of business. If it only extends to special kinds of business, occurring in the course of mercantile trade, it is deemed to include the power to enter into all transactions usually occurring in the case of such special kinds of business—HGB 54 (1). It does not, in the absence of an express declaration to the contrary, include a power to sell or mortgage immovables, to raise loans, or to conduct legal proceedings—HGB 54 (2). Other restrictions of the power do not operate against a third party unless he is aware of such restrictions, or would have been aware of them if he had applied proper care—HGB 54 (3).

A traveller authorized to transact business outside the place where the establishment by which he is employed is situate, comes under the same rules as other employees with ordinary powers of agency. He is, however, presumed to have power: (1) to collect the invoice amount of the goods sold by him; (2) to give credit for the periods of time usual in the particular trade; (3) *inter praesentes*—to receive declarations as to the defects in the goods sold by him (192)—HGB 55. As to the powers of persons employed in shops and stores, see HGB 56.

A mercantile power of agency may be conferred on an employee in the principal's establishment or on a 'mercantile agent' (*Handlungsagent*). A person is a mercantile agent who, without being an employee in the principal's establishment, is permanently employed in the transaction of business for the purposes of the principal's mercantile trade—HGB 84 (1). If a mercantile agent has power to transact business so as to bind the principal, he is, as regards his power of agency, in the same position as a mercantile employee; if, on the other hand, he has only powers to act as an intermediary between the principal and third parties, a transaction, entered upon by him on behalf of the principal, requires ratification; such a transaction is, however, deemed to be ratified, unless the principal, immediately on becoming aware of the same, repudiates it by notice communicated to the other party thereto—HGB 85.

A mercantile agent who is not acting as traveller is not, in the absence of a special authority to that effect, entitled to receive payments on behalf of the principal, he is, however, presumed to be authorized to receive notices as to defects of goods and other similar matters—HGB 86, 87.

c.   Effect of Absence of Authority.

aa.   *Ratification.*

120.   No question as to agency can arise under German law in the case of acts done on behalf of unnamed or undisclosed principals.   A person, who does not professedly act on behalf of a named principal, cannot be treated as an agent, and a person, who was not named as principal by the agent acting on his behalf, cannot be treated as principal by the other party—BGB 164 (1) ; 177 (1). ' If the intention to act on behalf of another is not made manifest, the absence of the intention of a person to act on his own behalf cannot be taken into consideration ' —BGB 164 (2).

The rules as to unauthorized agency, therefore, only refer to cases in which a person, without authority to do so, purports to act on behalf of a named principal.

(1)   *Ratification of Agreements.*

An agreement to which an unauthorized agent is a party, may be made operative by the ratification of the alleged principal which may be communicated to the agent or to the other party.   120

The right of the alleged principal to ratify the agreement is forfeited if, after being called upon by the other party to declare his intention, he fails to do so within two weeks from the date of the communication of the request; if such a request is made, the ratification is inoperative unless communicated to the party making it—BGB 177 (2).

If the other contracting party knew of the absence of authority, he is bound until the time for ratification has elapsed; if he was ignorant of the absence of authority, he may repudiate the contract at any time before the ratification has been communicated.   The repudiation may be addressed to the alleged principal or to the agent, and is subject to the ordinary rules as to the communication of declarations of intention (96)—BGB 178.

(2) *Ratification of Unilateral Acts.*

In the case of unilateral acts, the rules are somewhat different. The party, to whom the declaration of intention (*e. g.* a declaration containing a notice to determine a lease) is made on behalf of an alleged principal, may, unless the principal has informed him of the agent's authority, demand the production of a written power, and in the case of the non-production of this power may repudiate the transaction at once—BGB 174. If he fails to avail himself of this right and raises no question as to the alleged power of agency, or if knowing of its absence he acquiesces in that fact, the position of both parties is the same as in the case of an agreement—BGB 180.

If a unilateral declaration of intention is communicated to a person who consents to receive it on behalf of another, but has no authority to do so (*e. g.* if a notice to determine a lease is addressed to the lessor's solicitor without the lessor's authority), ratification may take place in the same way as in the case of an active act of agency—BGB 180.

bb. *Liabilities of Unauthorized Agent.*

121   **121.** Under English law a person who in good faith acts as agent for another, without authority to do so, is liable in damages by reason of his implied warranty of authority; on the other hand a person who in bad faith, and with knowledge of the absence of authority, acts as agent for another renders himself liable to an action of deceit. No liability is of course incurred if the absence of authority was known to the other party. The rules of German law are similar in effect but of a more elaborate nature.

No liability is incurred by the unauthorized agent:

(1) if the other party was, or, by the application of proper care, would have become aware of the absence of authority;

(2) if the unauthorized agent was a person of restricted capacity (94), and his statutory agent did not give the required assent—BGB 179 (3).

Subject to these exceptions a person alleging powers of agency, which he does not in fact possess, is liable to another party with whom he enters into an agreement on behalf of a principal in the following manner:

(1) if the alleged agent knew that he had no authority, the other party may at his option either proceed with the agreement, substituting the agent as a party

in the place of the alleged principal, or repudiate it and claim full damages;

(2) if the absence of authority was unknown to the alleged agent (*e. g.* if the withdrawal of the principal's authority had been declared in the manner authorized in the case of an absent addressee (96), and had not reached him; or if he excusably misunderstood the principal's intentions), the other party can only claim damages for his 'negative interest' in the agreement; —as to the distinction between full damages and the 'negative interest' in the agreement, see 169 rule (2)—BGB 179 (1, 2).

d.   Operation of Powers of Agency.

aa.   As between Principal and Third Party.

122. A declaration of intention, made by an agent on behalf of his principal and within the scope of his authority, is immediately operative for or against the principal.   It is immaterial for this purpose, whether the fact that the agent is   122 acting for a specified principal is stated expressly or is apparent from the surrounding circumstances—BGB 164 (1).

In a corresponding manner a declaration of intention communicated to an agent who receives it on behalf of his principal, and has authority to do so, is binding on the principal—BGB 164 (3).

The identity of the principal must be made known to the party dealing with the agent, but it is not necessary that his name should be expressly mentioned; (*e. g.* a salesman in a shop does not expressly state that he is selling the goods on behalf of his employer, yet his intention to do so appears clearly from the circumstances). [1]

The operation of the powers of agency is consequently dependent on the presence of two factors, *viz.* : (1) the principal's authority (either existing at the time of the act or supplied by subsequent ratification); (2) the communication of the fact that the act is done on the principal's behalf.

An act done on the principal's behalf, though binding on the principal, is the agent's act, and the rules as to the knowledge of facts, as to discrepancies between real and apparent intention (98, 99), and as to the influence of fraud (102), or unlawful threats (103), are therefore applied with reference to the

---

[1]   The general rule is contained in BGB 164 (1); a special rule to the same effect as to the acts of the managers of a limited partnership is laid down by LPA 36.

agent's, and not with reference to the principal's knowledge or mental condition. This rule is expressly declared by BGB 166 (1), and substantially agrees with the corresponding rule of English law.

It is, however, clear that such a rule, though in harmony with the technical character of agency, would, if it stood alone, give a wide opportunity for fraud. It would manifestly be unfair if a principal, with knowledge of a defect in the title to any property, could instruct his agent who was ignorant of it to purchase such property, and thus obtain the protection afforded to a purchaser without notice, by taking advantage of the agent's ignorance.   English law is somewhat uncertain on this subject (see Blackburn *v.* Vigors 12 A. C. 531), but, according to German law, a principal, who has given definite instructions to an agent appointed by his own act (117), cannot take advantage of the fact that such agent was ignorant of circumstances of which the principal was aware, or of which he would have become aware, if he had applied proper diligence [1] —BGB 166 (2).

123

Where the powers of agency are conferred by rules of law (116), or where the agent is not acting in pursuance of definite instructions, the difficulty is met by the rules as to fraudulent misrepresentation made by third parties (109), it being remembered that intentional non-disclosure of material facts is frequently deemed fraudulent misrepresentation.   If therefore a wife, acting under her statutory power of agency in good faith, buys goods known by her husband to be stolen goods, the husband cannot take advantage of the wife's ignorance, though she is not an agent appointed by his act, and though she was not acting under special instructions.

bb.   As between Agent and Third Party.

123. The rights available against an agent who enters into an unauthorized agreement have been referred to above (121).   Where an agent acts within his authority the other party acquires no contractual rights against him personally, but if the agent is guilty of fraudulent misrepresentation, the other party, in addition to his remedies against the principal, has a right of indemnity available against the agent under the general rules as to unlawful acts (287).

cc.   As between Principal and Agent.

124. The mutual rights and duties of the principal and the agent are partly determined by the particular nature of the relation which creates the power of

---

1   As to the application of this principle to marine insurance, see p. 293 note 1 and 2.

agency (*e. g.* agreement for services (221) , mandate (232) , partnership (259)) , but the following rules are applicable to all cases:

(1) An agent is liable in damages for any wilful default on his part, and also for omission to apply the degree of care incumbent upon him under the particular circumstances (148) ; this rule applies in a case where a restriction, which is ineffective as against third parties, has been disregarded by the agent (148, 252, 259, 412 sub (5) , 460, &c.).

(2) A transaction to which a person is a party, as agent for a principal, is void if the same person without the principal's permission is also a party thereto as principal or as agent for another principal [1] —BGB 181.

(Under English law a transaction of such a nature may at the principal's option be upheld or repudiated.)

e.   Termination of Agency.

aa.   Duration of Powers of Agency.

125. A power of agency as a general rule remains in force as long as the relation for the purposes of which it was created remains in existence (*e. g.* the duration of the contract for services, or of the partnership term, determines the duration of the servant's or partner's power of agency; the duration of the incapacity of a person under incapacity determines the duration of his statutory agent's power of agency)—BGB 168.   This rule is, however, subject to the provisions as to revocability referred to below.

bb.   Revocability of Agency.

126. The power of agency may be revoked by the principal before its duration under the rule stated above (125) has expired, unless it is apparent from the relations between the parties under which the power subsists, that such revocability was to be excluded—BGB 168.   A power of agency given for the agent's own security (*e. g.* a power to sell goods or to collect debts conferred by way of security for money advanced by the agent to the principal) , is deemed to continue while the security is required.   An express agreement by which a power of agency is made irrevocable, is valid under German law, unless under the special circumstances of the case such a stipulation would be deemed *contra bonos mores*; (*e. g.* if the

---

1   The rule is not applied in the case of an act consisting exclusively of the performance of an obligation—BGB 181.

principal gave the agent an irrevocable general power to manage all his affairs).

125   Under Roman law a power of agency was deemed to be revoked by the principal's or agent's death or supervening incapacity, but under the new German law the rule that the power of agency continues until the relation in connexion with which it was created ceases, is not departed from in the event of the death or supervening incapacity of the principal or of the agent.   Many of the relations in connexion with which powers of agency are conferred continue after the death or supervening incapacity of the principal, but cease on the death or supervening incapacity of the agent; —as to mandates and agreements for services, see 229 sub (3), 231, 232; as to the continuance of a mercantile power of procuration, see HGB 52 (3).

A power of agency conferred for the agent's own security, is after his death or supervening incapacity, exercisable by his heirs or his statutory agent (as the case may be), unless the contrary has been expressly agreed upon.

Under English law a power of attorney can be made irrevocable: (1) for twelve months in any case; (2) without limit of time as between the principal and a party dealing with the agent, in any case in which the power was obtained for valuable consideration (Conveyancing Act 1882, ss. 8, 9), but these provisions are less favourable to persons dealing with an agent on the faith of the continuance of his powers, than the above-mentioned rules of German law, which are supplemented by the rules as to the mode of revocation referred to below (128).

cc.   Mode of Revocation.

(1) As between Principal and Agent.

127. As between principal and agent the power of agency is deemed to be revoked by the act or event which puts an end to the relation under which the power was conferred.   Thus if such relation comes to an end by any event other than notice (e. g. death, lapse of time, completion of the business in which the agent was employed) such event also terminates the power of agency; if it comes to an end by notice, no further notice is required to terminate the agency.

126   In the case of the termination of a mandate (232) or partnership (262) in consequence of any act or event other than express notice, a mandatory or partner who is excusably ignorant of such termination is, as between himself and his principal or partner, entitled to continue the exercise of his power of agency until he becomes aware of the termination or would have become aware of it had he applied proper care—BGB 674, 729; see also 415 sub (3), 446 sub (6), 467.

(2) *As between Principal and Third Parties.*

128. The following rules are applied:

(*a*) if the power of agency was conferred on the agent by a declaration made by the principal to a third party, the revocation does not affect such third party before it is communicated to him by the principal—BGB 170;

(*b*) if a third party has been informed by the principal of the creation of the power of agency, the revocation does not affect such third party until he has been informed of it in the same manner—BGB 171;

(*c*) if the creation of the power of agency was made known by public announcement, the revocation of the power does not affect any third party until a similar public announcement of the revocation is made—BGB 171;

(*d*) if the existence of the power was notified to a third party by the production of a written document, the revocation of the power does not affect such third party before such written document is returned to the principal, or (in the event of its having been lost or mislaid) is declared inoperative by the order of a competent Court—BGB 172, 175, 176;

(*e*) the above rules are not applicable as between the principal and any third party, who, when entering upon the particular transaction as to which the question arises, was, or by the application of proper care would have become, aware of the termination of the power of agency—BGB 173;

(*f*) if a mandatory, or partner, authorized under the rule mentioned above (127) to continue the exercise of his powers of agency, notwithstanding the termination of the mandate or partnership, deals with a third party who is aware or ought to have become aware of such termination, such third party cannot, as between himself and the principal or the other partners, take advantage of the continuance of the power—BGB 169.

9. ASSENT OF THIRD PARTIES
(AUTHORIZATION AND RATIFICATION)

a. In what Cases Required.

129. The expression 'assent' (*Zustimmung*) is used by the BGB in a general sense, which includes both the authorization of an act-in-the-law (*Einwilligung*) and its ratification (*Genehmigung*)—BGB 183, 184.

Among the cases in which a party to an act requires the assent of another, the following are of special importance:

(1) as mentioned above (94), the statutory agent's assent is, as a general rule, required to any act done by a person of restricted capacity;

(2) in many cases an act done by a husband or wife requires the assent of the other spouse (see for instance 414 sub (4));

(3) in any case in which a right relating to an immovable is charged with an incumbrance, the release of the right subject to such incumbrance requires the assent of the incumbrancer (310);

(4) any disposition [1] relating to an object, made by a person without power to make such disposition, is operative if it is made with the assent of the person entitled to dispose of the object—BGB 185.

b.　Rules as to Communication of Assent.

130. The assent is not as a general rule required to be declared in any particular form; the declaration of assent may be addressed to the party who requires the assent, or to the other party to the transaction to which the assent is given; a party intended to be affected by a unilateral act requiring the assent of a third party may repudiate such act, unless a written assent is produced to him, or unless the assent has been communicated to him by the assenting party—BGB 182; (compare the analogous rules mentioned above—94, 120).

128　　The authorization of an act-in-the-law may be revoked at any time before it has been acted upon, except in a case in which, owing to the special relation between the parties, the assent was irrevocable (see for instance 330, 360 sub (3), 428). The revocation may be communicated to the party requiring the assent or to the other party—BGB 183.

In some cases the required assent cannot be refused (see 527, 542).

1　The expression 'disposition' (*Verfügung*) occurs very frequently, and includes every transaction by which a right is transferred to another, or charged or pledged in favour of another.

CHAPTER III
PRESCRIPTION

1. Historical Statement

131. It is obviously desirable in the public interest that a claim left dormant for a considerable time should cease to be enforceable; and conversely, that the title to property over which the rights of ownership have been exercised for a considerable period should no longer be questioned.

Roman law gave effect to these principles by introducing a special defence (*longi temporis praescriptio*) available in cases of belated assertion of rights, and by conferring the ownership of a thing on a person who in good faith had exercised the rights of ownership for a specified period (*usucapio*). Both effects of the lapse of time were described by mediaeval writers under the head of *praescriptio*, a distinction being made between *praescriptio extinctiva* and *praescriptio acquisitiva*.

Under English law the lapse of the prescribed period as regards land not only bars the action, but also confers rights of ownership on the person in whose favour the time has run (2 & 3 Will. 4 cap. 27, s. 34); as regards *chattels*, on the other hand, the effluxion of the period bars the action, but creates no change of ownership (see Miller *v*. Dell (1891) 1 Q. B. 468, 471).

The BGB maintains the distinction between *praescriptio extinctiva* (which it calls *Verjährung*) and *praescriptio acquisitiva* (which it calls *Ersitzung* and which will be discussed below—329, 330, 334). The term prescription in this treatise is used as the equivalent for *praescriptio extinctiva*.

2. Effect of Prescription

132. The following rules apply as to the effect of prescription:

(1) where the duty to do an act is barred by prescription, the party originally bound by such duty may refuse to do the act;

(2) a party who has paid any sum of money or delivered any object by way
of performance of an obligation barred by prescription, or who has made any
acknowledgment, or given any security in respect of any such obligation, cannot
subsequently recover such sum of money or object, or revoke such acknowledgment
or security on the ground that the obligation was barred by lapse of time, whether
he was acquainted with this fact or not;

(3) the fact that an obligation is barred by prescription does not prevent a
creditor from exercising his rights over any object, charged, delivered, or
transferred to him by way of security for the performance of such obligation; but
such security is not available in respect of any claim for arrears of interest or of
any other payments or deliveries due at periodical intervals, in so far as such
claim is barred by prescription;

(4) where the principal claim is barred by prescription all accessory claims
(*e. g.* claims for interest, costs, &c.) are equally barred;

(5) the period of prescription may be shortened by agreement between the
parties, but any agreement for lengthening such period, or excluding or restricting
the application of the rules as to prescription, is void—BGB 222–225.

3. RULES AS TO PERIOD OF PRESCRIPTION

a. Time from which Period runs.

133. The time from which the period of prescription runs, is determined by
the following rules:

(1) in the case of an obligation to do any act, the period runs from the time
fixed for performance; in the case of an obligation to abstain from doing any acts
of a specified description, the period runs from the first act of infringement; if,
however, the performance cannot be claimed before notice given, the period runs
from the time of the expiration of the notice—BGB 198, 199;

(2) in the case of a claim to recover a thing from a person deriving title
from a former possessor, the period runs from the time at which such former
possessor acquired the possession of such thing—BGB 221;

(3) in the case of a claim which depends upon the avoidance of a voidable
act (except an act voidable under the rules of family law) , the period runs from

the first moment at which the right of avoidance arises [1]—BGB 200;

(4) in the case of several kinds of claims separate rules are laid down as to the time at which the period begins to run; see, for instance, 192 sub (5), 296;

(5) in the case of any claim subject to the short period of prescription referred to below—134 sub (2)—the beginning of the period is postponed to the end of the calendar year during which it would—but for this rule—begin, and in certain specified events to the end of the next following calendar year—BGB 201.

b.   Length of Period.

134. The length of the period of prescription is determined by the following rules [2] :

(1) in the absence of any special provision to the contrary, the period of prescription (as under the general rule of Roman law) is thirty years—BGB 195;

(2) shorter periods are substituted as regards certain classes of claims [3] of which the following are the most important instances:

(*a*) in the case of claims of carriers for freight and passengers' fares, of innkeepers and restaurant keepers for food, drink, and lodging, of workmen and servants for wages, or of medical and legal practitioners for their fees, the period is two years;

(*b*) in the case of claims of mercantile traders, manufacturers, and artisans for goods, work, and commission and disbursements, the period is two years, unless the goods, work, or services on account of which the claim arises, were delivered or given for the purposes of a trade carried on by the debtor, in which event the period is extended to four years;

(*c*) in the case of claims of persons engaged in farming and forestry for farm produce, firewood, &c. , delivered to the debtor for his private consumption, the period is two years;

132

---

[1]   This rule constitutes an exception to the general rule stated sub (1).   Thus, for instance, the right to a statutory portion of the estate of a deceased person arises on the death of the deceased, but the right of a statutory heir to avoid a testamentary disposition which excludes him only arises at the moment at which he becomes aware of the ground of avoidance; the period of prescription in such a case runs from the latter date only; in the case of claims under family law the rule stated sub (1) is applied.

[2]   In the case of a claim which is established by judgment or has the force of such a claim, the period is thirty years, without regard to its original nature; where, however, a claim for periodical future performance is established in this manner, the ordinary rule is applied—BGB 218-220.

[3]   As to the beginning of the period in the case of these classes of claims, see 133 rule (5).

(*d*) in the case of claims for arrears of interest, rent, and other similar periodical payments, the period is four years—BGB 196, 197;

(3) in the case of several kinds of claims, the length of the period is determined by separate rules, which will be mentioned in their respective places— see, for instance, 192 sub (5), 214, 241 sub (6), 296.

c.   Effect of Disabilities.

135. The length of the period is extended in the following cases:

(1) in the case of a claim against any person who is under incapacity, or of restricted capacity, and cannot be sued, on the ground that, for the time being, he is without a statutory agent, [1] an additional period is allowed, which comes to an end six months after the appointment of a statutory agent for such person;

(2) in the case of a claim on behalf of or against the estate of a deceased person an additional period is allowed, which comes to an end six months after the acceptance of the inheritance on the part of the heirs (522), or of the executor's office on the part of the executor (526), or after the institution of bankruptcy proceedings against the estate (536), or after the appointment of a curator (519) or administrator (535) of the estate.

If in either case the period of prescription is less than six months, the length of the period of prescription is substituted for the six months—BGB 206, 207.

4.   Interruption and Suspension of Prescription

a.   Interruption.

136. The BGB distinguishes between the interruption (*Unterbrechung*) and the suspension (*Hemmung*) of the prescription.   Where the prescription is interrupted, the time which has run prior to the date of interruption is not counted if the same claim becomes again subject to prescription where the prescription is suspended, the time which has run before the date of such suspension is added to the time running after its cessation—BGB 205.

The prescription is *interrupted* :

133

------

1   A person under incapacity cannot under any circumstances be sued while he has no statutory agent, but a person of restricted capacity can sue or be sued without his statutory agent in respect of any transaction into which he can enter without the assent of his statutory agent (94)—CPO 52.

(1) by part payment, payment of interest, giving of security, or any other act by which the claim is acknowledged—BGB 208;

(2) by action brought for the establishment or satisfaction of the claim, and by certain other acts deemed to have the same effect (*e. g.* the institution of bankruptcy proceedings; service of a third party notice which has reference to the claim; set-off by way of defence in an action; institution of arbitration proceedings, &c.)—BGB 209, 210, 220.

In case (1) a new period begins to run from the date of the last act of acknowledgment; in case (2) the interruption continues until the proceedings are terminated, but if the claim is withdrawn, or dismissed by an order not affecting its validity (*e. g.* on the ground of the incompetence of the Court), the interruption is ineffective, unless fresh proceedings are instituted within six months [1]—BGB 211 (1), 212–217, 220; if the proceedings are discontinued by consent, or simply allowed to drop, the interruption comes to an end at the moment when the last step is taken in the proceedings—BGB 211 (2), 215 (1), 220.

Illustration: If fees become payable to a medical practitioner in 1904, the period of prescription comes to an end on the 31st December, 1906 (see 133, rule (5); 134, rule (2)).   If an action is begun on that day, the plea of prescription is not available; if the action is dismissed by reason of its not being brought in the proper Court, and a new action is begun on the 30th June, 1907, the result is the same; but if the new action is begun on the 1st July, the claim is barred.   If the action is brought in the proper Court, and pleadings are delivered but nothing further is done, then the two years begin again to run from the date at which the last pleading was delivered.

b.   Suspension.

137. Prescription is *suspended* during the following periods: 134

(1) during any additional time expressly allowed by the creditor for the satisfaction of a claim which has fallen due, or during a period of time within which the debtor, by reason of some temporary circumstance, is entitled to refuse

---

[1]   In so far as the six months fall within the last six months of the period of prescription, the prescription is suspended during that period; in the case of the disabilities referred to above (135), the period is extended in a manner corresponding to the extension there mentioned—BGB 212 (2).

satisfaction [1] —BGB 202 (1) ;

(2) during the last six months of the period of prescription, if during such time the claimant is prevented from taking proceedings by reason of the temporary cessation of the administration of justice (in consequence of war, revolution, &c.), or by reason of *vis major* (deprivation of liberty, interruption of means of communication, severe illness, &c.)—BGB 203;

(3) as regards any claim between spouses during the continuance of the marriage; as regards any claim between a parent and a child during the child's minority; as regards any claim between guardian and ward during the continuance of the guardian's office [2] —BGB 204.

---

[1]   This rule is not applied in any case in which the debtor's temporary right to refuse satisfaction is based on one of the following grounds: (*a*) on a right of lien (174) ; (*b*) on the *exceptio non adimpleti contractus* (159) ; (*c*) on one of the special grounds of defence open to a surety (273) ; (*d*) on one of the dilatory pleas open to an heir of the original debtor (539)—BGB 202 (2).

[2]   As to the suspension of prescription in the events mentioned in the note to 136, see p. 121 note 1.

SECOND BOOK

LAW OF OBLIGATIONS

FIRST DIVISION
GENERAL RULES

CHAPTER I
NATURE OF OBLIGATORY RIGHTS AND DUTIES

1. DEFINITION

138. THE term *Schuldverhältniss* (obligatory relation) was substituted by the
BGB for the term 'obligation', formerly used in Germany, and still retained in
the *Swiss Obligationenrecht*.   It denotes a relation between two persons which
entitles one of them to claim from the other some act or omission recognized as
capable of producing a legal effect—BGB 241.   The BGB describes such an act
or omission by the general term *Leistung* which in the course of this treatise will
be translated by 'performance'.

Some of the rights against definite persons which arise under family law (*e. g.*
the right to the custody of an infant, or the personal rights of one spouse against
another) are not usually included among obligatory rights (79), though strictly
speaking they would come under the definition.   A person who is entitled to the
performance of an obligation, whatever its nature may be, is, according to
German legal terminology, called the 'creditor' (*Gläubiger*), and the person
who is under the obligation is called the 'debtor' (*Schuldner*).   For the sake of
brevity, the terms 'creditor' and 'debtor' will be used in this sense, though in
ordinary English language they have a somewhat narrower meaning.

2. IMPERFECT OBLIGATIONS

139. Some obligatory relations have a limited legal effect, notwithstanding the
fact that they do not create any rights enforceable by action.   Thus, for instance,
the transactions characterized by BGB 762–764 as gaming or wagering transactions
(265), do not impose any liability enforceable by action on the losing party, but

a party who has paid the amount of his loss cannot recover it on the ground that he was under no legal liability to make the payment—BGB 762 (1). A similar rule exists with reference to marriage brokage—BGB 656.

As mentioned above—132 rule (2), the payment of a debt barred by prescription (131) cannot be recovered, even if it was made in ignorance of the fact that the debt had become barred by prescription—BGB 222 (2).

No return or reduction can be claimed in respect of any performance, made in satisfaction of any liability incapable of legal enforcement, if such performance was made in compliance with a moral duty or the rules of social propriety—BGB 814.

In all these cases there is no claim in the technical sense of the word; but, on the other hand, the performance is not deemed an *indebitum*. The term 'natural obligation' is used by some textbook writers to denote the obligations belonging to the class now referred to, while others apply the term 'imperfect obligation'.

CHAPTER II
CREATION OF OBLIGATIONS

1. AGREEMENTS

a. Generally.

140. As a general rule, an obligation cannot be created by any act-in-the-law except an agreement (*Vertrag*) between the parties—BGB 305. There are, however, certain unilateral acts which create obligations, the effect of which is expressly recognized (see 142).

Under English law an agreement, not made by deed under seal, is inoperative unless supported by valuable consideration, but no similar rule exists in German law.

An agreement is formed by offer and acceptance in the manner shown above (100, 101), subject to such rules as to form and other matters affecting the validity of acts-in-the-law as have also been mentioned above (89 to 106).

An act-in-the-law, constituted by concurrent declarations of at least two parties, is called an agreement (*Vertrag*), whether any obligation arises under it or not. An agreement creating an obligation on at least one side (which in English terminology is called a 'contract') is in German legal language called an 'obligatory agreement' (*obligatorischer Vertrag*).

Some of the rules contained in the part of the BGB dealing with the law of obligations are applicable to agreements which do not create obligatory relations (*e. g.* sales, exchanges, or gifts completed by immediate delivery or payment), and it will be understood that the expression 'agreement', as used in the further course of this treatise, will include both kinds of agreements.

An obligatory agreement may result in a unilateral obligation (*e. g.* the obligation to repay a loan) or in a bilateral obligatory relation. The creation of a bilateral obligatory relation may be intended by the parties, but even where the primary intention of the parties was the creation of a unilateral obligation only, an obligation may be created on the other side as an incidental result.   Thus, in the case of a mandate (232), the primary intention is to impose on the mandatary the duty to act according to his instructions; but the principal may incidentally come under an obligation to reimburse the mandatary for his expenses.   In such cases the Roman law gave to the party entitled to the performance of the primary obligation the *actio directa*, while the party entitled to the performance of the incidental obligation became entitled to the *actio contraria*.

Agreements intending to create obligations on both sides are called reciprocal agreements (*gegenseitige Verträge*).   Agreements primarily intended to create an obligation on one side only, but incidentally resulting in the creation of an obligation on the other side, are called imperfectly reciprocal obligations (*unvollkommene gegenseitige Verträge*).

b.   Agreements in favour of Third Parties.

141.   Roman law did not allow a person who was not a party to an agreement to assert any rights created thereby; but under Germanic law agreements giving enforceable rights to third parties were not unknown.   English law, according to the finally established doctrine on this subject, follows the rule of Roman law (see Tweddle *v*. Atkinson 1 B. & S. 393; Eley *v*. Positive &c. Co. 1 Ex. D. 88); but the effect of an agreement giving rights to a third party may be attained by the creation of a trust.   An ordinary ante-nuptial settlement, by which enforceable equitable rights are in this manner given to the unborn issue of the intending spouses, is an example of daily occurrence. [1]

The BGB expressly recognizes the principle that a performance may by agreement be stipulated for in favour of a third party, with the effect of giving a direct right to such third party to claim such performance—BGB 328 (1).

The question whether a third party for whose benefit an agreement is entered into, is to have an enforceable right, whether such right is to vest forthwith, or whether it is intended to be subject to any condition (111) or stipulation as to time (114), and, finally, whether such an agreement may be revoked or modified by the parties thereto without the concurrence of the third party, must, in default of any express declaration of intention on the subject, be ascertained from the circumstances, and more particularly from the object of the agreement—

---

[1]   See also Married Women's Property Act 1882, s. 11, as to a policy on a man's life effected for the benefit of his wife and children.

BGB 328 (2).

The following presumptions and rules of interpretation are applied, in so far as no contrary intention is shown by the agreement:

(1) a promise to the effect that the promisor will pay a debt owing by the promisee to a third party, does not, in the absence of any of the special circumstances referred to in the following rules, give such third party a right to claim payment of the debt from the promisor—BGB 329;

(2) a right in favour of a third party stipulated for in a life insurance policy (266) or annuity agreement (269) is enforceable by such third party—BGB 330; (as to the time of vesting, see rule (4));

(3) if any benefit is conferred on the promisor exclusively in consideration of a promise in favour of a third party, such third party has a right to claim performance of such promise—BGB 330;

(4) if the date of the promisee's death is to be the date of performance (*e. g.* if A insures his life for the benefit of B), the third party, for whose benefit the promise is made, does not acquire a vested interest until the date of such death—BGB 331 (1); such an agreement may, therefore, during the life of the promisee be rescinded without the third party's concurrence, and if the third party dies before the promisee, his representatives are not in any event entitled to claim performance on the death of the latter; if the third party is not as yet born on the promisee's death, the period of vesting is postponed to the time of his birth; the agreement cannot in such a case be rescinded between the date of the promisee's death and the date of the third party's birth—BGB 331 (2);

(5) if the promisee has reserved the right to substitute another for the third party named in the agreement, the right of substitution may be exercised by testamentary disposition as well as by act *inter vivos*—BGB 332;

(6) no act of acceptance is required on the part of the third party, but a renunciation on his part by declaration communicated to the promisor is effective—BGB 333;

(7) all defences available as between the promisor and the promisee are also available as between the promisor and the third party—BGB 334;   142

(8) in the absence of any stipulation to the contrary, the promisee, as well as the third party, has the right to enforce the claim—BGB 335. [1]

---

1   As to the rule contained in HGB 435 which is generally referred to as a special instance of the recognition of an agreement in favour of a third party enforceable by such third party, see 241 sub (3).

2.   Unilateral Acts-in-the-Law Creating Obligations

142. An obligation must of necessity inure in favour of another, but it is not necessary that such other should always be cognizant of the right conferred upon him, or that his acceptance should be a condition of the binding nature of the obligation.   Under English law a promise made by deed is binding though not accepted by the promisee (Xenos *v.* Wickham 2 H. L. 296), but a promise made by parol, owing to the requirement of consideration, cannot be binding unless accepted by the other party (from whom, of course, the consideration must pass).

German law recognizes the following kinds of acts as unilateral acts creating a binding obligation, without the necessity of acceptance on the part of another party:

(1) an act *inter vivos* providing for the constitution of an incorporated foundation (57) [1]; (2) the public offer of a reward (283); (3) the execution of an 'obligation to bearer' (281).

3.   Obligations Created Otherwise Than
by Act-in-the-Law

143. It was customary in the older textbooks to classify all obligations as being *ex contractu*, *quasi ex contractu*, *ex delicto*, *quasi ex delicto*; but this mode of classification has now been completely abandoned.

There is now a broad line of demarcation between obligatory rights created by act-in-the-law and other obligatory rights.   The latter may be subdivided under two principal heads, namely: (1) remedial obligatory rights; (2) obligatory rights conferred by outside circumstances.

A remedial obligatory right (79) may arise on the breach of an antecedent right (167), or on the commission of an unlawful act by which an absolute right is violated (284).   In both cases the remedial right is of an obligatory nature, and in both cases it is a right to receive compensation in accordance with the definition of that term given below (167).

---

[1]   The founder in such a case does not become bound until his scheme has been approved by the competent public authority; it is, therefore, by no means a forced construction to say that the transaction is in reality an agreement between the founder and the public authority for the benefit of a third party.

Among the obligations imposed by outside circumstances, those created by the rendering of voluntary services (*Geschäftsführung ohne Auftrag*, *negotiorum gestio*— 301) and those created by the receipt of unjustified benefits (*ungerechtfertigte Bereicherung*—(298); '*jure naturae aequum est neminem cum alterius detrimento et injuria fieri locupletiorem*' —Dig. 50. 17. 206) require special attention.

Mutual obligations also arise between parties who are joint owners of property, or subject to joint liabilities by reason of some act or event not brought about by their own agreement, *e. g.* co-heirs of a deceased person—(*Gemeinschaft*, *communio incidens*—304, 305).

There are finally the obligations which in this treatise are described as liabilities created 'by estoppel' (306), and the obligations imposed on finders of lost objects (307).

CHAPTER III
RULES OF INTERPRETATION AS TO
PERFORMANCE OF OBLIGATORY DUTIES

1. Miscellaneous Rules

144. As stated in the section dealing with the interpretation of acts-in-the-law (107), the general rules there mentioned are supplemented by the special rules stated below as to the manner in which obligatory duties must be carried out, in the absence of any express or implied agreement to the contrary. [1]

(1) *General Rule.*

The debtor is under an obligation to effect the promised performance in such manner as good faith between the parties requires, due regard being had to ordinary usage—BGB 242. (This rule simply extends to all obligations the provisions relating to agreements contained in BGB 157 referred to above (107).)

(2) *As to Quality of Things not specifically defined.*

A person who is under an obligation to deliver a generically defined thing (*eine der Gattung nach bestimmte Sache*) must deliver a thing of the promised description and of average kind and quality. As soon as the debtor has done everything required on his part for performing his obligation in this manner, his obligation is deemed to refer to the thing appropriated to the agreement—BGB 243. The appropriation of the thing to the performance of the obligation converts the generic into a specific obligation.

Where the obligation to deliver generically defined goods arises under a mercantile transaction (36), merchantable goods of average kind and quality must be delivered—HGB 360, and see HGB 345.

---

[1] These rules, as far as the nature of the case admits in each particular instance, are applied to obligations imposed by law (*e. g.* under the rules of family law), as well as to those created by act of the parties concerned.

(3) *As to Currency, Weight, and Measure.*

Where payment is stipulated for in a foreign currency the payment may be   145
made in German currency at the rate of exchange current at the time and place of
payment—BGB 244.

Where payment is stipulated for in a kind of coin not current at the time of
payment, the payment must be effected as if no such stipulation had been made—
BGB 245; in the case of a mercantile transaction (36), measurement, weight,
currency, time, and distance are determined in accordance with the rule prevailing in
the place where the agreement is to be performed—HGB 361, and see HGB 345.

(4) *As to Interest.*

Where interest is payable by virtue of any agreement or legal rule the rate,
unless otherwise specified, is 4 per cent. per annum—BGB 246.

Where a claim arises under a mercantile transaction between mercantile
traders, interest at the rate of 5 per cent. per annum is payable from the date of
maturity, even in the absence of any agreement to that effect—HGB 352, 353.

(5) *As to Accessories.*

An obligation to sell or charge a thing comprises an obligation to sell or
charge the accessories of such thing (76)—BGB 314.

(6) *As to Discretionary Mode of Performance.*

Where the mode of performance is to be determined by one of the contracting
parties or by a third party, [1] such determination must, in the absence of an
express stipulation allowing unfettered discretion, be made in an equitable
manner; if made by one of the parties it must be communicated to the other
party; if made by a third party, it must be communicated to one of the parties. [2]
Where an equitable determination is not made within a reasonable time the
aggrieved party may refer the matter to the determination of a competent Court—
BGB 315, 317 (1), 318 (1), 319 (1).

Where the value of the consideration to be given in exchange for the other   146
party's performance is not specified, such other party is entitled to determine the

---

[1]   For an example, see 499 sub (d).

[2]   As to determinations to be made by several third parties, see BGB 317 (2).   As to certain
determinations to be made by the purchaser in the case of a mercantile sale, see HGB 375.

nature of the consideration—BGB 316.

Where it is expressly stipulated that a third party is to determine the mode of performance in his unfettered discretion, and where such third party is unable or unwilling to determine the matter, or unduly delays such determination, the agreement becomes inoperative—BGB 319 (2).

The determination made by a third party may be impugned by one of the parties to the agreement on the ground of mistake (99), fraudulent misrepresentation (109), or unlawful threats (110)—BGB 318 (2).

(7) *As to Compensation for Outlay.*

The duty to compensate for outlay in money or in kind, whether arising by virtue of an act-in-the-law or under any rules of law—see, for instance, 231 rule (5), 252, 302, 544—includes a duty to pay interest—see above sub (4)—on the money spent, or on the value of the material used, as from the date of the outlay. If a person entitled to the reimbursement of outlay had the enjoyment of the fruits or profits (77) of the thing for which such outlay was incurred, the duty to pay interest only arises in so far as consideration was given for such fruits or profits—BGB 256.

If the duty to compensate for outlay is limited to the amount by which the value of the thing for which the outlay was incurred has been increased (see, for instance, 198), interest on outlay is payable only in so far as the aggregate amount of principal and interest does not exceed that amount. [1]

(8) *As to Obligations to render Accounts or to furnish Inventory.*

The duty to render accounts for receipts and disbursements (see, for instance, 231, 414, 467) includes the duty to furnish vouchers. Where there is reason to suspect that the accounts relating to the receipts have not been made out with the necessary amount of care, the person entitled to the accounts may, unless the matter is of small importance, require the accounting party to make a sworn declaration as to the accuracy and completeness of the account—BGB 259, 261.

In a similar way a person whose duty it is to deliver an aggregate of things (71), or to give information as to the component parts of such aggregate, must furnish an inventory of such component parts to the party entitled, and make a

147

---

[1] If a person, entitled to claim compensation for outlay made for a specific purpose, has incurred an obligation in order to effect such purpose, he is entitled to be released from the obligation or, in the case of an obligation the performance of which is not yet due, to receive security—BGB 257.

declaration on oath as to the completeness of the inventory if required to do so—BGB 260, 261.

The sworn declaration in any such case is called *Offenbarungseid* or *Manifestationseid*.

(9) *As to Exercise of ' Jus tollendi'*.

A person entitled to remove an article affixed to a thing which has to be delivered to another (see, for instance, 209 sub 4, 361, 378), must after effecting such removal restore the thing to its prior state.   He may exercise the right in question (frequently called *jus tollendi* by German writers) after the delivery of the thing, but the person to whom it was delivered may in such a case claim security for the damage which may be caused by the severance—BGB 258.

2.   ALTERNATIVE OBLIGATIONS

145. Where the debtor is under an obligation to perform one out of several specified acts, then, in the absence of any contrary agreement between the parties, the following rules apply:

(1) The election rests with the debtor—BGB 262.

(2) After the election has been made and communicated to the other party the selected performance is deemed to be the only performance stipulated for *ab initio*—BGB 263.

(3) If the debtor does not exercise his right of election, and the creditor's claim has to be enforced by judicial proceedings, judgment is given in an alternative form; such a judgment entitles the creditor to enforce such of the alternative obligations as he may think fit, but the debtor may, prior to the completion of such enforcement, satisfy his obligation by doing one of the alternative acts stipulated for by him—BGB 264 (1).

148

Illustration: *A* agrees to sell to *B* either his brown mare or his grey mare for the sum of £ 50 but fails to perform his agreement.   *B* obtains judgment directing *A* ' to deliver to *B* the said brown mare or the said grey mare against payment of the sum of £ 50 '.   *B* obtains an order enabling the official process-server to obtain possession of the grey mare, but before this order has been carried out *B* delivers the brown mare.   The claim is satisfied.

(4) If, according to the agreement between the parties, the creditor has the right to elect, and he delays his election, the debtor may request him to notify his election within a specified reasonable period of time; if after the lapse of the period the request remains unsatisfied, the right of election passes to the debtor—BGB 264 (2).

(5) If one of the promised alternative acts is, or becomes impossible (158), the obligation is deemed to refer to the other alternative act or acts; if however the impossibility was caused by the act or default of the non-electing party, the electing party may elect the impossible act. The result of such an election is that the electing party, if he is the debtor may consider his obligation satisfied; if he is the creditor he may claim damages for non-performance—BGB 265.

Illustration: If in the event mentioned in the illustration to rule (3) the grey mare is killed owing to *A*'s negligence, *B* may at his option accept the delivery of the brown mare in satisfaction of *A*'s promise, or claim damages for non-performance of the promise to deliver the grey mare.

Rules (1) and (2) and the first part of rule (5) correspond to the rules of English law on the same subject; as to rule (1), see judgment of Bovill J. in Deverill *v.* Burnell L. R. 8 C. P. 475, 478; as to rule (2) Co. Lit. 146 a; as to rule (5) MeIlquham *v.* Taylor (1895) 1 Ch. 53.

3. PLACE AND TIME OF PERFORMANCE

a. Place of Performance.

146. In the absence of any contractual stipulation as to the place of performance or of any special circumstances (such as the nature of the obligatory relation between the parties or any specific rule of law applicable thereto) from which the place of performance can be inferred, the following rules apply:

(1) if the obligation was incurred in the course of the debtor's trade, the debtor's place of business is the place of performance [1]—BGB 269 (2);

---

[1] The place of performance (*Erfüllungsort*, *Leistungsort*) must be distinguished from the place of destination (*Bestimmungsort*); if a vendor undertakes to deliver goods by forwarding them from one place to another, the place from which they are to be forwarded is, as a general rule, the place of performance for the vendor's obligation, whereas the place to which they are forwarded is the place of destination. The circumstance that the debtor has undertaken or is under a legal duty to pay the carriage does not in itself justify the conclusion that the place of destination is the place of performance—BGB 269 (3), 270 (4)—but such an intention may be gathered from other circumstances. In the case of a sale of goods the place of destination is, as a general rule, the place of performance for the *purchaser's* obligation to *receive* the goods,

(2) in every other case the place in which the debtor was domiciled at the time when the obligation was incurred by him is the place of performance [1]—BGB 269 (2) ;

For instances of cases in which the place of performance is fixed by specific rule of law applicable under the special circumstances, see 252, 379.

In the case of an agreement by which several obligations are undertaken, each obligation may of course have a separate place of performance.

The ascertainment of the place of performance is frequently of importance for the purpose of determining the choice of law, the interpretation of a particular expression—see, for instance, 144 rule (3), 147 rule (4), —or the jurisdiction of a particular court.   On the latter point, see CPO 29.

Under English law the debtor is generally bound to find the creditor—see Walton *v.* Mascall 13 M. & W. at p. 458; 67 R. R. at p. 676, and Bills of Exchange Act 1882, s. 52 (1), —but as regards the sale of goods the rule is similar to the above-mentioned rule of German law—see Sale of Goods Act 1893, s. 29 (1).   As to the ascertainment of the place of performance for the purposes of establishing the jurisdiction of the English High Court, see RSC, Order XI, rule 1 (*e*).

150

b. Time of Performance.

147. The following rules apply as to the time of performance, in the absence of any other expressed or implied stipulation:

(1) where no time is fixed, the performance of the obligation may be offered or claimed as soon as the obligation is incurred—BGB 271 (1) ;

(2) where a time is fixed the creditor cannot claim, but the debtor may offer

---

while the place of performance for the *vendor's* duty to *deliver* under the general rule is the vendor's place of business (see RGZ 49, 72) ; in the case of a money debt, the creditor's place of business is presumed to be the place of destination if the debt arose in the course of his business, and the place of his domicil is the place of destination in any other case, but the question, whether the place of destination is also the place of performance, is determined by the rules stated in the text—BGB 270 (1) (2) (4).   A debtor who owes a money debt is presumed to have undertaken the cost and risk of transmission, unless such cost and risk are increased by the fact that the creditor after the date of the creation of the obligation has removed his domicil or his place of business, in which event the increase of the cost and the whole risk has to be borne by the creditor—BGB 270 (1) (2) (3).

1   Rules (1) and (2) are also applied in cases in which an obligation is of a negative nature—RGZ 51, 312.

performance before the stipulated time; if the debt does not bear interest [1] a debtor who repays it before the stipulated time is not entitled to claim any abatement—BGB 271 (2), 272;

(3) the performance of any obligation incurred in the course of a mercantile transaction (36) cannot be claimed or offered except during the usual business hours—HGB 345, 358;

(4) if it is agreed that an obligation incurred in the course of any mercantile transaction is to be performed in 'the spring' or in the 'autumn', or at any similarly defined point of time, the meaning of any such expression is determined by the commercial usage prevalent in the place of performance—HGB 345, 359 (1). (For the general rules as to computation of time, see 108.)

---

[1] In the case of interest-bearing debts there is, as a general rule, an expressed or implied agreement not to repay before a stipulated time; in the absence of such an agreement interest is payable up to the date of payment only. As to the right to repay debts bearing more than 6 per cent. interest, see 106.

CHAPTER IV
CIRCUMSTANCES AFFECTING LIABILITY

1. ABSOLUTE LIABILITY AND LIABILITY FOR DEFAULT

a. General Rules.

148. A debtor may under a special legal rule applicable under the circumstances, or under the terms of his promise, be bound by his obligation, even if its performance becomes impossible without any default on his part; but, as a general rule, he is not liable for non-performance or incomplete performance if the performance or the complete performance was rendered impossible by any circumstance not brought about by his own default—BGB 275. The default may be wilful or negligent. The expression 'wilful default'[1] is used as an equivalent of *Vorsatz*, which term denotes any default made by the debtor with the consciousness of the consequences of his conduct, though not necessarily with the intention to violate his obligation; where an aggravated liability is attached to intentional default the BGB uses the word *Arglist* or *Böswilligkeit*, or some similar word—see, for instance, 157 b, 160 note 2 (p. 159 note 1), 185, 201 sub (4), 222 sub (3).

b. Degrees of Negligence and Diligence.

Negligence is called *Fahrlässigkeit*, and means the omission of the degree of diligence (*Sorgfalt*) which under the special circumstances of the case the debtor was bound to give. In the absence of any contrary legal rule applicable under the special circumstances, or of any express or implied stipulation, the diligence usual 'in ordinary intercourse' must be applied—BGB 276 (1). If a person is required to use diligence in a transaction which on his side is a mercantile transaction (36), 'the diligence of a careful mercantile trader' (*die Sorgfalt*

---

[1] As to the meaning of this expression in English law, see Bennett *v.* Stone (1903) 1 Ch. 509, 515, 519.

eines ordentlichen Kaufmanns) is required—HGB 347.

152 In certain specified cases it is sufficient to give the degree of care which the person concerned usually gives to his own affairs (*diligentia quam suis*)—see, for instance, 252, 259, 412 sub (8), 442—but a person whose liability is reduced in this manner is in any event liable for damage caused by gross negligence in the performance of his obligation—BGB 277.

Gross negligence (*grobe Fahrlässigkeit*) is not defined by the BGB, but the definition of Roman law still holds good: ' *Lata culpa est nimia negligentia , id est non intelligere quod omnes intelligunt* ' —Dig. 50. 16. 213. 2 (Ulpian).   To disregard a risk which is obvious to everybody constitutes gross negligence. [1] Damage done recklessly is called *bösliche Schädigung*. [2]   The word *böslich* must be distinguished from *böswillig*, which, as mentioned above, implies an intention to cause damage.

c.   Circumstances excluding Liability.

A person is not responsible for damage caused by any act done in a state of unconsciousness or during morbid disturbance of the mental faculties, excluding the free action of the power of volition, unless such unconsciousness or mental disturbance was brought about by culpable indulgence in stimulants or narcotics; [3] a deaf and dumb person or an infant between the ages of seven and eighteen [4] is not responsible for any damage caused by any act done by him while he did not possess the degree of intelligence required for enabling him to realize his responsibility.

Where the damage was caused by an unlawful act (284) for which compensation cannot be obtained from a third party under the rules stated below (150), the person by whom the act was done, though released from direct responsibility by the effect of the rules stated above, has to compensate the injured party in so far

---

[1]   The cases in which a debtor's responsibility is restricted to damage caused by his wilful default and gross negligence are exceptional; for examples, see 155, 201, 219, 301, 307.

[2]   See, for instance, HGB 202, which provides that where, on the formation of a company, shares are allotted for any consideration other than cash, the promoters are liable for any damage caused by them recklessly in connexion with such allotment.

[3]   If the act was done under the influence of culpable indulgence in stimulants or narcotics, the person by whom it was done is responsible as if he had been guilty of negligence—BGB 276 (1), 827.

[4]   An infant who has not attained the age of seven, being under total incapacity, is not in any event responsible for any damage caused by him.

as this appears equitable under the circumstances, regard being had to the   153
pecuniary position of the parties, and in so far as the payment of such compensation
does not deprive the party by whom the damaging act was done of the means for
his own maintenance and for the performance of his statutory duties as to the
maintenance of others (412 sub (9), 430, 431)—BGB 276 (1), 827–829.

d.   Comparison with English Law.

Under English law a promisor must, as a general rule, carry out his
promise, and is liable for its non-performance, even if he is not guilty of wilful
default or negligence.   At first sight this rule seems to be diametrically opposed
to the German rule, but as English law recognizes that under special circumstances,
such as those referred to in Taylor v. Caldwell 3 B. & S. 826, the non-performance
of an agreement is excused unless caused by the promisor's wilful or negligent
default, the difference between the two systems is not so great as it appears.

The distinction between various degrees of diligence, though sometimes
mentioned in English judgments, is not so consistently carried out as in German
law (see the dictum of Rolfe B. , in Wilson v. Brett 11 M. & W. on p. 114; 63
R. R. on p. 530, in which gross negligence is stated to be the same thing as
ordinary negligence 'with the addition of a vituperative epithet').

e.   Contractual Modification of Liability.

The degree of diligence which a person is bound to give under the circumstances
of any particular case may be modified by agreement between the parties concerned,
but the responsibility for the debtor's own wilful default cannot be excluded
beforehand by mutual agreement.   The responsibility for an agent's wilful default
may be excluded.   The creditor may, of course, after the occurrence of the default,
waive any rights to which he becomes entitled by reason thereof—BGB 276
(2), 278.

In certain cases where the debtor is liable without reference to any default on
his part, the performance is excused if it was prevented by *vis major* (*höhere
Gewalt*).   *Vis major* corresponds to the 'act of God' of English law, and is
assumed to exist in any case in which the non-performance, or the incompleteness
of the performance, of an obligation could not have been avoided, even if the
highest degree of diligence had been applied.

2.   CONTRIBUTORY DEFAULT OF PLAINTIFF

154   **149.** Under English law the plaintiff's contributory default affects the defendant's liability in the case of claims for damage done by unlawful acts; under the rules of the present German law the liability created by a contract or other act-in-the-law is affected in the same way by the contributory default of the other party as the liability for an unlawful act.   Under German as well as under English law, the proof of the plaintiff's own default is relevant only for the purpose of showing that the defendant's default was not the 'decisive' [1] or 'preponderant' (*vorwiegend*) cause of the damaging event, but while under English law the fact that the defendant's default was not the decisive cause deprives the plaintiff of his entire claim to compensation (except in cases coming under Admiralty law), German law leaves it to judicial discretion to determine whether the defendant's liability to make compensation is entirely destroyed or merely reduced by contributory default on the part of the plaintiff—BGB 254 (1).

Contributory default may be constituted by an omission as well as by a positive act (*e. g.* by the omission to call attention to the risk of an unusually serious loss)—BGB 254 (2).

The contributory default of a person for whose default the plaintiff is liable under the rules mentioned below (150) has the same effect as the plaintiff's own default.

3.   LIABILITY FOR THE DEFAULT OF OTHERS

a.   In respect of the performance of Obligations arising under an Act-in-the-law.

150. In the case of any act done by a person's statutory agent (116) on his behalf, the principal is liable for the agent's default in the same way as he would be liable for his own default if his capacity were unrestricted—BGB 278.

In the case of an act done by any other agent on behalf of a principal a distinction must be drawn between acts specially delegated to independent persons and acts done in the ordinary course by assistants (*Gehülfen*).

155   As regards independent persons the general rule is that the performance of

---

1   The expression 'decisive', which is used by Sir F. Pollock (see Law of Torts, 7th edition, p. 455), is clearer than the expression 'proximate' generally used in the English authorities.

an obligation undertaken by *A* may not, in the absence of express permission, be delegated by him to *B*.   If such delegation takes place *A* is liable for all consequences due to the unauthorized delegation of his duty.   If the debtor has authority from his creditor to delegate the performance of his obligation to another, the question as to the liability of the original debtor for the default of the substitute employed by him depends upon the agreement between the parties or the specific legal rules applicable under the particular circumstances—see, for instance, 231 rule (2).

As regards the employment of assistants, it is of course clear that many kinds of obligations cannot be carried out in detail by the promisor in person, but that the performance must be effected by servants or other employees working under his superintendence.   In such cases there is an implied authority to employ assistants, and where such implied authority exists (and also where the employment of assistants is expressly authorized) the debtor, in the absence of a special stipulation to the contrary, is answerable for any default on the part of his assistants as though it had been his own—BGB 278; if the principal is himself only liable for gross negligence he is only liable for gross negligence on the part of his assistants; if the principal is answerable for *diligentia quam suis* the assistants must show the degree of care which such principal bestows on his own affairs.

If the employment of assistants is unauthorized (*e. g.* if the promisor has agreed to perform the promise in person, or if the work is of a nature which according to ordinary custom is not handed over to assistants) the promisor commits a wilful default by such unauthorized employment of assistants, and is therefore liable for the consequences, whether attributable to the assistants' default or otherwise.

b.   As to Unlawful Acts.

aa.   *General statement.*

The question as to the liability of a person for the unlawful acts of servants, agents, or others who are under his control, is one which in all countries has given rise to considerable controversy.   French law imposes a general responsibility on parents, schoolmasters, and employers for the acts of any infant children, pupils, apprentices, and servants who are under their custody or control.   The responsibility, however, for a particular act is excluded by proof that such act could not have been prevented by the person exercising the control (Code Civil, art. 1384).

156

The Swiss Code of Obligations (ss. 61, 62) imposes a similar liability and recognizes a similar ground of exemption, with the modification that the responsibility is excused if it is proved that due diligence has been used for the purpose of preventing the damaging act.   Under English law there is no responsibility for the acts of children, pupils, or apprentices; but, subject to certain statutory modifications applicable in particular cases and subject to the anomalous doctrine of ' common employment' and the complicated provisions of the Workmen's Compensation Acts, there is a general rule that a master or principal is responsible for damage caused by any wilful or negligent act of a servant or agent acting within the scope of his employment (see Pollock on Torts, 7th ed., pp. 72–105).   The proof that the damaging act could not have been prevented by the master or principal is not of any avail, and to that extent the liability for the default of others goes further than in French or Swiss law.

In Germany the law on the subject is complicated by the fact that there are specific modifications of the general rules in the case of particular employments and trades (151), but, subject to such exceptional provisions, the rules are as follows:

(1) A person who employs another on any kind of work must compensate any third party for damage unlawfully inflicted upon him by his employee in the course of his employment, unless he can prove: (*a*) that he applied the degree of diligence usual under the circumstances in the selection of the employee, and, if it was his duty to supply appliances or tools, or to superintend the work, that he applied the same degree of diligence as regards such supply or superintendence; or (*b*) that the damage would have arisen notwithstanding the application of the proper degree of diligence on his part—BGB 831 (1).   A sub-contractor who has undertaken to supply the appliances or tools, or to superintend the work, is liable in a corresponding way—BGB 831 (2).   In so far as the sub-contractor is liable, the liability of the employer is excluded if the employment of a sub-contractor was authorized and the required diligence was applied in his selection; as to English law on this point, see Waldock *v.* Winfield (1901) 2 K. B. 596.

(2) Any person who is under a legal or contractual obligation to exercise supervision over another by reason of the infancy or bodily or mental infirmity of the latter is liable for all damage unlawfully inflicted upon any third party by the person requiring supervision, unless he has exercised proper diligence as to the duty of supervision—BGB 832.

Thus it will be seen that under German law the liability for acts of others is not so extensive as under French and Swiss law; that as regards rule (1) it is not so extensive as under English law, and that no rule corresponding to rule (2) exists in the latter system.

The rules as to the liability of the owner of animals or buildings for damage caused by such animals, or by the fall of such buildings, will be discussed below—294.

bb. Liability of corporate bodies and associations for acts of their agents.

In the case of corporate bodies or associations of persons, whose acts must of necessity be done by agents, the rule has been constantly recognized that all such bodies are liable for unlawful acts done by duly constituted agents in connexion with the performance of their functions as such agents—BGB 31; RGZ 32, 35; 57, 93.

4. SPECIAL LIABILITIES ATTACHING TO PARTICULAR EMPLOYMENTS

151. The general rule, that a person is liable for such damage only as is caused by his wilful or negligent default, is varied in the direction of greater severity in the case of persons engaged in certain kinds of employment. The stringency of the liability of *nautae*, *caupones*, *stabularii* under the Praetorian edict has been maintained more or less consistently in most countries.

Under German law special liabilities attach to innkeepers and carriers as to the safety of goods, and to the owners of railways as to the safety of human beings. On the other hand the liability of carriers by sea is modified by the anomalous rules as to the limitation of the risk of shipowners, which must be separately referred to.   158

a. Liability of Innkeepers.

An innkeeper, who in the regular course of trade gives sleeping accommodation to guests, is liable for the loss or deterioration of anything brought into his inn by a guest accommodated in the course of such trade, unless the loss or deterioration was caused (*a*) by the guest or any of his companions, or (*b*) by the condition of the thing itself, or (*c*) by *vis major*. In the case of money, negotiable instruments, or valuables not deposited for safe custody with special notice of their nature, the liability is limited to 1,000 marks; but if the innkeeper declines to take any such things into safe custody, or if the damage is caused by himself or any of his employees, the liability is unlimited. A notice posted in the inn repudiating the innkeeper's liability is ineffective, but an express agreement between innkeeper and guest excluding such liability is binding on the latter—

BGB 701, 702.   (As to the necessity of immediate notice of any loss suffered by the guest, see BGB 703.)

b.   Liability of Carriers.

The liabilities of carriers are discussed below in connexion with the special rules relating to agreements with carriers (241).   The general principles regulating such liabilities may be summed up as follows:

(1) An ordinary carrier by land or sea is not liable for any loss not caused by his default; but while, in the case of an ordinary obligation, a person who incurs a loss by reason of negligence on the debtor's part must prove such negligence, a carrier is liable for the deterioration or loss of goods entrusted to him, and for delay in their delivery, unless he can prove that the damaging event could not have been prevented by the application of the diligence of a careful carrier—HGB 429 (1), 606.

(2) The owners of a railway undertaking are responsible for the deterioration or loss of goods entrusted to their care irrespectively of any default on their part, or on the part of their employees, unless the damage was caused by the default of any person entitled to dispose of the goods, or by *vis major*, or by a defect in the goods, or by a hidden defect in the packing—HGB 456 (1).

(3) All carriers are liable for the default of their employees in the same manner as for their own default—HGB 431, 458, 485.

159   (4) Carriers are not liable for the loss of valuables, works of art, money, or negotiable instruments, unless proper notice of the value or nature of the goods is given when the goods are sent—HGB 429 (2), 456 (2), 607.

As to contractual modifications of a carrier's liabilities and other circumstances which modify the liability, see 241 sub (5); as to the limitation of the liability of shipowners, see below, sub (3).

c.   Special Rules as to Shipowners and Masters of Ships.

The liability of a shipowner under an agreement of affreightment is limited to the value of the ship by which the goods are carried and to the freight earned during the voyage, unless he is personally in default, or unless he has expressly made himself answerable for the performance of the carrying agreement—HGB 486.   The master of a ship is liable for all damage resulting from his failure to apply the diligence of a careful ship-master—HGB 511, 512.

d. Liability of Owners of Railways for Personal Injuries.

The owners of a railway undertaking are liable for the consequences of any bodily injury (whether resulting in death or otherwise) caused in the working of the railway to any human being, unless they can prove that such injury was caused by the default of the sufferer, or was due to *vis major*.   This liability cannot be excluded by agreement—*Haftpflichtgesetz* of 1871, ss. 1,5, as modified by EG 42.   As to the effect of insurance against accidents, see s. 4.

e. Comparison with English Law.

It will be seen that the liability of innkeepers in England is much less severe than in Germany, as the limitation of liability introduced by the Innkeepers' Act applies to all goods and not merely to goods of a particular kind, and the limit is also lower than under the German law.   Carriers other than owners of railway undertakings are, on the other hand, subject to a more stringent liability under English law, being excused by *vis major* only, and remaining liable even if they can prove that the circumstance causing the loss or deterioration of the goods was not due to want of diligence on their part.   The ship owner's limitation of liability in the case of loss of or damage to goods is similar in principle, but under English law the limit is not fixed by the value of the ship and freight, but by the fixed amount of £ 8 for each ton of the ship's tonnage (see Merchant Shipping Act 1894, s. 503).   The severe liability of railway companies for injuries to persons is peculiar to German law.

5. DELAY (*MORA*) AND *LIS PENDENS*

a. Debtor's Delay (*mora solvendi*).

aa. How constituted.

152. The following rules apply to this subject:

(1) a debtor is in *mora solvendi*[1] if the promised act remains unperformed at the time fixed for its performance ('the act of performance has fallen due') and after a demand on the creditor's part;

160

---

[1]   This term will be used as an equivalent of the German *Schuldner-Verzug*, as no convenient English expression can be found.

(2) the creditor's demand is dispensed with if the time of performance is either originally, or by notice after default, fixed with reference to the calendar year (*dies interpellat pro homine*), or if judicial proceedings for the enforcement of the claim have been resorted to—BGB 284;

(3) the debtor is not deemed to be in *mora* if the punctual performance of his obligation has been prevented by any circumstance for which he is not responsible under the rules stated sub 148 to 151—BGB 285.

bb.   Effect of mora solvendi.

153. A debtor who is in *mora* thereby subjects himself to an increased liability in accordance with the following rules:

(1) he must apply the highest degree of diligence, whatever degree of diligence was originally required; he is liable even for accidental damage to the subject-matter of the obligation, unless he can prove that such damage could not have been avoided by the punctual performance of his obligation—BGB 287;

(2) he is liable for all damage caused by the delay; in the case of a claim for money other than a claim for interest, interest runs from the time at which the delay begins, the rate being 4 per cent. in an ordinary case, and 5 per cent. in the case of a bilateral mercantile transaction (36)—BGB 286 (1), 288, 289, and HGB 352 (1);

(3) if the debtor has to pay compensation for an object which deteriorated or was destroyed while he was in *mora*, the creditor may claim interest on the amount of such compensation, from the date which serves as the basis for the assessment of such compensation—BGB 290;

(4) if the creditor can prove that the delay has rendered the performance useless to him, he may decline the performance and claim compensation in lieu thereof—BGB 286 (2).

As to the consequences of *mora solvendi* where time is ' of the essence ' — see 161.

b.   Creditor's Delay (*mora accipiendi*).

aa.   How constituted.

154. The creditor is in *mora accipiendi* [1] if he refuses to accept the performance

---

[1]   The term *mora accipiendi* is used in this treatise as the equivalent of the German expression *Gläubiger-Verzug.*

tendered by the debtor.   If the performance is tendered before it is due in any case in which the debtor is not entitled to anticipate the performance (147), the creditor is not deemed to be in *mora* [1]—BGB 293.

The performance must be effected in the manner in which the creditor is entitled to claim it, but a verbal tender is sufficient in the following cases: (1) if the creditor declares that he will not accept the performance; (2) if the completion of the performance depends on an act of the creditor (*e. g.* if it is the creditor's duty to carry away the thing which he is entitled to claim).   In the latter case a request on the debtor's part asking the creditor to do the required act is deemed equivalent to a verbal tender of the performance.   The request is unnecessary where the creditor's act has to be done at a time, or at the expiration of a notice, fixed by reference to the calendar—BGB 294, 295, 296.

The creditor is not in *mora*, if at the time of the tender, or at the time fixed for the creditor's act of acceptance, the debtor in fact is unable to perform the obligation—BGB 297.

In the case of reciprocal obligations the creditor is in *mora* if he is willing to accept the other party's performance, but fails to tender performance on his part—BGB 298.

bb.   *Effect of mora accipiendi.*

155. *Mora accipiendi* has the following effects:

(1) whatever degree of diligence the debtor may have been bound to apply up to the time when the delay began, he ceases as from such time to be responsible for any damage not caused by his wilful default or gross negligence—BGB 300 (1);

(2) if the obligation was to deliver a generically defined thing—144 rule (2)—the risk of the performance passes to the creditor [2], from the moment of the tender of a specific thing offered in satisfaction of the obligation—BGB 300 (2);

(3) interest on a debt bearing interest ceases as soon as *mora accipiendi* begins—BGB 301;

162

---

1   Where no time of performance is fixed, or where the debtor is entitled to anticipate the time of performance, a creditor who is temporarily unable to accept a tendered performance, is not thereby placed into *mora* unless the debtor has given him reasonable previous notice of his intended performance—BGB 299.

2   Before such tender the debtor bears the risk; he has to deliver a thing answering the description, whatever may happen to the thing which may have been appropriated by him for such delivery—BGB 279.

(4) a debtor who is under liability to hand over to the creditor the profits of a thing (77), is, as from the commencement of *mora accipiendi*, responsible only for such profits as are actually received—BGB 302;

(5) if the debtor is under an obligation to give up the possession of a parcel of land, he may abandon the possession as soon as the creditor's delay begins; but he must, if practicable, give previous notice of his intention to do so— BGB 303;

(6) the debtor is entitled to claim reimbursement of any expense incurred by the unsuccessful tender, or by the storage of the subject-matter of the obligation during the continuance of *mora*—BGB 304.   (As to the effect of the purchaser's *mora* in the case of a sale, see 193.)

c.   Effect of *Lis Pendens* (*Rechtshängigkeit*).

156. As a general rule the institution of judicial proceedings[1] places the debtor in *mora* and subjects him to the increased liability mentioned above, but as this rule is subject to certain exceptions—see 152 rule (3)—the effect of *lis pendens* apart from *mora* has to be considered.   The following provisions relate to this subject:

163   (1) interest runs from the date at which a claim is brought forward, but if the action is brought before the claim is due, interest runs from the date on which the claim becomes due[2]—BGB 291;

(2) if the claim is for the delivery of any specific object, the debtor is, as from the time of its assertion, under the same obligations, and entitled to the same rights as the possessor of a thing during the pendency of an action brought by the owner for the recovery of its possession (343, 344), except in so far as the special nature of the obligation or the debtor's *mora* places the creditor in a more favourable position—BGB 292.

---

[1]   The *Rechtshängigkeit* begins at the date of the service of the process by which the proceedings are instituted, or in the case of a supplemental claim brought forward at any hearing of the action, at the date of such hearing. —see CPO 253, 263, 281, 693, 695, 697.

[2]   Where a right to a periodical payment is in question, a declaration as to the right to future payments may be claimed in an action.

CHAPTER V
DISCHARGE OF OBLIGATIONS

1.   GENERAL RULES

a.   Mode of Performance.

157. THE mode of performance depends on the nature of the particular obligation;   164
if the obligation arises under an act-in-the-law, the mode of performance is in the
first instance regulated by the intention of the parties as shown by their
declarations of intention; if the obligation arises under a rule of law, applicable
under the particular circumstances of the case, the mode of performance depends
in the first instance on such rule of law; in either case the rules of interpretation
discussed 144 to 147 are applicable in so far as they are material.

b.   Acceptance of Performance.

The acceptance of a performance made in discharge of the debtor's obligation,
has the effect of shifting the burden of proof; if the creditor after such acceptance
alleges that the debtor's performance was not the performance promised by him, or
that it was incomplete, it is for him to prove these allegations—BGB 363.   In
some cases the acceptance may preclude all further question as to the completeness
of the discharge, but this fact must under the general rules be proved by the
debtor.   Special rules, however, are applicable in the case of any bilateral
mercantile sale.   In the case of any such sale the purchaser must, so far as
practicable, examine the goods immediately on delivery; defects noticeable on
such examination must be communicated to the vendor forthwith, defects not so
noticeable, immediately on discovery.   Failure to comply with these requirements,
in the absence of intentional (*arglistig*) concealment on the vendor's part,
deprives the purchaser of all claims on the ground of defective performance unless
the goods are so obviously different from the purchased goods, that the purchaser
cannot be deemed to have accepted them in performance of the agreement—HGB   165

377, 378.

It will be seen that German law in the case of mercantile sales is more favourable to the vendor than English law, as under English law a purchaser's claim for breach of warranty is not affected by the acceptance, though he may by such acceptance have lost his right to rescission; Sale of Goods Act 1893, s. 11.

c. Appropriation of Performance where several Obligations are outstanding.

Where several obligations of the same kind are outstanding, and where a performance on the debtor's part does not satisfy all such outstanding obligations, the debtor may determine in what order the obligations are to be deemed satisfied. In the absence of any such determination, priority must be given to claims which are due over those which are not due.   Among claims which are due, the following elements determine the priority in the order in which they are mentioned: (1) the security given for the performance of the obligation, (a less well secured obligation is satisfied before a better secured obligation); (2) the nature of the obligation, (a more onerous obligation is satisfied before a less onerous obligation); (3) the date of the creation of the obligation, (an obligation of older date is satisfied before an obligation of more recent date).   Where none of the indicated elements make a distinction possible, the outstanding obligations are deemed to be satisfied *pro rata* of their respective values—BGB 366.   Where an outstanding obligation includes a claim for interests and costs, the value of an act of performance is appropriated: first, to the claim for costs; secondly, to the claim for interest; and thirdly, to the principal claim.   If the debtor desires another mode of appropriation, the creditor may decline the performance—BGB 367.

It will be seen that the German rule is more favourable to the debtor than the rules of English law on the same subject.   The well-known rule in Clayton's Case (1 Mer. 572) only deals with banking accounts, where all the sums paid in form a blended fund.   Subject to that rule, the creditor has, in the absence of a direction on the debtor's part, the right to appropriate a payment received by him in such manner as he thinks fit, and this right of appropriation may be exercised ' up to the very last moment ' —see Seymour *v.* Pickett (1905) 1 K. B. 715 (C. A.).   In the absence of any appropriation on the debtor's or creditor's part, the law appropriates the payment to the earlier debt (Mills *v.* Fowkes 5 Bing. N. C. 455, 461; 50 R. R. 754, 756).

d.   Prohibition of Performance by Instalments.

The performance of a single obligation must be distinguished from the performance of an agreement involving a series of obligations.   The debtor is not entitled to perform a single obligation [1] by successive instalments—BGB 266.   An exception to this rule occurs in the case of bills of exchange and promissory notes; the holder of such an instrument is not entitled to refuse the payment of a part of the amount—WO 38, 98.

English law has the same general rule on the subject as German law, but does not admit the exception.   As to the consequences of partial impossibility of performance, see *post* 158.

e.   Performance for the Benefit of a Third Party.

As a general rule, an obligation is not deemed to be discharged unless the performance is made for the creditor's benefit; but if it is made for the benefit of a third party, with the creditor's assent (129), the debtor is discharged.   A person is presumed to be authorized to receive an object if he produces a receipt for such object signed by the person who is entitled to receive it—BGB 362, 370.

f.   Performance by a Third Party.

In any case in which the promised act is not from its nature required to be done by the debtor in person, [2] performance on the part of a third party must be accepted, unless the debtor expressly objects to such performance.   A creditor who refuses the performance offered by a third party in a case where no such objection has been raised by the debtor, renders himself liable to the consequences of *mora accipiendi* (155).   If the performance is accepted notwithstanding the objection, the debtor is discharged—BGB 267.

A third party entitled to any right over an object threatened with seizure by a judgment creditor of the debtor may avert such seizure by satisfying the judgment

167

---

1   This is so where the obligation is divisible as well as where it is indivisible.   An indivisible obligation is one which cannot be performed in separate parts without rendering the performance ineffective. A divisible obligation is one which can be effectively performed in separate parts (*e. g.* the obligation to pay a sum of money or to deliver fungibles of a specified weight and measure).

2   For instances of cases in which the debtor must perform in person, see 221, 231, 252.

debt on the debtor's behalf, or by giving security, or by means of set-off.   In so far as the creditor in such a case receives satisfaction for his claim, the third party is entitled to be subrogated to his rights as against the debtor—BGB 268.

Under English law a third party, who makes a payment on behalf of a debtor without his authority, does not acquire any rights against the debtor, nor does the creditor incur any liability by refusing the tender of a performance on the part of a person other than the original debtor—Walter *v.* James L. R. 6 Ex. 124.

g.   Debtor's Right to Written Acknowledgement.

A debtor who performs his obligation is entitled to a written acknowledgement of such performance, and to the return of any written acknowledgement of indebtedness given by him [1]—BGB 368, 371 (as to the costs of the acknowledgement, see BGB 369).

2.   IMPOSSIBILITY OF PERFORMANCE

a.   Generally.

158. Impossibility of performance may either exist *ab initio*, or be caused by an event occurring subsequently to the formation of the agreement.   In the first case the agreement is void; but a party who was ignorant of the impossibility is within certain limits entitled to compensation from the other party, if such other party knew, or ought to have known, of the impossibility—BGB 306, 307—see *post* 306.

An agreement, however, made with the implied or expressed condition that it shall become operative on the removal of the impossibility is binding if the impossibility can be removed—BGB 308 (1).   An agreement made subject to a condition precedent, or to a stipulation postponing its operation to a future date, is valid, if the impossibility is removed before the fulfilment of the condition or before the date fixed by the stipulation—BGB 308 (2).

Impossibility caused by an event subsequent to the creation of the obligation requires more detailed discussion, being of much greater practical importance than impossibility existing *ab initio*.

As mentioned above (148), a debtor as a general rule becomes released from

---

1   If the creditor is unable to return any such document the debtor is entitled to a publicly certified acknowledgement of the discharge of his obligation—BGB 371.

168

his obligation in so far as its performance becomes impossible by reason of any circumstance or event for which he is not responsible.   In the absence of a contractual stipulation, or a special rule of law providing otherwise for the particular case, he is only responsible for circumstances or events due to his wilful default or negligence—BGB 276 (1).   In case of dispute it is the debtor's duty to prove that the circumstance or event, by which the performance of the obligation has been rendered impossible, was one for which he was not responsible—BGB 282.

Where the debtor has undertaken to deliver a generically defined thing, his inability to deliver such thing, though not due to any default on his part, is not a ground of excuse, so long as the delivery of a thing belonging to the genus is possible—BGB 279.   The most obvious example of the application of this rule occurs where a debtor undertakes to pay money or to deliver fungibles (73), and is unable to do so because he does not possess the necessary funds; but the rule is applicable whether the promised thing is a fungible or otherwise.   The fact that the debtor has appropriated a specific thing to the performance of the obligation, and that such thing was subsequently destroyed without any default on his part, is not of any consequence, unless it can be shown that the creditor had agreed to accept such appropriations.

In so far as the performance of an obligation becomes impossible by reason of   169
a circumstance for which the debtor is responsible, the creditor is entitled to compensation (167) for the damage suffered through the non-performance of the obligation—BGB 280 (1).

As regards impossibility of performance in the case of reciprocal agreements, see 160.

b.   Partial Impossibility.

If, owing to any circumstance or event for which the debtor is responsible, the performance of his obligation becomes partially impossible, the creditor may decline to accept partial performance, and claim compensation for the non-performance of the whole agreement wherever partial performance is useless to him. [1]   If the creditor cannot prove that partial performance is useless to him, he must accept it, but has a right of compensation in respect of the incompleteness of the performance—BGB 280 (2).

---

[1]   The creditor's and debtor's mutual rights and duties are in such a case governed by the same rules as apply in the case of the rescission of an agreement—162 sub c.

Illustration: *A* has charge of a pair of horses for *B*.   One of the horses is killed by an event for which *A* is responsible.   If *B* can prove that he valued the two horses only as a pair, and that the remaining horse is of no use to him singly, he can refuse to take it back, and claim damages for the loss of the pair.   If this cannot be proved, he must take the remaining horse, and has a claim for damages in respect of the loss of the horse killed by *A*'s default.

c.   Creditor's Right of Subrogation in respect of Debtor's Claims for Indemnity.

If the circumstance or event by which the debtor's performance has been rendered impossible is one entitling him to partial or total indemnity from another (*e. g.* from an insurance company, which has taken the risk of such circumstance or event, or from a wrongdoer who is liable for the damage caused thereby), the creditor is entitled, in satisfaction *pro tanto* of his claim for compensation, to an assignment of the claim for indemnity, or to the delivery or payment of any object or sum of money received by the debtor in respect of such claim—BGB 281.

d.   Comparison with English Law.

170   Under English law an agreement is void if its performance is physically or legally impossible under any conceivable circumstances; if the impossibility of the performance is due to any special circumstances affecting the particular case, the agreement is not void on the ground of impossibility of performance (see Hills *v.* Sughrue 15 M. & W. 233; 71 R. R. 651).   As regards the effect of supervening impossibility, the contrast between English and German law has been pointed out above (148).

3.   PERFORMANCE OF RECIPROCAL AGREEMENTS

a.   Legal Character of Reciprocal Agreements.

159. In the case of a reciprocal agreement (see 140) there are three possibilities.   It may be intended: (1) that each party shall be bound independently of the question, whether the other party performs his promise or otherwise; or (2) that one party shall perform his part of the agreement before he has any claim for performance by the other; or (3) that both parties shall be contemporaneously willing and ready to perform their promises.   Under English law the last-mentioned intention is presumed in the case of an agreement for the sale of land (see Laird v. Pim 7 M. & W. 479; 56 R. R. 768) or of goods (Sale of Goods Act 1893, s. 28).   In the case of other kinds of agreements no legal presumption exists, and the intention of the parties must be ascertained in accordance with the ordinary rules of construction.

Under German law an agreement containing mutually independent promises in the manner stated above, sub (1), is not generally referred to as a reciprocal agreement, and will not in the further course of this treatise be so described.

Where, in the case of a reciprocal agreement, there is no express or implied stipulation to the contrary, each party is entitled to refuse performance, unless the other party is ready and willing to perform the whole of his promise at the same time.   This right of refusal is not affected by the counter-promise being made up of several distinct promises by different persons—BGB 320 (1).

Illustration: *A* makes an agreement with *B* and *C* for the purchase of a quantity of fungibles, it being agreed that *B* and *C* shall each be liable to deliver one half of the purchased quantity, and that each is to receive half of the purchase price; *B* tenders his half.   *A* is not required to pay *B*'s share of the purchase price, until *C* is ready and willing to deliver the remaining half.

171

A deviation from the general rule is authorized where the counter-promise has been partly performed, and where—owing to the fact that the outstanding part of the performance is of trifling importance, or to some other special circumstances—the refusal of the counter-performance would be a breach of good faith—BGB 320 (2).

Where, under the terms of an agreement, performance on the part of *A* must precede the performance on the part of *B*, *A* may nevertheless claim contemporaneous performance, if *B*'s financial position has become seriously weakened after the formation of the agreement, and if the performance of his promise has thereby been rendered insecure [1] —BGB 321.

As regards the form of the action in the case of the breach of a reciprocal agreement, see 167.

---

[1]   This provision may cause great hardship, as it enables unscrupulous persons to repudiate disadvantageous transactions; no doubt the repudiating party must prove his case, but the other party will frequently shrink from the public investigation of his financial position.

b. Impossibility of Performance in the case of Reciprocal Agreements.

160. Where, in the case of a reciprocal agreement between A and B, the impossibility of the performance of A's promise is caused by an event subsequent to the formation of the agreement, [1] such an event may be

(1) an event for which neither A nor B is responsible; or (2) an event for which B is responsible; or (3) an event for which A is responsible.

Illustration of case (1): A makes an agreement for the sale of a horse to B; the horse, before the completion of the sale and without any default on A's part, is accidentally killed;

172   Illustration of case (2): A undertakes to make a dress for B, for delivery on a given date (time being of the essence of the agreement), the terms being that B is to furnish the material, while A is to find the accessories and charge a lump sum for the whole; B does not furnish the material at the proper time and the completion of the dress on the agreed date becomes impossible;

Illustration of case (3): Facts, as in the case referred to in Illustration of case (1), except that the horse's death is due to A's negligence.

The consequences as to A's rights under the agreement are as follows:

In case (1) A has no right to the counter-performance if the performance is totally impossible; if the performance is partly impossible, the counter-performance is reduced *pro tanto*—BGB 323 (1).   If B avails himself of the rule mentioned above—158 sub c, —and obtains the assignment of A's right of indemnity against a third party, A has a claim to the counter-performance, but subject to reduction in so far as such counter-performance would be of greater value than the right of indemnity—BGB 323 (2).

Illustration: If in the case referred to in Illustration 1, A has insured the horse, and the insurance money exceeds the purchase price, B is entitled to the whole of the insurance money, and must pay the whole purchase price; if the insurance money is less than the purchase price, then the purchase money is reduced proportionately.

----

[1]   Where the performance of the promise of one of the parties is impossible *ab initio* the general rule stated above (158) is applied.

If *B* has performed his counter-promise to a larger extent than he is required to do under the rules stated above, he is entitled to recover the excess value of his performance under the rules as to unjustified benefits (298)—BGB 323 (3).

In case (2) *A* has a right to the counter-performance, but such counter-performance is reduced in so far as *A* in consequence of the non-performance of his promise saves any outlay, or uses the time which he would have applied to the performance of his promise, in some other profitable occupation [1]—BGB 324 (1).

Illustration: In the case referred to in Illustration 2, *A* is entitled to the agreed lump sum, but he must allow a deduction in respect of any saving of outlay for accessories which he would have incurred if he had made the dress, and for any remuneration which he receives, or by the application of proper diligence would have received, if he had employed the time intended for the making of the dress in some other work.

B is deemed responsible for the circumstance preventing the performance of *A*'s promise, whatever his original liability may have been, if he is in *mora accipiendi* (154)—BGB 324 (2).

Illustration: *A* has agreed to warehouse *B*'s furniture at a specified rent and for a specified period, and takes responsibility for the risk of fire; *B* refuses to take possession after the expiration of the period, and the furniture is subsequently destroyed by fire; *B* must pay the rent, and has no right to compensation from *A*.

In case (3) *B* may, at his option, exercise one of the following alternative rights: (*a*) he may claim compensation for non-performance; (*b*) he may rescind the agreement; [2] (*c*) he may exercise the rights which he would be able to

---

[1] Any income which he intentionally (*böswillig*) neglects to earn is, for this purpose, treated like income earned by him.

[2] The question as to the distinction between the remedies (*a*) and (*b*) has given rise to considerable controversy among German writers, many authors holding that compensation for non-performance cannot be claimed unless the plaintiff performs his own promise. The prevailing opinion, however, is against this view (RGZ 50, 266). The result is that the claim for compensation for non-performance is in most cases more advantageous than the claim for rescission, but in a case in which a reciprocal agreement has been partly performed, the party with whom the option lies may prefer rescission. (Illustration: *A* sells Whiteacre and Blackacre to *B* for £ 10, 000; the sale cannot be completed as *A*'s title proves unsatisfactory. If *B* simply rescinds he obtains no compensation for the loss of the bargain; if he claims compensation he may under the German rules as to damages be amply indemnified in that respect. If, however, a good title to Blackacre has been shown, and Blackacre has consequently been conveyed to *B* against payment of £ 5, 000 before the defect in the title to Whiteacre was discovered, *B*, if claiming compensation for non-performance,

exercise in case (1).

If the performance is partially impossible, *B*, if able to prove that partial performance will be useless to him, has the same rights as in the case of total impossibility; if he is unable to prove the uselessness of partial performance, he

174   must accept the partial performance, his own liability for counter-performance being rendered proportionately less (compare 158 sub b)—BGB 325 (1).[1]

c. *Mora solvendi* in the case of Reciprocal Agreements.

(1) *In ordinary cases.*

161. Where time is not of the essence of a reciprocal agreement (see below sub (2)) and one of the parties is in *mora solvendi* (152) , the other party's only remedy, as a general rule, is to claim performance and damages in respect of the delay, unless he can prove that the belated performance would be useless to him, in which event he may either claim compensation for non-performance or rescission as in the case mentioned above—160 case (3).

Time may be made of the essence of the agreement by a notice addressed to the party[2] who is in *mora solvendi* requiring him to perform within a specified reasonable period, and stating that after the lapse of the period the performance will no longer be accepted; if this notice is not complied with, the party by whom it was given may claim compensation for non-performance, or rescission, but his right to claim performance can no longer be exercised.   If, in any such case, the agreement is partly performed before the lapse of the period, the party by whom the notice was given has the same remedies as he would have had in the case of partial impossibility of performance brought about by the default of the other

---

could only claim compensation for the loss suffered by the non-conveyance of Whiteacre; it might, therefore, be advantageous to him to claim rescission instead of claiming compensation for incomplete performance; on such rescission he would reconvey Blackacre against repayment of the £ 5, 000 and have no further claim for compensation.)

1   A party to a reciprocal agreement who has obtained judgment directing the other party to perform his promise, may send a notice to such other party requiring him to perform within a specified period, and declaring that after the lapse of the period performance will no longer be accepted.   If the notice is not complied with the party by whom it was given has the remedies open to *B* in the event mentioned in the text—BGB 283, 325 (2).

2   In such a case two notices are required as a general rule: (1) the notice by which the debtor is placed in *mora solvendi*; (2) the notice declining performance after the lapse of a specified period.   The second notice is not required in a case in which the debtor has expressly refused to perform his promise— RGZ 57, 112.

party—see 160 case (3)—BGB 326.

(2) *In cases in which time is of the essence of the agreement.*

Apart from the cases in which time is made of the essence by notice in the manner stated above, sub (1), time, in the absence of any indication to the contrary, is deemed to be of the essence of a reciprocal agreement ' if it is stipulated that the promise of one of the parties is to be performed at an exact point of time, or within a strictly defined period'—BGB 361; HGB 376 (1). The mere mention of a time or period, at which, or within which, the promise must be performed, is not sufficient for this purpose; the stipulation in question must be ' so *essentially* an integral part of the transaction, that the performance or breach of the agreement on that point causes the transaction to stand or fall, and that, therefore, a performance after the agreed point of time is not to be deemed a performance of the agreement '—RGZ 51, 348.

175

An agreement as to which time is of the essence of the definition given above, is called a *Fixgeschäft*; if one of the parties to such an agreement does not perform his obligation punctually, the other party may rescind the agreement; if the transaction is a mercantile sale (36) of goods, or negotiable instruments, [1] he may, at his option, either rescind or claim compensation for non-performance—BGB 361; HGB 376 (1).

4.   RESCISSION

a.   Circumstances entitling a Party to Rescission.

162. As shown above (158, 160, 161) a party may, in certain events, instead of claiming the performance of an agreement, claim rescission either alternatively to the right to claim compensation for non-performance, or without such alternative right; the right of rescission in certain events may also be stipulated for between the parties; where an agreement provides that a debtor, in the event of the non-performance of his promise is to forfeit his contractual rights, the creditor on the happening of such event is entitled to rescission—BGB 360.

---

1   In the case of such a mercantile sale the mere lapse of the stipulated time has the effect of rescinding the agreement, unless the creditor immediately after the lapse of such time declares by notice communicated to the debtor that he insists on performance.   The alternative right to claim damages for non-performance only arises in so far as there is technical *mora solvendi.*

b. How Right exercised.

The following rules apply to this subject:

(1) the right to rescind is exercised by means of a notice communicated to the other party—BGB 349;

176   (2) where no time is fixed for the exercise of the right, the other party may, by notice, require the party entitled to the right to exercise it within a specified reasonable period; if the notice is not complied with before the lapse of the period the right is forfeited—BGB 355;

(3) where several parties are entitled to the right it must be exercised by all of them, and where several parties are subject to it, it must be exercised against all of them.   The forfeiture of the right by one of several parties operates against all of them—BGB 356;

(4) where the exercise of a contractual right of rescission is dependent on the payment of forfeit money, the right is forfeited unless such payment is made simultaneously with the communication of the notice of rescission, or immediately after the repudiation of the notice by the other party on the ground of such non-payment—BGB 359.

c. Effect of Rescission.

The following rules apply in any case in which a party exercises a right of rescission to which he is entitled under any legal rule or contractual stipulation— BGB 327:

(1) the parties must contemporaneously return to each other everything previously received in pursuance of the rescinded agreement;

(2) in so far as any services have been rendered or the use of a thing has been allowed, the money value of such services or of such use must be paid;

(3) a party who has to return a thing under rule (1) is under the same liability for the loss or deterioration of such thing and has to account for fruits and profits in the same way as a person who is in possession of a thing while an action for its recovery by the true owner is pending (343)—BGB 346–348.

d. Forfeiture of Right of Rescission.

The right of rescission is forfeited by the party entitled thereto (hereinafter called the rescinding party):

(1) if any object which ought to be returned under the rules stated sub c is destroyed, materially altered or deteriorated owing to the wilful default or negligence of the rescinding party, or of any party deriving title under him, or of   177 any party for whose default he is responsible according to the rules stated above (150)—BGB 350–353;

(2) if the rescinding party, after becoming subject to the effects of *mora solvendi* as to the return of the objects to be returned by him or of an essential part thereof, fails to comply with a notice requiring him to return such objects or such part thereof, within a reasonable time specified in such notice—BGB 354;

(3) if, in the case of a contractual right of rescission, the other party is in a position to discharge his obligation by set-off (165), and immediately on receiving the notice of rescission avails himself of his right of set-off—BGB 357.

5.   SUBSTITUTED MODES OF PERFORMANCE

a.   Performance in Lieu of Promised Performance.

163. An obligation is duly discharged if a creditor in lieu of the promised performance, accepts a different performance (*e. g.* if a lessor entitled to the return of the leased object in a state of good repair agrees to accept it in its actual state with compensation in money for the dilapidations)—BGB 364 (1).

The performance accepted in lieu of the promised performance may consist in the substitution of a new obligation for the obligation which has to be discharged (*Novation*); but the mere fact that a debtor undertakes a new obligation is not accepted as proof of an intention on the part of the parties to consider the old obligation as discharged—BGB 364 (2).

Illustration: If a promissory note is given by way of payment for a claim for sold goods, the claim for the sold goods, in the absence of an express agreement to the contrary, is not extinguished by the receipt of the promissory note.

Where the undertaking of a new obligation by the debtor does not operate as a discharge of the former obligation, such new obligation is said to be undertaken *erfüllungshalber* (on account of performance), but where the creditor accepts the substituted obligation in lieu of the promised act, the substituted obligation is said to be accepted *an Erfüllungsstatt* (in lieu of performance).

Where the creditor accepts any right or thing in lieu of the promised performance, the debtor is under the same duty as to warranty of title and quality   178 as a vendor (186, 187)—BGB 365.

b.   Lodgment with a Public Authority (*Hinterlegung*).

164. Under English law a debtor can under certain specified circumstances discharge his obligation by lodgment in Court (see for instance Land Clauses Act 1845, s. 69; Trustee Act 1893, s. 42); but there is no general rule on the subject, and a person who is liable to perform an obligation for the benefit of a person under disability or of uncertain address is sometimes placed at great disadvantage.   The BGB deals with this difficulty in a very comprehensive manner by establishing the following principles:

aa.   General rules.

(1) A person who is under an obligation to pay or deliver any money, negotiable instrument, valuable, or other similar object, [1] may, in any of the events mentioned below, lodge such object with any public authority authorized in that behalf by State regulation.   Such lodgment may be effected: (*a*) if the creditor is in *mora accipiendi* (154); (*b*) if the debtor, by reason of any personal disability of the creditor, is unable to perform his obligation (*e. g.* if the creditor is an infant and has at the time no statutory agent); (*c*) if the debtor is unable to perform his obligation with entire safety because through no fault of his own he is uncertain as to the creditor's identity (*e. g.* if the original creditor is dead, and the debtor, notwithstanding the application of proper diligence, has been unable to ascertain what persons represent his estate)—BGB 372.

(2) If the debtor is under an obligation to deliver a movable thing, not included among the objects which may be lodged with a public authority, he may, if the creditor is in *mora accipiendi*, sell such movable thing in the manner prescribed for that purpose, and deposit the proceeds of sale with the competent public authority; if the debtor cannot safely perform his obligation on account of any personal disability of the creditor, or of any doubt as to his identity, this right of sale may be exercised only in so far as the thing, which the debtor has to deliver, is of a perishable nature, or in so far as the expense of keeping it would be unreasonably great—BGB 383–386.

179

---

1   The class of objects may be defined by State regulation.

bb.   *Place of lodgment; duty to give notice.*

The lodgment must be effected in the place of performance (146), and notice must be given to the creditor as far as practicable.   The fact that the rule as to the place of lodgment or as to notice is disregarded does not deprive the lodgment of its legal effect, but the debtor is liable for any damage which the creditor may suffer as a result of such disregard—BGB 374.

cc.   *Transmission by post.*

The lodgment is not effective unless the object intended to be lodged actually comes into the possession of the public authority to whom it is intended to be delivered, but, in the case of transmission by post, the lodgment, if it becomes effective, operates as from the time of dispatch—BGB 375.

dd.   *Conditional lodgment.*

Where the debtor is not required to perform his obligation except after performance of some act on the creditor's part, the debtor may, on effecting the lodgment, stipulate, that the creditor is not to be entitled to receive the deposited object, unless he can produce evidence of the performance of his own obligation— BGB 373.

ee.   *Effect of lodgment.*

The deposited object may be withdrawn by the debtor at any time before the lodgment has become 'final'. [1]

The lodgment becomes final: (1) if the debtor waives his right of withdrawal; (2) if the creditor accepts the lodgment in full discharge of his claim; (3) if a final judgment in an action between the creditor and the debtor declares the lodgment to be in order. [2]   While the right of withdrawal subsists, the claim is undischarged, but the debtor can meet any demand on the creditor's part by reference to the lodgment; the creditor must bear the risk of the safety of the deposited object, and has no claim for interest or loss of profits.   If the debtor exercises the right of withdrawal the lodgment is without effect, and the costs of the lodgment (which would otherwise have to be borne by the creditor) must be

180

---

[1]   The right of withdrawal cannot be exercised during the debtor's bankruptcy, nor can the object be seized by a judgment creditor of the debtor—BGB 377.

[2]   The waiver or acceptance must be communicated, or the judgment produced to the public authority with whom the deposited object is lodged.

discharged by the debtor. As soon as the lodgment has become final the debtor is discharged to the same extent as if he had delivered the deposited object to the creditor at the time when the lodgment was made—BGB 376–379, 381.

ff. Declaration as to creditor's identity on payment or delivery out.

Where, according to the regulations of the public authority, the deposited object cannot be withdrawn without the debtor's authorization, the creditor may require the debtor to give such authorization, in the events in which he would have been entitled to claim the performance of the obligation if the lodgment had not taken place—BGB 380.

gg. Effect of lapse of time.

The creditor's right to the payment of the deposited amount, or to the delivery of the deposited object, is barred after the lapse of thirty years from the date at which notice of the lodgment was received by him, unless payment or delivery is demanded before the lapse of the period; as soon as the creditor's right is barred the debtor may withdraw the deposited object, notwithstanding a previous waiver of his right of withdrawal—BGB 382.

c. Set-off.

165. Under English law the right of set-off only arises in the course of an action; before action brought a debt is not extinguished *pro tanto* by reason of the fact that the debtor acquires a claim against the creditor (Searles *v.* Sadgrove 25 L. J. (Q. B.) 15). German law, on the other hand, recognizes an independent right of set-off (*Aufrechnung*) in respect of which the following rules apply:

(1) a claim may be set off against another of the same nature (*e. g.* a money claim may be set off against a money claim, a claim for delivery of stocks or debentures of a certain class, may be set off against a claim for stocks or debentures of the same class)—BGB 387;

(2) a debtor may set off a claim to which he is entitled against an obligation to which he is subject, if, at the time, he has both the right to demand satisfaction of the claim and to perform his obligation—BGB 387;

(3) the fact that the place of performance or destination (146) is not the same for two claims does not prevent their being set off against one another; but a party against whom the right of set-off is exercised under such circumstances may claim compensation for any loss suffered by him owing to the fact that he is unable

181

to perform his obligation, or to receive the other party's performance at the proper place; if it was specially agreed that one of the claims should be satisfied at a fixed time and place such claim cannot, in the absence of an indication to the contrary, be set off against an obligation which has to be performed in another place—BGB 391;

(4) a claim which can be met by a plea of confession and avoidance cannot be set off against another claim, but a claim barred by prescription may be set off against another claim, if it was not barred at the time when the right of set-off became available [1]—BGB 390;

(5) no claim belonging to any of the following classes can be set off against another:

(*a*) a claim arising from an unlawful act committed wilfully;

(*b*) a claim exempted from judicial attachment—176 sub (1) [2];

(*c*) a debt owing to any Imperial or State Revenue authority cannot be set off against a debt owing by such authority unless both debts concern the same local establishment of such authority [3]—BGB 393–396;

(6) the right of set-off is excluded under any of the following circumstances:

(*a*) a claim against a bankrupt acquired after the commencement of the bankruptcy, or with the knowledge of the bankrupt's insolvency cannot be set off against a debt owing to the bankrupt; a debt owing to the bankrupt incurred after the commencement of the bankruptcy cannot be set off against a claim against the bankrupt;

(*b*) a debtor, whose debt has been attached by a judgment creditor of the person to whom such debt is owing, cannot discharge such debt by setting off against it a claim against such person, if such claim was acquired by him after the attachment of his debt, or if such claim fell due after such debt and after the date of the attachment—KO 55; BGB 392;

(7) the right of set-off is exercised by declaration communicated to the other party, and must not be made subject to any condition or stipulation as to time

182

---

1   Under English law a plea of set-off is not available, if the claim to be set off is barred by prescription. (Walter *v*. Clements 15 Q. B. 1046.)

2   An exception to this rule occurs in the case of claims against public sick funds created under the laws as to compulsory insurance; arrears of subscriptions may be set off against each claim, though the claim is exempt from seizure—BGB 394.

3   The Revenue authorities in Germany have local establishments which collect the taxes for the districts respectively allotted to them.

(111, 114)—BGB 388;

(8) the two claims set off against one another become extinguished to the extent of the smaller claim as from the date at which they began to co-exist—BGB 389;

(9) a person exercising the right of set-off may determine which out of several contemporaneous claims is to be set off against his debt. In the absence of any declaration of intention on the subject, the rules as to the order of discharge of several co-existing obligations—157 c, are applied, *mutatis mutandis*—BGB 396.

d. Waiver.

166. Under English law the waiver by a creditor of his right to the performance of a contract is invalid, unless it is made for valuable consideration or in the special form of a deed under seal. German law, on the other hand, allows an obligation to be discharged by an informal and gratuitous agreement between the creditor and debtor—BGB 397 (1).

An agreement by which the creditor acknowledges that there is no obligatory relation between him and his debtor has the same effect—BGB 397 (2).

It is unnecessary to state the reason which induces the creditor to waive his claim. If, however, it can be shown that the agreement was made without any legal ground (*causa*), or that the object of the transaction was not attained, the party who has waived his right may claim restitution on the ground of ' unjustified benefits' (298)—BGB 812 (2).

183   The fact that the motive of the transaction was an intention on the creditor's part to make a gift to the debtor, is sufficient to exclude the operation of the rule as to unjustified benefits, but it subjects the transaction to the rules as to gifts (199).

A mutual waiver made with the object of putting an end to a dispute, or to a state of uncertainty, is called a compromise (*Vergleich*); such a compromise is inoperative if it was made under a mistaken assumption as to the facts, and if, but for such mistaken assumption, there would have been no dispute or uncertainty—BGB 779.

CHAPTER VI
REMEDIAL OBLIGATORY RIGHTS

1. RIGHT TO PERFORMANCE OR RESTITUTION IN KIND

167. I<small>T</small> is often stated that the remedies of ' specific performance ' and ' injunction ', introduced by the English Equity Courts by means of their power over the person of the defendant, have no equivalent in continental law, and that, under the continental law, as under English common law, the only remedial right is a right to pecuniary damages.   This assertion was incorrect as regards the former German law, and is equally incorrect as regards the present law.

The primary remedial right under German law is a right to performance [1] where the obligation results either from an act in the law, or from surrounding circumstances, and a right to compensation (*Schadenseratz*) where the obligation results from an unlawful act.

The right to compensation is not primarily a right to pecuniary damages.

' A person liable to make compensation is bound to restore the state of things which would have existed, if the event creating the liability had not happened. ' — BGB 249.   The right to receive compensation for damage suffered by reason of an unlawful act is therefore primarily a right to restitution in kind. [2]

The general rule that every obligation gives rise to a claim for specific performance or restitution in kind is subject to the following exceptions:

(1) on the grounds of public policy the following classes of claims cannot be specifically enforced [3] :

(*a*) a claim for personal services (221) ;

---

[1]   Where the obligation is of a negative character, the right to performance resolves itself into a right to prohibit any course of conduct by which such obligation is violated.

[2]   An order restraining a person guilty of unlawful conduct from a continuance of such conduct comes under the same head.

[3]   As to agreements restraining former employees from competition, see p. 175 note 1.

185   (*b*) a claim for the performance of a promise of marriage (407) [1]—BGB 1297;

(*c*) a claim for the restitution of conjugal rights (412) [2];

(2) in certain events a person entitled to the performance of an agreement may claim rescission in lieu of performance, see above, 160, 161, 162;

(3) in the events mentioned below (168) the right to performance or restitution in kind is transformed into a claim for pecuniary damages.

In any case, which comes under the general rule, the right to the performance of an obligation, or to restitution in kind, where damage has been inflicted by an unlawful act, can be enforced by threat of imprisonment or fine, or by other methods specified in CPO 883–892.

In the case of a claim for performance of the promise of one of the parties to a reciprocal agreement the remedial right is exercisable as follows:

(*a*) if under the reciprocal agreement the performance of the mutual promises is to be contemporaneous, the plaintiff may claim an order directing the defendant to perform contemporaneously (*Zug um Zug*) with the plaintiff's performance;

(*b*) if performance of the plaintiff's promise is under the agreement to precede the defendant's performance, and if the defendant is in *mora accipiendi* (154), the plaintiff may claim an order directing the performance of the defendant's promise; if the *mora accipiendi* continues, the plaintiff may enforce the performance of the defendant's promise without being first compelled to perform his own promise—BGB 322.

2.   RIGHT TO PECUNIARY DAMAGES

a.   Circumstances transforming Claim for Performance or Restitution into Claim for Pecuniary Damages.

168. Under certain specified circumstances the claim for performance or
186   restitution in kind is transformed, *ipso facto*, into a claim for pecuniary damages; under other specified circumstances, the creditor may at his option claim either performance, restitution, or pecuniary damages; and there are finally circumstances under which the debtor may substitute pecuniary compensation for restitution in

---

1   Under some of the old State laws, orders for the specific performance of a promise to marry were obtainable.

2   In cases (*a*) and (*c*) an order for performance may be made by the Court, but there are no means of enforcement—CPO 888 (2).

kind:

(1) the claim is transformed, *ipso facto*, if performance or restitution in kind is impossible, [1] or possible only in such a way as not to afford sufficient compensation to the creditor—BGB 251;

(2) the creditor may at his option claim pecuniary damages in place of performance or restitution in kind:

(*a*) where his claim is for personal injuries, or damage to a thing—BGB 249;

(*b*) where the debtor is in *mora solvendi* and belated performance is useless, or where time has by notice been made of the essence of an agreement, or is of the essence of a mercantile sale (152, 161)—BGB 250;

(*c*) where performance of an agreement is partially impossible and partial performance is useless (158, 161) ;

(3) a debtor may at his option compensate the creditor in money, if performance or restitution in kind would require an outlay out of proportion to the requirements of the case—BGB 251 (2).

b.   Damages in respect of Physical Pain or Mental Suffering.

168a. As a general rule damage which does not cause pecuniary loss can only give rise to a claim for performance or restitution in kind—BGB 253, but in the following cases compensation in money can be claimed in respect of physical pain or mental suffering:

(*a*) in the case of personal injuries; (*b*) in the case of unlawful imprisonment; (*c*) in the case of certain sexual offences against females—BGB 847, 1300.

c.   Measure of Damages.

169. Where pecuniary damages are payable they are assessed on the following principles: 187

(1) as a general rule compensation must be paid for loss of profit as well as for other loss.   Such profit as, according to the ordinary course of events, and in view of the preparations and precautions of the parties, might reasonably have been expected, is deemed to have been lost—BGB 252;

(2) in certain cases a party injured by the fact that anagreement is invalid,

---

1   In the case of impossibility of performance of an agreement, a claim to compensation only arises in so far as the impossibility is caused by a circumstance for which the debtor is responsible (158, 160).

has a claim to be indemnified for the actual loss suffered by him in consequence of his belief in its validity (306).

The interest in the agreement for which he is entitled to compensation is called the 'negative' interest in contradistinction to the 'positive' interest or 'interest in the performance' (*Erfüllungsinteresse*) to which a party is entitled in the case of a valid agreement [1]—BGB 122, 179, 307, 309;

(3) special rules are laid down as to the measure of damages on the breach of certain classes of agreements:

(*a*) in the case of the breach of a mercantile agreement for sale as to which time is of the essence (161), the amount of the difference between the sale price and the market price at the time and place at which the sale ought to have been completed, may be recovered by way of damages—HGB 376;

(*b*) where, on a sale, there is a breach of warranty of essential qualities, the compensation (if compensation is claimed) takes the shape of a reduction of the purchase price (*Minderung*), which is computed according to the method mentioned below—192;

(*c*) damages payable by a carrier, in respect of the deterioration or loss of the goods, are assessed as follows: full damages including loss of expected profit are payable if the loss or deterioration is caused by the wilful default or gross negligence of the carrier, or of any person for whose default he is responsible; where, however, the carrier, under the special rules as to his liability discussed below—241 sub (5), is liable for loss or deterioration not caused by wilful default or gross negligence, his liability does not extend beyond the payment of the value of the lost goods, or of the loss in value caused by the deterioration of the goods (the saving in outlay for duties or other charges being deducted in each case)—HGB 430, 457, 611, 613;

(*d*) damages payable by carriers by land in respect of delay in transmission are assessed as follows: full damages are payable in all cases in which an ordinary carrier is liable for the delay; but the owners of a railway undertaking, in the case of delay not brought about by wilful default or gross negligence, are

188

---

[1] If a party has not altered his position on the faith of the agreement, the value of the negative interest cannot exceed the expenses incurred by him in connexion with the formation of the agreement; if he has done any act in reliance on the validity of the agreement (*e. g.* if in the case of an invalid sale he has resold the article bought by him), he is entitled to claim the amount of the loss suffered in consequence of such act. Whatever the value of the negative interest no greater amount can be claimed in respect thereof than could have been claimed if the agreement had been valid and had been broken—BGB 122.

only liable to the extent of the amount declared for that purpose by the person for whom the goods are carried, and in the absence of any such declaration are only liable to the extent of the amount payable for carriage—HGB 429, 466;

(4) the damages payable in respect of an unlawful act which injures the person of another (including unlawful imprisonment, sexual misconduct, slander and libel) must compensate the injured person for all injurious effects on his earning power and success in life, caused by such unlawful act, and may in a case coming within the exceptional rules mentioned above—168a, include compensation for physical pain or mental suffering.   In some cases the damages are payable in the shape of an annuity—BGB 824, 842–844, 847;

(5) a person liable to return a thing taken away from another by means of an unlawful act, must compensate such other for all loss arising from the deterioration or loss of such thing, though not due to his default; he is also liable to pay interest on the amount of the damages from the date which serves as the basis for the calculation of the loss—BGB 848, 849.

The rules as to damages recoverable on breach of agreement are qualified by the provision mentioned above—149, according to which the omission to point out special circumstances involving the risk of an unusually serious loss is looked upon as contributory default, unless the special circumstances were known, or by the exercise of proper diligence would have become known to the other party; 'special' damages cannot, therefore, be recovered, unless the circumstances giving rise to them ought to have been contemplated.

189

It will be seen that in the result the rules of English law laid down in Hadley *v.* Baxendale 9 Ex. 341; Horne *v.* Midland Railway L. R. 8 C. P. 131, and similar cases are also applied in Germany, though this result is attained by a somewhat different method of reasoning.

Compensation in money must be distinguished from conventional and judicial penalties, as to which, see 170 and 171.

3.   Right of Subrogation

170. A person who compensates another for the loss of a thing or a right is entitled to the assignment of the claims which the person receiving compensation has against any third party, in respect of the thing or right for which compensation has been given—BGB 255.

Illustration: A bailee, who compensates the owner of the bailed goods wrongfully taken out of the bailee's custody, may ask for an assignment of the owner's right to recover the goods from their unlawful possessor.

A person who has compensated another for the loss of a right which through his negligence has been barred by prescription, may claim the assignment of such right, as it would be of value to him in the event of the debtor declining to avail himself of the defence of prescription.

4. ANCILLARY REMEDIAL RIGHTS

a. Penalties.

aa. Conventional penalties.

171. Under the English rules of equity a penalty, which a party to an agreement promises to pay in the event of the non-performance of his obligation, can only be recovered in so far as the penalty is deemed to have been intended as a contractual assessment of the damages recoverable on breach of the agreement (liquidated damages); where such a construction is impossible under the circumstances, a penalty exceeding the value of the damage cannot be awarded (see Willson *v.* Love (1896) 1 Q. B. 626). The rules of German law on this subject are entirely different. On principle the parties may agree to the payment of a penalty in addition to full damages, and it is only in a case in which the amount of the penalty seems out of proportion to the importance of the matter, that the Court may reduce the amount of the penalty to a reasonable amount, making, however, full allowance for all damage actually suffered whether pecuniary or otherwise—BGB 343.

A penalty agreed to be paid by a person who is a mercantile trader in the full sense of the word (36), cannot be reduced in any case—HGB 348, 351.

The German rules as to penalties distinguish two principal cases, namely (1) the case of a penalty payable in lieu of damages or on account of damages; (2) the case of a penalty payable irrespectively of the other rights to which the creditor is entitled. Where the debtor promises to pay the penalty in the event of his failing to perform his obligation, the agreement as to the penalty is deemed to have the effect mentioned sub (1); where the debtor promises to pay the penalty in the event of failing to perform his obligation in the agreed manner, or at the agreed time, the agreement is deemed to have the effect mentioned sub (2).

In the first case the agreement is similar to an English agreement as to liquidated damages, but the position of the German creditor is more favourable. He may at his option claim the performance of the agreement or the penalty, and, where he is entitled to compensation by reason of the breach, he may claim damages in excess of the amount of the penalty; the penalty only represents the minimum amount of the damages. [1]

In the second case the creditor may claim performance as well as the penalty, but if he accepts performance without reserving his right to the penalty, he forfeits his right to the penalty.   If he is entitled to damages for defective performance he may claim such damages in lieu of the penalty—BGB 340, 341.   If the penalty is to be satisfied otherwise than by the payment of money, damages cannot be claimed in addition to the penalty—BGB 342.

The penalty becomes payable as soon as the debtor is in *mora solvendi*   191 (152); where the obligation consists in the forbearance from certain acts, the penalty is payable as soon as any act in contravention of the obligation is committed—BGB 339.

As to the burden of proof, in the event of the debtor denying his liability to pay the penalty, see BGB 345.

No penalty is payable in respect of the breach of an obligation which is inoperative under any rule of law—BGB 344.

bb.   Judicial penalties.

172.   In certain specified cases a person convicted of a criminal offence may be ordered to pay a penalty to the injured person; the acceptance of such a penalty bars the right to further relief.   Penalties of this kind may be imposed for defamation which subjects a person to pecuniary loss, or endangers his future success in life, for unlawful wounding, and for certain infringements of patent rights or other similar rights—StGB 188, 231; German Patent Act, s. 37; Useful Designs Protection Act, s. 11; similar provisions are contained in other statutes on kindred subjects.

---

1   The rule stated in the text is not applied where under an agreement restraining a mercantile employee from competition with his principal after leaving the latter's service, a penalty is payable in the event of a breach; in such a case the principal has no remedy except the recovery of the penalty, and cannot obtain an injunction restraining a continuance of the breach.   An express stipulation to the contrary is void—HGB 75 (2), 76 (1).

b.   Earnest Money (*Draufgabe*, *Arrha*).

173. The payment of earnest money in the absence of any contrary agreement has two effects.   In the first place it is evidence of the formation of the agreement with reference to which it is made—BGB 336 (1); in the second place it is a security for the performance of the agreement.   If the performance of the obligation of the giver of the earnest money becomes impossible by reason of a circumstance for which he is responsible, or if the agreement is rescinded by reason of any default on his part, he forfeits the earnest money.   In the absence of a contrary agreement the earnest money cannot be retained, if the agreement is duly performed, or if damages for its breach are recovered.   It must either be accepted as part performance of the agreement, or part payment of the damages, or it must be returned.   If the agreement is rescinded without any default on the part of the giver, it must be returned—BGB 337, 338.

192   In the absence of a contrary agreement, earnest money is not in the nature of forfeit money (*Reugeld*), that is to say, the person giving it cannot release himself from his obligation by forfeiting the earnest money—BGB 336 (2).

The expression 'earnest money' has been used for the sake of brevity, but the rules given above are applicable, whether money or any other object be given in earnest to bind the bargain.

c.   Lien.

aa.   Ordinary lien.

174. The expression *Zurückbehaltungsrecht*, in the sense given to it by the BGB, has a somewhat wider meaning than the term 'lien' by which it is here translated.   The German right, though called a right of retention, not only enables the person entitled to it to retain a thing belonging to the debtor, but also to refuse the performance of any act which the debtor is entitled to claim until the debtor performs his own obligation.   With reference to reciprocal agreements requiring contemporaneous performance, this right is specially regulated, and has already been mentioned (159, 167), but the BGB confers the same right in a number of cases, where no reciprocal agreement, in the technical sense of the word, is in existence between the parties—*e. g.* where mutual obligations arise in the case of voluntary services (301), or unjustified benefits (298).

The right of lien is available: (1) in all cases in which the debtor has a

matured counterclaim arising out of the same legal relation as his own obligation;
(2) in all cases in which a person, who is under a duty to deliver an object not obtained by him by means of an unlawful act, has at the same time a matured claim in respect of any outlay incurred or damage suffered in respect of such object [1] —BGB 273.

The creditor may prevent the exercise of the right of lien by giving security (87), but personal security may be refused.   (As to the effect of the allegation of a right of lien by way of defence to an action, see BGB 274.)

bb.   Mercantile lien.

Mercantile lien is intended to secure the claims of a mercantile trader against another mercantile trader, in so far as they arise from transactions which are mercantile transactions on both sides (36).   It differs from ordinary lien in the following respects:

(1) it consists exclusively in the right to retain movable things and negotiable instruments which by virtue of any mercantile transaction have, with the debtor's consent, come into the creditor's possession, or under his control, and does not include the right to refuse the performance of any obligation, other than the obligation to deliver such movable things or negotiable instruments;

(2) it is available for the purpose of securing claims not connected with the objects which are to be retained;

(3) in certain exceptional events it may be exercised for the purpose of securing claims which have not as yet matured; these events are:

(*a*) the debtor's bankruptcy or the suspension of payment on his part;

(*b*) the fruitlessness of any execution proceedings for the recovery of a judgment debt;

(4) it is not merely a passive right; it enables the creditor to deal with the things retained by him in the same manner as if they had been pledged to him (402, 403);

(5) it is available, not only against the debtor but also against any person who acquires the ownership of the retained objects, while they are in the creditor's possession;

(6) the right may be excluded by a direction given by the debtor at the time of the delivery of an object or by an undertaking on the creditor's part, but if any

193

---

[1]   See, for instance, 307 rule (5), 344 sub a.

of the events mentioned sub (3) has occurred, and was unknown to the creditor at the time of the delivery, or of the undertaking, the direction or undertaking may be disregarded [1] —HGB 369–371—as to HGB 369 (2), see BGB 986 (2).

---

[1]   The ordinary lien of German law corresponds in a certain measure to the particular lien of English law, which is a right to retain goods belonging to the debtor in respect of a claim relating to such goods; the mercantile lien of German law corresponds in a certain measure to the general lien of English law, which is a right to retain certain kinds of property as security for the general balance of the account.   A particular lien exists in favour of persons who have expended labour or skill on goods or who are under a legal obligation to receive goods or under special statutory rules (*e. g.* innkeeper's lien, unpaid seller's lien) ; a general lien exists in favour of bankers, brokers, factors, and solicitors.   Neither kind of lien as a general rule confers a right of realization (see, however, Innkeepers Act 1878, s. 1, Railway Clauses Consolidation Act 1845, s. 97, Sale of Goods Act 1893, s. 48).   Both kinds of lien may be conferred by special agreement between the parties.   It will be seen that neither of them is as extensively available as the corresponding right conferred by German law.

CHAPTER VII
TRANSFER OF RIGHTS AND DUTIES

1. ASSIGNMENT OF RIGHTS

a. Historical Statement.

175. ROMAN law, like Germanic law and the older English law, did not on principle allow rights to be assigned, but under all systems numerous exceptions became gradually engrafted on the general rule, more particularly with reference to rights embodied in negotiable instruments, and even apart from such special cases the tendency to modify or depart from the general rule became more marked as time went on.

In England the rules of equity, and the provisions of the Judicature Act, have had the effect of practically abrogating the rule, and a similar development has taken place in Germany.   Modern German law recognizes the right to assign obligatory and other rights to the fullest extent.

b. Rules as to Mode and Effect of Assignment.

176. The following rules are primarily applicable to assignments of obligatory rights, but in so far as the nature of the case admits, and no express rule of law excludes their applicability, they also apply to assignments of other rights, and to transfers of rights effected by rule of law (see, for instances, 182 sub (4), 274, 417 sub (2))—BGB 412, 413.

(1) *What classes of rights can be assigned.*

A right belonging to any of the following classes cannot be assigned:

(*a*) a right which is exempt from attachment by a judgment creditor (*e. g.* a claim for wages, a claim for maintenance, an officer's claim for pay or pension up to a certain limit, a claim against a public sick fund, or similar public fund created under the laws as to compulsory insurance, &c. , see CPO 850);

195   (*b*) a right which by agreement between the debtor and creditor is declared to be incapable of assignment;

(*c*) an obligatory right which would alter in character if it was exercisable by any person other than the original creditor; [1]

All other rights, present or future, [2] may be validly assigned—BGB 398–400.

(2) *Form of assignment.*

Under English law, in so far as it depends on Judicature Act 1873, s. 25 (6), the assignment of a chose in action must be in writing.   Under German law no writing is required, except in the case of the transfer of a mortgage debt, which must be effected in the manner mentioned below (390).

Notwithstanding the validity of an informal assignment, the assignor is bound at any time at the request and cost of the assignee to deliver to the latter a publicly certified written assignment—BGB 403.

The technical expression used by the BGB for the assignment of a right is *Abtretung*, but the older expression *Cession* is still frequently used in textbooks and legal documents.

(3) *Notice of assignment.*

Under English law an assignment is not fully effective until notice is given to the debtor; no similar rule exists in German law.   The assignment is complete as soon as the agreement between the assignor and the assignee is complete, and in case of a conflict between several assignees the priorities depend entirely on the order of the dates of the several assignments—BGB 398.   The debtor is, however, as between himself and an assignee, duly discharged by payment to, or performance for the benefit of the assignor, if at the time of the payment or performance he was not aware of the assignment; the assignee is also bound by

196   any arrangement made between the debtor and the assignor, or by any judgment obtained by the assignor against the debtor unless the latter at the date of the arrangement, or of the institution of the action, was aware of the assignment—

---

[1]   The majority of cases which serve as illustrations of this rule are specially provided for, see, for instance, 198 sub A rule (1), 210 rule (6), 221, 231 rule (2), 261, 358, 432.

[2]   The doubt previously existing as to the possibility of assigning future debts, has now been removed—see RGZ 55, 334; as to the English rule on this subject, see Tailby *v.* Official Receiver 13. A. C. 523.

BGB 407, 408.   On the other hand, a creditor who has given notice of the assignment to the debtor cannot, as between himself and the debtor, deny the existence or the operativeness of the assignment, and he cannot withdraw the notice, except with the concurrence of the person named therein as the assignee— BGB 409.

A debtor who has not received a written notice of the assignment from the assignor may make his performance for the benefit of the assignee dependent upon the production of a written assignment signed by the assignor.   This must, in the case of the assignment of the assignable part of the salary or pension of a military or civil official, be publicly certified—BGB 410, 411.

(4) *Effect of assignment on securities.*

All securities for a debt, and all rights of priority to which the assignor is entitled, pass to the assignee by virtue of the assignment of the debt, unless expressly excluded from the assignment.   In the case of the transfer of a mortgage debt, the transfer of the security cannot be excluded—BGB 401, 1153 (but see BGB 1190 (4)).

(5) *Duties of assignor.*

The assignor is bound to furnish to the assignee all information required for the enforcement of the right assigned to the latter, and to deliver to him any documents in his possession which help to establish the claim—BGB 402.

(6) *Defences open to debtor.*

The debtor is entitled to avail himself of all defences and all rights of set-off against the assignee, which he could have used against the assignor at the time of the assignment; but a claim against the assignor acquired by the debtor after the receipt of the notice of the assignment, or falling due after the receipt of the notice of assignment, and after the maturity of the assigned debt, cannot be set off against the assignee—BGB 404, 406.

c.   Negotiable Instruments.

aa.   *Generally.*

177. Special rules are applicable to the assignment of rights embodied in   197
negotiable instruments.   A negotiable instrument is a document the lawful holder of which is entitled, as such, to claim the performance of the obligations referred

to therein, and which, upon the performance of such obligations, must be handed over to the party performing them—BGB 797; HGB 364 (3); WO 39.

(1) *Kinds of rights which may be embodied in negotiable instruments.*

The most important negotiable instruments (bills of exchange, cheques, bank-notes, obligations to bearer, &c.) embody obligatory rights, but under German law many instruments with all the characteristics of negotiability embody real rights—308—(*e. g.* bills of lading, certificates of charge issued to bearer (374), &c.).

(2) *Classification of negotiable instruments.*

Negotiable instruments are under German law divided into two classes:
(*a*) instruments passing by endorsement; (*b*) instruments to bearer; the special characteristics of each class are referred to below (178, 179).

(3) *Consequences of loss and defacement of a negotiable instrument.*

If a negotiable instrument is lost or defaced, an order may generally be obtained declaring the instrument to be inoperative (*Kraftloserklärung*, amortization), and after the issue of such an order the person entitled to the instrument may, subject to the regulations applicable to the particular case, enforce the rights embodied therein without the production or delivery of a document or obtain a fresh copy thereof (see, for instance, BGB 798–800; HGB 365 (2); WO 73).

(4) *Effect of assignment on debtor's defences and rights of set-off.*

198 The transferee of a negotiable instrument is in a much better position than an ordinary assignee of a claim. While the latter must submit to all the defences and rights of set-off available against the assignor (see 176 sub (6)), the transferee of a negotiable instrument, if in the position of a lawful holder, can only be met by the following defences:
(1) defences arising from the invalidity of the debtor's declaration expressed on the face of the instrument (*e. g.* want of authority of the person who signed the debtor's name on the instrument, incapacity, &c.);
(2) defences arising from the tenor of the instrument (*e. g.* formal defects);
(3) defences available as between the transferee and the debtor (*e. g.* a right of set-off operating between such transferee and the debtor)—BGB 796; HGB 364 (2); WO 82.

(5) *What constitutes a lawful holder.*

The indorsee of an instrument to order, in the absence of fraud or gross negligence, is a lawful holder if there is a continuous chain of indorsements down to the one under which he holds (even if any indorsement constituting a link in the chain is forged); the possessor of an instrument to bearer is, as between himself and the debtor, deemed to be the lawful holder, but if his possession is unlawful (311 sub (4)), the person entitled to possession can recover the instrument—BGB 793, 1007 (1, 2); HGB 365 (1); WO 36, 74, 75.

(6) *Comparison of German and English rules.*

Under English law certain documents which, under German law, possess the characteristics of negotiability (*e. g.* bills of lading, dock warrants, &c.), are not deemed negotiable instruments in the full sense of the word, but by virtue of the provisions of the Factors Act 1889, ss. 2, 9, some of the practical consequences of negotiability are attached to them. English law has only gradually recognized the negotiability of instruments to bearer, but as regards Government Bonds, which are treated as negotiable by the custom of the Stock Exchanges and debentures of companies, it is now fully established (Bechuanaland, &c. Co. *v.* London Trading Bank (1898) 2 Q. B. 658; Edelstein *v.* Schuler (1902) 2 K. B. 144). One important distinction between German and English law is to be found in the fact that, according to English law, the holder does not acquire the full rights of a lawful holder unless he is a holder for value. In German law this requirement does not exist. A person who in good faith acquires a negotiable instrument by way of gift, has the same rights thereunder as a purchaser for value. The rule of English law under which the negotiability of a cheque may be restricted by the holder for the time being (see Bills of Exchange Act 1882, s. 81) does not exist in German law.

199

bb. Negotiable instruments passing by indorsement.

178. The following classes of instruments pass by indorsement:

(1) bills of exchange and promissory notes—WO 36, 98;

(2) any written order or promise by which a mercantile trader is requested or undertakes to pay or deliver to the order of another a sum of money or a negotiable instrument or a fungible thing, provided that such payment or delivery is not made dependent on some counter-performance on the part of the holder—

HGB 363 (1); [1]

(3) bills of lading, carriers' receipts, warehousing receipts issued by any undertaking licensed for that purpose, bottomry bonds, policies against risks of carriage by land or sea if issued to order—HGB 363 (2);

(4) share certificates registered in the holder's name—HGB 222 (3). [2]

The indorsement of a negotiable instrument, if accompanied by its delivery to the indorsee, has the effect of transferring all rights conferred by the instrument from the indorser to the indorsee, and the debtor is not bound to perform his obligation unless the instrument, duly receipted by the last indorsee, is handed to him—HGB 364 (1, 3).

The rules of bill of exchange law as to the form of indorsement (280), the holder's title, and other similar matters apply to all negotiable instruments which pass by indorsement—HGB 222 (3), 365 (2).

cc.   Instruments to bearer.

200   **179.** The following classes of instruments to bearer are recognized by German law:

(1) obligations to bearer (*Schuldverschreibungen auf den Inhaber*) (279);
(2) share certificates issued to bearer—HGB 179, 183.

An obligation to bearer is a promise contained in a written instrument to make a payment or to perform an act for the benefit of the bearer of the instrument—BGB 793 (1). [3]   An obligation of this kind which promises the payment of a sum certain in money, if issued in Germany without government permission by any person or corporation other than the fiscal authorities of the German Empire, or of a German State, is invalid—BGB 795.

An obligation to bearer may have interest warrants (coupons) annexed to it, as to which special rules are laid down by BGB 803–805; it can be converted by the debtor into an obligation for the benefit of a named person if the holder requires this to be done, but the debtor is under no obligation to effect this conversion—BGB 806.

Tickets of admission to entertainments, or similar documents which confer

---

1   The instruments of the second class include cheques (which, according to German law, are not deemed bills of exchange), and delivery orders for goods of a fungible (73) kind.   The law as to cheques in Germany is still regulated by State legislation.

2   The law requires that the title to such certificates must pass by indorsement of bill.

3   Bank-notes fall within the definition but are regulated by special legislation.

rights on the holder without mentioning his name, are not instruments to bearer in the technical sense of the word; but if it appears from the circumstances that it was the intention of the person issuing any such document to promise the performance mentioned therein to any bearer thereof, [1] the rules as to negotiability, &c. , applicable to an instrument to bearer apply to such a document—BGB 807.

A document issued for the benefit of a named person ' or bearer' is, under the rules of English law, deemed a document to bearer (see the note to Bills of Exchange Act 1882, s. 8 (3) in Chalmers' edition) ; under German law, on the other hand, such a document is not deemed an instrument to bearer or even a negotiable instrument; the alternative is regarded as having been put in for the benefit of the debtor, and though he is duly discharged by payment or delivery to the bearer, the holder is not entitled to claim performance of the obligation embodied by the instrument unless the right to claim such performance has been validly assigned to him according to the general rules as to the assignment of obligatory rights (176)—BGB 808. [2]

201

2.   TRANSFER OF LIABILITY

180.   Under English law, as under Roman law, the assumption of the burden of an obligation by a new debtor in the place of the original debtor is looked upon as the creation of an entirely new obligation; according to this view the creditor, whose assent must of course be given, agrees to accept the benefit of a newly created claim in satisfaction of the old claim, and thereby joins in a transaction having the character of a ' novation'.

The new German law, on the other hand, following Germanic traditions, regards the transfer of a liability in the same way as the assignment of a claim, subject to the requirement of the creditor's assent.   The new debtor is deemed to take over the old obligation, and this transaction which is called the ' assumption of an obligation' (*Schuldübernahme*) is governed by the following rules:

(1) if the agreement is made between the new debtor and the creditor it becomes immediately operative—BGB 414;

---

[1]   In the case of railway tickets, transferability is generally expressly excluded; though they mention no name they are only available for the actual purchaser.

[2]   The debtor may, as in the case of a negotiable instrument, refuse to pay or deliver except against delivery of the document.   The document if lost or destroyed may be declared inoperative like a negotiable instrument.

(2) if the agreement is made between the original debtor and the new debtor, it must be ratified by the creditor in accordance with the ordinary rules as to ratification (130); the ratification is inoperative if made before notice of the agreement is actually received either from the original or the new debtor, and if such notice specifies a period of time within which the ratification must be made, it is deemed to be refused unless communicated to the new or to the original debtor within the specified period; [1] the parties may at any time before the ratification or repudiation of the agreement on the creditor's part, modify or rescind it; subject to this provision and to any stipulation to the contrary, the new debtor is as between himself and the original debtor, bound to satisfy the obligation while the ratification is being awaited, and also after its refusal—BGB 415;

202

(3) after the assumption of the obligation by the new debtor, he may avail himself of the same defences as the original debtor, but he is not entitled to avail himself of any right of set-off to which the original debtor would have been entitled—BGB 417 (1);

(4) a creditor who authorizes the transfer of the liability for a debt can no longer avail himself of the previously existing securities for such debt, unless the person who gave the security (*e. g.* a surety or a person who has charged or pledged any object as security) authorizes the assumption of the obligation by the new debtor—BGB 418;

(5) where a person by agreement takes over the whole of another person's property, [2] he becomes liable jointly with the transferor of the property for the whole of the debts of the latter, but only to the extent of the value of the property and of the rights conferred upon him by such agreement; the liability of the assignee cannot in such a case be excluded by agreement between him and the assignor—BGB 419;

---

1   Where the purchaser of mortgaged property agrees with the vendor to assume the personal liability for the mortgage debt, the rule is modified in the following manner: the notice must be given by the vendor, and cannot be effectively given before the purchaser is registered as owner of the property; the mortgagee is deemed to have accepted the substitution of the purchaser's for the vendor's liability, unless he notifies his refusal within a period of six months from the receipt of the notice.   The purchaser may compel the vendor to give the required notice, and the vendor is bound to inform the purchaser of the result of the notice as soon as such result is ascertained—BGB 416.   (Under English law the vendor remains liable, unless expressly released by the mortgagee; in such a case the purchaser usually indemnifies the vendor against his liability.)

2   An instance of such an agreement occurs where a father transfers his property to his children in consideration of an annuity charged on the immovables (*Altenteil*).   Where the property is transferred as a whole, the fact that some objects are excepted from the transfer is not material—RGZ 24, 260.

(6) where a mercantile business undertaking acquired by act *inter vivos* (purchase, gift, partition, &c.) is continued under the old firm name (with or without an indication as to the new owner being a successor of the former owner) the new owner of such undertaking becomes liable for all the obligations incurred by the former owner in connexion with the conduct of the business; any agreement   203 to the contrary is inoperative as against a third party to whom such agreement is not communicated, unless it is registered in the commercial register and published in the prescribed manner; where the old firm name is dropped, the new owner of a business undertaking is not liable for the obligations of the former owner, unless a public announcement in the usual form is made as to the liabilities having been taken over, or unless there is some other special ground imposing such liability on the new owner [1] —HGB 25.

---

[1]   As to the period of prescription, see HGB 26.

CHAPTER VIII
JOINT LIABILITIES AND JOINT RIGHTS

1. Historical Statement

204   **181.** The much discussed and somewhat obscure distinction existing in Roman law between debtors who are under a ' correal ' obligation and debtors who are under a ' solidary ' obligation, corresponds in a certain manner to the English distinction between ' joint debtors ' and debtors who are liable ' jointly and severally '.   In the later stages of both systems the distinction has lost in importance (as to English law, see R. S. C. , Order 16, rule 11), but according to English law there is still the important difference, that except in the case of a partnership liability (as to which, see Kendall *v.* Hamilton 4 A. C. 504; Partnership Act 1890, s. 9)—the liability of one of several joint debtors on his death becomes discharged *ipso facto*, while the obligation of one of several persons liable jointly and severally is binding on his estate.

Under Roman law there was also a distinction between ' correality ' and ' solidarity ' on the creditors' side, which, however, does not correspond with the English distinction between rights held ' jointly ' and rights held by several persons as ' tenants in common '.

Modern German law has not retained the distinction between correality and solidarity, either on the passive or on the active side; there is only one class of joint liabilities, while joint rights, as shown below, are divided into two classes, but the present classification has nothing in common with the classification of Roman law.

The BGB defines joint debtors (*Gesamtschuldner*) as persons ' whose liability to perform an obligation is such that each of them is bound to perform the whole obligation, while the creditor is not entitled to claim more than one performance of the obligation ' —BGB 421; in a corresponding way joint creditors

205   (*Gesamtgläubiger*) are defined as persons ' whose right to claim the performance of an obligation is such, that each of them is entitled to claim the whole

performance, whilst the debtor cannot be called upon to perform his obligation more than once' —BGB 428.

2.   JOINT LIABILITY

(1) *Presumption as to joint liability.*

182. Where several persons are liable for the performance of one obligation, they may be liable jointly [1] in accordance with the definition given above (181), or each may be liable in respect of part of the obligation only.

The question, which of the two kinds of liabilities is intended is determined by the following rules, which apply in the absence of an agreement between the parties, or of a special rule of law [2] providing otherwise:

(1) where the obligation is indivisible [3] the debtors are liable jointly—BGB 431;

(2) where the obligation is divisible the debtors are liable jointly, if they have undertaken a liability by the same agreement—BGB 427;

(3) where an obligation is divisible in any case which does not come under rule (2) [4] the debtors are liable in equal shares—BGB 420.

(2) *Special rules as to partnership liability.*

Under English law partners are jointly liable for the partnership debts (subject to the exceptional provision as to the estates of deceased partners, noted above).   Under German law a mercantile partnership firm is, like a Scotch firm, liable as a firm for the partnership debts (see above 68 and HGB 124); in addition to this the partners are jointly liable for such debts—HGB 128.   The   206 partners, are, as it were, joint sureties for the partnership.   In the case of a non-mercantile partnership the partnership as such cannot incur any liabilities, but where any contractual liabilities are incurred by the partners, or by a partner

---

1   The expression 'joint liability' will in the further course of this treatise be used as the equivalent of the liability arising under a *Gesamtschuldverhältniss*, which, according to the usual English terminology, would be described as a 'joint and several liability'.

2   For examples of such rules, see 275, 295.

3   As to the meaning of the term 'indivisible', see p. 153 note 1.

4   This may occur in a case where a person has claims against several persons in respect of voluntary services performed for their benefit (801), or in any case in which an obligation is imposed by the surrounding circumstances (297).

authorized to act on their behalf (67) , they are liable jointly under the rule mentioned above as to contractual liabilities incurred by several persons acting together.

(3) *Liability as between joint debtors and creditor.*

Where the liability is a joint liability under the rules stated above, the creditor may claim performance from each of the joint debtors wholly or in part. Until the complete performance of the obligation all the joint debtors remain liable—BGB 421.

After the death of one of the joint debtors the question whether his estate remains liable is determined by the same rules as if the liability had been exclusively his own. [1]

Illustration: If two artists enter into a joint agreement to produce a painting or a work of sculpture, the liability is a joint one; but in the event of the death of one of the artists before the time fixed for performance, his estate is not liable in damages for the breach of the obligation.

As regards the effect of the extinction of the liability of one of the joint debtors the following rules apply:

(*a*) performance by one of the joint debtors of the obligation, either according to its original tenor, or in some other manner accepted by the creditor (163) , or by set-off (165) , or by lodgment with a public authority (164) , operates in favour of the other joint debtors—BGB 422;

(*b*) a release of the debt, agreed upon between the creditor and one of the joint debtors, releases the other joint debtors only in so far as it can be shown that this was the intention of the parties to the agreement—BGB 423;

(*c*) the creditor's *mora accipiendi* upon the tender of the performance by one of the joint debtors operates in favour of the other joint debtors—BGB 424;

207   (*d*) other facts exonerating one of the debtors, or affecting his liability, do not exonerate the other joint debtors, or affect their liability; a notice given to one joint debtor does not affect the others; impossibility of performance (158) , prescription (132) , or its interruption (136) , or suspension (137) , or the fact that one of the joint debtors acquires the creditor's rights, whatever its effect on

---

[1]   As a general rule an obligation is not discharged by the debtor's death, but when the obligation is of a strictly personal nature its performance, on the debtor's death, is rendered impossible by an event for which he is not responsible; his estate is therefore discharged from liability (158).

the obligation of the debtor whom it concerns, does not alter the obligations of the other joint debtors—BGB 425.

Illustrations: (1) *A* takes an assignment of a debt for the payment of which *A* and *B* are jointly liable; *B* cannot allege that the debt has become extinguished by merger.   (2) The creditor takes proceedings against *A* for the enforcement of a debt for the payment of which *A* and B are jointly liable; he subsequently takes proceedings against *B*, after the period of prescription has run; the creditor cannot allege that the prescription in favour of *B* was interrupted by the proceedings against *A*.

(4) *Liability as between the several joint debtors.*

Joint debtors as between themselves, in the absence of a contrary agreement, are liable in equal shares [1] ; if the contribution of one of the joint debtors remains unsatisfied, the deficiency must be borne by the others.

In so far as a joint debtor, being entitled to contribution from the other joint debtors, satisfies the creditor, the creditor's right is *ipso facto* transferred to him, but the right so acquired must not be exercised to the detriment of the original creditor—BGB 426.

Illustration: The subrogated creditor, who has satisfied part of the debt, cannot, as regards the remaining part of the debt, claim any rights of priority to the prejudice of the original creditor.

3.   JOINT RIGHTS

183. Where several persons are entitled to the benefit of a right they are not deemed joint creditors (*Gesamtgläubiger*) except in cases specially provided for by law (see, for instance, 499), or by special agreement.

Where several creditors are entitled to the benefit of a right without being joint creditors in the technical sense of the word, the performance of the obligation is regulated as follows: if the obligation is divisible (see p. 153 note 1), the several creditors are entitled in equal shares; if the performance is indivisible it must be effected for the joint benefit of the creditors.   Where the obligation

208

---

[1]   This rule also applies as between several tort-feasors.   Under English law one out of several tort-feasors has no right of contribution against the others, if his participation in the unlawful act was wilful.

consists in the delivery of a movable thing, each creditor may require such thing to be lodged with a public authority (164); where it does not belong to the class of objects fit for such lodgment, each creditor may require it to be delivered to a judicially appointed receiver, the lodgment or delivery being made for the joint account of all the creditors—BGB 420, 432 (1).

Where, on the other hand, the creditors are joint creditors, the debtor, as mentioned above (181), can discharge his obligation by a performance for the exclusive benefit of one of them.   *Mora accipiendi* on the part of one out of several joint creditors operates against all, and if the debtor acquires the right of one of the joint creditors, the debt is extinguished by merger.   In all other respects the rules relating to joint liabilities (see 182) are applied, *mutatis mutandis*— BGB 429.

Joint creditors, as between themselves, are, in the absence of any special provision to the contrary, entitled in equal shares; if therefore one of them obtains satisfaction, each of the others is entitled to claim from him such part of the value of the benefit of the performance as corresponds to his share—BGB 430.

Persons who as joint owners of property (*Gesamthänder*) are entitled to assert claims arising by virtue of their common ownership, are not in the position of joint creditors—see 304; (as to co-ownership, see 325; as to claims forming part of the common property of partners, see 258).

SECOND DIVISION
RULES RELATING TO PARTICULAR KINDS OF OBLIGATIONS

FIRST SUB-DIVISION
OBLIGATIONS CREATED BY ACT-IN-THE-LAW

CHAPTER I
AGREEMENTS RELATING TO THE TRANSFER OF PROPERTY

1.   PURCHASE AND SALE

a.   General Rules.

(1) Distinction between Sale and Agreement for Sale.

184. UNDER English law a sale of goods has the effect of transferring the 209 property in the goods to the purchaser (Sale of Goods Act 1893 , s. 1 (3)). Under French law every sale relating to an existing and specified object of which the vendor at the time of the sale is the owner, has the same effect (Code Civil art. 1583, 1599). In both countries a ' sale ' must therefore be distinguished from an ' agreement to sell '.

Under German law the word ' sale ' means an ' agreement to sell ' ; the sale as such does not transfer the property.

(2) Subject-matter of agreement.

A sale under German law may refer to movable or immovable things, or to rights. It is not a necessary condition that the vendor should, at the time of the sale, be the owner of the purchased object, or that the purchased object should at that time be already in existence. [1]

210   Under English law a sale of goods may refer to existing goods owned or possessed by the seller, or to goods to be manufactured or acquired by the seller 'after the making of the contract' —Sale of Goods Act 1893, s. 5 (1). A contract for the sale of land is also valid without reference to the question whether, at the date of the contract, the vendor is the owner of the land or not.

(3) *Nature of agreement.*

The following rules apply to a sale under German law:

(*a*) the vendor of a movable or immovable thing is bound to deliver such movable or immovable thing, and to cause the ownership thereof to be vested in the purchaser;

(*b*) the vendor of a right is bound to cause such right to be vested in the purchaser, and, where the right involves the possession of a thing, to deliver such thing to the purchaser—BGB 433 (1); [2]

(*c*) the purchaser is bound to pay the purchase money, and, if the purchased object is a thing, to accept the delivery of such thing—BGB 433 (2).

(4) *Form of agreement.*

The sale of an immovable [3] and the sale of the estate of a deceased person or any share therein must be effected by public act (97 sub (1))—BGB 313, 2033, 2371.

Other sales do not require writing or any other form.

Under English law contracts for the sale of land, and, contracts for the sale of goods of the value of £ 10 or more, are, in the absence of part performance, required to be in writing—Statute of Frauds, s. 4; Sale of Goods Act 1893, s. 4 (1).

---

[1]   An agreement by which a contractor undertakes to manufacture or otherwise produce a specified object from material supplied by him is an agreement for work, but comes under all the rules relating to sales—BGB 651; HGB 381 (2).

[2]   Illustration: The vendor of a claim secured by pledge is bound to deliver the pledged object. See BGB 1251 (1).

[3]   If the immovable is duly conveyed and the transfer of ownership duly registered, an informal agreement becomes valid retrospectively—BGB 313.

b.   Mutual Duties of Parties on Formation of Agreement.

185. The vendor is bound to make full disclosure of defects of title, [1] and of defects in respect of essential qualities; an agreement excluding or restricting the   211 warranty of title or of essential qualities, which is otherwise implied by law, is inoperative if the vendor, with intent to deceive (*arglistig*), conceals a defect as to these—BGB 443, 476.

The purchaser has no claim for breach of warranty in respect of defects which were known to him on the formation of the agreement [2]; but the fact that he was aware of the existence of any incumbrance does not take away his right to claim its removal—BGB 439, 460.

Under the terminology of English law a German agreement for sale would be deemed a contract *uberrimae fidei*.

c.   Rules as to Purchase by a Person standing in a Fiduciary Relation to the Vendor.

186. In the same way as under English law, persons placed in a fiduciary relation to the parties for whose benefit a sale is effected (auctioneers, mortgagees, pledgees, &c.), are not allowed to purchase except with the assent (129, 130) of the beneficial owner.   Where in such a case a purchase has been effected without the required authority, the rules as to ratification are the same as in the case of the act of an unauthorized agent (120).   Where the assent is not obtained, the sale is inoperative, and, in the event of a second sale being effected, the unauthorized purchaser is liable for the costs of the abortive sale; if the amount of the proceeds of sale obtained in the effective sale is less than the amount which would have been obtained if the abortive sale had been effective, he is liable for the deficiency—BGB 456–458.   He may also be liable for further damages under BGB 823 (2); see 287.

---

1   The purchaser is not bound to inquire as to defects of title; but questions on such defects do not arise in the same way in Germany as they do in England, owing to the system of land registration.

2   Defects of quality of which the purchaser would have become aware, but for his gross negligence, are treated as defects which were known to him, unless they were fraudulently concealed by the vendor—BGB 460.

d. Implied Terms of Agreement.

aa. Warranty of title and warranty of essential qualities.

(1) *Warranty of title.*

187. A vendor, as shown above, is bound not only to deliver the sold object, but also to cause its ownership to be transferred to the purchaser.   The purchaser is entitled to acquire the sold object free from all incumbrances other than those in the nature of public charges—BGB 434, 436. [1]

In the case of the sale of an obligatory right the vendor guarantees the existence of the right; if the right is embodied in a negotiable instrument, he also guarantees that no application for an order declaring such negotiable instrument to be inoperative (177 sub (3)) is pending—BGB 437. [2]

The vendor's duty to deliver or transfer the purchased object, free from any defect of title or incumbrance, is more in the nature of a condition than of a warranty, within the meaning of the Sale of Goods Act 1893 as applied to England, but the expression ' warranty of title' is here used as a convenient expression, which in Scotland is applied in the sense here given to it, and is also in accordance with English popular language.   The German term corresponding to warranty, *Gewährleistung*, is only used with reference to the warranty of essential qualities.

Under English law an agreement for the sale of goods contains an implied *condition* as to the vendor's title, and an implied *warranty* of quiet possession and freedom of incumbrances (Sale of Goods Act 1893, s. 12); but an agreement for the sale of land only contains an implied condition, that a title to the satisfaction of the purchaser shall be deduced from the date stipulated for in the contract, or in the absence of any stipulation on the point, for a period of forty years (see Vendor and Purchaser Act 1874, s. 1).   The covenants for title which the purchaser, in the absence of any special agreement, has a right to claim from a

---

1   Where the object of the sale is an immovable, or a registered ship, the vendor must at his own expense procure the cancellation of all incumbrances which have remained on the register though they have ceased to be effective—BGB 435.   A lease is not considered an incumbrance according to German law. As to the effect of a sale of land which is subject to a lease, see 205, 215.

2   In the absence of an express stipulation the vendor does not guarantee the solvency of the debtor; where such a stipulation exists it is presumed to apply to the debtor's solvency at the date of the assignment— BGB 438.

vendor not being a trustee or mortgagee, only refer to interferences with the title created by the vendor or any person from whom he derives title ' otherwise than by purchase', while the covenants of a vendor being a trustee or mortgagee are still more restricted (see Conveyancing Act 1881, s. 7). The German law, as will be seen from the statement made above, gives much more extensive rights to the purchaser than English law, and this is specially the case with regard to the sale of land. 213

(2) *Warranty of essential qualities.*

The following rules are applied to the warranty of essential qualities:

(*a*) the vendor of a thing warrants, that, at the time when the risk passes to the purchaser (190), the purchased thing is free from defects impairing either its value or its fitness for its ordinary purposes, or for the purposes appearing from the agreement of sale, and that it has the qualities promised by such agreement— BGB 459;

(*b*) the dimensions stipulated for in an agreement for the sale of a parcel of land are deemed to be a promised quality within the meaning of rule (*a*) ; in the case of a sale of goods by sample, the qualities of the sample are deemed to be qualities promised by the agreement—BGB 468, 494;

(*c*) in the case of the sale of horses, mules, asses, and cattle, the warranty only extends to certain ' principal defects' (*Hauptmängel*) appearing within a specified period of warranty (*Gewährfrist*) ; the nature of the principal defects, and the length of the period of warranty, are determined by Imperial Order issued with the consent of the Federal Council, which may from time to time be supplemented or modified; the prescribed period of warranty may be extended or reduced by agreement between the parties—BGB 481–486, HGB 382;

(*d*) in the case of the sale by public auction of a thing pledged to or charged in favour of the vendor, no warranty of essential qualities is implied, if the fact that the vendor is selling as pledgee or mortgagee is expressly mentioned—BGB 461.

The provisions of English law, as to the implied warranty of essential qualities on the sale of goods, are of a somewhat more complicated and casuistic nature than the corresponding rules of German law (see Sale of Goods Act 1893, ss. 13– 15) ; their practical effect is, however, very similar.

bb.   Price and interest.

188. The following rules apply on this subject:

(1) where the price is not fixed by the agreement it must be determined by the vendor in an equitable manner;

214   (2) where the price is to be determined by the valuation of a third party, and such party fails to make such valuation, the sale is avoided[1];

(3) where the market price is to be paid, the market price prevailing at the agreed time (146) and place (147) of performance is presumed to be intended—BGB 453;

(4) where, in the case of a mercantile sale (36), the price is fixed by weight, the net weight is deemed to be intended in the absence of a special arrangement or special custom to the contrary—HGB 380;

(5) in the event of the purchase price not being paid at the stipulated time, interest at the rate payable in an ordinary case of *mora solvendi* (153) runs from the date at which the right to the profits of the purchased thing passes to the purchaser; if the purchase price is, by agreement between the parties, payable at a later date, interest runs from that date—BGB 452.

cc.   Duty to give information and supply documents of title.

189. The vendor must give full information to the purchaser as to the legal facts relating to the purchased object, including in the case of the sale of land, full information as to the boundaries, privileges, charges, and burdens; he must also deliver all documents of title relating to the purchased object which are in his possession and relate solely to such object; in so far as they relate to other matters, a publicly certified extract of the part relating to the purchased object must be delivered—BGB 444. [2]

dd.   Passing of risk to Purchaser.   Cost of delivery and transfer.

190. The rule of Roman law, *emptoris est periculum* (which as regards immovables, is also the rule of English law), has not been adopted by the new

---

[1]   Rules (1) and (2) follow from the general rule stated above 144 rule (6); rule (2) is, in the case of the sale of goods, also applied under English law (Sale of Goods Act 1893, s. 9 (1)).

[2]   Under English law a purchaser is only entitled to a statutory acknowledgement of the right to the production of documents remaining in the vendor's possession; if the purchaser requires a certified copy or extract the cost thereof is payable by him—Conveyancing Act 1881, s. 3 (6).

German law; the following rules apply on this subject [1] :

(1) subject to the exceptions mentioned below, the purchased thing remains at the vendor's risk until delivery—BGB 446 (1) [2] ;

(2) if upon the sale of an immovable the purchaser is registered as proprietor before delivery of possession, the risk passes to him from the time of the registration—BGB 446 (2) ;

(3) where the place of destination is not identical with the place of performance (146) , the risk passes to the purchaser, on delivery of the purchased thing to the forwarding agent or carrier by whom it is to be conveyed to the place of destination, but if the vendor unnecessarily deviates from the purchaser's instructions as to the mode of forwarding, he is liable for all damage arising from such disregard of his instructions—BGB 447;

(4) the costs of registering of a transfer of the ownership of an immovable or registered charge are payable by the purchaser, but all costs connected with the delivery of the purchased thing, whether movable or immovable (including the costs of measuring and weighing) , in any case where the place of destination is also the place of performance, fall on the vendor—BGB 448 (1) , 449;

(5) where the place of performance is not the place of destination, the costs of the additional carriage, and of the final delivery of the goods, is chargeable to the purchaser; all other costs are borne by the vendor—BGB 448 (1) ;

(6) the costs of the assignment of a right are payable by the vendor—BGB 448 (2);

(7) if in any case in which the risk passes to the purchaser before delivery (see above rules (2) and (3)) , the vendor has to incur any necessary outlay after the passing of the risk, he is entitled to reimbursement from the purchaser in the same way as if he had incurred that outlay under a mandate (231 , 232) from the purchaser; his right to the reimbursement of any other outlay is determined by the rules as to voluntary services (301)—BGB 450.

216

---

[1]   These rules also apply in respect of the risk relating to a thing required to be delivered on the transfer of a right (*e. g.* a pledge)—BGB 451.

[2]   Under English law the risk on the sale of goods passes to the buyer upon the transfer of the ownership, whether delivery has been made or not—Sale of Goods Act 1893, s. 20.

e.   Purchaser's Remedies in the case of Breach of Vendor's Duties.

aa.   Effect of breach of duty to deliver and of breach of warranty of title.

191. It will be remembered that the vendor's obligations make it incumbent on him: (*a*) to deliver the purchased object; (*b*) to transfer the ownership to the purchaser free from incumbrances.

If the delivery of the purchased object becomes impossible, or if the vendor as regards such delivery is in *mora solvendi* (152), the purchaser, as a party to a reciprocal agreement, is entitled to the remedies available in the particular event under the general rules mentioned above (159, 160).

If, after the delivery or transfer of the purchased object, a defect of title is discovered, the purchaser is in the position of a party to a reciprocal agreement which has been partly performed; he may therefore, if the vendor is unable to remove the defect or if he is in *mora solvendi* as to such removal, exercise the rights available in these events under the general rules, subject, however, to certain modifications which have been introduced for the vendor's benefit [1]—BGB 440 (1).

Owing to the provisions for the protection of purchasers in good faith (328, 333), a question as to defect of title can only arise in the case of stolen or lost movables.

bb.   Effect of breach of warranty of essential qualities.

(1)   *General statement.*

192. A question as to breach of warranty of essential qualities cannot arise before the time at which the purchased object is delivered to the purchaser, or until the risk has in some other manner passed to him (190).   If the vendor is unable to deliver a thing with the qualities specially guaranteed or required under the general rule, the ordinary rules applicable in the case of impossibility of performance of a reciprocal agreement (160) apply.

217

---

1   The modifications are as follows: (1) the defect of title must be proved by the vendor—BGB 442; (2) in the case of the sale of a movable in respect of which a third party has a paramount right, the right to compensation can only be exercised if the purchaser has delivered the purchased object to such third party or returned it to the vendor, or if such third party's claim has otherwise been satisfied by the purchaser or if the purchased thing was destroyed—BGB 440 (2) (3) (4).

After the time at which the risk passes to the purchaser, a purchaser aggrieved by a defect of quality can no longer avail himself of the general rules as to reciprocal agreements, the nature of his remedies being from that time determined by the following rules:

(*a*) in the case of the sale of a generically defined thing the purchaser may, at his option, either avail himself of one of the remedies mentioned in rule (*c*) or claim the delivery of a thing free from defects in the place of the thing which has been delivered by the vendor; if the thing delivered by the vendor was, at the time of the passing of the risk to the purchaser, deficient in any specially guaranteed quality, or if the vendor, with intent to deceive (*arglistig*), has concealed any defect, the purchaser may at his option claim damages for the non-performance of the agreement instead of availing himself of any of his other remedies—BGB 480, 491; this rule is subject to the provisions of rule (*d*) ;

(*b*) where a specific thing at the time of its sale was deficient in any of the specially guaranteed qualities, or where the vendor, with intent to deceive, concealed any defect, the purchaser may, at his option, either avail himself of one of the remedies mentioned in rule (*c*) or claim damages for the non-performance of the agreement—BGB 463; this rule is subject to the provisions of rule (*d*) ;

(*c*) in any case in which the thing delivered by the vendor is defective, the purchaser may, at his option, require the vendor to consent to a cancellation of the sale (*Wandelung*) [1] or to a reduction of the purchase price (*Minderung*) , [2]   218
in accordance with the rules mentioned below; the right to the cancellation of the sale of a parcel of land on the ground of deficient quantity cannot be exercised, unless the deficiency is so great that the maintenance of the sale would be useless to the purchaser; in the case of a sale of horses, mules, donkeys, cattle, &c. , the cancellation of the sale is the only remedy; as soon as the vendor has expressed his consent to the exercise of one of the alternative rights, the other alternative right is barred; if the purchaser informs the vendor of the existence of the defect

---

[1]   Where several things are sold together the right of cancellation can be exercised as to such of them only as are defective; if however the things so sold together were sold expressly as belonging together the purchaser may cancel the whole sale, and the vendor may require him to do so, if he does not avail himself of this right.   The cancellation of the sale of the principal thing involves the cancellation of the sale of any accessory, but if any accessory is defective the right of cancellation is confined to such accessory—BGB 469, 470.

[2]   The alternative right to cancellation or reduction of the purchase price on the ground of defects of a quality is derived from Roman law.   The action in question was introduced by the Aedile's edict.

without mentioning the remedy selected by him, the vendor may require him to declare within a specified reasonable period, whether he intends to make use of his right of cancellation, and if he fails to comply with this requirement his right to cancellation is forfeited—BGB 462, 465, 466, 468, 481, 487; the purchaser's rights under this rule are subject to the provisions of rule (*d*) ;

(*d*) if the purchaser accepts a defective thing with knowledge of the defect, [1] he cannot exercise any right otherwise available under rules (*a*), (*b*), and (*c*), unless on such acceptance he expressly reserves his rights; no express rule is laid down as to what constitutes acceptance in an ordinary case, [2] but, in the case of a bilateral mercantile sale (36), the purchaser is deemed to have accepted the goods, unless he examines them immediately on delivery and forthwith informs the vendor of any defect discovered on such examination, or unless the defect was not discovered on such examination; where a defect has thus escaped discovery the goods are deemed to be accepted unless the purchaser informs the vendor thereof immediately after its discovery, but the purchaser's rights are preserved if the notice of the defect is forwarded at the proper time; a vendor who, with intent to deceive, has concealed any defect is not entitled to plead the purchaser's acceptance of the goods; in the case of the sale of horses, &c., the purchaser, in the absence of fraudulent concealment on the vendor's part, is deemed to have accepted the purchased animal, unless he gives notice of any defect within two days from the expiration of the period of warranty (187 rule 3), or within two days from the animal's death, if such death takes place before the expiration of the period—BGB 464, 481, 485; HGB 377 (see also *ibidem* 378).

(2) *Legal nature of right to require cancellation of sale.*

The right to require cancellation must be distinguished from the right to rescission, to which a party to a reciprocal agreement is entitled in certain events (160, 161); the right to rescind is not in the nature of a claim against the other party, and therefore not subject to prescription; the right to cancellation is, on the other hand, in the nature of a claim against the vendor, and is subject to prescription—see below sub (4).   The effect of the cancellation of a sale under

---

1   As to the effect of the purchaser's knowledge of defects at the time of the sale, see 185.

2   The tests applied on the sale of goods under English law (express intimation; exercise of right of ownership; lapse of reasonable time without mention of defect—see Sale of Goods Act 1893, s. 35) would probably also be conclusive under German law.

the special rules here referred to is the same as that of rescission under the general rules (162), but subject to the following modifications [1] :

(*a*) the fact that the purchased thing has been transformed by the purchaser does not take away the right of cancellation, if the defect was discovered in the course of such transformation [2] ;

(*b*) the purchaser's costs of the agreement for sale must be refunded by the vendor—BGB 467;

(*c*) where, in the case of a sale of several things at a comprehensive price, the right of cancellation is exercised as to some of them only (see p. 201 note 1), a proportionate reduction of the price has to be effected—BGB 471.

(3)   *Reduction of purchase price.*

Where the purchaser makes use of his right to a reduction of the purchase price, such reduction is effected in accordance with the following rules:

(*a*) the reduced price must bear the same proportion to the original price as   220 the value of the purchased thing in its actual condition bears to the value which it would have had at the time of the agreement for sale, if it had been free from defects—BGB 472 (1);

(*b*) if the purchase price of one of several things purchased together has to be reduced the aggregate value of all the purchased things serves as the basis of the calculation—BGB 472 (2);

(*c*) if under the agreement for sale the purchaser has to do any act (not consisting in the delivery of fungibles) in addition to the payment of an agreed sum of money, the value of such act must be considered in estimating the purchase price; the amount of the reduction is then calculated under rule (*a*), and is deducted from the agreed sum of money—BGB 473.

Under English law the computation of the deduction, to be made in the case of breach of warranty of quality on the sale of goods, is not subject to any hard and fast rule, but, in the absence of evidence as to any loss directly and naturally resulting to the buyer by reason of the defect, the deduction is equal to the difference between the actual value of the goods as they are at the time of delivery, and the value which they would have had if they had been free from defects.

---

1   For the special rules applicable in the case of the sale of horses, &c. , see BGB 487, 488, 489, 492.

2   Where raw material is purchased its fitness for the purpose for which it was required is frequently not ascertainable before it has been worked upon, and consequently transformed.

(Sale of Goods Act 1893, s. 53 (2) (3).)

If x is the reduced price, p the original price, w the value of the non-defective goods, and v the value of the goods actually delivered, then, according to the German mode of computation, $x = \dfrac{p\,v}{w}$; according to the English mode $x = p + v - w$.

If the purchase price is below the actual value, the German mode of computation is more favourable to the vendor than the English mode, and *vice versa*. [1]

(4) *Effect of lapse of time on remedies for breach of warranty of quality.*

221   The remedies mentioned above sub (1) in rules (a), (b), and (c) are barred by the lapse of the short periods mentioned below, unless the vendor has, with intent to deceive, concealed the defect in respect of which they arise, in which event the period of prescription is thirty years.

These periods are:

(1) in the case of the sale of movable things other than horses, cattle, &c., six months from the date of delivery;

(2) in the case of the sale of horses, cattle, &c., six weeks from the expiration of the period of warranty;

(3) in the case of the sale of immovables, one year from the time of transfer of possession.

The periods may be extended by agreement between the parties; in other respects the ordinary rules as to prescription (see 131 to 137) are applicable, subject to small modifications. —BGB 477, 490. [2]

---

[1]   The comparison in the text disregards the complication created by the fact, that under English law the value at the time of delivery, and under German law the value at the time of the sale is made the basis of the calculation, but this discrepancy cannot affect the result to a material extent.

[2]   A purchaser who is entitled to avail himself of any of the remedies mentioned in the text, and who has not as yet paid the purchase money, may even after the lapse of the period of prescription withhold such payment in so far as he would otherwise be entitled to do so, if prior to the lapse of the period he has done one of the following things: (a) if he has forwarded a notice of the defect to the vendor; (b) if he has made an application to the court for the perpetuation of testimony as to such defect; (c) if in the course of an action between him and a subsequent purchaser relating to the defect he has served a third party notice on the vendor.   The purchase money may be withheld to the extent mentioned, without any such act done by the purchaser, if the defect has been concealed by the vendor with intent to deceive—BGB 478, 479, 490 (3).

f.   Vendor's Remedies in case of Breach of Purchaser's Duties.

193. The purchaser, as shown above—183, is bound to take delivery of the purchased thing when tendered to him, and to pay the purchase money upon such delivery (unless payment at another time has been agreed upon).   If he is in *mora accipiendi* as regards the delivery, or in *mora solvendi* as regards the payment, of the purchase money, the vendor may under the general rules avail himself of one of the following remedies: (1) he may claim performance of the agreement and compensation for the delay, including interest; (2) he may rescind the agreement if he can show that the belated performance of the agreement is useless to him, or if time is of the essence under the original agreement or has been made so by notice in the prescribed manner.   Where the purchased object has been delivered on the understanding that time should be allowed for the payment of the purchase money, the sale cannot be rescinded on non-payment of the purchase money at the agreed time, unless, in the case of the sale of a movable thing, it was stipulated that the ownership should not pass before payment of the purchase price (*pactum reservati dominii*) —BGB 454, 455.

222

In the case of a mercantile sale the vendor has the following additional remedies if the purchaser is in *mora accipiendi*: (1) he may store the goods at the purchaser's expense; (2) he may sell the goods for account of the purchaser by public auction or by private contract through an authorized broker, having previously given notice to the purchaser if practicable; where the goods are of a perishable nature the notice may be dispensed with; the vendor as well as the purchaser may bid at the public auction; the result of the sale, as far as practicable, must be communicated to the purchaser—HGB 373, 374.

The rules as to the vendor's rights under English law are not on the whole different from the German rules (as to goods, see Sale of Goods Act 1893, ss. 37–42), but no question of lien in the proper sense of the word can arise under German law, as the ownership does not in any event pass to the purchaser until the goods are delivered.

The *pactum reservati dominii* is permissible under English as under German law (see Sale of Goods Act 1893, s. 19 (1)).

On the sale of immovables an English vendor's rights go further in theory than a German vendor's rights, but the difference is not of much practical importance, as an English vendor does not as a rule rely on his equitable lien for unpaid purchase money, but secures himself by specific mortgage or charge if the purchase money is not paid contemporaneously with the conveyance of the land.

The claim for specific performance, which under German law may be asserted in the case of any sale, is not under English law available in the case of an agreement for the sale of movables (except under quite special circumstances).

223

g.   Rules as to Agreements similar to Agreements for Sale, Exchange, &c.

194. The rules as to sales are, *mutatis mutandis*, also applicable to exchanges— BGB 515.

The rules as to the duties of vendors and purchasers, and as to warranty of title and quality, are, *mutatis mutandis*, applicable to all agreements for the alienation or hypothecation of any property for valuable consideration (*e. g.* agreements for transfer of property by way of compromise, or in consideration of services, agreements to pledge or charge, &c.)—BGB 445, 493.   Partition agreements are specially provided for by BGB 757.

h.   Special kinds of Agreements for Sale.

aa.   Hire-purchase Agreements.

195. An agreement which in English phraseology is termed a 'hire-purchase' agreement, and in German is called *Abzahlungsgeschäft*, may either take the form of a hiring agreement which, after the payment of a certain number of instalments of rent, is converted into a sale, or it may, as is commonly the case in German practice, take the form of an immediate sale subject to the *pactum reservati dominii* until payment of the last instalment of the purchase price.

In order to check the many abuses to which transactions of this kind are apt to lead, an Imperial Act, passed in 1893 (*Gesetz betreffend die Abzahlungsgeschäfte*), has introduced the following special rules which are applicable either in the case of a sale, subject to the *pactum reservati dominii*, of any movable thing to any person other than a registered trader, for a purchase price payable by instalments, or in the case of an agreement embodying a similar transaction in another legal form:

(1) on the rescission of any sale or other agreement coming under the provisions of the Act, each party must return to the other party any property or money received by virtue of the agreement, and the purchaser must indemnify the vendor for any outlay made in pursuance of the agreement and for any damage caused by his default, or by any event for which he is responsible; he must also pay the amount representing the value of the use of the purchased thing, including its diminution in value during the time it was in the purchaser's possession; any agreement by which the purchaser's duties are extended is void;

(2) the payments and deliveries to be made by each party on the rescission of the agreement, must be made contemporaneously;

(3) if any penalty payable under the agreement, on the breach of any of the purchaser's obligations, is unreasonably high, it must be reduced to a reasonable amount;   224

(4) a stipulation accelerating the maturity of the balance of the purchase price in the event of a breach of the agreement is void, if it is to come into operation before at least two successive instalments are wholly or partly in arrear, and before the amount of arrears is equal to at least one-tenth of the purchase price.

bb.   Sale on approval.

196. A sale on approval (*Kauf auf Probe*) must be distinguished from a sale according to sample (*Kauf nach Probe*), which is an ordinary sale with a warranty of the qualities shown in the sample (187).

A sale on approval either begins to be operative on the approval of the goods by the purchaser (condition precedent) or ceases to be operative on the rejection of the goods (condition subsequent).   The following rules apply to such a sale:

(1) where no contrary intention is shown the approval is deemed to be a 'condition precedent' —BGB 495 (1);

(2) the vendor must allow the purchaser to inspect the thing purchased on approval—BGB 495 (2);

(3) the approval, in the absence of any stipulation in the agreement specifying the period, must be declared within such reasonable period as the vendor may determine—BGB 496;

(4) a purchaser to whom the purchased thing is handed for inspection, and who does not express his disapproval within the proper period, is deemed to have signified his approval—BGB 496. [1]

---

[1]   Where the approval is a condition precedent and the goods are delivered before approval the ownership does not pass until approval.   Compare Sale of Goods Act of 1893, s. 18 rule 4.

cc.   Redemption (' Wiederkauf ').

197. The English form of mortgage, by which the borrower conveys property to the lender, subject to a proviso for redemption on repayment of the debt, is unknown in Germany, but German practice has introduced a method by which the same object can be attained in another form.

A lender, who adopts that method, purchases an object belonging to the borrower with a stipulation enabling the borrower to repurchase it within a specified period at a specified price.   A person who makes it a regular business to purchase movable things, allowing the vendor such right of redemption, is subject to the regulations which by State law may be imposed upon pawnbrokers (*Gewerbeordnung*, *s*. 34 (2), EG 94).

The following rules are applied with reference to the right of redemption:

(1) the parties may fix such period for the exercise of the right of redemption as they may think fit; in the absence of any express stipulation on the subject, the right to redeem an immovable lapses after thirty years from the date of its creation, and a right to redeem either a movable or a right lapses after three years from the date of its creation—BGB 503;

(2) a declaration on the original vendor's part expressing his intention to exercise his right of redemption, if duly communicated to the original purchaser, creates an agreement for the sale of the object to which the right refers; the declaration is not required to be in the form necessary in the case of an ordinary purchase of an object of the same kind—BGB 497 (1);

(3) where no contrary intention is shown, the price payable on redemption is the original purchase price—BGB 497 (2);

(4) the person against whom the right of redemption is exercisable is under the following obligations: (*a*) he is liable for the destruction of, or any deterioration or material alteration in the purchased object attributable to any default on his part—BGB 498 (2); (*b*) if the purchased object is in existence at the time of the redemption he must hand it over to the person exercising the right of redemption with all accessories—BGB 498 (1); (*c*) if he has sold or incumbered the purchased object, or if the purchased object has been sold or incumbered by a judgment creditor or trustee in bankruptcy, he must recover it from the purchaser or remove the incumbrance—BGB 499; if this is impossible he is in the position of a debtor who cannot perform his obligation owing to an event or circumstance for which he is responsible (158, 160 sub (3))—BGB 499; (*d*) if the price payable on redemption, according to the agreement

between the parties, is determined by the value of the repurchased object at the time when the right of redemption is exercised, the person exercising the right of redemption is not entitled to any compensation under rule (*a*)—BGB 501;

(5) the person against whom the right of redemption is exercised is entitled to the *jus tollendi*—144 sub (9)—and to the reimbursement of any outlay by which the value of the repurchased object has been increased (except where the price of redemption is determined by the value of the repurchased object at the time of redemption)—BGB 500, 501;

(6) a right of redemption vested in several persons jointly, can only be exercised by all such persons acting jointly; where one of them has lost his right 226 by waiver, lapse of time, or otherwise, or is unwilling to exercise it, his concurrence is dispensed with—BGB 502;

(7) a right of redemption created under the general rules [1] is binding on the parties only, and does not affect any third party acquiring any right over the object to which it refers, even if such third party is aware of the existence of the right; where the right refers to an immovable the party entitled to it may register a 'caution' (319).

dd.   Right of Pre-emption (*Vorkauf*).

198. A party entitled to a right of pre-emption in respect of any object may, in the event of an agreement for the sale of such object being entered upon with a third party, prevent the completion of such sale, and become himself the purchaser in the place of the third party.

Statutory rights of pre-emption exist under Imperial law (see for instance 529), and under State law (see EG 67, 109); contractual rights of pre-emption may be created without restriction; a contractual right of pre-emption as a general rule is only operative as between the parties, but where such a right refers to an immovable it may be so constituted as to have the effect of a 'real right' (308). In the following rules, in which the effects of a 'personal' and of a 'real' right of pre-emption are stated separately, the person entitled to exercise the right is called 'the pre-emptor', and the person against whom the right can be exercised is called 'the pre-vendor', the object to which the right refers is called 'the property subject to pre-emption'.

---

[1]   State law may allow the creation of rights of redemption having the character of real rights (308); see for instance Prussian AG 29.

A.   *Personal Right of Pre-emption.*

(1) The right cannot, in the absence of a stipulation to the contrary, be transferred by assignment; if it is exercisable during a specified period, it is presumed to be transmissible on the death of the pre-emptor; in any other case, and in the absence of an express provision to the contrary in the statute or agreement by which the right is created, it lapses on the death of the pre-emptor—BGB 514;

(2) the pre-vendor is under an obligation to give notice to the pre-emptor of any agreement for the sale of the property subject to pre-emption; but a communication from the purchaser is deemed a performance of this obligation; the right is exercisable as soon as any such agreement has been made, and lapses unless exercised within a prescribed period commencing from the communication of the notice; this period, in the absence of any statutory or contractual provision to the contrary, is two months if the property subject to redemption is an immovable, and one week in every other case—BGB 510;

(3) the right is exercised by means of a declaration communicated to the pre-vendor, which is not required to be in the form otherwise necessary in the case of a sale of an object of the same kind; the communication of the declaration creates an agreement under which the pre-vendor is bound to sell and the pre-emptor is bound to purchase the property subject to pre-emption on the terms of the agreement made between the pre-vendor and the third party—BGB 504, 505;

(4) a provision in the agreement of sale between the pre-vendor and the third party, that the sale is to be rescinded in the event of the right of pre-emption being exercised, is inoperative as between the pre-vendor and the pre-emptor—BGB 506;

(5) where the consideration for the sale includes an act to be performed in addition to the payment of the purchase price, and the pre-emptor is unable to perform such act, the estimated value of the act must be added to the purchase price; if the value of the act cannot be estimated, the right of pre-emption cannot be exercised, unless the act is so unimportant that the sale would have been concluded even if it had not been promised—BGB 507;

(6) if the sale comprises any objects other than the property subject to pre-emption, the pre-emptor must pay a proportionate part of the agreed purchase price, but he may require the inclusion of any objects which cannot be severed from the property subject to pre-emption without disadvantage to him—BGB 508;

(7) a provision in the agreement with the third party, by which the payment of the purchase price is postponed, operates in favour of the pre-emptor only in so far as he gives security; on the purchase of an immovable a registered charge is sufficient security—BGB 509;

(8) the rules as to the exercise of joint rights of pre-emption are the same— *mutatis mutandis*—as the rules relating to the exercise of joint rights of redemption (197 sub (6))—BGB 513;

(9) in the absence of a stipulation to the contrary, the right of pre-emption cannot be exercised in the case of a sale of the property subject to pre-emption to any statutory heir (473) of the pre-vendor, if such sale is effected with reference to his right of inheritance—BGB 511;

Illustration: A father sells a house to a son for a purchase price payable on   228
the father's death by means of a deduction from the value of the son's share in the father's estate; the right of pre-emption cannot be exercised.

(10) the pre-emptor has no claim against a third party to whom the property subject to pre-emption is sold and delivered; on the other hand the third party, upon whose purchase the right is exercised, has no claim against the pre-emptor; the pre-vendor is of course liable for the breach of his agreement with the pre-emptor, or with the third party, but he may protect himself by making the sale to a third party subject to the exercise of the right of pre-emption. [1]

B.   *Real Right of Pre-emption.*

(1) A parcel of land [2] may be charged with a real right of pre-emption in favour of a named person, or in favour of the owner for the time being of another parcel of land; the creation of such a right must be registered, and is also subject to the other rules relating to the creation of real rights affecting immovables (310)—BGB 1094;

---

[1]   An exception to this rule, which results from the general principles of the German law of obligations, arises in the case of the statutory right of pre-emption exercisable on the sale of a share in any estate effected by one of the co-heirs (529); in such a case the right of pre-emption is after the transfer of the share to a purchaser exercisable against the purchaser—BGB 2035.

[2]   The owner of an undivided share may make such undivided share subject to a right of pre-emption, but the owner of the whole parcel cannot make an undivided share subject to the right.   The right in the absence of an indication to the contrary is deemed to extend to the accessories—BGB 1095, 1096.

(2) the effect of a real right of pre-emption as between the immediate parties is the same as the effect of a personal right of pre-emption [1]—BGB 1098 (1);

(3) the right may be made to extend to more than one sale, or to some specified sale; in the absence of any indication to the contrary it is deemed to extend to the first sale only—BGB 1097;

(4) any person who acquires any right relating to the property subject to pre-emption acquires such right, subject to the right of pre-emption; he is in the same position as if the right had actually been exercised, and the pre-emptor had caused a 'caution' (319) to be registered for the protection of his claims to the ownership—BGB 1098 (2);

229   (5) the right to give notice of a sale may be exercised by the owner for the time being of the property subject to pre-emption as well as by the pre-vendor; if the latter is not the owner, he is bound to give notice to such owner of the exercise of the right of pre-emption, or of the fact that such right has become barred by lapse of time—BGB 1099 [2];

(6) if, on a sale of the property subject to pre-emption to a third party, such property, notwithstanding the exercise of the right of pre-emption, is transferred to and registered in the name of the purchaser, or his successor in title, the registered owner may refuse to transfer the property into the pre-emptor's name except on repayment of any sum paid by him as purchase money; if the property is registered in the pre-emptor's name, but possession given to the purchaser or his successor in title, he may refuse delivery of possession in the same way; any payment which the pre-emptor has to make to the purchaser, or his successor in title, is deemed to be made in part satisfaction of the purchase money payable by him—BGB 1100, 1101;

(7) if the pre-emptor cannot be found, the right of pre-emption may be excluded by judicial order after the lapse of a period specified in a public citation; this rule is not applicable in any case in which the right of pre-emption

---

[1]   A personal right of pre-emption is not exercisable on any sale by a trustee in bankruptcy; a real right of pre-emption is exercisable on such a sale, if effected by private contract—BGB 512, 1098 (1).

[2]   Under rule A (2) the time within which the right of pre-emption may be exercised runs from the date of the notice of the sale communicated to the pre-emptor.   If the pre-vendor is not the owner of the property subject to pre-emption, the latter is interested in putting an end to the state of uncertainty; the rule in the text therefore allows him to give notice of the sale.   The right of pre-emption being exercised by a declaration communicated to the pre-vendor, the owner of the property is further protected by the rule under which the pre-vendor is bound to inform him, whether the right has been exercised, or has ceased to be exercisable.

is exercisable by the owner for the time being of a specified parcel of land—
BGB 1104.

2.   AGREEMENTS RELATING TO GIFTS *INTER VIVOS*

a.   General Statement.

199. It is proposed to compare the rules of German and English law with
respect to the following questions: (1) How is a gift effected? (2) How far can a
promise to make a gift be enforced? (3) In what events can a gift be revoked by
the donor? (4) In what events can the validity of a gift be contested on public or
private grounds? (5) What is the effect of a burden imposed upon the donee?

English law deals with these questions in the following manner:

(1) a gift may be effected by the transfer or delivery of the object to the   230
donee, or to another in trust for the donee, or by a declaration of trust on the
donor's part without delivery or transfer; a voluntary transfer of property from A to
B does not in itself constitute a gift from A to B; it is always necessary to ascertain
the intention of the parties; in some cases (*e. g.* in the case of a conveyance or
transfer to a wife or a child or to a person to whom the transferor stands in *loco
parentis*) the intention to make a gift is presumed; in some other cases (*e. g.* in
the case of a conveyance of land or a transfer of stock paid for by one person and
conveyed or transferred to another, not being the wife or child of the purchaser
or not being a person to whom he stands in *loco parentis*), it is presumed that
the grantee or transferee only takes as trustee for the purchaser; but it is not
necessary in any case that the gift should be the subject of an agreement
between the donor and the donee; it is possible to effect a gift without the
consent or knowledge of the donee (*e. g.* by the execution of a conveyance in
his favour);

(2) a promise to make a gift if made by deed under seal is enforceable at
law in all cases, unless vitiated by any circumstance which would also vitiate an
agreement for valuable consideration, and although the donee cannot avail himself
of the remedy of specific performance, he can claim the value of the gift by way
of damages;

(3) a donor, who does not expressly reserve a power of revocation, cannot
in any event revoke his gift; the rule as to the effect of the statute of 27 Elizabeth,
according to which a voluntary conveyance of land was revoked by a subsequent

conveyance for value of the same parcel, is repealed by the Voluntary Conveyances Act 1893;

(4) a gift of land or chattels is void under the statute of 13 Elizabeth if made with intent to defraud the donor's creditors; a voluntary settlement is voidable in certain events specified by the Bankruptcy Act 1883; a gift of land to a corporate body not authorized to hold land, and any other gift of land not within the classes of gifts sanctioned by the Mortmain and Charitable Uses Act 1888 causes the land to be forfeited to the Crown; subject to these exceptions a gift cannot be impugned or avoided as such on public or private grounds;

231

(5) a gift subject to a burden (*donatio sub modo*) is unknown to English law, but the purposes for which such a transaction is entered upon may be attained by a gratuitous transfer of property for the benefit of the transferee but subject to a specified trust in favour of another. [1]

The German rules on the same questions may be summarized as follows:

(1) a gift cannot be effected except by agreement between the donor and the donee (200);

(2) the promise of a gift, though made in the prescribed form, and not suffering from any of the defects which would invalidate an agreement for valuable consideration, ceases to be binding in certain specified events (201);

(3) a gift may be revoked by the donor in certain specified events (202);

(4) certain kinds of gifts are invalid on public grounds; the donor's statutory heirs (473) may in certain events claim a total or partial return of a gift interfering with their rights (203);

(5) there is a material difference between a German *donatio sub modo*, and an English gratuitous transfer of property upon specified trusts; under German law the donor can enforce the objects of the gift (204); under English law the donor has no further control over the matter, except in so far as the trusts are for his benefit; a gift subject to a burden must be distinguished from a transfer of property in consideration of a promise made by the transferee for the benefit of a third party. Such a promise under English law could be enforced by the transferor, but could not be enforced by the beneficiary.

---

[1]   A gift subject to a burden must be distinguished from a gift of onerous property (*e. g.* leaseholds or shares subject to calls).

b.   Definition and Mode of effecting Gifts.

200.   ' A transfer of property by means of which the donor out of his own property confers a benefit on the donee is a gift (*Schenkung*) if it is agreed between donor and donee that the transfer of the property is to be gratuitous. ' — BGB 516 (1).

' The non-exercise of a right to acquire property, or the waiver of a right   232 vested in interest, but not as yet vested in possession or the renunciation of a legacy or inheritance though intended to benefit another does not constitute a gift. ' —BGB 517.

Only a transfer of property under the donor's direct control comes within the definition.   The transfer is not required to be made to the donee himself.   A gratuitous payment made by the donor to a creditor of the donee, in payment of the donee's debt, is a gift from the donor to the donee.

An agreement relating to a gift is formed by offer and acceptance in accordance with the general rules, but where a transfer of property is effected without the donee's concurrence, the donor may require the donee to declare his acceptance within a specified period, and if the donee does not decline the gift within that period, he is deemed to have accepted it—BGB 516.

An agreement, by which a future gift is promised, is invalid unless made by public act (97) ; but the invalidity in such a case is removed by the performance of the promise, with the result that the act done in pursuance of the agreement is deemed to have been done in discharge of a valid obligation, and that the value of the benefit received by the donee cannot be recovered under the rules as to ' unjustified benefits' (298)—BGB 518.

c.   Effect of Promise of Future Gifts.

201.   A person who promises a future gift is under a less stringent liability than an ordinary debtor, as will be seen by the following rules:

(1) the donor may refuse the performance of his promise, in so far as such performance would, having regard to his other obligations, endanger his capability to maintain himself in accordance with his station in life, and to comply with his legal duties as to the maintenance of others (412 sub (9), 422 sub (3),

431) [1] ; where a donor who pleads this privilege has promised several gifts the priorities are determined by the respective dates of the several promises—BGB 519;

233   (2) if the performance of the promise becomes wholly or partly impossible by reason of any circumstance or event not due to the promisor's wilful default or gross negligence the promisor is under no liability—BGB 521;

(3) the ordinary rule under which a promisor has to pay interest from the time at which he is in *mora solvendi* (153) is not applied in the case of a promise of a gift—BGB 522;

(4) a donor who promises to give any specific thing which is in his possession at the date of the promise is not responsible for defects of title or quality except in so far as he has intentionally concealed such defects [2] —BGB 523, 524;

(5) if the donor promises any periodically recurrent payments, such payments, in the absence of a stipulation to the contrary, come to an end on the donor's death—BGB 520.

d.   Revocation of Gifts or Promises of Gifts by Donor.

202. The following rules as to the revocation of gifts or of promises of gifts are applicable in so far only as the particular gift or promise was not made in compliance with a moral duty or out of regard to social propriety—BGB 534:

(1) a donor who under the rule stated above—201 sub (1)—would be entitled to refuse the performance of the promise of a future gift may recover any object given to the donee, unless the donee provides such periodical payments as are necessary for the maintenance of the donor and of all persons entitled to be maintained by him (excluding, however, any illegitimate children); the right of recovery is barred in any of the following events: (a) if ten years have elapsed

---

1   This is the only remnant of the *beneficium competentiae* of Roman law.

2   Where the donor has promised a specific object, which was not in his possession at the date of the promise, the donee may claim compensation for non-performance in the event of such object being affected with a defect of title, which at the time when it was acquired by the donor was known, or, but for his gross negligence, would have been known to him.   Where the donor has promised a generically defined object, which was to be acquired by him subsequently to the date of the gift, the donee may in the event of the object given in performance of the promise being affected with any defect, which was known to the donor at the date of acquisition or would, but for his gross negligence, have been known to him, claim the delivery of an object without such defect in the place of the object given by the donor.   Where the donor with intent to deceive conceals any defects he is liable in damages—BGB 523, 524.

from the date of the gift; (*b*) if the donor has wilfully or by gross negligence caused his impoverishment; (*c*) if the return of the property would endanger the   234 donee's own maintenance or the maintenance of any person whom he is bound to maintain—BGB 528, 529;

(2) the donor may revoke the promise of a future gift, or recover property previously given, if the donee, by any serious offence committed against the donor or against one of the donor's near relations (*e. g.* physical maltreatment, insulting behaviour, wilful infliction of heavy financial loss, unlawful attempt to place the donor under guardianship), has shown gross ingratitude—BGB 530 (1);

(3) the donor's heirs may recover a gift or revoke a promise made by the donor if the donee has wilfully and unlawfully caused the donor's death, or if he has prevented him from exercising his right of revocation—BGB 530 (2);

(4) the right of revocation is barred: (*a*) by the lapse of one year from the time when the donee's offence became known to the donor; (*b*) by the donor's condonation of the offence or by waiver; (*c*) by the donor's death (except in a case in which rule (3) is applicable)—BGB 532, 533;

(5) on the breaking off of an engagement to marry, and on a divorce declaring one of the parties to be the exclusively guilty party, all gifts made by either party to the other during the subsistence of the engagement or marriage may be recovered in the manner specified below—407, 422 sub (6).

e.   Invalidity of Gifts on Public or Private Grounds.

aa.   Invalidity of gifts on public grounds.

203.   (1) Gifts to corporate bodies, the value of which exceeds 5,000 Marks, may be prohibited or restricted by State legislation, and are in fact inoperative in several German States, *e.g.* Prussia, if made without special government authorization (EG 86; Prussian AG art. 6 § 7);

(2) the donor's creditors may, in the event of his bankruptcy and in certain other events indicating his insolvency, recover or impugn any gift or promise of a gift made by him within a certain period prior to the date of any such event—KO 32, 37 (2) Number 4, 63; *Anfechtungsgesetz* 3 Numbers 3, 4; 7 (2).

bb.   Invalidity of gifts on private grounds.

(1) Gifts made with the intention of damaging a contractual heir or legatee   235 (507) may be recovered from the donee within three years from the date of the

vesting in possession of such heir or legatee's right[1]; a contractual legatee can proceed against the donee only in so far as he cannot obtain compensation from the heirs (509);

(2) on the computation of the compulsory portion of a statutory heir (510) all gifts made within the last ten years of the donor's life [1] must be added to the value of the estate, and any person entitled to a compulsory portion may claim the completion of his portion on the basis of such computation; the claim in the first instance must be satisfied by the testamentary or contractual heirs, but not so as to deprive them of their own compulsory portions (if any); any deficiency may be recovered from the donee; gifts made in accordance with a moral duty or social propriety cannot be recovered in this manner—see 511.

f.   Gifts subject to Burdens.

204. A gift subject to a burden (*Schenkung unter Auflage*) must be primarily intended to benefit the donee, and must therefore be distinguished from a transfer of property in exchange for a promise made by the transferee.   The burden may be imposed for the benefit of the donor or of a third party, or for some public object, or for the donee's own benefit. [2]

The following rules apply to gifts subject to burdens:

(1) the obligation imposed by the burden can, as soon as the gift has been completed, be enforced by the donor; a burden imposed for a public object may, after the donor's death, be enforced by the competent public authority—BGB 525;

236   (2) a third party for whose benefit a burden is imposed is entitled to enforce the performance of the donee's obligation, in the same way as a third party for whose benefit an agreement has been made (141)—BGB 330;

(3) in so far as, by reason of any defect of title or quality attaching to the object given to the donee, the value of the gift is not at least equal to the value of the outlay imposed upon the donee, the latter is entitled to repudiate the burden until the deficiency has been made up; if any outlay was incurred by the donee in

---

1   In the case of a gift to the donor's spouse, the ten years instead of running from the date of the gift, run from the date of the dissolution of the marriage.

2   Illustrations: (1) *A* gives his farm to *B* subject to the burden of allowing *A* to receive the produce of certain fields during *A*'s life; (2) *A* gives his park to *B* subject to the burden of allowing access to the public once a week; (3) *A* gives a sum of money to *B* subject to the burden of investing it in a prescribed manner and not changing the form of investment without the donor's permission.

ignorance of the defect, he is entitled to reimbursement in so far as the value of the outlay exceeds the value of the object given to him—BGB 526;

(4) if the donee does not perform the duty imposed upon him, the donor may revoke the gift in the manner and with the consequences prescribed in the case of the rescission of a reciprocal agreement (162); the right of revocation is excluded, if a third party is entitled to claim the performance of the donee's duty under rule (2)—BGB 527.

CHAPTER II
AGREEMENTS RELATING TO THE
TEMPORARY USE OF PROPERTY

1. LETTING AND HIRING AGREEMENTS

a. General Rules.

205. UNDER the present English law, letting and hiring agreements relating to chattels are of a purely contractual nature, while leases of land, besides establishing a contractual relation between the parties, confer a real right on the lessee; he takes 'an estate for years' in the land. Under German law, as under Roman law and the older English law, the letting of land only confers a contractual right on the lessee. The lease of a large block of houses for thirty years is an agreement, identical in its legal character with the letting of a horse or of a bicycle for an hour. There are of course a number of rules which have no meaning except in the case of a lease of land, but the general rules are applicable to both classes of agreements except in one important respect. Under the German common law the purchaser of a parcel of land was not bound by a lease of such parcel granted by his predecessor in title; in the event of his ejecting the lessee, the only remedy of the latter was a claim for damages against his lessor. This was a logical consequence of the purely contractual nature of the lease, but highly inconvenient, and after long debates the Second Commission decided to sacrifice logical consistency to practical convenience; the result is that, as a general rule, the transfer of the ownership of a parcel of land, brings about a transfer of the rights and liabilities arising under any lease to which such parcel is subject (215).

The lessee of an immovable, like the hirer of a chattel, is entitled, concurrently with the owner, to the possessory remedies against parties unlawfully disturbing his possession (315).

Leases of land in the nature of the building leases or mining leases in the form usual in England cannot be granted under German law, owing to the restriction as to duration referred to below (207) ; but the purposes for which such leases are granted under English law, can be attained by the creation of   238 heritable building rights (349) , or mining rights (350) , which are real rights (308) capable of registration, and different in their nature from the rights arising under a lease in the German sense of the word.

Having regard to the purely contractual nature of a lease under German law, leasehold interests are not registered in the land registry.

Under English law an estate for life in land, whether subject to the payment of rent or otherwise, is not considered a leasehold interest; under German law a lease (as shown below) may be granted for the life of the lessor or of the lessee.

For the sake of brevity the expression ' lease' will, in the course of this treatise, include letting agreements relating to chattels, and the expressions lessor and lessee will be applied in a corresponding manner.   The distinction between the different kinds of leases respectively called *Miete* and *Pacht* by the BGB will be explained below (206). The term ' lease of land' will in the course of this treatise include leases of buildings and tenements, and also of parts of buildings used as separate dwelling-places, or used separately for other purposes (see BGB 580).

b.   Distinction between an Ordinary Lease (*Mietvertrag*) and a Usufructuary Lease (*Pachtvertrag*).

206. The distinction between *Miete* and *Pacht* is of Germanic origin, both kinds of agreement being described in Roman law by the term *locatio conductio*. A lease by which the ' use of a thing' is accorded to the lessee during the continuance of the term is called *Mietvertrag*—BGB 535, and will in the course of this treatise be called ' an ordinary lease' ; a lease by which the ' use of an object and the enjoyment of its fruits' is accorded during the continuance of the term is called *Pachtvertrag*—BGB 581, and will in the course of this treatise be called ' a usufructuary lease'.   Where the term ' lease' is used without any addition both kinds of leases are referred to except where the context clearly indicates another meaning.

The expression 'term' will be used indiscriminately for the German expressions *Mietzeit* and *Pachtzeit*.

The definitions given above show that there are two points of difference between   239 an ordinary lease and a usufructuary lease: (1) an ordinary lease always refers to a ' thing ' , whereas a usufructuary lease may refer to a right as well as to a thing; (2) an ordinary lease only confers the right to the ' use ' of the leased object, while a usufructuary lease also confers the right to the fruits (77) ; the lease of a dwelling-house is always an ordinary lease; the lease of agricultural land is always a usufructuary lease; the lease of the sporting rights over land is a usufructuary lease of a right; an agreement to let a mare for the purpose of being ridden is an ordinary lease; an agreement to let a mare for breeding purposes is a usufructuary lease.

c.   Duration of Lease.

207. Under English law a letting agreement may extend over any length of time.   Leases of land for 1 , 000 years occur in actual practice.

Under German law the maximum duration of a lease is thirty years, or the life of the lessor or of the lessee.   A lease for more than thirty years can be terminated by notice in the same way as a lease for an indefinite term—BGB 567.

The following rules apply to the termination of leases:

(1) a lease for an indefinite term may be terminated by notice like a yearly tenancy under English law; the length of the notice varies according to the nature of the lease, the longest notice being necessary in the case of a usufructuary lease of land [1] , or of a right; such a notice must terminate at the end of a year of tenancy, and must be given at the latest on the first business day of the half year at the end of which the notice expires—BGB 564, 595 (1).   As to the length of notice in other cases, see BGB 565 (1) (2) (3) ;

(2) if the use of the leased object is continued after the expiration of the term, the parties are deemed to have agreed upon a lease for an indefinite period, unless notice of a contrary intention is given by either party within the prescribed time—BGB 568, 581 (2) ;

(3) a lease for a definite time comes to an end when the time is ended, but may be determined by notice before that time in any of the following events:

(*a*) in the event of any breach of agreement by the lessor or lessee entitling the other party to determine the lease under the rules stated below—213 sub

240

---

[1]   Under English law agricultural yearly tenancies (which correspond with German usufructuary leases of land for an indefinite term) also require longer notice than other yearly tenancies (see Agricultural Holdings Act 1883, s. 33).

(3), 214 sub (2)—by notice given by such other party;

(*b*) if the lessor refuses his consent to an assignment or underlease without any serious ground of objection against the person of the proposed assignee or underlessee—by notice given by the lessee—BGB 549 (1);

(*c*) in the event of the lessee's death—by notice given by the heirs of the lessee; (in the case of an ordinary lease notice may also be given by the lessor)—BGB 569, 596 (2);

(*d*) in the event of the removal to another town of a member of the armed forces, a public official, a minister of religion, or a public school teacher, being the lessee of any tenement occupied by him prior to such removal—by notice given by such lessee—BGB 570.

The length of the notice varies according to the nature of the event entitling the party concerned to give such notice, see BGB 549 (1), 565 (4), 569, 570, 595 (2).

No rules of law analogous to those entitling a party to a lease to determine it on the lessee's death, or on his removal to another place, exist in England.   The German rules on the subject seem of a somewhat arbitrary nature, and may have an effect exactly opposite to the one which was evidently intended, but as they may be varied by agreement between the parties, the matter is not of much practical importance.

d.   Form of Letting Agreements.

208. Under English law an agreement for a lease having more than three years to run, must be made in writing pursuant to the provisions of the Statute of Frauds.   Under German law an agreement to let an immovable for a term exceeding one year, unless embodied in a written document, is treated as a lease for an indefinite term (see 207 rule (1)) which cannot be terminated before the end of the first year—BGB 566.   Other letting agreements are not required to be in writing.

e.   Implied Terms of Agreements.

aa.   *Lessor's Duties.*

209. In the absence of any stipulation to the contrary the following rules apply as to the lessor's duties:

(1) the lessor in the case of an ordinary lease is bound to allow to the lessee

241

the use of the leased thing during the agreed term[1] ; in the case of a usufructuary lease he is bound to allow to the lessee the use of the leased object during the agreed term, as well as such fruits (77) as, in accordance with the rules of proper management, may be looked upon as income of the leased object—BGB 535, 581 (1);

(2) the lessor is bound to hand over the leased object to the lessee in a state which makes it fit[2] for the agreed use, and to preserve[3] it in that state during the agreed time—BGB 536, 581 (2);

242

(3) a stipulation by which the lessor's liability in respect of defects of quality or title impairing the agreed use is excluded or restricted, is void if any such defect has been concealed by the lessor with intent to deceive—BGB 540, 541, 581 (2);

(4) the lessor has to bear all outgoings, including rates and taxes—BGB 546, 581 (2);

(5) the lessor is bound to refund to the lessee all necessary outlay incurred for the preservation of the leased object—see 144 sub (7)[4] ; the reimbursement of any other outlay is governed by the rule as to voluntary services (301); the lessee is entitled to the *jus tollendi*—see 144 sub (9); the right to claim

---

1   The effect of this rule goes much further than the effects of the covenants implied by the use of the word 'demise', or the usual lessor's covenant for 'quiet enjoyment' in a lease governed by English law. If an English lessor has a smaller estate than the estate demised to the lessee (*e. g.* if a tenant for life grants a term extending beyond his life) the lessee only takes such smaller estate; if the lessor has no estate at all the lessee may acquire an interest by estoppel, but he does not in either case acquire the interest he bargained for, and yet he has no remedy against the lessor, unless the defect of title was due to the lessor's default, or to the default of any person claiming under him.   A German lessor is bound to give full compensation to the lessee if his possession is interfered with by any third party having a paramount title.

2   Under English law no warranty or condition of fitness at the time of letting and no covenant to preserve such fitness during the term is, as a general rule, implied by a letting agreement, but there are two exceptions to this rule: (1) where a furnished house or apartment is let, an undertaking that the demised premises are reasonably fit for the purposes of habitation is implied (Smith *v.* Marrable 11 M. & W. 5; Harrison *v.* Malet 3 Times L. R. 58); (2) in any contract made for letting a house for habitation by persons belonging to the working classes at a rent not exceeding a certain specified amount a condition is implied ' that the house is at the commencement of the holding in all respects reasonably fit for human habitation ' — Housing of the Working Classes Act 1890, s. 75.

3   The lessee of a parcel of land used for agriculture is bound to effect certain repairs, and to replace certain effects during his tenancy—BGB 582, 586.

4   A person who hires an animal must feed such animal at his own expense—BGB 547 (1); the lessee of a piece of land let for farming purposes is bound to do certain repairs at his own expense (210 rule (4)).

compensation for outlay and the *jus tollendi* are barred unless exercised within six months from the termination of the tenancy—BGB 547, 558, 581 (2);

(6) where the tenancy of a piece of land let for farming purposes comes to an end during the year of tenancy, the lessor must compensate the lessee for any outlay which he has properly incurred in respect of any fruits (77) not as yet reaped on the termination of the tenancy, but which in due course of husbandry will be severed during the year of tenancy, in so far as such outlay does not exceed the value of such fruits—BGB 592;

(7) where the usufructuary lease of a piece of land let for farming purposes includes furniture and farming implements, live stock, &c. , which objects are comprehensively described by the German word *Inventar* (translated in this treatise by the words ' appurtenant stock ') , the lessor must from time to time replace all such parts thereof as are lost or destroyed by any event for which the lessee is not responsible (excepting, however, such animals as, according to the rules of husbandry, are replaced by their offspring).   The lessee has a right of pledge (392) over the ' appurtenant stock ' by way of security for his claims against the lessor relating thereto, unless the lessor gives other security in respect of such claim—BGB 586 (2) , 590. [1]

bb.   Lessee's Duties.

210.   In the absence of any stipulation to the contrary the following rules apply   243 as to the lessee's duties:

(1) the lessee must pay the rent at such time, or by such instalments, as may be agreed upon; in the absence of any stipulation as to the time of payment the rent is payable ' at the end of each period for which it is payable ' ; the rent for a parcel of land not let for farming purposes is payable on the first business day after the end of each calendar quarter; the rent for a parcel of land let for farming purposes, if fixed by a yearly sum, is payable on the first business day after the end of each year of tenancy—BGB 535 (2) , 551, 584; the fact that the lessee, owing to a circumstance affecting him personally, is unable to use the object let to him, does not release him from his obligation to pay the agreed

---

1   The hirer of a movable thing has a lien for any claim against the person by whom it was let in accordance with the general rule (174) ; but, subject to the exception mentioned in the text, the lessee of an immovable has no lien or charge in respect of his claims against the lessor—BGB 556 (2).

rent, [1] but he may deduct the value of any advantage derived by the lessor from his failure to use the object let to him.

Illustration: *A* hires a motor-car from *B* to be used on a tour from the 1st August to the 1st September, *B* supplying all necessary fuel and the chauffeur's wages; *A* breaks his leg on the 1st August, and consequently has to abandon his tour; *A* must pay the agreed rent, but may deduct the estimated cost of the fuel and the chauffeur's wages in so far as *B* is not compelled to pay them; if *B* lets out the car during any time in August he must also deduct the net earnings resulting from such letting—BGB 552;

(2) the lessee must not use the leased object for any other than the agreed purpose—BGB 550;

(3) the lessee is responsible for any loss or deterioration caused by his wilful default or negligence, or by the wilful default or negligence of a third party whom he has permitted to use the leased object—BGB 549 (2); see also BGB 553 [2]; he is not, however, responsible for any alteration or deterioration resulting from the agreed use of the leased object (reasonable wear and tear)—BGB 548;

(4) the lessee of a piece of land let for farming purposes must do all the ordinary repairs at his own expense, and must particularly keep in repair the dwelling-house and farm buildings, roads, ditches, and fences; he must not, without the lessor's consent, effect any change by which the mode of cultivation would be altered for a period extending beyond the term—BGB 582, 583;

(5) where a piece of land is let for farming purposes together with the appurtenant stock—see 209 rule (7)—the lessee is under an obligation to preserve each unit forming part thereof; where, however, he takes over the appurtenant stock at a valuation, subject to the obligation to return it to the lessee at a new valuation [3] on the expiration of the lease, he is entitled to dispose of the

244

---

1   But for this special provision a lessor might under the rules stated above, 160 case (3), refuse the payment of the rent, if the event preventing him from using the hired object (*e. g.* his illness) was not due to his default.

2   The lessee's liability for loss caused by his own default results from the general principles of the law of obligations (148); the liability for the default of others is specially provided for; the last-mentioned liability is not avoided by the fact that the use of the leased object was accorded to another with the lessor's assent.

3   Such an agreement is sometimes called *Eisernviehvertrag*; the lessor retains the ownership of the appurtenant stock, but the lessee has a free right of disposition; each unit acquired by the lessee with the object of preserving the stock in the aggregate becomes the lessor's property as soon as it is added to the stock—BGB 588 (2).

individual units composing the stock, but must preserve the stock as a whole in accordance with the proper rules of husbandry, and is liable even for accidental destruction or deterioration—BGB 586 (1), 587, 588;

(6) the lessee must not, without the lessor's consent, do any act by virtue of which a third party becomes entitled to the use of the leased object—BGB 549 (1); but where the consent is unreasonably refused the lessee may, as mentioned above—207 rule (3) (b), give notice to determine the lease[1];

(7) if during the continuance of the term any defect of the leased object becomes apparent, or any preventive measure is required for the purpose of averting a danger which was unforeseen at the date of the lease, or if any third party claims a right over the leased object, the lessee must forthwith inform the lessor of   245
the occurrence—BGB 545 (1);

(8) on the termination of the lease the leased object must be delivered up to the lessor, who is also entitled to proceed against any third party to whom the use of the leased object was permitted by the lessee—BGB 556 (1), (3); the lessee of a piece of land let for farming purposes has to deliver up the leased object in the state in which it would be, had it been dealt with during the term in accordance with the proper rules of husbandry; if the leased object was a whole farm (*Landgut*) the lessee must also leave all manure produced thereon and being on the premises, on the termination of the lease, and so much of the other farm produce as is required for the continuance of the farming operations, during the period intervening between the termination of the lease and the time in which similar farm produce could be obtained from the farm; in so far as the quantity of such farm produce, other than manure, exceeds the quantity which the lessee found on the premises at the beginning of his tenancy, the lessor must pay compensation in respect thereof—BGB 591, 593;

(9) where the appurtenant stock was taken over at a valuation and has to be returned at a new valuation—see above rule (5)—the lessee is bound to return the whole of such stock, but the lessor may reject any units which are superfluous or too valuable; similar rules are applied in the case of a whole farm being taken over by the lessee in a corresponding manner—BGB 589, 593, 594.

---

1   The provision of BGB 226, according to which the exercise of a right with no other object than the infliction of damage on another is not permitted—see 79, may possibly enable the lessee to compel the lessor to withdraw his resistance, where such resistance is clearly unreasonable.   Under English law the unreasonable refusal of the lessor's consent to an assignment or under-lease may be disregarded in a case in which he is bound not to refuse his consent except on reasonable grounds.

f.   Lessor's Right of Pledge.

aa.   Comparison with English right of distress.

211. A German lessor's 'right of pledge' (*Pfandrecht*) bears some resemblance to an English landlord's right of distress, but there is a marked difference between the two kinds of rights in the following respects:

(1) an English landlord's right of distress serves exclusively as security for the payment of rent; a German lessor's right of pledge serves as security for the performance of all the lessee's obligations;

246   (2) an English landlord's right of distress is not available except in respect of overdue rent; a German lessor's right of pledge within the limits mentioned below sub *bb* rule (3) serves as security for future rent;

(3) an English landlord's right of distress—subject to the provisions of 34 & 35 Vict. cap. 79 for the protection of lodgers—extends to all the goods, not belonging to any specially exempted class, found on the demised premises; a German lessor's right extends only to goods of which the lessee is the owner.

bb.   Rules as to German lessor's right of pledge.

The lessor of an immovable is entitled to a statutory right of pledge over the lessee's goods in accordance with the following rules:

(1) the rules relating to a contractual right of pledge (392) are applicable except in so far as they involve the possession by the pledgee of the pledged thing, and except in so far as they are modified by the following rules—BGB 559, 581 (2), 1257;

(2) the right extends to all things brought on to the premises by the lessee of which he is the owner, including negotiable instruments, but it does not extend to documents, other than negotiable instruments, serving as evidence of rights (*e. g.* certificates of charge) and does not generally extend to goods exempt from seizure by a judgment creditor; in the case of a lease of a piece of land let for farming purposes the right of pledge extends to the severed fruits and also to certain kinds of stock and implements exempt from seizure by a judgment creditor—BGB 559, 585;

(3) the right of pledge, subject to the provisions of rule (5), is in all cases a security for overdue rent, and for the rent falling due in the current year of tenancy and in the year immediately following it; in the case of a lease of land let for farming purposes, it serves as security for the whole of the rent to fall due during the term; in all cases it serves also as a security for any claim for past breaches of obligations other than the obligation to pay rent—BGB 559, 585;

(4) the lessor must allow the removal of things subject to his right of pledge, in so far as it takes place in the regular course of business or in accordance with common practice, [1] and in so far as the goods remaining on the premises are sufficient for his protection; subject to this restriction, the lessor may forcibly prevent the removal of goods intended to be removed, or recover the possession of goods removed without his knowledge or contrary to his express direction; the right of pledge over goods lawfully removed is released by the fact of the removal; the right of pledge over goods unlawfully removed is released if the lessor fails to take judicial proceedings for their recovery within a month from his discovery of the removal—BGB 560, 561;

(5) where any goods subject to the lessor's right of pledge are seized by a judgment creditor, the lessor cannot, except in the case of a lease of land let for farming purposes, exercise his right of pledge, as against such judgment creditor, in respect of any rent which fell due more than a year prior to the date of the seizure—BGB 563, 585;

(6) the lessee may obtain a release of the right of pledge as to any individual thing subject thereto by giving specific security for the value of such thing—BGB 562.

g.   Effect of Breaches of Agreement.

aa.   Generally.

212. The general rules as to the effect of impossibility of performance, or of delay in performance of a promise forming part of a reciprocal agreement (see 159 to 162) are somewhat modified in the case of leases.   It will be remembered that a party to such a reciprocal agreement may in certain events, instead of claiming performance by the other party, claim compensation for non-performance, or rescission.

In the case of a lease, the rights which in similar events may be substituted for the right to performance are as regards the lessee: (1) the right to a temporary suspension of the obligation to pay rent or to a reduction of the rent, (2) the right

---

[1]   *E. g.* if goods are sold in the usual course by a shopkeeper, or farm produce or cattle is sold in the usual course by a farmer.

248   to pecuniary damages, (3) the termination of the lease; as regards the lessor:
(1) the right to pecuniary damages, (2) the right to terminate the lease.

bb.   *Lessee's remedies.*

(1) *Right to temporary suspension or reduction* of rent.

213. If the leased object, on delivery of possession to the lessee, is affected
with any defect destroying or impairing its fitness for the agreed use, or if it is
deficient in one of the agreed qualities, [1] the lessee is entitled to a remission or
reduction of the rent, while the defect continues to operate.

The total or partial withdrawal of the use of the leased object brought about
by a third party having a paramount right, has the same effect as a defect.

The reduction of the rent is calculated on the same principles as the reduction
of the purchase price in the case of a sale (192).

If the defect arises during the term, the consequences are the same as in the
event of its presence on delivery of possession—BGB 537, 541, 581 (2).

The right is not available if the defect was known [2] to the lessee on the
formation of the agreement, or if, in the event of a defect appearing during the
term, the lessor through delay in its notification was prevented from remedying
it—BGB 539, 545 (2).

(2) *Right to pecuniary damages.*

If a defect of the kind defined sub (1) is in existence on delivery of
possession, or if it arises subsequently in consequence of any event for which the
lessor is responsible, or if the lessor is in *mora solvendi* (152) in respect of his
obligation to remedy the defect, the lessee, instead of claiming the right
mentioned sub (1), may claim pecuniary damages for breach of agreement.

Where the lessor is in *mora solvendi*, the lessee may himself remedy the defect
and claim repayment of his outlay—BGB 538, 541.

(3) *Right to terminate lease.*

249   If the agreed use of the leased object is not accorded to the lessee at the
agreed time, or if, having been accorded, it is wholly or partly withdrawn, the

---

[1]   In the case of a lease of an immovable the promised dimensions are deemed an agreed quality of the
leased object—BGB 537 (2).

[2]   In certain cases ignorance resulting from gross carelessness is considered as equivalent to
knowledge—BGB 539.

lessee is entitled to terminate the lease, if the lessor fails to comply with a notice requiring him to remedy his breach of agreement within a specified period. [1]

In the following events the lessee may terminate the lease without giving the lessor a previous opportunity to remedy his breach of agreement:

(*a*) if 'time' is of the essence (162) in respect of the lessor's obligations [2] ;

(*b*) if in consequence of the breach in question the continuance of the lease is of no advantage to the lessee [3] ;

(*c*) if the leased premises, being intended as a place of habitation or occupation for human beings, are in a condition seriously endangering the health of such human beings—BGB 542 (1) (2) ; 544. [4]

Where a lease is terminated on one of the grounds mentioned above, any rent which has been paid in advance must be repaid by the lessor with interest from the date of payment, unless the circumstance justifying the rescission was one for which the lessor was not responsible, in which event the repayment can only be claimed under the rule as to unjustified benefits (298)—BGB 543 (2).

A lessor who disputes the lessee's right to terminate the lease, on the ground that he did in fact accord the use of the leased object at the proper time, or that he remedied his breach of agreement before the expiration of the notice, must prove his allegation—BGB 542 (4).   250

cc.   Lessor's remedies.

(1) Right to claim compensation for damage.

(a) Right to compensation for destruction or deterioration.

214. This right arises where the damage is caused by an unauthorized use of the leased object, or by the lessee's wilful default or negligence—210 rule (3).

---

1   If the agreed use is hindered or prevented to an unimportant extent only, the right to terminate the lease cannot be exercised except under special circumstances—BGB 542 (2).

2   This may be the case where the letting agreement refers to a movable object (*e. g.* where a horse is hired for a particular occasion) or where an immovable is let for a particular day (*e. g.* for the purpose of viewing a procession).

3   The lessee cannot allege this circumstance if owing to his failure to give immediate notice—210 rule (6)—the lessor was prevented from remedying the breach of agreement—BGB 545 (2).

4   The effect of a breach of agreement, by reason of which the agreed use of the whole leased object is not accorded to the lessee at the proper time or is withdrawn from him, in a case where the leased object comprises several things, or accessories, as well as a principal object, is determined by rules similar to those which, in the case of a sale, determine the effect of a breach of warranty affecting part only of the sold goods (192 sub (2))—BGB 543 (1).

It is barred by the lapse of six months from the date of the return of the leased object, and is lost if the lessor's right to the return of the leased object has lapsed by prescription under the general rules (131, 133)—BGB 558.

(b) Right to compensation for failure to redeliver.

Where the lessee fails to deliver up the leased object on the termination of the lease, the lessor is entitled, by way of damages, to claim the rent accruing during the time while the lessee's breach of duty continues, and in the case of a usufructuary lease he may claim rent proportionate to the profits which he might have derived had he enjoyed these profits from the time at which the leased object ought to have been delivered up.   The claim for rent by way of damages does not exclude a claim for further damages—BGB 557, 597.

(2) Right to terminate lease.

The lessor may terminate the lease: (a) in the event of the lessee being in *mora solvendi* as to two successive instalments of rent, and failing to comply with a notice requiring immediate payment [1] ; (b) in the event of an unauthorized use of the leased object by the lessee, or by any other person, being continued after the receipt of a notice requiring the discontinuance of such unauthorized use; (c) in the event of the lessee failing to apply the proper degree of diligence and thereby materially endangering the safety of the leased object—BGB 554.

251   A lessor who terminates the lease in any of the events mentioned sub (b) and (c) must repay any rent paid in advance, with interest from the date of payment—BGB 555, 581 (2).

It is open to the parties to provide that the breach of any covenant contained in the lease is to cause the forfeiture of the lease, and it may even be stipulated that in such an event the lessor may terminate the lease without giving the lessee an opportunity to remedy the breach.

In respect of the right to terminate the lease without previous warning, on non-payment of two instalments of rent or on any other breach of covenant causing a forfeiture of the lease under the terms of the agreement, [2] German law is more

---

[1]   If the lessee immediately on receipt of the notice declares that he is entitled to a right of set-off and succeeds in establishing such right the notice is inoperative.

[2]   Under English law the breach of a covenant against assignment or underletting causes the forfeiture of the lease, if this is provided by the agreement; but under German law this consequence may be attached to any breach of covenant.

favourable to the lessor than English law (see Common Law Procedure Act 1852, s. 210; Conveyancing Act 1881, s. 14 (9)).

The English rules as to relief against the forfeiture of leases derive their principal importance from the fact that in many cases (*e. g.* in the case of building leases) the annual rent (usually called the ground-rent) is considerably less than the annual value, and that, therefore, the forfeiture of the lease is frequently of considerable advantage to the lessor, and of considerable disadvantage to the lessee.   As under German law building leases do not exist, and consequently the lessee's pecuniary loss by reason of the forfeiture can never be very serious, it is less necessary to adopt elaborate precautions against an unfair exercise of the lessor's right to terminate the lease.

h.   Effects of Sales and other Dispositions on Lessee's Rights and Duties.

aa.   General Statement.

215. As mentioned above (205), the rule of Roman law under which the lessee of an immovable was liable to be ejected by a purchaser has not been adopted by the new German law which provides that, where the lessee or any person claiming under him is in possession of the demised premises at the time of the sale, the rights of the lessee are binding on the purchaser, but that, where neither the lessee nor any person claiming under him is in possession at the date of the sale, the purchaser, in the absence of an agreement to the contrary, is not bound by the lease—BGB 571, 578.   On any further sale the new purchaser is bound in the same way as the original purchaser, whose liability thereupon ceases, whilst the liability of the original lessor continues under the rules and subject to the restrictions mentioned below (216)—BGB 579.

252

If the lessor incumbers the leased object (*e. g.* if he grants a heritable building right, or a right of usufruct, or an easement to any third party), the incumbrancer is in a position corresponding to that of a purchaser.   Where the incumbrancer's right only partially conflicts with the lessee's rights, the incumbrancer must refrain from any exercise of his right which would prevent the lessee from using the leased object in the agreed manner—BGB 577.

For the sake of brevity the statement of the following rules will be made with exclusive reference to the effects of a sale, it being understood that they are also applicable, *mutatis mutandis*, to the effects of the creation of an incumbrance—

BGB 578.

bb.   Effect of sale on rights and liabilities of lessor and purchaser.

216. The purchaser, as between himself and the lessee for the time being, is entitled to the rights, and is subject to the liabilities, to which he would be entitled or liable if he were the lessor; he is entitled to the benefit of any security given by the lessee to the lessor, but he is not bound by the lessor's obligation to return to the lessee any objects given by way of security, unless such objects were handed over to him by the lessor, or unless in his agreement with the lessor, he expressly undertook to return them to the lessee—BGB 572 (1), 581 (2).

The lessor continues to be liable for the performance of the obligations to which the purchaser becomes subject under the rules stated above, in the same way as if he had originally undertaken such liability as surety for the purchaser, and renounced the *beneficium excussionis* (273); where notice of the sale is given to the lessee, the lessor is released from his liability unless the lessee gives notice to terminate the lease on the earliest possible date after the receipt of the notice of the sale—BGB 571 (2), 581 (2).

253

cc.   Effect of sale on prior assignment of future rent.

217. An assignment of the claim for rent payable in respect of the current quarter, or the next following quarter, is operative as between the original lessor and the purchaser, but any assignment of the claim for rent to accrue at any subsequent date is inoperative as against a purchaser without notice [1]—BGB 573.

---

1   A similar rule is applied to an arrangement between the original lessor and the lessee under which future rent is paid in advance; in such a case the arrangement does not remain operative beyond the quarter following the one in which the lessee receives notice of the passing of the property; if the lessee, when entering on the arrangement, is aware of the fact that the property has passed to the purchaser the arrangement is wholly inoperative; in so far as the arrangement is operative the lessee is entitled—subject to certain specified restrictions—instead of paying any instalment to which it refers, to set-off against such instalment any claim against the original lessor whether arising under the lease or otherwise—BGB 574, 575.

Illustrations: (1) on the 31st March a lessee prepays the instalments of rent due on the 30th June, 30th September, and 31st December; the house is sold and the property passes on the 1st June, but the fact does not become known to the lessee before the 1st July; he is not required to pay any rent to the purchaser in respect of the quarters paid for in advance.   (2) A lessee, paying rent quarterly on the same days as in illustration (1), sells goods to his lessor for an amount exceeding three instalments of rent and delivers them on the 15th April.   The facts as to the sale of the house, the passing of the property, and the notice to the lessee are the same as in the case of illustration (1).   The lessee can set-off the price of the goods against the instalments of rent payable on the 30th June, 30th September, and the 31st December.

The original lessor is, as between himself and the lessee, estopped from denying the validity of a sale of which he has informed the lessee—BGB 576, 581 (2).

dd. Special provisions as to sales of land seized by judgment creditors.

218. Where land subject to a lease has been seized by a judgment creditor and is publicly sold, the purchaser, notwithstanding the fact that the lease is for a definite term, can terminate the same by notice, as if it had been made for an indefinite term (see 207); the right is forfeited if it is not exercised at the earliest 254 opportunity.   Imperial Statute relating to Compulsory Sales of 1897, ss. 57, 59 (1) (2).

2. GRATUITOUS LOANS OF THINGS
(*Sachleihe, Commodatum*)

a. General Statement.

219. The gratuitous loan of a thing whether movable or immovable is called *Sachleihe*; a person who borrows the use of a house comes under the rules as to *Sachleihe*, as well as a person who borrows a book or an agricultural machine. An agreement for the gratuitous loan of a thing is not deemed a gift, though it may be of considerable pecuniary advantage to the borrower; on the other hand, the loan of a thing is deemed gratuitous notwithstanding the fact that it is made in exchange for a service rendered to the lender; (for an illustration, see Dig. 13. 6. 18 '*Si communem amicum ad cenam invitaverimus tuque eius rei curam suscepisses et ego tibi argentum commodaverim*').   According to English terminology a loan of such a description would be a loan for valuable consideration.

b. Lender's Rights and Duties.

An agreement for a gratuitous loan binds the lender to grant the borrower the use of the borrowed thing during the agreed time; if no time is fixed, the borrowed article must be returned as soon as the purpose for which it was borrowed has been accomplished, or as soon as a sufficient period of time has passed for allowing such purpose to be accomplished; if neither a time nor a purpose for the loan is agreed upon, the lender may claim the return of the borrowed thing at any time he may think fit.   The lender may also terminate the loan by notice: (*a*) if by reason of an unforeseen circumstance he requires the borrowed thing for his own use; (*b*) if the borrower makes an unauthorized use of the borrowed thing (*e. g.* by granting its use to a third party) or seriously endangers the safety of the borrowed thing by the neglect of his contractual duties; (*c*) on the borrower's death—BGB 598, 604, 605.   The lender's liabilities as to the safety of the borrowed article pending delivery to the borrower, and as to defects of title or quality, are similar to the liabilities of a donor in the case of an agreement for a gift (201)—BGB 599, 600.

c.   Borrower's Rights and Duties.

255   The borrower's duties as to the safe preservation of the borrowed thing, as to its proper use in accordance with the agreement, and as to its return at the proper time, are similar to the corresponding duties of a lessee in respect of the leased object—210 rules (3) (6) (8).   The cost of the preservation of the borrowed thing (including the cost of feeding a borrowed animal) must be borne by the borrower.   The right to the reimbursement of any other outlay is determined by the rules as to unjustified benefits—298—BGB 601–604 (1).

d.   Comparison with English Law.

Under English law an agreement for the loan of a thing made without consideration moving from the promisee, is not enforceable against the lender, nor could the latter in such a case be prevented from recovering the borrowed article at any time he might think fit.   The borrower according to English law is of course bound to bestow proper diligence in respect of its custody, and of its return to the lender at the agreed time.

3.   LOANS OF MONEY AND OTHER FUNGIBLES

a.   General Statement.

220. A loan of money or fungibles, whether gratuitous or otherwise, is called *Darlehen*, if according to the intention of the parties, the borrower becomes the owner of the borrowed things, and his obligation to return the same is satisfied by the delivery of the same quantity of things of the same kind and quality—BGB 607 (1), Cases are conceivable in which fungibles are lent with the intention of being returned in specie, but in any such case the fungibles become ' specific things' , *pro hac vice* and the transaction does not come within the definition of a *Darlehen*.

Illustration: A money-changer may for the purpose of decorating his shop window, borrow bank-notes and coins from another, subject to a stipulation that the identical notes and pieces are to be returned; this would not affect the rights of third parties without notice of the facts, but an unauthorized use of the borrowed things would, according to German law, be a criminal offence on the borrower's part, and would also render him liable to the other consequences of his unlawful conversion.

256

Where money or other fungibles are due from one person to another by virtue of any transaction not originally in the nature of a loan, it may be agreed between the parties that their mutual obligatory relations shall be determined by the rules relating to loan transactions—BGB 607 (2).

Illustration: (1) the vendor of 100 cwts. of coffee of a certain quality, having received the purchase money, agrees with the purchaser that the delivery of the coffee shall be postponed, and that he shall owe the 100 cwts. to the purchaser, as if they had been lent to him; (2) the coffee is delivered, and the parties agree that the payment of the purchase price is to be postponed, and that the purchaser shall owe the amount of the purchase price, as if it had been lent to him by the vendor.

b.   Agreement for future Loan of Money or other Fungibles.

According to German law (which in this respect materially differs from English law), a promise to lend money or other fungibles is enforceable like any other agreement, but the lender may, in so far as no contrary intention is shown, refuse the loan, if, between the date of the promise and the time for performance, the financial position of the intending borrower has been so weakened as to endanger the prospect of repayment [1] —BGB 610.

c.   Interest on Loans of Money.

A mercantile trader (36) is entitled to charge interest on any loan granted in

---

1   Compare the general rules as to reciprocal agreements (159); the specific rules relating to loans are more favourable to the borrower than the general rules, as the latter cannot be varied by agreement between the parties.

the course of his trade; subject to this exception the payment of interest is not an implied term of an agreement for a loan.   Where interest is stipulated for, and no time for the payment of interest is fixed, interest is payable at the end of each year during which the loan continues; if the loan was for a shorter period than a year the interest is payable on the repayment of the loan—BGB 608; HGB 354 (2); as to the rate of interest, see 144 sub (4).

d.   Repayment of Loan.

Where no time is fixed, either party may at any time give notice of repayment. In the case of a loan for an amount exceeding 300 Marks, at least three months' notice must be given; in the case of smaller loans one month's notice suffices. Loans not bearing interest may be repaid by the debtor at any time without notice—BGB 609; as to the repayment of loans bearing interest at a rate exceeding 6 per cent. , see 106.

CHAPTER III
AGREEMENTS RELATING TO WORK AND SERVICES

1. AGREEMENTS FOR REMUNERATED SERVICES

a. General Statement.

221. ANY agreement by which one party promises services for a remuneration 258
to be paid by the other party is an agreement for services (*Dienstvertrag*) ; on the
other hand an agreement by which the accomplishment of a definite result is
promised for a reward to be paid by the other party is an agreement for work
(*Werkvertrag*)—233.   The distinction is analogous to the Roman distinction
between *locatio operarum* and *locatio operis*.   A brokerage agreement (237) is
something between an agreement for services and an agreement for work.

An agreement for services may be of a more or less permanent nature, or
may relate to a single service to be rendered to or for the benefit of the person
paying the reward.   It may relate to services of any kind, for the old distinction
between *operae illiberales* and *operae liberales* has ceased to exist.   Nor is the
mode of payment material; the person giving his services may be paid by wages or
salary, by commission, or by sums dependent upon the extent and character of
his work or otherwise.   The main characteristic of the agreement for services
consists in the fact that services are promised on one side and reward on the
other—BGB 611.   In so far as no contrary intention appears, an agreement for
services is of a strictly personal nature; neither the claim for the services nor the
duty to perform the service can be transferred to another—BGB 613.

Agreements for services of a public or a quasi-public nature (*e. g.* agreements
for the services of government officials or the services of advocates, notaries,
&c.) are regulated by separate enactments which do not come within the scope of
this treatise.

The rules of the BGB relating to private agreements for services are
supplemented, and to a certain extent modified, as to particular kinds of employment 259

by other enactments. Thus the regulation of agreements relating to domestic service is (subject to certain restrictions imposed by EG 95) left to State legislation; provisions analogous to those of the English Factory Acts relating to the employment of persons working in factories and workshops are contained in the *Gewerbeordnung*; special provisions, as to particular classes of employees, are also contained in the HGB, the Imperial Statute relating to Seamen of 1902 (*Seemannsordnung*), and other Imperial Statutes.

Some of the special provisions relating to particular employments are referred to in the following statement of the law as to agreements for services, but it is, of course, impossible, within the space which can be allotted to the subject, to discuss the rules existing outside the Civil and Commercial Codes with any degree of completeness.

The expressions *der Dienstberechtigte* and *der zur Dienstleistung Verpflichtete* used by the BGB to designate 'the person entitled to the services' and 'the person bound to give the services' respectively, will, in the course of this treatise, be translated by the words 'employer' and 'employee' . [1]

b. Employer's Duties.

aa. *Payment of remuneration.*

(1) *General rules.*

222. The following rules apply on this subject:

(1) where a remuneration has been expressly agreed upon, the employer is bound to pay it, in accordance with the agreement;

(2) the promise to pay a remuneration is implied, where the particular services cannot under the special circumstances of the case be expected to be given gratuitously; (*e. g.* where a patient sends for a doctor, or a cab runner offers to carry luggage)—BGB 612 (1);

260   (3) where the scale of remuneration is not expressly agreed upon or fixed by any public tariff the scale established by custom is conclusive—BGB 612 (2); in

---

1   An apprenticeship agreement is an agreement for reciprocal services, the master's services constituting wholly or partly the remuneration for the apprentice's services and *vice versa*; where the master receives a premium and where the apprentice receives wages, this constitutes an additional remuneration. It will be understood that notwithstanding this reciprocity of services, the term employer in the case of an apprenticeship agreement is used for the master, and the term employee for the apprentice.

the absence of a special agreement, or of a tariff or general custom, the rule stated above with reference to the cases in which the mode of performance is left to the discretion of one of the parties—144 sub (6)—is applied, with the result that the employer has to determine the amount of the remuneration, but that the employee is not bound by this determination if it appears inequitable;

(4) a mercantile employee is entitled to remuneration in accordance with local custom; in the absence of any such local custom such remuneration as appears reasonable under the circumstances must be paid—HGB 59;

(5) where the rate of payment is fixed with reference to a specified period of time, the remuneration must be paid at the end of each such period; in all other cases the remuneration must be paid after the performance of the agreed services; in the case of mercantile employees payments at longer than monthly intervals are prohibited—BGB 614; HGB 64.

(2) *Payment in kind.*

As a general rule services may be rewarded by the payment of money or in any other way, but the Imperial *Gewerbeordnung*, following the example set by the English Truck Acts, restricts payment in kind to the employees coming under its provisions.   The wages of such employees (who in the course of this treatise will be referred to as 'industrial employees') must be paid in cash in Imperial German currency, and no set-off is allowed except in respect of certain specified objects (food, use of dwellings or land, fire, light, medical assistance, tools, material, &c.); the amount set off in respect of any such object must not, except in the case of tools and material supplied for contract work, exceed the cost price of any object supplied or the usual rent of any tenement of which the use is allowed to the employee—GO 115–118.

(3) *Effect of impossibility and mora accipiendi on the part of the employer.*

Where the acceptance of the services is impossible, the ordinary rules as to the effect of impossibility of performance in the case of reciprocal agreements apply (see 160).   Where the employer is in *mora accipiendi* the general rules stated above (161) are modified by the provision, that the remuneration must be paid for the services remaining unperformed by reason of such *mora accipiendi*, the employer not being entitled to claim any subsequent performance of such unperformed services, but having the right to deduct from the remuneration the value of any outlay saved by the employee in consequence of his non-performance, 261 or of any income which he has actually earned or might, but for his intentional neglect, have earned, by some other employment of his services—BGB 615.

Illustrations: *A* engages a gardener to work in his garden, in accordance with directions to be given by him, on a certain date.   The garden is destroyed by a landslip before the date arrives; the performance of the service having become impossible by reason of a circumstance for which neither the employer nor the employee is responsible, the gardener cannot claim the promised wages.   If on the other hand the work in the garden cannot be performed on the promised date by reason of the fact that *A* has failed to give the promised directions, the gardener may claim his wages; should other suitable work have been offered to him on the day in question, he must allow the deduction of the wages which he has or could have received for such work.   Under the general rules as to reciprocal agreements, the gardener would have had to request *A* to give him the directions within a specified time and would, if the request had been complied with, have had no claim in respect of the day wholly or partially lost, unless time had originally been made of the essence of the agreement.

Where an employer has to provide care and medical attendance in accordance with the rule stated below—223 sub (4)—the cost of such care and attendance may be deducted from the remuneration payable in respect of the time, during which the employee was unable to give his services—BGB 617.

(4) *Payment during temporary inability of employee* to *perform* services.

An employee engaged for continuous services, who is temporarily unable to perform them, is in the position of a person who finds it impossible to perform one of the obligations forming part of a reciprocal agreement.   Under the general rule he would, if the impossibility was due to a circumstance for which neither he nor 262 the employer was responsible, lose his claim for payment during the time within which he was disabled (see 160), but under a special provision relating to agreements for services, the claim of the employee for payment of his remuneration continues during the time of his disability, if it is of reasonably short duration, [1] and not due to any default on the part of the employee—BGB 616.   It is immaterial whether the disability was caused by illness or by any other cause; service on a jury or attendance before a Court as witness, and the compulsory per-

---

1   If the disability is of longer duration it comes under the ordinary rule.

formance of military duties are grounds of disability coming within the definition.

The rights of a mercantile employee prevented from working by reason of a disability not due to his own default go further than those of an ordinary employee; he is entitled to remuneration [1] for the whole period of his disability if such period does not extend beyond six weeks, and to six weeks' remuneration if the disability continues for a longer period, even if he is dismissed from his employment by reason thereof [2] —HGB 63 (1), 72 (2).

bb.   Duties as to health and morality of employees.

(1) As to place of work and appliances.

223. The conditions as to the place of work and the appliances used in connexion with services rendered under the employer's direction, must be so arranged as to protect the employee against any danger to life or health, in so far as this is possible having regard to the nature of the work—GO 120 (a); BGB 618 (1); HGB 62 (1).

(2) As to arrangements for employees residing with employer's family.

Such arrangements must be made as to dwelling and sleeping accommodation, and as to time of work and recreation, as are required to ensure the health, morality, and the due performance of the religious observances of the employee— 263 BGB 618 (2); HGB 62 (2).

For special rules relating to apprentices and young employees, see HGB 76 (3) (4); GO 120.

(3) As to holidays.

Industrial employees cannot be compelled to work on any Sunday or public holiday, unless the nature of the particular undertaking requires continuous work—GO 105 (a).

In other respects no general rules are laid down as to holidays, but employers as well as employees are subject to the local rules of public law as to Sunday observance.

---

1   In so far as the remuneration consists of salary, board, and lodging, he is entitled to the full remuneration; but he loses such part of his remuneration as consists of a commission or percentage of profits.

2   An ordinary employee must allow the deduction of any sick pay or other compensation received from a compulsory insurance fund; but a mercantile employee suffering under any disability of the nature described above, is entitled to his remuneration without the deduction of any insurance money, even if the contrary was expressly stipulated for in his agreement with the employer—BGB 616; HGB 63 (2).

(4) *As to care in case of sickness.*

A person employed in continuous services which absorb the whole or the principal part of his working time, who, while residing with the employer's family, is attacked by an illness not caused by his wilful neglect or gross carelessness, is entitled to proper nursing and medical attendance, either in the employer's house or in a public institution at the employer's expense for a period not exceeding six weeks.   The termination of the agreement for services in consequence of the illness does not affect the obligation to provide care and medical attendance.

Where the care and medical attendance are provided by any insurance fund or public authority the employer is released from his obligation—BGB 617.

(5) *General rules.*

Rules (1) (2) and (4) cannot be excluded or restricted by private agreement—BGB 619; HGB 62 (4).   Their non-observance has the ordinary consequence incident to the breach of a contractual obligation, and is subject to the same provision as to liability for the default of others (see 150).   In the event of the non-obselvance of rules (1) or (2) the damages are assessed as in the case of a claim for compensation for damages done by an unlawful act—BGB 618 (3); HGB 62 (3).   The power of State legislation to regulate the conditions of domestic service does not include an authorization to relax rules (2) and (4) in the employer's favour—EG 95.   Where the employee is a mercantile apprentice the infringement of rules (1) and (2) is punishable by fine—HGB 82 (1).

264

cc.   *Duty as to apprentices.*

224. The master must give theoretical and practical instruction to his apprentices, either personally or through an employee specially selected for the purpose—HGB 76 (2), GO 127; a person deprived by criminal sentence of his civil honorary functions, [1] is not allowed to take apprentices—HGB 81, 82 (2), GO 126.

dd.   *Duty to give testimonial.*

225. On the termination of an agreement for continuous services, the employee is entitled to a testimonial as to the length and nature of his services and as to his

---

[1]   A person deprived of such functions cannot sit on a jury or occupy any honorary public office.

conduct and efficiency—BGB 630; HGB 73, 80; GO 113.

c.   Employee's Duties.

aa.   Active duties.

226. The following rules apply to the employee's active duties:

(1) the employee must give the services stipulated for by the agreement; in the case of an agreement for mercantile employment containing no express provision on the subject, local custom determines the nature and extent of the services; in the absence of any local custom such services must be rendered as appear reasonable under the circumstance of the case—BGB 611; HGB 59;

(2) the services must be rendered by the employee in person except in so far as a contrary intention is shown; where the employment of substitutes or assistants is permitted by the agreement, the liability for the default of such assistants or substitutes is determined by the general rules on the subject; see 150—BGB 613;

(3) where the employee either expressly or by implication warrants special aptitude on his part for the promised services, the absence of such aptitude constitutes a breach of the agreement [1] ;

(4) a duty to obey the employer's directions, in so far as they do not go beyond the natural requirements of the employment, is expressly imposed on industrial employees (GO 121), and will in many other cases be implied from the nature of the agreement for services.

265

bb.   Passive duties.

227. Among the passive duties frequently imposed by agreement or custom, those relating to secrecy, and abstinence from acts betraying the employer's interests, are the most prominent.   Mercantile employees are subject to a statutory prohibition preventing them during the continuance of their employment from conducting any mercantile trade on their own account, and from entering into any transactions within the scope of the employer's business, except with the employer's express or implied permission.   If the employee, notwithstanding such prohibition, enters upon any transaction on his own account, the employer may, instead of claiming damages, take it over for his own account; if the employee

---

[1]   This rule results from the general principles of the German law of Obligations.

enters upon any transaction on account of a third party, the employer may claim the remuneration accruing to the employee from such transaction—HGB 60, 61; as to agreements prohibiting competition after termination of the agreement for service, see p. 92 note 1.

d.   Termination of Agreement for Services.

aa.   Normal termination.

228. The following rules apply on this subject:

(1) if the agreement for services is entered upon for a specified period not exceeding five years, the agreement expires at the end of such period; if the agreement is entered upon for a longer period or for the life of the employer or employee, the employee may at any time after the lapse of five years determine the agreement by giving six months previous notice of his intention in that behalf—BGB 620 (1), 624; [1]

(2) if the agreement is entered upon for an indefinite time, and the time of its termination cannot be gathered from the nature or object of the services, either party may give notice to terminate the agreement; the length of the notice generally depends upon the mode in which the payment of the remuneration is fixed, but special rules are laid down as to some kinds of employments [2]; if the remuneration is not payable with reference to a fixed period of time, the agreement may—except in so far as the special rules provide otherwise—be terminated at any time by either party, but where the employment occupies the whole or the greater part of the employee's time at least fourteen days' notice must be given—BGB 620 (1), 621, 623;

(3) if an employment is with the employer's knowledge continued by the employee beyond the time fixed for its duration by the agreement, such agreement is deemed to have been renewed for an indefinite time, unless the employer immediately objects to the continuation of the employment—BGB 625.

---

[1]   This is one of the rules which as to domestic service cannot be altered by State legislation—EG 95.

[2]   As to employees of a superior kind (tutors, private secretaries, companions, &c.) whose time is wholly or principally occupied by the duties undertaken under the agreement, see BGB 622; as to mercantile employees HGB 66–69; as to superior industrial employees—GO 133 a, 133 aa, 133 ab, 133 ac; as to ordinary industrial employees—GO 122.

bb. Termination on special grounds.

(a) Termination by act of one of the parties.

229. An agreement for services may be terminated without notice, and prior to the date of its natural termination, in the events and in the manner shown by the following rules:

(1) either party to any agreement for services not coming under the special provisions of rule (2) may determine such agreement on any cogent ground (*wichtiger Grund*) [1] —BGB 626; HGB 70, 71, 72 (1);

(2) an agreement for services, made between an industrial employee and his employer, may on certain specified grounds be terminated by the employer, and may on certain other specified grounds be terminated by the employee [2]; where any cogent ground exists which is not included among those specially enumerated, the agreement may be terminated by either party, if it was entered upon for more than four weeks, or if more than fourteen days' notice of termination is required by the agreement—GO 123, 124, 124 a;

(3) where services of a superior kind and involving special confidence in the employee, are not of a continuous nature and are not given for a fixed salary, the relation between the parties can be terminated by either party without previous notice—BGB 627 (1). [3]

267

---

[1] It is left to judicial discretion to determine what constitutes a 'cogent ground', but the instances of cogent grounds justifying the termination of an agreement for the service of a mercantile employee given by HGB 71, 72 (1) will serve as a guidance. Such an agreement may (*inter alia*) be terminated by the employer, if the employee is unfaithful or violates his duty as to refraining from competition (227), or if he persistently neglects his duties, or by reason of illness, criminal punishment, or military service for more than eight weeks, is prevented from the performance of his duties, or if he is guilty of certain specified offences against the employer or any person acting on his behalf. The employee may terminate the agreement (*inter alia*): if he becomes incapable of performing the services, or if he does not receive his promised remuneration, or if the employer does not perform the duties specified above—223 sub (1) and (2); or if he commits or does not prevent the commission of certain specified offences against the employee.

[2] The grounds are similar to those set out as examples of cogent grounds for the termination of agreements for mercantile services (see note 1), but some additional grounds are mentioned. Thus the employer may terminate the agreement if the employee has deceived him by a false statement or testimonial, or if he is careless in respect of precautions against fire, &c.; the employee may terminate the agreement, if a continuance of the employment is likely to endanger his life or health in a manner or to an extent which he was unable to discover upon entering upon the agreement; either party may terminate the agreement, if the other party incites him to do any unlawful or immoral act—GO 123, 124.

[3] If the employee terminates the relation without a cogent ground, in any case in which the employer is unable to procure the required services elsewhere, he is liable in damages—BGB 627 (2).

(b) Termination by death of one of the parties.

In the absence of a special stipulation to the contrary the employee's death terminates the agreement. [1]   On the other hand the employer's claim to the employee's services (though not, as a general rule, transmissible by assignment) passes on the employer's death to his heirs like any other obligatory right vested in him.   The employer's death may be a cogent ground enabling his heirs to terminate the agreement by notice to the employee.

cc.   Effects of termination of agreement.

230. If an agreement for services comes to an end by reason of the fact that the performance or acceptance of the promised services has become impossible, or if it is rescinded on the ground of either party being in *mora solvendi* or *mora accipiendi*, the ordinary rules, applicable in the case of the termination of a reciprocal agreement by reason of such fact—see 160, 161—come into operation.

If, on the other hand, an agreement is terminated by act of one of the parties, the following special rules apply:

(1) where a continuous employment is terminated by the act of the employer, a reasonable period after the time at which the employment would, but for this rule, have come to an end, must be allowed at the employee's request for the purpose of enabling him to find a new employment [2] —BGB 629 [3].

(2) where an agreement for services is terminated by the employer on any ground other than the employee's breach of agreement, and also where it is terminated by the employee on the ground of the employer's breach of agreement, the employee is entitled to a proportionate remuneration for the services rendered up to the date of the termination of the agreement; in any other case in which the agreement is terminated by the act of either party, such proportionate remuneration is not payable in so far as the services up to the date of termination were of

---

[1]   As to the duty of the employee's heirs in certain cases to continue the services until the employer has made other arrangements, see 231 rule (9).

[2]   This provision, which was introduced by the Commission of the Reichstag, is an instance of the bad effect of hurried alterations of well-matured schemes of legislation.   It seems an intolerable hardship that an employer should be forced to retain for even a short period, the services of an employee dismissed for gross intemperance, immorality, cruelty, or any other equally cogent ground.

[3]   As to the right of a mercantile employee disabled by illness to receive remuneration after the termination of his employment, see 222 sub (4) ; as to the right of an employee to receive medical care, &c. , in the same event, see 223 sub (4).

no advantage to the employer [1]—BGB 628 (1) ;

(3) if an agreement for services is terminated by either party by reason of a breach of agreement committed by the other party, such other party is liable to compensate the party terminating the agreement for all damage suffered in consequence of such termination—BGB 628 (2) ; HGB 70 (2).

e.   Special Rules as to Agreements involving Business Transactions for Account of Another.

231. The following rules apply in all cases in which business is transacted for another, whatever the nature of the agreement between employer and employee may be—BGB 675 [2] :   269

(1) the employee is in all cases liable for wilful default and negligence (148) ; if he is a mercantile agent (238) or a commission merchant (239) he must bestow the diligence of a careful mercantile trader—HGB 84 (1) , 384 (1) ;

(2) the employee, in the absence of express or implied authority, is not entitled to entrust the execution of the employer's orders to a third party; if authorized to do so, he is liable for any default in the transmission of the orders, but not otherwise—BGB 664 (1) ;

(3) the employee must follow instructions, unless he has reason to think that the employer would have altered the instructions, had he known the true state of the circumstances; in the last-mentioned event he may deviate from the instructions if delay involves risk; otherwise he must inform the employer and await fresh instructions—BGB 665; as to commission merchants, see also HGB 385, 386;

(4) the employee must keep the employer informed as to the execution of his orders, and render an account after the completion of such execution—BGB 666; HGB 84 (2) , 384 (2) ;

(5) the employee must surrender to the employer all benefits received by him in connexion with a transaction carried out on the employer's behalf—BGB 667; HGB 387; as to the right of commission merchants to act for their own benefit, see 239 rule (12) ; if any money for which the employee has to account to the employer is used by the employee for his own purposes, he must pay

---

[1]   As to the employee's duty to return any remuneration paid in advance, see BGB 628 (1).

[2]   The agreement may be one for remunerated services (221) , for unremunerated services (232) , or for work (233) ; they are dealt with together in this place for the sake of convenience.

interest at the legal rate from the date of such use—BGB 668;

(6) the employer must, if requested to do so, advance funds to the employee, for the purpose of enabling him to act, and must repay to him any outlay, the necessity of which he was entitled to assume—BGB 669, 670; as to 270 commission merchants, see HGB 396 (2); a broker or mercantile agent is, in the absence of a contrary agreement or special mercantile custom, not entitled to the reimbursement of his expenses—BGB 652 (2); HGB 90;

(7) if the employee terminates the agreement without any cogent ground and without giving the employer an opportunity to make other arrangements, the employee is liable for all damage resulting from the sudden termination of the agreement—BGB 671 (2);

(8) where the agreement is in the nature of an agreement for services, an agreement for work, a brokerage agreement, or an agreement with a mercantile agent, the rules as to remuneration applicable respectively in the case of such agreements—222 sub (1), 235 sub (2), 237 sub (4), 238—must be applied;

(9) unless a contrary intention is shown, the agreement is not terminated by the employer's death or incapacity, but it is terminated by the death of the employee; if, according to a contractual stipulation, the agreement is terminated by the employer's death or incapacity, the employee, if there is any risk in delay, must, notwithstanding such termination, continue the execution of the employer's orders until the employer's heirs have had an opportunity of making other arrangements; on the employee's death, his heirs must give immediate notice to the employer, and execute his orders until he has had an opportunity to make other arrangements; while the employee or his heirs continue to act in the aforesaid manner the agreement is deemed to continue—BGB 672, 673;

(10) in any case in which the agreement is terminated otherwise than by notice communicated to the employee, the employee is entitled to be treated as if the agreement had continued in force until he became aware or would, by the exercise of proper diligence, have become aware of its termination—BGB 674.

2. MANDATE (*Auftrag*)

232. A 'mandate' (*Auftrag*) is an agreement for unremunerated services involving the transaction of business for another.   The person who agrees to perform such services is called the 'mandatary' (*der Beauftragte*); the person at whose request the services are given is called the 'mandant' (*der Auftraggeber*)—

BGB 662.

Under English law the mandatary's promise to act in accordance with the   271
mandant's request would not be binding on him, except in the improbable event
of such promise being given under seal; but he would, of course, be entitled to
the reimbursement of any outlay incurred on the mandant's behalf.   Under
German law, a person who is asked by a friend to make a purchase or to effect a
sale on such friend's behalf, and who tacitly or expressly agrees to comply with
such request, is liable in damages for negligence in carrying out such purchase or
such sale in the same way as if he was employed as a paid agent, and his claim
for reimbursement of outlay does not go any further than it does under
English law.

The general rules relating to agreements involving the transaction of business
for others have been stated above—231.   The only rule specifically referring to a
' mandate ' agreement is that, in the absence of a contrary stipulation, it may at
any time be terminated by either party, while the mandatary is entitled to
terminate the agreement on any cogent ground, even though he has expressly
renounced such right—BGB 671 (1) (3).

3.   AGREEMENTS FOR WORK (*Werkvertrag*)

a.   General Characteristics.

233. An agreement for work and labour is distinguished from an agreement
for services by the fact that the result of work, and not the work as such, is
contracted for by the parties.   Every agreement by which the person promising
the work (*der Unternehmer*)—who in the course of this treatise will be called
' the contractor ' —undertakes to produce a certain result, and by which the
person ordering the work (*der Besteller*)—who in the course of this treatise will
be called ' the employer ' —undertakes to pay the agreed remuneration, comes
within the definition.   The work contracted for by such an agreement may consist
in the production or alteration of a thing, or in the bringing about of any other
result—BGB 631.

Under English law any agreement ultimately resulting in the delivery of a
chattel is deemed an agreement to sell (Lee *v.* Griffin 1 B. and S. 272), but
under German law an agreement resulting in the delivery of a chattel to be
produced by the contractor, is an agreement for work, though many of the rules   272

relating to sales are, as shown below—234, applied to such an agreement.   An agreement for work, within the German meaning of the word, is in many cases hardly distinguishable from a sale.

Illustration: A person who writes to a clock maker, ordering a clock of a certain description, does not know or care whether the clock is in stock or has to be specially made, the clockmaker when accepting the order remaining discreetly silent on the subject.   Under English law the agreement would in any event be a contract for the sale of goods—Sale of Goods Act 1893, s. 5.   Under German law it is uncertain whether the agreement is a sale or an agreement for work.

In the same way the distinction between an agreement for services and an agreement for work is frequently difficult to ascertain.

Illustration: Hercules undertakes to clean the stables of Augias for a fixed remuneration, but fails to complete the work owing to insuperable difficulties; Augias contends that there was an agreement for work and that no remuneration is payable, as the agreed result was not attained; Hercules, on the other hand, contends that there was an agreement for services, and that he had performed these services with proper diligence and with the promised skill, and was therefore entitled to the promised remuneration.

An agreement for services is on several grounds more to the advantage of the person undertaking any work than an agreement for work, and it is generally assumed that in any case of doubt the inclination of the Courts will be in favour of an agreement for services.

An agreement for work, if involving the undertaking of business transactions on behalf of the employer (e. g. an agreement with a mercantile agent who undertakes the sale of his principal's goods for payment of a commission on each sale effected by him) is subject to the special rules stated above—231.

b.   Rules as to Agreements for Work where Contractor supplies Material.

234. Where the contractor supplies the material the following special rules apply:

273   (1) the contractor is bound to deliver the thing produced by him to the employer, and to cause the ownership thereof to be vested in him—BGB 651 (1);

(2) where the thing to be supplied is a fungible (e. g. in a case in which

any metals sold by weight are ordered from the foundry or smelting works), the agreement is in all respects governed by the rules as to sales; where the thing to be supplied is not a fungible the following matters are determined by the rules as to agreements for work: (*a*) the mode of payment; (*b*) the passing of the risk; (*c*) the remedies for breach of warranty of quality; in respect of all other matters the rules as to sales apply—BGB 651 (1) ;

(3) if the agreement for work is a bilateral mercantile transaction (36) the special rules applicable in the case of mercantile sales—see, for instance, 192, 193—are applied—HGB 381 (2) ;

(4) the rules under which a contractor, by way of security for his claims, is entitled to a right of pledge or charge over the thing produced or altered by him— see 235 sub (7)—are not applied in any case in which the material is supplied by the contractor—BGB 651 (1) ;

(5) where the contractor only supplies accessories (*e. g.* where a dress-maker makes a dress out of material supplied to her, but furnishes the trimmings), the rules as to agreements for work are applied exclusively—BGB 651 (2).

c.   Rules as to other Agreements for Work.

235. In the case of any agreement for work not coming under the rules stated above—234, the following rules apply, subject to any modification agreed upon by the parties.

(1) *Duties of contractor.*

The contractor is under an obligation to perform the work in accordance with the agreement; he is not ordinarily bound to act personally, but if he agrees to do so, his personal work is a promised quality—BGB 631 (1), 633 (1).

(2) *Remuneration of contractor.*

The presumption as to remuneration and the mode of ascertaining the scale of remuneration is the same (*mutatis mutandis*) as in the case of an agreement for services—see 222; as in the case of an agreement of the latter kind, the remuneration is not necessarily payable in money; it must be paid or furnished as soon as the result of the work is delivered to the employer and accepted by him in satisfaction of his claim for performance; where delivery is excluded by the nature of the work (*e. g.* where the work consists in the removal of goods or the obtaining of orders) the completion of the work takes the place of delivery; where the remuneration is

274

payable in money, interest is payable from the time when payment ought to be made; where the work is to be done by instalments, a proportionate part of the remuneration must be paid or furnished on the delivery or completion of each instalment—BGB 632, 641, 646.

(3) *Warranty as to quality of work.*

Warranty of quality in the case of an agreement for work corresponds approximately with the warranty of quality on the sale of goods (187 sub (2)), but the remedies available in the two cases differ from each other considerably.

It will be remembered that, in the case of a sale, the primary remedy, as a general rule, is the right to require the cancellation of the sale or the reduction of the purchase price, but that the purchaser of a thing generically defined may, instead of availing himself of either alternative, demand the delivery of a thing free from any defect—192 sub (1). In the case of an agreement for work the primary remedy is the claim for the removal of the defect; but, where the defect materially diminishes the value of the work, the employer may require the contractor to consent to the cancellation of the sale, or to the reduction of his remuneration, in any of the following events:

(a) if the removal of the defect is impossible, or if the contractor refuses to remove it;

(b) if, under the circumstances of the case, immediate cancellation or reduction is of special importance to the employer;

(c) if the contractor fails to remedy the defect within a reasonable period of time, specified in a notice requiring him to do so—BGB 633 (2), 634 (1) (2) (3).

If the contractor is in *mora solvendi* (152) as to the correction of the defect, the employer may remedy the defect at the contractor's expense—BGB 633 (3).

275   A claim for compensation, instead of cancellation or reduction of the remuneration, arises where the defect is due to a circumstance for which the contractor is responsible (particularly in the case of negligence on his part or on the part of any person for whom he is responsible)—BGB 635.

The right to require the contractor's consent to the cancellation of the agreement has the same effect as the right to the cancellation of a sale—see 192 sub (2)—BGB 634 (4).

The rules as to the effect of fraudulent concealment, and of the employer's knowledge of defects at the time of the acceptance of the performance are the same as in the case of a sale—see 185, 192 (1)—BGB 637, 640 (2); as to prescription, see BGB 638, 639.

(4) *Effect of non-delivery of work at promised time.*

If the work is not completed at the promised time the employer may, in any case in which time is of the essence, or in which the contractor is in *mora solvendi*, avail himself of the remedies to which he is entitled in these circumstances under the rules as to reciprocal agreements—160, 161.   He may also, without reference to the question whether time is of the essence, or whether the contractor is in *mora solvendi*, rescind [1] the agreement or claim the reduction of the remuneration in any of the following events:

(*a*) if performance within a reasonable time is refused by the contractor or impossible;

(*b*) if under the circumstances of the case immediate rescission or reduction is of special importance to the employer;

(*c*) if, after the lapse of a reasonable time specified in a notice communicated to the contractor, the work remains unperformed—BGB 636.

(5) *Passing of risk.*

In the same way as the vendor of a movable thing bears the risk of the thing sold by him until delivery, the contractor bears the risk of the work contracted for by him and of the material used in connexion therewith, until delivery and acceptance, or completion to the employer's satisfaction.   If the employer supplies the material, the contractor must apply due diligence in its preservation, but he is not liable for accidental loss or deterioration; if such accidental loss or deterioration is caused by any defect in the material supplied by the employer, or if in consequence of any direction given by the employer and without any default on the contractor's part the work has been destroyed, deteriorated, or rendered impossible, the contractor is entitled to remuneration proportionate to the amount of labour bestowed on the work and to reimbursement of any outlay not allowed for in such remuneration, without prejudice to any claim for damages against the employer to which he may be entitled under the general rules.   The rules as to the risk of the transmission of the product of the work where such product is forwarded by the employer's direction to a destination other than the place of performance are the

276

---

1   As to the distinction between the right to require the contractor's consent to cancellation which is exercisable in some of the events mentioned sub (3) , and the right to rescission exercisable in some of the events mentioned sub (4) , see 192 sub (2).

same as in the case of a sale—see 190 rule (3)—BGB 644–646.

(6) *Effect of mora accipiendi.*

An employer who is in *mora accipiendi* bears the risk of the work from the time at which such *mora* begins; if the completion of the work depends upon any act to be done by him (*e. g.* sitting for a portrait), and the omission of such act places him in *mora accipiendi*, the contractor is entitled to reasonable compensation for any damage suffered thereby; in the last-mentioned event the contractor may declare that he will rescind the agreement if the employer fails to do the required act within a specified reasonable period; if the agreement is accordingly rescinded the contractor is entitled to compensation for his work and outlay—BGB 643, 644 (1); as to the quantum of damages, see BGB 642 (2).

(7) *Contractor's right of pledge and charge.*

A contractor, in addition to the right to which he is entitled under the general rules (159, 174) to make the delivery or completion of his work dependent on the payment of his remuneration, is entitled to the benefit of the following special rules:

277   (*a*) a contractor, who has produced a movable thing from material supplied to him by the employer, or has repaired a movable thing belonging to the employer, and has obtained possession of such thing on its production, or for the purpose of effecting the repairs, [1] is entitled to a right of pledge (392) over such movable thing by way of security for his contractual claims—BGB 647.

(*b*) a contractor who has undertaken the construction of a building or of a part of a building is entitled to the registration of a cautionary hypothecary charge (373) on such building, by way of security for his contractual claim; while the work is incomplete he may claim the registration of such a charge for a proportionate part of his remuneration, and for any outlay not allowed for in the remuneration—BGB 648.

(8) *Rescission where estimate is exceeded.*

An agreement for work may be rescinded by the employer in any case in which the contractor has made an estimate without guaranteeing its accuracy, and

---

1   Where the object has been produced or repaired on the employer's premises, it does not come into the contractor's possession; if in such a case he acquires the possession at a subsequent time he may exercise his right of lien under the general rules.

in which the work cannot be completed without largely exceeding such estimate; if the agreement is rescinded on this ground, the contractor is entitled to a remuneration proportionate to the amount of labour bestowed on the work, and to the reimbursement of any outlay not allowed for in the remuneration—BGB 650.

(9) Arbitrary rescission by employer.

The employer may at any time before the completion of the work rescind the agreement without alleging any reason; if he avails himself of this right, the contractor is entitled to the whole of the agreed remuneration, but subject to deduction of any saving of outlay, or of any earnings which he has received, or, but for his intentional neglect, might have received during the time saved in consequence of the rescission of the agreement—BGB 649.   (See the illustration given above, 222 sub (3).)

4.   SPECIAL KINDS OF AGREEMENTS INVOLVING WORK OR SERVICES

a.   General Statement.

236. Certain kinds of agreements involving work or services are specially   278
regulated by the BGB and the HGB.   In so far as such agreements are for services or for work, they come under the rules respectively relating to such agreements, and as they all involve the transaction of business for another, they also come under the rules relating to agreements involving the transaction of such business (231).   The special rules stated below are supplemental to the general rules.

b.   Brokerage Agreements (*Mäklervertrag*).

(1) Definition of term.

237. A brokerage agreement (*Mäklervertrag*) is an agreement by which the employer promises to pay the contractor a remuneration for acting as intermediary in the formation of an agreement with a third party, or for pointing out an opportunity for entering upon such an agreement.   The contractor in such a case is called a 'broker' (*Mäkler*).   The promise to pay remuneration is implied if the requested service cannot, under the circumstances, reasonably be expected to be performed without remuneration (*e. g.* where the request is addressed to a professional broker)—BGB 652 (1), 653 (1).

(2) *Classification of professional brokers.*

A person who professionally (*gewerbsmässig*) transacts business of the nature described is called a professional broker. A person who, without being in any continuous contractual relation with any particular employer, professionally acts as intermediary in the formation of agreements relating: (1) to the purchase or sale of merchandise or negotiable instruments; (2) to insurance; (3) to the carriage of goods, bottomry, and affreightment; or (4) to other objects of mercantile intercourse, is called a 'mercantile broker' (*Handelsmäkler*), and is in respect of any negotiations relating to any such agreement subject to the special rules applicable to mercantile brokers—HGB 93. [1]

279 Among non-mercantile brokers, land brokers and mortgage brokers are of special importance. The business of the former represents a large part of the business done in England by 'estate agents'. As to marriage brokage, see 139.

(3) *Rules as to brokers acting for both parties.*

Under English law, a broker under any circumstances commits a breach of duty by accepting any brokerage or commission in respect of any particular transaction from any party other than his employer in that transaction; under German law, on the other hand, a broker who acts for the other party as well as for his employer commits a breach of duty only in so far as such double employment violates the agreement with his employer; and the question whether this is the case or not depends upon the particular circumstances. A mercantile broker is presumed to act for both parties—HGB 99.

A broker who by acting for both parties violates his agreements forfeits his claim for remuneration and reimbursement of outlay—BGB 654.

(4) *Scale of remuneration.*

The scale of remuneration is determined by rules similar to those applicable in the case of an agreement for services, see 222 sub (1)—BGB 653 (2).

Where the brokerage agreed to be paid on the conclusion of an agreement for services appears unduly high the Court may at any time before payment reduce the

---

1 As to a mercantile broker's duty to deliver a written memorandum of any transaction brought about by his intervention; to preserve samples of goods; to keep a journal in the prescribed form; and as to his personal liability, see HGB 94–96, 98–104. Specific rules as to produce and Stock Exchange brokers are contained in the Imperial Bourse Law of 1896.

amount—BGB 655.

c.   Mercantile Agency Agreements.

238.   A person who, without being a commercial employee, is continuously employed by a principal for the purpose of bringing about business transactions connected with the principal's mercantile trade, or for the purpose of entering into such transactions on the principal's behalf, is called a ' mercantile agent ' (*Handlungsagent*).   His agreement with the principal is generally in the nature of an agreement for work, and subject to the special rules as to agreements involving the transaction of business for others stated above—231.   As to the powers of agency held by mercantile agents, see 119.

In the absence of any contractual stipulation, a mercantile agent is entitled to the usual remuneration on every transaction brought about by his intervention, and on every transaction which, but for the principal's unreasonable conduct, would have been so brought about.   Where the transaction is a sale the claim to commission does not, in the absence of a contrary stipulation, arise before payment of the invoice amount; if such invoice amount is paid in part, a proportionate part of the commission becomes payable.   If the agent is expressly appointed for a specified district, he is, in the absence of any indication to the contrary, entitled to a commission on all transactions entered upon by the principal within such district, and without regard to the question whether such transactions were brought about by his intervention or not. **280**

He is not, in the absence of an express stipulation providing otherwise, or of a special custom to the same effect, entitled to the reimbursement of any outlay incurred in the usual course of business.

He may, when settling his accounts with the principal, require the production of an extract from the principal's books showing the transactions brought about by his agency, or on which he is otherwise entitled to commission—HGB 88–91.

An agreement with a mercantile agent entered upon for an indefinite period may be terminated by either party by a six weeks' notice terminating at the end of a calendar quarter; where there is a cogent ground—see p. 247 note 1—such an agreement may be terminated without notice—HGB 92.

d.   Agreements between Commission Merchants and their Principals.

239.   A person who, in the regular course of his business, undertakes to purchase or sell goods or negotiable instruments in his own name, but upon the instruction of another, [1] is called a ' commission merchant ' (*Kommissionär*) — HGB 383.

An agreement between a commission merchant and his principal comes under the rules stated above—231—as to agreements involving the transaction of business for others, but is further subject to the following specific rules, [2] in the statement of which the party to whom the commission merchant sells or from whom he buys is called the purchaser or the vendor (as the case may be) :

281

(1) a commission merchant must do the business undertaken by him with the diligence of a careful mercantile trader; he must watch over his principal's interests and follow his instructions—HGB 384 (1) ;

(2) he must give all necessary information to his principal, and more particularly inform him as to the execution of his instructions—HGB 384 (2) ;

(3) he must render an account of every transaction entered upon on the principal's instructions, and hand over any money or other object received in connexion with any such transaction—HGB 384 (2) ;

(4) a commission merchant, who applies the required diligence, is not, as between himself and his principal, liable for the performance of the vendor's or purchaser's obligations, unless he expressly guarantees such performance, or unless such guarantee is implied by virtue of any local custom, [3] or unless he fails to mention the vendor's or purchaser's name when reporting the transaction to his principal; a commission merchant who is instructed to purchase a bill of exchange is bound to indorse it without making any reservations as to his liability—HGB 384 (3) , 394, 395;

(5) if the principal fails to give any instructions as to the disposal of goods forwarded to the commission merchant, the latter may take such measures, as to the storage or sale of the goods, as a mercantile vendor may take in a case in

---

1   The words ' upon the *instruction* of another' are used instead of the words ' for *account* of another' which are a more literal version of the German text.   A commission merchant as between himself and the party with whom he transacts business acts as principal and not as agent; as between himself and his principal the transaction is entered upon for the principal's account.

2   The specific rules in question are also applicable to commission merchants undertaking other mercantile business than the purchase or sale of the objects mentioned in the text, as well as to mercantile traders who, without being commission merchants within the meaning of the definition given above, undertake mercantile business on the instructions of others—HGB 406 (1) , but it is more convenient to state the rules with exclusive reference to commission merchants undertaking purchases and sales only.

3   In such a case he is entitled to a special *del credere* commission—HGB 394 (2) .

which the purchaser is in *mora accipiendi*, see 193—HGB 389 (see also 388 (2));

(6) a commission merchant who executes an order for the purchase of any negotiable instruments in the nature of stocks, shares, or debentures, or of any similar instruments, issued to bearer or passing by indorsement, is bound within a specified short period of time to give a list of the numbers or other distinguishing marks of the documents of title delivered to him by the vendor; a general waiver of the principal's right to receive such a list is inoperative (Imperial Statute of 1896 relating to the custody of negotiable instruments, ss. 3 and 4);

(7) a commission merchant is under the following liabilities as to goods which come into his custody for the principal's account:

(*a*) if goods forwarded to him are received in a defective condition, recognizable by their outward appearance, he must preserve all rights against the carriers of the goods, and take care to record the evidence as to their defective state, and forthwith inform the principal—HGB 388 (1);

282

(*b*) he is liable for the loss or deterioration of the goods, unless he can prove that such loss or deterioration could not have been avoided if he had applied the diligence of a diligent mercantile trader; he is, however, not bound to insure the goods, unless specially instructed to do so—HGB 390;

(8) if the principal is a mercantile trader, he is subject to the same duties as to the investigation of goods purchased for him by a commission merchant, as a mercantile purchaser—see 192 sub (1) (d); non-compliance with these duties bars his remedies against the commission merchant in the same way as if he were the purchaser, and the commission merchant the vendor—HGB 391;

(9) a commission merchant, who sells goods on credit without the principal's authority, unless such a course is sanctioned by local custom, becomes personally liable for the payment of what would have been the cash purchase price; the risk of an advance, made to a vendor of goods without the principal's authority, is borne by the commission merchant—HGB 393;

(10) a commission merchant must assign to the principal all claims arising from purchases or sales made on the principal's instructions; even before such assignment is made, such claims, as between the commission merchant and his principal, and also as between the commission merchant and his creditors, are deemed to be vested in the principal—HGB 392;

Illustration: *C*, a commission merchant, sells goods to *A* on credit on *P*'s instructions; a judgment creditor of *C* cannot seize the debt owing by *A* to *C* so as to defeat *P*'s claim [1] ;

(11) the commission merchant's claims against the principal in respect of commission, money lent, or obligations undertaken, or costs incurred in respect of the principal's goods, as well as any other claims arising on the current account with the principal, are secured by a right of pledge (392) over the goods, and over the principal's claims (if any) against the purchasers or vendors of the goods—HGB 397–399.

(12) a commission merchant, when instructed to purchase or sell any goods having a market value, or any securities officially quoted on any public exchange, may, in the absence of any direction to the contrary, himself become the purchaser or the vendor at the price most favourable to the principal, at which the order could have been executed on the particular day, without thereby forfeiting his right to commission or reimbursement of outlay, or his charge for the security of his claims against the principal; if the order is revoked, and the revocation reaches the commission merchant before he has dispatched his notification of the execution of the order, the right can no longer be exercised; a notification of a sale or purchase which does not expressly state that the commission merchant himself is the purchaser or vendor, is deemed to be a notification of the fact that the order was executed by agreement with a third party; the application of the last-mentioned rule, or of the legal rules, as to the price to be fixed in the case of any purchase or sale by the commission merchant, from or to himself, cannot be excluded by agreement between the parties—HGB 400–405.

e. Agreements between Forwarding Agents and their Principals.

240. A person who, in the regular course of his business, undertakes the forwarding of goods by the agency of carriers in his own name, but on the instructions of another, is called a forwarding agent (*Spedilteur*).   The rules relating to agreements between forwarding agents and their principals [2] are, to a great extent, the same as those regulating the relations between commission merchants and their principals (239).   Proper diligence must be applied not only to the

---

[1]   The rule does not operate as between the commission merchant and any third party taking an assignment of the claim without notice of the principal's rights.

[2]   Mercantile traders who are not forwarding agents within the definition of the term given above, but who in a particular case in the course of their trade undertake the forwarding of goods in the manner mentioned in the text, are subject to the same rules as regular forwarding agents—HGB 415.

forwarding of the goods but also to the selection of the carriers and sub-agents.   A sub-agent (*Zwischenspediteur*) employed by a forwarding agent, like the principal forwarding agent, is entitled to a statutory right of pledge (392); if the sub-agents' claims are satisfied by his immediate principal, such claims and all securities held in respect thereof become vested in such immediate principal—HGB 407–411.

A forwarding agent may, in the absence of any stipulation to the contrary, carry the goods himself; in such a case the rules as to a carrier's rights and duties (241) are applied as well as the rules relating to forwarding agents, the forwarding agent being entitled to his agency commission, as well as to the proper charge for freight or carriage; but in any of the following events a forwarding agent is, in the absence of an arrangement to the contrary, exclusively subject to the rules as to carriers, and not entitled to any agency commission:

(*a*) if he has agreed to forward the goods from place to place at a fixed charge;

(*b*) if he forwards the goods of any principal, together with goods belonging to other principals, on payment of a lump sum for freight and carriage for all the goods—HGB 412, 413.

284

Claims against forwarding agents in respect of the loss or deterioration of goods forwarded through them are subject to a shortened period of prescription—HGB 414.

f.   Agreements with Carriers.

(1) *General statement.*

241.   A carrier by land, by river, or by inland waters, is called *Frachtführer*, [1] a carrier by sea *Verfrachter*.   A person who, in his own name (whether as owner or as forwarding agent), makes an agreement with a carrier as to the forwarding of goods is called *Absender*, if the agreement is for carriage by land, and *Befrachter*, if the agreement is for carriage by sea.   In the following statement the expression ' carrier by land' will include carriers by river or inland waters, and the expression ' carrier' without any addition will include carriers both by

---

1   This expression is only applied to persons who undertake the carriage of goods in the regular course of their business; but the rules relating to carriers by land are also applicable to other mercantile traders in so far as in any particular case they undertake the business in question—HGB 425, 451.

sea and by land; the expression 'sender' will include all persons making agreements with carriers as to the forwarding of goods. The person to whom the goods are forwarded, and who according to the German terminology is designated as *Empfänger*, will be called 'the consignee'.

An agreement between a sender and a carrier is in the nature of an agreement for work (the work consisting in the receipt, carrying, custody, and delivery of goods, and the remuneration in the carriage or freight payable on delivery of the goods), but the general rules as to agreements for work (233) are modified as to carriers by land by HGB 425–473, and as to carriers by sea by HGB 556–663. [1]

A detailed statement of the rules relating to carriers' agreements would occupy too much space, but a few of their specially characteristic features must be mentioned.

(2) *Written documents relating to agreement.*

285   A written document embodying the agreement is unnecessary, but in the case of carriage by land the carrier has the right to demand the delivery of a letter of advice (*Frachtbrief*) by the sender, while in the case of carriage by sea the sender has a right to claim a bill of lading (*Konnossement*); this right, as a matter of practice, is always exercised—HGB 426 (1), 642.

A letter of advice is a letter addressed by the sender to the consignee, announcing the dispatch of the goods and the essential terms of the agreement with the carrier; a bill of lading, like an English document of the same description, acknowledges the shipment of the goods, and also embodies the essential terms of the agreement between the sender and the carrier—HGB 426 (2), 643.

Where goods are sent by rail, the sender may claim the endorsement of a receipt for the goods on a duplicate of the letter of advice—HGB 455 (1); where goods are sent by river, or any other inland water, the carrier may at his discretion issue a certificate of shipment (*Ladeschein*), which has the same effect

---

[1]   The railway regulations (*Eisenbahnverkehrsordnung*) issued from time to time by the Federal Council which have the force of law further modify and supplement the general rules—HGB 454, 472.   The rights of passengers by land are dealt with by these regulations exclusively; the rules as to the carriage of passengers by sea are contained in HGB 664–678.   An Imperial Statute of the 15th June, 1895 (amended in 1898), contains some special provisions relating to carriage of goods by river and inland waters.   The rules relating to carriers are not applicable to the postal authorities—HGB 452, 663.

as a bill of lading relating to goods sent by sea—HGB 444–446.

(3) *Consignee's rights in case of carriage by land.*

Where goods are carried by land, the agreement between the sender and the carrier is in the nature of an agreement for the benefit of a third party (141), namely, the consignee.   The consignee's rights are, however, subject to the sender's right to stop the goods or to change their destination at any time prior to their arrival and to the delivery of the letter of advice to the consignee. [1]   A sender of goods who has obtained an endorsement of the receipt of the goods on a duplicate of the letter of advice, cannot exercise the right of stoppage without production of such duplicate—HGB 433, 455 (2).

Subject to the above-mentioned right of stoppage by the sender, the consignee, by virtue of the agreement between the sender and the carrier, is entitled to the following rights:

(*a*) he may take measures for the protection of the goods prior to their arrival, and give directions in that behalf to the carrier;

(*b*) after the arrival of the goods he may claim delivery of the letter of advice and of the goods, and enforce all other obligations incurred by the carrier under the agreement, but he must himself perform all obligations resulting from such delivery, including the obligation to make all payments due to the carrier in accordance with the letter of advice—HGB 435, 436.

(4) *Right of holders of bills of lading or certificates of shipment.*

A bill of lading issued to order [2] has all the characteristics of a negotiable instrument (178), a lawful holder being entitled to the performance of the agreement embodied in the document—HGB 363, 651.

A sender who does not remain in possession of the full set of bills of lading

286

---

[1]   If the carrier fails to deliver the letter of advice after the arrival of the goods, the time of the institution of proceedings for the delivery of the letter of advice is substituted for the time of delivery—HGB 433 (2); the sender's right is analogous to the English right of stoppage in transit—see Sale of Goods Act 1893, ss. 44–46.   The assignee's insolvency is not a necessary condition of the exercise of the right conferred by German law.

[2]   A bill of lading is deemed issued to order, if it is issued 'to order' or to the order of a named person or to a named person or his order.   The sender is entitled to a bill of lading issued in one of these forms—HGB 644.

abandons all power over the goods. [1]   No right analogous to the English right of 'stoppage in transit' exists under German law as to goods carried by sea—HGB 659 (1).

A holder of the bill of lading, who accepts delivery of the goods, is bound to pay the freight and to perform all other obligations resulting from such delivery in accordance with the terms of the bill of lading—HGB 614.

The rules relating to certificates of shipment are similar to those relating to bills of lading—HGB 444–450.

(5) *Carrier's liability as to goods.*

(a) *As to time of dispatch and time and mode of delivery.*

In the absence of any specific agreement as to the time of dispatch and delivery, the duties in this respect of carriers by land are determined by local custom; in the absence of any special agreement or custom, the following rules apply:

(1) the goods must be forwarded and delivered within a reasonable time;

(2) if the beginning or completion of the carriage of goods by land is temporarily [2] prevented by circumstances for which the sender is not responsible, he may rescind the agreement; the carrier in such a case, if he is not himself in default, is entitled to compensation for his work and outlay—HGB 428;

287   (3) the owners of a railway undertaking must publish lists as to periods of delivery; these must not exceed the maximum periods fixed by the regulations of the Federal Council;

(4) the owners of a railway undertaking, on receiving goods addressed to a place situate at a distance from the railway, may agree to be liable as carriers for the carriage to the station nearest to the place of destination, and to be liable as forwarding agents for the further carriage of the goods—HGB 468;

(5) the owners of a railway undertaking are liable for the non-observance of their promise as to the time of delivery, unless they can prove that the delay was caused by a circumstance beyond the control of themselves or of any of their

---

1   A bill of lading is generally issued in three copies collectively called the full set; the holder of an incomplete set has no power of disposal while the goods are on their way; on the arrival of the goods at the place of destination the holder of one part of the set is entitled to the delivery of the goods—HGB 645 (1), 659 (2).

2   A permanent impediment would be in the nature of a supervening impossibility of performance, and would come under the general rules relating thereto (see 160).

employees; in the case of an ordinary carrier it is sufficient to prove that the delay could not have been prevented by him or his employees, if he or they had employed the diligence of a diligent carrier—HGB 429 (1), 431, 458, 466 (1). As to the quantum of damages, see 169 rule (3) (d).

(b) Liability for loss or deterioration of goods.

The grounds of liability are approximately the same as in the case of delay (see above), a railway undertaking being responsible for all damage not caused by *vis major*, or default on the sender's part, or defective condition of the goods, and an ordinary carrier being responsible for all damage which the diligence of a careful carrier could not have prevented—HGB 429 (1), 431, 456 (1), 467, 606.

Where valuable works of art, money, or negotiable instruments are forwarded, the carrier is not liable unless the nature or value of the goods is declared—HGB 429 (2), 456 (2), 607.

The owners of a railway undertaking are not liable for certain specified kinds of damage, unless such damage was caused by themselves or any of their employees—HGB 459, 460.

A maximum amount for the extent of the liability may be fixed by a railway undertaking: (a) as regards valuables, in so far as this is permitted by the regulations of the Federal Council; (b) generally, where exceptional conditions as to freight are accorded to the sender pursuant to the published tariffs; in neither case can the liability for wilful default or gross negligence be thus limited—HGB 461, 462.

A shipowner's liability is limited in accordance with the rules of maritime law; see 151 sub c—HGB 485.

As to the quantum of damages recoverable from a carrier in case of loss or deterioration of the goods, see 169 rule (3) (c).

(c) Liability of Sub-contractors.

In the case of carriage by land a carrier who takes the goods from the original carrier with the original letter of advice becomes liable for the performance of the agreement, and the sender or consignee may claim damages for breach of agreement either from the original carrier or from any such subsequent carrier.

Where the respective owners of several railway undertakings successively act as carriers, an action for damages can only be brought against the original carriers, or the last carriers who took the goods, or the carriers on whose line the damage

288

was caused.

Any carrier who has paid a claim for damages is entitled to be indemnified by the carrier by whose default the damage was actually caused; if it cannot be proved that the damage was caused by the default of any particular carrier, every carrier who cannot prove that the damage did not happen while he was in charge of the goods must contribute a share of the damages *pro rata* of his share in the total amount of the carriage—HGB 432, 469.

As to sub-contracts in the case of carriage by sea, see HGB 662.

(6) *Circumstances excluding liability.*

(a) *Contractual modification.*

An ordinary carrier can modify the legal rules as to his liability by agreement with the sender, but the liabilities of railway undertakings arising under the legal rules or the regulations issued by the Federal Council cannot be restricted by private arrangement—HGB 471.

(b) *Acceptance of the goods.*

The acceptance of goods carried by land and the payment of the carriage bars all claims for deterioration discoverable from the external condition of the goods, unless such deterioration was recognized by the official experts called in by the consignee prior to such acceptance; in the case of any deterioration not discoverable from the outward condition of the goods, the right to damages is preserved by an application for investigation by the official experts, if such application is made in the prescribed manner immediately on the discovery of the deterioration, but not later than eight days after the acceptance of the goods.

In the case of the carriage of goods by sea an application for investigation made within two days from the acceptance of the goods preserves the right to damages, whether the deterioration was outwardly visible or not.

289   Acceptance does not bar the claim in any case where the damage was caused by the wilful default or gross negligence of the carrier or of any of his employees—HGB 438, 464, 608, 609.

(c) *Prescription.*

The rules as to the effect of lapse of time on claims for compensation for loss or deterioration or delay are the same as in the case of similar claims against forwarding agents (240).

Claims for indemnity or contribution by one of several carriers against any of the others under the rules mentioned, sub (5) (c), are not subject to the short period of prescription to which the original claims are subject—HGB 439.

As to claims for the loss of passengers' luggage, see HGB 465.

(7) *Carrier's rights.*

(a) *Right to payment of carriage or freight and disbursements.*

No general rules are laid down as to the rates of carriage payable to ordinary carriers by land, but railway undertakings, in the same way as under English law, are bound to charge uniform rates, which must be publicly announced.   Carriers by sea, in the absence of any agreement as to the amount of the freight, are entitled to freight at the rate current at the time and place of shipment—HGB 619 (1).   As to the mode of calculation, see 619 (2), 621.

The carriage or freight is usually payable on delivery of the goods.   The carrier is entitled to the repayment of certain necessary disbursements (customs duties, storage charges, &c.)—HGB 440 (1).

Where, in the case of goods sent by railway, a mistake is made in the application of the tariff or the calculation of the amount, the claim for repayment of the difference is barred after the lapse of a year from the date of payment— HGB 470.

(b) *Rights as to documents.*

A carrier by land is entitled to receive from the sender all documents required by the carrier for the purpose of complying with the regulations of the customs, excise, and police authorities.   In so far as no default attaches to the carrier, the sender is liable for all damages resulting to the carrier from the insufficiency or inaccuracy of such documents—HGB 427.

(c) *Rights in case of sender's or consignee's default as to*
delivery or acceptance.

If the sender fails to deliver the goods, or the consignee or the holder of the   290 bill of lading fails to accept the goods and to pay the amount of the carriage or freight remaining outstanding at the time at which the delivery, acceptance, or payment ought to take place, the ordinary rules as to *mora solvendi* in the case of a reciprocal agreement—161—are applicable as between the carrier and the sender.

In the case of goods carried by sea, demurrage may also be payable by the sender or by the holder of the bill of lading under the rules of maritime law—

HGB 567.

Where the consignee of goods carried by land cannot be found, or refuses acceptance of the goods and payment of the freight, the carrier must, if possible, take the sender's instructions.   If this is not possible, or if the sender's instructions are delayed or impracticable, the carrier may store the goods at the sender's expense, or sell them in the events and in the manner in which a mercantile vendor may, under the rules stated above—193, sell goods where the purchaser is in *mora accipiendi*.

The sender and the consignee must be informed of the storage and sale in so far as this is practicable—HGB 437.

(d) Land carrier's right of pledge.

The claims of a carrier by land for freight and all disbursements incurred in pursuance of the agreement with the sender are secured by a right of pledge (392) on the goods carried by him, which right of pledge remains in force while such goods are in his possession or are represented by documents of title (bills of lading, certificates of shipment, warehouse receipts) which are in his possession. It continues to be operative after the delivery of the goods or documents, if the carrier, within three days after such delivery, makes an application for its judicial enforcement in the prescribed manner—HGB 440.

Where the goods pass successively through the hands of several persons being either carriers or forwarding agents, the following rules apply:

(1) the last carrier must exercise the rights of the carriers or forwarding agents through whose hands the goods have previously passed, and has to collect all their claims as agent on their behalf; if he has himself satisfied any such claim, the claim, and the right of pledge by which it is secured, become vested in him;

(2) if the last carrier delivers the goods without payment and fails to make an application for the judicial enforcement of the right of pledge within three days from the date of the delivery, he is liable to the other carriers or forwarding agents for the payment of their claims, and forfeits his right of recourse in respect of any claim previously satisfied by him;

(3) in the event of the goods being subject to conflicting legal rights of pledge in favour of any commission merchants (239), forwarding agents (240), or warehousemen (252 rule 11), the rights of pledge by which the forwarding charges and the carriage of the goods are secured take priority over those by

291

which other rights are secured (*e. g.* the claims of the commission merchant and warehousemen in respect of commission, warehouse rent, or outlay; the claims of forwarding agents and carriers in respect of advances).   Subject to this provision, the priorities are determined by the dates of the several rights of pledge in the ordinary way—HGB 443.

5.   Agreements between Authors and Publishers

a.   General Characteristics.

242. Publishing agreements are governed by the Imperial Statute of 1902 on Publishing Law (*Gesetz über das Verlagsrecht*), and also by the rules relating to agreements for sale (184) and for work (233), and the general rules as to reciprocal agreements (159, 160, 161) in so far as these in any particular case are applicable.

A publishing agreement, according to the statutory definition, is an agreement by which the author of a literary or musical work becomes bound to hand it over to the publisher for the purpose of being reproduced in a number of copies and published for the publisher's own account, and by which the publisher becomes bound to reproduce such work in a number of copies and to publish it— GVR 1.

The promise of a remuneration to the author is not an essential part of the agreement, but as in the case of an agreement for services (222), is presumed in any case, in which, under the special circumstances, the author was entitled to expect a remuneration; where the quantum of the remuneration is not fixed by the parties, a reasonable remuneration must be paid—GVR 22.

An agreement by which the publisher undertakes to bring out the work for the author's account on payment of a commission is not a publishing agreement within the meaning of the statute, and is governed by the rules as to agreements between commission merchants and their principals (239). [1]

The expression ' author' for the purposes of the statute, includes any person 292

---

1   A publisher is not a commission merchant, but he is a mercantile trader (36).   As mentioned above—p. 260 note 2, the rules relating to agreements between commission merchants and their principals are also applicable to agreements between any mercantile traders and their principals, in so far as they relate to business transacted by the mercantile trader in his own name, but on the instruction of a principal—HGB 406.

entitled to dispose of the author's right (83) , who enters into an agreement of the nature described with a publisher, whether such person be the actual producer of the work forming the subject of the agreement or not—GVR 48.

b.   Publisher's Rights.

243. The following rules apply, in so far as they are not modified by agreement between the parties:

(1) the publisher has the exclusive right to reproduce and circulate the original work, the author retaining the right to translate the work, to dramatize a narrative work, to reproduce the contents of a dramatic work in narrative form, to rearrange a musical work (otherwise than by mere extract or transposition) , and to reproduce and publish the result of such translation, transformation, or rearrangement—GVR 2 (2) [1] ;

(2) the publisher, as such, is not entitled to reproduce in a collective work, a work published separately or to publish separately a work first published in a collective work—GVR 4 ;

(3) the publisher in the absence of express authority is entitled to bring out one edition only; where he is authorized to bring out several editions the publication of each edition is subject to the same conditions and stipulations as the publication of the previous edition.   Where no agreement exists as to the number of copies, each edition may comprise 1, 000 copies in addition to a specified number of reserve copies and presentation copies—GVR 5–7 ;

(4) the publishing price, unless fixed by the agreement, may be fixed by the publisher; he may also reduce the price if such reduction does not interfere with any legitimate interest of the author, but he is not entitled to raise the price without the author's consent—GVR 21 ;

(5) the publishing right arises [2] on the delivery of the work to the publisher, and comes to an end on the termination of the publishing agreement; if the agreement refers to a definite number of editions, or a definite number of copies,

---

1   After the lapse of twenty years from the end of the calendar year in which the work was published, it may be included by the author in a collective work; the author of a gratuitous contribution to a collective work, may, after the lapse of one year from the end of the calendar year of publication, reproduce and publish such contribution—GVR 2 (3) , 3.

2   Before the delivery of the work the publisher has a claim to the delivery of the work, which is of a purely obligatory nature, and is available exclusively against the author; the publishing right, on the other hand, is an absolute right available against the whole world.

it ceases to be operative as soon as such editions or copies have been sold out; if   293
the agreement is to continue during a specified period of time, the publisher is
not entitled to sell any copies remaining unsold at the termination of such
period—GVR 9 (1), 29 (1) (3).

c.   Author's Duties.

aa.   *As to delivery of work and alterations therein.*

244. The following rules apply in the absence of any stipulation to the contrary:

(1) the work when delivered must be fit for reproduction—GVR 10;

(2) if the work is complete on the formation of the agreement it must be
delivered immediately—GVR 11 (1);

(3) a work which has to be produced or completed after the formation of the
agreement, must be delivered in sufficient time for the accomplishment of the
purpose for which its publication was intended; where no indication as to the time
of delivery can be gathered from the purpose which the work is to serve, the work
must be delivered within such period of time as would enable the author to complete
it, if he bestowed on it such part of his working time as may be expected under the
circumstances; the time which is taken up by other occupations must be taken
into consideration, if the publisher when entering upon the agreement was aware,
or by the application of proper diligence would have become aware, of such other
occupations—GVR 11;

(4) the author may, while the reproduction of the work is proceeding, make
such alterations as he thinks fit, but only in so far as they do not affect a legitimate
interest of the publisher; the cost of such alterations as exceed the usual limit must
be borne by the author, unless they are caused by events which have happened since
the commencement of the reproduction; an opportunity must be given to the author
to make alterations prior to the publication of each new edition; the publisher is
not entitled to make any alterations to which the author could reasonably object—
GVR 12, 13.

bb.   *Warranty as to title.*

The author is bound to cause the agreed right of reproduction and publication
to be vested in the publisher, and to enable the publisher, in so far as the author's
right becomes vested in him under the publishing agreement, to take the necessary
proceedings in the event of any infringement—GVR 8, 9 (2); if the author, with
intent to deceive, conceals the fact that the work was previously delivered to

another publisher, and published by him, he is under the same liabilities as a vendor who conceals a defect of title (185)—GVR 39 (2).

294   No warranty of title is implied in the case of a work as to which no author's right (83) exists; but the author himself is in such a case bound to abstain from competition with the publisher during the first six months after publication—GVR 39 (1) (3).

d.   Publisher's Duties.

aa.   *As to payment of author's remuneration.*

245. The following rules apply in the absence of any stipulation to the contrary:

(1) the remuneration, if consisting in a single payment of a fixed amount, must be paid on the delivery of the work; if the amount is uncertain, or if it is dependent on the size of the finished copy, it must be paid on completion of the reproduction; if it is dependent on the number of copies sold, a yearly account must be rendered—GVR 23, 24;

(2) the author is entitled to a specified number of presentation copies, and to the right to purchase any copies which are at the publisher's disposal, at the lowest trade price—GVR 25, 26;

(3) the author is entitled to the return of the manuscript, if he expressly reserves such right before the beginning of the reproduction—GVR 27;

(4) the accidental destruction of the work after delivery to the publisher has the effect of releasing both parties from their contractual obligations, except that the publisher's obligation to pay the author's remuneration remains; the publisher may require the author to produce another similar work for a reasonable remuneration if this can be done without much trouble; if non-delivery is due to the publisher's *mora accipiendi*, the work is considered as delivered—GVR 33;

(5) the publisher may rescind the agreement, if the object for which the publication was intended can no longer be attained; in such a case the author remains entitled to his remuneration—GVR 18.

bb.   *As to reproduction and publication.*

The following rules apply in the absence of any stipulation to the contrary:

(1) the publisher must, as to the mode of reproduction and get-up, pay regard to the contents and purpose of the work, and the custom of publishers—GVR 14;

(2) the reproduction must be commenced immediately on the delivery of the work, or such part thereof, as is to be published as a separate volume, or

instalment—GVR 15;

(3) the publisher is responsible for the correction of the proofs, but must submit such proofs to the author for approval; if the author raises no objection to the proofs of any particular part within a reasonable period, he is deemed to have given his sanction to the publication of such part in the form shown by the proofs—GVR 20;   295

(4) the publisher is bound to produce as many copies of each edition as he is entitled to produce under the rules mentioned above (243); the fact that he is entitled to produce a new edition, does not make it incumbent upon him to do so, but the author may rescind the agreement, if the publisher refuses, or fails to bring out a new edition when requested to do so by the author—GVR 17;

(5) on the publication of a new edition of a collective work, the publisher, if acting in concurrence with the editor, is entitled to omit any individual contribution which was included in a former edition—GVR 19.

e.   Transfer of Publisher's Right.

246. The publisher's right, in the absence of any contractual prohibition, is transferable, and transmissible on death; in the event of a transfer *inter vivos* of the publisher's whole business, and of transmission on death, the author's consent is not required, [1] in all other cases in which the right is intended to be transferred, the author's assent is required, but it may not be withheld except on a cogent ground, and is deemed to be given, if its refusal is not declared within two months from the receipt of the publisher's request.

The performance of the publisher's duties as to reproduction and publication by his successor in title is deemed to be a proper performance of the agreement; if the successor, as between himself and the original publisher, agrees to undertake such duties, he and the original publisher are liable, jointly and severally, for such performance—GVR 28.

f.   Author's Right to Rescind.

247. The author may, at any time before the commencement of the reproduction

---

1   Under English law the benefit of a publishing agreement is not under any circumstances assignable without the author's consent—Hole *v.* Bradbury (1879) 12 Ch. D. 886; Griffith *v.* Tower Publishing Co. (1897) 1 Ch. 21.

of the work, rescind the agreement if any event happens which could not have been foreseen at the time of the formation of the agreement, and the foreknowledge of which would have induced the author upon a judicious consideration of the circumstances to abandon the projected publication. The publisher is, in such a case, entitled to the reimbursement of any outlay incurred in view of the agreement, and if the work is published by another publisher within a year from the date of the rescission, he is also entitled to damages for breach of the agreement, unless a renewed offer was made to him and refused before the new publishing agreement was entered into—GVR 35.

296

g. Effect of Author's Death, or impossibility of completion of Author's Work.

248. As the author's obligation is of a strictly personal kind, it is extinguished by his death—see 157 f. If part of the work has been delivered before the author's death, the publisher may, by a declaration communicated to the author's heirs, uphold the agreement as to the delivered part; but he forfeits this right if, on being required by the author's heirs to declare his intention as to its exercise within a specified reasonable period, he fails to do so. Similar results follow if the author, owing to any circumstance or event for which he is not responsible, is unable to complete the work—GVR 34.

h. Effect of Publisher's Bankruptcy.

249. In the event of the publisher's bankruptcy, the trustee in bankruptcy may at his option adopt or disclaim the agreement; if he adopts the agreement and assigns the publisher's rights thereunder to a transferee, such transferee becomes liable as between himself and the author, in respect of the publisher's obligations; the publisher's estate in bankruptcy is liable in the same way as if such estate were a surety for the transferee who had waived the *beneficium excussionis* (273).

If the reproduction of the work has not commenced on the institution of the bankruptcy proceedings the author may rescind the agreement—GVR 36.

i. Remedies of Parties in case of Breach of Agreement.

250. The rights of either party, on the breach of any contractual stipulation on the part of the other party, are somewhat more extensive than they would be under the general rules stated above—160, 161—as to reciprocal agreements—

GVR 30–32.

The effect of the rescission of the agreement [1] is the same as under the rules stated above—162, but where the rescission takes place by reason of a circumstance for which the other party is not responsible, the duty of such other party as to the return of anything received in pursuance of the agreement, is governed by the rules as to unjustified benefits, and is not, therefore, as strict as under the general rule.   If the work has been partly or wholly delivered at the   297 time when the right of rescission is exercised, it depends upon the circumstances of the case whether the agreement is partly upheld—GVR 37, 38.

j.   Special Rules as to Contributions to Newspapers and Periodicals.

251. The general rules are, in the case of contributions to newspapers and periodicals, modified in the following manner, unless a contrary intention is shown:

(1) the author preserves the free right of disposal over his contribution; where the exclusive right of reproduction and publication is expressly conferred on the publisher the author's right of disposal revives, in the case of a contribution to a newspaper immediately after the publication of the issue to which such contribution was made, and in the case of a contribution to any other periodical after a year from the end of the calendar year in which it was published;

(2) the rule stated above—243 rule (3)—as to the number of copies is not applicable;

(3) the publisher may make such alterations in a contribution which is to be published without the author's name as are usually made by publishers of newspapers and periodicals of the same kind;

(4) the author is not entitled to claim performance of the agreement to publish his contribution, or damages for non-performance, unless the exact point of time for the appearance of the contribution was fixed by the publisher; if the contribution is not published within a year from the date of the delivery, the author may rescind the agreement without prejudice to his right to remuneration;

(5) the author is not entitled to obtain copies at the lowest trade price, and in the case of a contribution to a newspaper, is not entitled to any presentation

---

1   The effect is the same, where a publishing agreement is rescinded on any ground, other than a breach of agreement (see for instance 248, 249).

copies—GVR 42–46.

6. Agreements relating to the Custody of Movable Things

a.   General Statement.

252. While the *depositum* of Roman law implied the gratuitous assumption of the custody of a thing, the *Verwahrungsvertrag* of the German law is an agreement for the custody of a movable thing, whether for reward or otherwise—BGB 688.

The promise of a reward is implied if under the circumstances of the case the gratuitous assumption of the custody of the thing in question cannot be expected (*e. g.* if furniture is deposited with a trader whose usual business consists in the keeping of furniture for reward)—BGB 689.

298

The rules as to the duties of the bailor and the bailee bear a certain resemblance to the duties of employers and employees in the case of agreements involving business transactions for the account of another (231), and may be summed up as follows:

(1) an ordinary bailee, if rewarded, is liable for wilful default and negligence; in the absence of any reward it is sufficient for him to apply the diligence usually applied to his own affairs; a warehouseman (*Lagerhalter*), *viz.* 'a person who in the usual course of his trade undertakes the storage and custody of goods', is responsible for their loss or deterioration, unless he can prove that such loss or deterioration could not have been avoided by the application of the diligence of a diligent mercantile trader; he is not bound to insure the goods unless specially instructed to do so; a bailee is liable for the default of his employees to the same extent as for his own default—BGB 690, 691; HGB 416, 417.

(2) a bailee, in the absence of express or implied authority, is not entitled to place a thing deposited with him into the custody of another; if authorized to hand over the bailed object to a third party, he is liable for any default in the course of such handing over but not otherwise—BGB 691;

(3) as regards deviation from instructions a bailee is in the same position—*mutatis mutandis*—as a person transacting business on behalf of another—231 rule (2)—BGB 692;

(4) a bailee is entitled to the reimbursement of any outlay incurred in respect of the bailed object—BGB 693; HGB 420 (1);

(5) a bailor must indemnify the bailee in respect of any damage arising through any defect in the bailed object, unless he can prove: (*a*) that he did not in fact know the perilous nature of the defect, and would not have discovered it by the application of proper diligence, or (*b*) that the bailee was informed of the circumstances or otherwise aware of them—BGB 694;

(6) a warehouseman must allow a bailor at any time during business hours, to have access to goods deposited with him, for the purpose of making inspection, obtaining samples, or taking measures for the preservation of the same— HGB 418;

(7) a bailor may at any time withdraw the bailed object, subject, however, to the bailee's lien in respect of his remuneration or disbursements—BGB 695;

299

(8) an ordinary bailee may at any time require the bailor to withdraw the bailed object, unless the object was deposited for a fixed period, in which event the withdrawal before the expiration of such period cannot be claimed except on a cogent ground (*e. g.* the perilous nature of the goods); a warehouseman cannot— except on a cogent ground—claim the withdrawal of goods deposited for an indefinite time, unless at least three months have elapsed from the date of the lodgment, and unless at least one month's previous notice has been given—BGB 696; HGB 422;

(9) on the termination of the bailment, the bailor must himself remove the goods; he is not entitled to have them taken to his residence or place of business— BGB 697;

(10) no rule is laid down as to the measure of the reward payable to an ordinary bailee [1]; a warehouseman, in the absence of a special agreement on the subject, is entitled to the remuneration usual in the particular locality—HGB 420; as to the time of payment, see BGB 699; HGB 420 (2);

(11) an ordinary bailee has a lien for his disbursements and his remuneration; a warehouseman has a right of pledge (393)—HGB 421;

(12) the claims of a warehouseman are subject to the same short period of prescription as the claims of a forwarding agent (240)—HGB 423.

b.   Bailment in the nature of a Loan (*depositum irregulare*).

253. If fungibles are entrusted to the care of another without any special

---

[1]   In the absence of any agreement on the subject the rules as to a discretionary mode of performance— 144 sub (6)—have to be applied.

arrangement, the property in the bailed objects remains in the bailor, and the identical objects must be returned to him; if, on the other hand, a special arrangement is made to the effect that the ownership of the bailed objects is to pass to the bailee, and that the duty to return such objects will be sufficiently discharged by the return of similar things of the same quality and quantity, the rules as to loans of fungibles (220) are applicable; where the arrangement is 300 made while the fungibles are in the bailee's custody the transaction is treated as a loan, as from the time at which the bailee acquires the ownership of the bailed objects.   In any case the time and place of the return are, in the absence of any stipulation to the contrary, determined by the rules as to agreements for the custody of movables—BGB 700 (1).

The authorization enabling the bailee to appropriate the deposited fungibles may, as a general rule, be express or implied, but where negotiable instruments are deposited it is inoperative, unless made by express words; where shares or debentures are deposited by any person who does not carry on the business of a banker or money-changer, the authorization is invalid unless given by a written document specially referring to the particular transaction—BGB 700 (2); Imperial Statute of 1896 relating to the custody of negotiable instruments, s. 2 (1).

The most common example of a bailment in the nature of a loan occurs in the case of a 'banker's deposit'; the lending of stocks and shares in such manner that the borrower acquires the property, and has only to return stocks and shares of the same description and quantity, is a familiar Stock Exchange transaction, and metals and other goods having the nature of fungibles are also frequently lent on similar terms.

A transaction occupying an intermediate position between a bailment in the proper sense of the word and a loan of fungibles, occurs where a bailor authorizes a warehouseman with whom he stores fungibles to mix his goods with others of the same kind and quality belonging to other bailors.   Such an authority has the effect of transferring the ownership to the several bailors by whom respectively such an authority was given as tenants in common, in the proportions in which they have contributed to the total quantity of the goods, the warehouseman being authorized to deliver to each depositor a quantity proportionate to his share, without requiring the assent of the other depositors—HGB 419.

c.   Special Rules as to the bailment of Shares and Debentures.

254. Under the Imperial Statute of 1896 referred to above—253, any mercantile trader, who in the course of his business receives for safe custody, or 301 by way of security, debentures or shares issued to bearer or passing by indorsement, or other negotiable instruments of the same kind having the nature of fungibles, is bound to conform to the following rules:

(1) he must keep the instruments belonging to each depositor separately from those belonging to himself or to other depositors, and in such manner that each depositor's name is shown on the outside of each separate bundle;

(2) he must keep a special book in which all the details relating to the securities belonging to each depositor are separately recorded;

(3) he must give notice to any third party with whom the documents are deposited in his name that they are not his property (*ibid.* ss. 1, 8).

A mercantile trader who disregards any of these rules is in certain specified events subject to criminal punishment (*ibid.* s. 10).

d.   Comparison with English Law.

255. Under German law, as shown above, an unrewarded bailee has to bestow the amount of diligence which he is accustomed to give to his own affairs, but in any case he is liable for gross negligence.

In effect, this rule corresponds exactly with the rule of English law on the same subject (see the notes to Coggs *v.* Bernard 1 Sm. L. C. 11th ed. p. 173, and see the observations of Pollock C. B. in Beal *v.* South Devon Railway Company 3 H. & C. 337).

The question whether, for the purpose of making the bailee subject to a more stringent liability, it is necessary that a reward *ad hoc* should be stipulated for in respect of the custody of the bailed object, or whether it is sufficient that the bailment should occur in the course of transactions which, taken together, are a source of profit to the bailee (*e. g.* whether a banker who, in accordance with the ordinary custom of bankers, receives securities or valuables from a customer without making a special charge is subject to the liabilities of a rewarded bailee), is as undecided in German as it is in English law (see Giblin *v.* McMullen L. R. 2 P. C. 317; *re* United Service Company L. R. 6 Ch. 212).

CHAPTER IV
PARTNERSHIP AGREEMENTS

1. General Statement

256. A PARTNERSHIP agreement is an agreement by which two or more persons who are called the partners become mutually bound to further a common object in an agreed manner, and more particularly to furnish the agreed contributions— BGB 705.

The general characteristics of the several kinds of partnership recognized by German law, their nature as legal entities, and their relations to the outside world have already been discussed—65 to 70—as also has the nature of the liability of the partners as against partnership creditors—182 sub (2).

The relation of partners *inter se* are primarily governed by the partnership agreement, and the general legal rules are only applicable in the absence of special contractual stipulations on the points which they affect. [1]

A partnership agreement is not required to be in writing or subject to any other formal requirements; a disregard of the rules as to registration applicable in the case of mercantile partnership—see 68 sub (5)—does not prevent the formation of such a partnership, while, on the other hand, compliance with the rules, though creating an estoppel as between a person registered as a partner and third parties, does not necessarily bind the partners *inter se*.

Illustration: *A* in order to enable *B* to obtain credit makes an agreement with him, that the formation of a mercantile partnership between *A* and *B* is to be registered, but that as between *A* and *B* the business is to belong to *B* exclusively; *A* in such a case is liable as a partner as against third parties, but as between *A* and *B* there is no partnership.

---

[1]   As regards the rules contained in the HGB this is expressly provided by HGB 109; as regards the rules contained in the BGB it is generally indicated by the context.

The rules stated below apply to mercantile partnerships as well as to others except where the context shows that a particular kind of partnership is referred to.

2. PARTNERS' CONTRIBUTIONS

257. In the absence of any stipulation to the contrary the following rules apply: 303

(1) the contributions of the several partners must be equal in value; they may consist of services or of money, or other objects; where fungibles or consumable things are to be contributed it is presumed that the partners are intended to be co-owners [1] (325); where things of another kind are to be contributed the same presumption exists, if the contribution is to be made on the basis of a valuation, which is not exclusively intended for the purpose of fixing the proportions of the profits—BGB 706;

(2) a partner cannot be compelled to make any contributions beyond the contribution originally agreed upon, except where a deficiency arises on the dissolution of the partnership—BGB 707, 735;

(3) the partnership property includes the partners' contributions, and all objects acquired by virtue of any right forming part of the partnership property; a third party is not affected by the fact that any claim against him belongs to the partnership, unless he is aware of such fact—BGB 706, 718, 720.

3. CONDUCT OF PARTNERSHIP BUSINESS

258. The following rules apply in the absence of any stipulation to the contrary:

(1) in a non-mercantile partnership no act can be done without the unanimous assent of all the partners—BGB 709 (1); in a mercantile partnership, any act not belonging to the ordinary conduct of the partnership business, including the conferment of a power of procuration (118), requires such unanimous assent; a partner can act alone in respect of the conferment of a power of procuration, if there is danger in delay—HGB 115, 116, 119;

(2) in a mercantile partnership each authorized partner, [2] other than a commandite partner, has power to transact the ordinary partnership business, and   304

---

[1]   In the case of a non-mercantile partnership, the partnership property belongs to the partners as co-owners; a mercantile partnership can own property as a separate entity.

[2]   If the agreement provides that the partners must act together, a partner may nevertheless act alone, if there is danger in delay—HGB 115 (2).

is bound to give his services to it—HGB 114 (1);

(3) a commandite partner has no power to transact any business for the partnership, or to veto any act intended to be done by an ordinary partner, unless such act is outside the scope of the ordinary business of the partnership— HGB 164;

(4) where by the partnership agreement power to transact the partnership business is conferred on one partner or on several partners exclusively, the other partner or partners are not authorized to transact such business [1]—BGB 710; HGB 114 (2);

(5) where any authorized partner requests another authorized partner to abstain from any particular transaction, such request must be complied with—BGB 711; HGB 115 (1);

(6) where according to the partnership agreement a majority of the partners is required for the purpose of sanctioning any transaction, each partner is presumed to have one vote—BGB 709 (2);

(7) the absence of authority to transact the partnership business does not deprive a partner of the right to receive information as to the affairs of the partnership and to inspect the books, unless such right is excluded by the partnership agreement; even where the right is excluded, it may be exercised if there is any ground for assuming any dishonesty in the conduct of the partnership business— BGB 716; HGB 118;

(8) the power of any partner to transact the business of a non-mercantile partnership may be withdrawn by the other partners on any cogent ground, more particularly in the event of any breach of duty on the part of such partner or of his becoming incapable to properly conduct business; the partners must be unanimous in such a case unless the partnership agreement provides otherwise—BGB 712 (1); the power of a partner to transact the business of a mercantile partnership may on the same grounds be withdrawn by an order of a competent court made on the unanimous application of the other partners—HGB 117;

(9) if a partnership is dissolved otherwise than by notice (e. g. by the death
305   or bankruptcy of a partner) an authorized partner may continue to transact partnership business until he becomes (or by the application of proper diligence would have become) aware of the dissolution of the partnership—BGB 728; HGB 136.

---

1   As to the effect of such restriction on third parties, see 68.

Rule (3), according to which a commandite partner is not entitled to transact any business for the partnership, may, like all other rules enumerated under this head, be excluded by agreement between the partners; a commandite partner may therefore be authorized to transact partnership business without becoming a full partner; under the law of some of the American States which recognize commandite partnership under the name of ' special partnership ', a special partner who interferes in the partnership business thereby becomes liable as a full partner (see New York Partnership Law 1897, s. 37).

4. DUTIES OF PARTNERS *INTER SE*

259. The following rules apply in the absence of any stipulation to the contrary:

(1) a partner must in the performance of his duties bestow the same degree of diligence which he is accustomed to bestow on his own affairs—BGB 708;

(2) a partner authorized to transact partnership business is, as between himself and the other partners, entitled to the same rights and subject to the same duties as an employee under an agreement involving the transaction of business for another (231)—BGB 713;

(3) a partner in a mercantile partnership is entitled to be indemnified in respect of any outlay incurred on behalf of the partnership which, under the circumstances, he was entitled to consider necessary, with interest as from the date of the outlay, and also for any loss suffered in connexion with the conduct of the partnership business—HGB 110;

(4) a partner in a mercantile partnership who fails to pay at the proper time his contribution to the partnership capital, or any moneys received for the partnership, or who without authority withdraws any funds from the partnership, must pay interest as from the day on which the funds in question ought to have been paid in or were withdrawn—HGB 111;

(5) a partner in a mercantile partnership is not entitled, without the consent of the other partners, to transact for his own account any business of the kind usually transacted by the partnership, or to become a full partner in any other partnership which transacts such business; in the event of a breach of this duty by any partner, the other partners may expel him from the partnership and may also claim full compensation, or the transfer of all rights arising out of the unauthorized transaction—HGB 112, 113.

306

5. DIVISION OF PROFITS

260. The following rules apply in the absence of any stipulation to the contrary:

(1) the accounts of a non-mercantile partnership entered upon for a temporary object, must be made up and the profits and losses apportioned between the partners on the termination of the partnership—BGB 721 (1);

(2) the accounts of any other partnership must be made up, and the profits and losses apportioned between the partners at the end of each business year [1]— BGB 721 (2); HGB 120 (1);

(3) the profits and losses of a non-mercantile partnership are divided equally between the partners, whatever their contributions to the capital may be; where the agreement determines the shares of the partners in the profits, and is silent as to the division of the losses, the losses are divided in the same way as the profits—BGB 722;

(4) in a mercantile partnership, not being a commandite partnership, each partner is entitled to interest on his contribution to the partnership capital at the rate of four per cent.; if the profits are not sufficient for the payment of four per cent. , the rate of interest is reduced accordingly; the balance (if any) remaining after payment of interest is divided between the partners in equal shares; if there is a loss such loss is shared by the partners in equal shares—HGB 121;

(5) the sum due to each partner for interest and profit is credited to him on 307 capital account, and the sum drawn by him during the year is debited to the same account; each partner may in each year draw an amount equal to four per cent. on the sum standing to his credit on capital account at the beginning of the year; he may also draw the amount credited to him for the profit of the preceding year if practicable without obvious injury to the partnership business—HGB 120 (2), 122. (As to the division of profits in a commandite partnership, see HGB 167–169.)

---

[1]   In the case of a mercantile partnership, the partners are bound to conform to the general rule requiring mercantile traders to make up yearly balance sheets—whatever the provisions of the partnership agreement may determine—HGB 39.

6. Rules as to Assignment of Partner's Share in Partnership Assets

261. A partner cannot validly assign his share in the partnership assets, [1] or any claim against the other partners arising under the partnership agreement; he may, however, validly assign any of the following kinds of claims:

(1) any claim against the partnership which arises in the course of the management of the partnership business, and of which he may demand satisfaction before the winding-up of the partnership (*e. g.* a claim to reimbursement of outlay);

(2) the claim to his share in the ascertained profits;

(3) the claim to his share in the surplus assets remaining on the winding-up of the partnership—BGB 717, 719 (2).

7.   Effect of Death or Bankruptcy of a Partner

a.   Effect of a Partner's Death.

262. The death of a partner terminates the partnership unless the agreement provides otherwise—BGB 727 (1).   Where the rule applies and a partner's death occurs, the heirs of the deceased partner must immediately give notice to the other partners; if there is danger in delay they must continue the part of the management which was entrusted to the deceased, until new arrangements as to the conduct of the business can be made by the surviving partner; (see the corresponding provision in the case of agreements involving the transaction of business for another (231) rule (9)); the surviving partners must in such a case, pending such new arrangements, continue their part of the management, the partnership being deemed to remain in existence in the meantime—BGB 727 (2); HGB 131, 137 (1).   308

b.   Effect of a Partner's Bankruptcy.

The bankruptcy of a partner terminates the partnership.   Where a partner becomes a bankrupt the partnership business must be continued until new arrangements can be made, and in the meantime the partnership is deemed to

---

[1]   A person owing a debt to the partnership is not entitled to set off a claim against a partner—BGB 719 (2).

remain in existence—BGB 728; HGB 137 (2).

c.   Continuation of Partnership between other Partners.

If, in accordance with the partnership agreement, the partnership is, on the death or bankruptcy of a partner, to be continued between the other partners, the rules stated below (263) as applicable in the event of the retirement of a partner are applied *mutatis mutandis* [1]—BGB 736; HGB 138.

d.   Continuation of Partnership with Heirs of Deceased Partner.

If under the partnership agreement the partnership after the death of a partner is to be continued with his heirs, no change occurs except that the place of the deceased partner is taken by his heirs.   Where the deceased in any such case was a partner in a mercantile partnership, each of his heirs may require to be admitted as a 'commandite' partner; if the other partners refuse to comply with such request he may retire from the partnership without previous notice [2]—HGB 139.

8.   Retirement of a Partner

263. If the partnership agreement provides that, on the retirement of a partner, the partnership shall continue between the other partners, a retiring partner is, in the absence of any stipulation to the contrary, entitled to the following rights and subject to the following liabilities:

(1) his share in the partnership assets becomes vested in the other partners;

(2) he is entitled:

(*a*) to the return of all objects lent by him to the partnership;

(*b*) to the payment of such sum as would have been payable to him if the partnership had been wound up on his retirement;

(*c*) to be released from his liability for matured partnership debts, and to be indemnified and secured in respect of his liability for debts which may mature

---

1   In the case of the bankruptcy of a partner in a mercantile partnership, the same rules are applied if the other partners decide to continue the partnership among themselves, though the agreement has no provision to that effect; in the event of the bankruptcy of one of two partners the other partner may continue the partnership business—HGB 141 (2), 142 (2).

2   The heir's rights in this respect cannot be modified by the partnership agreement, except in so far as it may be agreed that in the event of an heir becoming a commandite partner, his share in the profits is to be reduced—HGB 139 (5).

after his retirement;

(3) if the partnership assets, at the time of his retirement, are insufficient for the payment of all the partnership debts and the repayment of the partners' contributions, he must pay his share of the deficiency;

(4) he is entitled to his share of the profit, and bound to bear his share in the loss arising from any transactions not finally closed at the time of his retirement, but cannot interfere in the management of such transactions; he is, however, entitled at the end of each year to receive an account of the transactions closed during the year, and the payment of his share in the profit on such transactions, as well as a report on those which are still pending—BGB 736, 738–740; HGB 138. [1]

9. REMOVAL OF A PARTNER

264. The removal of a partner in a mercantile partnership may be brought about in one of the following ways:

(1) in any event in which the dissolution of the partnership may be ordered by the Court on the ground of the misconduct of any partner or some other similar ground—see 68 sub (7)—the Court may, at the request of the other partners, instead of directing such dissolution, order the removal of such partner from the partnership. In such a case the same rules are applied as in the event of the continuance of a partnership after the retirement of a partner (263), the date of the institution of the judicial proceedings being deemed the date of the retirement—HGB 140;

310

(2) in the event of a judgment creditor of one of the partners giving notice to dissolve the partnership, in accordance with the provisions enabling him to do so in certain specified events, the other partners may declare that they will continue the partnership among themselves; the same rules are then applied as if the partner whose creditor gave the notice had retired from the partnership at the end of the business year during which the notice was given, and the partnership had been continued by the other partners—HGB 141 (1). [2]

---

[1] The results are analogous if a mercantile partnership agreement provides that on the death, retirement, or bankruptcy of one of two partners, the other is to take over the partnership business, or if one of two partners elects to take over the business on the bankruptcy of the other, in a case where the agreement is silent on the subject—HGB 142.

[2] If a partner is removed, and only one partner remains, such other partner may take over the partnership business; where the removal is ordered by the Court, this can only be done, in so far as the order contains a direction to that effect—HGB 142.

CHAPTER V
ALEATORY AGREEMENTS

1. GENERAL STATEMENT

311   **265.** THE expression ' aleatory agreement' is used to designate an agreement in the performance of which chance is intended to play an essential, though not necessarily the only, part. The circumstance that chance, as a matter of fact, affects the result of an agreement, does not give an aleatory character to a transaction. A betting transaction is not necessarily of an aleatory character, more especially if the bet refers to an existing fact, as to which each party backs his own opinion. Under Roman law a betting agreement was therefore deemed legitimate and enforceable by action (see Dig. 19. 5. 17. 5), while gaming transactions were, as a general rule, deemed void. This distinction was maintained in the German common law, and also to a limited extent in the Prussian Code (see ALR I, 11 § 579). Under English law the prohibition of gaming as well as of wagering transactions was introduced by statute; both kinds of transactions were valid at common law and no distinction was drawn between them.

    The new German law abolishes the distinction between gaming and wagering agreements, and declares that no obligation can be created by gaming or betting, but that nothing actually handed over to the winner can be recovered on the ground of the payment having been made without just cause. Special rules apply to insurance agreements and annuity agreements and to time bargains in stocks and produce—see 266–270.

    A promise made to the winner of a bet, to pay its amount to a third party is invalid, but the holder of a bill of exchange or promissory note issued to another in satisfaction of a gaming or wagering debt, has all the rights of a holder in due course, notwithstanding the fact that he is aware of the nature of the consideration for which the bill was issued—R. O. H. vol. 10, p. 387.

312   Agreements between the issuers and takers of lottery tickets are valid, if the lottery is sanctioned by the government of the State in which it is carried out—

BGB 763.

Under English law the amount of a gaming or wagering loss cannot be recovered after payment owing to the operation of the rule, ' *in pari delicto potior est conditio defendentis* '.   As to negotiable instruments issued in payment of a wagering debt, a distinction is drawn between wagers treated as ' illegal ' by virtue of 5 & 6 Will. IV c. 41, and wagers which are merely void under 8 & 9 Vict. c. 109.   The holder of a negotiable instrument issued in payment of a wager of the former kind has no claim unless he can prove that he gave value and was ignorant of the nature of the consideration for which the bill was issued.   The holder of an instrument of the latter kind is presumed to have given value, and the fact that he knew the bill to have been issued in payment of a wager does not affect his right—Bill of Exchange Act 1882, s. 30; Fitch *v.* Jones 5 E. & B. 245.   Lotteries are prohibited by statute.

2.   INSURANCE AGREEMENTS

a.   Generally.

266. An insurance agreement is an agreement by which the insurer, in consideration of a single payment or a series of periodical payments, undertakes the payment of a fixed sum on the happening of an event as to which it depends on chance either whether or when it will happen.   In no known system of law is an insurance agreement considered invalid by reason of its aleatory character if the insured has a so-called ' insurable interest ' which requires protection against the event to which the insurance relates; in other words, if the intention of the agreement is to reduce a loss which the insured expects to suffer in the event against which he insures himself. [1]

b.   Present state of German Insurance Law.

267. In Germany the law as to any kind of insurance other than marine insurance, in so far as it concerns the relations between insurer and insured, is at the present moment still governed by State law. [2]   The rules of public law as to   313

---

[1]   The fact that the insured must have an insurable interest, does not necessarily mean that the agreement must be an agreement ' of indemnity ' —as is the case with some kinds of insurance agreements. In the case of life insurance the insured sum may be entirely out of proportion to the pecuniary loss caused by the termination of the insured life.

[2]   The draft of an Imperial Statute on the subject is now (May, 1906) before the Reichstag.

the conduct of insurance business are governed by the Private Insurance Act of
1901—see 52, 58, 63—under which all insurance business is subject to
government permission and government control, and by virtue of which the
business of life insurance and insurance against accidents, employers' liability,
fire and hail, cannot lawfully be carried on in Germany by any person or association
of persons not incorporated as a share company or constituted as a mutual society
in the prescribed manner.

c.   German Rules as to Marine Insurance.

268. The rules of private law as to marine insurance contained in HGB 778–
905 are too complicated to be stated or even summarized in this treatise, but the
following statement deals with some of the more important matters:

(1) any interest in the safety of a ship or of a ship's cargo from the perils of
maritime navigation which can be estimated in money (excluding the claims of
the master or crew for pay or wages) can be the subject of marine insurance—
HGB 778–780;

(2) a marine insurance agreement may be made for the benefit of a third
party, who may be either named or unnamed (insurance for ' whom it may
concern '); the person who insures, whether insuring for his own account or for the
account of a third party, is called 'the insurance taker' (*Versicherungsnehmer*),
while a third party for whose account an insurance is taken is called ' the
insured' (*der Versicherte*)—HGB 781–783 [1];

(3) a marine insurance agreement is not required to be in writing or in any
particular form, but the insurer is compelled at the request of the insurance taker
to hand him a written statement called a policy (*Police*) setting forth the terms of
the agreement—HGB 784;

(4) a marine insurance agreement is not void on the ground that at the time
of its formation the possibility of loss was already excluded, or that the loss
against which the insurance was intended to provide had already happened,
unless such fact was known to both parties at the time of the formation of the
agreement; if one of the parties was aware of the fact, the agreement is not binding on the party to whom it was unknown; thus, if the insured was aware of the
loss, the insurer is entitled to the premium, notwithstanding the fact that he is not

---

[1]   Insurance by an independent party for account of a third party must be distinguished from insurance
by means of an agent.   In the former case the insured is not a party to the agreement; see HGB 783.

bound by the agreement—HGB 785;

(5) a marine insurance agreement is inoperative in so far as the amount of the insurance exceeds the value of the insured object; the parties may agree beforehand as to the proper insurance value of the insured object, in which case the policy is called a ' valued policy' (*taxirte Police*) , but even in such a case the insurer may obtain an order reducing the amount of the valuation if he can prove that it is excessive—HGB 786, 792, 793 [1] ;

(6) an insurance agreement does not bind the insurer, if the insurance taker fails to disclose, or makes a false statement as to, any material fact, unless the undisclosed fact was known to the insurer at the time of the formation of the agreement—HGB 806 [2] ;

(7) if the venture in respect of which the insurance was effected is totally or partially abandoned, or if the insured object or part thereof does not become exposed to the risk covered by the insurance, or if part of the insurance becomes inoperative by reason of over-insurance effected in good faith, the insured becomes entitled to the return of the premiums, or of a proportionate part thereof, subject to a deduction called ' *Ristornogebühr*' [3] —HGB 894 (1) , 895–897. [4]

---

[1]   These provisions secure the character of a marine policy as an ' agreement of indemnity' ; as to the apportionment of claims between several insurers, and as to the effect of several insurances taken out successively, see HGB 787–791; as to the assessment of the proper insurance value, see HGB 794–803.

[2]   The knowledge of an agent is deemed the principal's knowledge in all cases.   In the case of an agreement for account of a third party the knowledge of such third party or of an intermediary is deemed to be the knowledge of the insurance taker, unless the undisclosed fact became known to the party concerned at such a late stage, that he could not, without using unusual means of communication, have informed the insurance taker; if the concealment concerns only a part of the insured objects, the agreement operates as regards the other parts.   The full premium is payable in any event—HGB 807–811.   Concealment of a fact known to an agent or intermediary is material only in so far as the agent or intermediary was concerned in the particular transaction; in this respect German law is substantially the same as English law—see Blackburn *v.* Vigors 12 A. C. 531; Blackburn *v.* Haslam 21 Q. B. D. 144; Wilson *v.* Salamander Insurance Co. 88 L. T. 96.

[3]   As to the amount of the ' *Ristornogebühr*' see HGB 894 (2).

[4]   Detailed rules as to the payment of the premiums and the duties of the insurance taker and insured as to giving information as to the name of the ship in which the insured goods are shipped, and as to any mishap as to salvage, &c. , are contained in HGB 812–819; as to the nature and duration of the risks against which the insurance is available (including the provisions as to particular average, contributions to general average, time policies, &c.) in HGB 820–853; as to the circumstances, under which compensation for a total loss has to be paid and the events in which a declaration of abandonment may be made, and as to the method of assessing the damages in HGB 854–881; as to the mode of payment of the compensation in HGB 882–893; as to the effect of the insolvency of the insurer in HGB 898; as to the effect of the alienation of the insured object during the continuance of the insurance in HGB 899–900; and as to prescription in HGB 901–905.

3. ANNUITY AGREEMENTS

315   **269.** An agreement to pay money, or to do any other acts for the benefit of another at regular intervals during an indefinite period of time, is called '*Leibrentenvertrag*'. For the sake of brevity this expression is here translated 'annuity agreement'; though according to English usage the term 'annuity' is only applied to periodical payments of money.

An annuity agreement, in the absence of a conflicting statutory or contractual provision applicable in the particular case, must be made in writing—BGB 761, and is subject to the following rules:

(1) the annuity must be paid during the life of the annuitant;

(2) the stipulated amount is the amount payable in each year;

(3) each instalment must be paid in advance; money payments must be paid by quarterly instalments; where the annuity agreement stipulates for acts other than the payment of money, the instalments are determined by the nature and object of the acts;

(4) the whole of an instalment belongs to the annuitant if he was alive at the beginning of the period for which it was paid; (under English law the same rule is applied in a case in which the annuity is payable in advance—Trevalion *v.* Anderton 66 L. J. ; Q. B. 230; on appeal, *ibid.* 489)—BGB 759, 760, 761.

4. TIME BARGAINS IN STOCKS AND PRODUCE

    270. Where a time bargain in stocks and produce is made with the intention on both sides that no delivery shall take place, but that the difference between the agreed sale price and the market price at the time fixed for performance shall be paid by the vendor to the buyer in the event of the market price being higher than the sale price and *vice versa*, the transaction is clearly a wagering transaction, and it is void as such both under English and under German law. If, however, it is the intention of one of the parties that the agreement shall be carried out

316 literally, while the other party intends to turn it into a bargain for the payment of the difference between the market price and the sale price, the bargain is enforceable under English law, whether such intention was known to the first-mentioned party or otherwise (Thacker *v.* Hardy 4 Q. B. D. 685; Forget *v.* Ostigny (1895) A. C. 318). Under German law—BGB 764—on the other hand, a time bargain in stocks or produce entered upon by one of the parties thereto, with the intention

that it should ultimately result in the mere payment of a difference, is void if the other party is aware, or by the exercise of proper diligence would have become aware, of such intention, unless it comes within the exception created by s. 69 of the Bourse Law of 1896.

Under the above-quoted section the validity of a time bargain entered upon in accordance with the rules of any of the public exchanges cannot be questioned by a party thereto who is registered in the Bourse Register for the branch of business to which the particular bargain belongs.   Transactions between registered speculators are therefore valid, notwithstanding the fact that there was no intention of actual delivery on either side.   If one of the parties is not registered while the other is registered, the unregistered party can claim his profit if he wins, without having to pay his loss if he loses.   The law on the subject will probably be amended within a short time.

CHAPTER VI
AGREEMENTS OF SURETYSHIP

1. General Statement

271. An agreement of suretyship or guarantee (*Bürgschaft*) is defined as an agreement 'by which the surety (*Bürge*) binds himself to the creditor of a third party to answer for the performance of the obligation of such third party'. It may refer to a future or contingent obligation as well as to a present unconditional obligation—BGB 765.

A person who requests another to give credit to a third party is liable as surety for such third party to the extent of the credit given in accordance with such request; this form of suretyship, which is called *Creditauftrag* (*mandatum crediti*) is distinguishable in some ways from an ordinary guarantee; an ordinary guarantee is invalid unless the surety has bound himself in writing, or, being a mercantile trader in the full sense of the word (36), has given the guarantee in the course of a transaction which on his side is a mercantile transaction[1]; an instruction to give credit, on the other hand, imposes the liability of a surety on the person giving the instruction, though it was not given in writing[2]—BGB 766, 778; HGB 350, 351.

---

[1] If the surety satisfies the obligation incurred by an informal agreement, the agreement is treated as valid, with the result that the surety cannot recover such payment as an 'indebitum' (298), as he might have done, if the agreement had been invalid for all purposes—BGB 760.

[2] An instruction to give credit in the above-mentioned manner differs in its effects from a mere undertaking to pay for work done for another or for goods supplied to another, because such an undertaking is binding, even if the person for whom the work is done, or to whom the goods are supplied, does not become liable as principal debtor. Undertakings of the latter kind are, under English law, distinguished from guarantees, and do not therefore come within s. 4 of the Statute of Frauds (see Lakeman *v.* Mountstephen L. R. 7 H. L. 17), but an instruction to give credit to another on the understanding that the person to whom credit is to be given is to be the principal debtor, and the person who gives the instruction is to be liable as surety, would under English law come under the rules relating to guarantees, and would therefore be required to be in writing.

2.   EXTENT OF SURETY'S LIABILITY

272. The surety is liable to the same extent as the principal debtor, even in   318
so far as the liability of the latter is increased by reason of his default or *mora*
(252); the surety is not, however, liable in respect of such changes in the
principal debtor's liability as are brought about by any act-in-the-law done by the
principal debtor after the date of the guarantee—BGB 767 (1).

Illustration: If the surety guarantees that the principal debtor will return a
picture lent to him, and the picture is destroyed by fire without any default on the
part of the principal debtor, the surety is not liable if the principal debtor is not
in *mora solvendi* as to the return of the picture.   If he is in *mora solvendi*, and
consequently liable for accidental loss, the surety is equally liable.   If the time
for the return of the picture was extended after the date of the guarantee by agreement
between the principal debtor and the creditor, and the picture was destroyed
during such extended period, the surety is not in any event liable for the loss.

A surety is liable for the costs of enforcing the guaranteed claim against the
principal debtor—BGB 767 (2).

The rules stated above are, of course, applicable in so far only as the surety
has not limited his liability to an aliquot part of the guaranteed debt, or to a fixed
maximum amount.   They are also modified in the event of a continuous
guarantee being given to secure a fixed maximum amount of indebtedness.

3.   DEFENCES OPEN TO SURETY

273. The surety may avail himself of any defences and rights of avoidance
and of set-off to which the principal debtor is entitled as between himself and the
creditor [1]—BGB 768, 770.

In a case not coming under the exceptional rules stated below, a surety may
also avail himself of the *beneficium excussionis* (*Einrede der Vorausklage*), by
virtue of which he may require the creditor to prove that he has obtained a
judgment against the principal debtor, and that his attempt to enforce such
judgment was unsuccessful—BGB 771.

---

[1]   He may avail himself of a defence to which the principal debtor was originally entitled but which
was waived by him.   If the principal debtor is dead, the surety is not entitled to derive any advantage from
the fact that his heirs are liable to a limited extent only (533)—BGB 768.

319   The *beneficium excussionis*, a survival from Roman law, which has never penetrated into English law, is excluded in any of the following events:

(1) if the surety is a mercantile trader in the full sense of the word (36) and the guarantee was a mercantile transaction on his part—HGB 349, 351;

(2) if the surety has expressly waived the *beneficium excussionis*, or agreed to be liable as 'principal debtor' (*Selbstschuldner*)—BGB 773 (1), Nr. 1;

(3) if the difficulty of taking judicial proceedings against the principal debtor is materially increased by the fact that, since the date of the guarantee, he has removed his domicile, his business establishment, or his place of residence— BGB 773 (1), Nr. 2;

(4) if bankruptcy proceedings have been instituted against the principal debtor, or if it may be assumed from the circumstances that the enforcement of a judgment against him would not result in the discharge of the guaranteed debt, it being at the same time impossible to obtain satisfaction by the sale of any movable thing pledged to the creditor or subject to his right of lien—BGB 773 (1), Nrs. 3 and 4, 773 (2).

4. REMEDIES OF SURETY AGAINST PRINCIPAL DEBTOR

a. Right to obtain Release from Guarantee.

274. A person who becomes a surety at the principal debtor's request, or who has volunteered his suretyship under circumstances which, under the rules as to voluntary services (301), place him in the position of a mandatary (232), may require the principal debtor to procure his release from the suretyship in any of the following events:

(1) if a material deterioration of the principal debtor's financial position has taken place;

(2) if the difficulty of taking judicial proceedings against the principal debtor has been materially increased after the date of the guarantee by a change, of his domicile, place of business, or residence;

(3) if the principal debtor is in *mora solvendi* (152) in respect of the obligation guaranteed by the surety;

320   (4) if the creditor has obtained a final judgment against the surety for the performance of the guaranteed obligation.

Where the principal debtor's obligation has not as yet matured, the principal debtor may, instead of procuring the release, give security (87)—BGB 775.

b. Surety's Right of Subrogation.

In so far as the surety satisfies the creditor, the claim against the principal debtor, with all securities held by the creditor in respect thereof, becomes vested in the surety, *ipso facto*.   The surety is not entitled to use any right so becoming vested in him to the creditor's detriment—BGB 401, 774 (1).

Illustration: The creditor's claim is for £ 300, of which £ 200 are guaranteed; he also has a right of pledge on goods belonging to the principal debtor.   The surety pays the £ 200, and therefore the debt, to the extent of £ 200, becomes vested in him, and he also becomes entitled to a right of pledge over the goods, by way of security for his claim for £ 200.   As he must not use his rights to the creditor's detriment, he must allow the creditor to occupy the position which he would have occupied if the principal debtor had paid off the £ 200.   As this would not be the case if he claimed to rank *pari passu* with the creditor in respect of his right of pledge, his charge for £ 200 is postponed to the creditor's right of pledge for the remaining £ 100.

5. REMEDIES OF SURETY AGAINST CO-SURETIES

275. All persons who guarantee the performance of the same obligation are deemed co-sureties (*Mitbürgen*) whether any privity exists between them or not; the co-sureties are liable as joint debtors (182)—BGB 769.

The mutual rights of co-sureties are regulated by the general rules relating to the mutual rights of joint debtors—182 sub (4)—BGB 774 (2); they are less favourable to a co-surety who pays off the guaranteed debt than the corresponding rules of English law. [1]

---

[1]   Under German law a co-surety cannot proceed against the other co-sureties before he has satisfied the debt; under English law he can assert his claim for contribution as soon as the creditor has obtained judgment against him.   Under German law a creditor cannot in the first instance claim more from any individual co-surety than his share of the contribution, but if he cannot obtain payment in full from any particular co-surety, he can claim a share of the deficiency from each of the other co-sureties; under English law the full amount of the contribution may be claimed from each co-surety, provided that the claimant does not ultimately retain more than the amount due to him—see Mere. Law Am. Act 1856, s. 5; Wolmershausen *v.* Gullick (1893) 2 Ch. 514; in *re* Parker (1894) 3 Ch. 400.

6. DISCHARGE OF SURETY

a. Where the Guarantee is given for a Definite Time.

321   **276.** A surety who is entitled to the *beneficium excussionis* (273) becomes discharged, unless the creditor immediately on the termination of the period for which the guarantee is given, takes proceedings against the principal debtor, and immediately on the termination of such proceedings, informs the surety that he will assert his rights against him.

A surety who is not entitled to the *beneficium excussionis* is discharged on the termination of the period for which the guarantee is given, unless the creditor immediately on the expiration informs him, that he will assert his rights against him—BGB 777 (1).

b. Discharge brought about by Creditor's default.

If the creditor abandons a right of priority, or a charge, or a right of pledge, or a right against a co-surety serving as collateral security for the guaranteed debt, the surety is discharged to the extent of the benefit which he would have derived from the abandoned right, if it had not been abandoned [1]—BGB 776.

c. Discharge by Notice or Death.

The rule of English law under which a continuing guarantee entered upon for an indefinite time may, as to future transactions, be terminated at any time, unless the contrary is expressly stipulated (*re* Crace (1902) 1 Ch. 733), though not expressly laid down by any definite rule, would probably be upheld under German law, subject to certain safeguards as to the period of notice &c.

322 The surety's death does not, under German law, put an end to the guarantee; in the case of an instruction to give credit (271) the rules as to the effect of death on agreements involving the transaction of business for others (231) are applied. (As to the rules of English law on this subject, see Coulthart *v.* Clementson 5 Q. B. D. 42; *re* Silvester (1895) 1 Ch. 573.)

---

[1] Under English law any change in the relations between the creditor and the principal debtor brought about after the date of the guarantee has the effect of discharging the surety; under German law the surety's liability cannot be increased by reason of any such change (272), but the change in itself does not discharge the surety.

CHAPTER VII
ABSTRACT AGREEMENTS

1. GENERAL STATEMENT

277. An agreement by which one of the parties incurs a liability without 323 reference to the reason or motive inducing him to incur such liability is called an 'abstract agreement' (*abstrakter Vertrag*).

Under English law such an agreement if made under seal is not inoperative by reason of its abstract nature. Under German law the abstract nature of such an agreement is not in itself a ground of nullity, but if it does not come within the special rules enumerated below—278–282—its performance may be resisted under the rules as to 'unjustified benefits' (298).

2. ABSTRACT PROMISES AND ACKNOWLEDGMENT OF LIABILITY

278. An agreement, by which a performance is promised absolutely (*selbständig*), or by which the existence of an obligatory relation is acknowledged, is required to be in writing, unless the promise or acknowledgment is made in connexion with an agreed account, or with a compromise, or by a mercantile trader[1] (36) in connexion with a transaction which on his side is a mercantile transaction. If, according to the nature of the transaction, a more solemn form than mere writing is required (as in the case of the promise of a gift or of a promise to convey land) such other form must be used—BGB 780–782; HGB 350, 351. If the required form is observed the performance of the agreement cannot be resisted under the rules as to 'unjustified benefits'. An abstract promise is called *Schuldversprechen*; an abstract acknowledgment *Schuldanerkenntniss*.

---

[1] The rule is applicable only in the case of persons who are mercantile traders in the full sense of the word—BGB 351.

3. ORDERS TO PAY MONEY OR DELIVER FUNGIBLES; CHEQUES

a. Definitions.

324   **279.** An order to pay a sum of money, or to deliver a thing (*Anweisung*),
may mention the transaction with which the order is connected (as when *A* orders
B to pay *C* the sum of £ 10 'being the purchase price of a picture bought by *B*
from *A*'); but orders to pay are usually given absolutely, without any reference
to the *causa*.   Cheques (which under German law are not bills of exchange) and
mercantile delivery orders are the most important instances of abstract orders to
pay or deliver; bills of exchange, though of a similar nature, are not treated as
orders to pay or deliver, and will be referred to separately (280).   The
following rules are applicable to all written orders to pay or deliver, money,
negotiable instruments, or other fungibles.   The person to whom the payment or
delivery is to be made, is deemed authorized to receive such payment or delivery,
and the person to whom the order is addressed is deemed to be authorized to make
the payment or delivery to the person named in the order; but neither authority
becomes operative, before the order has been delivered to the person to whom, or
to whose order, the payment or delivery is to be made—BGB 783.   The person
issuing the order is called *der Anweisende* (drawer); the person to whom or to
whose order the payment or delivery is to be made is called *Anweisungsempfänger*
(payee); the person to whom the order is addressed is called *der Angewiesener*
(drawee).

b. Acceptance.

If the drawee accepts the order he is, as between himself and the payee,
bound to comply with its tenor, on delivery of the document on which the order is
written, and is not entitled to avail himself of any defences or rights of set-off,
except such as are available between him and the payee—BGB 784, 785.   The
payee's claim arising from the acceptance is barred after three years—BGB 786.

c. Transferability.

325   An order to pay or deliver, which is issued to the payee or his order and drawn
on a mercantile trader, and is not made conditional on any counter-performance on
the part of the payee, is, in the following observations, referred to as 'a mercantile

order to pay or deliver' ; such an order may be transferred by indorsement like a bill of exchange, with similar consequences as to the rights of the indorsees against the acceptor—see 280.

An order to pay or deliver which does not come within the definition of a mercantile order, can be transferred by assignment in writing followed by delivery to the assignee, unless the transferability is expressly excluded by the drawer. The drawer cannot, as between himself and the drawee, contend that the transferability of the order has been excluded, unless such exclusion is expressly mentioned in the text of the order, or has been communicated to the drawee.   If the drawee accepts such an order, while it is in the hands of an assignee, he cannot as against such assignee, make use of any defences available as between him and the payee; subject to this exception the assignee of a non-mercantile order is not in a better position than the assignee of an ordinary obligatory right (176)—HGB 363 (1), 364, 365; BGB 792 (3).

d.   Relations between Drawer and Payee.

As between the drawer and the payee, neither the transfer of the order nor its acceptance on the part of the drawee has the effect of a payment or delivery to the payee; the payee is not deemed to have received such payment or delivery from the drawer before the drawee has actually made such payment or delivery.

A payee who, on refusal of acceptance or payment or delivery by the drawee, fails to give immediate notice to the drawer is liable in damages; he is similarly liable if he fails to give immediate notice of his unwillingness or inability to present the order to the drawee—BGB 788, 789.

e.   Relations between Drawer and Drawee.

The mere fact that the drawee is indebted to the drawer does not bind him to accept the order, or to effect the payment or delivery to which it refers.   If the drawer's intention, when issuing the order, was to recover a debt owing to him by the drawee, payment of the order by the drawee to the extent of the debt has the effect of discharging the debt—BGB 787. 326

The drawer is entitled to revoke the order, as long as it is not either accepted or complied with by the drawee; such revocation is effective, even if it constitutes a breach of duty as between the drawer and the payee—BGB 790.

f.   Effect of Death or Supervening Incapacity.

The death or supervening incapacity of any party to an order of the above-mentioned description does not render it inoperative—BGB 791.

g.   Special Rules as to Cheques.

Special rules relating to cheques may be enacted by state law—EG (HG) 17; but except in Alsace-Lorraine, where the French Statute of 1865 as to cheques is still in force, no state legislation exists on the subject.   A cheque to order is therefore generally treated as an unconditional order to pay money on demand drawn on a mercantile trader, and therefore transferable by indorsement; the rights of the holder of a cheque under German law are much less extensive than under English law; an English holder of a dishonoured cheque has the same right of recourse as the holder of a dishonoured bill of exchange; under German law, on the other hand, the holder of a dishonoured cheque has no claim against the drawer as such, and has only such rights against his immediate predecessor in title as result from the particular transactions in connexion with which the cheque was indorsed to him—RGZ 44, 158.

h.   Mercantile Promises.

An unconditional promise made by a mercantile trader to pay or deliver money, negotiable instruments, or other fungibles which has not the required characteristics of a promissory note (280), is called *kaufmännischer Verpflichtungsschein*, and is transferable and negotiable like a mercantile order to pay or deliver—HGB 363 (1).

4.   BILLS OF EXCHANGE AND PROMISSORY NOTES

a.   Definitions.

327   **280.** A bill of exchange (*Wechsel*) is a mercantile order to pay which has specific characteristics, and is subject to specific rules of law.   It is differentiated under German law from the other classes of mercantile orders to pay or deliver by the following characteristics:

(1) the drawee is not required to be a mercantile trader;

(2) it must contain the statement that it is a bill of exchange;

(3) it must refer to the payment of a fixed sum of money, which must be mentioned in the document;

(4) it must indicate the time and place of payment;

(5) it must be intended to be discharged by one single payment on a specified date or at sight, or on the expiration of a specified period after the date of issue, or after sight, or at the time of a specified fair or market; (the other specific requirements, prescribed by Bills of Exchange Law, namely: indication of name of payee, signature of drawer, and name of drawee, are also essential to other mercantile orders to pay.)—WO 4.

A promissory note stands in the same relation to a mercantile promise to pay as a bill of exchange to a mercantile order to pay; the maker of a note, instead of instructing another to make a payment, promises a payment to be made by himself, which payment has to be effected at the place indicated in the note or, if no such place is indicated, at the place of issue; subject to the modifications necessitated by this difference, the essential requirements of a promissory note are the same as those of a bill of exchange—WO 96, 97.

b.   Liabilities and Rights of Parties to Bills of Exchange and Promissory Notes.

The special consequences resulting from the negotiability of bills of exchange and promissory notes have already been referred to (177, 178). The liability of every party to any such instrument according to the German theory is deemed to be the result of a unilateral act. The obligation of the acceptor of a bill to pay its amount to the lawful holder at maturity is deemed to be independent of the contractual relation between him and the drawer, or the person for whose account 328 the bill was drawn. In the same way, the liability of the drawer and every indorser of a bill to pay the amount of any claim to which a lawful holder may be entitled in the event of such bill being dishonoured is deemed to be independent of the contractual relation existing between the drawer and the payee, or between an indorser and his immediate indorsee. The act of accepting, drawing, or indorsing is accordingly looked upon as a unilateral act creating an obligation, the performance of which may be enforced by every lawful holder of the bill, not because he is the assignee of a contractual right, but independently of any contractual right.

Illustration: *A* accepts a bill drawn by *B*, payable at three months' date, on the understanding that *B* will put him into possession of the necessary funds before maturity. The bill is drawn to *B*'s own order and indorsed by him in blank. *C* obtains possession of the bill, and, without being authorized by *B*, negotiates it with *D*, who gives full value for it. *D* can claim payment from *A*, notwithstanding the fact that *B* has not put him into possession of funds. If *A* fails to pay at maturity *D* has a right of recourse against *B*, notwithstanding the fact that he did not receive any value for the bill and that the bill was negotiated against his will.

The holder of a bill of exchange has a right of recourse against the indorsers and the drawer, in the event of its non-payment at maturity, if he complies with the following rules [1] :

(1) the bill must be presented at the proper time;

(2) the fact of non-payment must be authenticated by a document called 'Protest', which must be drawn up by a notary or process-server, unless such document is dispensed with by an express statement on the face of the bill;

(3) notice of dishonour must be given within a specified short period to the holder's immediate predecessor in title—WO 41–43, 45–55.

329   The holder's right against the acceptor is not, as a general rule, lost by failure to present at the proper time, or to have a protest taken out in a case of non-payment; but where the bill is payable at the place of business or residence of any party other than the acceptor, the right against the latter is lost if the formalities as to presentation and protest are neglected—WO 43, 44.

The holder's rights against the several parties liable to him in case of non-payment are subject to specified short periods of prescription—WO 77–80.

Under English law similar rules are applied but presentation or protest is not, in the absence of an express stipulation to the contrary, required for the purpose of safeguarding the holder's right against the acceptor (Bills of Exchange Act 1882, s. 52), and there are no special rules as to prescription.

The rights and duties of parties to promissory notes are similar to the rights and duties of parties to bills of exchange. If a promissory note is payable at the place of business or residence of a person other than the maker, presentation and protest in case of non-payment are required for the purpose of safeguarding the

---

[1]   Under English law the holder has a right of recourse in the event of non-acceptance—BEA 1882, s. 43 (2)—but no similar right exists in German law. On the other hand German law empowers the holder, in the event of the acceptor's insolvency, to claim security—WO 29—which right does not exist in English law.

holder's rights against the maker, but subject to this exception the rights against the maker of a promissory note are not lost by reason of failure to present at the proper time or to make a protest—WO 98–100.   As to English law, see BEA 1882, s. 89.

5.   OBLIGATIONS TO BEARER

281. The definition of an obligation to bearer given above (179) shows that such an obligation, like a promissory note, binds the promisor to perform his promise for the benefit of the lawful holder of the instrument—BGB 793; but it is distinguished from a promissory note and from a mercantile promise to pay or deliver by the following characteristics:

(1) the promise need not refer to the payment of money or even to the delivery of a thing; thus a promise to cut the bearer's hair against delivery of the document containing the promise is an obligation to bearer within the meaning of German law;

(2) it may be made subject to the performance of a condition;

(3) periodical performance may be promised, and, in the case of an obligation for the payment of money, interest coupons may be attached;

(4) the time and place of performance need not be mentioned;

(5) the promise is not made to any particular payee on his order but to the bearer, which expression means the lawful holder of the instrument.

330

Any person who has a right of disposal over the instrument is deemed to be its lawful holder and entitled against delivery of the instrument to the performance of the obligation to which it refers; the promisor is, however, duly discharged even if he pays to a holder who has no right of disposal over the instrument—BGB 793 (1).

The promisor's obligation is created by the execution of the document [1]; if the instrument itself makes its validity dependent on a particular form of execution, such form must be complied with. [2]   In the absence of any express stipulation to

---

[1]   This shows that the act is, in its character, unilateral; if a document duly executed but not intended to be issued, comes into the hands of a lawful holder, he is entitled to avail himself of his rights as such lawful holder—BGB 794 (1).

[2]   State legislation may determine that, as regards obligations to bearer issued by the State, or certain public bodies, a particular form of execution is to be observed, and that an instrument to bearer executed in another form is to be invalid, notwithstanding the fact that the requirement as to form does not appear on the face of the instrument—EG 100.

the contrary, an obligation is deemed to be duly signed by the promisor if his signature is reproduced by mechanical process in accordance with his instructions—BGB 793 (2), 794.

An obligation to bearer has all the characteristics of a negotiable instrument (177).

Peculiar rules exist as to prescription, both as regards the principal obligation and also as to interest and similar accessories—BGB 801–803.

6.   MERCANTILE ACCOUNT STATED

282. It is usual for mercantile traders of a certain class to enter into a kind of agreement with their customers which in German terminology is called *Kontokorrent-Vertrag*; under such an agreement a customer's transactions are shown by successive entries on both sides of his account, a balance being struck at periodical intervals; as soon as the balance is struck the mutual claims resulting from the transactions shown by the previous entries are deemed to be discharged, and an abstract obligation to pay the balance is imposed on the party who is found to be the debtor thereof.   An account kept in this manner is called *Kontokorrent*, or *laufende Rechnung.* [1]

Notwithstanding the fact that the individual items of the account disappear as soon as the balance is struck, the securities for any individual claim are not thereby released.

If a judgment creditor of one of the parties has obtained an order attaching the balance due to such party on such current account, the other party to the account is precluded as between himself and the judgment creditor from setting off against such balance any subsequent items appearing on the account and resulting from business entered upon after the date of the attachment—HGB 355–357.

---

[1]   Interest may be charged on the balance of such an account, notwithstanding the fact that it is in the nature of compound interest—see 106.

CHAPTER VIII
PUBLIC OFFERS OF REWARD

283. UNDER English law a public offer of a reward is looked upon as an offer of an agreement which becomes binding by its acceptance, the acceptance being implied from the fact that a party to whom the offer was known performs the act for which the reward is promised (Carlill *v.* Carbolic Smoke Ball Company (1893) 1 Q. B. 256). German law, on the other hand, looks upon such a promise as a binding unilateral act. This is shown by the fact that a person performing the act for which the reward is promised has a claim against the promisor, notwithstanding the fact that the act was performed in ignorance of the offered reward—BGB 657.

The offer may be made irrevocable; an offer limited to a specified period is, in the absence of any contrary indication, deemed to be irrevocable during such time; where the offer is revocable, the revocation is ineffective unless it is published in the same way as the offer, or notified by direct communication to the party concerned; a revocation after the performance of the act is ineffectual, even if the promisor when revoking the offer was ignorant of the performance—BGB 658.

As between several parties claiming the reward, priority of performance is decisive; where the performance of several claimants is contemporaneous, the reward must be divided between them, unless it is in its nature indivisible (p. 153 note 1), in which event it must be decided by lot which party is to take the reward; if several persons have contributed to the result for which the reward is claimed, the promisor, on dividing the reward between them, must consider the comparative share of each claimant in the accomplishment of the result; the parties are not bound by a manifestly unjust decision, and may in such a case ask for lodgment of the reward with a public authority (164)—BGB 659, 660.

The offer of a prize to be competed for by several parties is not binding unless a time is fixed for the closing of the competition. The decision on the award rests with the umpire or umpires named in the public announcement, and if no such umpire is named, with the promisor; in the case of equality of merit the question is decided by drawing of lots.   The promisor is not entitled to claim any proprietary right in any work for which the prize is offered, unless this is expressly stipulated for in the announcement of the competition—BGB 661.

SECOND SUB-DIVISION
OBLIGATIONS CREATED OTHERWISE THAN
BY ACT-IN-THE-LAW

CHAPTER I
UNLAWFUL ACTS

1. GENERAL STATEMENT

284. UNDER Roman law there was no general rule by virtue of which a person injured by an unlawful act was entitled to claim compensation from the wrongdoer. A liability was imposed in respect of certain specified injuries to the person or property, but the satisfaction to the injured person was more in the nature of a penalty than of compensation for the damage suffered by him, and this penal character of the liability for torts was demonstrated by various results, as for instance by the rule according to which, in the case of some kinds of torts, each of several wrongdoers had to pay the full penalty ('*nam ex lege Aquilia guod alius praestitit alium non relevat cum sit poena*' , Dig. 9. 2. 11. 2), and above all by the rule as to the extinction of the claim on the death of the wrongdoers or of the injured person, [1] which to a certain extent is still preserved in English law.

The German common law gradually substituted the principle of compensation for the principle of punishment, and consistently with that principle made the heirs of the wrongdoer liable for the compensation to the extent of the value of the wrongdoer's estate; the claims of the injured person did not, however, pass to his heirs, unless an action for their enforcement was commenced in his lifetime.

The Prussian Code for the first time established a general liability for every

---

[1] Under Roman law the heir of the wrongdoer was not, however, allowed to profit by the wrong (Dig. 50. 17. 38), and the Canon law (cap 5 x de raptoribus 5, 17) made the heir liable even where the estate had derived no benefit from the tort.

335   act done wilfully or negligently by which a person's health, liberty, honour, or property was injured—ALR 16, 1–10—and the Code Napoléon has similar general enactments (ss. 1382, 1383).

The BGB has a general clause imposing liability for damage done by unlawful acts, and a number of subsidiary clauses dealing with particular instances; certain special kinds of damage done by unlawful acts are further provided for by separate statutes.

The right to compensation for pecuniary loss does not, under the present law, become extinguished either by the death of the wrongdoer or by the death of the injured person; but the right to damages for physical or mental suffering, which, as mentioned above—168a—is recognized in certain classes of cases, does not pass to the heirs of the injured person—BGB 847.

Under English law, actions in respect of torts are frequently brought for the sole purpose of asserting a right (as in actions for trespass) or merely for vindicating the plaintiff's character (as in actions for libel and slander); under German law damages are not awarded unless a claim for substantial compensation can be proved; a judgment for nominal damages in an action founded on an unlawful act is therefore impossible, but the relief granted in such an action may, as shown above—148—consist in restitution in kind.

The rules determining liability for the unlawful acts of others, and the rules as to the nature of the compensation to which the injured person is entitled have been discussed above—150 sub b, 168, 169.   The rules as to contributory default are referred to sub 149.

2.   CAPACITY TO COMMIT UNLAWFUL ACTS

285. As mentioned above—92—the capacity for committing unlawful acts is regulated by rules entirely distinct from the rules governing the capacity for acts-in-the-law.   A person belonging to one of the following classes is not generally responsible for damage inflicted by an unlawful act:

(1) an infant under the age of 7—BGB 828 (1);

(2) an infant between the ages of 7 and 18, or a deaf and dumb person, who at the time of the commission of the act did not possess the degree of intelligence necessary for realizing his responsibility—BGB 828 (2);

336   (3) a person committing the unlawful act in a state of unconsciousness, or in a state of morbid disturbance of the intellectual faculties excluding the free

exercise of the powers of volition [1]—BGB 829.

If compensation cannot be recovered from a person liable for the unlawful act of the incapable person under the rules mentioned above—150 sub b—the Court may order the incapable person to pay such compensation as seems equitable under the circumstances, having regard especially to the relative pecuniary situations of the parties, and so that the party ordered to pay compensation shall not in any event be deprived of the means of maintaining himself in accordance with his station in life, or of complying with his legal duties as to the maintenance of others—412 sub (9), 430, 431—BGB 829. [2]

There is an apparent difference between the rules of German and English law as to the capacity for unlawful acts, which, however, on closer examination, proves unimportant.   Under English law, neither infancy nor any other ground of incapacity affects the liability for torts, but as a tort must be committed either wilfully or negligently, a person, who, without any default on his part, is in a mental condition—whether permanent or temporary—which prevents him from foreseeing the probable consequences of any particular act, is not under any circumstances liable in tort for the consequences of such act.   The principal difference between the rules of German and English law as to the responsibility of infants and mentally deficient persons for torts lies in the fact that under German law the general mental condition may be inquired into in the case of persons not having attained the age of 18, and deaf and dumb persons, while under English law a party, whatever his age or general mental condition may be, is not released from his liability for damaging acts, unless he can prove that the mental condition under which the particular act was done made him incapable of foreseeing its probable consequences.   The absolute incapacity of infants under the age of 7 337 existing under German law is of no practical importance, as it is hardly conceivable that a child of such tender age would be held liable for a tort in any country.

3.   PARTIES ENTITLED TO CLAIM COMPENSATION

286. An unlawful act frequently injures persons other than the immediate

---

1   If the disturbance was temporary and brought about by the voluntary use of stimulants, or narcotics, the person suffering thereunder is responsible in the same way as if the damage had resulted from his negligence—BGB 829.

2   This obligation can hardly be characterized as an obligation 'ex delicto'; it rather belongs to the group of obligations created by outside circumstances referred to below (297).

victim. The immediate victim is always entitled to compensation, but German law also recognizes the rights of the following classes of persons:

(1) the person whose duty it is to pay the funeral expenses of a person killed by an unlawful act is entitled to the reimbursement of such expenses—BGB 844 (1);

(2) any person entitled to be maintained by a person killed by an unlawful act, or who would have been so entitled if the death had not taken place (including any *nasciturus* in existence, but unborn at the time of such death) has a claim to be compensated for the loss of maintenance during the time during which the right to maintenance would have continued to be operative, having regard to the probable duration of the life of the person killed by such unlawful act; the compensation is payable by means of periodical payments—BGB 844 (2);

(3) any person entitled by law to the services [1] of a person killed or injured by an unlawful act is entitled to compensation in respect of the loss of such services—BGB 845.

The rights to which the classes of persons severally mentioned above are entitled in the event of the death of the direct victim of an unlawful act are of course entirely distinct from any rights which his heirs may have as representatives of his estate. Thus a right to compensation for the medical expenses, and loss of income during the period preceding the death, may be asserted by the heirs concurrently with the claims of persons injured by loss of maintenance or loss of services.

The fact that the injury to the indirect victims of the unlawful act is treated as an independent tort, giving rise to a separate claim for compensation, would logically lead to the conclusion that the contributory default (149) of the direct victim does not bar or reduce the claims of such indirect victims; it is, however, expressly provided that such contributory default has the same effect on the claims of the indirect victims, as on those of the direct victim, or of his heirs—BGB 846.

The right of the indirect victims of an unlawful act to obtain compensation for damage suffered thereby is recognized in English law to a very limited extent. Under Lord Campbell's Act certain relatives of persons killed by a wrongful act, neglect, or default, are entitled to compensation, and in cases of seduction the person entitled to the services of the seduced female (whether under any contract

338

---

1   Rights to services arise under family law—see 412, 440.

for services or otherwise) is entitled to damages; but, while under German law the obligation to compensate the person indirectly injured exists concurrently with the obligation to compensate the direct victim of the unlawful act or his estate, English law, wherever the right of an indirect victim is recognized, deprives the direct victim or his estate of his right to compensation.

4. DEFINITION AND CLASSIFICATION OF UNLAWFUL ACTS CONFERRING RIGHT OF COMPENSATION

a. General Rules as to Unlawful Acts.

287. Any unlawful act coming under one of the following heads gives rise to a claim for damages under the general rules:

(1) any act done wilfully or negligently by means of which a right belonging to certain specified classes of absolute rights is infringed—BGB 823 (1);

(2) any act done wilfully or negligently by means of which an express provision of law intended for the protection of others is infringed—BGB 823 (2);

(3) any act done wilfully by means of which damage is done to another in a manner *contra bonos mores*—BGB 826.

The absolute rights referred to under the first head are: the right to freedom from violence, the right to health, the right to liberty, the right of ownership, and other rights similar to the right of ownership. [1]   An obligatory right is not within the rights mentioned under the first head.   Therefore the fact that *C* induces *A* to break an agreement entered upon between *A* and *B*, does not in itself entitle *B* to claim damages from *C*. (RGZ 57, 138; 57, 353)   An act violating one of these specified rights is unlawful, if it is not done in exercise of any right to which the person doing the act is entitled (*e. g.* the right of self-defence, or self-help) , or by virtue of any authority conferred by public law (*e. g.* the authority of public officers to restrain the liberty of individuals or to remove property in certain events) , or with the consent of the injured person.   The consent of the injured person is, however, inoperative if, having regard to the nature of the act, the giving of such consent is *contra bonos mores*.

The acts coming under the second head are acts infringing absolute rights

339

---

[1]   The expression *sonstiges Recht* is somewhat freely translated by ' right similar to the right of ownership' , but the translation is warranted by the interpretation put on the original words by the authoritative legal tribunals and textbook writers.

protected by statutory provisions, but not included in the specified rights mentioned above (*e. g.* acts wilfully or negligently disturbing possessory rights or the enjoyment of servitudes, both rights being protected by express provisions of law)—311, 351.

The acts coming under the third head are damaging acts of any kind done wilfully and so as to be *contra bonos mores*. The expression 'wilful' (*vorsätzlich*), as mentioned above (148), is not synonymous with 'intentional'. A person causes damage 'wilfully' if the act or omission causing the damage is done with the consciousness of its damaging effect (see RGZ 57, 241). An act done with no other intention than of causing damage to another would clearly be an act *contra bonos mores*, and come under the third head on that ground; but even where there is no such intention an act may be *contra bonos mores*. In a recent case which came before the RG, an association, comprising the whole of the employers belonging to a particular branch of industry, passed a resolution preventing the further employment of a particular workman by any member of the association; it was held that the resolution constituted an unlawful act, as it was *contra bonos mores* to deprive a workman of the possibility of earning his living in the branch of industry for which he was specially qualified, without a sufficient reason (which in the case before the Court was held to be absent)—RGZ 57, 418. A person inducing another to break an agreement, though not violating one of the rights enumerated under the first head, may yet commit an unlawful act if his conduct can be regarded as *contra bonos mores*.

340

Conspiracy with regard to an act not unlawful in itself is not theoretically noticed in German law, but the combination of several persons in an act causing serious damage to another would no doubt be looked upon in most cases as an aggravating element.

In the result the general rules of German law as to responsibility for damage done by acts lawful in themselves, but becoming unlawful by reason of the motive for which or the manner in which they are done, do not materially differ from the rules of English law as established by the recent cases, Allen *v.* Flood (1898) A. C. 1; Quinn *v.* Leathem (1901) A. C. 495; Giblan *v.* National Labourers' Union (1903) 2 K. B. 600 (see particularly the judgment of Romer L. J. on pp. 619, 620, which expresses the same principles as those contained in the last-mentioned decision of the RG).

Actions for personal injuries, false imprisonment, and trespass relate to the class of acts described above sub (1), as also do actions for the infringement of rights relating to firm names, trade marks, and similar rights, in so far as they are not protected by special statutes; actions for deceit, misappropriation, wrongful conversion, and defamation, relate to the class of acts described sub (2), in so far as the damaging act is dealt with by criminal law; in so far as this is not the case, the manner in which the act is committed may bring it under class (3).

b.   Rules as to Specific Classes of Unlawful Acts.

aa.   Defamation.

288. Wilful defamation is an offence against the criminal law (StGB 186, 187), and therefore also an unlawful act entitling the injured party to compensation; this, where no pecuniary damage is inflicted, means restitution (167); where pecuniary damage is inflicted the injured party may either claim a judicial penalty (172) not exceeding 6, 000 Marks—StGB 188—or damages.

Negligent defamation is not, as a general rule, deemed an unlawful act, but a person who makes or publishes an untrue statement which is likely to injure the credit of another, or to curtail his earning powers, is liable to compensate such other; ignorance of the untruth of the statement is no ground of excuse if such untruth would have been discovered by the exercise of proper care—BGB 824 (1). (As to defamation by a competitor in trade, see *post* sub (4).)   The compensation must not exceed the pecuniary loss, and ought not to include a solatium for wounded feelings or annoyance (168a).

341

If the person making, or the person receiving, the libellous statement is justifiably interested in the information conveyed thereby, no compensation can be claimed if the person making the allegation was ignorant of its untruth—BGB 824 (2).

The principal characteristics differentiating German from English law, as to claims for compensation arising in cases of defamation may be summarized as follows:

(1) there is no distinction in German law between slander and libel;

(2) no action lies under German law for negligent defamation, unless the plaintiff has suffered pecuniary loss, and no damages can be awarded except in respect of such pecuniary loss;

(3) the distinction between absolute and qualified privilege does not exist in German law; wilful defamation is not privileged under any circumstances; negligent defamation is excused in every case in which the utterer or the recipient

of the defamatory statement had a legitimate interest in its contents.

bb.   Seduction.

289. Seduction, in the popular sense, is a cause of action if the seducer and the seduced were under an engagement to marry and the marriage was broken off by reason of the seducer's default—BGB 1300 (1).   Apart from this rule, a female who has been induced by deceit or threats, or by the abuse of her dependent position in relation to the seducer to have illicit intercourse with him, is entitled to claim compensation for all damage resulting from such illicit intercourse—BGB 825.   In both cases compensation may be awarded for damage not resulting in pecuniary loss (168a)—BGB 847 (2), 1300 (2).

The German action for seduction is, of course, entirely different from the corresponding English action, with regard to which the fiction of a loss of services has to be introduced, and which cannot in any case be brought by the victim of the seduction.   On the other hand vindictive damages, which may be awarded in the English action, are out of the question under the German rules, as even the damages in respect of mental suffering or loss of reputation, are assessed with the sole object of giving a reasonable compensation to the injured female.

cc.   Default in the performance of official duties.

290. The duties of public officials are imposed on them by statutory provisions intended for the protection of others; a person injured by the wilful or negligent violation of such duties is therefore entitled to compensation under the general rules as to unlawful acts (287).   The liability of an official guilty of any such violation of duty is, however, somewhat mitigated by the following special rules:

(1) a party injured by an official's negligence has no claim against him, if he can obtain compensation elsewhere (*e. g.* from the public authority represented by the negligent official)—BGB 839 (1);

(2) a judge, who violates his official duties as regards any judgment delivered in an action, is liable for the damage caused thereby, in so far only as his default is in the nature of a criminal offence—BGB 839 (2);

(3) an official is not in any event liable for damage caused by his default if the injured party could have averted such damage by appealing to a higher authority, and has wilfully or negligently omitted to do so—BGB 839 (3).

dd.   Unfair competition.

291. The application of the general principles as to unlawful acts to unfair trade competition was first introduced by the French Courts, and followed in Germany, in a somewhat hesitating manner.   It was therefore thought expedient to pass a special Imperial Statute on the subject, which came into force on the 1st July, 1896, and remained in force, after the introduction of the BGB, by virtue of EG 32.   Some acts of unfair competition which cannot be dealt with under that statute may possibly come under the general rules as to acts *contra bonos mores* referred to above—287.

The statute provides a remedy in the case of:

(1) any untrue allegation made in a public announcement, by which it is intended to create the impression of a specially favourable offer—ss. 1–4;

(2) any untrue allegation concerning a competitor, or any of his employees, which is likely to injure his trade or his credit—ss. 6, 7;

(3) any misleading use of a firm name or business designation—s. 8.

A competitor injured by any of these three kinds of offences, may obtain an order prohibiting its continuation, without proving that the offender was guilty of wilful default, or negligence.

In the case of the offence mentioned sub (1) full compensation may be obtained if it can be proved that the offender was aware, or ought to have been aware, of the untruth of his allegation; in the case of the offences mentioned sub (2) and (3) full compensation may be obtained, even if the offender acted in good faith and was not guilty of negligence, but in the case of the offence mentioned sub (2) the ordinary rule as to privileged communications—288—is applicable.

Any person who is wittingly guilty of any offence referred to sub (1) and (2) commits a criminal offence; the injured party may in such a case, instead of asserting his right to compensation claim the award of a judicial penalty (172) not exceeding 10, 000 Marks—ss. 4, 7, 14.

Under English law unfair competition as such does not constitute a cause of action.   The assumption, that ' apart from fraud, intimidation, molestation, or obstruction... there is some natural standard of fairness ' or ' reasonableness ... beyond which competition ought not, in law, to go' is repudiated by the Courts (*per* Bowen L. J. in Mogul Steamship Co. *v.* McGregor 23 Q. B. D. 598).   Some of the acts which are dealt with by the German Statute as to unfair competition would, however, be treated as unlawful acts under English law on other grounds; thus titles of literary works and trade names which are likely to deceive the public are forbidden—see Metzler *v.* Wood 8 Ch. D. 606, Reddaway *v.* Banham (1896)

343

A. C. 199; and disparagement of goods is a special kind of libel—see Western Counties &c. *v.* Lawes &c. L. R. 9 Ex. 218; White *v.* Mellin (1895) A. C. 154.

ee.   Liability of owners of mines, quarries, and factories, for personal injuries.

292.   Under the *Haftpflichtgesetz* of 1871 (as amended by EG 42) [1] the owner of a mine, quarry, or factory is liable for the damage suffered by a person killed or injured in consequence of such owner's default, or of the default of any representative of such owner, or of any person entrusted by such owner with the superintendence of the undertaking, or of the workmen in his employment.   The mode of compensation is similar to the mode of compensation in respect of injuries to life and limb prescribed under the general rules—see 169 rule (4), 286.   The owner's liability cannot be excluded by agreement.   The general rules as to the consequences of contributory default (149) do not apply in the case of a claim under the statute; the English doctrine of 'common employment' has never been adopted in Germany.

The practical importance of the above-mentioned provisions has been very much diminished by the operation of the law as to compulsory insurance. [2]

344

---

1   The special liability of railway undertakings under the statute mentioned in the text has been referred to above—151 sub (4); no further reference is made to it in this place, as it is not in any sense a liability *ex delicto.*

2   The several statutes as to compulsory insurance against accidents successively enacted since 1884, and all republished in 1900 in an amended form, deal with the following classes of workmen and employees:

(1) the Industrial Accidents Insurance Statute deals with persons employed: (*a*) in mines, quarries, &c.; (*b*) in certain specified trades connected with building and other works; (*c*) in the postal service or on telegraphs and railways; (*d*) in the carriage of goods or persons, and the forwarding and storage of goods;

(2) the Agriculture and Forestry Accident Insurance Statute deals with persons employed in agriculture and forestry;

(3) the Building Works Accident Insurance Statute deals with persons employed in building works not provided for by the statutes mentioned sub (1) and (2);

(4) the Maritime Navigation Accidents Insurance Statute deals with persons engaged in the occupations denoted by its title.

All workmen and employees engaged in the occupations enumerated above whose annual earnings do not exceed 3,000 Marks are compelled to insure against accidents, and in some cases the compulsion extends to employees whose annual earnings exceed 3,000 Marks, and also to persons working on their own account. The liability of an employer in respect of damage to life and limb, or to health, suffered by a person employed by him, is as to persons insured under the compulsory system modified as follows:

(1) neither the insured nor any of the persons benefiting by the insurance has a claim against any person who, but for the compulsory law, would be liable under the Statute of 1871 in respect of damage to life or limb or health, unless it is proved in the course of a criminal trial—or in some exceptional cases without such trial—that the damaging event was wilfully caused by any such person; where such proof has

ff.   Liability of shipowners in respect of damage done by collisions.

293. The following rules apply on this subject:

(1) if the collision is caused exclusively by the default of the crew of one of the ships, the owner of such ship is liable, as well as the persons by whose default the collision was caused;

(2) if the crew of neither ship was in default, neither shipowner is liable;

(3) if both the crews were in default, the question as to the liability for the damage and as to the amount of the compensation depends on all the material circumstances, more particularly on the question as to whose default had the preponderating influence [1];

(4) if the damage is caused by a compulsory pilot the shipowner is not liable—HGB 734–739.

gg.   Liability in respect of danger arising from animals and buildings.

294. There is no general rule of German law corresponding to the rule of English law, under which a person who brings a dangerous object on to his land, is liable in damages, if he fails to use proper precautions for preventing the danger (Fletcher *v.* Rylands L. R. 1 Ex. 265).   The following rules apply as to certain specific sources of danger:

345

346

---

been furnished the difference between the value of the compensation which would have been payable to a person not subject to compulsory insurance, and the value of the compensation received under the compulsory insurance law may be claimed;

(2) an insurance association, other than a compulsory insurance association, which has paid any compensation to a direct or indirect victim of the damaging event, has a claim for compensation against any person who, but for the compulsory insurance law, would have been liable under the Statute of 1871 for such damaging event, if it is proved in the course of criminal trial—or in some exceptional cases without such trial—that the damaging event was caused by the wilful default of such person, or by his omission to give the degree of attention which he was bound to give in accordance with the requirements of his office or calling;

(3) a compulsory insurance association is entitled to the claim for compensation mentioned sub (2) without being in any case compelled to resort to a criminal trial in order to prove the facts on which the claim depends; the association is not bound to assert a claim founded on mere negligence, and the person against whom it is intended to assert such a claim may require a general meeting of the association to be summoned for the purpose of deciding, whether the majority wish the claim to be enforced;

(4) a compulsory insurance association is subrogated to any right of compensation to which any party entitled to compensation from its funds is entitled, otherwise than under the Statute of 1871, to the extent of the value of the compensation to which such party is entitled out of its funds. —See Trade Accident Insurance Statute, ss. 135–140, and the corresponding sections in the other compulsory insurance statutes.

1   Under art. 737 of the old HGB neither shipowner was liable where the damage was caused by both crews; under English law the damages are divided in such a case.

(1) *Liability for damage done by animals.* [1]

Where an animal causes injury to the life or limb or health of a human being, or damage to a thing, any person who would have been entitled to compensation if the damage had been caused by an unlawful act (286) is entitled to claim compensation for such injury from the person keeping the animal, whether there was any default on his part or not; a person so entitled may also claim compensation from any person who was placed in charge of the animal by the person keeping it, unless he can prove that he applied the degree of diligence usual under the circumstances, or that the damaging event could not have been avoided by the application of such diligence [2]—BGB 833, 834.

(2) *Liability for damage done by game.*

Where the sporting rights over any parcel of land are vested in any person other than the owner of such parcel, [3] the person in whom the sporting rights are vested is bound to compensate the owner for all damage done to the land or to any produce severed therefrom, but remaining thereon, by certain specified kinds of game (fallow, red, and roe deer, elk, wild boar, or pheasants).

(3) *Liability for damage done by the collapse of buildings.*

347   If by the collapse of a building or other erection, or by the severance of any part thereof from the main part, the life or limb, or health of a human being is injured, any person who would have been entitled to compensation if the damage had been caused by an unlawful act (286) may claim compensation for such injury from any person who is liable in respect thereof, under the following rules:

(1) the proprietary possessor (311) of the parcel of land on which the building or erection is situate is liable if the damaging event was caused by

---

[1]   There is considerable discontent among the agricultural classes in Germany about the rules on this subject, and amending legislation is now (November 1906) before the Reichstag.

[2]   As to the apportionment of the liability between the several persons liable to compensate the injured party, see 295.

[3]   Where the sporting rights over two adjoining estates cannot be exercised separately, and the owner of one of the estates leases the sporting rights over his land to the owner of the other estate, the sporting rights over both estates are deemed to be vested in the latter; in any other case of a lease of sporting rights, the lessee is not deemed the person in whom the sporting rights are vested.   If, under any statutory provisions, the several owners of all the holdings comprised in any district exercise their sporting rights jointly their liability for the damage done by the game is apportioned in proportion to the size of their respective properties—BGB 835.

defective construction, or insufficient repairs, unless he can prove that he applied the diligence usual under the circumstances for averting the danger—BGB 836 (1) (3); if any person other than the possessor of the land is in possession of the building, or erection, by virtue of any right in respect thereof—e. g. by virtue of a heritable building right (348, 349)—he is liable in the place of the possessor of the land—BGB 837;

(2) any person who by agreement with the possessor undertakes to keep the building or erection in repair, or has to keep it in repair by virtue of any right of user vested in him, is liable in the same way as the possessor—BGB 838;

(3) a former proprietary possessor is liable if the damaging event occurred within a year from the termination of his possession, unless he can prove that he applied the diligence usual under the circumstances while he was in possession, or that a subsequent possessor by the application of such diligence might have averted the danger—BGB 836 (2). [1]

(4) *General observations.*

The special rules stated above do not exclude the general liability for damage to life or limb or health, caused by dangerous animals or defective buildings; thus a person injured by reason of the bad condition of a staircase leading to a Court of Law in which such person had to attend, is entitled to damages from the Government of the State to which the Court belongs if the danger could have been avoided by the application of proper diligence (Prussian ' *Justizministerialblatt*' , 1904, p. 321).

Under the general rules, the plaintiff must always prove that the defendant 348 was in default, but under the special rules the liability sometimes arises apart from any question of default on the part of the defendant, and in all cases where the application ofthe proper degree of diligence affords a ground of excuse, the defendant must prove that such diligence was applied by him.

c.   Apportionment of Liability between several persons.

295. Where several persons have together committed an unlawful act, [2] or are

---

[1]   As to the apportionment of the liability between several persons liable together under the rules, see 295.

[2]   A person by whom the act was incited or assisted is for the purposes of the rule deemed a person acting together with the person doing the act—BGB 830 (2).

liable under any specific rule of law for damage caused by an unlawful act—see for instance 293 sub (1) and (3), they are liable as joint debtors—BGB 830 (1), 840 (1) [1]; the rules as to contributions—182 sub (4)—are, as between such joint tort-feasors, modified in the following manner:

(1) where a person is liable for the unlawful act of another for which such other is also liable (150), the party who has committed the act is, as between himself and the party liable for his act, answerable for the whole of the compensation—BGB 840 (2);

(2) where in the case of damage done by animals, or the collapse of buildings, &c., any person other than the person liable under the special rules mentioned above (294) is responsible for the damage (e. g. a builder through whose negligence the building has collapsed), such third party, as between himself and the person liable under the special rules, must bear the whole of the compensation—BGB 840 (3);

(3) where a public official, who is under a duty to appoint or control another entrusted with the care of a third party's affairs, [2] is liable for loss caused to such third party by the neglect of such duty, and the person appointed or controlled by him is also liable for the same loss, the latter as between himself and the official must bear the whole loss—BGB 840, 841.

The rules as to the apportionment of the compensation may in some cases be modified by agreement between the parties; thus a party who undertakes the care of an animal or of a building may agree with the person keeping the animal, or the possessor of the buildings, to undertake the whole of the liability.

d.   Prescription.

296. A claim to compensation for damage caused by an unlawful act is barred after the lapse of three years, reckoned from the time at which the party entitled to compensation becomes aware of the damage, and of the identity of the party liable in respect thereof; such a claim cannot in any event be asserted after the

---

[1]   An exception exists in the case of several persons jointly exercising sporting rights, who as to damage done by game are liable only *pro rata* of their respective interests in the land over which the sporting rights are exercised. —See p. 322 note 3—BGB 840 (1).

[2]   Illustration: The judge of a Guardianship Court has to appoint the guardian for any person within his jurisdiction requiring a guardian, and to control the exercise of such guardian's powers (451); the judge as well as the guardian are liable to the ward for loss caused by the neglect of their respective duties.

lapse of thirty years from the time of the commission of the unlawful act—BGB 852 (1).

A party liable to give compensation must, even after the lapse of the period of prescription, restore any benefit acquired by the commission of the unlawful act, in accordance with the rules as to unjustified benefits (298)—BGB 852 (2).

If a person by means of an unlawful act acquires a personal claim against another (e. g. if he extorts a promise by fraud), the latter may refuse satisfaction of the claim, even after the date at which the right to rescind the transaction has become barred by prescription—BGB 853.

The claims arising under the law as to unfair competition (see 291 and s. 11 of the statute there referred to), and the claims against railway undertakings and owners of mines, quarries, and factories in respect of personal injuries (see 292 and s. 8 of the statute there referred to), are subject to shorter periods of prescription.

CHAPTER II
OBLIGATIONS IMPOSED BY SURROUNDING CIRCUMSTANCES

1. COMPARATIVE STATEMENT

350   **297.** In all systems of law certain classes of obligations are recognized which neither result from an act-in-the-law nor from an unlawful act done by the debtor, but which are imposed upon him where, owing to some accident, mistake, or other circumstance, he becomes entitled to a benefit at the expense of another.

Under Roman law the obligations arising by reason of *negotiorum gestio* and those enforceable by the various kinds of *conditiones* (*condictio indebiti*, &c.) are instances of such classes of obligations.   Under English law they are not so common, but the actions ' for money had and received' and ' for money received to the use of another' may be referred to as instances of their recognition, as well as the rules of maritime law as to voluntary salvage and towage and the rules of equity as to 'resulting uses' and 'resulting trusts'.

The rules as to 'unjustified benefits' (298) and 'voluntary services' (301) forming part of the new German law give a general recognition to the principle that a person benefited by accident or mistake at the expense of another is bound to restore such benefit or to compensate the other for his sacrifice; the rules as to obligations arising by community of interests (304, 305) and by estoppel (306) illustrate the same principle in a less direct way.

2. UNJUSTIFIED BENEFITS

a. General Rule.

298. An ' unjustified benefit' (*ungerechtfertigte Bereicherung*) is a benefit received without a sufficient legal ground (*ohne rechtlichen Grund*).   The expression 'legal ground' is the equivalent of the Roman *causa*, which has a

more extensive meaning than the English term ' consideration ' in its usual
narrower sense; thus the *animus donandi* is a good legal ground, though it is not   351
a ' valuable consideration '.

Any person who receives a benefit at the expense of another without a
sufficient legal ground must restore such benefit to the person at whose expense it
was received.

Where the benefit was received on a sufficient legal ground, which has
subsequently ceased to operate, or by virtue of an act-in-the-law the purpose of
which has not been accomplished, the person at whose expense such benefit was
received has a right to the restoration of the *status quo ante* in the same way as if
no sufficient legal ground had ever been in existence; if it was, however, known
to him *ab initio* that the accomplishment of the purpose of the transaction was
impossible, or if such accomplishment was prevented by any unfair conduct on
his part, he forfeits his claim to restoration—BGB 812, 815.

Illustrations: 1. *A* makes a gift of a house to his son *B*.   *B* is guilty of
conduct entitling *A* to revoke the gift; upon the exercise of such right *A* is entitled
to claim the retransfer of the ownership by reason of the fact that the legal
ground, on which such ownership was transferred to *B*, has ceased to operate.

2. *A* pays *B* for the use of a window on a date on which the coronation
procession is to pass it; the procession does not pass, owing to the King's illness.
A may recover the amount paid by him because the purpose of the hiring
agreement under which it was paid was not accomplished; if *A* knew that the
procession on the day in question could not possibly take place, he has no right to
recover the amount paid by him.

The general rule as to unjustified benefits stated above is supplemented by
some special rules of which the effect is stated in the following section.

b.   Special Rules.

(1)   *Recovery of objects delivered in discharge of a non-existent*
obligation (condictio indebiti).

299. A person who pays money or delivers an object under the mistaken
impression that he is discharging an obligation may, under the general rule stated
above (298), recover such money or such object on finding that the assumed
obligation was non-existent; he has the same right if, at the time of making the
payment or delivery, he was in a position to resist a claim for the performance of

352   the obligation intended to be discharged, by means of any defence or set-off other than the plea of prescription. [1]

The mere fact that the performance of the obligation was not due at the time when the payment or delivery was made does not entitle the party making it to recover the money or object paid or delivered prematurely, or to demand interest for the intermediate period.

The right to recover any money or object paid or delivered for the purpose of discharging an obligation which in fact was non-existent or unenforceable is excluded if the payment or delivery was made with the knowledge of the invalidity of the obligation or of the existence of a valid defence, or in compliance with a moral duty, or with the requirements of social propriety—BGB 813, 814.

(2) *Claims for indemnity in respect of unauthorized alienations of property.*

If any person makes any disposition of a thing or right which is binding upon the true owner, though unauthorized by him (see for instance 333), such true owner is entitled to claim from the person making such unauthorized disposition any benefit received in consideration thereof or in connexion therewith [2]—BGB 816 (1).

If the person by whom the unauthorized disposition was made did not himself receive any benefit in return therefor or in connexion therewith, any other person by whom a direct benefit was derived in consequence of such disposition is liable in his place—BGB 816 (2).

If any payment or delivery was made to a person who was not entitled thereto, but with the result that the person making such payment or delivery was

353   duly discharged thereby (see for instance 175), the person who was entitled to such payment or delivery may claim from the person by whom it was received the surrender of all benefits derived therefrom—BGB 816 (2).

---

[1]   This rule corresponds to the English rule as to the recovery of money paid under a mistake of fact, but under the German law other objects may be recovered as well as money, and no distinction is drawn between a mistake of fact and a mistake of law.

[2]   If the disposition was in the nature of an unlawful act, the true owner is of course entitled to full compensation under the rules as to unlawful acts, but if the act was done in good faith and without negligence, nothing more can be claimed than the restitution of any benefit received by the transaction. Illustration: If a sheriff's officer without any default on his part sells goods not belonging to the judgment debtor to a purchaser, who in good faith acquires the ownership, the true owner has a claim against him only in so far as the proceeds of sale are in his hands.

(3) *Claims for return of payments and deliveries made in consideration of prohibited or immoral acts (condictio ob turpem causam).*

If the purpose of the transfer or delivery of any object to another is of such a nature as to constitute its acceptance a prohibited act, or an act *contra bonos mores*, the party making the transfer or delivery may recover such object unless he was *in pari delicto*.   If any obligation is incurred for any purpose of the nature described, the party incurring such obligation may claim to be released therefrom, even if both parties were *in pari delicto*—BGB 817.

Illustration: *A* receives £ 100 from *B* for the disclosure of a secret chemical process; the disclosure was a gross breach of confidence, and therefore *contra bonos mores*; if *B* was not aware of this circumstance he may recover the £ 100; if the circumstances were known to him he has no claim for a return of his payment; if instead of paying the £ 100 he had promised to pay them at a future date, he might have refused such payment and claimed to be released therefrom in any event.

(4) *Claims against parties to bills of exchange in respect of rights lost by informality or prescription.*

The holder of a bill of exchange who has forfeited his right of recourse against the drawer by his failure to comply with the requirements as to presentation or notice of dishonour, may claim the surrender of any 'unjustified benefit' accruing to such drawer by reason of the forfeiture of the right of recourse.   Similar rules are applied, as to claims barred by prescription, against acceptors of bills of exchange or makers of promissory notes—WO 83, 98, Nr. 10.

Illustration: *A*, the acceptor of a bill for £ 100, has refused payment; *H*, the holder, omits to send proper notice of dishonour to the drawer *D*, and consequently loses his right of recourse against *D*; the bill had been accepted by *A* for *D's* accommodation, and *D* had remitted no funds to *A*; *H* can recover from *D* the amount which he received on negotiating the bill.

c.   Nature of Claim for surrender of unjustified benefits.

300. The rules as to 'unjustified benefits' are intended to prevent the person concerned from reaping an unmerited advantage at the expense of another, but it is not their object to indemnify the claimant.   For this reason the person having to return the benefit is not *ab initio* bound to exercise any diligence as to the preservation of any object which he may be liable to return; if such object is

354

destroyed before he becomes aware of his duty to return it, the loss falls on the claimant.   The recipient has to return the object received by him, and all profits received therefrom, as well as any object received in its place or by way of compensation for its loss or destruction; if the return of any object is impossible, its value must be paid to the claimant, in so far as the benefit of such value is still retained by the claimant—BGB 818 (1) (2) (3). [1]

The restriction as to the recipient's liability ceases to operate after action brought; from that time the stricter liability brought about under the general rules as to the effect of *lis pendens* (156) is imposed upon the recipient—BGB 818 (4); in the following events such stricter liability begins to operate at an earlier date:

(1) where the recipient, on the receipt of the benefit, is aware of the absence of a legal ground the stricter liability begins as from the receipt of the benefit; where he becomes aware of the absence of a legal ground at some later date, the stricter liability begins as from such later date—BGB 819 (1);

(2) where the acceptance of the benefit infringes a legal prohibition or is *contra bonos mores*, the stricter liability begins as from the time of such acceptance—BGB 819 (2);

(3) where the legal ground originally existing ceases to operate, or where the purpose of the act by which the benefit was conferred is not attained, the recipient, if at the time of the receipt of the benefit he was aware of the possibility of the cesser of the legal ground, or of the uncertainty of the attainment of the purpose, comes under the more stringent liability as from such time; in either of the last-mentioned events interest cannot be claimed from a period anterior to the time at which the right to recover the benefit is established; the return of profits can be demanded in so far only as the recipient is still benefited thereby at such time—BGB 820.

If the recipient of a benefit transfers such benefit gratuitously to another, the transferee becomes liable in the place of the original recipient, in so far as the liability of the latter is excluded by reason of the transfer—BGB 822. [2]

The claim to recover any unjustified benefit, or to be released from an

---

1   If the recipient has consumed the value, he is deemed to have retained its benefit.

2   If at the time of the transfer the original recipient was under the stricter liability, the remedy is available against him only; but as long as the stricter liability does not operate, the recipient ceases to be liable as soon as he transfers the object to another, except in so far as he receives any benefit by reason of the transfer or retains the benefit derived from the use of the object.

obligation incurred without a sufficient legal ground, is subject to the ordinary rules as to prescription, but the performance of an obligation incurred without a sufficient legal ground may be refused, notwithstanding the fact that the claim to be released from such obligation is barred by prescription—BGB 821.

3.   Voluntary Services

a.   Generally.

301. The claims of persons rendering voluntary services are recognized by the rules ' as to conduct of business on behalf of another without his request ' (*Geschäftsführung ohne Auftrag*) , which correspond to the rules of Roman law as to *negotiorum gestio*; the same principle is also applied in the special rules relating to maritime salvage or assistance (*Bergung und Hülfeleistung*).

A person who volunteers his services has, in certain events, a claim for reimbursement of outlay, but under the specific rules as to salvage and assistance a reasonable reward may be claimed, as well as the reimbursement of outlay.

English law maintains the maxim that no one can make himself the creditor of another against his will, and therefore does not generally give a claim for the reimbursement of outlay voluntarily incurred, though such outlay may have been beneficial to another, but the rules of maritime law as to claims for salvage are similar to those of German law (Merchant Shipping Act, ss. 544–571).   356

b.   Voluntary Conduct of Business on behalf of another.

302. A person, who conducts business on behalf of another without his request, and without being otherwise entitled to act on his behalf, is described by the German expression *Geschäftsführer*, the person for whom he acts being described as the *Geschäftsherr*, which expressions in the further course of this treatise will respectively be reproduced by the English terms ' voluntary agent ' and ' involuntary principal ' .

The following rules are applied as to the duties of a voluntary agent:

(1) he must, as soon as practicable, give notice of his intervention to the involuntary principal, and must, unless there is danger in delay, await the reply to such notice before proceeding any further—BGB 681;

(2) he must conduct the involuntary principal's business in accordance with his interest, and pay regard to his actual or presumable wishes—BGB 677;

(3) subject to rule (6), he is liable for wilful default or negligence in the same way as if he were acting under an agreement involving the transaction of business for another (231)—BGB 681;

(4) if, in any case not coming under rule (5), the voluntary agent's intervention was in opposition to the actual or presumable wishes of the involuntary principal, he is also answerable for accidental damage—BGB 678;

(5) the fact that the voluntary agent's intervention is opposed to the involuntary principal's wishes is disregarded in any case in which failure to intervene would have prevented the performance at the proper time of a duty imposed on the principal in the public interest, or incumbent upon him with reference to the maintenance of any relative (412 (9), 430)—BGB 679;

(6) if the voluntary agent's intervention had for its object the prevention of an urgent danger threatening the involuntary principal, the voluntary agent is not liable for any default extending beyond wilful default and gross negligence—BGB 680;

357   (7) if the voluntary agent is under incapacity or restricted capacity he is not liable for any default on his part, except in so far as any liability arises under the rules as to unlawful acts (287) or as to unjustified benefits (298)—BGB 682;

(8) the voluntary agent is entitled to the reimbursement of his outlay in accordance with rule (9), unless it can be shown that at the time of his intervention he did not intend to claim reimbursement; where a person provides maintenance for any ancestor or issue it is presumed that he does not intend to claim reimbursement—BGB 685;

(9) the voluntary agent is entitled to reimbursement of outlay in every case in which the intervention was in the principal's interest, and in accordance with his expressed or presumable wishes, or was ratified by him, [1] or comes under rule (5); in every other case the voluntary agent has no claim in respect of his intervention, except in so far as the involuntary principal is liable under the rules as to unjustified benefits—BGB 683, 684;

(10) the fact that the voluntary agent is under a mistake as to the identity of the involuntary principal does not affect the mutual position of the parties; the

---

[1] A person who pays the expense of having the snow swept away in front of an absent relative's house in accordance with a police regulation, or who pays the overdue allowance of the absent relative's son, is therefore entitled to reimbursement, notwithstanding the fact that he was requested not to make any such payments.

person on whose behalf the intervention is made is entitled to the rights and subject to the duties of an involuntary principal, even if the voluntary agent intended to act for another person—BGB 686;

(11) if a person who believes that he is acting on his own behalf is in fact acting on behalf of another, [1] he is not entitled to the rights, or subject to the duties of an involuntary agent—BGB 687 (1);

(12) if a person transacts any business as his own knowing it to be the business of another, the person on whose behalf he is acting may at his option assume or decline the position of an involuntary principal—BGB 687 (2).

c.   Maritime Salvage and Assistance.

303. A person who renders services to a ship in distress or assists in saving her cargo has a right to the reimbursement of his outlay and to a reasonable reward which is recognized in different ways by the maritime law of all countries. Under English law only one kind of claim, *viz.* the claim for salvage, is admitted; under German law, on the other hand, a distinction is drawn between salvage (*Bergung*) and maritime assistance (*Hülfeleistung*), the reward being described as *Bergelohn* in the case of salvage, and as *Hülfslohn* in the case of maritime assistance.   Salvage relates to an abandoned ship or cargo; maritime assistance relates to a ship in distress—HGB 740.   (Compare Merchant Shipping Act 1894, s. 546.)

Under English law the rights of persons rendering services in saving life are specially safeguarded (Merch. Sh. A. 1894, ss. 544, 545), but under German law the saving of life is not taken into consideration, except in cases in which the ship or the cargo, or part of the cargo, is saved; where this is done the persons saving life rank *pari passu*, as to the claim for reward, with the persons saving property—HGB 748 (2).

The reward for salvage or assistance is calculated so as to include reimbursement of outlay, and is assessed and apportioned among the several persons entitled thereto in accordance with the principles laid down in HGB 742–749, as modified by s. 1 of the Imperial Statute of 1902 on the same subject.   The reward for assistance is always assessed at a lower figure than the reward for salvage would have been under the same circumstances; for the purpose of the computation of

358

---

1   Rule (11) and rule (12) may be applicable in a case in which a person deals with property which he believes to be his own, or intends to treat as his own, while another person is the true owner.

the reward, the value of the saved objects is an entirely subordinate element—HGB 747.

The following classes of persons are not entitled to any reward for salvage or assistance:

(1) the crew of the ship which is abandoned or in distress—HGB 740;

(2) any person who obtrudes his services unnecessarily, and more particularly any person who, while the master remains on the ship, boards the ship without his permission;

359 (3) any person who fails to inform the master or the owner or the competent authority of the existence of the saved objects—HGB 750.

The claim for reward is primarily a claim charged on the ship and cargo, but a master delivering any goods charged with a claim for salvage or assistance, and any person receiving any such goods with notice of the charge, becomes personally liable to the extent to which the ship is liable; the shipowner is liable to the same extent as the master if the master delivers the goods on such owner's instructions—HGB 751-753.

If the reward was fixed by the agreement, either while the ship was in distress or otherwise, the agreement overrides the legal rules as to its assessment, but in the first-mentioned event a reduction of the agreed amount may be claimed if it is unduly high under the circumstances—HGB 741.

4. OBLIGATIONS ARISING FROM COMMUNITY OF PROPERTY OR LOSS

a. Community of Ownership.

304. The distinction familiar to English lawyers between joint tenancy and tenancy in common does not exist in German law, as the rule of survivorship which characterizes the English joint tenancy is not recognized under the German system.   German law distinguishes between the more intimate community (*Gemeinschaft zur gesamten Hand*) [1] , of which the common ownership of partners in a non-mercantile partnership (67), the community of goods between husband and wife (417) , and the community subsisting between co-heirs (529) are conspicuous examples, and the less intimate ' community by undivided shares '

---

1   The persons participating in such a community are called *Gesamthänder.*

(*Gemeinschaft nach Bruchteilen*), which represents the ordinary type of common ownership; each of the participants in a 'community by undivided shares' may alienate his undivided share without the concurrence of the others, while in the case of the *Gemeinschaft zur gesamten Hand* this cannot be done. [1]

The rules as to the management of property held by one of the more intimate communities, and as to the rights and duties of the individual participants, are laid down separately as to each kind of community; where no such separate rules are laid down, the rules, which regulate the rights and duties of the several participants in a community by undivided shares, are applicable—BGB 741; these rules may be summarized as follows:

360

(1) in the absence of evidence to the contrary, the shares of the participants in the common property are deemed to be equal; the shares in the fruits (77) are equal to the shares in the common property; each of the participants may use or enjoy the property, but so as not to interfere with the use or enjoyment of the others—BGB 742, 743;

(2) the participants who own the major portion of the common property may make such arrangements as to its management as is suitable to its nature, but so as not to cause any essential change and not to interfere with the right of any individual to his share in the income; in the absence of any such arrangement, no act of management is operative unless it has the concurrence of all the participants or unless it is necessary for the preservation of the property—BGB 744, 745;

(3) each of the participants is under an obligation, as between himself and the others, to contribute such part of the expenses and outgoings as corresponds to his share in the common property—BGB 748;

(4) a partition in accordance with the specific rules laid down by the BGB 752–757 may at any time be claimed by any one participant, except in so far as such claim is excluded by agreement; partition may be claimed, notwithstanding any agreement to the contrary, if there is any cogent ground—see p. 247 note 1; a stipulation excluding partition during a fixed period is revoked by the death of a participant, unless the contrary is expressly provided; an agreement between the parties excluding the right to partition is not binding on any person who, as judgment creditor of any participant, has seized his share, or on the person who administers the estate of any participant in bankruptcy; the right to partition is not in any event barred by prescription—BGB 749–751, 758; KO 16 (2);

---

1   As to the right of a co-heir to sell his share in the estate, see 529.

(5) the common property cannot be alienated except with the concurrence of all the participants, but each participant may alienate his share without the assent of the others [1] —BGB 747.

361   The special rules laid down by HGB 489–509 as to the common ownership of ships (*Rhederei*), in cases where the owners are not partners in the ordinary sense of the word, are not of great practical importance.

b.   Community of Loss.

305. Community of loss exists under the rules of maritime law as to general average (*grosse Haverei*) which are derived from the *lex Rhodia de jactu*, and the general principles of which are universally adopted.   The provisions of German law on the subject may be summarized as follows :

If the master of a ship, in order to avert a danger threatening both ship and cargo, sacrifices some part of the cargo or of the ship, or incurs any special outlay, the loss or outlay is shared by ship, freight, and cargo in their proper proportions.   The statement as to the amounts respectively payable by the several parties concerned is made out by public officials who are called *Dispacheure* (average staters).   The persons whose property was sacrificed have no personal remedy against the parties liable to contribute to their loss, but are entitled to a right of pledge (393) over the objects in respect of which the contribution is payable ; this right of pledge does not affect *bona fide* purchasers, but any person who receives goods charged with such average contribution with notice of such charge becomes personally liable for the amount of the contribution if he delivers the goods to a third party ; a party who has taken possession of the goods in good faith and without notice of the right of pledge is not affected thereby—HGB 700– 733.   Analogous provisions exist as to inland navigation—Statute as to Inland Navigation, ss. 78–91.

5.   Obligations created by Estoppel

306. The principle of ' estoppel ', which plays a very important part in English law, is not known as such in Germany, but certain classes of obligations recognized

---

[1]   An agreement as to the mode of management as well as an agreement excluding the right to partition, either permanently or during a fixed period, or making it dependent upon notice, is binding on the successors in title of any participant—BGB 746, 751.

by German law are based on principles similar to those of English law of estoppel,
and may conveniently be classed together under that head.

According to the English law, a person who induces another to act on the   362
assumption that a certain state of facts is in existence must, in the cases to which
the rules as to estoppel are applicable, allow the relations between him and such
other person to be regulated by the 'conventional state of facts' thus created,
and cannot, as between himself and such other person, derive any advantage
from the circumstance that the real state of facts was different (see Lord
Blackburn's judgment in Burkinshaw v. Nicolls 3 A. C. 1004, 1025). The
German law in the cases in which the same principle is applied does not go quite
so far, but it gives a right to the party who relies on the existence of a state of
things, which does not in fact exist, to receive compensation from the party whose
representation caused his mistaken assumption. The principle is applied as
follows: (1) where a declaration of intention is void on the ground of not having
been intended seriously (98), or is avoided on the ground of mistake (99), the
party to whom the declaration was communicated is entitled to compensation for
the damage suffered by him, owing to his reliance on the effectiveness of the
declaration; where the declaration was one not required to be communicated to
another party (95), any person suffering damage by relying on its effectiveness is
entitled to compensation—BGB 122; (2) where an agreement is void on the
ground that it was impossible *ab initio* (158), or on the ground of immorality or
illegality (102), the party who at the time of the apparent formation of the
agreement was aware of its nullity must compensate the other party for any
damage suffered by his reliance on the validity of the agreement unless the nullity
was, or ought to have been, known to such other party—BGB 307–309.

The damages recoverable in either case are damages for the 'negative
interest' in the effectiveness of the declaration or the validity of the agreement
(169).

6. OBLIGATIONS AND RIGHTS OF FINDERS OF LOST OBJECTS

307. A person who finds an object lost by another and takes it into his
possession is subject to the duties and entitled to the rights appearing from the
following rules:

(1) the finder of an object of which the value exceeds three Marks must give
immediate notice to the loser, or to any person entitled to receive the lost object;   363

where this cannot be done, notice must be given to the competent police authority;

(2) the finder must keep the object in his custody unless he prefers to deliver it to the competent police authority, or unless the police authority requires him to deliver it; he is not liable for any damage to the found object caused otherwise than by his wilful default or gross negligence;

(3) if the found object is of a perishable nature, or if the expense of its preservation is excessive, the finder must sell it by public auction, having previously given notice of the intended sale to the police authority;

(4) the finder must, on demand, hand over the object or the proceeds of its sale to the loser, or to any other person entitled to receive it; by his delivery to any such person he is discharged from all further claims;

(5) the finder is entitled to the reimbursement of any reasonably necessary outlay made in connexion with the custody or preservation of the found object, as well as to a reward, calculated according to the value of the found object;

(6) if, after the lapse of a year from the communication of the notice to the police authority, no claim has been lodged with such police authority, the identity of the loser or owner remaining unknown to the finder, the finder acquires the ownership of the found object or of its proceeds of sale, unless he waives his claim thereto; if he waives his claim the parochial authority steps into his shoes. Any person suffering loss by such transfer of ownership may, within three years, claim restitution under the rules as to unjustified benefits (298).   If the value of the found object is below three Marks, the ownership is acquired after a year from the date of the finding, unless such finding is deliberately concealed [1]—BGB 965–977.

As to treasure-trove, see 341.

---

[1]   As to objects found in buildings and by public authorities, see BGB 978–983.

THIRD BOOK

LAW OF THINGS

CHAPTER I
GENERAL SURVEY

1. NATURE OF REAL RIGHTS

308. THE third book of the BGB deals mainly with 'real rights', though it also   367
incidentally contains rules referring to obligatory relations arising in connexion
with the ownership or possession of things or similar matters (see 79).

A real right is a right affecting a thing available against all the world, and
not merely against a particular person.

The most complete real right is the right of ownership, but a real right may
also concern a thing owned by another; a person entitled to a real right over a
thing owned by another may, by virtue of such right, be enabled to exercise some
of the privileges of ownership in lieu of the owner, or to restrain the owner from
exercising some of the privileges of ownership.

While obligatory rights may, within certain limits, be created at the unfettered
discretion of the parties concerned, real rights are inoperative unless they conform
to certain types defined by law.

Real rights affecting *immovables* are classified as follows: (1) ownership
rights (323); (2) rights akin to ownership rights (*e. g.* heritable building rights,
mining rights, &c. (348); (3) rights of user over land owned by others, and
rights of restraining the owner's rights of user, *viz.* servitudes (352) and
perpetual charges (366); (4) rights granted by way of security (372). Real
rights affecting *movables* are classified as follows: (1) ownership rights (323);
(2) usufruct (358); (3) rights of pledge (392).

The rights derived from possession are not real rights, but they are closely
connected with real rights, inasmuch as possession frequently assists the acquisition
or assertion of a real right. Registration is another factor by which the acquisition
and assertion of a real right may be assisted, but it only affects immovables and
registered ships.

The general law as to real rights may, as to certain specified matters (*e. g.*   368 family settlements, entails, transmission of immovables on owner's death; rights relating to rivers, springs, mines, and minerals; sporting rights; neighbour's rights, servitudes and perpetual charges; compulsory purchase and compulsory consolidation and subdivision of land; rights of aliens and corporate bodies to hold land, &c.) and within certain specified limits, be modified by State law— EG 57–69, 73, 74, 88, 109–131.

2. Rules as to the Creation, Transfer, and Extinction of Real Rights by Act-in-the-Law

a. Generally.

309. A real right is, as a general rule, created, transferred, or extinguished by an agreement between the parties concerned called a ' real agreement ' (*dinglicher Vertrag* [1]) , by which the person by whom the right is to be created, modified, or transferred declares his intention in that behalf, and by which the person in whose favour such right is to be created, modified, or transferred declares his acceptance. A real agreement must be distinguished from an obligatory agreement concerning a real right.   A ' real' agreement is intended to effect the change to which it refers by its own operation, whereas by an obligatory agreement concerning a real right one of the parties undertakes to effect such change by a subsequent transaction.   The difference between a ' real agreement' and an ' obligatory agreement concerning a real right' is analogous to the difference between a ' sale of goods' and an ' agreement to sell goods' —Sale of Goods Act 1893, s. 1 (3)—or between a ' conveyance on sale of land' and an ' agreement for the sale of land' under English law.

A ' real agreement ' , though intended by its own operation to create, modify, transfer, or extinguish the real right which it concerns, is not operative as a general rule unless accompanied, followed, or preceded by a prescribed outward act (transfer of possession or registration).   Under English law, a sale of movables or a conveyance of land, as a general rule, operates immediately and completely without the necessity of any transfer of possession or registration, but in some exceptional cases an additional outward act is required, as under German law, for the purpose of making the sale or conveyance completely effective (*e. g.*

369

---

1   The BGB uses the term *Einigung* in the place of *dinglicher Vertrag*; the textbooks use the latter expression, which is more convenient and more familiar to German readers.

in the case of a transfer of registered land—Land Transfer Act 1875, ss. 30–34—or of a bill of sale given by way of security for the payment of a debt—Bills of Sale Act 1882, s. 8).

b.   As to Immovables and Registered Ships.

310. The following special rules apply as to immovables [1] :

(1) The transfer of ownership or the creation or modification of a right affecting an immovable, or the transfer of ownership, or of any such right, or the creation or modification of any right affecting such a right is effected by the combined operation of two acts, namely: (*a*) a real agreement (309) between the parties; (*b*) compliance with the rules as to registration.

The real agreement is not binding on the parties before registration, [2] unless it is made by public act declared in the presence of the Registrar or by a written document filed in the Registry, or unless the party whose right is affected by the transaction has delivered to the other party [3] a document in the prescribed form authorizing the registration of the change (318)—BGB 873, 876, 877.

(2) The release of a right is effected by the combined operation of two acts, namely (*a*) a declaration by the releasing party communicated to the party in whose favour the release is intended to operate, or made before the Registrar; (*b*) the cancellation of the right on the register.

The declaration mentioned sub (*a*) is not binding before the cancellation has been effected, unless made before the Registrar, or unless the releasing party has delivered to the other party a document in the prescribed form authorizing the cancellation (318).   If the right intended to be released is subject to the right of another, such other must declare his assent (130) [4] —BGB 875, 876.

370

---

[1]   The rules given in the text are not applicable in the districts in which the new system of registration is not as yet operative, or as to immovables, which under the provisions of State law are exempt from registration (see 315).

[2]   After registration the agreement is binding though not made in the prescribed form.

[3]   A declaration made by one of the parties to any transaction of the above-mentioned nature is not invalidated by the fact that, subsequently to the time at which such declaration has become binding on the declarant, and after the filing of the application for registration, but before registration, the declarant's powers of alienation have become subject to any restraint (*e. g.* by his bankruptcy), see 104—BGB 878.

[4]   In the case of the release of a charge on an immovable the owner's assent is required (391).   The release is not invalidated by the fact that a restraint on the power of disposition of the releasing party is imposed after the filing of the application for registration—BGB 878.

(3) In certain specified cases a real right is created, transferred, or extinguished *ipso facto* in connexion with another event. [1]   See, for instance, p. 364 note 1.

(4) In the case of registered ships registration is not required except on the creation of rights of pledge; these require registration in a similar way as charges on immovables—BGB 1260.

---

[1]   In any such case the event by which the change is produced has the effect of creating a discrepancy between the true state of things and the state of things recorded in the register, and it is to the interest of the party benefited by the change to apply for a rectification of the register (321).

CHAPTER II
POSSESSION AND REGISTRATION

1. POSSESSION

a. Definition of Technical Terms.

311. POSSESSION means 'the actual control' (*tatsächliche Gewalt*) over the thing to which it refers—BGB 854 (1). The distinction between detention and possession, which is familiar to the students of Roman law, and which was preserved in the first draft of the BGB, has now disappeared. Under Roman law possession in the legal sense was not recognized unless the possessor had the intention of dealing with the thing possessed by him as if he were its owner; a bailee or lessee was deemed 'detentor' and not a 'possessor' of the bailed or leased object. In the terminology of the new German law, as in the terminology of English law, the term 'possession' is used in every case in which actual control exists, without regard to the purpose for which it is exercised. This definition is, however, subject to the following rules, by which it is supplemented and qualified:

(1) *Possession by clerks or servants.*

Where any person who has a thing under his control exercises such control for another in his household or business, or under any other circumstances requiring him to follow the directions of such other with regard thereto, such other is alone deemed to be the possessor thereof—BGB 855. A person who in this manner has control on behalf of another is called *Besitzdiener* or *Besitzgehilfe* ('possessor's servant' or 'possessor's assistant').

(2) *Direct and indirect possession.*

Where possession is obtained for a period of time by virtue of any contractual or other relation between the person authorizing the possession and the person obtaining it (*e. g.* under a lease or bailment, or by virtue of a right of pledge, or

372   of a right of usufruct, or under an agency agreement) the person authorizing the possession and the person exercising actual control are both deemed to be in possession; the possession of the person exercising actual control is called 'direct possession' (*unmittelbarer Besitz*), the possession of the person authorizing the control is called 'indirect possession' (*mittelbarer Besitz*)—BGB 868.

(3) *Proprietary possession.*

A person who is in possession of a thing intending to deal with it as owner is called 'proprietary possessor' (*Eigenbesitzer*)—BGB 872.

(4) *Faulty possession.*

Possession obtained against the former possessor's will, and without the sanction of any rule of law, is called 'faulty possession' (*fehlerhafter Besitz*)—BGB 858 (2).

(5) *Joint possession.*

Several persons together may be in possession of a thing in a manner corresponding to the manner in which several persons may be co-owners of a thing (325).   Such possession is called *Mitbesitz*, and will in this treatise be described as 'joint possession' .

(6) *Part possession.*

Separate possession of any specified part of a thing, more particularly of any specified part of a building, is called *Teilbesitz* (part possession—see BGB 865).

b.   Acquisition of Possession.

312. Possession is acquired by the assumption of the actual control over a thing delivered or abandoned or lost by a former possessor, or acquired originally by the new possessor.

(1) *Delivery.*

The transfer of the possession of a movable thing may be effected by the delivery of such thing into the hands of the transferee or into a place or receptacle of which the transferee has control (as when coals are deposited on a truck belonging to the purchaser).

373   The transfer of the possession of an immovable is effected by any outward act by which the transferee is enabled to obtain access to such immovable (*e. g.* by

the delivery of the key).

In any case in which a ' real agreement' (309) is concluded between the transferor and the transferee as to the transfer of the possession of a movable or immovable thing, such transfer is deemed to have taken place as soon as the transferee obtains control over such thing—BGB 854 (2).

The indirect possession (311 sub (2)) of a thing may be transferred by the assignment of the claim to its delivery—BGB 870.

In the case of goods represented by a negotiable instrument (bill of lading, dock warrant, warehouse receipt, &c.), the transfer of the document of title operates as a transfer of the right to obtain possession—see HGB 424, 450, 647—and has, therefore, the effect of giving the transferee the indirect possession of the goods.

Symbolical delivery, which played a great part in mediaeval law, has ceased to exist in modern German law; the delivery of a key is not in the nature of a symbolical delivery if it enables the transferee to exercise control over the thing of which the possession is to be transferred; if it does not attain that object it has no legal effect whatever.

(2) *Assumption of control after abandonment or loss by former possessor.*

A person who assumes possession of a thing of which the control was voluntarily abandoned or involuntarily lost by another—see 313—acquires the possession of such thing. [1]

(3) *Assumption of control over things not previously possessed by another.*

Possession of a thing not previously possessed by another is acquired: (1) by any person who severs a component part (75) from a thing possessed by him and obtains control over such severed part; (2) by any person who appropriates any wild animal or any fish caught by him in the sea.

c.   Termination of Possession.

313. The possession of a thing is terminated by the loss of the control over such thing either by delivery to another or by abandonment or loss—BGB 856 (1).

The possession of a thing is not deemed to have been abandoned or lost if the

374

---

[1]   Where control is acquired by means of an unlawful act the possession is faulty, and has not the same effects as lawful possession, see 315, 334.

circumstance preventing the exercise of actual control is by its nature of a merely temporary character.

Illustrations: Possession of a plot of land is not lost if, owing to a flood or a landslip, the access to it is for the time being prevented; possession of a horse is not lost while it has temporarily strayed out of the paddock in which it is kept— BGB 856 (2).

d.   Transmission of Possession on Death.

314. The possession of all things possessed by any person at the time of his death becomes, *ipso facto*, vested in his heirs—see 470 sub (1)—BGB 857.

The possession thus devolving on the heirs is different in its nature from ordinary possession, though it is not called by another name; where the heirs, owing to absence or some other cause, are unable to exercise actual control, their possession is of a merely fictitious nature, but it has many of the effects of physical possession. [1]

e.   Possessory Remedies. [2]

(1) Self-help.

315. The act of a person who unlawfully deprives another of his possession, or disturbs him therein, is described as ' unlawful interference ' (*verbotene Eigenmacht*)—BGB 858 (1).

A person whose possession is disturbed by unlawful interference may defend his right by force, and may use force for the recovery of a movable thing from a person apprehended *in flagranti delicto*.   A person who by unlawful interference is ousted from the possession of an immovable may, immediately after being ousted, use force for the recovery of possession—BGB 859 (1) (2) (3).

The right of self-defence may be exercised by any person who has actual control

---

[1]   For an express recognition of the distinction between the heirs' fictitious possession and their actual possession, see BGB 2025, 2027.   As regards the meaning of the expression ' of the possessor of the inheritance ' (*Erbschaftsbesitzer*), see p. 601 note 1.

[2]   A person wilfully or negligently and unlawfully disturbing the possession of another is liable to compensate such other under the general rules as to unlawful acts (287).   The claim for compensation is in such a case available as well as the possessory remedies, but as compensation primarily means restitution (167) the two remedies may frequently coincide.

on the possessor's behalf, and against the heirs of the person guilty of unlawful interference, as well as against any other person deriving title under him with notice of the faulty nature of the possession [1]—BGB 859 (4), 860.

(2) *Legal remedies against unlawful interference.*

The rule of English law, according to which ' bare possession constitutes a sufficient title to enable a party enjoying it to obtain legal remedy against a mere wrongdoer' (see Notes to Armory *v.* Delamirie 1 Sm. L. C., 11th edition, on p. 357), is also recognized by the present German law.

A person who is ousted from possession may claim recovery of possession from any person who, as against him, is in faulty possession—311 sub (4)— BGB 861 (1).

A person who is disturbed in his possession by unlawful interference may claim a removal of the disturbance, and, where further disturbance is impending, may obtain a perpetual injunction against the wrongdoer—BGB 862 (1).

Neither remedy is available if the aggrieved person was himself in faulty possession as against the wrongdoer or as against his predecessor in title, and if such faulty possession was obtained within a year prior to the ouster or disturbance—BGB 861 (2), 862 (2).

Illustration: *A* claims the delivery of a horse which *B* unlawfully took out of *A*'s stable. *B* proves that six months before the removal of the horse *A* had similarly removed it from his stable. The claim is dismissed, notwithstanding the fact that *B*'s act was unlawful. If *B* had taken the horse more than a year after it had been taken from him, *A*'s action would have been successful.

Either of the above-mentioned possessory remedies is forfeited:

(1) by the lapse of a year from the time of the unlawful interference—BGB 864 (1);   376

(2) by a final judgment obtained in a separate action [2] declaring the person guilty of the interference entitled to the right of possession or to the commission of the disturbing act—BGB 864 (2).

---

[1]   As to the right of the possessor of a thing to remove it from a parcel of land possessed by another, see BGB 867.

[2]   In an action for the recovery of possession or the removal of a disturbance brought on the ground of unlawful interference, the defendant cannot assert his own right to possession or to commit the disturbing act, except for the purpose of proving that he was not guilty of unlawful interference—BGB 863.

(3) *Legal remedies for establishing right to possession.*

The remedies described above, sub (2), are available only in case of unlawful interference; the remedies referred to below, on the other hand, are available in such cases, and also in any case in which the person who wishes to establish his right to possession was not ousted or disturbed by any unlawful interference.   The following rules apply on this subject:

(1) the former possessor of a movable thing may recover its possession from the actual possessor if the latter when acquiring possession was not acting in good faith—BGB 1007 (1);

(2) if any movable thing, other than money or a negotiable ins trument issued to bearer, was stolen from the former possessor, or lost by him, he may recover its possession from the actual possessor, even if such possessor when acquiring possession was acting in good faith—BGB 1007 (2) [1];

(3) a former possessor, who, when acquiring possession, was not acting in good faith, or who has voluntarily abandoned the possession of a thing which has since come into the possession of another, is not entitled to recover its possession from such other—BGB 1007 (3).

f.   Effect of Possession as to Proof of Ownership and as to Right to Profits.

(1) *Presumption of ownership.*

316. A person who is in proprietary possession—311 sub (3)—of a movable thing is presumed to be its owner; any person who, as defendant or plaintiff in an action, wishes to dispute such ownership must prove his allegation.   This presumption is not, however, available against the former possessor of a movable thing other than money, or an instrument to bearer, from whom such movable thing was stolen, or by whom it was lost.

A former possessor of a movable thing is presumed to have been the owner of such thing while he was in possession thereof.   Where the possession is divided between a direct possessor and an indirect possessor—311 sub (2)—the presumption operates in favour of the latter—BGB 1006.

377

---

1   This rule is not applicable if the actual possessor is also the owner of the thing lost or stolen from a former possessor.

(2) *Right to fruits and profits.*

A person in possession of a thing—whether movable or immovable—is entitled to the fruits (77) of such thing if he, in good faith, believes himself to be the owner of such thing or entitled to the usufruct thereof, and if his title to possession was acquired for valuable consideration; if he is ejected by the true owner, he is not bound to account for any fruits received up to the time of the commencement of the owner's action; if the possession was acquired in good faith, but without valuable consideration, the possessor must account for the fruits under the rules as to unjustified benefits (298)—BGB 987, 988, 993; see also below—339.

2.   REGISTRATION OF RIGHTS RELATING TO IMMOVABLES

a.   General Statement.

317. At the date of the coming into force of the BGB registers on the model required by the new law existed in most Prussian districts, but in other parts of Germany considerable diversity prevailed.   The time and manner of the introduction of registers arranged according to the new system was, by EG 186, left to the discretion of each local sovereign; the establishment of new registers in those States in which the previously existing registers were unfit for adoption under the new system, is now proceeding gradually in accordance with the Orders in Council issued on the subject in the several States which they concern.   The mode of introduction generally resembles the mode in which the Prussian system was originally introduced; that is to say, the whole of the parcels of land situate within each registration district are registered by the registration authorities *proprio*   378 *motu*, with the incumbrances thereon, on the information derived from the land-tax registers and maps, or from the old registers as supplemented by the depositions of the parties concerned; that being done, a period of time for the presentation of claims adverse to the registered rights is fixed and announced by public notice; a party who fails to present his claim within the stipulated period of time is in the same position as a party who fails to register a right to which he is entitled in a district in which the register is finally established.   After the lapse of the period, and after a further period allowed for dealing with adverse claims which have been presented, the register is deemed to be established, and an official announcement is made to that effect.

In those German districts in which registers arranged in accordance with the provisions of the new law have not as yet become operative, the old local law, as to the acquisition and loss of the ownership of immovables, and as to the creation, transfer, hypothecation, and discharge of other rights relating to immovables and certain other cognate matters is still in force—EG 189 (1).

State legislation may exempt certain kinds of immovables (*e. g.* immovables belonging to public authorities) from the rules as to registration, and may also provide that servitudes affecting such immovables may be created without being registered—EG 127, 128; GBO 90.

The following statement refers to the law of those districts in which the new registers are in operation, and to such immovables as are not exempt from registration under the rule stated above.

Each German state is divided into registration districts, and every parcel of land, as a general rule, has a separate folio (*Grundbuchsblatt*) in the register of the district; but for particular reasons several independent parcels may be registered on the same folio—GBO 2, 3, 4, 86–89.

Each folio, in addition to the heading and the description of the property, has three separate divisions, the first being intended for the registration, names, and descriptions of the successive owners, the second for the registration of incumbrances other than charges granted by way of security (*e. g.* servitudes, perpetual charges, heritable building rights, mining rights, &c.), the third for the registration of charges granted by way of security.

A lease, as mentioned above (205), does not confer any real right on the lessee, and is, therefore, incapable of registration, but a heritable building right (349), which, if granted for a limited time, corresponds in its effect to an English lease, requires registration as an incumbrance on the parcel which it affects; a heritable building right may also be registered on the owner's application on a separate folio, in the same way as a parcel of land, and must in any case be registered in such a manner in the event of any transfer of ownership or hypothecation—GBO 7. [1]

The same rule is applied to such mining rights, and other heritable rights similar to rights of ownership, as under the provisions of any State law are dealt with as immovables (348, 350).

---

[1] A similar rule prevails under the English Land Transfer Acts as to leases exceeding a certain duration; they are registered as incumbrances on the freehold title and may be registered separately on the leasehold register; in a compulsory district the leasehold title must be registered on any sale.

Registration under German law does not in any case confer an absolute title on the person registered as owner; the distinction between registration with an absolute title and registration with a possessory or qualified title, which exists in England, is therefore unknown in Germany.

A further difference between the English and the German system of registration arises from the fact that, subject to the exceptions referred to above, every parcel of land *must* be registered, while in England, even in the districts in which registration is compulsory, only such parcels are required to be registered as are sold after the date of the introduction of compulsion.

b.   Procedure on Registration.

318. As mentioned above (310) the creation, transfer, or modification of any right affecting an immovable is effected by the combined operation of a real agreement between the parties and the registration of the effect of such agreement, while the release of a right is effected by the combined operation of the releasing 380 declaration and the cancellation on the register of the right intended to be released.   The registration authorities are, except in the event of the transfer of ownership (327) or the creation or transfer of a right similar to ownership (348), not bound to inquire into the existence or validity of the real agreement or of the releasing declaration; if the agreement or release acted upon by the registration authorities is invalid, the consequent state of the register does not represent the true facts, and any party whose rights are injuriously affected by such incorrect state of the register may obtain its rectification (321).

The only evidence required by the Registrar in cases not coming under the above-mentioned exceptions is a written authorization to make the required entry or cancellation, executed in the prescribed form by the party whose right is to be incumbered, transferred, modified, or released by such registration or cancellation. In the case of the transfer of a certificated charge (374) the production of the transfer deed (390) is sufficient.   An authorization to register the grant, modification, or transfer of a right is called ' an authority for registration ' (*Eintragungsbewilligung*); an authorization to register the release of a right is called ' an authority for cancellation ' (*Löschungsbewilligung*) [1] —GBO 19, 21−29.

The original or an authenticated copy of every document filed in support of

---

1   As to the Registrar's right to enter a reference to the ' registration authorization ' in lieu of the full definition of the right requiring registration, see BGB 874.

the application for registration must be retained at the registry; the documents so retained are called *Grundakten.*

The register and all documents referred to in any entry are open to the inspection of any person who can prove a legitimate interest—GBO 9, 11.

c.   Registration of Cautions and Objections.

(1) *Cautions*

319. Under English law any person claiming to be interested in any registered land may lodge a caution with the Registrar, accompanied by an affidavit as to the nature of his interest and subject to liability in damages in the event of his acting without reasonable cause.   The effect of such lodgment is that no dealing can be registered without the cautioner's consent in respect of the land to which the caution applies before the expiration of the period specified in a notice which has to be served on the cautioner—Land Transfer Act 1875, ss. 53–56.

The rules of German law as to cautions differ from the English rules in the following respects:

(1) a caution (*Vormerkung*) [1] cannot be registered without the authorization of the person whose right it affects, or an order from the competent court obtained on summary application—BGB 885;

(2) the registration of a caution does not prevent any dealings with the immovable or right affected thereby, but any such dealing (including the seizure of the immovable or right by any judgment creditor or trustee in bankruptcy) which takes place after the registration of the caution is inoperative, in so far as it would, if operative, frustrate or restrict the cautioner's claim [2] —BGB 883 (2);

(3) if the person whose right is affected by the registration of the caution is entitled to any defence permanently excluding the cautioner's claim, he is entitled to demand the cancellation of the caution—BGB 886;

---

[1]   A caution is registered for the benefit of a person who is entitled to an obligatory right affecting an immovable.   An obligatory right of such a nature would according to English terminology be described as an equitable interest in the immovable.

[2]   Illustration: *A* by an obligatory agreement undertakes to transfer the ownership of Whiteacre to *B* on a specified future date; *B* registers a caution for securing his right; *A* subsequently transfers the ownership to *C*; the right acquired by *C* is subject to *B*'s right.   Under a further special provision contained in BGB 888, *C* is bound to give his assent to the registration of *B* as owner on the completion of his agreement with *A*. The caution, in so far as it is operative, is binding on any heir of a deceased person whose right it affects, notwithstanding any restriction as to the liability of such heir for the debts of the estate of the deceased (533).

(4) if the person who is for the time being entitled to the benefit of the caution cannot be found, the cancellation of the caution may be effected after the lapse of a specified period in the same way—*mutatis mutandis*—as the cancellation of a charge in a case in which the mortgagee cannot be found (387)—BGB 887.

(2) *Objections.*

The registration of an objection (*Widerspruch*) to the correctness of the   382
register may be effected (in a similar way as the registration of a caution) by any party claiming a light to the rectification of the register (321) [1] —BGB 899.

If the person who has caused the objection to be registered succeeds in his application for rectification, any third party whose right was registered subsequently to the registration of the objection is bound to submit to the rectification.

d.   Effect of Registration.

(1) *As to presumption of right.*

320. In the same way as the possession of a movable creates a presumption of its ownership (316), the registration of a right affecting an immovable creates a presumption of the validity of the right and the title of the person in whose favour it is registered; the cancellation of any such right on the register creates a presumption of the release or extinction of such right—BGB 891.

(2) *As to priorities.*

As between incumbrances registered in the same division of the register the priorities are determined by order of registration; as between incumbrances registered in different divisions the priorities are determined by the date of the entry; incumbrances registered in different divisions as from the same date rank *pari passu*—BGB 879.

Illustration: A right of usufruct and two hypothecary charges are registered on the same date.   Both hypothecary charges rank *pari passu* with the right of usufruct, but the charge registered in the first place ranks in priority to the charge registered in the second place.

The priorities may be altered by subsequent agreement between the parties

---

1   As to a case in which the registration of an objection may be effected without the concurrence of the party concerned, or the intervention of the Court, see p. 408 note 1.

383 concerned.   In such a case there must be a real agreement between the incumbrancer whose right obtains priority and the incumbrancer whose right is postponed, and the change must be registered.   If the right intended to be postponed is an hypothecary charge, land charge, or annuity charge (372), the owner of the mortgaged property must give his assent; if the right intended to be postponed is itself subject to the right of another, such other must give his assent—BGB 880. On the creation of any incumbrance the owner of the immovable which it affects may reserve to himself the right to create other incumbrances within specified limits having priority over the first-mentioned incumbrance—BGB 881. [1]

e.   Rectification of Register.

321. If any right relating to an immovable or to any charge or other incumbrance on any immovable exists without being registered, or is incorrectly registered or incorrectly cancelled, or if any charge or incumbrance, caution or objection which ought to have been cancelled has not been cancelled, the person affected by the incorrect state of the register may apply for a rectification of the register, and may compel any person whose rights would be affected by such rectification to give his assent thereto, and to procure any registration required for the purpose of making such assent effective.

If the production of any certificate of charge (374) is required for the purpose of obtaining the rectification of the register, the possessor of the certificate may be compelled by the person entitled to rectification to produce such certificate.   The costs of the rectification must be borne by the applicant, except in so far as a contrary result follows from the circumstances under which the right to rectification arises [2] —BGB 894–897.

3.   REGISTRATION OF SHIPS

384 **322.** Every German ship must be registered with the owner's name and other particulars under the Imperial Statute of 1899 relating to the right of the flag of

---

1   The reservation must be registered as a qualification of the incumbrance which it concerns—BGB 881.

2   If any right is wrongly registered in favour of a person by whose default the inaccurate registration was brought about, he is, of course, bound to consent to the rectification of the register and to pay the incidental costs; in many cases the incorrect state of the register is not due to the default of any person; thus, if owing to the fulfilment of a condition, the ownership of an immovable is transferred from *A* to *B*, *B* has a claim to the rectification of the register, but he must pay the costs.

merchant ships, and all changes affecting the registered particulars must equally be registered.   Non-compliance with the provisions as to registration of any rights other than incumbrances does not affect the rights of the parties concerned; incumbrances affecting ships are subject to the same rule as to registration and priorities, and as to the circumstances entitling a party to claim the rectification of the register, as incumbrances on immovables—BGB 1259–1263, 1267.

CHAPTER III
OWNERSHIP

1. DEFINITION OF OWNERSHIP; EXTENT OF OWNER'S RIGHTS; CO-OWNERSHIP

a. Definition.

385   **323.** UNDER English law the ownership of a parcel of land is frequently split up among several persons, of whom each is entitled to an 'estate' in such parcel, and who severally and in succession to each other become entitled to the possession or to the rents and profits of such parcel; where the ownership is not split up into several estates the owner is called a tenant in fee simple. A German owner of land is in all cases a tenant in fee simple. [1]

Ownership in its complete form, like liberty in its complete form, is existent in human thought but not in reality. The complete dominion which the term ownership implies is restricted by the rights of the community, and also by the private rights of others; this restricted character of ownership finds expression in the definition contained in BGB 903, which declares that the owner of a thing may, *in so far as the rules of law and the rights of third parties admit*, deal with such thing as he pleases and restrain the interference of others.

The provisions of State law restricting proprietary rights in the public interest are expressly maintained by EG 111, and the general rule of the present German law, according to which the exercise of a right is prohibited if it can have no object except the infliction of damage on another (79), also imposes a limit to the exercise of the rights of ownership.

The power of the owner of an immovable to restrain the interference of others
386   enables him to prevent the construction or maintenance on an adjoining immovable

---

[1]   As to the creation of successive interests by the grant of a right of usufruct, or by the appointment of a 'reversionary heir' taking in succession to a 'limited heir', see 358, 494.

of erections, [1] the existence or use of which would with reasonable certainty lead to an interference with his rights of ownership—BGB 907 (1) ; he is also, in the event of the threatened collapse of a building situated on an adjoining immovable, entitled to compel the person who would be liable for the damage caused by such collapse (294) to take the steps necessary for averting the danger—BGB 908.

The owner of a thing is not, however, entitled to restrain any interference with such thing on the part of another who is compelled to have recourse to it for the purpose of averting an impending danger of a much more serious nature than the damage caused by his act—BGB 904.

Certain kinds of interference with the rights of ownership must be tolerated, because they belong to the ordinary conditions of life in industrial communities. The owner of a parcel of land of which the enjoyment is interfered with by gases, vapours, smells, smoke, soot, warmth, noises, vibration, or any similar disturbing influence proceeding from another piece of land, is without a remedy, in so far as the interference with the enjoyment of his own land is not of any material importance, or in so far as the disturbing influence is brought about by a use of the land from which it proceeds which under the local circumstances is not contrary to usage. The immission of any gases or vapours, &c., by means of specially constructed pipes may be restrained—BGB 906.

b.   Local Extension of Ownership Rights.

324. As under English law, the ownership of land extends upwards *usque ad coelum*, and downwards *usque ad inferos*, but under the rules of modern German law the owner is not entitled to restrain any interferences with his right which takes place at an altitude so high, or at a depth so low, that no damage is caused thereby—BGB 905.

Interferences disturbing the amenities of a piece of land (as, for instance,   387 telegraph wires obstructing the view of the sky) are deemed damaging interferences, but aerial navigation at a considerable altitude comes within the statutory qualification.

As regards the land below the surface the ownership rights are subject to the right of third parties to win minerals under the conditions imposed by State law

---

1   Trees or bushes are not ' erections' within the meaning of the rule—BGB 907 (2)—but it may be provided by State law that they must be kept at a certain distance from the boundary—EG 124; see also p. 361 note 1; GO 26; EG 125.

(350)—EG 67.

c. Co-ownership.

325. The co-ownership (*Miteigentum*) of German law is analogous to the 'tenancy in common' of English law, [1] and governed by the following rules:

(1) a thing held in co-ownership may be incumbered in favour of one of the co-owners;

(2) a parcel of land held in co-ownership may be incumbered in favour of the owner for the time being of another parcel of land, notwithstanding the fact that the actual owner of such other parcel is one of the co-owners;

(3) a parcel of land may be incumbered in favour of the owners for the time being of a parcel of land held in co-ownership, notwithstanding the fact that the owner of the parcel subject to such incumbrance is one of the co-owners of the parcel entitled to its benefit;

(4) an arrangement between the co-owners of a parcel of land as to management, user, partition, or other similar matters is not binding on the successor in title of any co-owner, unless registered as an incumbrance on the land register;

(5) a claim enforceable, on the partition of a parcel of land, by one of the co-owners against the others is binding on the successors in title of any co-owner only in so far as it is registered on the land register [2].

(6) each of the co-owners of a thing may assert the rights of ownership over such thing as against third parties; a claim for the delivery of a thing held in co-ownership cannot, however, be satisfied except by delivery to all the co-owners jointly, or by lodgment with a public authority (164), or delivery to a judicially appointed Receiver—BGB 432 (1), 1008–1011.

388

2.   MUTUAL RIGHTS OF NEIGHBOURING OWNERS

326. The mutual rights of neighbouring owners are governed by the following rules:

---

[1]   The expression 'co-ownership' is used with reference to the community of the more intimate kind (*Eigentum zur gesamten Hand*) as well as with reference to the ordinary community by divided shares (*Gemeinschaft nach Bruchteilen*)—see 304.

[2]   Such a claim would have to be registered as an hypothecary charge (373).

(1) *Rights to lateral support.*

A parcel of land must not be excavated so as to take away the support of a neighbouring parcel of land unless some other method of support is provided—BGB 909.

(2) *Rights as to projecting roots and branches.*

Projecting roots may, in so far as they interfere with the enjoyment of a parcel of land, be removed by the owner of such parcel of land; projecting branches interfering with such enjoyment may be removed if their owner fails to do so within a reasonable period specified in a notice communicated to him [1]—BGB 910.

(3) *Rights as to fruits falling across boundary.*

Fruits falling from a tree or bush standing on a neighbouring piece of land, not being a piece of land used for public purposes, are deemed to be fruits of the piece of land on which they fall—BGB 911.

(4) *Rights as to overlapping buildings.*

If the owner of a parcel of land, without being guilty of wilful default or gross negligence, has constructed a building overlapping his boundary, the owner of the land on which such building overlaps, who has failed to raise an immediate objection, must suffer such overlapping building to remain on his land, but he is entitled to the payment of rent for the use of the space occupied thereby, and the rent so payable is a charge on the building taking priority over all other charges; 389 the party for the time being entitled to such rent may at any time require the person for the time being liable to pay the same to purchase the space occupied by the overlapping building at a reasonable price [2]—BGB 912-915.

---

[1]   The rules on this subject may be modified by State legislation—EG 122, 124.   Many State laws provide that trees and bushes must be kept beyond a certain distance from the boundary.   Special provisions also exist as regards fruit trees; in Württemberg the right to remove branches and roots projecting from land used for farming purposes or from public roads is much restricted. —Württemberg AG 241-245.

[2]   If the overlapping building interferes with a heritable building right (349), or a servitude (354), affecting the land occupied thereby, the person for the time being entitled to the benefit of such building right or servitude has the same privileges—*mutatis mutandis*—as the owner of the parcel of land would have had, had such building right or servitude not been in existence—BGB 916.

(5) *Rights as to way of necessity.*

Under German law, as under English law, a right of way of necessity arises when a piece of land is severed from a larger piece, and thereby cut off from communication with the outside world; in such a case the owner of the 'land-locked' piece of land has a right of way over the piece of land which retains the communication, without being required to pay any compensation to the owner of such piece of land.

A right of way, subject to the payment of compensation, arises under German law in every case in which a parcel of land is without such communication with a public highway as is required for its proper enjoyment. The compensation payable to the owners of the land over which the right is exercised is a rent payable in a similar way as the rent payable in respect of the space occupied by an overlapping building—see above, sub (4).

A right of way of necessity does not arise in any case in which the cutting off from communication of the land-locked piece of land was brought about by its owner's own arbitrary act [1]—BGB 917, 918.

(6) *Rights as to boundaries.*

Either of two adjoining owners may require the other to concur in the erection or restoration of a boundary mark in the manner required by State law or local custom, the expense being shared by both equally, unless another mode of division results from the relations between the parties—BGB 919.

If two plots of land are separated by an intervening plot, ditch, wall, hedge, fence, or similar appliance serving for the benefit of both plots, it is presumed that the owners of both plots are entitled to the common use of such intervening plot or appliance, unless it is apparent from outward signs that it belongs exclusively to one of the two owners. [2] The common right of user entitles either of the two owners to such use as will not hinder the use of the other, the costs of maintenance being borne by the two owners in equal shares—BGB 921, 922.

The fruits of a tree or bush standing on the boundary plot belong to both owners in equal shares; either owner may demand the removal of the tree or bush

---

[1] State legislation may extend the rules as to ways of necessity so as to provide for access to a railway line or river—EG 123—but this privilege has not been exercised up to the present.

[2] A similar presumption exists in English law as to party walls—see Cubitt *v.* Porter 8 B. & C. 257; 32 R. R. 374.

at the joint cost of both owners; if the other owner waives his interest in the tree or bush the owner who removes it has to bear the whole cost, but acquires the exclusive ownership of the severed tree or bush.   The claim to the removal of the tree or bush is excluded in a case in which it serves as a boundary mark, and cannot conveniently be replaced by another mark—BGB 923.

In the event of any dispute as to the exact boundary the mode of possession is the determining factor; if the mode of possession cannot be accurately established, each of the plots separated by the disputed plot is increased by a plot equal in size to one-half of the disputed plot, unless such result would contradict ascertained facts; in the last-mentioned event the division has to be made in such manner as appears equitable under the circumstances—BGB 920.

(7) *Rights derived under State law.*

(a) *As to windows and light.*

The rules as to the mutual rights of neighbours concerning windows and access of light (*Fensterrecht und Lichtrecht*) which are governed by State law—EG 124—vary considerably.   Under the provisions of the Prussian Code, which remain in force in a large part of the kingdom of Prussia, two kinds of rights are recognized:

(*aa*) the occupier of a parcel of land is entitled to demand that all windows in the wall immediately adjoining such land should be barred, and also placed at a certain height above the ground—ALR I. 8 § 138;

(*bb*) the occupier of a house is entitled to prohibit the erection of any building depriving the windows of such house of light, if such windows have been in existence for a period of ten years; if the building to which such windows belong receives its light exclusively from the side on which they are placed, the new building must be erected at a sufficient distance to allow the sky to be seen from an unopened window on the ground floor; if the building in which such windows are placed also receives light from another side, it is sufficient for the sky to be seen from an unopened window on the first floor—ALR I. 8 § § 142, 143.

Under German common law no such prescriptive right to light exists.

Prussian and English law resemble each other in respect of the rules as to deprivation of light, but under English law the period of prescription is twenty years instead of ten years, and there is no absolute rule as to the quantity of light to which the owner of land becomes entitled by prescription.   'Any substantial interference with his comfortable use and enjoyment of his house according to the

391

usage of ordinary persons in that locality is actionable as a nuisance at common law. ' —Farwell J. in Higgins *v.* Betts (1905) 2 Ch. 210, 214.

(*b*) *As to other matters.*

Among other neighbours' rights recognized by certain State laws and remaining in force the following may be mentioned :

(*aa*) the right to demand that cesspools be kept at a certain distance from the boundary ;

(*bb*) the right to prevent the planting of trees interfering with the wind necessary to drive a windmill ;

(*cc*) the right of the owner of a parcel of land to have access to the neighbouring land for the purpose of affixing planks to buildings standing on his own land (*Hammerschlagrecht*).

3.　Acquisition and Loss of Ownership

A.　As to Immovables

a.　Derivative Acquisition from True Owner. [1]

392　　**327.** A real agreement (309) intended to transfer the ownership of an immovable is called *Auflassung*, and will, in the course of this treatise, be called a ' conveyance by agreement ' ; whereas other transactions affecting immovables can be effected by successive declarations of the parties, a conveyance by agreement must be effected by contemporaneous declarations of the parties or their attorneys

---

[1]　The text deals exclusively with the transfer of ownership by act-in-the-law, but the ownership of an immovable is frequently transferred from one person to another without the necessity of any such act.　Thus on the marriage of spouses who have made an ante-nuptial marriage contract providing for community of goods—217, all property not having the character of privileged or separate property, which was vested in either spouse at the time of the marriage, is *ipso facto* transferred to both spouses as co-owners; where the community of goods is provided for by a post-nuptial marriage contract, the transfer of ownership takes place on the execution of such contract; the ownership of after-acquired property in either case becomes vested in both spouses on acquisition.　Where any such property consists of any immovable, or any right relating to an immovable, either of the spouses can compel the other to concur in the application for the registration of the change of ownership—BGB 1438, 1519, 1549.　The death of a person has the effect of transferring the ownership of his property to his heirs—BGB 1922, 1942.　In the case of bankruptcy the property of the bankrupt does not, as under English law, become vested in a trustee, but remains vested in the bankrupt, who, however, becomes incapable of alienation, whilst, on the other hand, the trustee in bankruptcy acquires certain powers of disposition relating to such property—KO 6; RGZ 29, 29.

before the Registrar; a conveyance by agreement which is made subject to any condition (111) or to any stipulation as to time (114) is inoperative—BGB 925.

The production of an 'authority for registration' (318) is not sufficient evidence for the registration of the transfer of ownership; the registrar is required to satisfy himself as to the proper observance of the formalities prescribed for a conveyance by agreement.

In the absence of any evidence showing a contrary intention the transfer of the ownership of the principal thing has the effect of transferring the ownership of all accessories (76) belonging to the transferor at the time of the transfer.   If, in consequence of the alienation of the principal thing, any accessories not belonging to the transferor, or subject to the rights of any third party, come into the possession of the transferee, the same rules are applied as in the case of an alienation of a movable thing by a person without title or with an imperfect title (333), the question as to the good faith of the transferee being decided with reference to the state of his knowledge at the time of the transfer of possession—BGB 926.

b.   Derivative Acquisition of Ownership from Persons without Title or with Imperfect Title.

328. A party to a conveyance by agreement acquires the ownership of the parcel conveyed thereby in conformity with the state of the title appearing from the register, subject to the cautions and objections entered thereon, and subject also to such restrictions or qualifications not appearing on the register as are known to the transferor at the time when he files his application for the registration of the transfer.

A restraint on the transferor's powers of alienation, intended for the protection of any particular persons (104), but not entered on the register or known to the transferee at the time when the application is filed, does not affect his rights— BGB 892.

The above-mentioned rules apply in the case of a voluntary conveyance as well as in the case of a conveyance on sale, but in the case of a voluntary conveyance the true owner is entitled to compensation from the transferee under the rules as to 'unjustified benefits'—see 299 sub (2).

Illustrations: 1. *A* is erroneously registered as the heir of the deceased owner of Whiteacre, *B* being the true heir; *A* sells and conveys Whiteacre to *C*, who is not acquainted with *B*'s rights; *B* cannot claim the rectification of the register or otherwise dispute *C*'s title, or claim any compensation from him.   If *A* had made a voluntary transfer of the ownership to C, B would not be entitled to contest his right of ownership, but he would be entitled to a claim for compensation under the rules as to 'unjustified benefits'.

2. A purchases an immovable as to which no charge is registered, an objection having, however, been registered on the application of B, who subsequently shows that he is entitled to a charge; A must allow the charge to be registered.

c. Acquisition of Ownership by Long Possession (*Ersitzung*).

(1) Where the registered owner is in continuous possession.

394 **329.** A person who has been registered as owner of a piece of land continuously for thirty years, and during the same period of time was in continuous proprietary possession, acquires the ownership of such piece of land by virtue of such registration and such long possession.

For the purpose of ascertaining whether a person was in continuous possession for thirty years the following rules apply:

(1) possession at the beginning and at the end of the period creates a presumption in favour of continuous possession during the whole period;

(2) the time during which a predecessor in title is registered and in possession runs in favour of his successor in title;

(3) the time during which property belonging to the estate of a deceased person is in the possession of any person other than the heirs (528) runs in favour of the heirs;

(4) a loss of possession brought about against the possessor's will is not deemed to interrupt the continuity of the period in any case in which the possession is recovered within a year from the date of such loss, or by means of an action brought within such period;

(5) the rules as to the suspension or interruption of the period are similar to the rules as to the suspension and interruption of the period of prescription (136, 137)—BGB 900 (1), 938–944.   (As to the extinction of incumbrances by lapse of time, see BGB 901.)

(2) Where a person other than the registered owner
is in Continuous posssession.

330. Thirty years' continuous proprietary possession by a person not registered as owner does not in itself exclude the rights of the former owner, but such long possession enables the possessor to obtain a judicial order made after a proceeding by public citation (*Aufgebotsverfahren*)—see CPO 977–981—declaring the rights of the former owner to be forfeited; on production of such order the possessor is entitled to be registered as owner.

If the former owner is registered as such, an order declaring his rights to be 395 forfeited cannot be made, unless he is dead or untraceable (44), no entry requiring the owner's concurrence having been made within thirty years prior to the date of the order.

If, before the promulgation of the order declaring the rights of the former owner to be forfeited, a third party is registered as owner, or has caused any objection to be entered against the state of the register, the order is inoperative as against such third party—BGB 927.

d. Original Acquisition of Ownership.

331. The rules as to alluvion, newly-formed islands and dried-up river beds, are left to State regulation (EG 65).   The law on the subject is generally derived from the rules of Roman law as to *insula in flumine nata*, *alveus derelictus*, *alluvio*, and *avulsio*.   (See *Dernburg*, *Pandekten*, vol. 1, § 207; *Stobbe*, *Deutsches Privatrecht*, vol. 2, § 91.)

The possibility of acquiring by *occupatio* the ownership of pieces of land relinquished by the former owner, which existed in Roman law (see *Dernburg*, *Pandekten*, vol. 1, § 203), is not recognized under the present law.

If the owner of a piece of land makes a declaration before a competent officer of the land registry, by which he renounces his rights to the ownership of such piece of land, and if such renunciation is thereupon entered on the register, the abandoned piece of land may be appropriated by the treasury authorities of the State in which it is situate, except in so far as the State law provides that the right of appropriation belongs to some other public authority or private person; the appropriation is effected by registration—BGB 928; EG 129.

In certain parts of Germany the right of appropriating abandoned parcels of land has been transferred to the communal authorities.

As to the original acquisition of the ownership of mines and minerals, see 350.

B. As to Movables

a. Derivative Acquisition from True Owner. [1]

396   **332.** On the transfer of the ownership of an immovable by act-in-the-law two requirements must, as shown above—327, be complied with, namely, a real agreement between the parties, and the registration of the transfer of ownership in the land registry.   On the transfer of the ownership of movables a real agreement between the parties is equally necessary, but a transfer of possession, as a general rule, takes the place of registration—BGB 929.

Whereas a conveyance by agreement (327) of an immovable made subject to any condition or stipulation as to time is in operative, the transfer of the ownership of a movable thing is not invalid by reason of its being made subject to any condition or stipulation as to time (*e. g.* the *pactum reservati dominii*—193).

The transfer of possession required under the general rule is dispensed with in any of the following events:

(*a*) if the transferee at the time of the formation of the agreement is already in possession, *e. g.* as bailee or pawnee of the movable of which the ownership is transferred to him, (*traditio brevi manu*)—BGB 929;

(*b*) if the transferor retains the direct possession, whilst the transferee acquires the indirect possession, *e. g.* if a vendor becomes bailee for the purchaser, (*constitutum possessorium*)—BGB 930;

(*c*) if neither the transferor nor the transferee is in possession, but the right to possession is assigned by the transferor to the transferee—BGB 931;

(*d*) if on the sale of a registered ship or any share therein it is agreed between the parties that the property is to pass forthwith from the vendor to the purchaser—HBG 474.

(As to the transfer of the possession of goods represented by a bill of lading or other negotiable instrument, see 312 sub (1).)

b. Derivative Acquisition of the Ownership of Movables from Persons without Title or with Defective Title.

397   **333.** The effect of the possession of a movable thing is not quite as far reaching as the effect of the registration of a right affecting an immovable thing.   Three

---

1   See p. 364 note 1.

classes of movables must be distinguished:

(1) money, bank-notes, and other instruments payable to bearer, and things sold by public auction, whatever their nature may be;

(2) things not included in the classes of things enumerated sub (1), which have not been stolen from, or lost by the true owner (*e. g.* things sold by an unauthorized agent);

(3) things not included in the classes enumerated sub (1), which have been stolen from or lost by the true owner.

The transfer of the possession of a thing belonging to any of the classes of things enumerated sub (1) and (2), if accompanied or preceded by a real agreement for the transfer of its ownership to the transferee, has the effect of conferring such ownership upon the transferee free from any incumbrance, notwithstanding any defect in the transferor's title, or the existence of any undisclosed charge or right of pledge, provided that at the time of the transfer of possession the transferee is in good faith in accordance with the rules stated below—BGB 932 (1), 936.

In the events in which the ownership is transferred, under the rules stated above (332), without any transfer of possession, the following rules are applied:

(1) in the case of *traditio brevi manu* the ownership passes at the time of the formation of the real agreement, if at such time the transferee is in good faith, and if the possession was originally acquired by delivery from the transferor— BGB 932 (1), 936;

(2) in the case of *constitutum possessorium* the ownership does not pass before the actual delivery of possession, and only if the transferee is in good faith at the time at which such delivery takes place—BGB 933, 936.

(3) in the case of the assignment of the right to possession the ownership passes at the time of such assignment, if at that time the assignor is in indirect possession, and if the transferee at the same time is in good faith; if the assignor is not in indirect possession the ownership does not pass before the actual delivery of possession, and only in so far as the transferee is in good faith at the time of such delivery—BGB 934, 936.

A person is not deemed to be in good faith, if he knows the thing of which the ownership is intended to be transferred does not belong to the transferor or is subject to any incumbrance, or if his ignorance on the subject is due to gross negligence—BGB 932 (2), 936 (2).   The fact that a transferee, though aware of the fact that the transferor is not the true owner, has some reason to assume

398

that he is transferring the ownership under the owner's authority, does not as a general rule entitle such transferee to claim the privilege of good faith; but, where goods are sold by a mercantile trader (36) in the regular course of his business, the purchaser is deemed to be in good faith, notwithstanding the knowledge of the fact that the vendor is not the owner, unless he knows, or but for his gross negligence would have known, that the vendor had no authority to sell the goods on the owner's behalf—HGB 366.

In the case of the sale to a banker or money-changer of stolen or lost instruments payable to bearer, not being bank-notes or other similar notes payable on demand, or interest coupons payable at an early date, the banker or money-changer is not deemed to be in good faith, if within a year prior to the sale, the particulars of the stolen or lost instrument were published in the *Imperial Gazette*; the rule is not applied if the person concerned by reason of any special circumstance did not, and by the application of proper care would not have, become aware of the publication of the particulars—HBG 367.

Where a movable thing, not being either money or an instrument payable to bearer or a thing purchased at a sale by public auction, has been stolen or lost, its ownership cannot be acquired from any person other than the true owner—BGB 935.

A comparison of the provisions of English law on the subject of the acquisition of property from persons with defective title, with the rules enumerated above leads to the following results:

(1) as regards money and negotiable instruments the German and English rules are similar to each other, except that under English law the good faith of a banker or money-changer is not necessarily excluded, if the particulars of the loss have been published and remained unnoticed by such banker or money-changer; there is also the material difference, that under English law only a holder for value acquires a good title from a transferor whose title is defective (see Bills of Exchange Act 1882, ss. 29 (1), 38 (3)), while under German law the holder of a negotiable instrument obtaining its proprietary possession in good faith, even by way of gift, acquires an indefeasible title, subject, however, to the rule as to unjustified benefits mentioned above—299 sub (2);

(2) the English rule about goods bought in 'market overt' corresponds with the German rule about things bought at a sale by public auction (except in so far as sales by public auction cover a much wider ground than sales in 'market overt' under the English rules), but whereas under English law the property in

stolen goods bought in market overt reverts to the true owner after the conviction of the thief (see Sale of Goods Act 1893, s. 24 (1)) , a German purchaser who in good faith purchases goods at a public auction, without notice of the fact that they were stolen goods, acquires an indefeasible title;

(3) the general rules of German law under which the ownership of a movable thing, not stolen from or lost by its owner, passes to a person who acquires such thing in good faith, notwithstanding a defect in the title of the person from whom it was acquired, are intended to serve the same purpose as the English enactments contained in the Sale of Goods Act, the Factors Acts, and other Statutes enabling the apparent owner or the person having apparent authority to sell the goods, to dispose of them as if they were the true owners (see Sale of Goods Act 1893, ss. 21 (2) , 25). [1]

c. Acquisition of Ownership by Long Possession (*Ersitzung*).

334. The ownership of a movable thing is acquired after ten years' proprietary possession by a person who at the time of acquiring such possession was under the honest belief that he was the owner, and did not, prior to the effluxion of the period, discover that this belief was erroneous.

Illustration: *A* takes possession of certain chattels, to which he thinks himself entitled as next of kin of a person whom he believes to have died intestate; 400 a will is subsequently discovered by which the chattels are bequeathed to *B*; if the contents of the will do not come to the knowledge of *A* before the expiration of the ten years, *A* acquires an indefeasible title.

The rules as to the computation of the period, and as to its suspension or interruption, are the same as in the case of the acquisition of the ownership of immovables—329—BGB 937-944.

The undisclosed rights of an incumbrancer are extinguished by long possession, in the same way as the rights of an owner, and subject to the corresponding requirements as to good faith—BGB 945.

---

1   The English enactments as in the case of the other rules to which reference has been made are intended for the exclusive protection of purchasers for value, whilst German law protects any transferor who is in good faith, but subject to the rules as to unjustified benefits (298).

d.   Original Modes of Acquisition

aa.   Accession.

(1) *General rules.*

335. The ownership of a movable thing is lost, if by becoming attached to or combined with another thing, it ceases to be an independent unit.

A movable thing ceases to be an independent unit, by becoming attached to another thing (incorporation)—336, or by being mixed up or blended together with another thing (*commixtio*, *confusio*)—337, or by being transformed by work (*specificatio*)—338.   In the case of incorporation by attachment to an immovable or to another movable thing which on such attachment becomes the principal thing—76, the owner of such immovable, or of such principal movable thing becomes the owner of the thing attached thereto; in the case of ' specification ', the person by whom the transformation is effected, as a general rule, acquires the ownership; in all other cases to which reference has been made the owners of the several things joined together become co-owners (325) of the combined thing, in shares proportionate to the value of the things respectively contributed by them— BGB 946–948, 950 (1).

In so far as the ownership of a thing attached to another or transformed by work is lost by its former owner, all incumbrances affecting such thing are discharged; in so far as the former separate owners become co-owners of the combined thing, the share in the combined thing of every co-owner becomes subject to the incumbrances to which the thing formerly owned by him in severalty was subject; an incumbrance affecting an immovable or a principal movable thing extends to any movable thing becoming part thereof by incorporation—BGB 949, 950 (2).

A person who, under the above-mentioned rules, becomes deprived of any right is entitled to claim compensation in money from any person benefiting by his loss in accordance with the rules as to unjustified benefits (298) ; he cannot, however, claim the restoration of the original state of things unless he is under the circumstances entitled to the *jus tollendi*—144 sub (9) , or unless the event by which he was deprived of his right was brought about by an unlawful act—BGB 951.

(2) *Incorporation (Verbindung).*

336. The expression ' incorporation ' (*Verbindung*) is used whenever two things are so attached together that the identity of one of them or of both is lost.

This happens:

(*a*) if a movable thing is attached to a parcel of land in such manner as to form an essential component part (75) thereof;

(*b*) if a movable thing is attached as accessory to another movable thing so as to form an essential component part of the principal thing;

(*c*) if two movable things are attached together so as to form essential component parts of the combined thing, neither of them being an accessory of the other.

As mentioned above—335, the owner of a thing attached to another in the manner mentioned sub (*a*) or (*b*) loses his right of ownership, while the owner of a thing attached to another in the manner mentioned sub (*c*) acquires a right of co-ownership in the combined thing—BGB 947.

Under English law certain 'fixtures' attached to land by lessees or tenants for life for purposes of ornament, trade, or agriculture, remain in the ownership of the person by whom they were attached to the land, and the rule making them part of the land is only applied if they are not removed within the particular period of time allowed in each case; under German law such fixtures follow the general rule, but the rights of lessees or usufructuaries or other persons entitled to the temporary possession of land are safeguarded by the *jus tollendi*—see 144 sub (9), which, as   402 a general rule, is a better protection to a person attaching tenant's fixtures to the land than the right of ownership reserved to such a person under English law. [1]

(3) *Commixtio, Confusio.*

337. If movable things are mixed up together (*Vermischung*), or blended together (*Vermengung*), in such manner as not to be severable from one another, or as to be severable only by a process causing an expense out of proportion to the value of the result, the ownership in the separate things, as mentioned above—335, is lost, and the several owners become co-owners of the combined thing—BGB 947.

(4) *Specification.*

338. A person who creates a new movable thing by working up or transforming material supplied by another becomes the owner of such new thing, unless the

---

[1]   The fact that under German law the landlord becomes owner of the tenant's fixtures, while under English law the tenant retains the ownership, is not, however, without practical importance; an English tenant may give a valid charge on such fixtures (see Meux *v.* Jacobs L. R. 7 H. L. 481), while this would be impossible under German law.

value of the work of transformation is considerably inferior to the value of the materials. Writing, drawing, painting, printing, engraving, or any other similar work done on the surface of any material is deemed to be work done on such material—BGB 950 (1).

The same rule would probably be applied under English law, but the fact that there seems to be no reported case on the subject shows that it is not of much practical importance. A manufacturer, or artist, or author generally uses material purchased by himself; where the material is supplied by the person ordering the work (as, for instance, in the case of a dressmaker who works up the stuff supplied by her customer), the material is generally more important than the work.

bb. Appropriation of products or other component parts of a thing.

339. As we have seen above (335) the ownership of a thing is lost if it becomes the component part of another thing; in a corresponding manner a fresh right of ownership is created whenever a component part of a thing is severed from such thing. The component part so becoming severed may either be in the nature of a product (e. g. the produce of land or the offspring of cattle), or it may be part of the substance of the thing from which it is severed (e. g. a fixture removed by a person entitled to the *jus tollendi*); the following rules refer to both kinds of component parts in so far as the contrary does not appear from the context:

(1) the owner of a thing from which a component part is severed, subject to rules (2) and (3), acquires the ownership of the severed part, unless such severed part by virtue of any real right—e. g. a right of usufruct (358), or an antichretic right of pledge (398)—becomes vested in any other person—BGB 953, 954;

(2) the rights of any person referred to sub (1), in so far as they relate to any fruits (77), are postponed to the rights of a proprietary possessor of the thing from which such fruits are severed, who at the time of obtaining possession believed himself entitled thereto and to the enjoyment of the fruits, and did not at any subsequent time before severance become aware of any defect in his title; a person who is in possession by virtue of any real right of user is dealt with in the same way as a proprietary possessor [1]—BGB 955 (1) (2);

(3) the rights of any person referred to sub (2) are again postponed to the

---

[1]   A person ousted from possession but recovering possession within a year from the date of its loss, or by virtue of an action brought within that period, is in respect of his right to the severed parts deemed to have been in continuous possession—BGB 955 (3) ; confer 329.

rights of any person who, by permission on the part of the owner, or of any person having real or apparent authority to grant such permission, is entitled to appropriate any component part of the thing to which such permission relates (*e. g.* a lessee under a usufructuary lease—205, 206; a purchaser of any growing crops or of any part of a demolished building)—BGB 956, 957;

(4) the ownership in a severed component part vests in the person entitled thereto immediately on severance, but a person entitled to appropriate a severed part under rule (3), who, at the time of severance is not in possession of the thing from which such part is severed, does not acquire the ownership of the severed part before taking possession thereof—BGB 956.

404

cc.   Acquisition of ownership by occupancy (Aneignung).

(1)   *General rules.*

340. A thing is deemed to have no owner if it never had any owner (as in the case of a wild animal in a state of liberty), or if its owner has abandoned its possession with the intention of abandoning its ownership—BGB 959.

The ownership of a thing having no owner is acquired by any person who obtains proprietary possession thereof, unless possession was obtained by the infringement of a legal prohibition or of another person's right of appropriation— BGB 958. [1]

(2)   *As to things lost by their owner (treasure trove, wreckage).*

341. The loss of a thing by its owner frequently produces results similar to those of the abandonment of its ownership; the finder of a lost thing—as mentioned above (307)—acquires the ownership thereof if during a certain specified period no notice of the loss is given to him or to the local police authority; the absence of such a notice during the prescribed time has, therefore, the same effect as the

---

[1]   A person acquiring the ownership possession of a wild animal, killed during a time of the year during which the killing of the particular animal is forbidden, does not acquire its ownership; in a similar way a poacher does not acquire the ownership of any game or fish taken in violation of the sporting rights of another; subject to these exceptions the ownership of any wild animal which is in a state of liberty is acquired by any person who acquires its proprietary possession.   A wild animal kept in any private park and a fish kept in a private pond are not deemed to be in a state of liberty.   If a wild animal which was in a state of captivity escapes therefrom, it is deemed to be ownerless unless it is immediately pursued by its owner; if it is pursued it is deemed to be ownerless as soon as the pursuit is abandoned.   A tame animal is deemed to be ownerless if it loses the habit of returning to a particular spot—BGB 960.   As to the ownership of bees leaving their hives and invading other hives, see BGB 961–964.

abandonment of the ownership.

405   Where any thing has been hidden for so long that its owner cannot be found any more, the ownership, as to one moiety, passes to the finder, and as to the other moiety to the owner of the thing within which the secreted thing was found; one moiety of a thing dug out of the earth consequently belongs to the owner of the land; on the other hand one moiety of a thing found in a cupboard or wardrobe belongs to the owner of such cupboard or wardrobe—BGB 984.

If any objects are saved from a wreck public notice of the fact must be given, with a request to the owners of such objects to present their claims within a prescribed period; where no claim is made on the part of any owner, the ownership is disposed of in accordance with the following rules:

(1) wreckage and goods saved from stranded ships or found on the beach (*strandtriftige Güter*) belong to the State;

(2) wreckage and goods taken on a vessel after having been found at the bottom of the sea or floating on the surface, or taken out of an abandoned ship (*seetriftige Güter*), belong to the salvor, but his right is forfeited if he has failed to give immediate notice of the facts in accordance with the statutory requirements (*Strandungsordnung* of 1874, as amended in 1901, ss. 4–19, 20, 21, 35); as to the salvor's right of pledge in respect of his claim for remuneration and reimbursement of outlay, see 303.

Under English law treasure trove (that is to say ' gold or silver in coin, plate, or bullion, concealed in a house or in the earth or other private place, the owner thereof being unknown '), as well as all wreckage, &c. (jetsam, flotsam, ligan, wreck of the sea), belongs to the Crown or to the grantee of the Crown entitled in the particular locality to the franchise of treasure trove, &c. (see Attorney-Gen. *v.* Moore (1893) 1 Ch. 676).

4.   OWNER'S CLAIMS AGAINST PERSONS INTERFERING WITH RIGHTS OF OWNERSHIP

a.   Claims against Possessor.

aa.   Claim to recover possession.

342. The legal remedies for the recovery of possession referred to above
406   (315) are intended to protect a former possessor as such and without reference to the right of ownership; an owner as such is entitled to claim possession by an

action similar to the Roman *vindicatio*, which is available in any case in which an immovable or movable thing is withheld from the owner. [1]   The plaintiff succeeds in such an action if he can prove his right of ownership, unless the defendant can prove that he or the indirect possessor—311 sub (2)—from whom he derives his right to possession, has a right to possession available against the owner.

If an indirect possessor has a right to possession as against the owner, but was not authorized to transfer such right of possession to another, the owner is entitled to a judgment ordering the direct possessor to deliver possession to such indirect possessor, and directing delivery to the owner in the event of such indirect possessor being unable or unwilling to take possession.

A person who is in possession of a movable thing, of which the ownership was transferred by means of an assignment of the right to possession—332 sub (c)—may, as against the assignee, avail himself of any defence which he would be entitled to use against the assignor—BGB 985, 986.

Illustrations:

1. *A* lets his house to *B*; *B*, not having a right to underlet, underlets to *C*; *A* may bring an action against *C*, claiming an order directing *C* to give up possession to *B*, and directing that in the event of *B* failing to take possession, possession should be given to *A*.

2. *A* has let a horse to *B* for a month; during the month *A* sells the horse to *C*, and transfers the ownership by the assignment of his right to possession.   *B* may refuse delivery to *C* before the expiration of the month.

bb.   Mutual claims for compensation.

(1)   Owner's claims against possessor.

343. As mentioned above (339), a person who, in good faith, is in proprietary possession of a thing, or who, in good faith, is in possession of such thing by virtue of a real right of user, acquires the ownership of all fruits of such thing severed during the time of his possession.   A possessor, who is not in good faith, does not acquire the ownership of any fruits or other component parts of the thing possessed by him, but, after having severed such component parts, he may of course confer a good title on a purchaser acquiring any such component part

407

---

[1]   An owner who merely wants to assert his right of ownership may do so without claiming possession by an action asking for a declaration as to his right—CPO 256; the owner of an immovable may assert his right by claiming the rectification of the register (321).

without any notice of the defect in the vendor's title.

The mutual rights and liabilities of an owner who recovers the possession of a thing from another, and of such other, are governed by the following rules:

(a) As to compensation for fruits and profits.

(1) The person from whom possession is recovered is not liable to compensate the owner in respect of fruits, severed by him while he was in good faith, [1] before the commencement of the owner's action, except under the following rules:

(aa) he is liable in respect of fruits which would not have been won if the proper course of husbandry or management had been followed—BGB 993;

(bb) if his title to possession was not obtained for valuable consideration he is liable in accordance with the rules as to unjustified benefits (298)—BGB 988.

(2) If he was in bad faith when obtaining possession he has to account for all profits earned by him during the continuance of his possession; if he ceased to be in good faith at any time after taking possession, he has to account for all profits earned by him after such time—BGB 990.

(3) He must account for the whole of the profits earned by him during the pendency of the action as well as for all profits which, but for his default, would during such time have been earned in the usual course of husbandry or management—BGB 987.

(b) As to other claims.

408   If the thing, which is the subject-matter of the action, is deteriorated or destroyed, or cannot be delivered to the owner, the liabilities of the person against whom the owner's right to possession is established are governed by the following rules:

(1) if he was in good faith he is not liable in respect of any damaging event which has happened before the commencement of the action, except under the circumstances mentioned sub (2);

(2) if his title to possession was derived from an indirect possessor, he is liable in respect of any of the above-mentioned damaging events due to any default on his part in so far as he is liable to such indirect possessor;

(3) he is liable in respect of any loss caused by any of the above-mentioned damaging events due to any default on his part which has happened during the pendency of the action;

---

1   A possessor who in good faith derives his title from an indirect possessor is deemed to be in good faith, notwithstanding the bad faith of such indirect possessor—BGB 999 (1).

(4) if he was not in good faith when obtaining possession, he is liable in respect of any of the above-mentioned damaging events due to any default on his part which has happened while he was in possession; if he ceased to be in good faith at any time after taking possession, he is under the same liability as from such time; if he is in bad faith and also in *mora solvendi* in respect of his obligation to yield possession to the owner he becomes subject to the more stringent liability brought about by that circumstance—153;

(5) if possession was obtained by means of unlawful interference (315) or of any criminal act, the owner is entitled to full compensation under the rules as to unlawful acts—169 sub (5)—BGB 989–992.

(2) *Counterclaims of possessor.*

344. The person from whom possession is recovered is entitled to certain claims against the owner, which are governed by the following rules:

(a) *Right to compensation for outlay.*

(1) Necessary outlay incurred by him before the commencement of the action, and while he was in good faith, must be repaid by the owner, except in so far as it was incurred for the preservation of any thing of which he enjoyed the profits—BGB 994 (1); see also BGB 995;

(2) necessary outlay incurred during the pendency of the action, or while he was in bad faith, must be repaid by the owner in so far only as the rules as to voluntary services (301) prescribe such payment—BGB 994 (2); 409

(3) compensation in respect of unnecessary outlay incurred before the commencement of the action, or before knowledge of the fact that the possession was unauthorized, may be claimed, in so far as the thing, for the preservation or improvement of which such outlay was incurred, has, in consequence thereof, an increased value at the time at which the owner recovers possession—BGB 996;

(4) where the owner recovers a plot of land used for agriculture, the cost of raising any crop to be reaped before the expiration of the agricultural year must be repaid by the owner, if it was incurred in the usual course of husbandry and does not exceed the value of such crop—BGB 998;

(5) the right to the reimbursement of outlay may be exercised by a successor in title of the party making the outlay, and against a successor in title of the person who, at the time when the outlay was incurred, was the owner of the thing for which it was incurred—BGB 999.

(*b*) *Jus tollendi.*

The person from whom possession is recovered is entitled to the *jus tollendi*—144 sub 9—except as regards:

(1) any thing which was affixed for the purpose of increasing the profits to which he was entitled as possessor;

(2) any thing of which the removal is useless to him;

(3) any thing for which the owner offers adequate compensation in money—BGB 997;

(3) *Comparison with English law.*

345. The rules of German law are much more favourable to the person from whom possession is recovered, and less favourable to the owner, than the corresponding rules of English law.   Under English law an owner of land is entitled to mesne profits for the whole time while he was entitled to possession, and the claim of the owner of a chattel in an action of detinue is for the delivery of the chattel and damages in respect of the detention.   The possessor has not in either case to account for any profits actually received by him, but the amount awarded for mesne profits or damages, as a general rule, exceeds any such profits to a considerable extent.

410

b.   Claims in respect of Interference with Rights other than Right of Possession.

346. As the owner's action for the recovery of possession corresponds to the Roman *vindicatio*, so the action in respect of interferences with rights, other than the right of possession, corresponds to the Roman *actio negatoria.*   The Roman *actio negatoria* was applied principally in cases in which the defendant claimed to be entitled to do the act complained of by virtue of a servitude affecting the owner's land (352), but the BGB confers the right of action on any person whose rights of ownership are disturbed, otherwise than by interference with the right of possession.   In any such case the owner may claim the removal of the disturbing factor; if further interferences are to be apprehended, he may also obtain an injunction restraining such further interferences—BGB 1004 (1).

The disturbance must be one of a permanent or recurrent nature (*e. g.* the erection of a building obstructing the owner's light, or the frequent use of a private road); isolated acts of interference give rise to an action for damages, but do not constitute a ground of action justifying the above-mentioned proceedings.   If the act complained of is one which the owner is bound to suffer, he has no right of action—BGB 1004 (2).

c.   Claim to remove a Thing from Land in the Possession of Another.

347. A person, out of whose possession a thing has been removed to the land of another, may, subject to certain restrictions, enter upon such land for the purpose of searching for and taking away such thing—see p. 349 note 1; in the same way, and subject to the same restrictions, the owner of a thing, situate upon land which is in the possession of another, may enter upon such land for the purpose of searching for and removing such thing—BGB 1005.

5.   RIGHTS SIMILAR TO OWNERSHIP RIGHTS

a.   General Survey.

348. A number of rights exist in German law which, though in the nature of *jura in re aliena*, and treated as such, are also in themselves treated as immovables, capable of being registered and alienated as such, and of being made subject to servitudes and other burdens.   The most prominent among them are the rights of ' *superficies* ' and ' *emphyteusis* '.   These rights were created by Roman law, in order to facilitate the exploitation of State lands and Crown lands by tenants whose position as mere lessees would have been too insecure; a lessee under Roman law had a mere contractual right against the lessor, and was unable to protect himself against interference on the part of others, but a person entitled to build on land by virtue of a grant of ' *superficies* ', or to cultivate land under a grant of ' *emphyteusis* ', was entitled to remedies for the protection of his rights similar to the remedies available for the protection of ownership rights; the right of ' *superficies* ' or of ' *emphyteusis* ' was, moreover, transmissible *inter vivos*, and formed part of the owner's estate on his death, while a lessor's right was a strictly personal right.

The *Erbpacht* (heritable lease), which was similar in its nature, though not identical with the Roman ' *emphyteusis* ', and a number of other rights connected with the tenure of land and similar in their nature to rights of ownership, were recognized by Germanic law.

411

The present German law deals with the rights now under discussion in the following manner:

(1) the modern equivalent of '*superficies*' is recognized throughout the Empire and withdrawn from the competence of State legislation; it is now known under the designation of *Erbbaurecht* (heritable building right)—349;

(2) the Germanic *Erbpacht* (heritable lease) and its special varieties known as *Büdnerrecht* and *Häuslerrecht* are preserved in the several States in which they were recognized prior to the coming into force of the BGB; where such a right is preserved it is made subject to the rules of Imperial law relating to immovables (*e. g.* the rules as to registration) in so far as they are applicable thereto, but in so far as the rules of Imperial law leave any gap, such gap is filled up by State law—EG 63;

(3) in respect of certain other rights affecting land it is left to State law to determine whether they are to be subject to the rules of Imperial law relating to immovables or whether they are to be governed by State law; these rights include feudal rights—EG 59; rights relating to the use of water (*e. g.* the right to have a water-mill)—EG 65; and sporting rights—EG 69;

(4) mining rights, which are also left to State law, are discussed below (350);

(5) an alienable and heritable right relating to land not belonging to one of the above-mentioned classes cannot be created, but any right which was in existence on January 1, 1900, is upheld, it being left to State law to determine whether such right is to be made subject to the Imperial rules relating to immovables, or whether it is to be governed by State law—EG 184, 196.

b.   Rules as to Heritable Building Rights.

349. A heritable building right is 'an incumbrance on a parcel of land, by virtue of which the grantee acquires a right capable of alienation, and transmissible on death, to erect a building on or below the surface of such parcel of land'—BGB 1012.   A right of this nature is granted for the objects for which a building lease is granted under English law; a German lease, owing to its purely contractual nature and uncertain duration (207), would not give a builder sufficient security.

The grant of a heritable building right may be perpetual and need not be subject to the payment of rent, but as a rule such a right is granted with a limited duration and subject to the payment of a yearly sum.

A heritable building right is registered as an incumbrance on the land which it affects, and may at the grantee's option be registered as an independent parcel immediately on its creation; its registration as an independent parcel is compulsory on any alienation or hypothecation—GBO 7.

Land not required for building purposes may be included in the grant, if such inclusion is advantageous for the purposes of the use of the building; the grant   413 cannot be limited to one particular story of a building [1]—BGB 1013, 1014.

A real agreement as to the grant of a heritable building right is subject to the same formal requirements as an agreement for the transfer of the ownership of an immovable (327), but the rule excluding conditions and stipulations as to time, does not apply to grants of heritable building rights—BGB 1015.

The destruction of the building erected by virtue of a heritable building right does not terminate the right—BGB 1016.

In all other respects all rules relating to immovables are—*mutatis mutandis*—applicable to heritable building rights—BGB 1017.

c.   Mining Rights.

350. The rules of public and private law as to mines and minerals, which, under EG 67, are left to State legislation, are in all German States, excepting the kingdom of Saxony, regulated on the model of the Prussian rules introduced by the *Allgemeines Berggesetz* of 1865.   Under these rules special mining authorities are created, who superintend the administration of the law.   The main feature of German mining law is found in the fact that minerals do not belong to the surface owner as such, but to the first finder who complies with the prescribed formalities, whether he be the surface owner or a stranger.

A person wishing to win minerals under land owned by a stranger must, in the first instance, acquire the right of search (*Schürfrecht*).

If no private agreement can be arrived at between the parties, the mining authority fixes the conditions, subject to which the right of search may be exercised, more particularly the compensation to be paid in respect of the damage done to the surface.

---

[1]   Under some of the former German laws a right of ownership in a particular story of a building (*Stockwerkseigentum*) was recognized, and rights of that nature which were in existence on the coming into force of the BGB are recognized in accordance with the rules of the old law—EG 182.

Any person who finds minerals, whether as owner of the land or by virtue of the exercise of the right of search, may file a claim (*Mutung*) with the mining authority for a grant of the mining rights in accordance with a plan showing the

414   exact position and the dimensions of the mine intended to be acquired (*Feldesstreckung*).   The date of the filing of the claims is conclusive as to the priority of the claimant.   The mining authority is bound to make the grant if it does not refer to land under which mines are forbidden (dwelling-houses, burial-places, roads, &c.), and if the prescribed formalities are complied with.

The grant (*Verleihung*) is made subject to the right (if any) of third parties, but the rights of such third parties are barred unless asserted within a specified short period.   The grantee obtains a right, capable of alienation and transmission on death, to win the minerals specified therein.   This right is for all purposes dealt with as an immovable, and is subject to the same rules as to registration, &c. , as an immovable.   The grantee of the mining rights is entitled to purchase compulsorily so much of the surface as is required for the purposes of the mine.   On the other hand, the owner of the surface is entitled to full compensation for all damage. [1]

In the kingdom of Saxony the general mining law applies only to metals; coal, clay, chalk, and other similar minerals, belong to the surface owner; he may, however, grant the right to win such minerals to another, in which event such a right is dealt with as an immovable—EG 68.

The rule of law allowing a stranger to obtain mining rights by occupancy exists as to certain mines in Cornwall (tin bounding) and in many colonies and foreign countries.

---

[1]   Full particulars as to Prussian mining law are given by Dernburg, *Bürgerliches Recht*, vol. 3, pp. 499–551; as to the method of computing the compensation for damage, see EG 67 (2).

CHAPTER1 IV
RIGHTS OF USER OVER PROPERTY OWNED BY OTHERS, AND RIGHTS OF RESTRAINING OWNER'S RIGHTS OF USER

1. GENERAL SURVEY

351. THE present chapter only deals with real rights; the rights of user, existing by virtue of contractual relations (*e. g.* the rights of lessees) , have been dealt with in connexion with the law of obligations; heritable building rights and other similar rights, though, strictly speaking, rights of user over land owned by others, have been referred to in the chapter dealing with the rights of ownership, as they are treated as independent objects of ownership, capable of being registered and dealt with like immovables; rights of user conferred by way of security will be dealt with in the chapter relating to real rights conferred by way of security; there remain the rights classed as 'servitudes' (*Dienstbarkeiten*) under Roman and German law (which include the 'easements' and *profits à prendre* of English law, as well as a number of other rights) , and the 'perpetual charges on land' described in German terminology as *Reallasten*, which are akin to servitudes, though they differ from them in one important respect—see 366.

2. SERVITUDES GENERALLY

a. Classification.

352. A limited right to the use of a thing belonging to another, or a right to restrain such other from exercising some of his rights of ownership, is called a 'servitude' under Roman and German law; the person who grants a servitude takes away from his own rights of ownership and increases the rights of the grantee—*jus suum deminuit, alterius auxit, hoc est servitutem aedibus suis imposuit*—Dig. 39. 1. 5. 9. Where such a right exists for the benefit of the owner for the time being

416 of a specified immovable it is called a 'real servitude' (*Grunddienstbarkeit*) [1];
where it exists for the benefit of a specified person it is called a personal servitude
(*persönliche Dienstbarkeit*).

The right of usufruct is the only personal servitude by virtue of which the
grantee obtains an unrestricted right of user over the property subject thereto; all
other personal servitudes are called 'restricted personal servitudes' (*beschränkte
persönliche Dienstbarkeiten*).

The burden of all real servitudes and of all restricted personal servitudes is
borne by the owner for the time being of an immovable; a right of usufruct may, on
the other hand, be charged on a movable thing or a right as well as on an immovable.

The benefit of a real servitude being, as mentioned above, vested in the
owner for the time being of a specified immovable, passes from one person to
another on each change of ownership; a personal servitude, on the other hand,
cannot be transferred by act *inter vivos*, and comes to an end on the grantee's
death; the grantee may, however, subject to certain restrictions, authorize
another to exercise his rights [2]—BGB 1059, 1092.

In the following statement the immovable upon which the burden of a
servitude is imposed will be called 'the servient tenement', while the immovable,
for the benefit of which a servitude is created, will be called the 'dominant
tenement'. [3]

b.   Creation of Servitudes.

aa.   By act-in-the-law.

353. A servitude charged on an immovable may be created by act-in-the-law
under the general rules as to the creation of real rights (309). [4]

417 A right of usufruct affecting a movable thing is created by the combined
operation of a real agreement between the parties and of the delivery of such

---

[1]   As heritable rights, mining rights, and other similar rights, are treated as independent immovables
(348), the benefit of a real servitude (*e. g.* a right of way) may be attached to such a right.

[2]   A person entitled to the usufruct of land may grant a usufructuary lease—206—to a tenant.

[3]   The corresponding expressions *dienendes Grundstück* and *herrschendes Grundstück* are also used by
German writers; the BGB calls the servient tenement *belastetes Grundstück*, but the dominant tenement is
called *Grundstück des Berechtigten*.

[4]   A real servitude, which was in existence in any registration district at the time when the new system
of registration came into force in that district, remains operative, though unregistered, unless State legislation
provides otherwise—EG 187.

movable thing to the grantee; the usufruct of a right is granted in accordance with the rules applicable to the assignment of such right—BGB 1032, 1069 (1). [1]

bb.   Creation of servitudes by prescription.

A personal servitude affecting an immovable cannot be acquired by prescription.

The usufruct of a movable thing is acquired by prescription in the same way—*mutatis mutandis*—as the ownership of a movable thing is acquired by long possession—334; as the person who acquires the ownership of a movable thing by long possession must during the prescribed period be in proprietary possession, so the person who acquires the usufruct by prescription must during the prescribed period exercise the rights of a person entitled to the usufruct—BGB 1033.

A title to a real servitude, registered as a component part of the dominant tenement, [2] is acquired by prescription in the same way as a prescriptive title to the ownership of land is acquired by the person registered as owner—329—BGB 900 (2).

The right to light, as shown above—326 sub (7), according to some State laws, is acquired by ten years' user.

3.   REAL SERVITUDES

a.   Comparative Statement.

354. The rule of Roman law: *impedit servitutem medium praedium quod non servit*—Dig. 8. 3. 7. 1—has not been adopted by the present German law; a real servitude is not inoperative on the ground that the dominant and the servient tenement do not adjoin each other.

Under English law there are a limited number of specifically defined easements and *profits à prendre.*   German law, on the other hand, gives a general definition as to the nature of real servitudes, which admits of the creation of a number of rights which under English law would not be classed either as easements or as *profits à prendre*, and of which the burden would therefore not 'run with the land'.

418

---

[1]   There can be no usufruct of a right which is incapable of assignment; see 176 sub (1)—BGB 1069 (2).

[2]   A real servitude is not effective unless registered as an incumbrance of the servient tenement; but it may also, on the application of the owner of the dominant tenement or of any incumbrancer, be registered as a component part of the dominant tenement.

Thus under English law building restrictions or restrictions as to the use of buildings, which do not result from any recognized easements, are not binding on any purchaser who has not covenanted to observe them, or is not affected with notice of any existing covenant.   Under German law, on the other hand, a real servitude restricting the use of land in any way which may be of advantage to the dominant tenement, and is not prohibited by any rule of State law, is binding on every successive owner of the servient tenement.

Illustration: A servitude may be imposed on a parcel of land by which the erection of any shop or factory on such parcel of land or the obstruction of the view enjoyed from the dominant tenement is prevented.

State law may narrow the limits within which real servitudes may be created, and regulate the operation of certain specified real servitudes, but it cannot extend the limits imposed by Imperial law on the creation of such servitudes—EG 115.   All servitudes which were in existence on the 1st January, 1900, remain in force, but their operation is to a large extent made subject to the provisions of the new law—EG 184.

b.   Statement of Rules.

(1) *Limits within which real servitudes may be created.*

355. A real servitude may consist:

(*a*) of the right to use the servient tenement for some specified purpose connected with the use of the dominant tenement;

(*b*) of the right to restrain the doing of certain specified acts on the servient tenement;

(*c*) of the right to restrain the exercise of some specified right resulting from the ownership of the servient tenement which would otherwise be available against the dominant tenement—BGB 1018.

419   A right of way, or a right of pasture, is an example of the servitudes described sub (*a*); a right to restrain the erection of a building obstructing the light of the dominant tenement, of those described sub (*b*); a right to restrain the owner of the servient tenement from objecting to an obstruction of his own light, of those described sub (*c*).

No burden must in any event be imposed upon the servient tenement, which is not of advantage to the dominant tenement.   As in Roman law the servitude must be *fundo utilis*, and the right conferred by the servitude must be exercised *civiliter*, and with a proper regard to the interests of the owner of the servient tenement—BGB 1019, 1020.

(2) *Active duties imposed on owner of servient tenement.*

The rule of Roman law under which a servitude could not be created, *ut aliquid faciat quis*, [1] has not penetrated into the new German law; a burden may now be imposed upon the servient tenement imposing an active duty on its owner for the time being; where the burden so imposed consists *exclusively* of the performance of such active duty, the right is called a *Reallast* (perpetual charge)—366—and is not included in the servitudes; but where the burden consists of a negative as well as of a positive duty the term ' servitude ' is applied to it; (*e. g.* where the duty to keep a road in repair is imposed on the owner of a tenement over which a right of way is granted).

Where any structure is required on the servient tenement, for the purpose of enabling the owner of the dominant tenement to exercise a right of support, the duty to keep such structure in repair is, in the absence of an agreement to the contrary, imposed on the owner of the servient tenement, but no similar duty is implied in any other case in which any structure or other appliance is erected on the servient tenement for the purpose of assisting the exercise of the rights resulting from a real servitude [2] —BGB 1022.

(3) *Right of transference.*

Where the exercise of a right resulting from a servitude exclusively affects a particular part of the servient tenement, and thereby causes great inconvenience to the owner of the servient tenement, the latter may require the owner of the dominant tenement to transfer the exercise of his right to another part of such tenement, provided that such other part is equally convenient for the exercise of the right.   This privilege cannot be waived or restricted by agreement—BGB 1023.

420

---

1   *ut aliquid faciat quis* 意思为 "使某人为某种行为"。Dig. 8. 1. 15. 1: Servitutium non ea natura est, *ut aliquid faciat quis*, veluti viridia tollat aut amoeniorem prospectum praestet, aut in hoc utin suo pingat, sed ut aliquid patiatur aut non faciat. 役权，本质上并非要求供役地所有权人为某种行为，譬如移除草木以使景色更宜人，或者为此目的而在供役地（的建筑物上）绘画，而是要求供役地所有权人容忍他人为一定行为，或者要求供役地所有权人不为一定行为。——校勘者注

2   A structure which is not required in connexion with a right of support must be maintained by the owner of the dominant tenement unless the contrary is agreed upon between the parties—BGB 1020, 1021.

(4) *Rule as to conflict of real servitudes.*

Where two real servitudes having the same right of priority conflict with one another, the owner of either of the dominant tenements may require the owner of the other to come to an arrangement with him, giving effect to the respective rights of both parties in an equitable manner—BGB 1024.

(5) *Effect of sub-division of dominant or servient tenement.*

On a sub-division of the dominant tenement, the owner of each section may continue the exercise of the right previously enjoyed by the owner of the whole tenement, in so far as he derives any advantage from such exercise; but in the absence of an agreement to the contrary, the exercise of the rights of the several owners must be so arranged as not to cause greater inconvenience to the owner of the servient tenement, than was caused by the previous exercise of the right by one owner—BGB 1025.

On a sub-division of the servient tenement the servitude, in so far as it affects only a particular part of such tenement, remains a burden on such part only. If the servitude affects the whole tenement its burden is imposed on each separate section—BGB 1026.

Illustration: A right of way does not affect the sections through which the path or road does not go. A right of pasturage, on the other hand, continues to be exercised over the whole area.

c.   Remedies for the Protection of Real Servitudes.

(1) *Possessory remedies.*

356. Under German common law a person who exercised a right which could have resulted from a real servitude, *nec vi*, *nec clam*, *nec precario*, was deemed to be a 'quasi-possessor' of such right, and as such entitled to certain possessory remedies. The new German law does not recognize the quasi-possession of any servitude, unless it is registered as a component part of the dominant tenement; if the possessor of an immovable for the benefit of which a real servitude is registered in this manner is disturbed in the exercise of the right resulting from such servitude, and has exercised such right within a year prior to the disturbance, he is entitled to remedies corresponding to the remedies of a possessor disturbed by unlawful interference—315—BGB 1029. [1]

(2)   *Assertion of right.*

The owner of a thing, whose rights of ownership are interfered with otherwise than by interference with his possession, may, as mentioned above (346), assert his right of ownership by proceedings similar to the *actio negatoria* of Roman law. Analogous proceedings may be taken for the assertion of the right to a real servitude—BGB 1027.

d.   Loss of Real Servitudes by Prescription.

357. The general rule under which a right registered as an incumbrance on an immovable cannot become barred by prescription—BGB 902—is subject to the exception mentioned below.

If any structure or appliance, hindering the exercise of a right resulting from a real servitude, is affixed to the servient tenement, the claim to remove such structure or appliance may be barred by lapse of time under the ordinary rules as to prescription (131–137), notwithstanding the fact that the servitude is registered as an incumbrance of the servient tenement—BGB 1028. [2]

4.   Usufruct

a.   General Statement.

358. The usufruct of Roman and German law corresponds in a certain manner to the limited ownership enjoyed under English law by a person who, whether for life or for any other limited period, is entitled to the possession of a specified object of property, and to the appropriation of all profits derived from it in the ordinary course of management; but, while under English law, the person entitled to this limited ownership has a proprietary right in such object, the right   422

---

1   The possessory remedies cannot be exercised as to unregistered servitudes, unless the absence of registration is due to the fact that the new system of registration is not as yet completed in the particular district, or unless the dominant tenement belongs to the class of tenements not requiring registration under State law.   In any such case a limited protection is granted—see EG 191.

2   Illustration: If the use of a right of way is prevented by a locked gate the owner of the dominant tenement has a claim for the removal of such gate, which claim may become barred under the general rules as to prescription; as soon as the claim is barred, the right of way is lost, though it still appears on the register.

under Roman and German law is deemed a *jus in re aliena*. The usufruct of a movable thing, or of a right capable of assignment under German law, may be granted as well as the usufruct of an immovable. The grantee, who is called the 'usufructuary' (*Niessbraucher*), is entitled to reap and appropriate the profits (77) of the object of which the usufruct (*Niessbrauch*) has been granted to him, which object in the further course of this treatise will be described as 'the usufructuary object'—BGB 1030, 1068, 1069 (2).

A usufruct may be granted to a natural person or to a corporate body for a specified time, or subject to a condition subsequent (*e. g.* the re-marriage of a testator's widow), but it cannot under any circumstances be granted for a period exceeding the life or corporate existence of the usufructuary—BGB 1061.

If the usufruct is granted in consideration of an annual payment the position of the usufructuary is somewhat analogous to that of a lessee under a usufructuary lease (206), but whereas a lessee has only a personal right against the lessor, a usufructuary has a real right affecting the usufructuary object, for the protection of which the same remedies are available as for the protection of the right of ownership (342, 346)—BGB 1065.

The rules as to usufruct refer primarily to rights of usufruct created by act-in-the-law or acquired by prescription; but certain rights of usufruct arising under family law (*e. g.* the father's right of usufruct of his infant child's property (447), and the husband's right of usufruct of his wife's property under the statutory régime—414 sub (5), are governed by similar rules.

b.   Rules as to Usufructuary Object.

359. The usufructuary object, as mentioned above (358), may be a movable or an immovable thing, or a right. The usufruct of an aggregate of things, or of an aggregate of things and rights, may also be granted, but in such a case the objects comprised in such aggregate must be specifically referred to; a grant of the usufruct of a person's whole property or of his whole estate, [1] without special reference to the objects comprised in it, is inoperative—BGB 1085, 1089.

The grant of the usufruct of an immovable includes the usufruct of the accessories in the same way as the transfer of the ownership of an immovable transfers the ownership of the accessories (327)—BGB 1031.

---

[1]   A testator may by his will give the usufruct of his estate to a legatee; this gives the legatee a right to claim from the testator's heirs a grant of the usufruct of the individual objects comprised in such estate.

The grant of the usufruct of an undivided share, confers upon the usufructuary the grantor's rights of participation in the management and enjoyment of the property held in co-ownership; the right to demand partition (304) cannot, however, be exercised without the grantor's concurrence; after partition the usufructuary becomes entitled to the usufruct of the property appropriated to the grantor—BGB 1066.

The owner of the usufructuary object, as well as the usufructuary, are entitled at any time to demand an expert report on the state of the usufructuary object; where it consists of an aggregate of objects, each of them may claim the taking of an inventory—BGB 1034, 1035, 1067.

The usufruct of fungibles (73) is a somewhat anomalous kind of usufruct. [1] The so-called usufructuary of fungibles acquires the ownership thereof, the grantor being entitled, on the expiration of the so-called usufruct, to receive the value of the fungibles which were subject thereto; if the claim for the restitution of the value is endangered the grantor may claim security.   In practice the usufruct of fungibles is only granted in connexion with the grant of the usufruct of other objects; as for instance on the grant of the usufruct of a business [2] —BGB 1067,   424 1075 (2), 1084; HBG 22 (1).

c.   Rights and Duties of Usufructuary.

360. Usufructuary's real rights in respect of the usufructuary object, are supplemented by personal rights available against the owner for the time being of such object, [3] who in his turn is entitled to certain personal rights available against the usufructuary.   The nature of these rights and duties appears from the following statement:

(1) *Right to possession.*

The usufructuary is entitled to the possession of the usufructuary object, in

---

[1]   The quasi-usufruct of Roman law ('*usus fructus earum rerum quae usu consumuntur vel minuuntur*' — Dig. 7. 5) and the bailment of fungibles (*depositum irregulare*) referred to above (253) have similar characteristics.

[2]   Where the usufruct of a stocked farm is granted the ownership of the stock does not pass to the usufructuary, but he obtains powers as to the alienation and purchase of such stock, similar to those of a lessor who takes over the 'appurtenant stock' at a valuation (p. 226 note 3)—BGB 1048.

[3]   As between the owner and the usufructuary, the latter is entitled to assume, in the absence of express notice to the contrary, that the grantor of the usufruct is the owner of the usufructuary object—BGB 1058.

so far as it consists of movable or immovable things—BGB 1036 (1).

Where the usufructuary object is a right embodied in an instrument payable to bearer or indorsed in blank, such instrument itself must be lodged with a public authority (164) in the joint names of the usufructuary and the owner, but the usufructuary is entitled to the exclusive possession of any coupon sheets or dividend sheets belonging to such instrument [1]—BGB 1081, 1082.

Where the usufructuary object is a money claim not bearing interest, or a claim for the delivery of a specific object, the usufructuary is entitled to collect the claim, and where the maturity of the claim depends upon notice requiring payment or delivery, he is entitled to give such notice; the money or object received by him in satisfaction of the claim becomes subject to the usufruct—BGB 1074, 1075.

425   Where the usufructuary object is a money claim bearing interest, any payment out of corpus must be made to the creditor and the usufructuary jointly; if one of them claims lodgment with a public authority in the joint names such lodgment must be effected; the creditor must concur in giving the directions required for the investment of the money—BGB 1076–1080. [2]

(2) Right to profits.

The usufructuary is of course entitled to the profits of the usufructuary object, but certain classes of profits may be excluded by agreement—BGB 1030 (2), 1068 (2).

The profits to which the usufructuary is entitled do not include any fruits which are won in violation of the proper rules of management or husbandry; the ownership of such fruits vests in the usufructuary, as they are severed from the thing by which they are produced, but the owner is entitled to compensation on the termination of the usufruct—BGB 1039.

Where the usufructuary object is the right to receive an annual or other

---

[1]   Government securities and the debentures and shares of Companies, are, in most Continental countries, represented by instruments to bearer or indorsable instruments to which the so-called coupon-sheets or dividend-sheets are annexed: the holder collects each instalment of interest and each dividend by detaching the ' coupon' representing it, from the sheet to which it belongs, and presenting it to the banker by whom the interest or dividend is paid.

[2]   As regards the defences and rights of set-off open to the debtor, the usufructuary is in the same position as an assignee of the right would be—176 sub (6).   The grantor of the usufruct cannot effectively waive any such right by act-in-the-law, or consent to its modification in a manner detrimental to the usufructuary's interests without the consent of the latter—BGB 1071.

periodical payment, each instalment is deemed a profit to which the usufructuary is entitled—BGB 1073.

The owner's share in any treasure trove (341) found on land subject to a right of usufruct, is not deemed a profit to which the usufructuary is entitled— BGB 1040. [1]

(3) *Rules as to management of usufructuary object.*

The following rules apply on this subject:

(1) the right to win profits must be exercised in a proper course of management or husbandry, and so as to preserve the fitness of the usufructuary object for the economic purposes, for which it was previously intended, and as to prevent the loss of any of its essential characteristics [2] —BGB 1036 (2), 1037 (1), 1041;   426

(2) the usufructuary has to bear the cost of the ordinary repairs and renewals, but he is not responsible for any deterioration caused by the proper exercise of his rights—BGB 1041, 1050;

(3) immediate notice must be given to the owner of the usufructuary object of any actual or impending damaging event, and of any threat of interference on the part of any stranger—BGB 1042;

(4) a usufructuary whose right relates to a parcel of land may use any component part thereof for the purpose of effecting any repairs and renewals, which are not chargeable against him; if he does not himself effect such repairs or renewals, he must allow the owner to use such component parts for the same purpose—BGB 1043, 1044;

(5) where the usufructuary incurs any voluntary outlay for the benefit of the usufructuary object, his right to reimbursement is governed by the rules as to voluntary services (301);

(6) where the usufructuary object is a matured claim to the payment of money or to the delivery of a specific thing, the creditor and the usufructuary are under a mutual obligation to concur with each other in all steps necessary for the realization and enforcement of such claim—BGB 1078, 1083;

---

1   The usufructuary's right to profits derived from land is subject to the payment on his part of the ordinary rates and taxes and of the interest on all incumbrances existing at the date of the creation of the usufruct; the insurance against fire or other damaging events must be provided for by the usufructuary in so far as such insurance has to be provided for in accordance with the proper course of management—BGB 1045–1047.

2   As to the special rules relating to the winning of stones, clay, peat, and other component parts of the soil, and to the management of forests and mines, see BGB 1037 (2), 1038.

(7) in the event of a conflict between several rights of usufruct the same rule is applied as in the event of a conflict between several real servitudes—355 sub (4)—BGB 1060.

d. Mutual Rights on Termination of Usufruct.

361. The following rules apply on this subject:

(1) on the termination of the usufruct, the usufructuary must return the usufructuary object to its owner;

(2) the usufructuary is entitled to the *jus tollendi*—144 sub (9);

(3) where the usufructuary object is a piece of land used for farming purposes or a whole farm, the rules as to the mutual rights of lessor and lessee on the termination of the tenancy—209 rule (6), 210 rule (8) apply—*mutatis mutandis*—BGB 1049 (2), 1055;

(4) if the usufruct of an immovable let on lease [1] comes to an end before the expiration of the lease, the rules as to the rights of lessees on a sale of the leased object—215 to 218—are applied, *mutatis mutandis*; but the rules relating to the owner's right to give notice to terminate the lease are somewhat different from those regulating the lessor's right under the corresponding circumstances—BGB 1056;

(5) the owner's claims in respect of outlay and the *jus tollendi* are barred after the lapse of six months from the termination of the usufruct—BGB 1057.

e. Owner's Remedies against Usufructuary.

362. The owner has the following remedies:

(1) in the event of the continuance on the part of the usufructuary of any unauthorized use of the usufructuary object, after the receipt of a notice requiring him to discontinue such unauthorized use, a judicial order may be obtained restraining him from continuing such unauthorized use—BGB 1053;

(2) in the event of any conduct on the part of the usufructuary, justifying the apprehension of a material violation of the owner's rights, a judicial order may be obtained directing the usufructuary to give security (87); if the usufructuary fails to comply with such an order within a specified time, the owner may ask for the appointment of a judicial Receiver to whom the management of the usufructuary

---

1   As mentioned above (352), the right of usufruct cannot be assigned to another, but the usufructuary may authorize another to exercise the right; this enables him to grant a lease.

object is then handed over—BGB 1051, 1052;

(3) in the event of the continuance of any conduct on the part of the usufructuary constituting a material violation of the owner's rights, after the receipt of notice requiring him to discontinue such conduct, a judicial Receiver may be appointed having the same powers as a judicial Receiver appointed under the rule stated sub (2)—BGB 1054.

f.   Rules for the Protection of Owner's Creditors.

363. Where the usufruct of a person's whole property, or of the estate of a   428 deceased person, has been granted or bequeathed (359), the grantor's or testator's creditors, in so far as their claims arose before the constitution of the usufruct, may enforce their rights against the usufructuary object in accordance with the special rules contained in BGB 1085–1089.

5.   RESTRICTED PERSONAL SERVITUDES

364. A restricted personal servitude entitles the grantee to use an immovable for certain specified purposes, or to exercise rights over the same similar to the rights resulting from a real servitude—BGB 1090.   A restricted personal servitude always affects a servient tenement, and its benefit is always vested in a specified person; it resembles the right called a ' profit in gross ' under English law, but whilst such a profit in gross is alienable and transmissible on death, a restricted personal servitude like the right of usufruct is incapable of assignment, and comes to an end on the grantee's death.

Where the extent of the grantee's right resulting from a restricted personal servitude is not specifically defined, such right is not deemed to go beyond his personal wants—BGB 1091.

Illustration: The grantee of a right to cut wood is not authorized, in the absence of a stipulation to the contrary, to cut any wood for the purpose of sale.

One of the best known restricted personal servitudes is the right to the sole occupation of a building, or of part of a building.   Where such a right is granted, the grantee may use the space allocated to him for his family and such servants and attendants as are usually required for persons in his station of life.   Where the use of a part of a house is given, the grantee is entitled to use in common with the other inhabitants of such house all appliances and conveniences intended for the common use of its inhabitants—BGB 1093.

6. Extinction of Servitudes

a. Release by Act-in-the-Law.

365. A real servitude may be released by the owner for the time being of the dominant tenement; a personal servitude may be released by the grantee.

429   The release of a servitude affecting an immovable is governed by the general rules as to the release of rights affecting immovables—310 rule (2). The release of the usufruct of an immovable is, in the absence of evidence to the contrary, deemed to include a release of the usufruct of the accessories—BGB 1062.

The release of the usufruct of a movable or of a right is effected by a declaration made by the usufructuary and communicated to the owner of the usufructuary object or to the grantor of the usufruct; a declaration addressed to the latter is sufficient, even if the usufructuary is aware of the fact that he is no longer the owner of the usufructuary object—BGB 1064, 1072.

b. Extinction by Natural Events.

A servitude, granted for a definite period of time or subject to a condition subsequent, is released by the expiration of the period or the fulfilment of the condition.

A real servitude comes to an end by the destruction of the servient tenement or of the dominant tenement.

A personal servitude comes to an end by the death of the grantee, or, in the event of the grantee being a corporate body, by the termination of its corporate existence—BGB 1061, 1068, 1090 (2).

c. Extinction by Prescription.

A real servitude, as well as a restricted personal servitude, becomes extinguished by prescription, as soon as the claim to remove an appliance, preventing the exercise of the rights of the party benefited by such servitude, is barred by lapse of time (see the Illustration—p. 391 note 2)—BGB 1028, 1090.

d. Extinction by Merger.

The usufruct of a movable becomes extinguished by merger, if the usufructuary acquires the ownership of the usufructuary object, unless the continuance of the usufruct confers a legal advantage on him [1] —BGB 1063.

A servitude affecting an immovable does not in any case become extinguished by merger—BGB 889.

e.   Extinction by other Causes.

A servitude becomes extinguished by the public sale of the servient tenement 430 on the application of an execution creditor, unless such sale is made subject to the servitude—ZVG 91, but see EG (ZVG) 9.

The rules of State law may provide that, on the compulsory purchase of any immovable required for any public purpose, all servitudes affecting such immovable are to be extinguished—EG 109.

7.   PERPETUAL CHARGES ON LAND (*Reallasten*)

a.   General Characteristics.

366. Under Roman law it was impossible to create a perpetual charge imposing an active duty upon the owner for the time being of an immovable.   Such a charge would have violated the rule *servitus in faciendo consistere nequit*.   As mentioned above—355 sub (2)—the new German law has abandoned this rule.

A servitude may be created by which an active as well as a passive duty is imposed on the owner for the time being of the servient tenement; but where the duty imposed by any such incumbrance is exclusively of an active nature, the Germanic designation: *Reallast* (translated in this treatise by the expression ' perpetual charge') is applied to it.   Manorial rights, tithes, chief rents, and other charges arising under ancient customs or in connexion with the tenure of land are the best known historical examples of charges of this kind, but an annuity charged on land under the provisions of a modern marriage contract, or of a will, also comes within the definition of a *Reallast*. [2]

Readers of German works of fiction will remember the custom prevalent among peasant proprietors in many parts of Germany, under which the owner of a tenement, on ceasing to be fit for arduous farm work, transfers the ownership to a

---

[1]   If another right of usufruct exists, ranking behind or *pari passu* with the owner's right of usufruct, it is obviously to his advantage to keep the last-mentioned right alive.

[2]   As to the difference between an annuity charged as a *Reallast* and an annuity charged as an ' annuity charge' (*Rentenschuld*), see p. 406 note 1.

son, in consideration of a provision for his benefit charged upon the tenement and described as the ' old man's part ' (*Altenteil*); this custom serves as a useful paradigma of the rights of usufruct, restricted personal servitudes, and permanent
431   charges on land.   The provision for the old man generally consists in the 'usufruct' of a reserved plot, the 'use' of a cottage, and of a 'perpetual charge' on the surrendered tenement, securing recurrent payments and deliveries of money, articles of food, firewood, &c. , and labour on the reserved plot, to be given for a certain number of days in each year. [1]

Any charge on land which is intended to secure the performance of duties of a recurrent kind—BGB 1105 (1)—is within the definition of a perpetual charge. It is not necessary that the times for the performance of the duties should recur on fixed dates; thus, for instance, a charge on a manorial estate by virtue of which churches and school buildings for the use of the population residing within its area have to be provided and kept in repair, comes within the definition, notwithstanding the fact that the duty is only to be performed when a particular need arises.

State legislation may provide for the compulsory redemption of existing perpetual charges—EG 113—, and prohibit the creation of new ones—EG 115. [2]

b.   Creation and Extinction of Perpetual Charges.

367. A perpetual charge may be created by act-in-the-law under the rules as to the creation of rights affecting immovables [3]—315, 317.

A perpetual charge becomes extinguished:
432   (1) by a release on the part of the beneficiary effected in conformity with

---

[1]   State legislation may lay down special rules as to making provisions for the old man's part—EG 96. Several of the *Ausführungsgesetze* deal with it.   See, for instance, Prussian AG 15; Bavarian AG 32–48; Saxon AG 31; Baden AG 9.   A particular kind of perpetual charge has been introduced by the Prussian legislation, intended to extend the system of peasant proprietorship by the creation of special authorities with powers for the compulsory purchase of large estates, which are subsequently sub-divided among small owners in consideration of a perpetual rent charged on each separate parcel (*Rentengüter*).   The rent charge can be redeemed on special terms.   See EG 62, 118 (Prussian Statute of 1890).

[2]   In Prussia it is not allowed to create perpetual charges extending beyond the life of the grantee, except for the purpose of securing periodical payments of money; charges created for the last-mentioned purpose may be redeemed on specified terms by the owner of the immovable on which they are charged—Prussian Statutes of 1850, 1862, 1872, 1873, and 1876, Prussian AG 30.   In Bavaria the law is similar (Bavarian AG 85).   In *Württemberg Reallasten* of all kinds are forbidden (Statute of 1848).

[3]   A perpetual charge of a nature prohibited by State law cannot be validly created; the Registrar is bound to refuse the registration of such a charge.

the general rules as to the release of rights affecting immovables—310 sub (2);

(2) by redemption in accordance with the rules of State law;

(3) on any sale by public auction made for the benefit of an execution creditor [1] (ZVG 91);

(4) by order of the Court in any case in which the beneficiary cannot be found after proceedings analogous to the proceedings which may be taken where a mortgagee cannot be found—387—BGB 1112.

c.   Burden and Benefit of Perpetual Charges.

368. The burden of a perpetual charge cannot be imposed on a specific part of the immovable which it affects, but it may be imposed on a co-owner's undivided share—BGB 1106.

The performance of the duties arising under a perpetual charge may be enforced by judicial sale or by the appointment of a Receiver, in the same way as the payment of the interest of a mortgage debt may be enforced—389—BGB 1105 (1), 1107.

The owner of an immovable which is subject to a perpetual charge is also personally liable for the performance of all acts required to be done while the ownership is vested in him, unless such personal liability is expressly excluded—BGB 1108 (1).

The benefit of a perpetual charge may be vested in a specified person or in the owner for the time being of a specified immovable—BGB 1105 (2).

A charge for the benefit of a specified person is called 'subjectively personal' (*subjektiv persönlich*); a charge for the benefit of the owner for the time being of a specified immovable is called 'subjectively real' (*subjektiv dinglich*).

The benefit of a subjectively real charge may, by the entry of a note in that behalf on the register, be appropriated to a locally defined part of the immovable, but such benefit cannot in any event be transferred to any specified person or to the owner for the time being of any other immovable—BGB 1109 (2), 1110.

A subjectively personal charge cannot in any event be transformed into a subjectively real charge—BGB 1111 (1).

---

[1]   The provisions made for securing the 'old man's part' (see 366) remain in force notwithstanding such public sale—EG (ZVG 9).

d.   Transmissibility of Benefit of Perpetual Charge.

433   **369.** The benefit of a subjectively personal charge cannot be transferred by the original grantee, unless the right to the performance of any individual act secured by such charge is a right capable of assignment under the rules as to the assignment of obligatory rights—176—BGB 1111 (2).

The benefit of a subjectively real charge is transferred as a matter of course by the transfer of the ownership of the immovable for the benefit of which it is created.

e.   Consequences of sub-division of Servient or Dominant Tenement.

370. On the sub-division of an immovable subject to the burden of a perpetual charge, each separate part becomes subject to the burden of the whole charge, except in so far as State legislation enables the charge to be divided and apportioned among the several parts severed from each other—EG 120 (2) Nr. 1, 121.   The respective owners of the several parts are in the position of joint debtors (182)— BGB 1108 (2).

On the sub-division of an immovable, entitled to the benefit of a perpetual charge, the owners for the time being of the several parts become together entitled to the benefit of the charge.   If the benefit is divisible (as in the case of a claim for money payments) each owner becomes entitled *pro rata* of the size of his part; if the benefit is not divisible they are in the position of creditors entitled to the benefit of a right without being joint creditors (183).   These rules are subject to the following exceptions:

(1) if the charge is of exclusive advantage to a locally defined part of the sub-divided immovable, or if the owner has annexed its benefit to a locally defined part, such locally defined part retains the benefit of the charge to the exclusion of the other parts;

(2) if, in a case in which the benefit of the charge has not been annexed to a locally defined part, the owner sells a part of the dominant tenement but retains the other part the benefit of the charge becomes annexed to the part retained by him—BGB 1109.

CHAPTER V
REAL RIGHTS GRANTED BY WAY OF SECURITY

A. CHARGES ON IMMOVABLES

1. GENERAL CHARACTERISTICS

371. UNDER English law a mortgagee is the legal owner of the property   434
conveyed to him by way of security for the mortgagor's debt, the mortgagor being
entitled to remain in possession of such property and to have the same re-conveyed
to him on repayment of the mortgage debt and all accessories thereof (which last-
mentioned right is called the equity of redemption).   If the mortgagor makes
default in respect of any of his obligations, the mortgagee may, unless prevented
from doing so by the terms of the mortgage deed, take possession of the mortgaged
property or collect the rents and profits by means of a Receiver, or sell the
mortgaged property for the mortgagor's account, retaining the amount of his own
claim out of the proceeds of sale, or obtain an order foreclosing the mortgagor's
equity of redemption.   The proprietor of a registered charge under the Land
Transfer Acts 1875 and 1897 is not the legal owner of the mortgaged property,
but he has otherwise the same rights as a legal mortgagee.

Under German law a creditor secured by a charge on an immovable is not in
any event entitled to take possession of the property, and cannot bring about the
appointment of a Receiver or the sale of the mortgaged property without an order
of the Court; he cannot in any event become absolute owner of the mortgaged
property by means of foreclosure proceedings.

Both under German and English law an agreement made before the maturity
of the mortgage debt between the mortgagor and mortgagee, and providing that the
absolute ownership of the mortgaged property is, in certain events, to pass to the
mortgagee, is void. [1]   Under German law an agreement made before the maturity   435

---

[1]   The English rule of equity providing for this is expressed by the maxim ' once a mortgage always a
mortgage '.

of the mortgage debt is also void if it gives the mortgagee an extra-judicial power of sale—BGB 1149; a covenant on the part of the owner of the mortgaged property not to sell or further charge the property while the first charge subsists is equally inoperative—BGB 1136.

It will be seen from a comparison of the rules stated above that the remedies of a person entitled to a charge on an immovable under German law are much less extensive than the remedies to which an English mortgagee is entitled; on the other hand, the German system of registration gives many advantages to a German incumbrancer, more particularly if his charge ranks after another charge. An English second mortgagee runs many risks which are non-existent under German law.

For the sake of convenience, the expression 'mortgagee' is used in this treatise for the designation of a creditor entitled to a charge on an immovable created by way of security under German law, the expression 'the mortgaged property' for the designation of the property subject to the charge, the expression 'mortgage debt' as the designation for the sum charged on the mortgaged property, it being, however, understood, after the explanation given above, that the position of the person described as mortgagee is entirely different from that of an English mortgagee.

The expression 'charge' [1] is used as a general term for three distinct kinds of charges, respectively termed 'hypothecary charge' (*Hypothek*), 'land charge' (*Grundschuld*), and 'annuity charge' (*Rentenschuld*), of which the characteristics are described below (372). There is no recognized collective German name for the three kinds of charges, [2] but as many of the provisions explained in this chapter are applicable to each of them, it will be convenient to describe them by a common designation.

State legislation may impose a limit of value, beyond which an immovable cannot be charged in favour of a mortgagee—EG 117 (1), but up to the present time no such limit appears to have been imposed by the law of any German State.

2. CLASSIFICATION OF CHARGES

a. Hypothecary Charges, Land Charges, and Annuity Charges.

436   **372.** The Roman 'hypotheca' was essentially an accessory to a debt. The

---

[1] A charge given by way of security must, of course, be distinguished from a perpetual charge imposed on a servient tenement in accordance with the rules stated above, 367.

[2] Dernburg uses the expression *Grundstückpfandrechte*.

mortgagee's rights were only available in so far as a debt was in existence; a transferee of the 'hypotheca' took the debt as well as the security, subject to all the defences open to the debtor; in so far as the debt had been repaid before the transfer was effected, he was not entitled to retain the security.   An English mortgage, though in other respects differing from the Roman hypotheca, resembles it in respect of its accessory character.

The rules of Roman law carrying out to its full extent the accessory character of charges on immovables [1] were gradually modified in many parts of Germany; the old Prussian Code already took a decided step in that direction, and a Prussian statute passed in 1871 created a new form of charge called 'land charge' (*Grundschuld*), which was made entirely independent of the existence of a debt, being enforceable without proof of the mortgage debt, as long as it remained on the register as an incumbrance on the immovable which it affected.

The accessory charge known as 'hypothecary charge' (*Hypothek*) remained in existence by the side of the land charge, it being left to the agreement of the parties to select either form of security, but even the accessory charge was more favourable to the creditor than the Roman hypotheca.

The new German law has in all essential points followed the Prussian system.   It defines an hypothecary charge as a charge on an immovable by which the payment of a specified sum, 'in satisfaction of an existing or future certain or contingent debt', is secured—BGB 1113—whereas a land charge is defined as a charge on an immovable by which the payment of a specified sum is secured— BGB 1191.   In the case of an hypothecary charge the mortgaged property is pledged to secure the repayment of a debt, and the creditor can, on principle, enforce his rights only in so far as there is a debt; in the case of a land charge the mortgaged property serves as security for the payment of a specified sum of money, without reference to the question whether its owner or any other person is under any liability as to the payment of such sum.   The practical effects of the distinction are, however, not so important as the theoretical differences between the two kinds of charges.

Under the rules stated below (373) the transferee of an hypothecary charge can frequently enforce his right to the payment of the sum secured thereby, notwithstanding the fact that the debt which it was intended to secure is not a

---

[1]   The hypotheca of Roman law also applied to movables, but in most parts of Germany hypothecary charges on movables were gradually discontinued.

valid debt or was discharged in some other way; on the other hand, a land charge is frequently given as collateral security for a personal debt, and, as between the immediate parties, the invalidity or discharge of such a debt would in the event of an attempt to enforce the charge give rise to a counterclaim.

In actual practice hypothecary charges are much more common than land charges; the latter are principally used as security for loans to trading companies, in the same way as mortgage debentures are used as securities for loans to English companies.

An hypothecary charge may at any time be converted into a land charge, and a land charge may at any time be converted into an hypothecary charge if such a change is agreed upon between the mortgagor and the mortgagee, and assented to by any prior mortgagee—BGB 1198.

An annuity charge (*Rentenschuld*) is a land charge securing a succession of periodical payments instead of the payment of a specified single sum; on the creation of an annuity charge a specified sum, called the redemption sum (*Ablösungssumme*), must be agreed upon, on payment of which the charge can at any time after notice given in the prescribed manner be redeemed by the owner of the mortgaged property; the mortgagee is not entitled to the payment of the redemption sum unless the safety of the charge is endangered by a deterioration of the mortgaged property.

An annuity charge may be converted into an ordinary land charge and *vice versa* in the same way as an hypothecary charge may be converted into a land charge [1] —BGB 1199–1203.

---

[1]   As an annuity charge in some respects resembles a perpetual charge on land securing periodical money payments (366), it may be convenient to call attention to the differences between the two kinds of charges:

(1) in the case of a perpetual charge the owner of the servient tenement is personally liable for the instalments falling due, while he is owner; in the case of an annuity charge there is no personal liability, unless expressly undertaken;

(2) a perpetual charge is not redeemable except possibly under the provisions of State law; an irredeemable annuity charge cannot be created in any event;

(3) an annuity charge can, but a perpetual charge cannot, be converted into a land charge;

(4) the benefit of a perpetual charge can, but the benefit of an annuity charge cannot, be annexed to an immovable.

b.   Ordinary Hypothecary Charges and Cautionary Hypothecary Charges.

(1)   Ordinary hypothecary charge.

373. If the accessory character of an hypothecary charge had been consistently   438
maintained, the principle of the conclusiveness of the register would have been
sacrificed; this was avoided by the enactment of the following rules:

(1) a mortgagee is presumed to be entitled to the amount of the mortgage
debt which appears on the register; it is not for him to prove the existence of the
debt, but for the debtor to prove its non-existence or reduction by part payment,
set-off, or otherwise—BGB 891, 1138;

(2) the fact that the mortgage debt is barred by prescription does not
prevent the enforcement of the charge against the mortgaged property—BGB 223
(1);

(3) the maturity of a mortgage debt falling due on the termination of a
specified period after notice is, as against the owner of the mortgaged property, [1]
determined by notice given to or by him; as against the personal debtor the
maturity of the debt is determined by notice given to or by him [2] —BGB 1141
(1);

Illustration: *A* charges Whiteacre with a debt owing by him to *B*, repayable
six months after notice; *C* purchases Whiteacre subject to the charge but without   439
undertaking any personal liability in respect thereof; *B* gives notice to *C* claiming
repayment of the mortgage debt, but omits to give notice to *A*; on the expiration
of the notice he may obtain an order for the judicial sale of Whiteacre, but he
cannot enforce *A*'s personal covenant;

(4) a transferee of the registered mortgaged debt, who claims payment
thereof out of the proceeds of sale of the mortgaged property, is not affected by
any defences or rights of set-off which are not disclosed on the register, except in
so far as the existence of such defences or rights of set-off was known to him at the
date of the transfer; such defences and rights of set-off are available in an action

---

[1]   It is presumed in favour of the mortgagee that the person registered as owner is the owner—BGB
1141 (1).

[2]   If the owner is not domiciled in the German Empire, or if the creditor is excusably ignorant of his
identity, or if he cannot be found, the local Court of the district in which the immovable is situate may, on
the creditor's application, appoint a person to whom notices may be addressed—BGB 1141 (2).

brought by the transferee for the enforcement of the debtor's personal covenant [1] —
BGB 1137, 1138, 1156, 1157.

Illustration: A mortgage debt is registered as amounting to £ 1000; the
debtor has paid off £ 500, but has omitted to have the payment entered on the
register; the mortgagee transfers the debt for £ 1000.   The transferee brings an
action against the debtor claiming:

(a) satisfaction out of the mortgaged property;

(b) a personal judgment against the debtor.

He will obtain judgment for £ 1000 as to claim (a), and for £ 500 as to
claim (b), subject to the restriction that the amount recovered by the enforcement
of either claim is *pro tanto* to be deemed in satisfaction of the other claim; if,
therefore, the proceeds of the sale of the mortgaged property amount to £ 600 he
cannot claim anything by virtue of the personal judgment against the debtor.

(2) *Cautionary hypothecary charge.*

The rules stated above sub (1) show that the accessory character of an
ordinary hypothecary charge has been abandoned to a considerable extent for the
purpose of upholding the principle of the conclusive character of the entries
appearing on the Land Register; in the case of a ' cautionary hypothecary
charge' (*Sicherheitshypothek*) the accessory character of the charge is, on the
other hand, strictly maintained; the remedies against the mortgaged property are
only available in so far as the existence of a personal debt can be proved—BGB
1184 (1), 1185 (2).

The form of a cautionary hypothecary charge has to be adopted in all cases in
which the balance for the time being owing on a current account has to be
secured, as well as in all cases in which the payment of any bond payable to
bearer, or any other negotiable instrument, is to be secured by a charge on land.

An hypothecary charge is deemed a cautionary hypothecary charge:

(1) if it is entered as such on the register—BGB 1184 (2);

440

---

1   The rule stated in the text is subject to the following exception: the owner of an immovable on
which an uncertificated charge (374) is registered, by way of security for an advance which in fact has not
been made, may, within a month from the date of the registration, without the intervention of the Court,
procure the entry of an objection on the register (319); such an objection, even against a transferee who
took his transfer before it was registered, is deemed to have been registered simultaneously with the charge—
BGB 1139.   A person who takes the transfer of an uncertificated charge within the first month of its
existence, consequently runs the risk of the subsequent registration of such an objection.

(2) if it is expressed to be created as a security for any debt owing to the mortgagee by the debtor up to a specified maximum amount [1]—BGB 1190 (1) (3);

(3) if it is created as a collateral security for the payment of any negotiable instrument [2]—BGB 1187.

A cautionary hypothecary charge may be converted into an ordinary hypothecary charge and *vice versa*, in the same way as an hypothecary charge may be converted into a land charge (372)—BGB 1186.

c.   Certificated Charges and Uncertificated Charges.

374. In the case of a cautionary hypothecary charge a certificate of charge cannot be issued; in the case of any other kind of charge a certificate of charge may be issued, unless a stipulation to the contrary is agreed upon between the mortgagee and the owner of the mortgaged property, with the assent of all interested parties, and entered on the register—BGB 1116 (1) (2), 1185   441 (1), 1192.

A charge, of which a certificate may be issued, is called *Briefhypothek* or *Briefgrundschuld*, and will, in the course of this treatise, be described as a ' certificated charge ' .

A charge as to which a certificate cannot be issued is called *Buchhypothek* or *Buchgrundschuld*, and will, in the course of this treatise, be described as an ' uncertificated charge ' .

Certificates of land charges [3] may be issued to bearer (subject, of course, to the restrictions imposed generally on the issue of instruments to bearer—179).

Where the benefit of one certificated charge is sub-divided among several

---

[1]   Where such a debt bears interest the accrued interest is taken into consideration on the computation of the total amount of indebtedness—BGB 1190 (2).

[2]   As mentioned above (372), trading companies in Germany issue land charges for the same purpose as English companies issue debentures; for the same purpose they also frequently issue bonds to bearer, secured by a cautionary hypothecary charge; where a cautionary hypothecary charge is created for such a purpose, the owner of the mortgaged property may cause a specified person to be registered as trustee for the bondholders with power to act on their behalf in all matters—BGB 1189.

[3]   Certificates of land charges issued to bearer are frequently used by trading companies for the purposes for which debentures are issued by English companies.   As in the case of a cautionary hypothecary charge registered to secure bonds issued for the same purpose—see p. 409 note 2—the name of a trustee may be registered who acts on behalf of the holders of such certificates—BGB 1189, 1195.

persons, each of them is entitled to a certificate relating to his share: (*Teilhypothekenbrief*, *Teilgrundschuldbrief*).   The certificate relating to the share takes the place of the original certificate as regards such share.   The fact that any such part certificate has been issued must be indorsed on the certificate relating to the undivided charge—BGB 1152; GBO 61.

A certificate of charge gives an extract from the register which must contain:

(1) particulars of the mortgaged property;

(2) the owner's name and address;

(3) the entries relating to the nature of the charge and the contents of any documents referred to in such entries;

(4) a summary statement as to prior charges.

If the debt secured by the charge is evidenced by any written instrument, such written instrument or a certified copy of such parts thereof as relate to the debt must be annexed to the certificate—GBO 57, 58.

Where a certificate of charge has been issued, it must be produced before any entry relating to the charge which it represents can be made on the register. [1] A copy of the entry made on the production of a certificate must be indorsed thereon—GBO 42 (1), 43, 62.

In so far as the contents of a certificate of charge and of the indorsements thereon are not in agreement with the entries in the register, the holder of such certificate is not entitled to rely on the correctness of the entries on the register— BGB 1140.

If a certificate of charge is lost or destroyed proceedings may be taken for its annulment by judicial order, which being obtained, a new certificate may be issued.   The filing of an application for a new certificate by a person who has obtained a judicial order for the annulment of the old one is deemed equivalent to the production of the certificate—BGB 1162; GBO 42 (2), 67, 68.

An uncertificated charge may be converted into a certificated charge by the registration of an agreement to that effect between the creditor and the owner of the mortgaged property, assented to by all other interested parties—BGB 1116 (3).

442

---

[1] There are two exceptions to this rule: (1) an objection against the validity of a charge, directed to be entered by an interlocutory order of a competent Court, may be registered without the production of the certificate; (2) where land charge certificates to bearer have been issued an authorization signed by the registered trustee replaces the production of the certificate—GBO 42 (1), 43.

3.   CREATION AND MODIFICATION OF CHARGES

a.   Creation.

375. The general rules relating to the creation of real rights (309) apply to the creation of charges of every kind, but on the creation of a cautionary hypothecary charge created as a collateral security for bearer debentures, or of a land charge represented by bearer certificates, or of a land charge in favour of the owner of the mortgaged property (377), a declaration made by the owner of the mortgaged property, and communicated to the registration authorities, takes the place of the real agreement required in other cases [1]—BGB 1188, 1192, 1195, 1196.

Full particulars must be entered on the register, specifying the mortgagee's name, the amount of the mortgage debt, and the rate of interest if the mortgage debt is to bear interest.   The entry in the register may refer to the ' authority for registration' (318) if the latter contains further details as to the nature of the mortgage debt—BGB 1115.

443

The registered mortgagee does not in any event become entitled to the benefit of the charge registered in his favour before the debt which such charge was intended to secure has come into existence; where the charge is a certificated charge he does not become entitled until the certificate is delivered to him. [2]

During the period intervening between the registration of the charge and the time at which the registered mortgagee becomes entitled to its benefit, the owner of the mortgaged property is deemed to be entitled to the benefit of the charge (377)—BGB 1117, 1163, 1192.

The registered charge is a security for the original mortgage debt, and for such interest and other accessories as are specified on the register, as well as for all interest which may become payable under any rule of law, *e. g.* as a consequence of *mora solvendi* (153), or after judgment, and for all costs which may be lawfully incurred in connexion with the enforcement of the claim—BGB 1118.

---

[1]   A charge in favour of a judgment creditor may be registered on his application (see, for instance, CPO 866, 867) ; State legislation may also authorize the registration of cautionary hypothecary charges in favour of certain public authorities—EG 91.

[2]   As a general rule the certificate is issued to the owner of the mortgaged property, who hands it to the mortgagee against payment of the sum intended to be secured thereby, but the issue to the mortgagee may be agreed upon; in that event his title accrues immediately on registration.

b. Modification.

376. Under the general rules as to modification of rights affecting immovables, any modification of the terms of a registered charge requires the assent of all interested parties.

Special rules apply in the following cases:

(1) where the mortgage debt under the original agreement does not bear interest, or bears interest at a rate below five per cent., an agreement charging the mortgaged property with interest at a rate not exceeding five per cent. may be registered without the assent of any mortgagees ranking *pari passu* with, or behind the mortgagee in whose favour the change is made—BGB 1119 (1);

(2) where the date or place of repayment is altered the assent of any mortgagee ranking *pari passu* with, or behind the mortgagee agreeing to such alteration, is not required—BGB 1119 (2);

(3) where the benefit of a charge is sub-divided among several persons, an arrangement, under which any one of such persons takes priority over the others, does not require the assent of the owner of the mortgaged property—BGB 1151;

(4) where an hypothecary charge, serving originally as security for a specified debt, is to become security for another debt, a real agreement between the mortgagee and the owner of the mortgaged property, assented to by all interested parties, is required; if such an arrangement is made in connexion with a transfer of the charge to a new mortgagee, the former mortgagee must assent [1]—BGB 1180.

4. RULES AS TO CHARGES BECOMING VESTED IN THE OWNER OF THE MORTGAGED PROPERTY

377. Under the strict rules as to merger, prevailing in Roman law and also under English common law, it is deemed impossible that a person should be creditor and debtor at the same time; a charge is therefore under these rules deemed to be extinguished whenever the mortgagor becomes entitled to the mortgage debt, or whenever such debt is paid off by him. The practical inconvenience of this rule is obvious in a case where the charge which is paid off ranks before another charge, which, in consequence of the extinction of the prior charge,

---

[1] This provision is intended to save trouble and costs; if the change could not be effected in the manner described in the text, it would be necessary to cancel the original charge and register a new charge.

becomes the first charge on the property, though arranged on terms corresponding to the smaller security offered by a second charge.

In modern English law the inconvenience is avoided by the rules of equity, under which there is a presumption against merger on payment of a mortgage debt in any case in which it is to the mortgagor's interest to keep the debt alive. [1]

The new German law, following in the footsteps of the Prussian law, does not recognize the principle of merger in respects of rights affecting immovables; under the rules which are now in force an incumbrance affecting an immovable is not extinguished by its transfer to the owner of such immovable, or by the fact that the incumbrancer acquires the ownership of the immovable—BGB 889; the possibility of the same person being mortgagee and mortgagor is therefore recognized in a manner which obviates the necessity of a resort to legal fictions or conveyancers' devices.

445

A charge in favour of the owner of the mortgaged property is known by the name of *Eigentümerhypothek* or *Eigentümergrundschuld* (owner's charge). A 'land charge' may be created as 'owner's charge' *ab initio* [2]—BGB 1196.

A charge in the owner's favour also arises:

(1) during the time intervening between the first registration and the accrual of the mortgagee's rights (375);

(2) on the discharge of the mortgage debt by payment or otherwise—382, 383, 385, 386—BGB 1163 (1). [3]

While the owner is entitled to the benefit of a charge, it always has the character of a land charge, except in a case in which, on payment of the mortgage debt by the owner of the mortgaged property, the claim against the personal debtor is transferred to such owner—382 sub (b). [4]

---

[1]   Before this rule was established, the device of having the mortgage debt assigned to a third party as trustee for the mortgagor had to be resorted to.

[2]   There are several reasons which may induce the owner of an immovable to register a charge in his own favour, *e. g.* he may be able at a particular moment to obtain a second charge on comparatively easy terms; by registering himself as first mortgagee he preserves the possibility of selecting the most favourable time for obtaining a first charge.

[3]   In some exceptional cases the charge becomes extinguished on repayment; for a recapitulation of these cases, see p. 426 note 1.

[4]   Where a charge registered as an hypothecary charge is converted into a land charge by the effect of the rule mentioned in the text, the stipulations as to interest, notices, times, and places of payment registered in respect of the personal debt, are applied as if they had been registered in respect of the sum secured by the land charge—BGB 1177.

A charge which becomes vested in the owner of the mortgaged property remains effective exclusively as a security for the principal debt; in so far as the charge is a security for arrears of interest, costs, or other accessories, it becomes extinguished on becoming vested in the owner of the mortgaged property, except in so far as any third party has any right relating thereto—BGB 1178 (1).

446 The owner of the mortgaged property may covenant with any third party that he or any other owner for the time being of the mortgaged property will at any time at which a charge thereon becomes vested in him take the necessary steps for procuring the cancellation of such charge; a caution stating the terms of such an agreement may be entered on the register—BGB 1179. [1]

5. RULES AS TO PROPERTY SUBJECT TO CHARGE

(1) *Objects added to mortgaged property.*

378. The charge extends to the following classes of objects, notwithstanding the fact that they are not component parts of the immovable expressed to be subject thereto:

(*a*) severed component parts and accessories of the mortgaged property, except such of them as under the rules stated sub 339 become vested in any person other than the owner or proprietary possessor of the mortgaged property, or have been lawfully removed from the mortgaged property before having been seized by the mortgagee—BGB 1120–1122; [2]

(*b*) moneys or other objects payable or deliverable at recurrent dates by way of rent for, or otherwise in respect of, the mortgaged property or any part thereof, excepting however any instalment which the mortgagee fails to seize within a year after maturity—BGB 1123–1126;

(*c*) insurance claims, except in so far as the object in respect of which a claim arises is restored or replaced [3] —BGB 1127–1130;

---

1   Such a covenant may be made for the benefit of a second mortgagee, who, on the cancellation of the charge, becomes first mortgagee, whereas, under the ordinary rule, the owner of the mortgaged property would, on discharging the first charge, become first mortgagee, with power to transfer the first mortgage to another at any time that he may think fit.

2   As to what constitutes lawful removal, see BGB 1121, 1122.

3   The rules as to the mortgagee's right in respect of the classes of objects mentioned sub (a), (b), and (c), are subject to certain qualifications introduced for the protection of third parties, which cannot be enumerated in detail.

(*d*) any parcel added on the register[1] to the parcel originally subject to the charge—BGB 1131.

(2) *As to charges affecting a part of an immovable.*

Each co-owner (325) of an immovable may charge his undivided share, but the sole owner of an immovable cannot charge a fraction thereof—BGB 1114.   447

A locally defined part of an immovable can be charged, if such part is converted into a separate parcel by being severed in the register from the parcel to which it belongs, and registered as an independent parcel on a separate folio.

(3) *As to charges affecting several parcels collectively.*

If several independent parcels are charged together with the payment of one specified debt, or of one specified sum, each parcel is deemed to be charged with the payment of the whole debt or of the whole sum.   A charge of this nature is called a 'collective charge' (*Gesamthypothek*, *Gesamtgrundschuld*).   A mortgagee entitled to the benefit of a collective charge may at any time apportion the charge among the several parcels, and thus convert the collective charge into as many charges as there are parcels.   Such a conversion must be registered on the folio of each parcel in the same way as the release of a right affecting such parcel— BGB 1132.

The questions arising on the repayment of a collective charge, in any case in which the several parcels subject to the charge belong to separate owners, will be discussed below—383.

6.   DISCHARGE OF MORTGAGEE'S CLAIMS

a.   Payment of Mortgage Debt.

aa.   General rules.

379. The conditions as to the time and place of the repayment of a debt secured by an hypothecary charge, if not expressly agreed upon by the parties, are determined upon by the general rules relating to the time and place of the

---

1   A parcel, appearing as an independent parcel in the register, is treated as a separate entity, and any parcel added to it is looked upon as an accretion to that entity—BGB 890.   An addition must be distinguished from a consolidation of two separate parcels by entry on one folio; in the case of consolidation each parcel is entered separately on the new folio with the charges to which it is subject.   On a sub-division of a parcel into two separate parcels, each separate parcel is registered as subject to the whole charge.

performance of obligations (146, 147). [1]

448   The time for repayment may be a fixed date or depend upon the expiration of a notice given by one of the parties or by either party, and it may also be stipulated that the mortgage debt shall fall due on non-compliance with the stipulation as to payment of interest or any other stipulation.

Certain modifications, arising in the case of the personal debtor and the owner of the mortgaged property not being the same person, are referred to below—380.

The conditions as to the time and place of payment of the sum secured by a land charge are not binding on the respective successors in title of the original parties unless entered on the register; in the absence of any registered agreement, six months' notice claiming payment may at any time be given by the mortgagee, and six months' notice announcing payment may at any time be given by the owner of the mortgaged property; upon the expiration of such notice the payment becomes due, and must be effected in the place in which the mortgaged property is registered—BGB 1193, 1194.

bb. Payment by personal debtor.

380. In the case of an hypothecary charge the owner of the mortgaged property is not necessarily the personal debtor. Thus if *A* sells Whiteacre to *B*, subject to a mortgage in favour of *C*, and if *C* declines to accept *B* as personal debtor in lieu of *A*, *A* remains the personal debtor, while *B* becomes the owner of the mortgaged property.

Where, in any case in which the personal debtor is a person other than the owner of the mortgaged property, the maturity of the debt depends upon notice, there may, as shown above—373, be two distinct maturities—one affecting the personal debtor, and the other affecting the owner of the mortgaged property. [2]   In any other case the mortgage debt falls due on the same date as against both parties.

The statement that the mortgage debt falls due as against the owner of the

---

1   State legislation may impose restrictions as to the limit of time during which a charge may be made irredeemable by the parties; such restrictions exist in several States (*e. g.* in Prussia, where the creditor's right to give six months' notice to redeem any kind of charge cannot be suspended for more than twenty years from the date of the creation of the charge—Prussian AG 32).   The Imperial Statute of 1899 relating to Mortgage Banks also imposes certain restrictions as to the time for the repayment of loans made by such banks on the security of charges on immovables (see ss. 18–21).

2   A notice to the owner of the mortgaged property is not effectual in the case of a certificated charge unless it is accompanied by the production of the certificate of charge; if the mortgagee is an unregistered transferee of a registered mortgage the transfer deed or deeds under which he derives his title must also be produced—BGB 1160 (1).

mortgaged property does not mean that he comes under any personal liability; it only means that from the date at which the debt is said to fall due against him the   449 mortgagee may use his remedies against the mortgaged property, and that he is deemed to be in *mora solvendi*—152—at the date at which he would have been in *mora solvendi* if he had become personally liable on the day on which the debt is said to fall due against him.   Interest recoverable in consequence of such *mora solvendi* may be recovered out of the property—BGB 1146.

The owner of the mortgaged property is entitled to repay the mortgage debt as soon as it falls due either as against him or as against the personal debtor.   He may satisfy the debt by lodgment with a public authority—164—or by set-off— BGB 1142.

cc.   Payment by a third party.

381. Any third party, whose rights would be affected by a compulsory sale of the mortgaged property (*e. g.* a subsequent mortgagee or lessee), may, as soon as the mortgagee threatens proceedings for enforcing his rights against the property, repay the mortgage debt and thereby step into the shoes of the mortgagee—BGB 1150. [1]

dd.   Effect of repayment.

(1) In ordinary cases.

382. Where the charge is not a collective charge the following rules apply:

(*a*) if a debt secured by an hypothecary charge is repaid by the owner of the mortgaged property who is at the same time the personal debtor, the charge, as shown above (377), becomes vested in him, but takes the character of a land charge; if the sum secured by a land charge is paid by the owner of the mortgaged property, the charge becomes vested in him—BGB 1163 (1), 1192;

(*b*) if a debt secured by an hypothecary charge is repaid by the owner of the property, another person being the personal debtor, the debt, as well as the charge, becomes vested in the owner of the mortgaged property; as between himself and the personal debtor he is in the position which a surety after payment of the debt   450 guaranteed by him occupies towards the principal debtor—274 sub b—BGB 1143 (1), 1163 (1);

---

1   Under English law every incumbrancer is entitled to redeem the mortgage debt and to demand either a reconveyance to himself or an assignment of the mortgage debt and conveyance of the mortgaged property to any third person—Conveyancing Act 1881, s. 12.

(c) if a debt secured by an hypothecary charge is repaid by the personal debtor, another person being the owner of the mortgaged property, the charge becomes vested in the personal debtor in so far as he is entitled to be indemnified by the owner of the mortgaged property; if, on the other hand, no claim to indemnity exists, [1] the ordinary rule as to the result of the discharge of the mortgage debt (377) is applied, and the charge becomes a land charge in favour of the owner of the mortgaged property [2] —BGB 1163 (1), 1164 (1);

(d) if the mortgage debt is repaid by a third party, see 381, such third party becomes entitled to the claim against the personal debtor (if any) and to the benefit of the charge—BGB 1150, 1153;

(e) if the mortgage debt is satisfied out of the proceeds of a judicial sale or out of the income received by a judicially appointed Receiver (389) the charge is extinguished—BGB 1181 (1) (3).

The repayment of the mortgage debt is, for the purposes of the rules stated above, deemed to be effected in all cases in which the mortgagee's claim is satisfied by release, set-off, or lodgment with a public authority, or by the fact that the debt and the claim become united in the same person [3] —BGB 1142 (2), 1150, 1164 (2).

(2) *In the case of a collective charge.*

383. The following rules apply as to the effect of the payment of a mortgage debt secured by a collective charge:

(a) where a debt secured by an hypothecary collective charge is repaid by the owner of one of the parcels subject to such charge, who is at the same time

---

[1]   In an ordinary case in which mortgaged property is sold, and in which the mortgagee refuses to allow the purchaser's personal liability to be substituted for that of the vendor, the vendor is entitled to be indemnified by the purchaser; but where the vendor, as between himself and the purchaser, undertakes the liability for the mortgage debt, no such claim to indemnity exists.

[2]   If the owner of the mortgaged property, not being the personal debtor, or the personal debtor, not being the owner of the mortgaged property, or a third party pays part of the mortgage debt, a part of the charge proportionate to such payment becomes vested in the person in whom the whole charge would have become vested if the whole amount had been paid; but the partial charge, so becoming vested in such person, ranks behind the mortgagee's remaining charge—BGB 1143 (1), 1150, 1176.   If the personal debtor who pays off the mortgage debt has only a partial right of indemnity against the owner of the mortgaged property, a partial charge proportionate to the amount of the payment becomes vested in him, but such *partial charge takes priority over the owner's remaining charge*—BGB 1164.

[3]   In so far as the claim secured by the charge consists of arrears of interest and accessories, the charge is extinguished, if it becomes vested in the debtor. —BGB 1178 (1).

personally liable for the whole mortgage debt, he becomes entitled to a land charge over his own parcel; if the debt is repaid by an owner who is not personally liable for the mortgage debt, he acquires the claim against the personal debtor, and an hypothecary charge over his own parcel as security for such claim; in either case the charge affecting the other parcels is extinguished, unless the party making the payment is entitled to indemnity from the owner of another parcel, in which event he becomes entitled to a collective charge over his own parcel and over the parcel out of which he claims indemnity [1]—BGB 1143 (2), 1173;

Illustration: *V*, being the owner of Whiteacre and Blackacre, which are both subject to a charge in favour of *M*, sells Blackacre to *D*, and indemnifies him against the charge; *D*, on repayment of the mortgage debt, acquires *M*'s personal claim against *V*, as well as an hypothecary collective charge affecting Whiteacre and Blackacre;

(*b*) where a mortgage debt secured by an hypothecary collective charge is repaid by the personal debtor, who does not own any of the parcels subject to the charge, the owners of such parcels become jointly entitled to the benefit of the charge, unless the personal debtor is entitled to indemnity from the owner of one of the parcels; in the last-mentioned event, he acquires a land charge on the parcel out of which he claims indemnity; the charge affecting the other parcels is extinguished—BGB 1172 (1), 1174;

(*c*) where several owners become jointly entitled to the benefit of a collective charge, each of them may, in the absence of an agreement to the contrary, elect to take a reduced charge on his own parcel in the place of his share in the collective charge [2]—BGB 1172 (2).   452

---

[1]   In the case of a partial claim to indemnity the rules (*a*) and (*b*) are modified in the same way—*mutatis mutandis*—as in the case referred to above, p. 418 note 2.

[2]   A complication arises in a case, where the personal debtor having repaid the amount of the mortgage debt, is entitled to a partial indemnity out of one of the parcels.   In such a case he acquires a separate charge on that parcel to the extent of his right to indemnity, and the collective charge is reduced *pro tanto*; if he elects to take a reduced charge on his own parcel in lieu of his share in the collective charge, the original amount secured by the collective charge is divided among the owners *pro rata* of the value of their respective parcels, and the amount of the separate charge of the personal debtor is then deducted from the amount apportioned to the owner of the parcel which it affects.   Illustration: *A*, being the owner of Whiteacre (worth £ 4, 000) and Blackacre (worth £ 2, 000) subject to a collective charge securing £ 3, 000, sells Whiteacre to *B* and Blackacre to *C*, remaining personally liable for the mortgage debt, but so that as between *A* and *B* the charge is to be borne by *B* to the extent of £ 1, 000, while as between *A* and *C*, the whole of the charge is to be borne by *A*.   *A*, on repayment of the mortgage debt acquires a charge for

(*d*) where a debt secured by a collective charge is paid out of the proceeds of a judicial sale of one of the parcels, or out of the income received in respect of one of the parcels by a judicially appointed Receiver (389) the whole of the charge is extinguished, but in so far as the owner of the parcel which was sold or managed by a Receiver is entitled to indemnity from the owner of another parcel he acquires a charge on that parcel—see p. 424 note 2.

see p. 424 note 2.

ee.   Rights as to delivery of documents.

384. If a mortgage debt secured by a certificated charge is discharged by the owner of the mortgaged property, he is entitled to the delivery of the certificate of charge, and of all other documents required for the purpose of enabling him to cause the proper entries or cancellations to be made on the register.

If a mortgage debt secured by a certificated charge is partially discharged, the mortgagee must indorse the payment on the certificate and produce the same at the registry for the purpose of having the part payment recorded on the register, or of enabling the issue of a part certificate to the owner representing the charge to which he is entitled by virtue of such part payment (374)—BGB 1144, 1145 (1).

453

If a personal debtor, who is not the owner of the mortgaged property, pays off the mortgage debt under circumstances which cause the charge to be vested in him, or confer upon him some other right entitling him to a rectification of the register, he is entitled to the same rights as to delivery of documents as an owner who pays off the mortgage debts—BGB 1167.

b.   Other Methods of Discharge.

aa.   General rules.

385. If a debt secured by an hypothecary charge becomes extinguished otherwise than by payment or by any of the acts or events deemed equivalent to payment under the rules mentioned above (382), or those specially discussed below (386, 387), the charge is converted into a land charge and becomes vested in the owner of the mortgaged property—BGB 1163 (1), 1177 (1).

The means by which a debt becomes extinguished otherwise than by payment or by the equivalent acts or events are of a varied kind, and have been discussed in their several places (see, for instance, 111, 114, 158, 160, 162).

£ 1, 000 on Blackacre, *B* and *C* become entitled to a collective charge on both parcels for £ 2, 000.   On an apportionment *B*'s share is £ 2, 000 less £ 1, 000 = £ 1, 000; *C*'s share is £ 1, 000.

bb.   Renunciation of a charge.

386. A mortgagee may renounce the benefit of a charge by declaration communicated to the Registration Authorities or to the owner of the mortgaged property, followed by registration in the ordinary course.   A charge, of which the benefit has been renounced by the mortgagee, becomes vested in the owner of the mortgaged property; if it was originally an hypothecary charge it is converted into a land charge—BGB 1168 (1) (2).

A mortgagee who partly renounces a certificated charge must indorse such partial renunciation on the certificate, and produce the same at the Land Registry in the same way as on the partial payment of the claim (384) [1] —BGB 1168 (3).

In the case of the renunciation of a collective charge the owners of the several   454 parcels previously subject thereto become jointly entitled to the charge; if, however, the mortgagee renounces his right only as to one of the parcels, the charge on such parcel becomes extinguished—BGB 1175 (1).

If the owner of any mortgaged property is entitled to a defence—other than the defence of prescription—permanently preventing the assertion of the mortgagee's claim, he may compel the mortgagee to renounce his charge in the above-mentioned manner—BGB 1169.

cc.   Forfeiture of rights where the mortgagee cannot be found.

387. If a mortgagee cannot be found, [2] the owner of the mortgaged property may institute proceedings by public citation (*Aufgebotsverfahren*) for the purpose of obtaining an order declaring the mortgagee's rights to be forfeited.   The order is made, if either of the following requirements is complied with:

---

[1]   The renunciation of a charge must be distinguished from the release of the debt secured by the charge; the release of the debt causes the charge to be vested in the person in whom it would vest on payment of the debt by the personal debtor (382); the renunciation of the charge, on the other hand, does not on principle affect the personal claim; it is however provided, that a personal debtor, who on payment of the debt would have had a right of indemnity against the owner of the mortgaged property, or against any of his predecessors in title, is, on the renunciation of the charge, released from his obligation to the extent of his right to indemnity—BGB 1165.

[2]   The expression ' cannot be found ', which occurs in English Statutes (*e. g.* Trustee Act 1893, s. 26), conveys the intended meaning more completely than the expression used by the BGB which usually means ' is unknown ' .   The proceedings in question are applicable, if the identity of the mortgagee cannot be ascertained (*e. g.* if the registered mortgagee is dead and it is impossible to ascertain who are his heirs), and also if it is unknown whether the registered mortgagee is alive or dead.

455

(1) if within ten years [1] prior to the date of the date of the application no entry has been made on the register affecting the charge in question, and if within such period the owner of the mortgaged property has not acknowledged the validity of the charge in a manner, which, if it were a question of prescription, would be deemed to interrupt the period of prescription (136)—BGB 1170 (1), 1192;

(2) if the owner of the mortgaged property, at a time at which he was entitled to repay the mortgage debt or to give notice promising repayment, has lodged the amount of the mortgage debt with a public authority (164) waiving at the same time the right to withdraw the deposited amount [2]—BGB 1171 (1), 1192.

A mortgagee whose rights are declared to be forfeited on the above-mentioned ground loses the benefit of the charge, [3] and the charge thereupon becomes vested in the owner of the mortgaged property; the certificate of the charge (if any) becomes void—BGB 1170 (2), 1171 (2).

If the application for a declaration of the forfeiture of the rights resulting from a collective charge is not made by all the owners of the parcels subject thereto, the forfeiture only relates to the charge affecting the parcels belonging to the applicants—BGB 1175 (2).

7. MORTGAGEE'S REMEDIES

a. In Case of Security being endangered.

388. English law offers no assistance to a mortgagee whose security has become

---

[1] In the case of an hypothecary cautionary charge, registered as collateral security for the payment of debentures to bearer—p. 409 note 2—, the forfeiture of rights cannot be declared in respect of any particular debenture, unless thirty years have elapsed from the date fixed for repayment. If within that time the debenture has been presented, or judicial proceedings for its enforcement have been commenced, the order cannot be made before the period of prescription has run from the date of the presentation or the commencement of the proceedings—BGB 1188 (2).

[2] Arrears of interest are not required to be lodged, unless the rate of interest is entered on the register; and it is unnecessary in any case to lodge arrears of interest having fallen due more than four years prior to the date of the order declaring the mortgagee's rights to be forfeited—BGB 1171 (1).

[3] Where the owner has lodged the amount of the debt with a public authority, the mortgagee may apply for payment—out of such amount within thirty years from the date of the order declaring his right to the charge to be forfeited; if he does not claim the amount within that time, the person by whom it was lodged may withdraw it, notwithstanding the fact that he has waived the right of withdrawal—BGB 1171 (3).

endangered by a deterioration of the mortgaged property. [1] German law, on the other hand, in such an event, provides the following remedies:

(1) where any act done by the owner of the mortgaged property or by any other person, justifies the apprehension that it will lead to any deterioration of the mortgaged property endangering the mortgagee's security, or that any accessories subject to the charge will be removed in violation of the proper rules of management or husbandry, the mortgagee may obtain an order restraining such act; where any such act is done by the owner of the mortgaged property, or where, owing to his omission to take proper precautions, any deterioration of the mortgaged property is to be apprehended, the Court may itself direct the necessary precautionary measures—BGB 1134, 1135, 1192;

(2) where the security has actually become endangered by any of the acts or omissions referred to sub (1), the mortgagee may serve a notice upon the owner of the mortgaged property, requiring him to take such remedying steps or to give such further charges on other property as will restore the sufficiency of the security; if the notice is not complied with within a reasonable period specified therein, the mortgagee may immediately enforce the charge against the mortgaged property in the same way as if the mortgage debt had fallen due (389); where the mortgage debt bears no interest the mortgagee must allow the deduction of interest at the legal rate from the date of payment down to the date of maturity—BGB 1133, 1135.

b. In case of mortgagor's default as to payment of principal or interest at the stipulated dates.

389. If the mortgage debt, or any interest thereon, remains unpaid after maturity, the mortgagee may obtain an order of the competent Court for payment of the overdue amount out of the proceeds of a judicial sale of the mortgaged property, or out of the income received by a judicially appointed Receiver [2] — BGB 1147; CPO 869; ZVG 1, 15, 146.

The action for the enforcement of the charge must be brought against the

---

1 As a general rule he can call in the mortgage debt by giving six months' notice to the mortgagor, but in many cases the mortgagee covenants not to call in the mortgage debt before a fixed date.

2 A mortgagee secured by a certificated charge cannot obtain such an order without production of the certificate of charge; if he is an unregistered transferee he must also produce the transfer deeds under which he derives his title—BGB 1160.

person registered as owner of the mortgaged property, [1] who, subject to the rules for the protection of transferees who in good faith rely on the correctness of the register—373 (1) rule (4)—may avail himself of any defences or rights of set-off to which he is entitled as against the actual or against the original mortgagee— BGB 1157.

If the charge is an hypothecary charge the owner of the mortgaged property may also, in a case in which he is not the personal debtor, avail himself of any defence or right of set-off to which the personal debtor is entitled, subject also to the above-mentioned rules for the protection of transferees, who in good faith rely on the facts appearing from the register—BGB 1137.

If the mortgagee's whole claim is satisfied out of the proceeds of the public sale or out of the rents and profits collected by the Receiver, the charge is extinguished—see 382 rule (e), 383 rule (d). [2]

8. TRANSFER OF CHARGES

390. A land charge or annuity charge can be transferred independently of any debt which it may be intended to secure.   The transfer of an hypothecary charge without the contemporaneous assignment of the debt for which it serves as a security is, on the other hand, impossible, and the assignment of a debt secured by an hypothecary charge operates at the same time as a transfer of the charge and is subject to the rules regulating the transfer of charges—BGB 401, 1153.

458   A certificated charge is transferred by a written transfer deed [3] accompanied or followed by the delivery of the certificate of charge; registration of the transfer on the Land Registry has the same effect as a written transfer.   An uncertificated

---

[1]   If the registered owner is not the true owner, the latter may intervene as co-defendant, and as such bring forward any defence or right of set-off to which he may be entitled—BGB 1148.

[2]   A collective charge is extinguished altogether, notwithstanding the fact that the claim is satisfied out of one of the parcels exclusively; if, however, the person against whose parcel the claim was enforced, has a right of indemnity against the owner of any other parcel, or against any of his predecessors in title, a charge on such other parcel to the extent of his claim for indemnity becomes vested in him.   Such a charge in the event of the partial satisfaction of the mortgagee's claim ranks behind the mortgagee's remaining charge; a charge on the parcel out of which indemnity is claimed, ranking *pari passu* with or behind the charge of the mortgagee who has obtained satisfaction, takes priority over the charge becoming vested by virtue of the right to indemnity—BGB 1181, 1182.

[3]   The transfer deed is not required to be executed in any particular form, but the transferee may, if he is willing to bear the cost, demand a public certification of the transferor's execution—BGB 1154 (1).

charge is transferred in the same way as any other right affecting an immovable (310)—BGB 1154.

A transferee of a certificated charge who is in possession of the certificate of charge, and can prove his title by an unbroken chain of publicly certified transfer deeds, of which the first is executed by the registered mortgagee, [1] is in the same position in every respect as if he were registered as mortgagee—BGB 1155.

The protection accorded to the transferee of an hypothecary charge who in good faith relies on the registered facts, against defences or rights of set-off available against the original mortgagee, or against the personal debtor, has already been referred to—373 (1) rule (4).   A transferee who relies on the facts recorded on the register is not prejudiced by any event not so recorded at the time of the transfer, whether happening before or after such time; he is, however, affected by any notice announcing payment of the mortgage debt given by the owner of the mortgaged property to the transferor after the date of the transfer, unless the transfer was known to such owner or entered upon the register [2] —BGB 1156.

9.   EXTINCTION OF CHARGES

391. It has been shown (379) that, as a general rule, the discharge of the mortgage debt or the renunciation of the mortgagee's rights does not extinguish the charge, but causes it to vest in the owner of the mortgaged property or some other   459 person.

In some exceptional cases, however, referred to separately—382 rule (e),

---

[1]   A judicial vesting order or a publicly authenticated acknowledgment of the fact, that the charge has become vested by law in any particular transferee, is deemed a publicly certified transfer deed—BGB 1155.

[2]   Special rules apply as regards the transfer of the claim for interest and accessories; a claim for arrears of interest may be assigned with or without the benefit of the charge, under the ordinary rules as to the assignment of obligatory rights; the assignee of any claim for interest or accessories falling due within the quarter during which the owner of the mortgaged property receives notice of the assignment and during the next following quarter takes such claim subject to all defences and rights of set-off which are available against the assignee of an unsecured claim—BGB 1158, 1159.

and p. 418 note 3, 383 rule (*d*), 386, [1] a charge becomes extinguished *ipso facto* by the discharge of the mortgage debt.

Where it is intended that a charge should be extinguished in any other case, this must be done by release and cancellation on the register in accordance with the general rules as to the release of rights affecting immovables (310) ; the owner of the mortgaged property must give his assent to the cancellation—BGB 1183.

B. RIGHTS OF PLEDGE RELATING TO MOVABLE THINGS AND RIGHTS

1. GENERAL CHARACTERISTICS

392. Under Roman law two kinds of charges were recognized : (1) charges on things—whether movable or immovable—remaining in the debtor's possession ; (2) charges on movable things handed over to the creditor for his security.   A charge of the former kind was called *hypotheca*, whilst a charge of the latter kind was described as *pignus*.   Germanic law distinguishes between charges on immovables and charges on movables, and allows the latter to be granted exclusively in the form of *pignus* (*Faustpfand*).   The same distinction is maintained by the present German law, which, however, extends the scope of *pignus*, by allowing a right, as well as a movable thing, to be placed under the creditor's control for the purpose of securing the performance of an obligation incurred by the person pledging such right or thing, and which, in the exceptional cases referred to below, also recognizes rights of pledge as to objects outside of the creditor's control. The technical name for this kind of charge is ' right of pledge ' (*Pfandrecht*), which, though used by some writers in a general way so as to include also charges on immovables, is, in the text of the Codes, applied exclusively to charges on movables and rights.

Certain statutory rights of pledge as to movable things outside of the creditor's

460

---

1   It may be convenient to recapitulate these exceptional cases : (1) where a mortgage debt secured by a collective charge is discharged by the owner of one of the parcels, the charge on the other parcels is extinguished, except in so far as the person discharging the debt has a right of indemnity against another parcel ; (2) if a mortgagee secured by a collective charge renounces his rights as to one of the parcels, the charge, in so far as it affects such parcel becomes extinguished ; (3) if a mortgage debt is satisfied out of the proceeds of a judicial sale or out of the income received by a judicially appointed Receiver the charge is extinguished ; (4) in so far as a charge secures arrears of interest and other accessories it is extinguished by merger or renunciation.

control (*e. g.* charges on registered ships; charges on freight and cargo created by bottomry bonds—HGB 679; the lessor's statutory right of pledge (211); the statutory rights of pledge of commission merchants, forwarding agents, and carriers—239, 240, 241 sub (7), are recognized, but a contractual right of pledge cannot be created except as to things placed under the creditor's control. [1]

The rule, ' once a mortgage always a mortgage ', which, as mentioned above—371, is applied under German law to charges on immovables, is also expressly declared in respect of rights of pledge relating to movables.   Any agreement, made between the pledgor and the pledgee, before the time at which the pledgee's right of sale has arisen, providing for the transfer of the ownership of the pledged object to the pledgee in the event of non-performance or unpunctual performance of the pledgor's obligation, is void—BGB 1229.

The rules as to contractual rights of pledge are, in so far as practicable, also applied to statutory rights of pledge, and to the rights of execution creditors in respect of movable objects seized by them (such seizure being described by the expression *Pfändung*)—BGB 1257; CPO 804.

A right of pledge of an anomalous kind, having some affinity with the *depositum irregulare* of Roman law (253), [2] is recognized as to bearer instruments, and instruments passing by indorsement deposited with a banker as security for a loan, but so that the ownership passes to the banker, the pledgor being entitled on repayment of the loan to the redelivery of instruments of the same kind and of the same aggregate amount as those delivered by him originally (Imperial Statute of 1896, commonly called *Bankdepotgesetz*). 461

Special regulations relating to the business of pawnbrokers—resembling the rules of the English Pawnbrokers Act—have been made in the more important German States, [3] pursuant to EG 94.

---

[1]   The exigencies of life, which in England have brought about the introduction of Bills of Sale by way of security for debt, have recently led to the use of a similar expedient in Germany, known under the term of *Sicherheitsübereignung* (transfer of ownership by way of security).   A transaction of this nature, though not specially authorized by any statutory rule, is considered valid and binding on the parties.   The abuses, which in England have led to the stringent rules about registration, have not as yet had time to show themselves sufficiently in Germany, but will no doubt gradually bring about legislation for the protection of general creditors.   The right of a creditor, to whom the ownership of any movable is transferred in the manner indicated in this rule, by way of security for a debt, differs entirely from the right of a pledge described in the text.

[2]   See also 359 as to the usufruct of fungibles granted in a similar manner.

[3]   See Prussian AG 41; Bavarian AG 911; Saxon AG 51; Baden AG 29.

2. LEGAL CHARACTER OF RIGHT OF PLEDGE

393. The right of pledge (*Pfandrecht*), relating to a movable thing or right, is, like a cautionary hypothecary charge—373, of a strictly accessory nature; it is a charge on a movable thing or on a right, created for the purpose of securing the performance of an existing or future, certain or contingent, obligation, entitling the ' pledgee' (*Pfandgläubiger*) to obtain satisfaction of such claim out of the pledged object (*Pfand*) [1] —BGB 1204, 1273.

As in the case of immovables, it may happen that the personal debtor is not the owner of the pledged object; the expression ' pledgor' (*Verpfänder*) denotes the person by whom the pledge was constituted, or his successor in title as owner or possessor of the pledged object, whether he be the personal debtor or otherwise. [2]

462   A right of pledge does not merely secure the principal claim, but extends to all claims for interest, costs, and other accessories; if the pledgor is not the personal debtor, the charge on the pledged object cannot be increased by any agreement between the pledgee and the personal debtor, entered upon after the creation of the right of pledge [3] —BGB 1210.

A pledgor, who is not at the same time the personal debtor, may, as between himself and the pledgee, make use of any defences or rights of set-off to which the personal debtor is entitled (including defences expressly waived by the personal debtor) and also of any defences to which a surety is entitled [4] —BGB 1211.

The pledgee's rights against the pledged object are not affected by the fact that the claim secured by the pledge is barred by prescription [5] —BGB 223.

---

[1]   A right of pledge affecting a registered ship may be granted as security for a maximum amount of indebtedness in the same way as a cautionary hypothecary charge on an immovable—BGB 1271.   An exception from the general rule, as to the accessory nature of rights of pledge, arises in the case of a bottomry bond which confers right against the pledged object in a similar way as a land charge confers a right against the immovable subject thereto—HGB 679.

[2]   If the pledged object is sold, the vendor remaining liable for the debt, the vendor is the personal debtor and the purchaser is his successor in title as pledgor; where a person pledges a thing owned by him to secure a debt owing by another, he is the pledgor and such other is the personal debtor.

[3]   Where a registered ship is pledged, the charge does not in any event cover an amount exceeding the registered amount—BGB 1259, 1264.

[4]   In accordance with the principle applied in other similar cases, the pledgor cannot take advantage of the fact that the original personal debtor is dead, and that his heirs are under limited liability (533) as to the debts of the deceased.

[5]   In so far as any claim to interest or any other recurrent payment or delivery is barred by prescription, the charge does not extend to such claim.

The pledgee has a 'real right' in respect of the pledged object, for the protection of which the same remedies are available—*mutatis mutandis*—as for the protection of the rights of ownership—342–346.   The pledgee of a movable thing placed under his control is, of course, also entitled to the possessory remedies—315.

3.   CREATION OF RIGHTS OF PLEDGE [1]

a.   As to Movables other than Registered Ships.

394. A right of pledge affecting a movable thing other than a registered ship, or affecting a negotiable instrument, is created by a real agreement (309) between the parties, accompanied or followed by the delivery of the pledged object; where the pledged object is a negotiable instrument passing by indorsement, such instrument on delivery must be indorsed in blank or to the pledgee's order.

463

Where the pledged object is in the pledgor's indirect possession—311 sub (2), the delivery is replaced by a notice to the person who is in direct possession; the delivery to the pledgee may also be replaced by a delivery, which brings the pledged object into the joint possession—309 sub (5), or under the joint control of the pledgor and the pledgee—BGB 1205, 1206, 1292, 1293.

Where the pledgor is without a title to the pledged object, or where his title is defective, the rules as to the acquisition of the ownership of a movable from a person without title or with a defective title—333, are applied—*mutatis mutandis*.   Where the pledged object is subject to the right of another (*e. g.* where the pledgor is not the owner but a pledgee of the pledged object) the pledgee's right takes priority over the right with which the pledged object is charged, unless the pledgee at the time of the creation of his right of pledge was not in good faith. The rules as to what constitutes good faith are the same—*mutatis mutandis*—as in the case of a transfer of ownership—333—BGB 1207, 1208, 1293.

Among several rights of pledge, the one which is created at a prior time takes priority, even if it was constituted as a security for a future or for a contingent claim—BGB 1209.

---

1   By a bottomry bond, a right of pledge can be created as to movable things (cargo), registered ships, and rights (freight) without delivery of the pledged object or of its registration.   The mode of creation as well as the right is of an anomalous nature, and is only mentioned here for the sake of completeness—HGB 679–699.

b.   As to Registered Ships.

395. A right of pledge affecting a registered ship, or a share therein, is created by real agreement between the pledgor and the pledgee, accompanied or followed by registration in the register of ships—322.   The rules as to the assent of third parties and as to priorities are the same—*mutatis mutandis*—as in the case of charges affecting immovables.

If a pledgor's rights are not correctly registered, or erroneously cancelled, he has similar rights as to the rectification of the register, and as to the entry of objections, as a mortgagee entitled to a charge on an immovable—BGB 1263, 1272.

464 A right of pledge affecting a registered ship, granted as a collateral security for the payment of bonds to bearer or other negotiable instruments, may be created in a similar manner as a charge on an immovable granted for the same purpose—see p. 409 note 2, and a trustee for the holders of the instruments secured by such right of pledge may be appointed in a corresponding manner—BGB 1270.

c.   As to Rights.

396. Any real or obligatory right, or any right relating to an immaterial object (82) capable of assignment or transfer, is also capable of being pledged [1]—BGB 1274 (2).

The formalities required for pledging a right are the same as would be required on the transfer or assignment of such right—BGB 1274 (1).   A real right is therefore pledged by means of a real agreement accompanied or followed by registration.   If the transfer of a right is incomplete without the delivery of a movable thing (*e. g.* of a certificate of charge), the same modes of delivery must be used as in the case of the pledging of a movable thing—394—BGB 1274 (1).

A personal claim capable of transfer by informal assignment cannot be validly pledged without notice to the debtor—BGB 1279, 1280.

---

[1]   A right of usufruct or a restricted personal servitude not being capable of assignment cannot be the object of a right of pledge; a land charge or an annuity charge is capable of being pledged—BGB 1291; an hypothecary charge cannot be pledged apart from the claim which it is intended to secure.   A share in a partnership or a claim to personal services cannot be pledged, as it cannot be assigned.

4. PROPERTY SUBJECT TO RIGHT OF PLEDGE

397. The right of pledge extends to all products severed from the pledged object; where the pledged object is a personal claim or land charge, or an annuity charge bearing interest, the right extends to the interest—BGB 1212, 1289, 1291; where the pledged object is a bond or a share certificate to bearer, or passing by indorsement with dividend or interest coupons attached thereto, the right of pledge extends to such coupons, in so far as they are delivered to the pledgee; the pledgor may, in the absence of an agreement to the contrary, demand the delivery of each coupon as it falls due, but he forfeits this right as soon as the pledgee's right of sale (402) comes into operation—BGB 1293, 1296.

A right of pledge affecting a registered ship extends to all accessories of which the ownership is vested in the shipowner—BGB 1265.   465

The pledgee of an undivided share in a movable is entitled to exercise the pledgor's rights as to participation in the management and as to the use of the pledged object, but the right to partition cannot be exercised without the pledgor's assent, unless the pledgee's right of sale—402, 403—has come into operation, in which event such assent is no longer required.   On partition the part which is appropriated to the pledged share becomes subject to the right of pledge—BGB 1258.

A share in a registered ship can be pledged as a separate object—BGB 1272.

Where a right of pledge refers to several objects, each object is deemed to be charged with the whole debt—BGB 1222, 1266, 1273.

5. ANTICHRETIC RIGHT OF PLEDGE (*Antichresis*)

398. Antichretic charges are institutions of Germanic law not unknown in the older English law.   The expression 'mortgage' used in England was originally used in contradistinction to *vif-gage* [1], which term was applied for a charge enabling the creditor to take possession of the property pledged to him, and to obtain payment of his debt with interest by the collection of the rents and profits.   A charge of this nature (*antichresis*, *Nutzungspfandrecht*) is invalid under modern German

---

1   vif-gage,（英格兰古法）活质；英文 living pledge，拉丁文 vadium vivum（亦作 vivum vadium）。活质，相对于"死质"（英文 dead pledge，拉丁文 vadium mortuum，亦作 mortuum vadium）。参见薛波主编：《元照英美法词典》，法律出版社 2003 年版，第 1394、1403 页。——校勘者注

law if it is intended to affect an immovable, but a movable thing or a right may be validly pledged under an agreement entitling the pledgee to appropriate the profits of the pledged object—BGB 1213 (1); where a naturally fruit-bearing movable thing is the pledged object, such an agreement is presumed in the absence of evidence to the contrary.   The presumption is not applied where the pledged object is a right—BGB 1213 (2), 1273 (2).

Where a pledgee is entitled to appropriate the profits of the pledged object, he is, in the absence of any express agreement to the contrary, subject to the following duties, in addition to the ordinary duties of a pledgee (399):

(1) he must exercise proper diligence in obtaining the profits;

466   (2) he must apply the net profits towards the satisfaction of the interest or costs (if any) secured by the charge, and subject thereto apply the same towards the satisfaction of the principal claim—BGB 1214.

6.   PLEDGEE'S DUTIES AND RIGHTS AS TO PLEDGED OBJECT

a.   As to Movable Things and Instruments to Bearer.

399. In any case in which the pledged object is a movable thing (other than a registered ship) or an instrument to bearer the pledgee has the following duties:

(1) in so far as he is in direct possession of the pledged object he has to use the same degree of diligence in respect of its custody as if he had agreed to undertake its custody (252)—BGB 1215, 1293;

(2) if by any dealings with the pledged object he infringes the pledgor's rights to any material extent, and continues such infringement notwithstanding the pledgor's request to discontinue the same, the pledgor may demand the lodgment of the pledged object with a public authority (164), or its delivery to a Receiver appointed by the Court, or the re-delivery to himself against payment of the debt secured thereby [1]—BGB 1217, 1293;

(3) if the deterioration of the pledged object or an essential diminution of its value is to be apprehended the pledgor may demand the re-delivery of the pledged object against any authorized security (87) other than the personal guarantee of a

---

[1]   Where the debt secured by the pledge does not bear interest and has not matured, interest at the legal rate may in the event mentioned in the text be deducted from the date of the payment down to the date of the maturity of the debt—BGB 1217 (2).

surety—BGB 1218 (1), 1293;

(4) if the pledgee, knowing that a material deterioration of the pledged object is impending, fails to give immediate notice thereof to the pledgor, in so far as such notice is practicable, he is liable in damages for the consequences of such failure to give notice—BGB 1218 (2), 1293;

(5) the pledgee is not, under any circumstances, bound to incur any expense for the preservation of the pledged object; if he incurs any such expense his claim to reimbursement is determined by the rules as to voluntary services—301; he is in any event entitled to the *jus tollendi*—144 sub (9)—BGB 1216, 1293;

467

(6) the pledgee is bound to re-deliver the pledged object on the extinction of his right of pledge (406)—BGB 1223, 1293;

(7) the pledgor's claims against the pledgee, arising under rules (1) and (4) in respect of any alteration or deterioration of the pledged object, are barred by prescription after the lapse of six months from the date of re-delivery; they are also barred by prescription in any case in which the right to re-delivery is barred by prescription—BGB 1226, 1293.

The rules stated above cannot of course be applied in any case in which a registered ship is the pledged object, as a pledged ship always remains in the pledgor's possession.   On the extinction of a right of pledge affecting a pledged ship the pledgor may demand the delivery of all documents enabling him to effect the cancellation of the charge on the register; where the pledgor and the personal debtor are different persons, the personal debtor has the same right if the cancellation of the right of pledge is to his advantage—BGB 1267.

b.   As to Rights.

400. The rights and duties of the pledgee of a right are (subject to certain modifications and exceptions) [1] regulated by the same rules as the rights and duties of the pledgee of a movable thing, and also by the following further rules:

(1) the pledgee of an obligatory right, or of a land charge, or of an annuity

---

1   Rules (1) (6) and (7) are applicable as regards the custody or delivery of any movable thing handed to the pledgee on the transfer of the right by way of pledge (*e. g.* a certificate of charge, a bill of exchange); rule (2) is applicable where the pledged object is an obligatory right; a pledgor availing himself of the privilege conferred by the rule would require the assignment of the right to a judicially appointed Receiver (see BGB 1275); rule (3) is applicable in the case of any diminution of value; rule (4) is not applicable; rule (5) is applicable.

charge, or of any right imposing an active duty on the owner for the time being of an immovable (*e. g.* a perpetual charge on land), is in the same position towards the debtor[1] as a transferee of the pledged right would be, but he cannot enforce

468   the pledged right before his right against the pledgee has become enforceable (404), except in the manner and subject to the conditions mentioned below in rule (3)—BGB 1277;

(2) a pledged right cannot be extinguished or modified so as to prejudice the pledgee's right without the pledgee's assent—BGB 1276;

(3) an obligatory right, or a land charge, or annuity charge, assigned or transferred to a pledgee by way of security, may be enforced in the following manner, even before the pledgor's claim against the pledgee has become enforceable:

(*a*) in the absence of any stipulation to the contrary, the pledgor, as well as the pledgee, may demand performance or payment for their joint benefit or lodgment with a public authority or with a judicially appointed Receiver; if the maturity of the pledged right depends upon a notice, a notice claiming performance may, except in the case of an antichretic pledge, be given by the pledgor without the pledgee's concurrence; a notice from the debtor announcing performance is inoperative unless given to the pledgee as well as to the pledgor;

(*b*) where the pledged right is embodied in a negotiable instrument delivered to the pledgee, the pledgee alone is entitled to claim payment or delivery, or to give notice claiming repayment or delivery in any case in which such notice is required—BGB 1279, 1281, 1283 (1) (2), 1291, 1294;

(*c*) where performance or payment has to be made for the joint benefit of the pledgor and the pledgee, each of them is bound to concur in any act required for the purpose of obtaining such performance or agreement; where the pledgee alone is entitled to demand performance or payment, he must apply due diligence in claiming such performance or payment, and on obtaining the same must give immediate notice thereof to the pledgor, in so far as this is practicable; where the maturity of the claim depends upon notice, the party, who under the general rule, or under any special agreement, has to give notice or to concur therein, may be required by the other party to give or concur in the notice if the security of the claim would be endangered by delay in the notice—BGB 1285, 1286, 1291;

---

[1]   The expression 'debtor' as used in the statement of the rules appearing in the text means the person against whom the pledged right is enforceable.

where in the case of a money claim payment for the joint account of the pledgor and the pledgee has been obtained, each of them is bound to concur with the other in procuring the investment of the amount standing to the credit of such joint account in trustee securities to be selected by the pledgor—BGB 1288 (1) ;

469

(*d*) the ownership of any object delivered under rule (*a*) for the joint benefit of the pledgor and pledgee passes to the pledgor, subject to the pledgee's right of pledge; where the pledged right is a right to obtain the transfer of the ownership of an immovable, the pledgee acquires a cautionary hypothecary charge (373) on such immovable—BGB 1287.

7.   PLEDGOR'S RIGHT TO REDEEM

401. The pledgor is entitled to satisfy the pledgee's claim, and to demand re-delivery of the pledged object at any time after the maturity of the claim.   The satisfaction of the claim may be effected by lodgment with a public authority (164), or by set-off (165)—BGB 1223, 1224.   If the pledgor, who redeems a pledge, is not the personal debtor, the claim against the latter on such redemption becomes vested in the pledgor, in the same way as the claim against the principal debtor becomes vested in the surety on repayment of the guaranteed debt (274 sub b)—BGB 1225.

The pledge may be redeemed by any third party entitled to any right affecting the pledged object which would be forfeited on its sale by the pledgee (*e. g.* by a subsequent pledgee).   This right of redemption may be exercised as soon as the pledgee's claim has matured.   The redeeming party on redemption acquires the claim against the personal debtor[1]—BGB 1249.

8.   PLEDGEE'S REMEDIES

a.   In Case of Security being endangered.

402. If at any time the pledgee's security is endangered by the impending deterioration of the pledged object, or by a justifiable apprehension of a serious diminution in its value, the pledgee of a movable thing (other than a registered ship), or of an instrument to bearer, has the following rights:

---

[1]   See the analogous rule as to the redemption of charges on immovables—381.

470   (1) where any deterioration is impending he may sell the pledged object in the manner stated below in rule (3), after having first given notice to the pledgor of his intention to do so; the notice is unnecessary if its service is impracticable, or if there would be any danger in delay;

(2) where a serious diminution in the value of the pledged object is apprehended, he may sell the pledged object, in the manner stated below in rule (3), if the pledgor fails to give sufficient further security within a reasonable period, specified in a notice requiring him to do so; the notice is unnecessary if its service is impracticable;

(3) the sale must be effected by public auction, unless the pledged object is quoted on the Stock Exchange, or has a market value; in either of the last-mentioned events a private sale by a publicly authorized broker or auctioneer at the current price is allowed; the fact that the sale has taken place must, if practicable, be notified to the pledgor without delay;

(4) the proceeds of the sale take the place of the pledged object; the pledgor may demand their lodgment with a public authority (164)—BGB 1219—1221, 1293.

No similar rules apply where the pledged object is a registered ship or a right, or a negotiable instrument passing by indorsement—BGB 1266, 1273.

b.   In Case of Pledgor's default as to discharge of obligation.

aa.   Where pledged object is a movable thing or negotiable instrument.

403. A pledgee, who does not obtain satisfaction of a matured liquidated claim secured by the pledge of a movable thing (not being a registered ship), [1] may enforce his right against the pledged object by selling the same without taking judicial proceedings in the manner appearing from the rules stated below.

Where the claim secured by the pledge is not originally a claim for the payment 471 of money, the right of sale does not arise before the claim has been converted into a money claim [2]—BGB 1228.

---

[1]   Where the pledged object is a registered ship, the right of sale is similar to the right of sale to which the mortgagee of an immovable is entitled; see 389—BGB 1268.

[2]   In some cases such conversion may take place without a judicial order, *e. g.* where a conventional penalty (171) has to be paid on non-performance of the debtor's obligations, but, as a general rule, a claim for the performance of an act other than the payment of money, can only be turned into a money claim by a judicial order converting the claim for performance into a claim for pecuniary damages.

The pledgee of an instrument to bearer, or of an indorsable instrument quoted on any Stock Exchange or having a market value, has the same power of sale as the pledgee of a movable thing.   The powers of the pledgees of other negotiable instruments are governed by the rules applicable as to pledged rights—BGB 1293, 1295.

The exercise of the right of sale is governed by the following rules [1] :

(1) where there are several pledgees the right can be exercised by any one of them, but a prior pledgee is not bound to deliver the pledged object to a subsequent pledgee for the purpose of enabling him to exercise the right of sale; if the prior pledgee is not in possession of the pledged object (*e. g.* if it is held by a third party for account of both pledgees) he is not entitled to oppose a sale for account of a subsequent pledgee, unless he wishes himself to exercise the right of sale—BGB 1232;

(2) where the pledged object is in the joint possession, or under the joint control of the pledgor and the pledgee, the pledgee may, as soon as the right of sale is exercisable, require the pledged object to be taken entirely out of the pledgor's control; the pledgor may in such a case require the pledged object to be delivered to a third party, who must undertake to keep it ready for delivery to the purchaser—BGB 1231;

(3) where several objects are pledged as security for one claim the pledgee is entitled, in the absence of an agreement to the contrary, to sell such of them as he may select, but he is not entitled to sell more objects than are required for the satisfaction of his claim—BGB 1230;

(4) the pledgee must inform the owner of the pledged object of his intention to sell the same, and of the amount of the claim intended to be satisfied by such sale; the notification is not required in any case in which it is impracticable— BGB 1233, 1234 (1);

(5) a month must elapse between the date of the notification and the date of the sale; if the notification is impracticable a month must elapse between the date at which the right of sale arises and the date of the sale; where the right of pledge was constituted by a mercantile transaction (36), or arose under the statutory rules relating to commission merchants (239), forwarding agents (240), warehousemen (252), or carriers (241), the period of a week is substituted for

472

---

1   Where the pledgee is a judgment creditor he may exercise the right of sale in the same manner as if he had seized the pledged object as such judgment creditor—BGB 1233 (2).

the period of a month [1]—BGB 1234 (2); HGB 368;

(6) the time and the place of sale must be publicly announced, and also separately notified to the owner of the pledged object and to any third party interested therein, in so far as such notification is practicable—BGB 1237;

(7) complicated regulations as to the place of the sale, the conditions of payment, and as to bids by interested parties must be observed—BGB 1236, 1238, 1239;

(8) the sale must be effected by public auction, unless the pledged object is quoted on the Stock Exchange or has a market value, in which event a private sale at the current price, through the agency of a publicly authorized broker or auctioneer, is permitted; if the pledged object is an article made of gold or silver a reserve price must be fixed equal to its melting value; if such reserve price cannot be obtained at a public sale, the pledged object may be sold privately at a price equal at least to such reserve price—BGB 1235, 1240;

(9) in any case in which a sale by the pledgee is lawfully effected in accordance with rule (10), the purchaser acquires the same rights as if he had purchased the pledged object from the true owner; this rule is also applied in a case in which the pledgee himself purchases the pledged object; all rights of pledge relating to the pledged object are extinguished by the sale, though known to the purchaser; a right of usufruct is extinguished unless it ranks in priority to all rights of pledge [2]—BGB 1242, 1244;

473

(10) a sale by the pledgee is deemed lawfully effected if the right of sale has arisen, and if rules (3) (6) and (8) have been observed, even if the other rules, or some of them, have been disregarded; if the pledgee has disregarded any of the other rules he is liable in damages if such disregard was due to any default on his part—BGB 1243;

(11) for all the purposes connected with the sale, the pledgee is entitled to assume that the pledgor is the true owner, unless the contrary is known to him—BGB 1248;

(12) an agreement made at any time before the right of sale has arisen,

---

[1]   This rule is generally applied in so far only as the transaction by which the pledge was constituted, or by virtue of which the statutory right arose was a mercantile transaction, as well on the pledgor's as on the pledgee's side, but as regards a carrier's or forwarding agent's statutory right, it is applied even where such a transaction is a mercantile transaction on his side only—HGB 368 (2).

[2]   A purchaser buying from a pledgee who has not disregarded any of the essential rules is, therefore, in a much better position than an ordinary purchaser.

under which the pledgee is authorized to disregard rules (6) and (8), is invalid, but in all other respects the rules as to the exercise of the power of sale may be modified by agreement between the pledgor and the pledgee, assented to by all other interested parties—BGB 1245;

(13) where the right of sale has arisen, either party may require the other to consent to a mode of sale differing from the authorized mode of sale, if such modified mode of sale on an equitable appreciation of the circumstances appears to the advantage of the interested parties; where such consent is refused, the modified mode of sale may be ordered by the Court—BGB 1246;

(14) in so far as the proceeds of sale satisfy the pledgee's claim, such claim is deemed to be discharged by the sale; in so far as this is not the case the proceeds of sale take the place of the pledged object which they represent—BGB 1247.

bb.   Where the pledged object is a right.

404. In the absence of any special agreement to the contrary the pledgee of a right has no power of sale or alienation; an agreement conferring such power is subject to the same restrictions as an agreement modifying the power of sale concerning a movable—403 rule (12)—BGB 1277, 1282 (2); in the absence of a contractual power of sale, the power to enforce the pledged right   474 takes the place of the power of sale to which the pledgee of a movable thing is entitled.

The pledgee of a right other than an obligatory right, land charge, or annuity charge cannot, in the absence of an agreement to the contrary, enforce the pledged right before having obtained judgment against the pledgor.

The pledgee of an obligatory right or of a land charge, or of an annuity charge, may enforce such right or charge without first obtaining a judgment against the pledgor in the same events in which the pledgee of a movable thing may exercise his power of sale [1]—BGB 1279, 1282 (1), 1284, 1291.

Where the enforcement of the right of pledge results in the payment of money,

---

[1]   In so far as the pledged right is a claim for the payment of money, the pledgee is not entitled to demand an amount exceeding the amount of his claim against the pledgor; in order to avoid the necessity of proving the extent of his claim, he may demand from the pledgor an absolute assignment of the claim to the required extent—BGB 1282 (1), 1291.   Where an obligatory right, or land charge, or annuity charge is subject to several rights of pledge, the right or charge is only enforceable by a pledgee whose right of pledge ranks in priority to the other rights of pledge—BGB 1290, 1291.

the amount received is appropriated towards the satisfaction of the pledgee's claim; where it results in the delivery of any object other than money, the ownership of such object becomes vested in the pledgor, but subject to a right of pledge for the pledgee's benefit; where the claim enforced by the pledgee is a claim for the transfer of the ownership of an immovable, the ownership of such immovable is transferred to the pledgor, subject to a cautionary hypothecary charge for the pledgee's benefit—BGB 1287, 1288 (2).

9.   TRANSFER OF RIGHT OF PLEDGE

405. On the transfer of any claim secured by a pledge, whether by assignment or under any rule of law (*e. g.* on death or bankruptcy, or seizure by a judgment creditor), the right of pledge becomes vested in the transferee.   The right of pledge cannot be transferred apart from the claim; if the claim is transferred with the express stipulation that the right of pledge is not to pass to the transferee, the right of pledge is thereby extinguished—BGB 1250.

475   The transferee may claim the delivery or assignment of the pledged object— BGB 1251 (1), 1273.

The pledgee's duties as to the pledged object (399, 400) pass to the transferee; if the transfer is effected by assignment the transferor continues liable for their performance as a surety for the transferee and without the *beneficium excussionis* (273)—BGB 1251 (2).

10.   EXTINCTION OF RIGHT OF PLEDGE

406. A right of pledge is extinguished:

(1) by the destruction of the pledged object, or by the fact that a third party, without notice of the pledge, acquires a good title thereto;

(2) by the discharge of the claim secured by the pledge—BGB 1252 [1];

---

1   The extinction of the right of pledge is not caused by the fact that the claim intended to be secured thereby is barred by prescription, or that the pledgor is entitled to any defence or right of set-off against the pledgee; if the pledgor is entitled to any defence permanently barring the claim, he may demand the re-delivery of the pledged object, or, in the case of the pledged object being a registered ship or a right, the release of the right of pledge—BGB 1254, 1266, 1273.   The discharge of the claim by merger causes the right of pledge to be extinguished, except where a third party is interested in the right, or where it is to the owner's advantage to keep the right of pledge alive—BGB 1256.

(3) by re-delivery [1] to the pledgor—BGB 1253 (1);

(4) by a releasing declaration communicated by the pledgee to the pledgor, or to the owner of the pledged object, assented to by any third party interested in the right of pledge—BGB 1255.

---

[1]   Where the pledged object (not being a registered ship) is in the pledgor's or owner's possession re-delivery by the pledgee is presumed; the same presumption is applied where a third party, after the creation of the right of pledge, has obtained possession from the pledgor or from the owner of the pledged object—BGB 1253 (2).

FOURTH BOOK

FAMILY LAW

CHAPTER I
HUSBAND AND WIFE

1. AGREEMENT TO MARRY

407. MUTUAL promises of marriage constitute an agreement between the parties described by the expression *Verlöbniss* (betrothal), which, as regards the conditions of its validity and some of its consequences, is subject to the ordinary rules as to obligatory agreements. The remedies on breach of the agreement are, however, modified in the following manner:

(1) an agreement to marry cannot be specifically enforced; a claim for pecuniary compensation arises, as a general rule, on breach of the agreement by one of the parties;

(2) the pecuniary compensation is—except under the circumstances mentioned below sub (4)—limited to an amount indemnifying the aggrieved party for any disbursements made or undertaken in contemplation of the marriage, or for any loss incurred through any steps taken by such party in contemplation of the promised marriage affecting his property or occupation; the compensation is payable in so far only as the disbursements or steps in question were reasonable under the circumstances; a promise to pay a penalty in the event of a breach of the agreement is void;

(3) the claim for compensation does not arise if the breach of promise is due to a cogent ground (*e. g.* the discovery of a legal impediment to the marriage, or of a circumstance which after the marriage would justify a decree of nullity or a divorce); if the ground justifying the breach of promise is a culpable act of the other party the party refusing to perform the promise is entitled to compensation from the party guilty of such culpable act; the rule as to the measure of damages is the same as in the events mentioned sub (2);

(4) if an intending wife of previously unblemished moral character has been seduced by the intending husband, she may, in the event of her being entitled to compensation for her pecuniary loss on either of the grounds stated sub (2) or

480   (3), claim damages in respect of the seduction, in addition to the compensation
for pecuniary loss; the claim for damages cannot be assigned to another and is not
transmissible on death, except in so far as it has been admitted by express
agreement or asserted by the institution of legal proceedings;

(5) in any case in which the promised marriage from any cause whatsoever
does not take place, either party—whether entitled to compensation or damages
under any of the rules stated above or otherwise—may claim from the other party
a return of all gifts and of all tokens symbolic of the engagement in accordance
with the rules as to unjustified benefits (298), unless the contrary has been
agreed upon; such an agreement to the contrary is presumed in any case in which
the death of one of the parties prevents the marriage;

(6) all claims for compensation, damages, or return of gifts or tokens, are
barred after the lapse of two years from the date of the rescission of the agreement [1]—
BGB 1297–1302.

2. RULES AS TO CELEBRATION OF MARRIAGE

408. The German rules as to the celebration of marriages are applicable to
all marriages celebrated within the German Empire, whether the spouses be of
German nationality or otherwise [2]—EG 13 (3).

The same rules apply to marriages between Germans celebrated outside of
the German Empire by German consuls or other officials authorized to celebrate
marriages under the Imperial Statute of 1870 (as modified by EG 40).

481   On the other hand, German law considers the marriage of a German celebrated
outside the German Empire as duly celebrated, if it is celebrated in accordance

---

[1] A somewhat anomalous rule entitles the parents of the aggrieved party, or any other persons acting
in their place, to compensation for any disbursements made or undertaken in connexion with the promised
marriage—BGB 1298 (1).   The cost of the wedding dress and of the wedding cake must be repaid to the
bride or to her parents, but the bride's wounded feelings—except in the case of seduction—are not heeded by
German law.

[2] There are certain international treaties sanctioning the celebration of marriages in Germany between
parties of whom neither is a German subject by the diplomatic agent or consul of the country of which one of
the parties is a subject.   No such treaty exists between Germany and Great Britain.   The marriage between
two subjects of any State which is a party to the Hague Convention, celebrated before the consul or diplomatic
representative of such State, is also recognized, subject to certain restrictions (see Art. 6 of the Convention
as to form of marriage).

with the law of the place of celebration [1]—EG 11 (1).

The German rules [2] recognize civil marriage exclusively.   The marriage is effected by the declaration of the parties made before the competent registration official (*Standesbeamter* [3]), and in the presence of each other expressing their intention to be married to each other.   The parties must make these declarations in person, and they must be unconditional and not subject to any stipulation as to time.   The registration official must be willing to receive the declarations.   Two witnesses of full age must be present.   The official must ask each of the parties whether he or she will marry the other, and on their answer in the affirmative declare them duly married spouses, and make the appropriate entry in the register—BGB 1317, 1318.

The marriage must be preceded by a public notice (*Aufgebot*) to be effected in the prescribed manner and subject to the previous presentation of certain prescribed documents—BGB 1316. [4]

In the majority of cases a religious marriage ceremony follows the civil marriage, but the celebration of a religious marriage ceremony by any clergyman or minister who has not satisfied himself of the fact that the civil marriage has taken place is a criminal offence, except in a case in which one of the parties is mortally ill—Personal Status Act of 1875, s. 67, as modified by EG 46. III.

482

The rules of the BGB as to marriage are not intended to interfere with the duties imposed by any religious denomination on its members—BGB 1588. The refusal of one of the parties to allow a religious marriage ceremony to be

---

1   As shown below a marriage celebrated in Germany must be solemnized before a competent civil official, but a marriage celebrated outside Germany before a minister of religion or even in the irregular Pre-Tridentine (Scotch) form is not invalid on the ground of informality if it is solemnized in a form which is lawful in the place of celebration.

2   As to the effect of a disregard of any of the rules, see 410.

3   He must be a duly appointed registration official; but a person publicly exercising the functions of such an official, without having been appointed as such, is deemed competent unless the absence of authority is known to both parties—BGB 1319.   The registration official must also have local jurisdiction, but the absence of such jurisdiction is not deemed one of the fatal defects by which the marriage is invalidated—BGB 1320, 1321, and see BGB 1324 (1).

4   The special requirements as to the public notice, and as to certain other matters connected with the celebration of marriages and its registration, are contained in the Personal Status Act of 1875, ss. 44–50. A member of the armed forces, or an official who according to the law of his State cannot marry without the permission of the competent authority, must produce such permission.   A foreigner who, according to the law of the German State in which the marriage is celebrated, requires any licence or testimonial on the part of his home authorities must produce such licence or testimonial—BGB 1315.

performed is therefore a 'cogent ground' entitling the other party to refuse the performance of the agreement to marry—407 rule (3) ; if the refusal to take part in a religious ceremony is not communicated to the other party before the celebration of the civil marriage, it may entitle such other party to obtain a decree of nullity on the ground mentioned sub 411 (2) (*d*).

The simplicity of the German rules as to the celebration of marriage contrasts very favourably with the complicated rules of English law, which allow four distinct forms of marriage : (1) marriage according to the rites of the Church of England; (2) marriage according to the usages of Jews or Quakers; (3) marriage before a duly authorized Roman Catholic Priest or Nonconformist Minister in a registered building; (4) marriage at a Superintendent Registrar's Office without religious ceremony; there being also considerable variety as to the mode of obtaining the preliminary authorization to marriage.

3.   CIRCUMSTANCES AFFECTING THE VALIDITY OF MARRIAGES

a.   General Observations.

409. The circumstances which affect the validity of a marriage according to German law may be divided into three classes : (1) fatal defects in the marriage ceremony; (2) public severing impediments (*viz.* impediments which give rise to proceedings for nullity by the public authorities if they come to their notice) ; (3) private severing impediments (*viz.* impediments which do not give rise to nullity proceedings unless one of the spouses takes proceedings).

The impediments called 'hindering impediments' do not in any case affect the validity of a marriage after its celebration.

(1)   *Absolute nullity.*

A fatal defect in the marriage ceremony brings about the nullity of the marriage in the sense in which the word 'nullity' is generally used in German (90) and in English law.   This nullity may be described as 'absolute' nullity—BGB 1324.

(2)   *Relative nullity.*

A public severing impediment brings about a nullity of an entirely different kind, which may be described as 'relative' nullity; an absolutely void marriage is of no effect, and may be disregarded for all purposes; a marriage relatively void has the following important effects :

483

(a) the nullity cannot be alleged in any judicial proceedings, before it has been established by a judgment of the competent Matrimonial Court, obtained on a petition for nullity—BGB 1329; CPO 606;

(b) any child of a relatively void marriage which otherwise satisfies the requirements of legitimacy (425), is deemed legitimate, unless the relative nullity of the marriage was known to both spouses at the time of such marriage—BGB 1699;

(c) re-marriage by one of the parties before the pronouncement of the nullity decree constitutes the crime of bigamy (StGB 171 as modified by EG 34 V);

(d) a third party who before the pronouncement of the decree of nullity without being aware of the relative nullity of the marriage enters upon any transaction to which one of the spouses is a party cannot be prejudiced by the effect of the decree—BGB 1344;

Illustration: The wife pledges her husband's credit in a case in which a lawful wife has authority to do so.   The husband is bound notwithstanding the fact that at a subsequent period the marriage is declared void;

(e) if one of the spouses at the time of the marriage is aware of the relative nullity, while the other is not aware of it (e.g. if a husband at the age of 20 allows the wife to believe that he is of full age), the innocent party is, on the pronouncement of the nullity of the marriage, entitled to the same pecuniary rights as an innocent spouse on the pronouncement of a divorce decree—422 sub (3)—BGB 1345. [1]

In all other respects a marriage relatively void is after the pronouncement of the nullity treated as if it had been void *ab initio*.   484

According to ordinary English terminology the nullity which I have described as relative nullity would be described as 'voidability', but German law reserves the equivalent of that expression (*Anfechtbarkeit*) for cases where the impediment is of a private nature, and remains unnoticed unless one of the spouses takes proceedings. [2]

---

[1]   If a spouse, entitled to the right mentioned in the text, exercises the same, he or she cannot avail himself or herself of the other pecuniary consequences of the nullity of the marriage and *vice versa*.   The spouse against whom the right is available may require the other spouse to decide within a specified reasonable period, whether he or she wishes to be treated as a divorced person or to abide by the ordinary consequences of nullity—BGB 1347.

[2]   As regards English marriages the term 'nullity' is sometimes used in an ambiguous sense.   Thus impotence is stated to be a ground of 'nullity', whilst such an impediment in reality only causes voidability (see Cavell *v.* Prince L. R. 1 Ex. 246).

The characteristic feature of relative nullity as distinguished from voidability is the fact, that proceedings for nullity can be taken by the public prosecutor as vindicator of the public interest, as well as by either spouse and by other interested parties—CPO 632.

(3) *Voidability*.

A private severing impediment causes a marriage to be voidable at the option of the spouse who has the right of avoidance or of the statutory agent of such spouse.   The right to avoidance is lost by the death of the party entitled thereto or by the lapse of six months from a date which varies according to the nature of the impediment.   During the lifetime of the spouse affected by the impediment it is exercised by means of proceedings in the Matrimonial Court; after the death of such spouse a declaration on the part of the avoiding party communicated to the competent Probate Court—468 sub (7)—is sufficient [1]—BGB 1338, 1339, 1340, 1341, 1342.

If the avoidance is duly effected, the consequences are the same in every respect as the consequences of a decree of nullity pronounced in the case of a relatively void marriage; the marriage is treated as if it had been void *ab initio*—
485   BGB 1343 (1).   The knowledge of the voidability has the same effect as the knowledge of the relative nullity. [2]

b.   Fatal Defects in Marriage Ceremony.

410. The following irregularities are deemed fatal defects in the case of any marriage celebrated in Germany:

(*a*) disregard of the rule that the declarations of the parties must be made before a person deemed to be a competent official under the rule stated above—p. 447 note 3;

---

[1]   After the communication of the declaration to the competent Probate Court the marriage may be treated as invalid, in so far as the declarant was in fact entitled to avoid the marriage; but it is open to any other party to contest the validity of the avoidance; in a case in which proceedings in the Matrimonial Court are necessary the marriage cannot be treated as voidable or void before judgment—BGB 1313 (2).

[2]   A party avoiding the marriage on the ground of his consent having been extorted by unlawful threats, has the same rights as the innocent party in a case of nullity known to the other party at the time of the marriage—see above sub (2) (*e*); if on the other hand the marriage is avoided on the ground of mistake the rights in question inure in favour of the person about whose identity or qualities the mistake was made—BGB 1346.

(*b*) disregard of the rule requiring the parties to make their declarations in person and in the presence of each other;

(*c*) disregard of the rule that the registration official must be willing to receive the declarations [1]—BGB 1324 (1).

If, however, the marriage is registered, notwithstanding any of the above-mentioned irregularities, the fatal defect is cured by the continuous cohabitation of the parties as husband and wife during a prescribed period of time [2] ; the period ceases to run on the institution of nullity proceedings—BGB 1324 (2).

c. Impediments.

(1) *Public severing impediments.*

411. The following impediments cause the ' relative nullity ' of a marriage:

(*a*) the incapacity (93) or temporary mental aberration of one of the parties   486
at the time of the marriage [3]—BGB 1323 , 1325;

(*b*) the subsistence at the time of the marriage of a previous valid marriage between one of the parties and another person [4]—BGB 1309 , 1323 , 1326;

---

1   The fact that the declarations are not made in the prescribed locality is not a fatal defect; if therefore a registration official declares himself willing to receive the declaration of the parties in any place of entertainment or in the open air, the parties if making the required declaration are validly married; the official would of course be subject to severe punishment for his disregard of the rules.   The non-observance of any of the rules as to the celebration of the marriage other than those mentioned above (*e. g.* the rules as to public notice, as to the local jurisdiction of the official, as to the place of celebration, as to the presence of witnesses, as to the question to be addressed to the parties, and as to the official's duty to declare them husband and wife) does not constitute a fatal defect.

2   The normal period is ten years, but if one of the parties dies before the lapse of ten years, the period down to such death is deemed sufficient, if at least three years have elapsed from the date of the marriage—BGB 1324 (2).

3   The marriage is deemed valid *ab initio*, if confirmed after the cesser of the incapacity, or mental aberration, and before the pronouncement of the decree of nullity, or of the dissolution of the marriage—BGB 1325 (2) ; if the confirming party is of restricted capacity and confirms without the authorization of the statutory agent the marriage ceases to be void and becomes voidable—BGB 1331.

4   If such other person has been judicially declared to be dead (45) and one of the parties at least is ignorant of the fact that the person declared dead is actually living, the re-marriage is not rendered void by such fact; the re-marriage in such a case has the effect of dissolving the former marriage.   Either of the parties to the second marriage, not having at the time of such marriage been aware of the fact that the person declared dead was living, may within six months from the time of becoming aware of such fact take proceedings

(*c*) certain specified kinds of relationship between the parties[1]—BGB 1310 (1) (3), 1323, 1327;

(*d*) the previous adultery of the parties, if the former marriage of one of them was dissolved on the ground of such adultery[2]—BGB 1312 (1), 1323, 1328.

(2) *Private severing impediments.*

The following impediments cause the voidability of a marriage:

487   (*a*) the absence of the authorization of the statutory agent of one of the parties where such party is of restricted capacity (94) at the time of the marriage—BGB 1304, 1330, 1331[3];

(*b*) the ignorance of one of the parties as to the nature of the ceremony or as to the effect of the declaration made before the registration official—BGB 1330, 1332;

(*c*) the mistake of one of the parties as to essential personal qualities of the other party[4]—BGB 1330, 1333;

(*d*) the fact that one of the parties was induced to marry the other under the influence of misrepresentation as to essential circumstances[5] (not being circumstances

---

for the avoidance of the second marriage.   If such proceedings are successful the other party, if equally innocent, is entitled to alimony in the same way as an innocent divorced person—422 sub (3) —BGB 1348, 1350, 1351. —As to the effect of an action claiming the annulment of a judicial declaration of death, see BGB 1349.

1   Marriages between the following classes of relatives are relatively void: Descendant and ascendant; relatives by marriage (424) in the ascending or descending line; brother and sister of the whole or half blood.   An illegitimate child and his issue are deemed to be descendants of the putative father and of his ancestors for the purpose of this rule—BGB 1310 (1) (3).   Marriages between certain other classes of relatives are also forbidden, but in their case the impediment is merely of a hindering nature (see p. 454 note 3).

2   The Government of the State of which the divorced party is a subject may grant dispensation from this impediment.   If the dispensation is granted after the re-marriage it has a retrospective effect—BGB 1312 (2), 1322, 1328 (2).

3   Confirmation of the marriage by the statutory agent while the restriction continues, or by the party concerned after its removal, bars the right of avoidance.   The confirmation by the statutory agent may in certain events be replaced by judicial confirmation—BGB 1337.

4   Only such personal qualities are considered essential as would on a proper consideration of the matter have induced the party concerned to refuse the marriage.   (Impotence is not in itself an impediment, but the ignorance of the other party as to its existence would be deemed a mistake as to an essential personal quality.)

5   The definition of what is essential is the same as that given above in respect of essential qualities; misrepresentation as to outside circumstances (*e. g.* as to the consent of the parents of one of the spouses or as to the intention to have a religious marriage) may be essential.

of a pecuniary nature) made by or with the knowledge of the other party, or of unlawful threats on the part of the other party or any other person—BGB 1330, 1334, 1335;

(e) the fact that a party to a previous marriage who was judicially declared to be dead (45) and believed to be dead at the time of the marriage is subsequently found to be living (see p. 451 note 4)—BGB 1330, 1350.

The right of avoidance may be exercised as follows: (1) in the cases mentioned sub (a) and (b) by the party under disability; (2) in the cases mentioned sub (c) and (d) by the party induced by mistake, misrepresentation, or unlawful threats; (3) in the case mentioned sub (e) by either party [1]—BGB 1331–1335, 1350.

The right to avoid a marriage on the ground of the absence of the authorization of the statutory agent can, while the disability continues, be exercised exclusively by the statutory agent.   Thus a father, whose infant son has married without his authorization, can alone exercise the right of avoidance while the son remains   488 under age [2]—BGB 1336 (2).

(3) Hindering impediments.

The following impediments ought, if discovered, to prevent the celebration of a marriage, but do not affect the validity of a marriage which has been solemnized notwithstanding their existence: (a) insufficient age [3]; (b) the absence of the required parental authorization in the case of persons below the age of 21 [4]; (c) the insufficiency of the time of widowhood in the case of a woman

---

1   Confirmation of the marriage after knowledge of the true facts, as well as the death of one of the parties, bars the right in the last-mentioned case—BGB 1350 (2).

2   If a person under total incapacity is on any ground entitled to avoid his marriage, his statutory agent may act on his behalf.   If a person of restricted capacity is on any ground other than the absence of the required authorization entitled to avoid his marriage he may exercise such right without the concurrence of the statutory agent—BGB 1336.

3   A man may not marry during infancy, a woman may not marry before attaining the age of 16; this rule is independent of the rule as to the necessity of the authorization of the statutory agent; even with such authorization the marriage ought not to be solemnized if either party is under the required age.   In the case of a woman dispensation from the rule as to age may be granted by the Government of the State of which she is a subject—BGB 1303, 1322 (1).

4   The father or adoptor of a child who has not attained the age of 21 must give his authorization to the marriage; in certain specified events the mother is substituted for the father.   As a general rule the person required to give the authorization is also the statutory agent and the two requirements coincide in such a case; but where the parental power of the parent in question is suspended or has been forfeited (442), his

previously married[1]; (*d*) the non-observance of the rules for the protection of the
property of the children of a previous marriage[2]; (*e*) the absence of the licence
or certificate required under the law of the particular State to the marriage of a
member of the armed forces, or of a public official, or of the subject of a foreign
State; (*f*) the existence of certain specified kinds of relationship between the
parties other than those constituting severing impediments[3]—BGB 1310–1315.

(4) *Comparison between English and German law.*

The following table shows the effect of the several impediments according to
English and according to German laws[4]:

---

authorization is required as well as that of the statutory agent.   A man who has been declared to be of full
age before having attained the age of 21 years (see 27) may marry without the authorization of any statutory
agent, but as long as he has not attained the age of 21 years the marriage ought not to be solemnized without
the parental authorization.   The absence of the authorization of the statutory agent in any case in which it is
required makes the marriage voidable, as mentioned above, but the absence of the parental authorization as
such is merely in the nature of a hindering impediment.   It may be replaced by an order of the Guardianship Court—BGB 1305–1308.

1   A woman is not allowed to re-marry before the expiration of ten months after the dissolution of her
previous marriage or after the date of the order declaring the nullity of such previous marriage—BGB 1313
(1).   Dispensation may be granted by the Government authorities of the State of which the woman is a
subject—BGB 1313 (2), 1322.

2   A widower or widow who re-marries must in certain events make certain prescribed arrangements for
the benefit of the issue of the previous marriage—see 446 sub (3)—and must in every case produce a
certificate from the Guardianship Court showing either that the prescribed arrangements have been made or
that they are unnecessary—BGB 1314.

3   The marriage between persons of whom one has had any illicit sexual connexion with any ancestor or
issue of the other is prohibited; marriage with an adopted child is prohibited, while the relationship created
by the adoption remains in existence—BGB 1310 (2), 1311.

4   I have purposely refrained from comparing the rules as to defects in the marriage ceremony or in the
preliminary notices, or banns, as they are of much smaller practical importance than the impediments.
According to English law, the *lex fori* decides what is a defect in the ceremony and what is an impediment
(Simonin *v.* Mallac 2 Sw. & Tr. 67; Sottomayor *v.* de Barros 3 P. D. 1), but according to German law an
impediment considered as such by the personal law of the party concerned must be considered an impediment
whatever the view of the *lex fori* may be on the subject.

Impediments.	Effect according to English law.	Effect according to German law.	
Incapacity. [1]	Absolute nullity.	Relative nullity.	
Absence of required authorization. [2]	Hindering impediment.	Voidability.	
Bigamy.	Absolute nullity.	Relative nullity.	
Kinship or affinity within forbidden degrees. [3]	Absolute nullity.	Relative nullity.	
Previous adultery of parties.	No effect.	Relative nullity.	490
Ignorance as to nature of ceremony. [4]	Absolute nullity.	Voidability.	
Mistake as to essential personal qualities.	No effect.	Voidability.	
Impotence.	Voidability.	No effect.	
Fraudulent misrepresentation as to essential facts. [5]	No effect.	Voidability.	
Duress.	Absolute nullity.	Voidability.	
Insufficiency of interval after previous marriage.	No effect.	Hindering impediment.	
Disregard of rule for protection of children of previous marriage.	No effect.	Hindering impediment.	

---

[1]   Incapacity due to mental decease is recognized as an impediment in both countries; in respect to the incapacity resulting from deficiency of age, it will be remembered that in Germany total incapacity ceases at the age of 7, but that a marriage entered upon during the period between that age and the attainment of full age (being the period of restricted capacity) is voidable unless authorized or confirmed by the statutory agent.   According to English law infancy is not a severing impediment as to males having attained the age of 14, or females having attained the age of 12 at the time of the marriage.

[2]   As shown above the absence of the authorization of the statutory agent to the marriage of a person of restricted capacity is a private severing impediment; the absence of the parental authorization in a case where the parent is not the statutory agent, or where the party in question, though not having attained the age of 21, has been declared of full age is merely a hindering impediment; the absence of the licence or certificate required in the case of the marriage of a member of the armed forces, or of a public official, or of a foreigner, is not a severing impediment in any case.

[3]   The kinds of relationship which render a marriage void according to English law cover a much wider ground than those which have the corresponding effect under German law; English law forbids, and German law allows, a marriage between an uncle and his niece, or his nephew's widow; between an aunt and her nephew or her niece's former husband; between a widower and his deceased wife's sister, or his deceased brother's wife; between a widow and her deceased sister's husband or her deceased husband's brother.

[4]   English law sees in such ignorance evidence of the fact that there was no true consent.

[5]   See Moss v. Moss (1897) P. D. 263.

(5) *Conflict of laws as to impediments.*

In the view of German law the effect of an impediment is, as to each of the spouses, determined by the law of the State of which such spouse is a subject at the time of the marriage. [1]   In so far as the law of such State refers back to German law, German law is to be applied.

Illustration: A British subject domiciled in Germany marries his deceased wife's sister, who at the time of the marriage is a German subject.   German law asks in the first instance: How would an English Court decide as to the validity of the marriage under the circumstances of the case?   The answer would be that an English Court would decide according to the law of the domicil, *viz.* German law.   The German Court would therefore apply German law, and declare the marriage valid.

491   According to the general rule of English law the effect of an impediment is, as to each spouse, determined by the law of the place in which such spouse is domiciled at the time of the marriage.

Illustration: A German domiciled in England marries his deceased wife's sister being also of German nationality.   In the view of English law the marriage would be invalid.

The general rule of English law is, however, subject to certain important modifications, owing to the fact that, according to English law, the *lex fori* may prevent the application of the personal law.   English Courts hold that the *lex fori* and not the personal law decides the question whether the violation of a particular rule constitutes a severing impediment or is merely a defect in the marriage ceremony, and it has been decided accordingly that the absence of the consent required by the personal law of either spouse is not deemed a ground of nullity by an English Court though treated as such by the personal law of the party concerned (Simonin *v.* Mallac 2 Sw. & Tr. 67—see Sottomayor *v.* Barros 3 P. D. 1, 7).

Illustration: A German subject of the age of 20, without the authorization of his father (being his statutory agent), marries a German, both parties being domiciled in Germany.   The father obtains a declaration of nullity in the Competent

---

1   This rule is laid down as to Germans wherever married and as to foreign subjects married in Germany by EG 13 (1), and as to subjects of States belonging to The Hague Convention by the Convention relating to marriage art. 1 (see however articles 2 and 3).

German Court.   An English Court would hold the marriage to be valid.

The *lex fori* may further, according to the view held in England, prevent the application of the personal law, if the personal law recognizes impediments of a kind to which English Courts refuse recognition (Dicey, *Conflict of Laws*, p. 647).   Thus English Courts do not recognize impediments of a penal nature, though recognized as such by the law which would otherwise be applicable (Scott *v.* Attorney-General 11 P. D. 128, as explained by Warter *v.* Warter 15 P. D. 152).

Illustration: *A*, having been divorced from his wife on the ground of his adultery with *B*, marries *B*, both *A* and *B* being Germans domiciled in Germany at the time of the marriage.   A German Court would hold such a marriage to be void; an English Court would hold it to be valid.

4.   EFFECTS OF MARRIAGE

A.   GENERAL EFFECTS

412. The effects of marriage are treated under two heads; the general effects being distinguished from the effects described under the collective name of matrimonial régime (*eheliches Güterrecht*).

The following are the general effects:

(1) *Conjugal community.*

Both spouses are bound to live together in conjugal community (*eheliche Lebensgemeinschaft*), which includes not only physical cohabitation but also a joint participation in all the affairs of life (*consortium omnis vitae*)—BGB 1353 (1). [1]   An action for the restitution of the conjugal community is therefore the proper remedy in all cases in which one of the spouses fails to perform any general duty owing by one spouse to another (RGZ 51, 185).   A demand for the restitution of the conjugal community may be resisted so far as under the circumstances it constitutes an abuse of the right, or in so far as the spouse to whom the demand is addressed is entitled to claim a divorce—BGB 1353.

A judgment for the restitution of the conjugal community has an effect similar to that of an English decree for restitution of conjugal rights (see Matrimonial Causes Act 1884).   Such a judgment cannot be enforced by attachment or otherwise, but failure to comply with it, if wilfully persisted in for a year, is

492

---

[1]   An agreement for separation between the spouses is void, as being *contra bonos mores*.

deemed wilful desertion—CPO 888 (2); BGB 1567.

(2) Wife's duty of obedience.

In all matters relating to the common affairs of life, including the choice of the place of abode, the husband's decision is binding on the wife, but so that the wife is not bound to obey in so far as the husband's decision constitutes an abuse of his rights—BGB 1354.

(3) Wife's surname.

493   The wife is entitled to, and bound to, assume the husband's surname—BGB 1355.   If, however, she continues the use of her maiden name under any circumstances under which it is customary to do so (e. g. if she has a professional or literary reputation under her maiden name and continues to use the name in the exercise of her profession or calling), the husband's insistence on the use of his name would constitute an abuse of his right.

(4) Wife's right to manage household matters.

Notwithstanding the husband's power to decide the general questions mentioned sub (2), the wife is entitled and bound to direct the affairs concerning the joint household.   She is bound to give her personal services in household matters, and also in her husband's business, in so far as such services are usually given under the circumstances under which the spouses are living—BGB 1356.

(5) Wife's implied power of agency.

The wife has an implied power to bind the husband's credit in all matters within the scope of her household management, unless the contrary is apparent from the surrounding circumstances.   This power is technically described as the 'power of the keys' (Schlüsselgewalt).   The power of the keys may, as between the husband and wife, be restricted or excluded in such manner as the husband thinks fit, but the restriction or exclusion of the power may be removed by an order of the Guardianship Court if it constitutes an abuse of the husband's rights. Third parties are not affected by any restriction or exclusion of the right unless the same is duly registered in the marriage property register (413)—BGB 1357.

(6) Wife's power of contracting.

The restrictions as to power of a married woman to bind herself by contracts which were in existence prior to 1900 in several parts of Germany, and which still exist in France (see Code Civil, s. 1125), have been entirely repealed by the

BGB Whatever the matrimonial régime may be, a wife has unrestricted powers to   494
incur obligations, but an obligation incurred without the husband's concurrence
cannot, as a general rule, be enforced against any property which under the
matrimonial régime affecting the particular parties comes under the husband's
management.

(7) Husband's power to determine wife's agreements for personal services.

The Guardianship Court may authorize a husband to determine, without
previous notice, any agreement for personal services on the wife's part if, in the
view of the Court, the wife's continuing to give such service would injure the
conjugal interests, but an agreement entered upon with the husband's assent or,
in the case of his absence, incapacity, or unreasonable refusal, with the leave of
the Guardianship Court, cannot be terminated in this manner—BGB 1358.

(8) Diligence to be applied by spouses.

Each of the spouses must in the performance of the duties incident to the
conjugal relation apply the same degree of diligence as he is accustomed to give to
his own affairs (148)—BGB 1359.

(9) Mutual duties as to maintenance.

The husband must maintain his wife in accordance with his station in life,
his means, and his earning powers.   The wife, in the event of the husband being
unable to maintain himself, must maintain him in accordance with his station in
life, in so far as this can be done having regard to her means and earning powers.
If the husband and wife are living together, maintenance has to be supplied in
kind in the manner suitable to the circumstances of the conjugal community. [1]   If
the husband and wife are justifiably living apart (*e. g.* in a case where the claim
for the restitution of the conjugal community would be an abuse of the rights of the
party asserting the claim), maintenance has to be supplied by means of the
payment of an annuity, and the husband has in such a case also to supply the   495
wife—as far as possible and necessary—with the household utensils required by
her.   The husband of a wife living apart from him may be wholly or partly
dispensed from his duty to maintain his wife, in so far as such dispensation seems
equitable under their mutual circumstances—BGB 1360, 1361.

---

1   The rules as to past and future maintenance, and as to funeral expenses, are the same as those
applicable in the case of kindred entitled to maintenance (433)—BGB 1360 (3).

(10) *Presumption as to property.*

It is presumed as between the husband and his creditors that all movable things not serving exclusively for the wife's personal use or ornament, and all negotiable instruments issued to bearer, or issued to order and indorsed in blank, being in the possession of one of the spouses or in their joint possession, belong to the husband.   Things serving exclusively for the wife's personal use and ornament are as between husband and wife, and also as between the husband and wife and their respective creditors, presumed to belong to the wife—BGB 1362.

(11) *Rule as to conflict of laws.*

The general effects of marriage in the view of German law depend on the law of the State of which the husband is a subject for the time being; they are therefore modified by a change of nationality, but they are not affected by a mere change of domicil.   An exception from the rule occurs where a husband leaves his wife under circumstances in which she is not bound to follow him, and loses his German nationality while the wife retains it.   In such a case a German Court before which any question arises as to the general effects of the marriage of the spouses applies German law—EG 14.

B. MATRIMONIAL RÉGIME

a. General Rules.

(1) *Meaning of expression.*

413. The expression 'matrimonial régime' (*eheliches Güterrecht, Ehegüterrecht*) is a collective description of the effect of a marriage on the property owned by each of the spouses at the date of the marriage or acquired at a subsequent time. These effects, in so far as they are determined by the statutory provisions on the subject, are collectively described as 'statutory régime' (*gesetzliches Güterrecht*); in so far as the statutory effect is displaced by marriage contract (*Ehevertrag*) the expression 'contractual régime' (*vertragsmässiges Güterrecht*) is used.

(2) *Distinction between rights acquired under matrimonial régime and rights acquired under law of inheritance.*

The rights acquired by each of the spouses under the matrimonial régime must be distinguished from the rights acquired under the law of inheritance.   The rights of one of the spouses under the matrimonial régime are in many cases without

496

practical effect before the death of the other spouse; at the same time such rights are vested rights *ab initio*, while the rights acquired under the law of inheritance, as a matter of course, do not come into being before the death of the predeceasing spouse.

Illustration: *H* (Husband) and *W* (Wife) by marriage contract become subject to the régime of 'community of movables', *H* being possessed of movables of the aggregate value of £ 10, 000; *W* being possessed of movables of the aggregate value of £ 5, 000; by virtue of the contract and the marriage the property of *H* and the property of *W* form one fund of the aggregate value of £ 15, 000, each of the spouses being entitled to one moiety of the common fund, but during *H*'s life the movables included in the common fund are in *H*'s power, he alone being entitled to receive the income and to deal with the corpus.   *H* dies without leaving issue, having by his will given his whole estate to a brother; *W* by the law of inheritance is entitled to a compulsory portion equal to one half of *H*'s estate.   Assuming the corpus of the property not to have increased or decreased during the marriage, and assuming all debts to have been paid in *H*'s lifetime, *W* on *H*'s death, by virtue of the marriage contract, becomes entitled in possession to her moiety of the common fund, while under the law of inheritance she becomes entitled to half the remaining moiety which belongs to her husband's estate. [1]

(3) *Matrimonial régime as to persons married before* 1900.

The matrimonial régime affecting the property of any spouses married before   497 January 1, 1900, is on principle determined by the law which was in force at the

---

[1]   The distinction is important from the point of view of private international law, inasmuch as the matrimonial régime is determined in accordance with the husband's personal law at the time of the marriage, while the rights arising under the law of inheritance are determined according to the personal law, to which the deceased spouse is subject at the time of his death.   Illustration: If *H* and *W* under the circumstances mentioned above had, after their marriage, become and remained domiciled in England and acquired British nationality, then, in the German, as well as the English view of the case, *W* would (notwithstanding the change of nationality and domicil) be entitled to her moiety of the common fund—EG 15; de Nicols *v.* Curlier (1900) A. C. 21; but her right to a compulsory portion of the husband's estate, being the other moiety, would have come to an end.   The distinction between rights derived from the law of inheritance and rights derived from the matrimonial régime under the present German law is clear under any circumstances, but under some of the old German systems, it was frequently difficult to determine to which class a particular right belonged.

time of the marriage in the place in which the husband was then domiciled,¹ but statutory modifications in the existing régime may be introduced by State Legislation—EG 218.   In all the more important German States such statutory modifications of the régimes affecting parties married before 1900 have been brought about.   It will be understood that the rules as to matrimonial régime stated below are those referring to spouses married on or after January 1, 1900, or to such spouses as have placed themselves under the present law by post-nuptial marriage contract.

(4) *Relation of statutory régime to contractual régime.*

The rules of the statutory régime apply except in so far as they are modified by marriage contract (*Ehevertrag*).²   If the contract deals with all the matters provided for by the rules of the statutory régime, the latter are not applied; but all matters not dealt with by the contract are governed by the statutory rules, unless the contract—as it may do—expressly stipulates, that the statutory rules are to be excluded.   The statutory rules as to effect of marriage on property belonging to German spouses may be compared to the regulations of an English company, which are those laid down by statute (Table A in the first schedule to

498   Companies Act 1862) except in so far as they are expressly excluded or modified by the articles of the company.

Any third party is, as between himself and either of the spouses, entitled to assume that the statutory rules apply, unless at the time when the particular transaction is entered upon, the modification or exclusion of the statutory régime is registered in the prescribed manner in the marriage property register³ (*Güter-rechtsregister*) of the district in which the husband is domiciled at such time, or unless such modification or exclusion of the statutory régime is known to such third party—BGB 1435, 1558–1563.

(5) *Rules as to conflict of laws.*

(*a*) If the husband at the date of the marriage is a German subject the

---

¹   The new law allows the régime to be altered by post-nuptial marriage contract.   This rule is maintained even in cases where under the rules originally applicable post-nuptial modifications were prohibited—as was the case in the German districts governed by French law—see French Civil Code, s. 1395; EG 200.

²   Every contract—ante-nuptial or post-nuptial—dealing with the mutual rights of the spouses as to any property owned by either of them is called a 'marriage contract'.

³   The marriage property register is entirely distinct from the register of births, marriages, and deaths, in which the marriage is registered.

régime is determined by German law;

(b) if the husband, after the date of the marriage, becomes a German subject or establishes his domicil within the German Empire, the matrimonial régime is determined by the law of the State of which the husband was a subject at the date of the marriage, but this rule is subject to the following qualifications:

(α) a post-nuptial marriage contract is held valid notwithstanding the fact that, according to the governing law (as, for instance, is the case in French law), the statutory régime cannot be modified by post-nuptial contract;

(β) in so far as the governing law refers back to German law (as, for instance, would be the case according to English law, if the husband at the date of the marriage had been a British subject domiciled in Germany), the matrimonial régime is governed by German law;

(γ) the foreign law cannot be invoked by either spouse as against any third party, unless the régime established by such law is duly registered in Germany—see above sub (4);

(δ) if the wife carries on business in Germany independently of her husband, the rules of German law—414 sub (4) (e) (α)—are applied in favour of a third party in so far as they are more favourable to such third party.

(c) in any case in which the German law is applicable, it does not affect   499
objects locally situate outside of the German Empire in so far as the *lex situs*
would exclude the application of the German law—EG 15, 16, 27, 28.

Illustration: If a wife who marries a German subject, and who by marriage contract adopts the régime of community of goods, has real property situate in England, such real property does not, *ipso facto*, become vested in the two spouses as co-owners, as it would according to German law.

b.   Statutory Régime.

aa.   Normal effects.

(1) *General characteristics.*

414. The wife's position under German law is much less favourable than the position of a wife under the English Married Women's Property Act 1882.   While an English wife coming under the provisions of that statute can freely manage her property and sell or mortgage the same and appropriate the income for her own purposes, a German wife, in the absence of a contrary agreement, must allow her husband to take into his possession and under his management the whole of her property in so far as it is not specially exempted under the rules stated sub (2), and to appropriate its income. [1]   Under special circumstances the husband's powers may be removed and the modifications described below (415) come into being, but proceedings involving such consequences are only instituted in extreme cases, and presuppose very strained relations between the spouses.

(2) *Non-privileged property and privileged property.*

500

The property which under normal circumstances comes under the husband's powers of management is called ' *eingebrachtes Gut* ' , and will in the course of this treatise be referred to as ' non-privileged property ' .   All the wife's property which is not deemed privileged property (*Vorbehaltsgut*) under the rules stated below is comprised in the non-privileged property.   The wife's privileged property consists of: (1) things intended exclusively for the wife's personal use, more particularly clothes, personal ornaments and appliances required for the wife's work; (2) property acquired by the wife's work or by any trade carried on by her independently of her husband; (3) property declared to be privileged property by the marriage contract; (4) property given as privileged property by a testator or donor; (5) property acquired by virtue of a right included in the privileged property or by way of substitution for any destroyed, damaged or withdrawn objects previously forming part of the privileged property, or by virtue of any act-in-the-law having reference to the privileged property—BGB 1365–1370.

The wife's non-privileged property, though under the husband's control and in his possession, remains vested in her, and all movable things or rights relating to movable things acquired by the husband out of funds belonging to such property (including negotiable instruments issued to bearer or indorsed in blank) become equally vested in the wife, and are added to her non-privileged property, unless it can be proved that the husband intended to acquire them for himself. [2]   Household

---

[1]   The normal statutory régime of the present German law is an adaptation of the Germanic system described on the *lucus a non lucendo* principle as *Verwaltungsgemeinschaft*.   It resembles the Roman dotal system to some extent; but according to that system everything was separate property, which was not specially given as *dos*, whereas under the German system everything goes into the husband's possession which is not characterized as privileged property.   On the other hand, the objects forming the *dos* passed into the husband's ownership, while under the present German law the wife's non-privileged property remains in her ownership.

[2]   In the last-mentioned event the ownership would vest in the husband, but the wife would be entitled to claim their transfer to her.

articles acquired in substitution for others belonging to the non-privileged property become part of such property in any case—BGB 1381, 1382.   Either spouse may at any time demand an inventory of the wife's non-privileged property or a report on the condition of the several things forming part thereof—BGB 1372.

(3) Husband's powers of management and disposition as to wife's non-privileged property.

The husband is entitled to take possession of the wife's non-privileged property and to manage it in due course of management, giving information as to the state thereof whenever required to do so by the wife.   In so far as necessary for the proper management, he may dispose of money or other consumable things [1] (74),   501 allow sums due to the wife to be set off against debts payable out of the wife's non-privileged property, and deliver any object comprised in such property to any party to whom the wife is bound to deliver it [2]; subject to these exceptions the husband cannot dispose of any part of the wife's non-privileged property without her assent (129), which assent may, however, in certain events (including the wife's unreasonable unwillingness to give it), be replaced by the sanction of the Guardianship Court [3]—BGB 1363, 1373–1376, 1377 (1), 1379.

The husband cannot alone give a valid discharge in respect of any property over which he has no independent disposing power.

The husband has no powers of management or disposition in respect of the wife's privileged property—BGB 1371.

The husband cannot assign or transfer his powers of management to any third party.   If he is under guardianship, his powers of management and disposition relating to the wife's non-privileged property are exercised by his guardian; this rule applies even in a case in which the wife herself is the guardian—BGB 1408, 1409.

(4) Wife's powers in respect of non-privileged property.

The wife has complete powers of disposition over her privileged property; as

---

[1]   If any money comes into his possession he must invest it in trustee securities, retaining only so much as may be required to meet expenses.   Other consumable things may be used or sold by the husband for his own purposes, but he must account for their value on the termination of his powers of management— BGB 1377 (2) (3).

[2]   The husband's rights and duties concerning the appurtenant stock of a parcel of land forming part of the wife's non-privileged property are the same as those of a usufructuary—360, 361 rule (3)—BGB 1378.

[3]   As to the husband's right to sue on the wife's behalf, see BGB 1380.

regards her non-privileged property the rules stated below sub (*a*) to (*d*) apply in cases not coming under the exceptions mentioned sub (*e*):

(*a*) any disposition relating to the non-privileged property made by agreement with a third party is inoperative, unless authorized or ratified by the husband; any disposition relating to such property made by unilateral act is inoperative unless authorized by the husband; subsequent ratification is ineffectual—BGB 1395–1398;

502   (*b*) a contractual obligation incurred by the wife is enforceable against the non-privileged property, if entered upon with the husband's assent; in the absence of such assent it is not enforceable against the non-privileged property, unless such non-privileged property is benefited thereby, in which event the rules as to 'unjustified benefits' (298) apply—BGB 1399 [1];

(*c*) the husband's assent though otherwise required under the rules stated sub (*a*) and (*b*) may be dispensed with, if by reason of illness or absence he is unable to give it, and if the intended transaction cannot be delayed without danger; if the husband unreasonably refuses his assent to any transaction required for the proper management of the wife's personal affairs, such assent may be replaced by the leave of the Guardianship Court—BGB 1401, 1402 [2];

(*d*) the restrictions as to dispositions affecting the non-privileged property are binding on third parties even if they are not aware of the fact that the wife is a married woman—BGB 1404;

(*e*) the following kinds of transactions may be entered into by the wife so as to bind the non-privileged property without the husband's assent:

(α) any transaction connected with the management of any trade or business carried on by the wife with her husband's authorization or knowledge

---

[1]   A married woman is generally capable of suing and being sued—CPO 52 (2)—but she cannot be plaintiff in an action for the enforcement of any right (not belonging to one of the excepted classes mentioned below) forming part of the non-privileged property except with the husband's assent.   A judgment obtained in any action in which the wife is a party without the husband's assent cannot be enforced against the non-privileged property—BGB 1400.   The following classes of rights may be enforced by the wife without the husband's assent: (1) rights as to which an action brought by the wife was pending at the date of the wife's marriage; (2) rights against the husband; (3) rights available against third parties of which the husband has disposed, without the wife's required assent; (4) rights of objection against any judicial seizure of property—BGB 1407.

[2]   As to unilateral transactions entered into by third parties relating to the non-privileged property or to obligations incurred by the wife, see BGB 1403.

and without any objection on his part [1] ;

(β) the acceptance or disclaimer of any right of inheritance (522) or   503
legacy (525) or the renunciation of any compulsory portion (510) or the
filing of an inventory of an estate to which the wife is entitled (533);

(γ) any transaction by which the offer of an agreement or of a gift is
refused;

(δ) any transaction between the wife and the husband—BGB 1405,
1406.

(5) Husband's right of usufruct.

The husband becomes entitled to the usufruct of the wife's non-privileged
property in the same way as the usufructuary of an aggregate of things or rights—
359.

In return for the right of usufruct he has to bear the expenses of the joint
household and certain specified outgoings incident to the management of the wife's
non-privileged property.   The nett income of the non-privileged property must,
at the wife's request, be applied in the first place to the maintenance of herself
and the children of the marriage—BGB 1363, 1383–1389.   If the husband defrays
any outgoings not chargeable against him which under the circumstances seem
required for the proper management of the non-privileged property, he is entitled
to re-imbursement out of corpus—BGB 1390.

The husband cannot assign his right of usufruct to any third party.   If he is
under guardianship (449), the right of usufruct is exercised by his guardian on
his behalf, even where the wife herself is the guardian—BGB 1408, 1409.

(6) Wife's rights in case of improper exercise of husband's rights.

The wife cannot as a general rule, while the husband's powers of management and usufruct continue, claim compensation from the husband in respect of
any unauthorized use of such powers; such claims under ordinary circumstances
remain in abeyance until the powers come to an end by death or otherwise. [2]

If, however, the husband's conduct justifies the fear that the wife's rights will   504
be infringed in a manner seriously endangering the safety of the non-privileged

---

1   The withdrawal of the authorization or the raising of an objection does not affect third parties unless
recorded in the marriage property register—BGB 1405 (3).

2   The claim for the wife's and the children's maintenance under the rules stated sub (5) can be
asserted at any time—BGB 1394.

property or of her claims for compensation against the husband, the wife is entitled to the following rights [1] :

(1) she may claim security (87);

(2) she may claim lodgment with a public authority in the joint names of husband and wife (164) of all instruments to bearer not being bank notes or dividend coupons, or other instruments classed as consumable things (74), which form part of the non-privileged property;

(3) she may assert her rights to compensation for losses caused by improper management, notwithstanding the fact that the husband's powers of management and usufruct continue—BGB 1391–1394.

(7) Liability for debts.

(a) As between spouses and creditors.

The husband's creditors have no right against the wife's non-privileged property.

The wife's creditors may, notwithstanding the husband's rights of management and usufruct, enforce their claims against the wife's non-privileged property unless they belong to one of the following classes [2] :

(1) claims in respect of transactions entered into without the husband's assent, in so far as such assent was required under the rules stated sub (4) [3] ;

(2) claims in respect of any liability of the wife incurred after the date of the marriage in connexion with any transaction affecting the privileged property (including liabilities incurred by the acceptance of any right of inheritance or legacy accruing after the date of the marriage under the will of any testator, but not including liabilities incurred in the course of any trade or business carried on with the husband's authorization or acquiescence)—BGB 1410, 1411 (1), 1412 (1), 1413, 1414.

It will be seen that the classes of excepted claims do not include:

(1) claims in respect of unlawful acts committed by the wife either before or during the subsistence of the marriage;

505

---

1   The rights mentioned in this place are those exercisable whilst the husband's powers continue; the grounds on which the revocation of the husband's powers may be demanded will be discussed below (415).

2   If the husband has alienated or consumed any consumable things under the power in that behalf mentioned sub (3), the creditors may compel him to replace their value—BGB 1411 (2).

3   The costs of any action to which the wife is a party are payable out of the non-privileged property, notwithstanding the fact that the judgment is otherwise not enforceable against the non-privileged property— BGB 1412 (2).

(2) claims in respect of any contractual liability incurred by the wife before the date of the marriage, or claims in respect of any liability incurred after the date of the marriage in connexion with any transaction not affecting the privileged property at the time at which the liability was incurred. [1]

These claims may therefore be enforced against the non-privileged property.

The wife's creditors may of course proceed against the privileged property in respect of all their claims.

(b) As between husband and wife.

As between husband and wife the following classes of claims must be borne by the privileged property [2] :

(1) claims in respect of unlawful acts committed by the wife after the date of the marriage;

(2) claims in respect of liabilities incurred after the date of the marriage in respect of rights or things becoming subsequently part of the privileged property.

If any such claim is satisfied out of the non-privileged property the husband may require the wife to transfer from the privileged property funds of sufficient value to make up the deficiency.   In the same way the wife may require the husband to transfer out of the non-privileged property funds of sufficient value to make up any deficiency in the privileged property caused by her having satisfied thereout any liability which, as between husband and wife, ought to be borne by the non-privileged property.   If, in either case, the property from which the deficiency is to be made up is insufficient to do so in full, the husband's or wife's claim is deemed to be satisfied by the transfer of such funds as are available— BGB 1415, 1417.

bb.   Modifications brought about by exceptional circumstances.

(1) Circumstances causing forfeiture of husband's rights ab initio.

415. The husband's rights of management or usufruct may of course be excluded   506 or modified by marriage contract; in so far as this is done the régime is a contractual régime, and does not come under the statutory rules.   There is, however, one case in which the husband's rights are forfeited *ab initio*, though not excluded by

---

1   As shown below (416) a post-nuptial marriage contract has the same effect as an ante-nuptial one. Any part of the non-privileged property can therefore at any time be turned into privileged property and *vice versa*.

2   As to costs of litigation, see BGB 1415 Nr. 3; BGB 1416.

marriage contract; this occurs, where a husband marries a wife of restricted capacity without the authorization of her statutory agent.   Such a marriage, as shown above—411 sub (2)—may within a certain period be avoided; if the period elapses without such avoidance of the marriage, its validity can no longer be impugned, but the husband has no light of management or usufruct as to any of the wife's property—BGB 1364.

(2) Circumstances causing revocation of rights.

The husband's rights of management and usufruct are revoked *ipso facto*:

(a) on the dissolution of the marriage by death or divorce, or on a judicial separation of the spouses;

(b) on the husband being adjudged a bankrupt;

(c) on the husband being judicially declared to be dead (45).

The rights may be revoked by the Court on the wife's application on one of the following grounds:

(a) on any of the grounds on which the wife is entitled to require security under the rules stated above—414 sub (6);

(b) on the ground that the husband has failed to comply with his duties as to the maintenance of the wife and children of the marriage, and that there is a reasonable cause for apprehension as to the safety of the claim for future maintenance;

(c) on the ground that the husband has been placed under guardianship (449), or has had a curator appointed for the management of his affairs (454)[1] — BGB 1418–20.

507   The husband's rights of management and usufruct may also be revoked by post-nuptial marriage contract.

(3) Husband's duties on revocation of rights.

On the revocation of the rights of management and usufruct the husband has to hand over the whole of the non-privileged property to the wife or her heirs, and at the same time to render an account of his management. [2]   If ignorant of the revocation he is entitled to continue the exercise of his rights until the time at which it becomes known to him, or would have become known to him if he had used proper care.   If the revocation is caused by the wife's death the husband is bound to continue

---

[1]   If a curator absentis has been appointed for the husband, the husband's rights of management and usufruct are not revoked unless the appointment is likely to remain in force for some time—BGB 1418 Nr. 5.

[2]   For particulars, see BGB 1421–1423.

such acts as are necessary for the management of the non-privileged property until
the wife's heirs are enabled to make proper arrangements—BGB 1424.

(4) Effect of revocation of rights of management and
usufruct (separation of goods).

Where a husband has forfeited or lost his rights of management and usufruct
on any ground mentioned sub (1) or (2) (excepting the ground of the dissolution
of the marriage, or of a pronouncement of judicial separation), the matrimonial
régime of 'separation of goods' (Gütertrennung) is established between the
spouses.   The effect of the régime of 'separation of goods' is as follows:

(a) each of the spouses has a free right of disposal as to his property;

(b) the husband has to bear the expenses of the joint household, but he is
entitled to such contribution from the wife's income or earnings as appears
reasonable under the circumstances; if the husband is under guardianship, or has
a curator appointed for the management of his affairs, or if the wife's or the
children's claim to maintenance is endangered, the wife may retain such part of
her contribution as may be required to provide for such maintenance;

(c) in the event of the wife incurring any expense for the purposes of the
joint household it is assumed, in the absence of evidence to the contrary, that she
does not intend to require re-imbursement from the husband;

(d) the husband may, in the absence of any direction to the contrary, retain   508
for his own purposes the income of any property of which the management is by
the wife's voluntary act entrusted to him, except in so far as such income is required
for the costs of management, or for the satisfaction of such of the wife's liabilities
as would in the ordinary course of management be satisfied out of the wife's
income—BGB 1426–1430. [1]

The separation of goods is not effective as between the spouses and any third

---

[1]   The rules as to the effect of the régime of separation of goods, besides being applicable in the
events mentioned above, are also applied in any case in which any of the three kinds of community of
goods—see 416 sub (3)—is dissolved by the Court, or in which separation of goods has been stipulated for
by marriage contract, or in which the husband's right of management and usufruct is excluded, or revoked by
marriage contract, or in which a previously existing community of goods is revoked by marriage contract,
unless the contract itself provides otherwise; they are also applied in all cases in respect of such part of the
wife's property as has the character of privileged property, but where there is any non-privileged property under
the husband's management the wife is not under any duty to contribute to the household expenses in so far as
the income of such non-privileged property represents a sufficient contribution—BGB 1371, 1436, 1470 (1),
1545 (1), 1549.

party unless it is registered in the marriage property register at the time which is material for the particular transaction, or unless it is known to such third party— BGB 1431 (1).

(5) *Reinstatement of the husband's rights of management and usufruct.*

The Court may, on the husband's application, reinstate his rights of management and usufruct in any of the following events:

(a) if the appointment of a guardian or a curator by which the revocation of the right was caused is set aside or rescinded;

(b) if a husband who has been judicially declared to be dead is found to be living.

Where the Court reinstates the right, such part of the wife's property as before the revocation of the husband's right had the character of privileged property, or has in the meantime assumed that character, becomes privileged property *ipso facto*. The rule as to registration is the same, *mutatis mutandis*, as on the separation of goods—BGB 1425, 1431 (2).

c.   Contractual régime.

aa.   *General rules.*

509   **416.** The relations between the contractual and the statutory régime have been explained above—413 sub (4).   The following general rules apply to marriage contracts:

(1) *Nature of contract.*

German law—differing in that respect from French law—allows modifications of the matrimonial régime to be made by post-nuptial contract—BGB 1432.

(2) *Form of contract.*

A marriage contract executed within the German Empire must be solemnized by contemporaneous declarations of the parties before a German Court or a German notary.   If not solemnized in such a form it is void and of no effect—BGB 1434. A marriage contract executed outside the German Empire may either be executed in the German form, [1] or in the form in which contracts of a similar nature are executed

---

[1]   A German consul is deemed a German notary, in so far as the parties appearing before him are German subjects.   If one of the parties is not a German subject the contract cannot be executed in the German form in any place outside the German Empire.

under the law of the place at which such contract is executed—EG 11.

As to the registration of a marriage contract excluding the statutory régime, see 413 sub (4). [1]

(3) *Modes of describing matrimonial régime.*

The matrimonial régime adopted in marriage contracts, as a general rule,   510
has the characteristics of one of several types known in the former German law or
in French law (*e. g.* dotal régime, general community of goods, community of
acquisitions, &c.).   These types under the former German law were subject to
considerable local variations, and were generally described by some special name,
or by the name of the Code by which they were defined (*e. g.* the community of the
Prussian Code, the community of movables of the French Code).   It was usual
in marriage contracts simply to state the name of the type to which the parties
desired to submit without going into any further details.

The BGB forbids all references to any system of law, which is no longer in
force, or to any system of foreign law, but if the husband at the material date is
domiciled in a foreign country, a general reference to the law of that country is
permitted; the material date is the date of the marriage in the case of an ante-nuptial
contract, and the date of the contract in the case of a post-nuptial contract—BGB
1433.

The only general types which are now recognized by German law, and which
are allowed to be described by their general names, are ' separation of goods '—
415 sub (4), ' general community of goods '—417, ' community of income and
profits '—418, and ' community of movables '—419.   A contract excluding the
husband's rights of management and usufruct, or revoking of one of the three

---

[1]   An ante-nuptial contract between parties of whom one is under total incapacity is inconceivable;
but a post-nuptial contract modifying the statutory or contractual régime in the case of one of the parties becoming
of unsound mind may frequently be desirable; in such a case the statutory agent executes the contract on
behalf of the incapable party.   A statutory agent has, however, no authority to execute a contract providing
for or revoking the régime of general community of goods, or excluding or re-introducing the continuance of
such community after the death of one of the spouses—417 sub (8).   A party to a marriage contract who is
of restricted capacity can in all cases execute it with the assent of his statutory agent.   (This happens in
any case in which an infant who marries with the statutory agent's authorization, enters into a marriage
contract.)   Where the contract provides for or revokes the régime of general community of goods or excludes
or re-introduces the continuance of the community after the death of one of the spouses, the statutory agent,
if he is a guardian, must obtain the leave of the Guardianship Court; if he is one of the parents no such leave
is required—BGB 1437, 1508 (2).

régimes of community of goods, is deemed to be a contract providing for separation of goods unless the contrary appears—BGB 1436.

The contract may, of course, instead of describing the régime by the name of a general type, set out the rights of the parties *in extenso*; where this is done the statutory régime is applied in so far as any point is left open.   One of the defined types may also be adopted by the contract, but made subject to modifications set out specifically.   To this rule there is only one exception.   The so-called 'continued community of goods'—417 sub (8)—if adopted at all, must conform to the statutory regulations; see BGB 1518.

bb.   General community of goods (Allgemeine Gütergemeinschaft).

(1) *General characteristics.*

417. The principal characteristic of all systems of community of goods is that the whole or certain parts of the property of each spouse by virtue of the adoption of the régime becomes vested in the two spouses as co-owners (*Gesamthänder*—304), in equal moieties, but so that the common property is managed by the husband, and that he also receives the income as manager of the community. [1]   The community is, as a general rule, dissolved by the dissolution of the marriage, and may also be dissolved on certain other grounds mentioned below sub (7).   If, however, on the death of one of the spouses any issue of the marriage are in existence the community may, under the régime of general community of goods, and also under the régime of community of movables, be continued, in certain events, between the surviving spouse and the issue of the marriage in the manner explained below sub (8).

(2) *Distinction between several kinds of property.*

The common property (*Gesamtgut*) consists of the whole property of both spouses which is not the separate property of one of them.   Where a general community of goods has been stipulated for by ante-nuptial marriage contract the property vested in each of the spouses at the date of the marriage, in so far as it has not the character of separate property, becomes vested in both spouses as co-owners immediately on the marriage, and all property acquired subsequently to

---

[1]   Neither of the spouses can, while the community subsists, assign or charge his undivided share in the common property or demand a partition.   A debtor is not entitled to set off a claim against either of the spouses against a debt owing to the common fund, unless such claim is enforceable against the common property—BGB 1442.

the marriage by one of the spouses, and not having the character of separate property, becomes vested in both spouses as co-owners immediately on acquisition. Where a general community of goods is established by post-nuptial contract a corresponding rule is applied, the date of the contract being substituted for the date of the marriage—BGB 1438.

The separate property is either privileged (*Vorbehaltsgut*) or non-privileged (*Sondergut*); the non-privileged separate property consists of objects of which the ownership cannot be transferred by act-in-the-law (*e. g.* property held under any feudal tenure, rights of usufruct, &c.)—BGB 1439; the privileged property   512
includes the same classes of property as are included in the privileged property under the statutory régime—414 sub (2), excepting, however, property consisting of things intended for the wife's personal use and property acquired by the wife's personal work, or in the course of her trade; the last-mentioned classes of property form part of the common fund—BGB 1440.

(3) *Husband's rights of management and disposition.*

(a) *As regards common property.*

The husband's rights of management and disposition in respect of the common property go much further than the corresponding rights in respect of the non-privileged property under the statutory régime.   As a general rule he has free powers of disposition in respect of any right or thing included in the common property. [1]

The following classes of transactions, however, require the wife's assent:

(1) agreements or dispositions relating to the whole or an aliquot part of the common property;

(2) agreements or dispositions relating to immovables;

(3) promises of gifts, or gifts which are not made or given for the purpose of satisfying a moral duty, or in compliance with the rules of social propriety.

In cases (1) and (3) a disposition made in satisfaction of an obligation undertaken with the wife's assent, can be made by the husband alone.

The leave of the Court takes the place of the wife's assent in the same events

---

[1]   Under the statutory régime the husband is bound to exercise due diligence and to render an account of his management—BGB 1374.   Under the régime of general community of goods, no such liability exists, as a general rule.   The husband must, however, replace the value: (1) of any intentional diminution of the common property; (2) of any diminution brought about by a transaction requiring the wife's assent and entered into without such assent—BGB 1456.

as under the statutory régime—414 sub (3)—BGB 1443–1447.

(b) As to separate non-privileged property.

The husband retains the management of his own non-privileged separate property, [1] and has the same powers in respect of the wife's non-privileged separate property, as in the case of the statutory régime—414 sub (3)—BGB 1439.

(c) As to privileged property.

513   The husband has of course full powers of management and disposition as to his own privileged property [2]; he has no powers whatsoever over the wife's privileged property.

If the husband is under guardianship his powers of management and disposition are exercisable by his guardian, even where the wife is the guardian—BGB 1457.

(4) Wife's powers of disposition.

(a) As regards common property.

The wife as a general rule has no power of disposition in respect of the common property, but the common property may become bound by transactions entered upon by her with or without her husband's assent (or with the leave of the Court in lieu of the husband's assent) in a similar way as the non-privileged property may under the statutory régime become bound by such transactions—414 sub (4)—BGB 1449–1455.

(b) As regards separate property.

As regards the non-privileged and privileged separate property the wife has the same powers of disposition respectively as those exercisable respectively over the non-privileged and privileged property under the statutory régime—BGB 1439, 1441. [3]

(5) Rules as to receipt and disposal of income.

(a) As to common property.

The income belongs to both spouses as tenants in common as part of the

---

1   As to promises of gifts, see BGB 1446.

2   As to promises of gifts, see BGB 1446.

3   A husband having privileged property is bound to provide for the wife's maintenance independently of the nature of the matrimonial régime; see 412 sub (9).

common property, but the husband by virtue of his powers of management is entitled to receive it; the expenses of the household are payable out of the common property—BGB 1458.   The debts which are enforceable against the corpus—see below sub (6)—are of course also enforceable against the income.

(b) As to non-privileged separate property.

The income of the non-privileged separate property of both spouses accrues to the common property—BGB 1439, 1525.

(c) As to privileged property.

Each spouse is entitled to receive the income of the privileged property belonging to him; but in so far as the income of the common property and of the non-privileged separate property is insufficient to provide for the household expenses, the wife must contribute a reasonable part of such expenses from the income of her privileged property—BGB 1441.

(6) Liability for debts.

(a) Creditor's rights as to common property.

The husband's creditors may enforce their claims against the common property in all cases.   The wife's creditors may, as a general rule, enforce their claims against the common property, but the same classes of liabilities which under the statutory régime are not binding on the non-privileged property, are under the régime of general community of goods not binding on the common property.   The liabilities which are binding on the common property are called 'common property liabilities' (Gesamtgutverbindlichkeiten)—BGB 1459 (1), 1460–1462.

(b) Creditor's rights as to separate property.

The husband's creditors may enforce their claims against his non-privileged, as well as against his privileged separate property.   The wife's creditors may enforce their claims against the wife's privileged property in all cases—BGB 1441; their remedies against the wife's non-privileged separate property are regulated by the same rules as the creditor's rights against the wife's non-privileged property under the statutory régime—BGB 1439, 1525.

(c) Personal liability of spouses.

Each spouse is of course personally liable for his own debts.   The husband is also liable severally and jointly with the wife for such of her liabilities as are binding on the common property under the rules stated sub (*a*). The last-mentioned liability ceases on the dissolution of the community—see below sub (7), in respect of such debts as are—as between the spouses—chargeable against the wife under the rules stated sub (*d*)—BGB 1459 (2).

(*d*) Apportionment of liabilities as between husband and wife.

Some of the common property liabilities are, as between husband and wife, chargeable on the privileged property of the spouse through whom the liability arose. This rule applies to all the classes of liabilities which under the statutory régime must, as between husband and wife, be borne by the wife's privileged property. [1]

515   If the husband applies any part of the common property for the benefit of his privileged property, he must make up the deficiency; on the other hand, he can claim compensation from the common property for the value of any part of his privileged property applied by him for the benefit of the common property.

Claims for a proper apportionment of the burdens respectively falling on the several funds cannot, as a general rule, be enforced before the dissolution of the community, but in so far as the wife's privileged property is sufficient to pay any matured debts chargeable against her, the claims against her privileged property may be enforced as they arise—BGB 1463–1467.

(7) Dissolution of community.

(*a*) Grounds of dissolution.

The community is dissolved *ipso facto* in either of the following events :

(1) on the dissolution of the marriage by death in any case in which the issue of the marriage do not take the place of the deceased spouse under the rules stated sub (8)—BGB 1482, 1483;

(2) on the dissolution of the marriage by divorce or on the judicial separation of the parties—BGB 1564, 1586. [2]

---

1   There is also a special provision as to the chargeability of the cost of an outfit for a child of the marriage, or for a child of one of the spouses, provided by the husband out of the common property; see BGB 1465.

2   The same consequence follows in any case in which the marriage is dissolved by the re-marriage of one of the spouses after a judicial order declaring the other spouse to be dead—p. 451 note 4.   If the re-marriage is subsequently avoided the general community of goods is *ipso facto* reinstated.   If, on the other hand, the conjugal community is reinstated after an order of judicial separation the separation of goods continues, unless a new marriage contract providing for the reinstatement of the community of goods is made—BGB 1587.

The community may be dissolved by order of the Court on the wife's application in any of the following events:

(1) if the husband has without the wife's assent disposed of any part of the wife's property by any transaction requiring such assent and the wife's interests are seriously endangered thereby [1] ;

(2) if the husband has wilfully reduced the common property;

(3) if the husband fails to perform his duties as to the maintenance of the wife or of the issue of the marriage, and if their future maintenance is seriously endangered;

(4) if the husband is placed under guardianship on the ground of extravagance [2] ;

(5) if, by reason of the obligations incurred by the husband, the common property is charged with debts to such an extent that serious risk arises as to the wife's after-acquired property.

If, owing to the wife's liabilities, a similar risk arises as to the husband's after-acquired property, the community may be dissolved by the Court on the husband's application—BGB 1468, 1469.

The community may also be dissolved by post-nuptial marriage contract.

(b) Effect of dissolution.

On the dissolution of the community either spouse is entitled to claim a partition of the common property (*Auseinandersetzung*) in accordance with the rules mentioned below [3] ; the spouses are henceforth deemed to live under the régime of 'separation of goods'—415 sub (4), each spouse taking, as his property, the property apportioned to him on such partition or acquired after the date from which the dissolution operates. [4]   The rule as to the registration of the change of régime is the same as in the case of the revocation of the husband's right

---

1   Such a transaction would, as between husband and wife, be invalid, but it might be valid as between the husband and an innocent third party (this would happen if an immovable forming part of the common property had been registered in the land register in the husband's sole name and transferred by him to a *bona fide* purchaser).

2   If the husband is placed under guardianship on any other ground the community continues, the husband's guardian managing the common property in his place.

3   Where the dissolution of the community is ordered by the Court, the applicant may require the partition to operate as from the date of the application—BGB 1479.   As to partition by the Court, see *Gesetz über freiwillige Gerichtsbarkeit*, s. 99.

4   Property acquired, by way of substitution for any part of the common property, between the date of the dissolution and the date of the completion of the partition, accrues to the common property—BGB 1473.

of management and usufruct under the statutory régime.

During the period between the dissolution and the completion of the partition the management of the common property is vested in both spouses jointly.   The property must in the first instance be applied towards the payment of the common property liabilities [1] ; the residue is divided between the spouses in equal parts, but each spouse may claim the specific appropriation of certain specified kinds of objects contributed by him to the common property in part satisfaction of his share.   The rule as to the equal division of the residue is departed from in a case where on a divorce or judicial separation one of the spouses is declared to be the exclusively guilty party—422 sub (2).   In such a case the innocent party is entitled, at his option, either to claim a half share of the residue or a return of the value of his contributions to the common property; if a return of the contribution is claimed and its full value cannot be restored the deficiency is borne by the spouses in equal shares [2] —BGB 1470–1478.

517

In any case in which the death of one of the spouses causes the dissolution of the community, the part of the common property appropriated to his share forms part of his estate—BGB 1482, 1484 (3), 1510.

(8) Continuance of community after death of one of the spouses.

(a) General rules.

If, on the death of one of the spouses, any issue of the marriage between him and the surviving spouse are living, the community is continued between the surviving spouse and such issue, unless the continuance is excluded or prevented in one of the ways mentioned below—BGB 1483 (1).

If the community is continued the share of the deceased spouse is not deemed to belong to his estate, but passes to the issue in the same way as if under English law it had been settled upon the deceased spouse for life, with remainder to the issue surviving him. [3]

---

[1]   As to unmatured or disputed liabilities, and as to liabilities which, as between the spouses, are chargeable against one of them exclusively, see BGB 1475; as to the personal liability of the spouses after the partition of the common property, see BGB 1480, 1481.

[2]   Illustration: *H*, who has contributed £ 50, 000 to the common property, is divorced on *W*'s petition, he being declared the guilty party.   *W*, having contributed nothing will of course adopt the first alternative.   If she had contributed the £ 50, 000 and *H* had contributed nothing, she would have adopted the second alternative; if in such a case the value of the common property available for partition had amounted to £ 40, 000 she would obtain £ 40, 000 and have a personal claim against *H* for £ 5, 000.

[3]   This continuance of the community is of Germanic origin; it does not exist in French law.

The continuance of the community may be *excluded*: (1) by express provision in the contract providing for the general community of goods or in a subsequent contract; (2) by a testamentary disposition made by the spouse by whose death the marriage is dissolved; but such a disposition is inoperative, unless the testator was at its date entitled to deprive the surviving spouse of his compulsory portion (516) , or to obtain a judicial order for the dissolution of the community—BGB 1508, 1509.

The continuance of the community may in all cases be *prevented* by the refusal of the surviving spouse to accept such continuance—BGB 1484.

(b) Rights of issue.

If on the death of one of the spouses no issue other than issue of the marriage between the deceased spouse and the surviving spouse are living, the share of the deceased spouse becomes vested in such of the issue as are deemed his statutory heirs (475) .   The community, as from the death of the predeceasing spouse, is in such a case called a ' continued community ' *(fortgesezte Gütergemeinschaft)*.

If any issue of the deceased spouse other than the issue of the marriage between him and the surviving spouse are living such issue are entitled to the same rights as if the share of the deceased spouse belonged to his or her estate, and may claim satisfaction of their portions out of the common property, in so far as the separate property of the deceased spouse is insufficient for that purpose—BGB 1483.

Illustration 1: *W* dies intestate, leaving her surviving her husband *H*, and *A*, a child of the marriage, and *B*, a child by a former marriage.   She leaves no privileged or non-privileged separate property; the common property after payment of debts is valued at £ 8, 000.   Under the law of intestacy *B* is entitled to three-eighths of his mother's estate.   The value of the estate is deemed to be one-half of the net value of the common property.   *B* therefore receives objects of the value of £ 1, 500 out of the common property; the residue is the common property of *H* and *A*.

Either spouse may by a testamentary disposition assented to by the other spouse deprive any issue of his share in the continued community; the issue so deprived of his share may claim a compulsory portion out of the share of the deceased in the common property, without prejudice to his claims against the separate estate of such deceased—BGB 1511.

Illustration 2: *H* dies, leaving him surviving his wife *W*, and three children of the marriage, A, B, and C; H, by a testamentary disposition assented to by W, has excluded C from the continued community, but has made no testamentary disposition as to the distribution of his separate estate; the net value of the separate estate is £4, 000, and one-half of the net value of the common property £8, 000. C's statutory portion is one-fourth, his compulsory portion one-eighth of H's estate; he therefore receives £1, 000 out of the separate estate and £1, 000 out of the common property. [1]

(c) Alterations as to constitution of common property.

519   As shown above, the common property may be diminished by the claims of any issue of the deceased spouse, not being issue of his marriage with the surviving spouse, and also by the claims of any issue of that marriage excluded by testamentary disposition; on the other hand, the common property is increased by the following classes of property: (1) property accruing to the surviving spouse out of the separate estate of the deceased spouse [2]; (2) property accruing to the surviving spouse after the death of the deceased spouse—BGB 1485.

The rules as to what constitutes privileged or non-privileged property of the surviving spouse are not modified by the continuance of the community—BGB 1486.

(d) Rules as to management of common property and liability for debts.

The rules on these subjects which are applicable during the original community also apply during the continuance, but so that the surviving spouse takes the husband's place—BGB 1487.   The common property liabilities of the deceased spouse, as well as all the liabilities of the surviving spouse, are enforceable against the common property [3]—BGB 1488.

---

[1]   The claims of the issue of a former marriage are different in kind from the claims of any excluded issue.   Claimants of the first-mentioned class are entitled to an apportionment of objects representing their share in the property; in the case of claimants of the second class, the claim is for a sum of money representing the compulsory portion.

[2]   Illustration: In the case mentioned in Illustration 2 given above sub (b) W is entitled to one-fourth of H's separate estate; this one-fourth part having the value of £1, 000 is added to the common property. It follows that in that particular case the value of the common property remains as it was before, the £1, 000 paid out to C being counterbalanced by the £1, 000 newly contributed by W.

[3]   The liabilities of the participating issue are not charged on the common property, nor are they personally liable for the debts of the deceased or the surviving spouse—BGB 1489 (3).   As to the personal liability of the surviving spouse, see BGB 1489 (1) (2).

(e) Effect of death or renunciation of participating issue.

On the death of any participating issue during the continuance of the community, his issue (if any) are substituted in his place; the share of any participating issue who has died without leaving issue accrues to the surviving participating issue; if no participating issue survive, the whole of the common property becomes vested in the surviving spouse.   The share of any deceased issue is not deemed to form part of his estate—BGB 1490.

Any participating issue may renounce his share by declaration before the competent Court, or by agreement with the other participants. [1]   If the person   520 wishing to renounce his share is under parental power (441) or under guardianship (449) the leave of the Guardianship Court must be obtained in the first instance.   The renunciation has the same effect as the death without issue of the renouncing party—BGB 1491.

(f) Dissolution of continued community.

The continued community may be dissolved by the surviving spouse at any time, and is dissolved *ipso facto* by the re-marriage or death of the surviving spouse. The community may also be dissolved by the Court, on the application of any participating issue: (1) on grounds similar to those on which a community of goods between husband and wife may be dissolved on the application of one of the spouses—see above sub (7) (a) ; (2) on the ground that the surviving spouse has forfeited his parental power (442) in respect of the applicant or would have forfeited it if he had been entitled thereto—BGB 1492–1496.

The rules as to the effect of the dissolution are similar to those applied in the case of the dissolution of a community between husband and wife [2]—BGB 1497, 1498.

The surviving spouse takes one-half of the common property; the other half is divided among the participating issue on the same principles, as if such half were the residuary estate of the predeceasing spouse, and as if such spouse had

---

1   In such a case a payment may be made out of the common property in consideration of the renunciation.

2   As to the apportionment of the liabilities as between the parties, see BGB 1499, 1500, 1504.   As to the appropriation of specific objects, see BGB 1502, 1515.

died intestate, leaving no issue other than the participating issue [1] —BGB 1503 (1).

The predeceasing spouse may, by testamentary disposition made with the assent of the surviving spouse, reduce the share of any issue in the common property to a half of the statutory share, and may also on the same grounds as those on which a person entitled to a compulsory portion may be deprived thereof (516) deprive any issue of the whole of such share.   Any issue declared ' unworthy to inherit' (*erbunwürdig*)—480—forfeits his share in the continued community— BGB 1506, 1512–1514, 1516. [2]

cc.   Community of income and profits.

418. The régime of community of income and profits (*Errungenschaftsgemeinschaft*, *Communauté réduite aux acquêts*), as defined by the BGB, resembles the various systems which under the same name before 1900 formed the statutory régime in many parts of Germany; the same name is also given to one of the contractual régimes specially defined by the French Code, ss. 1498, 1499.   The main characteristic of this régime as defined by the BGB is that the common property is constituted exclusively by the earnings, profits, and income accruing to the spouses during the subsistence of the marriage (excluding, however, the income of the wife's privileged property and such other kinds of income as are excluded from the community by marriage contract).   All other property belonging to either spouse at the commencement of the community or accruing during its continuance, otherwise than by way of income, remains the separate property of such spouse.   Privileged separate property is only recognized in the wife's case and is formed of the same classes of property as constitute the wife's privileged property under the régime of general community of goods.   All other property belonging or accruing to either spouse not being in the nature of income is deemed non-privileged

---

1   Advances received during the lifetime of the predeceasing spouse must, as between the participating issue *inter se* be brought into hotchpot; any payment made out of the common property during the subsistence of the community in consideration of the renunciation of a share is deemed to have been made in part satisfaction of the moiety belonging to the issue; as between the issue *inter se* such payment is deemed to be made in part satisfaction of the claims of those who are benefited by the renunciation—BGB 1501, 1503.   As to the right of the participating issue to the restoration of gifts made by the spouses during their joint lives, for the purpose of supplementing their compulsory portions, see BGB 1505.

2   Any issue may also in the lifetime of both spouses renounce his right to a share in the continued community in the same manner as a share in an estate may be renounced in the lifetime of a testator or intestate—479, 485 (1) (*a*)—BGB 1517.

separate property of such spouse, with the effect that the income of such property becomes common property.   All property which cannot be proved to be separate property is deemed to be included in the common property—BGB 1519–1524, 1526, 1527. [1]

The management of the common property is governed by the same rules as under the régime of general community of goods—417 sub (3) (4)—BGB 1519 (2).

The wife's non-privileged property is managed by the husband as in the case of the statutory régime—BGB 1525.

The expenses of the household and all outgoings affecting either the common property or the non-privileged property of either spouse are payable out of the common property.   The husband's creditors can enforce their claims against the common property in the same way as under the régime of general community.

The rights of the wife's creditors in respect of the common property are more restricted than under the régime of general community of goods; thus, for instance, claims in respect of the wife's unlawful acts and claims in respect of liabilities incurred by her before the commencement of the community cannot be enforced against the common property—BGB 1529–1534.   The rules as to the apportionment of the liabilities as between the spouses also differ somewhat from the rules applicable under the régime of general community of goods—BGB 1535–1538, 1541. [2]

The husband as well as the wife may obtain a judicial order for the dissolution of the community on the same grounds as under the régime of general community of goods.   The wife may also obtain a judicial order for the dissolution of the community on the grounds on which, under the statutory régime, she may obtain an order for the revocation of the husband's rights of management and usufruct. The community is dissolved *ipso facto* on the grounds on which a general community of goods is dissolved *ipso facto*, [3] and also on the grounds on which the husband's powers are revoked *ipso facto* under the statutory régime—BGB 1542–1544.   It may also be dissolved by post-nuptial marriage contract.

---

[1]   As to the right of each spouse to claim an inventory of the non-privileged property, see BGB 1528.

[2]   In so far as the common property is benefited at the expense of the non-privileged separate property of either spouse or *vice versa*, the deficiency must on the dissolution of the community be made up out of the benefited property—BGB 1539.   As to the presumption in respect of consumable things withdrawn from the non-privileged separate property of either spouse, see BGB 1540.

[3]   The death of a spouse always dissolves the community of profits; a continued community cannot be stipulated for under this régime.

The rules as to the effects of the dissolution of the community are the same as under the régime of general community of goods; as regards the wife's non-privileged property the rules applicable on the revocation of the husband's rights of management and usufruct under the statutory régime apply.   If the dissolution of the community is brought about by any event other than the dissolution of the marriage by death or divorce, the régime of 'separation of goods' takes the place of the régime terminated by the dissolution—BGB 1545, 1546.

The reinstatement of the community of income and profits may be brought about on the same grounds as the reinstatement of the husband's rights of management and usufruct under the statutory régime; the wife may obtain a judicial order for the reinstatement of the community in any case in which it has been dissolved by reason of the husband's bankruptcy—BGB 1547, 1548.

dd.   Community of movables.

523   **419.** The 'community of movables and of income and profits' (*Gemeinschaft des beweglichen Vermögens und der Errungenschaft*)—generally described by the shorter name of 'community of movables' (*Fahrnissgemeinschaft*)—is an adaptation of the French statutory régime (*communauté légale*), which prior to 1900 formed the statutory régime in many parts of Germany. [1]   Under this régime the common property consists of all movables belonging to either spouse at the commencement of the community or acquired subsequently, whether in the nature of capital or of income (with the exception of the classes of objects mentioned below) and of all objects movable or immovable acquired in substitution for objects included in the common property.   All immovable property, [2] on the other hand, belonging to either spouse at the commencement of the community or accruing to him during its continuance remains separate property.

The separate property also includes: (1) inalienable objects; (2) objects declared to be separate property by marriage contract; (3) objects directed to be held as separate property by the testator or donor from whom they are derived. Privileged separate property is only recognized in the wife's case; it consists of such objects as are declared to have that character by marriage contract or by the

---

[1]   Under the French system immovables acquired after the marriage are included in the common property; under the new German system immovables are not included, unless they are acquired in substitution for any common property.

[2]   The expression 'immovable property' for this purpose includes all rights relating to immovables other than hypothecatory charges, land charges, and annuity charges—BGB 1551 (2).

testator or donor from whom they are derived, and of all objects acquired from the income of the privileged property, or in substitution for any objects forming part thereof.

A continuance of the community after the death of one of the spouses, in the event of there being any surviving issue, may be stipulated for by marriage contract, but while under the régime of general community of goods the continuance takes place unless excluded, the community under the régime now under discussion is dissolved on the death of one of the spouses, unless the contrary has been expressly provided.   In all other respects the rules as to the general community of goods are also applicable to the community of movables [1] —BGB 1549–1557.

5.   DIVORCE AND JUDICIAL SEPARATION [2]

a.   General Survey; Conflict of Laws.

420. The possibility of obtaining a divorce *a vinculo* did not become universal   524 in Germany before 1876.   In many parts of Germany (*e. g.* in Bavaria and Saxony) the only relief which a petitioner belonging to the Roman Catholic persuasion was able to obtain in respect of any matrimonial offence was 'perpetual separation' (*a mensa et toro*).   The Personal Status Act 1875 (which came into force on January 1, 1876) abolished perpetual separation orders and enacted that a divorce decree should be granted in any case in which a petitioner would under the former law have been entitled to a perpetual separation order.   Each of the two Drafting Commissions refused to alter this rule, but under the pressure of the Roman Catholic party a modified perpetual separation under the new name of 'dissolution of the conjugal community' (*Aufhebung der ehelichen Gemeinschaft*) was introduced into German law by the Reichstag, but so as to be convertible into a dissolution of the marriage at the option of either party (see 423).   In this treatise the term 'judicial separation' is used, though not a literal reproduction of the German term.

Under English law a judicial separation may be obtained on grounds which

---

[1]   As to the apportionment of liabilities between the separate property and the common property, see BGB 1556.

[2]   There are three ways in which marriage can be dissolved according to German law: (1) death; (2) divorce; (3) re-marriage in a case in which the other spouse though judicially declared to be dead is in fact living (see p. 451 note 4).

would not entitle the petitioner to a divorce; under German law a judicial separation cannot be obtained on any ground which would not be sufficient to establish a case for a divorce. The remedy is not intended as a minor remedy for minor offences, but as an alternative enabling petitioners to obtain matrimonial relief without a complete severance of the marriage tie.

The grounds on which a divorce or a judicial separation may be granted by a German Court, and the effects of a divorce decree or a separation order, are determined by the law of the State of which the husband is a subject at the date of the petition, but this rule is subject to four qualifications:

525 (1) the grounds must in any event be of a kind which would justify a divorce under German law; (2) a fact which has happened while the husband was a subject of a foreign State is not recognized as a ground for the relief claimed unless it would entitle the petitioner to obtain a divorce or separation under the law of such foreign State; (3) if the husband has ceased to be a German subject under circumstances under which the wife remains a German subject (39), German law is applied exclusively; (4) if the law, which under the principal rule is the governing law, refers back to German law, German law is applied exclusively—EG 17, 27.

Illustrations: 1. A German Court tries a petition brought by the wife of a French subject on the ground of a fact which under French law constitutes *injure grave*, but which is not a matrimonial offence under German law; the petition is dismissed. 2. The wife of a naturalized German subject claims a divorce on the ground of her husband's adultery committed while he was an Italian subject. The petition is successful, inasmuch as adultery, according to Italian law, though not a ground of divorce, is a ground of separation. 3. A Catholic husband has emigrated from Germany to Austria under circumstances under which his wife, being also a Catholic, was not bound to follow him, and having lost his German nationality by ten years' absence, has become naturalized in Austria. The wife claims a divorce in a German Court on a ground which is recognized as a ground of divorce by German law. Austrian law does not in any case allow Catholics to be divorced. The wife is entitled to a divorce. 4. A British subject domiciled in Germany petitions for a divorce in a German Court on the ground of the wife's wilful desertion. As according to English law the right to a divorce is entirely governed by the *lex fori* the case is determined by German law.

b.   Grounds of Divorce or Judicial Separation.

421. The grounds which entitle a petitioner to obtain a divorce or a judicial separation are sub-divided into 'absolute' and 'relative' grounds.   Where the facts constituting an absolute ground are established the petitioner is entitled to the order prayed for; in the case of a relative ground it is left to judicial discretion whether, under the special circumstances of the case, the relief ought to be granted.

The absolute grounds are: 526

(1) adultery, bigamy, and sodomy—BGB 1565 (1);

(2) attempts against the petitioner's life—BGB 1566;

(3) wilful desertion [1]—BGB 1567 (1).

The relative grounds are:

(1) any facts, by which the marital relation owing to any grave breach of marital duty, [2] or dishonourable or immoral conduct on the respondent's part, is disturbed to such an extent, that the petitioner cannot fairly be expected to continue the marriage—BGB 1568;

(2) insanity, having continued for more than three years during the marriage, and being of a kind so severe that the intellectual community between the spouses has ceased and that there is no hope of its re-establishment—BGB 1569.

The right to obtain a divorce on any ground other than the respondent's insanity is barred by condonation and may also be barred by lapse of time [3]; connivance in the case of adultery, bigamy or sodomy also bars the right—BGB 1565 (2), 1570–1573.   Facts which cannot, owing to lapse of time, form the foundation of a claim for divorce may be used for the purpose of corroborating other facts brought forward in support of the petition—BGB 1573.

---

[1]   Either of the following facts is deemed to constitute wilful desertion: (a) intentional disobedience to an order for the restitution of the conjugal community—412 sub (1)—continued for more than a year against the wishes of the other spouse; (b) intentional absence from the conjugal home against the wishes of the other spouse, continued for more than a year under circumstances under which personal service of any judicial process is impossible—BGB 1567 (2).

[2]   Gross ill-treatment is deemed a grave breach of duty within the meaning of the section.

[3]   The petition must be filed within six months reckoned from the time at which the petitioner became aware of the fact constituting a ground of divorce and at the latest within ten years after the happening of the fact—BGB 1571 (1); see also BGB 1571 (2) (3) (4), 1572.

c.   Effect of Divorce Decree. [1]

(1) *Dissolution of marriage.*

422. A divorce decree has the effect of dissolving the marriage as from the date on which it ceases to be appealable—BGB 1564.   From that date the spouses cease to be husband and wife and the general effects of marriage as well as the effects of the matrimonial régime come to an end, but new duties may spring up between the parties under the rules stated below.

(2) *Special liabilities of guilty party.*

If a marriage is dissolved on any ground other than the respondent's insanity the divorce decree must declare the dissolution of the marriage to be due to the respondent's fault; where in any such a case a cross-petition on the respondent's part is equally successful or where facts are proved, which show that the respondent would have been successful if he had filed a cross-petition, or that condonation or lapse of time would have been the only reason preventing his success, the decree must on the respondent's application also declare the petitioner to be in fault— BGB 1574.   If only one of the spouses is declared to be the guilty party, he incurs certain liabilities and becomes subject to certain disabilities—see below sub (3) to (6).   For the sake of brevity the party declared to be guilty to the exclusion of the other will in the further course of this treatise be described as the 'exclusively guilty party'.

(3) *Right of innocent party to alimony.*

If the former husband is the exclusively guilty party he must supply the former wife with maintenance suitable to her station in life, in so far as she is unable to obtain such maintenance from the income of her property or from her earnings. [2]

If the former wife is the exclusively guilty party, she must supply the husband

---

1   The effects referred to sub (2) to (6) also result in the case of an order for judicial separation— see 423.

2   The wife's earnings are taken into consideration in so far only as under the special circumstances under which the spouses have been living it is usual for the wife to earn money by her work—BGB 1578 (1). As to the reduction or removal of the liability to supply maintenance in case of the poverty of the exclusively guilty party, see BGB 1579; as to the manner in which maintenance has to be supplied, see BGB 1580 and 432.

with maintenance in accordance with his station in life, in so far as he is unable to maintain himself.

A petitioner, who obtains a divorce on the ground of the respondent's insanity, is under the same liability in respect of the maintenance of the latter, as   528 if he were the exclusively guilty party in the case of a divorce obtained on any other ground.

The right to receive maintenance is forfeited by re-marriage. [1]

On the death of the exclusively guilty party his heirs become liable in his place—BGB 1578, 1581 (1), 1582 (1), 1583.

(4) *Family name of divorced wife.*

A divorced wife, if not the exclusively guilty party, is entitled to retain her former husband's family name; if she is the exclusively guilty party the former husband may compel her to resume her maiden name; she may do so in any event.   She may also, in any case in which she is not the exclusively guilty party, resume the name which she had immediately before the marriage with the husband from whom she is divorced—BGB 1577.

(5) *Custody and maintenance of infant children.*

If the marriage is dissolved on any ground other than the insanity of one of the spouses, and either spouse is declared the exclusively guilty party, the custody and care of the infant children belong to the innocent party; if both parties are declared to be guilty, the mother has the custody and care of the sons, who have not attained the age of six years, and of all the infant daughters; the father in such a case has the custody and care of the infant sons who have attained the age of six years.   The Guardianship Court may provide differently, if a modification of the ordinary rule appears desirable in the infants' interest.   A parent who is deprived of the care and custody of any child is entitled to have access to such child; the manner in which such access is to be given may be regulated by the Guardianship Court—BGB 1635, 1636.

No special provision is made as regards cases in which a marriage is dissolved on the ground of the insanity of one of the spouses, as insanity would in any event cause the suspension of any parental power which might otherwise be   529

---

1   The re-marriage of the guilty party may have the effect of increasing or reducing the liability, as his or her financial position may improve or deteriorate by the re-marriage—see BGB 1581 (2).

vested in such spouse (442).¹

The duties of the spouses as to the maintenance of their children (431, 432) are not modified by the divorce; where such duty falls on the husband, and the maintenance cannot be supplied out of the children's own income, the wife has to contribute a reasonable part of her income and earnings.   If the maintenance of any child who is in the wife's custody is endangered, she may retain her contribution for the purpose of providing for such maintenance—BGB 1585.

(6) *As to the restoration of gifts.*

The right of the innocent party to revoke gifts made to the guilty party has been referred to above—202 rule (5)—BGB 1584.

d. Judicial Separation.

423. A spouse, who is entitled to petition for a divorce, may claim judicial separation in lieu of divorce.   The order obtained on any such petition must declare the separation to be due to the fault of one or both of the parties in the same manner as on a petition for divorce.   If the respondent requires the Court to grant a divorce decree in the place of the judicial separation claimed in the petition the Court must give effect to his application.   While the parties are living apart under an order for judicial separation, either of them is at any time entitled to obtain a divorce decree—BGB 1575, 1576 (1).

An order for judicial separation has all the effects of a divorce decree except the dissolution of the marriage.   The parties may at any time restore the conjugal community, in which event the effects of the separation are removed *ipso facto*, but the property of the spouses is, on the resumption of the conjugal community, held under the régime of separation of goods—415 sub (4), whatever the previously existing régime may have been—BGB 1576, 1586, 1587.

---

1   Where a marriage is dissolved by the re-marriage of one of the spouses while the other, though judicially declared to be dead, is living, the same rules are applied as in a case where a divorce is declared to be due to the fault of both parties—BGB 1637.

CHAPTER II
PARENT AND CHILD

1. KINSHIP AND AFFINITY

a. General Rules.

424. Two persons, of whom one is a descendant of the other, are deemed to 530 be kindred in the direct line (*in gerader Linie verwandt*). Two persons, not being kindred in the direct line, but having a common ancestor, are kindred in the collateral line (*in der Seitenlinie verwandt*). The degree of kinship is determined by the number of the births by which the connexion between the two persons concerned is effected. [1]

According to English law there can be no kinship between a person born out of wedlock and any other person except his issue; according to German law, on the other hand, there is kinship between an illegitimate child and its mother, and consequently also between the child and the mother's kindred. There is, however, no kinship between an illegitimate child and its father.

In the case of husband and wife, the kindred of one are deemed to be relatives by marriage (*verschwägert*) of the other. A person thus related by marriage to one of two spouses, is deemed to be related to him in the line and the degree in which he is related to the spouse to whose kindred he belongs—BGB 1589, 1590.

b. Rules as to establishment of Paternity and Legitimacy.

aa. As to children born in wedlock.

425. In the same way as under English law, a child is presumed to be the

---

1 Where the kinship is in the collateral line, it is necessary to go back to the common ancestor; thus brothers are kindred in the second degree, first cousins are kindred in the fourth degree, nephews in the third degree, &c. The rules on this subject are those of the Roman civil law, which have also been adopted in England and which differ from those of the Canon law.

legitimate issue of a marriage, if born during the subsistence of such marriage,

531   without regard to the length of the period which has elapsed between the marriage and the birth, and a child born after the dissolution of a marriage is presumed to be the legitimate issue of such marriage, if the date of the birth is not too far removed from the date of the dissolution of the marriage.

Under English law there is no fixed presumption as to the length of the period of gestation, but German law presumes that such period is not shorter than 181 days or longer than 302 days. [1]   The time intervening between the 302nd day and the 181st day before the birth is called 'the period of possible conception' (*Empfängnisszeit*)—BGB 1592 (1).

The particulars of the German rules on the presumption of legitimacy are as follows:

(1) a child born in wedlock is legitimate, whether conceived before or after the marriage, if the husband during the period of possible conception has cohabited with the wife, unless it is clearly impossible under the particular circumstances that the husband is the child's father [2]—BGB 1591 (1);

(2) in so far as the period of possible conception falls within the time of the subsistence of the marriage, cohabitation between the spouses is presumed—BGB 1591 (2);

(3) in so far as the period of possible conception falls within a period of time preceding the marriage, cohabitation is presumed if the husband dies prior to the birth of the child without having taken proceedings to dispute its legitimacy—BGB 1591 (2);

(4) the illegitimacy of a child born during wedlock, or within 302 days after the dissolution of the marriage between its mother and her husband, cannot be alleged for any purpose, unless the husband has within the prescribed period taken proceedings for disputing the legitimacy or has died before the expiration of

532   that period.   The husband forfeits his right to take such proceedings if at any time

---

[1]   If it can be proved by evidence that a child was conceived more than 302 days before the date of its birth such proof is accepted for the purpose of establishing the child's legitimacy. —BGB 1592 (2).

[2]   Under English law the child of a mother who re-marries after the dissolution of the first marriage, born at a time at which it might be the child of either husband, is called 'more than ordinarily legitimate', and can, according to some authorities, select its father on attaining full age (Kerr's Blackstone, 4th ed., vol. i, p. 432).   Under German law a child born under such circumstances is deemed to be the child of the first husband if born within a period of 270 days from the time of the dissolution of the marriage; if born at any later time it is deemed to be the second husband's child. —BGB 1600.

after the child's birth he acknowledges the child as his child [1]—BGB 1593–1598 (1) (2).

bb.   As to children born out of wedlock.

426. A child born out of wedlock may be legitimated in one of the modes specified below (427); unless and until this is done, such a child is an illegitimate child, and, as mentioned above, is not deemed to belong to its father's kindred. Notwithstanding this fact the father is under certain liabilities both as regards the child and the child's mother, and for this purpose certain rules are laid down by which the paternity of an illegitimate child is determined. [2]   These rules are as follows:

(1) any person who, during the period of possible conception, has co-habited with the mother of an illegitimate child is deemed to be the father of such child unless this is clearly impossible under the particular circumstances, or unless it can be proved that another person also cohabited with the mother during the same period (*exceptio plurium concumbentium*) [3] —BGB 1717;

(2) a person who by public act (97), executed after the birth of an illegitimate child, acknowledges himself to be the father of such child can no longer avail himself of the *exceptio plurium concumbentium*—BGB 1718.

cc.   Legitimation.

(1) By subsequent marriage of parents.

427. *Legitimatio per subsequens matrimonium* is a mode of legitimation introduced by the Canon law and recognized in most civilized countries except in England and certain colonies and countries in which the English law on the   533 subject has been introduced and retained.   The German rules on the subject are as follows:

(1) an illegitimate child on the marriage of its father with its mother takes

---

[1]   As to the time for taking proceedings and the nature of the proceedings, see BGB 1594–1597; as to the formal and material requirements for the validity of the acknowledgment of the child's legitimacy, see BGB 1598 (3), 1599.

[2]   Under French law the well-known rule *la recherche de la paternité est interdite*—Code Civil, s. 340—prevents inquiries as to the paternity of an illegitimate child, but an illegitimate child formally acknowledged by its father becomes entitled to certain rights, see Code Civil, ss. 334–338, 756–766.

[3]   The *exceptio plurium concumbentium* can be rebutted by proof of the fact that the other person concerned cannot possibly be the father—BGB 1717 (1).

the status of a legitimate child in relation to its parents as well as to their kindred [1] ;

(2) the mother's husband is deemed to be the father of the illegitimate child if he has cohabited with the child's mother during the ' period of possible conception', unless it is clear under the particular circumstances of the case that the child could not have been conceived during such cohabitation;

(3) if the mother's husband acknowledges the child after its birth by public act (97), his cohabitation with the mother during the ' period of possible conception' is presumed;

(4) if the marriage between the child's parents is relatively void, the child is in the same position as a child born during the subsistence of a relatively void marriage—409 sub (2) rule (b);

(5) the issue of any child who dies before the date of its parents' marriage are by such marriage placed in the position in which they would have been if such child had survived the date of the marriage—BGB 1719–1722.

(2) *Legitimation by order of a public authority.*

The legitimation by order of a public authority (*Ehelichkeitserklärung*)— which corresponds to the *legitimatio per rescriptum principis* of Roman law—enables the father of an illegitimate child to give such child the status of legitimacy without marrying the mother, and even while married to a wife other than the mother of the legitimated child.   The rules on this subject are as follows:

534   (1) the public authority, designated for that purpose by the Government of the State of which the child's father is a subject, may make the order on the father's application; it is left entirely to the discretion of the competent authority to grant or to refuse the application, but the order cannot in any case be made unless the requirements mentioned below are complied with; the order must be unconditional and immediately operative;

(2) the father in his application must acknowledge the child as his child, but the validity of the legitimation cannot be impugned on the ground that the applicant is not truly the child's father;

---

[1]   In the case of princely and certain noble families, and also with respect to the right of succession as regards entailed estates or family settlements, this rule may be altered by State legislation—EG 58, 59. English law, though recognizing the legitimacy of a child legitimated by the marriage of its parents in accordance with the law of the father's domicil at the date of the child's birth, does not allow a child born out of wedlock to become entitled by descent to land situate in England.   Birtwhistle *v.* Vardill 2 Cl. & F. 571, 7 Cl. & F. 895, 51 R. R. 139.

(3) the following persons must give their authorization: (*a*) the child; (*b*) the child's mother if the child's age is less than 21 years; (*c*) the father's wife, if he is married [1];

(4) legitimation cannot take place if at the time of the conception of the child its parents were unable to contract a valid marriage on the ground of closeness of kinship or affinity;

(5) legitimation cannot take place after the death of the child; it can take place after the father's death if the application was made prior to such death;

(6) the effects of an order of legitimation are not quite so extensive as the effects of legitimation by subsequent marriage; the order establishes ties of kinship between the father and the child and the child's issue, but it does not establish ties of kinship between the child and the father's kindred, or ties of affinity between the child and the father's wife, or between the father and the child's spouse;

(7) the legitimation deprives the child's mother of her parental power, which, however, is restored in certain specified events; the mother is not bound to maintain the child, in so far as maintenance is supplied by the father;

(8) If the father wishes to marry while the legitimated child is under his parental power, he has to comply with the same rules as the father of a child born in wedlock who wishes to re-marry—446 sub (3)—BGB 1723–1725, 1726 (1), 1732–1740. [2]

(3) *Conflict of laws as to legitimation.*

The question whether and in what manner legitimation can be effected—in   535
the view of German law—depends on the law of the father's nationality at the time of the intended legitimation, but where the child intended to be legitimated is a German subject, the legitimation is inoperative, unless the consent of such child and of its mother—as required by German law—is obtained—EG 22.

Illustrations: 1. A British subject marries the German mother of his child in Germany.   The child is not legitimated by the marriage.   2. The subject of a country, in which a child can be legitimated by a public authority without the child's or mother's consent, obtains an order in his own country legitimating his

---

[1]   The mother's, and also the wife's authorization is dispensed with in certain events; if the mother refuses her authorization it may be replaced by the leave of the Guardianship Court in any case in which the child would be unduly injured by the failure of the attempted legitimation—BGB 1726 (3), 1727, 1735.

[2]   As to certain details connected with the procedure on an application for an order of legitimation, see BGB 1726 (2), 1728–1731.

infant child, being the child of a German mother, without obtaining the consent required by German law.   The child is not deemed legitimate by a German Court.

Under English law a child legitimated by the subsequent marriage of its parents is deemed to be legitimate, if such legitimation is authorized by the law of the place in which the child's father was domiciled at the date of the child's birth as well as by the law of the place in which he was domiciled at the date of his marriage with the child's mother—*In re* Grove 40 Ch. D. 216.   English law does not, however, give full effect to the legitimation brought about under the rules of foreign law; for though recognizing the status of a legitimated child under the particular circumstances of any case, it does not in any event allow a child born out of wedlock to inherit English realty as heir—see p. 496 note 1.

dd.   *Adoption.*

(1) *General rules.*

428. Adoption enables the adoptor to place the child of another into the same position as if it were his own.   A husband and his wife may together adopt a child as their joint adopted child.   Adoption is effected by a contract between the adoptor or the joint adoptors of the one part and the adopted child of the other part, which, however, requires the confirmation of the competent Court; the confirmation cannot be refused if the statutory requirements are complied with— BGB 1741, 1749, 1754.

(2) *Statutory requirements.* [1]

(*a*) *As to person of adoptor.*

A person having natural legitimate issue cannot adopt a child, but the fact that another child has been previously adopted is no impediment.   The adoptor must be at least 50 years old, and be at least 18 years older than the adopted child [2] —BGB 1741, 1743, 1744.

(*b*) *As to authorization.*

A married adoptor as well as a married adopted child requires his spouse's authorization; where a child below the age of 21 years is adopted, the authorization

536

---

[1]   In the case of joint adoption each adoptor has to conform with the requirements which according to the statement in the text have to be conformed with by the adoptor.

[2]   Dispensation may—within certain limits—be granted as to the requirements in respect of age—see BGB 1745.

of the parents is also required; if the child is illegitimate the mother's authorization is sufficient [1] —BGB 1746, 1747.

(c) As to contract.

The declarations of the parties must be made by them respectively in person, but if the adopted child has not attained the age of 14, its statutory agent may, with the leave of the Guardianship Court, make the required declaration on the child's behalf.   If either the adoptor or the adopted child is of restricted capacity the leave of the Guardianship Court must be obtained in addition to the assent of the statutory agent [2] —BGB 1750, 1751.   The contract must be unconditional and intended to be immediately operative—BGB 1742.   The contracting parties are bound by the contract, but the child does not acquire the status of an adopted child before the confirmation of the contract by the Court; the contract becomes inoperative if the child dies before its confirmation, or if the adoptor dies before having filed his application for confirmation—BGB 1753, 1754 (1).

537

(3) Effect of adoption. [3]

(a) As between the adoptor and the adopted child.

A child adopted by a single adoptor acquires the adoptor's name and the status of a legitimate child of such adoptor [4]; a child adopted by a husband and wife jointly acquires the husband's name and the status of a legitimate child of both spouses.   Any issue of the adopted child living at the time of the adoption, who are not parties to the contract of adoption, and any after-born issue of such issue are excluded from the effects of the adoption; all other issue of the adopted child acquire the same status, as if the adopted child were a legitimate child of the adoptor or adoptors.   No ties of kinship are created between the adopted child and the adoptor's kindred, and no tie of affinity is created between the adopted child and a single adoptor's spouse, or between an adoptor and the adopted

---

[1]   As to the events in which the authorization is dispensed with, see BGB 1746, 1747; as to the manner in which it has to be declared, see BGB 1748.

[2]   As to the conditions on which leave is dependent in a case where a guardian wishes to adopt his ward or his former ward, see BGB 1752; as to the effect of a voidable contract or voidable authorization, see BGB 1755.

[3]   The contract may exclude the adoptor's right to the usufruct of the child's property or the child's rights of inheritance; subject to these exceptions the effect of adoption cannot be modified by contract—BGB 1767.

[4]   A child adopted by a married woman takes the name which such married woman had before her marriage—BGB 1758.

child's spouse—BGB 1757, 1758, 1762, 1763.

An adoptor does not by virtue of the adoption become entitled to any right of inheritance in respect of the child's property.   A single adoptor has the same rights during the adopted child's infancy as a father entitled to the exercise of the parental power (441) [1] ; in case of his marriage the same rules are applicable— *mutatis mutandis*—as on the re-marriage of a person having legitimate issue by a former marriage—446 sub 3; joint adoptors are during the child's infancy in the position of parents—BGB 1757, 1759, 1761.

(b) *As between the adopted child and its natural kindred.*

538   By virtue of the adoption the natural parents of an adopted legitimate child lose their parental power, and the natural mother of an adopted illegitimate child loses the custody and care of the child, but the parental power, custody, and care are restored in certain specified events.   The natural kindred of the adopted child are not liable for its maintenance in so far as such maintenance is supplied by the adoptor or adoptors.   In all other respects the rights and duties arising from the kinship between the adopted child and its natural kindred are not modified by the adoption—BGB 1764, 1765, 1766.

(4) *Revocation of adoption.*

The adoption may at any time during the child's lifetime be revoked by contract between the adoptor or adoptors [2] of the one part and the child of the other part; after the child's death this may be done by contract between the adoptor or adoptors of the one part and the other persons affected by the adoption of the other part.   The revocation is subject to the same rules—*mutatis mutandis*—, as to its confirmation by the Court and otherwise, as the contract of adoption—BGB 1768 (1) (2), 1769, 1770.

The contract of adoption is revoked *ipso facto* by a marriage between the adoptor and the adopted child—BGB 1771.

The revocation of the adoption cancels the effects of the adoption. [3]

---

1   As to the duty to submit an inventory to the Guardianship Court, see BGB 1760.

2   Where two spouses are the adoptors, the right of revocation is exercised by them jointly during their joint lives and by the survivor after the death of one of them—BGB 1768 (3), 1769.

3   As to the change of name brought about by the revocation, see BGB 1772.

(5) *Conflict of laws.*

The rules as to conflict of laws are the same—*mutatis mutandis*—as those relating to legitimation—EG 22.

2. MUTUAL RIGHTS AND DUTIES AS TO MAINTENANCE (*Unterhaltspflicht*)

a.   As between Kindred.

aa.   Comparison between German and English law.

429. The rules as to the duty of kindred to supply maintenance to each other differ materially from the corresponding rules of English law.   Under English law   539 the person entitled to maintenance has no direct claim against the person bound to maintain him; the failure to provide maintenance where, in any case, it can be provided, and ought to be provided, is a criminal offence, but the right to maintenance cannot be enforced by civil proceedings.   Under German law, on the other hand, the right to maintenance can be enforced like an obligatory right.

A material difference also exists between the two systems of law, as to the kind of maintenance which has to be supplied; under English law a person bound to supply maintenance has done his duty as long as he keeps the persons dependent on him 'out of the workhouse' or—to speak more correctly—as long as such persons are not in need of parochial relief; under German law, on the other hand, the maintenance to be supplied must, as a general rule, enable the recipient to live in accordance with his station in life.

bb.   Persons liable to supply maintenance.

430. Any person able to support himself in accordance with his station in life [1] is bound to supply maintenance to any of his kindred in the direct line who are

---

1   For the purpose of ascertaining a wife's or an infant's ability to supply maintenance to any kindred the income of the wife's non-privileged property—414 sub (2)—is deemed the wife's income, and the income of the infant's property is deemed the infant's income (447), notwithstanding the husband's or parents' usufruct—414 sub (5), 447.   The income of any property common to the spouses under the contractual régime (417) is, for the purpose of the rules deemed to be the income of the spouse liable to supply maintenance to his kindred—BGB 1604, 1605.   A husband who has the usufruct of his wife's non-privileged property is liable jointly with his wife in respect of any maintenance payable out of such property—BGB 1386, 1388. Where there is common property the corpus of such common property is liable for the husband's and wife's liabilities as to maintenance, and the husband is also liable jointly with the wife in respect of her liabilities—BGB 1459, 1530 (2), 1534, 1549.

unable to support themselves (431).   Parents are liable to maintain their unmarried infant children, even if they have to reduce their standard of life for that purpose, unless some other person liable to supply maintenance is able to maintain such children, or unless such children's maintenance can be supplied out of the income or corpus of their property.   In so far as any person otherwise liable to supply maintenance is excused on the ground of the insufficiency of his means, the person who is next in order as to the duty to supply maintenance to the necessitous kindred becomes subject to the liability of the person so excused. [1] If the spouse of the person requiring maintenance [2] is able to supply such maintenance without imperilling his own means of subsistence, having regard to his station in life, his liability ranks before the liability of the kindred; if he would have to reduce his standard of life for the purpose of supplying the maintenance, the kindred are liable in the first instance.   Among the kindred the liabilities rank as follows: (a) the issue are liable before the ancestors; among the issue such of them as on the death of the necessitous relative would be entitled to statutory portions (475) are liable to supply the required maintenance collectively, each of them contributing a share corresponding to his statutory portion; (b) among the ancestors those of nearer degree are liable before those of remoter degree; those of the same degree are liable in equal shares [3] —BGB 1601, 1603, 1606, 1607 (1), 1608 (1).

Illustration: (1) W, being unable to maintain herself is married to H, who is unable to work, and whose income is only sufficient to allow him to support himself in accordance with his station in life; the issue consist of A, a son, and B and C, sons of a deceased daughter, all being able to supply maintenance to W; A's contribution is half of the sum required, B and C contribute the other half in equal shares; (2) if W, in the case mentioned in Ill. 1, has no issue and no parents living at the time in question, but her paternal grandfather and grandmother, and her maternal grandfather are living, and able respectively to supply the

---

[1]   The person who is next in order is also liable if the party liable in the first place cannot conveniently be sued in a German Court—BGB 1607 (2).

[2]   A divorced or separated spouse liable to supply maintenance, or a former spouse liable to supply maintenance under the rule stated above—p. 451 note 4, is for the purpose of the rule in the same position as a spouse—BGB 1608 (2).

[3]   The father's liability, by way of exception from the general rule, ranks before the mother's liability, unless the mother has the usufruct of the necessitous child's property, in which event the order is reversed— BGB 1606 (2).

maintenance, each has to contribute one third.

cc.   *Persons entitled to maintenance.*

431. Only such persons are, as a general rule, entitled to be supplied with   541
maintenance, as are unable to maintain themselves either by their earnings or
from the income or corpus of their property.   A person who in his station in life
is not expected to earn his own living (*e. g.* a lady belonging to the leisured
classes, a person preparing himself for the government service, or for one of the
learned professions) is deemed to be unable to obtain any earnings.   An
unmarried infant may claim maintenance from its parents before resorting to the
corpus of its property, except in so far as the parents if providing such maintenance
would have to lower their standard of life—BGB 1602.

dd.   *Nature of maintenance to be supplied.*

432. As mentioned above, the nature of the maintenance depends, as a
general rule, upon the station in life of the recipient, and must be suitable to
such station (*standesmässiger Unterhalt*).   It includes the whole cost of living
and, in the case of persons requiring education, also the cost of such education,
and of the preparation for any profession or calling.   The maintenance is, however,
reduced to the bare necessaries of life, if the condition of the person concerned
was caused by his own misconduct.   The same result happens if the person
requiring maintenance has committed certain specified offences affecting the
kindred liable to supply maintenance—BGB 1610, 1611.

As a general rule the maintenance has to be supplied by means of a fixed
annuity payable in advance by quarterly instalments; but where the parents of an
unmarried child are liable to supply such maintenance they may determine in
what manner it is to be provided, unless the Guardianship Court on any special
ground directs otherwise—BGB 1612.

ee.   *As to past and future maintenance.*

433. The expenses of past maintenance can only be claimed as from the date
at which the person liable to supply it was in *mora solvendi* (152), or at which
proceedings for the assertion of the right to maintenance were instituted.

An agreement waiving the claim to future maintenance is void. [1]   542

The right to maintenance becomes extinguished by the death of the person

---

1   As to any payment made before maturity, see BGB 1614.

entitled thereto, and also by the death of the person liable to supply it, except as regards such claims for past maintenance as are admissible under the rule stated above, or such instalments payable in advance as have fallen due prior to the death [1]—BGB 1613, 1614.

ff.   Conflict of laws.

434. The reciprocal duties as to maintenance between the parents and any legitimate child, and between the mother and an illegitimate child, are determined by German law if the parent, whose nationality is decisive, is a German.   In the case of a legitimate child the father's nationality is decisive as long as the father is living; if he is dead the mother's nationality is decisive.   In the case of an illegitimate child the mother's nationality is decisive.   Where the parent, whose nationality is decisive, has ceased to be a German subject, German law is still applied by German Courts, in so far as the child, whose right or duty as to maintenance is in question, remains a German subject—EG 19, 20.   No statutory rule exists as to the choice of law in any case in which the rights or duties as to the maintenance of any remoter kindred are in question.

b.   Liability of an Illegitimate Child's Father.

aa.   As to the child's maintenance.

435. The father of an illegitimate child (426) is bound to supply such child with maintenance in accordance with the mother's station in life (including the cost of education, as in the case of a legitimate child) from the date of its birth down to the completion of its sixteenth year; the maintenance is to be continued after that time, if the child, by reason of physical or mental defects, is unable to support itself; the father is released from the last-mentioned liability in so far as its discharge would deprive him of his own means of subsistence, having regard to his station in life.   The father's liability to maintain the illegitimate child ranks before the liability of the mother and her kindred. [2]   The maintenance must be

543

---

[1]   The funeral expenses of a necessitous relative have to be paid by the party liable to supply maintenance in so far as the payment of such expenses cannot be obtained from the heirs of the deceased—BGB 1615 (2).

[2]   The mother and her kindred are kindred of the illegitimate child (424) and therefore come under the ordinary rules.

supplied by means of an annuity payable in advance by quarterly instalments. [1] The claim is not extinguished by the father's death, even if such death comes before the child's birth, but the father's heirs may compound for the liability of the deceased by paying to the illegitimate child an amount equal to the compulsory portion (513) which such child would have taken, if it had been a legitimate child.   The cost of past maintenance may be claimed; a gratuitous renunciation of the claim for future maintenance is void; a renunciation for valuable consideration requires the sanction of the Guardianship Court—BGB 1708-1714.

A child deemed illegitimate on the ground that its parents' marriage was declared void [2] on any ground other than a fatal defect in the marriage ceremony (410) is entitled to maintenance from its father in the same manner as a legitimate child—BGB 1703.

bb.   As to maintenance of child's mother during confinement.

436. The father must pay to the mother the cost of the confinement and of her maintenance during the six weeks following the confinement, and must also repay to her any special outlay incurred by reason of her pregnancy or her confinement. The claim is not extinguished by the death of the father prior to the child's birth, or by the fact that the child is stillborn [3]—BGB 1715.

cc.   Conflict of laws.

437. The father's duties both as regards the maintenance of an illegitimate child, and as to the maintenance of the child's mother during her confinement,   544 are determined by the law of the State of which the mother is a subject at the date of the child's birth; a German Court will not, however, in any case enforce claims as to the maintenance of any illegitimate child or of its mother which go beyond the claims allowed by German law—EG 21.

---

[1]   As to proceedings before the birth of the child, see BGB 1716.

[2]   This can only happen, if the nullity or voidability of the marriage was known to both parties; if it was unknown to one of them, or if one of them was under duress, the children of the marriage, as mentioned above (409) are legitimate, notwithstanding the nullity of the marriage—BGB 1699.

[3]   It will be seen that the liabilities of the father of an illegitimate child are, under German law, of a much more extensive nature than under English law.

3. OTHER RIGHTS AND DUTIES ARISING FROM
PARENTAL RELATION

a. General statement.

438. The parental relation creates a number of miscellaneous rights and duties which have some similarity to the rights and duties which exist between husband and wife as part of the general effects of marriage (412).   These miscellaneous rights and duties are supplemented by certain definite rights exercisable by one of the parents (generally the father) as to the person and property of infant children, which rights are collectively described by the term ' parental power' (*Elterliche Gewalt*) , and which, in so far as they relate to the children's property, may fitly be compared with the husband's rights arising under the matrimonial régime (413).

b. Conflict of laws.

439. The rules as to the conflict of laws, as regards both the miscellaneous rights and duties and the parental power, are the same as those regulating the conflict of laws as to maintenance (434)—EG 19, 20.

c. Miscellaneous Rights and Duties.

(1) *As to family name.*

440. A legitimate child takes the father's family name.   An illegitimate child takes the mother's family name unless the mother's name has been changed by her marriage, in which case the child takes the mother's former name; the husband may, however, with the mother's and child's authorization, give the child his own name by a publicly certified act (97) before a competent authority—BGB 1616, 1706.

(2) *As to assistance in household work and business.*

545   A child, while residing in the parental home and educated and maintained by its parents, [1] is bound to render them such services in the household work or

---

[1]   An illegitimate child stands in the same position to the mother as a legitimate child to the parents— BGB 1705.   For the sake of brevity the rules in the text are expressed with reference to legitimate children and their relations to their parents, but it will be understood that they also refer to illegitimate children and their relations to their mother, unless the contrary appears from the context.

business as may reasonably be expected, having regard to the child's ability to render services, and the station in life of the parents concerned—BGB 1617.

(3) As to property.

The rules as to the management of the property of infant children come under the head of parental power.   As regards children of full age remaining in the parental home, the following rules are applied: (a) any outlay for the benefit of the household or of the parents is presumed to be made without the expectation of repayment; (b) if the whole or part of any child's property is handed over to one of the parents for the purpose of being managed by him, he is presumed to have the right to appropriate the net income remaining after the discharge of necessary outgoings—BGB 1618, 1619.

(4) As to outfit and advancement. [1]

A father is bound to supply any daughter who marries with an ' outfit ', suitable to her station in life, if he can do so without imperilling his own means of subsistence having regard to his station in life, and in so far as the daughter's own property is insufficient for the purpose.   If the father is dead or unable to supply the outfit, the duty to supply the outfit is transferred to the mother.   The right to receive an outfit is not transferable, and is barred after the lapse of a year from the date of the marriage.   The outfit may be refused: (a) if a daughter marries without the required parental authorization; (b) if she commits certain specified offences affecting the person liable to supply the outfit; (c) if she has received an outfit on the occasion of a previous marriage—BGB 1620–1623.

The transfer of any property to any child by way of ' advancement ', whether made in satisfaction of any legal obligation or otherwise, is not deemed a ' gift ' (200), except in so far as its value appears excessive under the special circumstances; but as regards warranty of title and quality, the rules relating to

546

---

1   The term ' outfit' is used as an equivalent for the German term ' Aussteuer' which comprises the whole of the furniture and household implements required on the foundation of a home as well as the wife's so-called ' trousseau '.   It is customary in Germany for the wife's father to supply the whole outfit.   The term ' advancement ' is used as an equivalent for the German term ' Ausstattung ' which includes any property transferred to a child by its father or mother, for the purpose of founding or preserving a home, or establishing a position in life for such child.   The term ' advancement ' therefore comprises the ' outfit ' given to a daughter as well as any dowry given to her, or any sum of money or other property given to a son on his marriage, or on his acquiring the ownership of a business, or joining a partnership or being admitted to a profession.

gifts are applied in all cases—BGB 1624.

Where the parent who, under the rules as to parental power, has the management of an infant child's property, transfers any property to such child by way of advancement, the intention to provide such advancement out of such child's property is presumed—BGB 1625.

d.   Parental Power.

aa.   Introductory observations.

441. The rules of the BGB as to 'parental power' represent a compromise between the principles governing the *patria potestas* of Roman law and the ideas underlying the Germanic 'right of wardship' over infant children.   The Roman paterfamilias who had powers over the issue under his *potestas*, whether infants or of full age, had to surrender some of his privileges in the later stages of Roman law, but he always retained the right of usufruct over the property of such issue. As regards infant children, this right is preserved by the BGB; subject to this exception, the main principle of Germanic law which looked upon the father's privileges not as rights exercisable for his own benefit, but as means for enabling him to protect the children's interests, is also the main principle of the new law. The expression 'parental' power indicates that the exclusive rule of the father has been abandoned; as a general rule the power is exercised by the father, but even where this is the case some of the functions have to be exercised by him with the mother's concurrence, and on the father's death, and in certain other events the mother takes his place.

The parental power is exercised over all the children during their infancy, and comprises the following rights and duties: (1) power of agency; (2) care of the children's person; (3) care of the children's property; (4) right of usufruct.

The exercise of the parental power is not subject to the same kind of control as the exercise of the office of a guardian (451); but, as will be seen below (446), the powers of interference of the Guardianship Court are very extensive, and may to a certain extent be exercised by the Court of its own motion.   A local authority also exists in each commune, called the 'Communal Orphan Council' (*Gemeindewaisenrath*), whose functions include the duty to give notice to the Guardianship Court of any fact relating to the exercise of the parental power which comes to its knowledge and calls for the interference of the Court.   A child subject to parental power has a claim for damages against the judge of the

Guardianship Court if he wilfully or negligently fails in the performance of any duty imposed upon him by law in such child's interest—BGB 1674, 1675.

bb.   Father's exercise of parental power.

442. The parental power is vested in the father until his death or judicial declaration of death, [1] unless it is suspended or forfeited on any of the grounds mentioned below; the father may also be deprived of the care of the child's person (445), or of the management of the child's property (446), by order of the Guardianship Court under the circumstances specified in the sections respectively dealing with these matters; his powers do not in any case extend to matters as to which a curator has been appointed (454), or to objects given by any testator or donor with directions excluding the parental power of management; [2] the father's power of agency is also restricted in certain other ways specified below.

The rights and duties connected with the care of a child's person are   548 exercisable and have to be performed jointly with the mother, but in the case of any difference of opinion the father has a preponderating voice.   The parents cease to exercise any power over the person of an infant daughter after her marriage, but the power of agency and the powers relating to her property in such a case remain vested in the person exercising the parental power—BGB 1626, 1627, 1628, 1633, 1634, 1638.

The father's parental power is *suspended* [3] in any of the following events: (1) in the event of his being or becoming subject to incapacity or restricted capacity; (2) in the event of the appointment of a curator of his affairs on the ground of any physical disability (454); (3) in the event of it being established by a declaration of the Guardianship Court that some fact exists which prevents him from exercising the power for a considerable period of time [4] —BGB 1676, 1677 (1).

The father's parental power is *forfeited* in the event of his being sentenced to

---

[1]   As to the consequences of divorce and judicial separation, see 422 sub (5).

[2]   Such a direction does not exclude the parental right of usufruct, unless such exclusion is expressly provided for—BGB 1651.

[3]   The suspension of the power does not involve the loss of the usufruct over the child's property— BGB 1678.

[4]   The suspension comes to an end when the incapacity or restriction ceases; in the event referred to, sub (3), the suspension does not cease until the Court declares that the reason preventing the exercise of the power has ceased to exist—BGB 1677 (2).

penal servitude or imprisonment extending over six months on the ground of any offence affecting the child—BGB 1680.

If the father, though entitled to exercise the parental power, is in fact unable to do so, and if the mother does not exercise her right of taking his place (443), the Guardianship Court has to make such arrangements as may appear necessary in the child's interest [1]—BGB 1665.

If, during the suspension, or after the forfeiture of the father's parental power, the power cannot be exercised by the mother, a guardian of the child must be appointed [2]—BGB 1773.

549   In all matters relating to the exercise of the power the father must apply such diligence as he gives to his own affairs—BGB 1664.

He is entitled to the re-imbursement of any outlay reasonably incurred in connexion with the care of the child's person or property, except where such outlay is under some special rule chargeable against him—BGB 1648.

cc.   Mother's exercise of parental power.

443. The parental power, including the right of usufruct, *becomes vested* in the mother in any of the following events: (1) on the father's death; (2) on a judicial declaration declaring the father to be dead [3]; (3) on the forfeiture by the father of the parental power, in any case in which the conjugal community has previously been dissolved by divorce, or judicial separation [4]—BGB 1684.

The mother *may exercise* [5] the parental power temporarily: (1) during the subsistence of the conjugal community in any case in which the father's power is suspended, or in which he is temporarily prevented from acting; (2) after the termination of the conjugal community by divorce or judicial separation if

---

1   As a general rule a curator is appointed under such circumstances—BGB 1909.

2   The guardian steps into the father's place; if the mother is living she acts concurrently with the guardian in all matters relating to the child's person—BGB 1698.

3   If the father in such a case is in fact living, he may resume his parental power after making a declaration of his intention to do so addressed to the Guardianship Court—BGB 1679 (2).

4   If the parental power is forfeited during the subsistence of the marriage, the mother does not acquire it; in such a case a guardian has to be appointed; if subsequently to such appointment the father and mother are divorced or judicially separated, the mother acquires the parental power and the guardianship comes to an end *ipso facto*—BGB 1882.

5   The right to exercise the power must be distinguished from the formal possession of the power; where the mother has only the right to exercise the power, the father's power revives as soon as the ground for the suspension of his power disappears.

authorized to do so by the Guardianship Court; the authority may be given if the father's power is suspended, and there is no prospect of a speedy termination of the suspension.   In the event mentioned sub (1), the usufruct in the child's property remains vested in the father—BGB 1685.

The mother's powers in an ordinary case are the same as those of the father, and subject to the same rule as to suspension, [1] forfeiture, and termination (448), except that the mother's powers are terminated by re-marriage, as well as by death or judicial declaration of death.   An assistant guardian (*Beistand*) having power to control the exercise of the mother's powers as to all or some of the matters included therein, may be appointed by the Guardianship Court under any of the following circumstances: (1) in pursuance of a testamentary direction on the father's part; such a direction is operative, if the father at the time of his death was in full enjoyment of the parental power; (2) on the mother's own application; (3) in any case in which the Court for special reasons deems such an appointment desirable [2] —BGB 1686, 1687.

550

The mother of an illegitimate child is not entitled to the parental power; such a child must in any case be protected by the appointment of a guardian (449). The mother, however, has the care of the child's person, the guardian exercising in that respect the powers of an assistant guardian—BGB 1707.

dd.   Powers of statutory agency.

444. The person exercising the parental power is the statutory agent (116) of each child subject to the power, and, as such, has authority to act on behalf of any incapable infant child, or to give the required assent to the acts of any infant child whose capacity is restricted.   This power of acting on behalf of, or concurrently with, any child subject to the parental power cannot, however, be exercised with reference to certain specified matters, as to which a conflict of interest between the child on one side and the father, or certain near relations of his, on the other side is possible.   The Guardianship Court may also withdraw the power of agency in respect of any other matter as to which it can be shown that such a conflict of interests exists to a material extent.   In such a case a curator

---

[1]   Where the mother's parental power is suspended by reason of her infancy, she retains the duties and rights as to the child's person, but subject to the control of the child's guardian; the same rule is applied where the power is terminated by reason of her re-marriage—BGB 1696, 1697.

[2]   As to the assistant guardian's powers and functions and as to the possibility of his removal, see BGB 1688–1695.

(454) must be appointed for the purpose of acting as the child's statutory agent—BGB 1630.   The restrictions on the powers of agency which arise with reference to the management of the child's property will be discussed below (446).

ee. Care of child's person.

551   **445.** The care of the person comprises: (1) the right and duty to educate [1] and control the child; (2) the right and duty to determine its place of residence; (3) the right to demand the restitution of the custody of the child from any person unlawfully detaining it—BGB 1631, 1632.

The rules as to the right of determining in what religion a child is to be brought up are left to State Law—EG 134.

The Guardianship Court may order a child to be removed from the parents' custody and sent to a suitable family, or to a school or reformatory on any of the following grounds [2] : (1) on the ground that the child's physical or moral welfare is imperilled by the abuse on the part of the parent exercising the parental power of his right to take care of the child's person, or on the ground of dishonourable or immoral conduct on the part of such parent—BGB 1666 (1); (2) in the case of a child under the age of twelve years on the ground that such child has committed a criminal offence [3] ; (3) on the ground that such removal appears necessary to prevent the child's complete moral depravation [4] —EG 135.

The removal to some educational or correctional establishment of a young person over the age of twelve, but under the age of eighteen years, may be ordered by any Court convicting such person of a criminal offence, if the Court is of opinion that he is not possessed of sufficient insight for the discernment of the criminality of the act of which he is convicted—StGB 56.

---

[1]   The right of education includes the right of inflicting reasonable chastisement, which may be extended by order of the Guardianship Court—BGB 1631 (2).

[2]   The Guardianship Court before making such an order must give a hearing to the parent exercising parental power; the other parent and the child's near relatives must also be heard, if this can be done without great delay and expense—BGB 1673.

[3]   Ordinary criminal proceedings cannot be taken against a child under the age of twelve years—StGB 55.

[4]   The removal in the events mentioned sub (2) and (3) is not permissible unless specially authorized by State law; as regards Prussia it is authorized under a Statute of 1900 known as the *Fürsorgerziehungsgesetz*.

ff.   Management of child's property.

(1) *Nature of powers of management.*

446. The power of management exercised by virtue of the parental power over   552
a child's property is similar in its nature to the power of management exercised by
a husband over his wife's non-privileged property under the statutory régime (414),
but a parent's power of management is much more extensive than a husband's
power.   The power is not necessarily exercised over the whole of the child's
property, owing to the fact that a testator or donor may, as mentioned above
(442), exclude it as to any objects given by him.   A testator or donor may also
give special directions as to the management of any objects not so excluded, and
these directions must be followed, unless the Guardianship Court gives leave to
disregard them, on the ground that the interests of the child would otherwise be
endangered [1]—BGB 1639.   The following statement must be taken to refer
exclusively to the management of property in respect of which the parental power
has not been excluded or made subject to special directions.

(2) *Rules as to management.*

The power of management includes the rights: (*a*) to take possession of,
and to give a valid discharge for, all sums of money or other property to which the
child is entitled; (*b*) to sell, charge, or otherwise dispose of any property belonging
to the child, but subject, as regards certain specified kinds of property, to the
leave of the Guardianship Court.

Transactions relating to immovables, or to the whole property under the
parent's management, or to any right of inheritance to which the child is entitled,
or to the purchase or sale of a business, to leases extending over a year, borrowing
transactions, or to the issue or indorsement of negotiable instruments, &c. , are
among those for which the leave of the Court is required. [2]

Gifts cannot be made on the child's behalf, except for the purpose of satisfying a   553
moral obligation or the requirements of social propriety—BGB 1641, 1643.

Objects which cannot be sold without the leave of the Court cannot be

---

[1]   Where the donor is living his assent to a deviation is sufficient, and if he is prevented by permanent
incapacity or absence the Guardianship Court may assent in his place—BGB 1639 (2), 1803 (3).

[2]   As regards certain kinds of these transactions a general authorization may be given—BGB 1643
(3), 1825.   As to the manner in which the leave of the Court is given and as to the effect of a transaction
entered into without such leave, see BGB 1828–1831.

delivered to the child without such leave—BGB 1644.

Any money requiring investment must be invested in trustee securities, unless the Guardianship Court on any special ground allows a deviation from this rule—BGB 1642.   A new business cannot be started on the child's behalf without the leave of the Guardianship Court [1]—BGB 1645.

(3) *Special duties of surviving parent.*

While both parents are living the Guardianship Court does not exercise any control over the management of the child's property, except in the events mentioned sub (4) and (5).   On the death of one of the parents the surviving parent must comply with the following requirements: (*a*) he must make an inventory of the whole of the property belonging to any child then subject to the parental power; if no such property exists he must file a declaration to that effect; (*b*) he must from time to time make and file an inventory of any property subsequently accruing to any child subject to the parental power; (*c*) if he intends to contract another marriage the Guardianship Court must be informed of such intention, and an inventory of the property subject to his management must be filed before the re-marriage; if any child is a participant in a continued community of goods—417 sub (8), a partition must be effected before the re-marriage, unless the Court gives leave to postpone this step [2]—BGB 1640, 1669.

(4) *Supervision of power of management.*

The parental power of management may be made subject to the control of the Guardianship Court in any case in which the child's property is endangered, either by a neglect of the duties incumbent on the parent exercising the parental power, or by the pecuniary embarrassments of such parent.

554

In such a case the Court may require an inventory to be filed and an account to be rendered, and may direct the lodgment with a public authority (164) of bearer securities, instruments indorsed in blank, and valuables, in such manner that they cannot be withdrawn or transferred without the leave of the Guardianship Court, or may take certain other precautionary measures of the same nature; if

---

[1]   The rule, as to the vesting of the ownership of movables acquired out of the child's funds, is the same—*mutatis mutandis*—as the rule as to movables acquired by a husband out of the wife's funds under the statutory régime—414—BGB 1646.

[2]   These rules are also applicable on the re-marriage of a divorced parent.   Failure to comply with them constitutes a 'hindering impediment' to the re-marriage—411.

these steps appear insufficient the parent may be ordered to give adequate security (87).   The Court may from time to time modify any such order or direction—BGB 1667, 1668, 1671, 1672.

(5) Withdrawal and termination of power of management.

The Guardianship Court may withdraw the power of management as to the property of any child: (a) in the event of a disregard of the provisions mentioned sub (3), or of disobedience to an order made under the rules stated sub (4) [1]; (b) in any case in which the parent exercising the parental power neglects his duties as to the maintenance of the child in such a manner that his future maintenance appears endangered—BGB 1666 (2), 1670.

The powers of management cease *ipso facto* if the parent exercising the parental power is adjudged a bankrupt; on the termination of the bankruptcy they can be restored by an order of the Guardianship Court—BGB 1647.

(6) Parent's duties on cessation of power of management.

If a parent loses his power of management as to a child's property in any manner mentioned sub (5), or by reason of the suspension, forfeiture, or termination of the parental power, such parent or his heirs must deliver the property previously managed by him to the statutory agent of the child, and at the same time render an account of the management.   If the power is terminated by the coming of age of the child to whom the property belongs, the property and the account must be delivered to the child—BGB 1681.

gg.   Right of usufruct.

(1) Nature of right.

447. A parent exercising the parental power over a child is entitled to the usufruct of all property, except ' free property' , belonging to such child. [2]   The free property (*freies Vermögen*) consists of: (a) objects intended for the child's personal use; (b) the child's earnings; (c) any property given as ' free

555

---

1   The rule as to hearing the parent intended to be deprived of his power of management, and the other parent, and the relatives, is the same as in the case of an application for an order withdrawing the care of the child's person—BGB 1673.

2   The parent is of course bound to maintain the child, but the surplus after the discharge of the outgoings belongs to the parent absolutely.   This constitutes a material difference between German and English law. If a parent carries on any business on a child's behalf the net profits belong to such parent, but any loss has to be made up out of the profits of the subsequent years—BGB 1655.

property' by a testator or donor. In so far as any property is withdrawn from his management, the parent exercising the parental power is not entitled to the direct exercise of the right of usufruct, but may claim the net income after the discharge of all outgoings. [1] The rules for the exercise of the right of usufruct are, subject to certain unimportant divergences, the same—*mutatis mutandis*—as those relating to the husband's usufruct over the wife's non-privileged property under the statutory régime—414—BGB 1649–1654, 1656–1660, 1663.

(2) *Termination of right of usufruct.*

The right of usufruct in respect of the property of an infant child comes to an end on such child's marriage with the parents' authorization. It may also be terminated: (1) by order of the Guardianship Court in any case in which the parent has failed to comply with his duty as to the child's maintenance, and in which the future maintenance is endangered [2]; (2) by the parent's renunciation—BGB 1661, 1662, 1666 (2).

hh. *Termination of parental power.*

556   **448.** The parental power is terminated: (1) by the death or judicial declaration of death of the parent exercising the power; (2) by the death of the child; (3) by forfeiture (442); (4) in the case of the mother by re-marriage (443); (5) by the child's coming of age. The rule as to the exercise of a parent's power during the period between the termination or suspension of the power, and the time at which such termination or suspension comes, or ought to come to his knowledge, is the same—*mutatis mutandis*—as the rule applicable on the termination of a husband's power of management under the statutory régime (414). If the parental power comes to an end by reason of a child's death, the parent is bound to attend to any matter, which could not safely be postponed, until the child's heirs have had time to make the necessary arrangements—BGB 1682, 1683.

---

[1]   If the parental power is suspended, or if the care of the person and the property has been withdrawn from the parent, the cost of the child's maintenance, in so far as it is chargeable against the parent, is treated as an outgoing—BGB 1656 (2).

[2]   The usufruct, as a matter of course, comes to an end on the termination or forfeiture of the parental power; on the suspension of the parental power it does not come to an end except in a case in which the power is transferred to the mother after the divorce or judicial separation of the parents—p. 510 note 4.

CHAPTER III
GUARDIAN AND WARD

1.   GENERAL RULES

a.   Cases in which Guardian is appointed.

449. UNDER German law at least one guardian (*Vormund*) must be appointed 557
for: (1) any infant, who is not subject to parental power, or whose person and
property are not under the care and management of either parent; (2) any adult
who has been placed under guardianship by reason of mental disorder,
extravagance, or dipsomania (28–31)—BGB 1773, 1896.   The functions of such
a guardian, and more particularly his powers to act on behalf of the ward (*Mündel*),
are strictly defined and extensive; in this respect, German has the advantage over
English law, under which the powers of the guardian of an infant's estate or person
are in some respects vague, and in many respects restricted, while a committee
who acts in lieu of a guardian for a person of unsound mind is only appointed in the
exceptional cases where the lunatic is so found by inquisition. [1]

An English guardian may be appointed by will; a German guardian is always
appointed by the Guardianship Court, which must select him in accordance with
the rules stated below (456).

b.   Cases in which a Supervising Guardian is appointed.

450. A supervising guardian (*Gegenvormund*) may be appointed in any case
which does not come within the exceptions mentioned below, and must be
appointed in every case not coming within the exceptions if the ward's property is
of more than trifling value, and if only one guardian has been appointed.   (See
456 sub (5).)

---

[1]   The powers of a person appointed under s. 116 of the Lunacy Act 1890 correspond to the powers of
a German 'curator' appointed for a special purpose.

A supervising guardian is not appointed:

(1) where the father or mother, having nominated a guardian in the manner
558   mentioned below (456 sub 2), has forbidden the appointment of a supervising
guardian.   In such a case the guardianship is called an 'exempted guardianship'
(*Befreite Vormundschaft*)—BGB 1792, 1852 (1), 1855;

(2) where either parent is appointed guardian of a legitimate adult child and
would, if the child were an infant, have the power of managing its property [1]—
BGB 1903, 1904.

c.   Functions of Guardianship Court and Family Council.

451. The duties and powers of the Guardianship Court as to the control of the
exercise of the guardianship are much more extensive than the similar duties and
powers with reference to the exercise of the parental power.   It is the duty of the
Court to supervise the exercise of the powers of the guardian, and of the supervising
guardian, and to prevent breaches of duty on the part of either of them, and it may
impose fines if its directions are disobeyed—BGB 1837, 1897 (see also 464).

The judge of the Court is under the same liability with reference to any
breach of this duty, as he is with reference to any breach of duty in respect of his
control over the parental power (441)—BGB 1848.   If either legitimate parent
so directs [2] a family council consisting of the judge of the Guardianship Court and
two to six other members is appointed; in such a case all the functions otherwise
exercised by the Guardianship Court are exercised by the family council—BGB
1858, 1860, 1872, 1897, 1905.

d.   Functions of Communal Orphan Council.

452. The Communal Orphan Council (441) has to nominate fit persons for the
559   office of guardian, supervising guardian, and for membership of the family council

---

[1]   If the mother is the guardian, a supervising guardian is appointed by her wish, or where any
special circumstance makes such appointment desirable—BGB 1904.

[2]   Where the ward is an infant, a family council may also be appointed on the application of any
kindred or relative by marriage, unless forbidden by either parent, in so far as the Guardianship Court
holds such appointment to be expedient in the ward's interest—BGB 1859.   As to the composition of the
family council, the regulations of its meetings, the appointment of substitutes, the power of the Court over
the members, and the circumstances under which its removal may be ordered, see BGB 1861 – 1881,
1905.

in so far as they are required.   It is bound concurrently with the Guardianship Court or family council to supervise the exercise of the guardians' functions, and to give information to the Court, or to the family council as to any breaches of duty coming under its notice.   On the other hand the Court or family council has to give notice to the Communal Orphan Council of the appointment of any guardian or assistant guardian for a ward residing in the district [1] —BGB 1849, 1850, 1851 (1), 1897.

e.   Interim Guardianship.

453. Where an application is made for placing any adult under guardianship an interim guardian (*vorläufiger Vormund*) may be appointed by the Court, if the Court holds such appointment necessary for the purpose of averting a material danger to the person or property of such adult.   The interim guardianship comes to an end on the proper guardian's appointment, or on the dismissal of the application—BGB 1906–1908.

f.   Cases for the appointment of a ' curator'.

454. The distinction of Roman law between the *tutela* over the younger infants, and the *cura* over those of riper age is not maintained in German law; the functions of a ' curator' (*Pfleger*) are intended to meet: (1) cases in which there is a parent or guardian who, under the particular circumstances, is incapable of acting; (2) cases in which, for various reasons, it is required that some one should act on behalf of a person who is not under parental power or guardianship.   The particular instances of the second class of cases are as follows:

(*a*) a curator may be appointed for the person and property of an adult not under guardianship who, by reason of any physical defect (*e. g.* deafness or blindness), is incapable of managing his affairs, and who consents to the curator's appointment;

(*b*) a curator may be appointed for some particular matters, or for some particular classes of matters, to which an adult, not under guardianship, cannot   560 attend himself, owing to any physical or mental defect; in this case also the consent of the person concerned is required;

---

1   Where the ward's residence is changed, the guardian has to give notice of such change to the Orphan Council of the district in which the former residence was situate, which in its turn has to communicate such notice to the Orphan Council of the new district—BGB 1851 (2).

(c) a curator may be appointed for an absent adult whose place of abode is unknown, [1] or who is prevented from returning and from attending to the management of his property;

(d) a *curator ventris* is appointed, if such appointment is required for the preservation of any future rights to which the *nasciturus* may become entitled after his birth [2] ;

(e) a curator may be appointed for an unascertained person, if the interests of such person require immediate protection (*e. g.* where the vesting of a reversionary interest which requires protection depends upon a contingent event) ;

(f) a curator may be appointed for the purpose of administering a fund collected for a temporary purpose, if the persons originally appointed for the management and distribution of such fund have died or ceased to act [3] —BGB 1909–1914.

g.   Cases in which Guardians and Curators are appointed for Subjects of other Countries.

455. A German Guardianship Court has power to appoint a guardian or curator for the subject of a foreign State, in any case in which the authorities of such State have failed to make adequate provision, and in which the person concerned either requires the care of a guardian or curator under his own law, or was originally placed under guardianship by a German Court.   Provisional measures may be ordered pending the appointment—EG 23.   An alien who is domiciled or resident in Germany may be placed under guardianship by a German Court—EG 8.

---

[1]   A *curator absentis* may be appointed, notwithstanding the fact that the absent person has appointed an attorney capable of acting on his behalf, if any circumstances exist which render the revocation of the power of attorney desirable—BGB 1911 (1).

[2]   If either parent would have exercised the parental power over the child if it had been born such parent is entitled to act, and the appointment of a curator is unnecessary.

[3]   As to the appointment of a curator for the estate of a deceased person, see 521.

2.   SELECTION AND APPOINTMENT OF GUARDIAN, SUPERVISING GUARDIAN, OR CURATOR

a.   Principle of Selection.

(1) *General principle.*

456. The Court in its selection of a guardian, supervising guardian, or curator   561
must follow a prescribed order of priority as between the persons who by law are
'called upon' (*berufen*) to act.   The Court is not authorized to disregard this
order of priority, except on one of the following grounds: (1) the consent of the
person passed over; (2) the incapacity or disqualification (457) of the person
passed over; (3) the existence of special impediments preventing the acceptance
of the office [1] ; (4) delay in acceptance on the part of the person passed over;
(5) the fact that in the opinion of the Court the appointment of the person passed
over would have been detrimental to the ward's interest—BGB 1778 (1) (2),
1897.

(2) *Order of priority where ward is an infant.*

The following classes of persons are called upon to act as guardian of an
infant in the order in which they are mentioned:

(1) the person (male or female) nominated as guardian by a testamentary
disposition of the ward's father [2] ;

(2) the person (male or female) nominated by a testamentary disposition of
the ward's legitimate mother [3] ;

(3) the ward's paternal grandfather [4] ;

(4) the ward's maternal grandfather.

---

[1]   If the impediments are of a temporary nature, the person passed over must, after their removal, be
appointed in the place of the originally appointed guardian—BGB 1778 (2).

[2]   Under English law the mother is statutory guardian after the father's death; in Germany such a
provision is unnecessary, because the mother, if she is capable of exercising the parental power, obtains the
care of the infant children and of their property by virtue of such power; the appointment of a guardian is
consequently not required in such a case.

[3]   Neither parent is entitled to nominate a guardian, if at the time of his death he is not entitled to
exercise the parental power or to act on behalf of the child in matters affecting its person or property—BGB
1777 (1).

[4]   Where the ward has been adopted by any person other than his father's or mother's spouse, neither
grandfather is called upon—BGB 1776 (2).

562   Where the ward is a married woman, the Court may pass over all the persons otherwise called upon in favour of her husband; where the ward is an illegitimate child, the grandparents may be passed over in favour of the mother—BGB 1776, 1777.

(3) *Order of priority where ward is of age.*

Where the ward is of age, the order of priority between the persons called upon to act as guardians is as follows:
(1) the ward's father;
(2) the ward's legitimate mother [1];
(3) the ward's paternal grandfather;
(4) the ward's maternal grandfather.

Where the ward is married, the Court may pass over all the persons otherwise called upon in favour of the ward's husband or wife; where the ward is an illegitimate child the grandparents may be passed over in favour of the mother—BGB 1897, 1898, 1899 (1).

(4) *Selection where no person called upon by law is available.*

Where no person called upon by law to act as guardian is available, the Court must select a proper person, male or female, married or unmarried, after hearing the Communal Orphan Council. Preference must be given to kindred or relations by marriage, and the ward's religious faith must be taken into consideration— BGB 1779, 1897.

(5) *Rules as to number of guardians.*

In the absence of any special ground justifying the appointment of several guardians (*e. g.* the nomination of several guardians in a testamentary disposition), only one is appointed for each ward; where several brothers and sisters (whether of the whole or half blood) require guardians a single guardian is, as a general rule, appointed for them collectively. Where, for any special reason, several guardians are appointed for one ward, each of such guardians may be appointed for a separate sphere of duties, *e. g.* one of them may be appointed as guardian of

---

[1] The order is somewhat varied in a case where the ward is an adopted child or the legitimate child of an invalid marriage—409 sub (2) (*b*)—BGB 1899 (2) (3), 1900 (2).

the person and another as guardian of the property [1]—BGB 1775, 1797 (2),   563
and see 1798.

(6) *Selection of supervising guardian and curator.*

A supervising guardian is selected in accordance with the same rules as those
regulating the selection of an ordinary guardian—BGB 1792 (4).   The selection of
a curator, in a case where such curator has to act in the place of the parent exercising
the parental power, or of the guardian, is left to the discretion of the Court [2] ; in
all other cases the selection of a curator is, as far as practicable, governed by the
same principles as the selection of a guardian—BGB 1915, 1916.

b.   Incapacity and Disqualification for Office.

457. A person may either be incapable of being appointed as a guardian or
merely disqualified.   If a person incapable of being appointed is appointed, such
appointment is void, *ab initio*; a disqualified person ought not to be appointed,
but if the prohibition has been disregarded the appointment is operative; the Court,
however, is bound to dismiss the disqualified person as soon as the disqualification
is brought to its knowledge.

A person under incapacity (93), or a person placed under guardianship by reason
of mental debility, extravagance, or dipsomania, is incapable of being appointed.

A minor who has attained the age of seven years, a person under interim
guardianship (453), or one whose property is being managed by a curator, an
undischarged bankrupt or a person deprived of civic rights by criminal sentence,
is disqualified, as well as a person expressly excluded by a testamentary disposition
of the ward's father or legitimate mother, [3] or a person who has not obtained the   564

---

1   Where several guardians are appointed, without distinction of spheres of action, they must act
jointly.   In cases of difference of opinion between the guardians the Guardianship Court decides, unless on
the appointment of such guardians other directions have been given.   The Court must follow any directions
given by an infant ward's parent as to the decision on differences of opinion between guardians nominated by
such parent, unless such directions appear to endanger the ward's interests—BGB 1797, 1798.

2   Where a curator has to be appointed for the management of any property given by a testator or donor
to a person subject to the parental power or under guardianship with directions that it should be withdrawn
from the management of the parent or guardian, the person (if any) nominated by such testator or donor as
curator must be appointed—BGB 1917 (1).

3   The mother cannot exclude a person nominated by the father; neither parent has the right of exclusion
in any case, in which he is deprived of the right of nomination under the rule stated above—p. 521 note 3—
BGB 1782, 1897.

required consent. The husband's consent is required, where his wife is appointed as guardian for a person other than himself or any child of his; the consent of the competent authority is required in any case, in which a public official or minister of religion is appointed—BGB 1780–1784, 1792 (4), 1897, 1900 (1).

c.   Duty to accept Office.

458. Every male German is bound to accept the office of guardian, supervising guardian, or curator, if not excused on one of the prescribed grounds.   A person who culpably declines the office without lawful excuse is liable for any damage suffered by the ward by reason of the consequent delay in the appointment and may be fined for his refusal. [1]

A person who has attained the age of sixty years, or who has more than four legitimate children, [2] or who is hindered by disease or infirmities, or who resides at an inconvenient distance from the office of the Guardianship Court, or who holds not less than two guardianships under previous appointments, is entitled to refuse the office.   The office may also be refused in any case, in which several guardians are to be appointed—456 sub (5)—or in which the guardian is directed by the Court to give security (459)—BGB 1785–1788.

d.   Procedure on Appointment.

459. It is the duty of the Guardianship Court to effect the appointment of a guardian, supervising guardian, or curator of its own motion whenever such appointment is required. [3]   The person appointed must declare before the Court that he will faithfully and conscientiously discharge the duties of his office and must confirm this declaration by clasp of hand (*Handschlag*) in lieu of oath.

The Court may order the guardian to give security (87) if such a precaution is required on any special ground.

The appointment may be made terminable on the happening of a special event.   A certificate of the appointment (*Bestallung*) is handed to the person appointed; it must contain the following particulars: (1) the ward's name and

565

---

[1]   The fine may not exceed 300 Marks and only three successive fines can be imposed; in this manner exemption from fines may be purchased at the cost of about £ 45.   The liability for damages, however, remains.

[2]   Adopted children are not counted.

[3]   Where a guardian has to be appointed for an infant the Court may, pending such appointment, make such preliminary orders as may be required in the ward's interest.

date of birth; (2) the guardian's, supervising guardian's, or curator's name; (3) the names of the other guardian or guardians (if any) or of the supervising guardian (if any); (4) details of the distribution of functions between several guardians where such a distribution is made; (5) a statement as to the appointment of a family Council where such an appointment has been made—BGB 1774, 1789, 1791, 1792 (4), 1844, 1897, 1915.

3.   RIGHTS AND DUTIES OF GUARDIAN, SUPERVISING GUARDIAN, AND CURATOR

a.   General Survey.

(1) *Guardian's rights and duties.*

460. A guardian has the same rights and duties as a parent exercising the parental power (excepting the right of usufruct), but is subject to much greater restrictions than a parent, more particularly in any case in which a supervising guardian is appointed.   The powers of a guardian, like those of a parent—442, do not extend to matters as to which a curator has been appointed, and, as in the case of a parent, the powers may be modified by direction of the Guardianship Court, or of a donor or testator from whom the ward receives property—BGB 1793, 1794, 1803, 1853, 1897.

(2) *Supervising guardian's rights and duties.*

The supervising guardian has to control the exercise of the guardian's office, and to give information to the Guardianship Court of any circumstances requiring its intervention (*e. g.* the guardian's death, or the happening of any event justifying his dismissal)—BGB 1799.   The necessity of his authorization for certain acts relating to the management of the ward's property will be referred to below—463 rules (2) and (3).

(3) *Curator's rights and duties.*

The rights and duties of a curator are determined by the purpose for which he   566 is appointed.   Within the scope of such purpose, he has the same powers and is subject to the same restrictions as a guardian—BGB 1915.

(4) *Liabilities of guardian, supervising guardian, and curator; right to remuneration.*

A guardian, supervising guardian, or curator is liable for all damage caused to the ward by his wilful or negligent default. [1]   Where several are in default they are liable jointly and severally, but where the default consists merely in the neglect of the duty of supervision, the guardian, as between himself and the supervising guardian, is liable exclusively.   A guardian or curator who employs any funds belonging to the ward for his own purposes has to pay interest thereon. [2] The duties of a guardian, supervising guardian, or curator must be performed without remuneration, unless the Court on any special grounds directs otherwise, *e. g.* where the extent of the property and the difficulties of its management justify such remuneration [3]—BGB 1833, 1834, 1836, 1897, 1915.

b.   Statutory Agency.

461. A guardian or curator is the ward's statutory agent.   The restrictions on the powers of agency are the same as those to which a parent who exercises the parental power is subject—444—BGB 1795, 1796, 1897, 1915.

c.   Care of Ward's Person.

462. The rules as to the care of an infant ward's person are the same as those applicable to the care of a child subject to the parental power—445, except that: (1) the Guardianship Court may order the removal of the ward into a family or school or reformatory, even in the absence of the grounds on which a child under parental power may be removed out of the parental custody, [4] and that (2) the care of the ward's religious education may be withdrawn from the guardian, if his religious faith is not the same as that in which the ward is to be educated—BGB 1800, 1801, 1838, 1915.

The guardian or curator of an adult has the care of the ward's person only in

567

---

[1]   The rule as to the sufficiency of the amount of diligence which the person concerned gives to his own affairs which applies in the case of a parent—446—is not applied in the case of a guardian, &c.

[2]   As to the right to be reimbursed for any outlay, see BGB 1835.

[3]   As to the remuneration of executors, see 526.

[4]   Where the ward is in the custody of either parent the rule is the same as where a child is under the parental power—BGB 1838.

so far as this is necessitated by the object of the guardianship or curatorship—
BGB 1901, 1915.

d.   Management of Ward's Property.

463. The rules as to the guardian's power of management over the ward's
property are similar to the rules as to a parent's power of management over his
infant child's property—446; in the same way as under the last-mentioned rules
the property given by a testator or donor must be managed in accordance with his
directions (if any) unless the Court in the ward's interest and subject to the donor's
assent (if living and capable of assenting) authorizes any deviation therefrom—
BGB 1793, 1803.

The following points of difference between a guardian's and a parent's powers
of management require mention:

(1) a parent, if entitled to the usufruct of the child's property, can use the
income for his or her own purposes, and can even, within certain limits, use
consumable things forming part of the corpus; a guardian cannot use any part of
the income or of the corpus of the ward's property for his or her own purposes and
must invest all income not required for the payment of necessary outgoings—BGB
1805, 1806, 1897;

(2) a parent is free to select any investments from within the range allowed
to him; a guardian selecting an investment must obtain the authorization of the
supervising guardian, or the leave of the Court—BGB 1810, 1821, 1897;

(3) a parent, exercising parental power, can dispose of or give a valid
discharge for any personal claim or negotiable instrument forming part of the
child's property; a guardian is, as a general rule, unable to do so without the
concurrence or ratification of the supervising guardian, or the leave of the Court
(such leave may, however, be given in respect of a whole class of transactions   568
together) [1] —BGB 1809, 1812, 1813, 1825, 1832, 1897, 1902;

(4) a parent, exercising parental power, retains the whole of the child's
property in his custody or under his control except under the special circumstances mentioned above—446 sub (4); a guardian, on the other hand, is required
to lodge with a public authority (164), or register, bearer securities, and instruments
indorsed in blank, and in such manner, that they cannot be withdrawn or transferred

---

[1]   As to the manner in which a transaction is authorized or ratified, see BGB 1828–1832.   As to the
parties to be heard, see BGB 1826, 1827.

without the leave of the Guardianship Court; other similar precautionary measures may also be ordered on any special ground; a guardian may on special grounds be allowed to retain the custody or control of the property requiring lodgment or registration under the general rule—BGB 1814–1820, 1897;

(5) the range of transactions requiring the leave of the Guardianship Court is considerably wider in the case of a guardian acting on behalf of a ward than in the case of a parent acting on behalf of a child—446 sub (2); for some kinds of transactions a general leave may be given—BGB 1821–1823, 1825, 1897; the rules about gifts, and about the delivery to the child or ward of objects which cannot be sold or charged without the consent of the supervising guardian, or the leave of the Court, are the same in both cases—BGB 1804, 1824, 1897.

The powers of a curator as to the management of any property entrusted to him are the same as those of a guardian—BGB 1915.

e.   Returns to be made to Guardianship Court.

464. The following rules apply:

(1) on the assumption of his office a guardian must with the assistance of the supervising guardian, if there is one, prepare an inventory of the ward's property, and similar inventories must be prepared on the subsequent acquisition of any property by the ward; if the inventory is deemed insufficient the Court may direct some other person or authority to take an inventory—BGB 1802, 1897;

569

(2) the guardian whenever requested to do so, must give information to the Court as to the conduct of the guardianship and the circumstances of the ward—BGB 1839, 1897;

(3) annual accounts must be prepared and placed before the Court; such accounts must first be submitted to the supervising guardian, if there is one, who must add such observations as may occur to him; the Court has to examine the accounts and to cause them to be amended or supplemented if necessary [1]—BGB 1840–1843 (1), 1897; see however BGB 1854;

(4) if the ward's father or legitimate mother is the child's guardian [2] and

---

[1]   Any disputed claim arising between the guardian and ward may be tried at once by action before the competent Court—BGB 1843 (2).

[2]   Where the ward is an adult the parent is frequently appointed guardian, but where the ward is an infant the parent in question would generally exercise the parental power; a parent, however, who has forfeited the parental power (e. g. a mother who re-marries) may be appointed guardian.

re-marries, he or she is under the same obligations as a parent exercising the parental power who re-marries—446 sub (3)—BGB 1845, 1897.

The rules as to returns and accounts are also applicable to a curator, in so far as they can be applied under the special circumstances—BGB 1915.

4. Termination of Guardianship or Curatorship and Vacation of Guardian's or Curator's Office

a. Circumstances causing Termination of Guardianship or Curatorship.

465. The guardianship ceases *ipso facto* in any of the following events:

(1) on the ward's death or declaration of death [1] (45);

(2) in the case of an infant ward not placed under guardianship on any ground other than infancy (*e. g.* lunacy, mental debility, dipsomania, extravagance): (*a*) on his attainment of full age; (*b*) on his becoming subject to parental power (*e. g.* by the restoration of a suspended parental power or by legitimation, [2] or adoption);

A guardianship ordered on the ground of any disability other than infancy is   570 terminated by the Guardianship Court if the ward ceases to be affected by such disability—BGB 1882, 1884 (2), 1897.

A curatorship comes to an end *ipso facto*: (1) in the case of a curator appointed for a person under parental power or guardianship, by the termination of such parental power or guardianship; (2) in the case of a *curator ventris* by the child's birth; (3) in the case of a curator appointed for a single transaction (*e. g.* a transaction as to which the ward's and the guardian's interests are conflicting) by the completion of the transaction; (4) on the declaration of the death of an absent person for whom a curator has been appointed.

A curatorship may be terminated by the Court:

(1) in the case of a curator appointed for a person incapable of managing his affairs on the ground of physical or mental defects, on the application of such person;

---

[1] If a ward, who is untraceable, has not been declared to be dead, the Court may terminate the guardianship—BGB 1884 (1).

[2] If in the case of legitimation by subsequent marriage the father's paternity is not established by judicial order, the guardianship continues until terminated by the Guardianship Court—BGB 1883.

(2) in the case of a *curator absentis* on the return of the absent person or on the cessation of the causes which prevented him from attending to his affairs or on his death;

(3) in any case in which the ground necessitating the appointment of a curator has ceased to exist—BGB 1918–1921.

b.   Circumstances causing Vacation of Guardian's or Curator's Office.

466. The office of any particular guardian or supervising guardian is vacated *ipso facto* by the death or judicial declaration of death of such person, or by his being himself placed under guardianship.   Notice of a guardian's or supervising guardian's death must be given by his heirs to the Guardianship Court.   A guardian must give notice of the death of a supervising guardian or joint guardian and *vice versa*—BGB 1885, 1894, 1895, 1897.

A guardian or supervising guardian is dismissed by the Court in any of the following events:

(1) if in consequence of his misconduct or of any other circumstance his retention of the office would, in the opinion of the Court, endanger the ward's interests, or if he is found to be disqualified—457;

571   (2) if he has not obtained the consent to his appointment required in his case under the rules stated above—457, or if such consent is revoked [1];

(3) if he desires to vacate the office on any cogent ground, more particularly on the ground that some circumstance has arisen which, if it had been in existence at the date of his appointment, would have entitled him to refuse the office—BGB 1886–1889, 1895, 1897.

A curator's office is vacated on the same grounds as a guardian's office— BGB 1915.

c.   Consequences of Termination of Guardianship or Curatorship, or of Vacation of Office of Guardian or Curator.

467. A guardian, supervising guardian, or curator must, on the termination

---

1   The Guardianship Court may in its discretion dismiss a female guardian or supervising guardian on her marriage, whether her husband consents to her retention of the office or not—BGB 1887 (1), 1895, 1897.

of the guardianship or curatorship, or on the vacation of his office, do the following things, in so far as they are compatible with the nature of his office:

(1) he must deliver or transfer the property under his care to the ward if *sui juris*, or to his statutory agent if he is under parental control or guardianship;

(2) he must prepare an account of the management of the ward's property which, if there is a supervising guardian, has to be examined by him, and with the written observations made by the latter, to be submitted to the Guardianship Court for examination; if the account is found to be in order, the Court issues a certificate to that effect;

(3) the certificate of appointment must be returned to the Court.

If the person concerned is dead the duty otherwise incumbent on him has to be performed by his heirs.

The rights and duties of a guardian, or curator, during the period intervening between the termination or vacation of his office and the receipt of the notice of such termination or vacation, or between the ward's death and the time at which the ward's heirs can take charge of the ward's estate, are regulated by the same rules—*mutatis mutandis*—as those applicable under the corresponding circumstances on the termination of the parental power—448—BGB 1890–1895, 1897, 1915.

FIFTH BOOK

LAW OF INHERITANCE

CHAPTER I
GENERAL SURVEY

1. SUMMARY OF PRINCIPLES

468. THE several branches of the law of inheritance are so closely connected with one another that it is impossible to understand the details of the particular rules without having some previous knowledge of the general principles governing the whole subject. The following summary is intended to meet this requirement:

(1) *Title to the estate of a deceased person.*

The title to the estate of a deceased person may be derived under a statutory rule or under a disposition made by the deceased. This fact is frequently expressed by the statement that the right of the persons taking the estate is acquired under the intestacy or under the will of the deceased, but this form of expression seems to assume that testamentary succession represents the normal, succession *ab intestato* the exceptional state of things. The authors of the BGB in its final shape were anxious to repudiate this view, which, though characteristic of the later developments of Roman law, is unhistorical and not in accordance with Germanic ideas. The statutory right of succession is therefore chiefly emphasized, and any right derived under a disposition of the deceased is looked upon as a modification of, or addition to, the statutory right. The rule of Roman law: *nemo pro parte testatus pro parte intestatus decedere potest*, has accordingly ceased to exist. The present rule is that the statutory heir succeeds, except in so far as he is displaced by any disposition of the deceased intended to become operative on his death. Such a disposition may be a testamentary disposition or a contractual disposition, the BGB having given recognition to the Germanic 'contract of inheritance', which was unknown to Roman law.

The statutory, testamentary, or contractual right to a share in the estate of a deceased person may be abandoned by renunciation in the lifetime of such person 576 (*Erbverzicht*), or forfeited by the committal of certain offences which render the person committing them 'unworthy to inherit' (*erbunwürdig*).

The share to which any statutory heir is entitled in the absence of any testamentary or contractual provision is called his 'statutory portion' (*gesetzlicher Erbteil*) ; the estate, as a whole, is called the 'inheritance' (*Erbschaft*).   The inheritance vests in the heirs immediately on the death of the deceased, subject to being divested as to the whole, or as to the share of any co-heir, by disclaimer within the period allowed by law; by the operation of such disclaimer the inheritance or the share disclaimed by any co-heir becomes, *ipso facto*, vested in the person next entitled.

(2) *Rights and liabilities of heirs.*

According to the principle of universal succession adopted by Roman law the heir took the place of the deceased person in every respect, becoming entitled to his rights and subject to his liabilities.   The *beneficium inventarii* introduced by Justinian enabled an heir to have an inventory of the estate taken in a specified manner and within a specified period, and thereby to limit his liability for the debts of the deceased to the value of the estate.   Under the new German law an heir who has not forfeited the privilege by certain specified acts or omissions, can at any time limit his liability in one of the ways mentioned below (532) , but an heir who either forfeits the privilege, or fails to take the steps required for the purpose of limiting his liability remains personally liable to the full extent.

No distinction exists between movables and immovables; on the death of the deceased the whole of the estate vests in the heir or heirs.

Where there are several heirs they stand to each other in the relation of co-heirs (*Miterben*).   Thus where several persons take the estate of the deceased as his next of kin, they take it as statutory co-heirs, and similarly several persons appointed as heirs by will or contract of inheritance are testamentary or contractual co-heirs.   If the testamentary or contractual heirs do not take the whole estate, the statutory heirs take the remaining part of the estate as co-heirs with the testamentary or contractual heirs.

577

(3) *Reversionary heirs and substitutional heirs.*

A will or contract of inheritance may appoint several persons as heirs in succession, one of them becoming entitled for a specified period, or until the happening of a specified event, and the other of them becoming entitled in possession at the end of such period or on the happening of such event.   The heir taking first is called *Vorerbe*, and will, in the further course of this treatise, be described as 'limited heir'; the heir taking in the last place is called *Nacherbe*, and will, in the further course of this treatise, be described as 'reversionary heir'.

A reversionary heir must be distinguished from a substitutional heir (*Ersatzerbe*), being a person appointed by a testator or contractor to take the place of the primarily appointed heir in the event of the latter being unable or unwilling to accept the inheritance.

(4) *Executors.*

Executors were unknown to Roman law; they were introduced into Germany under the influence of Germanic ideas fostered and assisted by the Canon law, but their position was vague and unsatisfactory in most German districts until 1900.   The BGB has regularized and defined their position in a very complete manner.   The powers of executors depend to a large extent on the provisions of the testamentary disposition by which they are appointed.   The estate does not in any case become vested in them, but they may be given the amplest powers of disposition and alienation, and their appointment may correspondingly deprive the heir of such powers.   The functions of a German executor are not necessarily exhausted by the payment of the testator's debts and the distribution of the residuary estate.   The powers of managing and alienating the testator's estate for the benefit of the heir, or of managing the portion of one particular co-heir, may be continued during such heir's or co-heir's life, or for a specified period not exceeding thirty years.   The functions of a German executor are in such a case more like those of an English trustee than like those of an English executor.

(5) *Legacies and testamentary burdens.*

The expression 'legacy' is here used as the equivalent of the German *Vermächtniss*, which comprises any gift out of the estate of a deceased person other than a gift of a share in the inheritance.   Such a gift may consist of a sum of money, or of a specific thing, movable or immovable.   Under the later Roman law the ownership of any thing specifically bequeathed became vested in the legatee as soon as the estate as a whole became vested in the heirs, but under the new German law a legatee does not acquire any right of ownership, but merely a personal right to the payment or delivery of the object bequeathed to him.   As a general rule, the heirs are bound to pay or deliver the bequeathed object, but the duty to satisfy a legacy may also be imposed upon a particular legatee.   Reversionary

578

and substitutional legacies may be given in a manner corresponding to the manner in which reversionary and substitutional heirs may be appointed, and legacies generally may be given by will or by contract.

A legacy must be distinguished from a burden (*Auflage*) imposed upon the heir or a legatee for the benefit of any person or object.   The person for whose benefit a burden is imposed on an heir or legatee has no right to enforce such benefit, the enforcement being left to the heir or executor, or to some public authority.

(6) *Compulsory right of succession.*

The so-called 'formal' right of inheritance of Roman law, which made it necessary for a testator to appoint every one of his natural heirs as heir, or to disinherit him on one or more of the recognized grounds of disinheritance, has not been adopted by the BGB, but the 'material' right of inheritance, which is the right of every statutory heir who has not either renounced his claim, or been declared 'unworthy to inherit' , or deprived of his share on some lawful ground, to a part of his statutory portion, is retained.   The portion of which a statutory heir cannot generally be deprived is called the compulsory portion (*Pflichtteil*) , and is equal to one-half of the statutory portion.   If less than the compulsory portion is left to a statutory heir—who is not excluded on one of the grounds mentioned above—he may require the testamentary or contractual heirs to make up the deficiency; if the compulsory portion or even a larger share is left subject to any restriction (*e. g.* the appointment of an executor with managing powers, or the appointment of a reversionary heir) , the statutory heir may at his option claim his compulsory portion free from any restriction in lieu of the benefit intended to be given to him, or abide by the provisions of the will or contract.

(7) *Functions of competent Probate Court.*

In the same way, as the Guardianship Court of a district has functions in respect of many matters relating to the matrimonial régime (413) , parental power (441) , and guardianship and curatorship (451) , the Court or authority described by the BGB as the 'Court dealing with the estates of deceased persons' (*Nachlassgericht*) , and which for the sake of brevity is here described as 'the competent Probate Court' , is entrusted with important powers relating to the custody and publication of testamentary instruments, and the distribution of the estates of deceased persons.   The competent Probate Court as a general rule is the local Court of the district in which the deceased was domiciled at the time of his death (FGG 72, 73 (1)), but, by virtue of EG 147, other authorities, more particularly notaries and communal authorities, may be entrusted by State legislation with its functions. [1]

2.   LOCAL DEVIATION FROM THE GENERAL LAW OF INHERITANCE

469. Certain classes of property may be exempted from the general rules of the law of inheritance by State legislation.   These are:

(1) property belonging to certain princely and noble families—EG 57, 58;

(2) property included in family settlements or held under feudal tenures— EG 59;

(3) parcels of land used for agricultural purposes or forestry, in districts where the right of a single heir can be established under the local law (*Anerbenrecht*)—EG 64 (1). [2]

The State law cannot, however, as regards any property referred to sub (3)   580 interfere with the owner's right to dispose of such property by testamentary disposition or contract of inheritance or bequest—EG 64 (2).

3.   COMPARISON WITH ENGLISH LAW

470. The comparison of the rules of the law of inheritance respectively applied in England and Germany ought to be preceded by the comparison of the practice as to dispositions *inter vivos* prevailing in each of the two countries.   A large part of the real property situate in England is entirely withdrawn from testamentary disposition, being comprised in family settlements, which are perpetually renewed; English personal property is also frequently tied up for several generations by marriage settlements and settlements created by will.   Thus the property of a married woman, through the effect of an after-acquired property clause contained in her marriage settlement, becomes frequently in its entirety subject to the trusts of that settlement.   In Germany, on the other hand, real property settlements, similar to those usual in England, cannot, generally, be made without government

---

[1]   This has been done in the Kingdom of Württemberg and the Grand Duchy of Baden.

[2]   This may be done in many districts of the provinces of Hanover and Westphalia, also in Prussian Poland under the colonization scheme introduced in 1890 now regulated by a Prussian Statute passed in 1896.

permission, and are comparatively rare, while marriage settlements and wills, by virtue of which property becomes vested in trustees for the benefit of several persons in succession, are not made at all.

This difference in the habits of the two countries has created the necessity of some institutions in German law which are unnecessary in England.   The 'continued community of goods', which, as mentioned above, may be stipulated for by marriage contract—417 sub (8), bears some resemblance to an English marriage settlement, inasmuch as one-half of the common property, on the death of the predeceasing spouse, goes to the issue by virtue of the marriage contract and not under the law of inheritance; in other respects there are, however, considerable diversities, more particularly owing to the fact, that the common property in which the issue are eventually entitled to share is not vested in trustees, but remains under the uncontrolled management of one of the spouses, and is subject to the debts of both spouses.   Moreover, the continued community of goods is not of frequent occurrence in the majority of German districts.

581

A German testator, who wishes to protect a son against his improvidence, or a daughter against her husband's business risks, can do this under the new law, by giving the issue of the child who requires protection a reversionary interest in such child's share, and by entrusting the management of such share to an executor during the child's life.   He may make such an arrangement either by his will or by contract of inheritance; if it is made in the latter form on a daughter's marriage, it bears a strong resemblance to an English marriage settlement by which the intended wife's father covenants to bequeath a certain sum to be held upon the trusts of the settlement.

As regards the purely legal differences between the German and the English law of inheritance, the following points call for observation:

(1) The etymological equivalent of the expression 'heir', as used in continental law, has an essentially different meaning from that which the expression has in English law.   Up to 1897 the English heir-at-law was in the position of a German statutory heir, but only in respect of real property; but under the present English law, the whole estate of a deceased person vests in a representative, who, in so far as he takes personalty, is called 'personal representative', and in so far as he takes realty, is called 'real representative'. The personal representative, like the German heir, takes the legal interest in the estate of the deceased; but while the German heir may become personally liable for the whole of the debts of the deceased, the real or personal representative of

English law does not come under any personal liability, except by reason of some default on his part.   The English real or personal representative, as such, takes no beneficial interest in the estate, whilst the German heir, as regards the beneficial interest is, at the worst, in the position of an English residuary legatee; if he is one of the statutory heirs he is, as a general rule, in a much better position, as his compulsory portion takes priority over legacies.   A German heir must therefore—leaving aside special circumstances under which an exception may arise—be a beneficiary as well as a representative.

(2) Under English law the representation of the estate cannot be given to several persons in succession; after the death of the representatives originally appointed, the representation is continued by the executor of the last surviving representative, or by an administrator appointed by the Court; a reversionary residuary legatee or devisee may, on the other hand, be appointed by an English will, but in so far as the residue given to him consists of personalty, the legal interest therein would not pass to him, *ipso facto*, on the termination of the prior beneficial interest.   Under German law, on the other hand, the legal interest in the whole estate may be made to pass to the reversionary heir, immediately on the termination of the interest of the limited heir.

(3) The 'heirs' of German law, for practical purposes, correspond to the residuary legatees of English law, but under English law the residuary legatees as such receive nothing before the debts and other legacies have been discharged, whereas the German heirs take the whole estate and pay the debts and legacies, being at the same time real and personal representatives and residuary legatees.

(4) An English executor who accepts the office, is, as regards the vesting of the testator's estate, in the same position as a German heir; the estate does not become vested in a German executor; but, as a German executor with full powers of management has complete control of the estate, third parties dealing with him are, as a general rule, as safe as third parties dealing with an English executor.

(5) Compulsory portions, though originally prescribed by English law, and still a feature of Scotch law, are now unknown in England.   The absolute liberty of testamentary disposition, which prevails at the present time, does not, however, go as far in its practical effects as might be supposed, as a large part of the property which a person enjoys during his life is frequently comprised in a settlement providing for his issue on his death.

582

4.   CONFLICT OF LAWS

471. The rules on this subject may be summarized as follows:

(1) The devolution of the estate of a person who, at the time of his death, was of German nationality—wherever situate, and whether consisting of movables or immovables, or of both—is on principle determined by German law; any question, therefore, as to the validity of a testamentary or contractual disposition affecting the estate, or as to the rights of the statutory or testamentary heirs, or of any legatee or creditor, is determined by German law, if the deceased, at the time of his death, was of German nationality, whatever his domicil may have been at such time—EG 24 (1).

This rule is, however, subject to the following qualifications:

(*a*) a testamentary disposition, or a contract of inheritance, though not executed in the form required by German law, is deemed duly executed if executed in the form required according to the law of the place of execution, or in the form required by the law of the State, of which the testator or contractor was a subject at the date of execution; if the testator or contractor was the subject of a non-German State at the date of execution, and was capable, according to the law of such State, of making a will, or becoming a party to a contract of inheritance, the validity of such will or contract is not affected by the fact that at the date of execution he was under the age prescribed by German law—EG 11 (1), 24 (3);

(*b*) if the last domicil of the deceased was outside the German Empire the heir may, as between himself and the creditors of the estate (532), require the law of such last domicil to be applied—EG 24 (2);

(*c*) the rule is not applicable in respect of any classes of objects of which the devolution, according to the *lex situs*, is determined by special rules—EG 28.

Illustration: A German by a will made in German form, and not attested by two witnesses, disposes of realty situate in England. As in England the devolution of the beneficial interest in realty is determined by special rules, a German Court would take the same view as an English Court, and hold that the beneficial interest in the English realty is not disposed of by the will, but passes to the person who is heir-at-law according to English law—EG 28.

(2) The devolution of the estate of a person not of German nationality, who

at the time of his death was domiciled in Germany, [1] is governed by the law of the State of which such person was a subject at the time of his death; but if the law of such State refers back to German law, German law governs the matter [2] —EG 25, 27.

584

This rule is subject to the following qualifications:

(*a*) the qualification as to objects situate outside Germany, and subject to special rules by the *lex situs*, is the same as that stated with reference to rule (1) sub (*c*) ;

(*b*) a German is entitled to make claims against the estate of a person who dies domiciled in Germany [3] if such claims are justified by German law, and notwithstanding the fact that they are not justified by the law of the nationality of the deceased—EG 25, 27. [4]

Illustration: A British subject *T* dies a widower domiciled in Germany, leaving as his sole issue two sons, *A*, who is a German subject, and *B*, who is a British subject; his residuary estate consists of immovables situate in England of the value of £ 5, 000, and personal estate situate in Germany of the value of £ 5, 000.   By a will made in English form, *T* gives his whole residuary estate to *B*; *A*, being a German, is entitled to claim one quarter of *T*'s whole estate as his compulsory portion (510) ; the German Courts will therefore allow him to retain £ 2, 500 out of the personal estate.

---

[1]   The Codes and Statutes are silent as to the devolution of the estates of testators or intestates, who are neither of German nationality nor domiciled in Germany.

[2]   The law which has to be applied is the law which in the country in question would be applied under the particular circumstances of the case, which law may be the law of the domicil, *viz.* German law.   But for the qualification of the German rule the game of battledoor and shuttlecock would proceed *ad infinitum.*   A somewhat difficult question arises with reference to the form of execution of a testamentary instrument; *i. e.* whether the general German rule, that the form prescribed by the law of the place of execution is sufficient is applicable in all cases or only in cases in which German law has to be applied in the first instance.   In the writer's opinion the rule of the law of the State of which the testator was a subject at the time of his death has to be ascertained; if that law declares that a will, wherever executed, is invalid unless its own rule as to execution is observed, a German Court would hold a will invalid if such rule has been disregarded.

[3]   Though nationality is the test as to the law which has to be applied, the *forum administrationis* is determined by the last domicil of the deceased. —CPO 27.

[4]   This rule is not applied in any case in which the deceased at the time of his death was the subject of any State which applies German law exclusively as to the devolution of the estate of a German dying domiciled within its territory—EG 25.

(3) If any property or money, forming part of an estate administered outside
585   Germany, is transmitted to Germany, by the intervention of any German public
authority, for the purpose of being delivered or paid to any heir or legatee of the
deceased, such delivery or payment cannot be stopped by any person claiming to
be entitled to such property as heir or legatee under German law—EG 26.

Illustration: *T*, a German subject having bequeathed the whole of his residuary
estate to *A* who is resident in Germany, dies domiciled outside of Germany; the
person administering the estate in the place in which *T* was domiciled, transmits
the whole property to a German public authority, with instructions to hand it over
to *A*; *B* though entitled to a compulsory portion in *T*'s estate under German law
(which according to rule (1) is decisive) cannot prevent the delivery of the
property to *A*, but he may as soon as *A* has received the property, take proceedings
against him for the purpose of obtaining payment of his compulsory portion.

CHAPTER II
STATUTORY RIGHT OF INHERITANCE

1.   GENERAL RULES

a.   Accrual of Inheritance.

472. THE word 'inheritance' (*Erbschaft*), as mentioned above—468 sub (1),   586
means the estate as a whole, but the rules applicable to the inheritance as a
whole are also applicable to the share of any particular co-heir—BGB 1922.

It will therefore be understood that any rule stated below which refers to the
'heir' and to 'the estate' or to 'the inheritance', is equally applicable to any
co-heir and to his share in the estate.

The accrual of the inheritance, which is designated as *Erbfall*, takes place
immediately on the death of the deceased.   An heir must be a living person at
the date of accrual, but a *nasciturus* conceived at the date of accrual and
subsequently born alive, is for this purpose deemed a person living at the date of
accrual—BGB 1923, 1942.

If the heir disclaims the inheritance it is deemed to have vested, as from the
date of accrual, in the person accepting it in his place—BGB 1953.

b.   Relation of Statutory Heirs to Testamentary and Contractual Heirs.

473. The persons who between them are entitled to the inheritance, except in
so far as it is validly disposed of by any testamentary or contractual disposition,
are called the 'statutory heirs' (*gesetzliche Erben*).   The testator may by
testamentary disposition deprive a statutory heir of his right of inheritance without
appointing another heir in his place.   The estate is then, subject to the rules as
to compulsory portions (512), administered as if the person so deprived had not
been living at the date of accrual.   If no natural person entitled to the rights of a
statutory heir is living, or deemed to be living at the date of accrual, the treasury   587

authority of the State of which the deceased was a subject [1] becomes the statutory
heir [2] —BGB 1936, 1937, 1938.

c.   Circumstances causing Forfeiture of Inheritance.

474. As mentioned above—473, a statutory heir may be deprived of his right
of inheritance by testamentary disposition; a right of inheritance may also be
forfeited in one of the following ways: (1) by formal renunciation in the lifetime
of the deceased (479); (2) by disclaimer on the part of the person entitled
(522); (3) by a judicial declaration establishing the ʻunworthinessʼ of the
party concerned (480).   Persons who have forfeited a right of inheritance are,
subject as to compulsory portions (512), deemed not to be living at the date of
the accrual—BGB 1953 (2), 2344 (2), 2346 (1).

d.   Mode of determining Statutory Heirs.

aa.   General rules.

475. The next of kin and the surviving spouse (if any) in so far as they have
not been deprived of their right or forfeited it, are the statutory heirs of the
deceased, and, as such, take the whole estate, or such part thereof as is not
disposed of by testamentary disposition or contract of inheritance.   For the purpose
of ascertaining who are the next of kin, the kindred are divided into classes
following each other in a prescribed order; if any member of a prior class is living
or deemed to be living, the members of the subsequent classes do not belong to
the next of kin.   If the next of kin are beyond a specified degree of kindred, the
surviving spouse, in addition to his share of the inheritance, is entitled to all
household articles, and all wedding presents.   This additional benefit is called
the ʻpreferential benefitʼ (*Voraus*).   If neither issue, nor parents or their issue,
nor grandparents, become entitled as statutory heirs, the surviving spouse takes the
whole inheritance.   A surviving spouse, against whom justifiable divorce or separation
proceedings were pending at the date of accrual, on the ground of any matrimonial
offence committed by him, forfeits his right of inheritance as well as the preferential
benefit.   If neither the surviving spouse nor any kindred become entitled as statutory
heirs, the treasury authority of the State of which the deceased was a subject

588

---

1   As to a possible conflict between several States, see BGB 1936.
2   The German treasury authorities are corporate bodies.

takes the place of the statutory heir—BGB 1930–1933, 1936.

bb.   Rules for determining order in which kindred are entitled and division among kindred.

476. The rules determining the order in which the kindred are entitled are based on the following principle.   The kindred are divided into classes, each class being called a *Parentel*; the first class consists of the issue of the deceased, the second of his parents and their issue, the third of his grandparents and their respective issues, each subsequent class consisting of the ancestors next in remoteness and their respective issues.   The members of the first class are called *Verwandte erster Ordnung*; those of the second class *Verwandte zweiter Ordnung* and so forth.   Among the members of each class those nearest in degree (424) to the deceased take priority over those further removed, but in the first class any deceased issue of the deceased is represented by his issue, and in the second and third classes any deceased ancestor of the deceased is represented by his issue, the division being *per stirpes* among issue and by lines among ancestors [1]; in the fourth class and the following classes there is no right of representation, and the nearest in degree take *per capita* —BGB 1924–1929.

These rules may be illustrated by examples as follows, it being assumed in all cases that the deceased does not leave any spouse surviving:

(1) First class: *D* leaves one child *A* who has issue, and two grandchildren *B* and *C*, children of a deceased child; *A*, *B*, and *C* are the next of kin, *A* takes $\frac{1}{2}$, *B* $\frac{1}{4}$, and *C* $\frac{1}{4}$; the issue of *A* are excluded.

(2) Second class: *D* dies without issue, and leaves a mother *M*, one brother of the whole blood *F*, one brother of the half-blood *G*, who is a son of *M* by a prior marriage, and another brother of the half-blood *H*, who is a son of *D*'s deceased father by a prior marriage.   *M*, *F*, and *H* are the next of kin, *M* in her own right, and *F* and *H* as representatives of their deceased father; *G* is excluded; *M* takes $\frac{1}{2}$, *F* $\frac{1}{4}$, and *H* $\frac{1}{4}$.

(3) Third class: *D* dies leaving no kindred belonging to the first or second class, but leaving him surviving in the third class, *P. A.* his paternal grandmother, *M. A.* his maternal grandmother, and *A* and *C* issue of the deceased paternal grandfather, *A* being an uncle of *D*, and *C* a cousin of *D* (the son of a deceased

589

---

[1]   Any member of the first, second, or third classes who belongs to several *stirpes* (e. g. , if his father and mother are cousins) takes a separate share in respect of each *stirps*—BGB 1927.

uncle).   Out of the half belonging to the paternal line *P. A.* takes $\frac{1}{4}$ in her own right, and *A* and *C* each take $\frac{1}{8}$ as representatives of their deceased ancestor; the half belonging to the maternal line goes entirely to *M. A.*

(4) Fourth class: the deceased dies without leaving any kindred belonging to the first three classes but one great-uncle *A*, and one second cousin *B*, being the grandson of another great-uncle; *A* alone is nearest of kin.

    cc. Rules for determining division as between surviving spouse and nearest of kin.

    477. The share of the surviving spouse is shown by the following table:

Nearest of kin being:	*Spouse takes:*
1. Issue of deceased	$\frac{1}{4}$
2. Parents of deceased or issue of parents	$\frac{1}{2}$
3. Grandparents exclusively	$\frac{1}{2}$
4. Surviving grandparents and issue of one of deceased grandparents	$\frac{5}{8}$
5. Surviving grandparents and issue of two deceased grandparents	$\frac{3}{4}$
6. One grandparent and issue of three deceased grandparents	$\frac{7}{8}$
7. More distant kindred	the whole.

In cases 4, 5, and 6, the share belonging to the next of kin goes entirely to the surviving grandparents.

In cases 2–6 the spouse also takes the spouse's preferential benefit (475)— BGB 1931, 1932.

Illustration: The deceased leaves no issue but a widow, his mother, and three brothers being sons of his deceased father. The widow takes the preferential benefit and one-half of the residue; out of the other half of the residue the mother takes one-quarter, and each of the brothers take one-twelfth.

e.   Equalization of Shares between Issue (Hotchpot provisions).

590   **478.** Such of the issue of the deceased as are statutory heirs must, on the division of the estate, as between themselves, account for certain kinds of gifts received from the deceased during his life in the manner known in English law as 'bringing

into hotchpot'. [1]   The liability to account for such gifts is called *Ausgleichungspflicht* (hotchpot liability).   The gifts to be accounted for in this manner are:

(1) gifts received by way of advancement—p. 507 note 1, unless expressly exempted from 'hotchpot liability'; (2) allowances or contributions to the expense of the preparation for a profession, in so far as their amount was out of proportion to the means of the giver; (3) gifts made expressly subject to 'hotchpot liability'.

The amounts to be accounted for under the rule stated above are added to the amount representing the net value of the part of the testator's estate divisible among issue.   The statutory portions are then calculated as if the value of the estate was equal to the aggregate amount formed by this addition, and the value of the gifts received by each descendant entitled to a share is deducted from the statutory portion of such descendant; if the value of the gifts received by any descendant exceeds the amount of his portion, such descendant is excluded from the division.

Examples.

The statutory heirs are W, the widow, and three sons, A, B, and C; the value of the estate actually left is ·   ·   ·   ·   ·   ·   ·   £20,000

W receives $\frac{1}{4}$· ·   ·   ·   ·   ·   ·   = 5,000

£15,000

A has to account for £8,000, B for £1,000, C for £3,000, together ·   ·   ·   ·   ·   ·   ·   = 12,000

£27,000

The share of A is £9,000 – £8,000 ·   ·   ·   = £1,000
The share of B is £9,000 – £1,000 ·   ·   ·   = 8,000
The share of C is £9,000 – £3,000 ·   ·   ·   = 6,000

£15,000

If A had to account for £10,000 he would be left out of account; £4,000 (being the aggregate value of gifts made to B and C) would be added to £15,000, making ·   ·   ·   ·   ·   ·   £19,000   591

B would receive £9,500 – £1,000 ·   ·   ·   = 8,500
C would receive £9,500 – £3,000 ·   ·   ·   = 6,500

£15,000

---

[1]   A gift made to any descendant of the deceased who would have been a statutory heir, if the deceased had died at the date of the gift, but who is represented, on the division of the estate, by his issue, must be brought into hotchpot by such issue; on the other hand, a gift made to any descendant who, if the deceased had died at the date of the gift, would not have been a statutory heir, is not, in the absence of a contrary direction, to be brought into hotchpot—BGB 2051 (1), 2053.

Any person who has to bring gifts into hotchpot must give information to all interested persons as to the particulars of such gifts—BGB 2050, 2055–2057. [1]

Where several shares are received by one person under separate titles (*e. g.* where any issue represents several *stirpes*), the hotchpot liability is considered separately for each share; the addition to a share, brought about by the lapse or forfeiture of another share, is for this purpose deemed a separate share—BGB 1935.

2. RENUNCIATION OF STATUTORY RIGHT OF INHERITANCE

479. Any person may by a publicly certified agreement with another renounce his rights to a statutory portion in the estate of such other. [2]   Such an agreement is called *Erbverzicht* (renunciation of inheritance).   Where the renouncing party is one of the kindred of the party to whose estate the renunciation refers, the renunciation extends to the issue of the renouncing party unless the contrary is shown.   Where the renunciation is made in favour of any other person it is, in the absence of a contrary stipulation, inoperative in the event of such other person being deprived of or forfeiting his own right; where a general renunciation is made by any issue of the person to whose estate the renunciation refers, it is presumed to be made in favour of the other issue, and of the spouse of such person.   An agreement between the parties, by which the renunciation is revoked, is subject to the same formal requirements as the original agreement—BGB 2346–2351.

3. FORFEITURE BY DECLARATION OF UNWORTHINESS

480. A statutory or testamentary heir may, on the application of any person who would benefit by his forfeiture of the inheritance, be declared 'unworthy to inherit' (*erbunwürdig*): (*a*) if by any wilful and unlawful act he has caused or attempted to cause the death of the deceased, or has brought him to a condition, by reason of which he became incapable, down to the date of his death, of making or revoking a testamentary disposition; (*b*) if by fraud or unlawful threats

---

1   As to gifts made out of common property by spouses living under any regime of community of goods, see BGB 2054.

2   The party to whose estate the renunciation refers must execute the agreement in person, unless he is incapable (93), in which case his statutory agent may act on his behalf; if he is of restricted capacity the concurrence of the statutory agent is dispensed with.   If either party is under guardianship the leave of the Court is required; if either party is under parental control, the leave is required unless the parties are spouses or intending spouses.

he has prevented the deceased from making or revoking a testamentary disposition, or compelled him to make or revoke a testamentary disposition; (c) if he has forged or destroyed any testamentary instrument made, or purporting to have been made, by the deceased which would, if genuine or existing, be operative at the date of the death of the deceased, or if he has knowingly used any such forged instrument.

If it can be shown that the deceased has condoned the offence, the declaration cannot be made.

The right of inheritance of the person declared unworthy becomes vested, as from the date of accrual, in such person or persons as would have been entitled to such right if the person declared unworthy had predeceased the deceased—BGB 2339–2344.

CHAPTER III
TESTAMENTARY RIGHT OF INHERITANCE

1. Introductory Observations

a. Nature of Testamentary Disposition.

481. Under Roman law a ' testament' was distinguished from a codicil; it was of the essence of a testament that it should contain the appointment of the testator's heirs, whereas a codicil only gave legacies without appointing heirs. The formalities of execution were much more stringent in the case of a testament than in the case of a codicil. Under English law there is no legal difference between a will and a codicil, but it is customary, in a case in which a testator executes several successive testamentary instruments intended to be read together, to designate the instrument first made as the will, and all subsequent ones as codicils to such will. Modern German law has abolished the word "*codicil*' and its German equivalent, (*Nachzettel*, *Nachtrag*, &c.) as savouring of the old distinction. Every instrument containing a testamentary disposition (*letztwillige Verfügung*) is called a will ('testament'), and no such disposition is valid unless the prescribed formalities as to the execution of a will have been observed. The expression 'disposition operative on death' (*Verfügung von Todes wegen*) is used as a general term, comprising wills as well as contracts of inheritance (504)—BGB 1937, 1941.

It is not of the essence of a will that it should appoint heirs or purport to dispose of the whole of the testator's estate or even of any part of it. An instrument containing nothing except the exclusion of particular persons from their statutory right of inheritance is called a will in the same way as an instrument disposing of the whole estate.

b. Joint Wills of Spouses.

482. Joint wills of spouses, and even of persons betrothed to each other, were permitted in those German districts in which the German common law was

applied, though such wills were unknown to Roman law, and prohibited in those   594
parts of Germany in which the law was based on the French Code Civil (see
s. 968).   Under the new law a joint will (*gemeinschaftliches Testament*) is only
permissible as between spouses—BGB 2265.   Such a will usually appoints the
surviving spouse as heir of the predeceasing spouse and the issue of the two
spouses as heirs of the survivor—see BGB 2269.   As to 'correspective dispositions'
in joint wills, see 483.

c.   Circumstances rendering Testamentary Dispositions inoperative.

aa.   General rules.

483. A testamentary disposition may be or become inoperative: (*a*) on the
ground of some defect in the tenor or expression of the disposition (484); (*b*) on
the ground of some act or event done by or affecting the testator or a testamentary
heir or legatee (485).   A testamentary disposition which is vitiated by one of
the defects mentioned sub (*a*) may either be void *ab initio* or only voidable at the
option of some person who would benefit by its avoidance; a disposition which is
rendered inoperative by any act or event referred to sub (*b*) may be rendered
inoperative for all purposes or only as regards a particular person.

Where a disposition is altogether inoperative it is treated as non-existent;
where it is inoperative as regards a particular person, it enures to the benefit of
the substitutional heir or heirs (493) or legatees (496 rule (6)), or of the
person or persons entitled by virtue of the right of survivorship (492), or of the
statutory heirs (473), as the case may be—BGB 2096, 2190.

If the tenor of a testamentary disposition admits of several interpretations,
one of which would render it inoperative while the other would make it operative,
such interpretation as will render the disposition operative is, in the absence of
any indication to the contrary, to be preferred—BGB 2084.

Several dispositions contained in one testamentary instrument may be so
interdependent that the invalidity of one also prevents the operation of one or more
of the others.   This is deemed to be the case if it can be shown that the testator
would not have made a particular disposition, if he had known of the invalidity of   595
another disposition.   In the absence of such proof the invalidity of one of the
dispositions does not affect the validity of the others—BGB 2085.   In the case of
a joint will made by spouses (482), dispositions so deemed to be mutually
interdependent are called 'correspective dispositions' (*korrespective Verfügungen*).
Dispositions by which the spouses confer mutual benefits on each other are, in the

absence of any indication to the contrary, deemed correspective dispositions—BGB 2270.

bb.   Defects cauing nullity or voidability of testamentary dispositions.

484. The following rules apply on this subject:

(1) all the dispositions contained in any will are void:

(*a*) if the testator was incapable of making a testamentary disposition (486) ;

(*b*) if the prescribed formalities (487, 488) have been disregarded [1] ;

(2) a testamentary disposition is void:

(*a*) if it is in favour of the judge, or notary, or of any witness taking part in the formalities of the execution of the will, or of any person related, by ties of kindred or affinity within certain degrees, to such judge, notary, or witness—BGB 2235;

(*b*) if its tenor is unintelligible or incomplete [2] ;

(*c*) if the testator makes its validity depend upon the determination of another, or if he empowers another to appoint an heir or legatee, or to select the object which is to go to a particular legatee; it is, however, permissible to bequeath a legacy to a class, with power to any person nominated by the testator to apportion the bequeathed objects among the class, or to appoint the whole to one or more members of the class, [3] or to give alternative legacies; the appointment of an executor may also be left to the discretion of a nominee—BGB 2065, 2151, 2153, 2154, 2193, 2198;

(3) a testamentary disposition vitiated by any of the following defects may be avoided within a specified period after the testator's death: (*a*) mistake on the testator's part as to its tenor [4] ; (*b*) a mistaken assumption or expectation on the

596

---

[1]   A testamentary disposition executed with the easier formalities allowed under certain special circumstances (488) becomes inoperative after a specified period reckoned from the date at which the special circumstances cease to exist.

[2]   The fact that the testator refers to a future supplemental direction, which he fails to give before his death, does not render the disposition inoperative, unless it can be shown that this was the testator's intention—BGB 2086.

[3]   The rule in the text shows that German law forbids the granting of a '*general* power of appointment' but allows the granting of a '*special* power of appointment' in respect of property bequeathed by will.

[4]   See 99; generally a declaration of intention is not voidable on the ground of mistake as to the tenor of the declaration, unless it can be shown that the declarant would not have made it had he known the true facts *and given reasonable consideration to the matter*; in the case of a testamentary disposition it is sufficient to show that the testator, being the man he was, would not have made the disposition, had he known the true facts.   Compare BGB 119 (1) with BGB 2078 (1).

part of the testator as to any fact or event, present or future; (c) the passing over any person entitled to a compulsory portion (510) of whose existence the testator was ignorant, or who was born or became entitled to a compulsory portion (e. g. by legitimation or adoption) subsequently to the date of the disposition; (d) the influence of unlawful threats.

The right of avoidance of a voidable testamentary disposition may, as a general rule, be exercised by any person benefited by such avoidance, but where a mistake as to any particular person forms the ground of avoidance, such person alone is entitled to exercise the right; where the passing over of any person entitled to a compulsory portion is the ground of avoidance, the person so passed over alone has a right of avoidance.   A disposition is not voidable on any ground mentioned sub (3) if it can be shown that the testator would have made the same disposition if he had known the true facts [1]—BGB 2078–2080, 2082.

An heir or legatee on whom any liability is imposed by a voidable disposition may refuse to discharge such liability, notwithstanding the fact that the right of avoidance has been barred by lapse of time—BGB 2083.

cc.   Acts and events preventing the operation of a testamentary disposition.

485. A testamentary disposition may be rendered wholly or partially inoperative   597 by the testator's revocation (489), or by any of the following acts and events:

(1) *Acts done or events happening before the testator's death.*

The following rules apply:

(a) a disposition conferring a benefit on a particular person is inoperative as regards such person if he or she renounces such benefit by agreement with the testator [2]—BGB 2352;

(b) a disposition in favour of an intended spouse is inoperative as regards such intended spouse if the engagement was broken off before the testator's death—BGB 2077 (2);

(c) a disposition in favour of a spouse is inoperative as regards such spouse if the marriage was declared void or dissolved before the testator's death, or if justifiable divorce or separation proceedings were pending on the ground of any

---

[1]   As to the manner in which the avoidance must be declared, see BGB 2081, which somewhat modifies the general rule on the subject (91).

[2]   This may in some cases be more convenient for the testator than the revocation of the whole will.   The formal requirements are the same as in the case of the renunciation of a statutory right of inheritance (479).

matrimonial offence committed by the surviving spouse—BGB 2077 (1) ; in this case as well as in case (b) the disposition remains operative if it can be shown that the fact in question would not have induced the testator to revoke the disposition—BGB 2077 (3) ; see also BGB 2268;

(d) a disposition in favour of any person who predeceases the testator is inoperative; but where a testamentary heir or legatee who predeceases the testator is a child or remoter issue of the testator, and leaves issue surviving the testator, it is presumed, in the absence of evidence to the contrary, that the issue, who would have taken the place of the deceased child or issue if the testator had died intestate, are intended to take as substitutional heirs or legatees [1]—BGB 1923 (1), 2069, 2160.

(2) *Acts done or events happening after the testator's death.*

The following rules apply:

(a) if any *nasciturus* deemed to be living at the testator's death under the general rule (472) is not subsequently born alive, a testamentary disposition in his favour becomes inoperative—BGB 1923;

(b) if any person appointed as testamentary heir is not as yet living or deemed to be living at the time of the testator's death, the disposition in his favour is inoperative, unless it can be interpreted as the gift of a reversionary right of inheritance (494) ; a legacy, on the other hand, does not lapse merely by reason of the fact that the legatee is not *in esse* at the time of the testator's death (500) [2] —BGB 2101, 2162 (2);

(c) if any heir or legatee is declared unworthy to inherit (480) or disclaims his right of inheritance (522) or a legacy in his favour (525), the disposition by which such right of inheritance or legacy is given is inoperative as regards such heir or legatee, and is deemed to be made in favour of such person or persons as would have been entitled, had the original heir or legatee predeceased the testator—BGB 1953 (1) (2), 2180 (1), 2371, 2377;

(d) if any descendant of the testator is appointed as reversionary heir

---

[1]   The same rule is applied if any benefit is conferred on the testator's ' children ' generally, and any of them predeceases the testator leaving issue surviving the testator—BGB 2068.   Under English law the benefit conferred on a child predeceasing the testator but leaving issue passes to the estate of the deceased child—Wills Act, s. 33.

[2]   A reversionary right given by a testator's will is forfeited unless it becomes vested within the prescribed period of time (494)—BGB 2109, 2163.

(494), so as to become entitled on the death of a limited heir who at the date of the will had no issue, or had issue whose existence was unknown to the testator, the disposition in favour of such reversionary heir becomes inoperative if the limited heir leaves any issue surviving him—BGB 2107.

2. The Formation and Revocation of Testamentary Dispositions

a. Testamentary Capacity.

486. An incapable person (93), or a person placed under guardianship by reason of mental debility, extravagance, or dipsomania, is incapable of making a will [1]; a person who has attained the age of 16 years, and whose capacity is not restricted (94) on any ground other than that of his infancy, can make a will by oral declaration before a judge or a public notary without the concurrence of his statutory agent, but a holograph will or a publicly executed written will (487) cannot validly be made by any person under age, nor can such a will be validly made by a person of full age who is unable to read written characters—BGB 2229, 2238 (2), 2247.

599

b. Formalities of Execution.

aa. *In ordinary cases.*

487. The several drafts of the Code prepared by the two Commissions and by the Federal Council did not recognize the validity of ' private wills' —whether in the nature of holograph wills or of wills executed by the testator in the presence of unofficial witnesses—it being desired that the system existing in some parts of Germany (*e. g.* the older provinces of Prussia), which required all testamentary instruments to be executed before a public authority, should be made universal. The discontent caused by this restriction in those German districts, in which the French law had taken root, induced the Reichstag to authorize holograph wills as

---

1 If the person placed under guardianship survives the date at which the order placing him under guardianship ceases to be appealable, the incapacity begins retrospectively from the date of the application, but the will of a person who dies before the order ceases to be appealable, is not invalid by reason of the order.   The will of a person under guardianship made during the pendency of an application for the removal of the guardianship is not invalid by reason of the existence of the guardianship if the application is successful—BGB 2229 (3), 2230.

well as wills executed in the form recognized by the several drafts; the BGB therefore deals with (1) holograph wills—being the only surviving instances of private wills; (2) publicly declared wills.   A will must in all cases be executed by the testator in person—BGB 2064.

(1) *Holograph wills.*

A holograph will (*eigenhändiges Testament*) is a document containing a direction of any kind intended to be operative on the writer's death, written and signed by the testator and indicating its date, and the name of the place at which it is written.   It is not necessary that the document should be described as a testamentary instrument, or should be strictly confined to testamentary directions. A testamentary disposition contained in an ordinary letter would be deemed a holograph will.   In the case of a joint holograph will the form is sufficiently observed, if one of the sponses writes out the will, and the other spouse adds a declaration in his own handwriting, with the required indication as to date and place, to the effect that he wishes the will to be treated also as his will—BGB 2231 Nr. 2, 2267.

600

A holograph will may be lodged with a public authority; if the public authority with whom it is lodged is not a Court of Law, or if the will at the date of the testator's death is lodged with a private person, such authority or person must on receiving notice of the death deliver the will to the Competent Probate Court—468 (7)—BGB 2248, 2259.

(2) *Publicly declared wills.*

A will executed in public form must be declared before a judge, or a public notary, [1] in one of the following ways: (*a*) the contents of the will may be declared orally before the judge or the notary; (*b*) a writing—sealed or open— may be handed to the judge or notary with an oral declaration to the effect that such writing contains the declarant's will; the declaration must in either case be made by the testator in person; the execution must also be attested by two additional witnesses, or by the Registrar of the Court, or another notary as a single additional witness.

The witnesses or witness must be present during the whole proceedings.

A will is void on the ground of informality: (*a*) if the judge or notary,

---

1   A German consul as regards German subjects has the same functions as a notary.

before whom it is declared or any additional witness, is related to the testator by ties of kindred or affinity within certain specified degrees; (b) if any one of the additional witnesses is related to the officiating judge or notary by ties of kindred or affinity within the same degrees. [1]

Minutes of the proceedings (*Errichtungs-Protokoll*) in the German language must be taken recording: (1) the date and place of the proceedings; (2) the names of the testator, of the officiating judge or notary, and of the additional witnesses or witness; (3) of the declaration made by the testator; (4) the fact that a written document was delivered (if this was done). 601

The minutes must be read out to the testator, and signed by him and the officiating judge, or notary, and the additional witnesses or witness.   If the testator declares that he cannot write, his signature is replaced by a record of such declaration in the minutes. [2]

The minutes of the proceedings, and the documents referred to therein, more particularly the writing (if any) delivered to the judge or notary, are placed in a parcel sealed with the official seal and taken into official custody.   The indorsement describing the will must be signed by the judge or notary.   If the public authority in whose custody the will is placed is not a Court of Law, the will must as soon as such public authority becomes aware of the testator's death be delivered to the Competent Probate Court—468 (7)—BGB 2231 Nr. 1, 2232–2242, 2246, 2259 (2).

bb.   *Relaxation of formalities in special cases.*

488. The principle of the Roman *testamentum militare*, which allowed the testamentary formalities to be relaxed in special cases, which is also recognized in England, has been adopted and considerably extended by the present German law.

Easier formalities are allowed in any of the following cases: (a) where a testator believes his death to be approaching so fast that he would not have time to

---

[1]   Infants, persons deprived of civil rights, persons who have been convicted of perjury, and persons in the service of the officiating judge or notary are improper witnesses, but the fact that any such person acts as a witness does not invalidate the will—BGB 2237; as to the nullity of any dispositions in favour of any person taking part in the formalities of execution or of any near relation of any such person, see 484 rule (2) (a).

[2]   As to declarations by testators unable to speak, and declarations by testators unable to express themselves in the German language, see BGB 2243–2245.

make a declaration before a judge or notary [1] ; (b) where the testator's place of residence is, by reason of an epidemic or of other exceptional circumstances, isolated from the outer world to such an extent that a declaration before a judge or notary is rendered impossible or exceptionally difficult; (c) where the testator, being a member of the armed forces in time of war or under a state of siege, is impeded by one of certain specified hindrances, from making a will in one of the ordinary forms; (d) in any case in which the testator is on board any German ship other than a warship while such ship is not in any German port.

602

In any of the cases referred to sub (a) and (b) the chief communal officer (*Gemeindevorsteher*) may officiate in the place of a judge or notary; in any of the cases mentioned sub (b) and (c) an oral declaration (which has to be recorded in writing) may be made before three unofficial witnesses; in any of the cases mentioned sub (d) a written will signed by the testator in the presence of an officer and two witnesses, or an oral declaration made before an officer and two witnesses and duly recorded, is sufficient.

Any will, executed in one of the easier forms under the rules mentioned above, becomes inoperative after the lapse of a certain specified period reckoned from the date at which the circumstances justifying the relaxation cease to exist— BGB 2249–2252; Imperial Military Law of 1874, s. 44; EG 44.

c.   Revocation of Testamentary Dispositions.

489. The capacity to revoke a testamentary disposition is governed by the same rules as the capacity to make such a disposition, subject, however, to the qualification that a person under guardianship on the ground of mental debility, extravagance, or dipsomania, may, notwithstanding such disability, revoke a testamentary disposition made before he was placed under guardianship—BGB 2253.

The revocation may refer to the whole of the contents of a will or to a particular disposition contained therein, and may be effected in one of the following ways:

(1) by a will [2] either expressly revoking the will or disposition intended to

---

1   A joint will can be executed in the simplified form, if one of the spouses is in the condition described in the text—BGB 2266.

2   Where in a joint will there are any correspective dispositions—483, the revocation of any of them by one of the spouses has the effect of revoking the corresponding dispositions of the other spouse.   This can only be done during the joint lives of the spouses, and must be done by a publicly authenticated written declaration.   Revocation by will is ineffectual in such a case—BGB 2270, 2271 (1) (2).

be revoked, or containing some disposition inconsistent with the disposition intended to be revoked [1] ;

(2) by the destruction of the will, or by the cancellation or alteration of any   603
testamentary disposition, effected by the testator in person, with the intention of revoking the will so destroyed or the disposition so cancelled or altered; this intention is presumed in the absence of any evidence to the contrary;

(3) a will declared before a judge or public notary is revoked by its removal out of the official custody, which may at any time be effected by personal delivery to the testator, or in the case of a joint will by delivery to the testators jointly at their joint request; a holograph will is not revoked by its removal out of the official custody [2] ;

(4) a testamentary disposition may be revoked by any stipulation contained in any contract of inheritance (504) which is inconsistent with such testamentary disposition [3] —BGB 2253–2258, 2272, 2289 (2).

3. TENOR AND EFFECT OF TESTAMENTARY DISPOSITIONS

a.   Appointment of Heirs.

aa.   Mode of appoiniment.

490. It is unnecessary to appoint the heirs, as such, by express words.   Any person to whom the testator gives the whole, or an aliquot part of his estate, is thereby deemed to be the testator's heir, or one of his heirs.   This presumption is not applied in a case in which the testator bequeaths the 'compulsory portion' to one of the statutory heirs, without stating that the beneficiary is to take such portion as one of the testator's heirs.   On the other hand a person to whom any specific object is given, though described as heir, is deemed to be a legatee, and not an heir, unless it is shown by other indications that it was the testator's

---

1   If a second will, revoking a previous will, is itself revoked, the dispositions of the previous will become operative again, as though they had never been revoked—BGB 2258 (2).

2   The fact that a will remains in the official custody on the testator's death does not prove that such will or the whole of the dispositions contained therein remain unrevoked; the revocation may have been made by a holograph will remaining in private custody, or by a publicly declared will placed in some other official custody, or by contract of inheritance.

3   German law has no rule similar to the rule of English law (Wills Act, s. 18) under which a testator's marriage revokes his will.

intention to appoint him as heir in the technical sense—BGB 2087.

bb. *Ascertainment of shares.*

604   **491.** The following rules apply in any case in which the testator's directions leave any doubt:

(1) if only one person is appointed as heir, and not more than an aliquot part of the testator's estate is given to him, the remaining part of the estate goes to the statutory heirs;

(2) if several persons are appointed as heirs and the shares given to them do not, in the aggregate, exhaust the whole estate, there are two possibilities:

(*a*) if it is clear from the directions contained in the will that the persons appointed are intended to take the whole estate (*e. g.* if the will says: I give the whole of my estate to A, B, and C, in the following proportions: three-tenths to A, two-tenths to B, and four-tenths to C) the shares are increased rateably; (A, in the example given, takes three-ninths, B two-ninths, and C four-ninths);

(*b*) if the will does not show that the persons appointed as heirs are to take the whole estate the part of the estate which is not disposed of goes to the statutory heirs;

(3) if several persons are appointed as heirs and the shares given to them, in the aggregate, exceed the whole estate, the shares abate rateably;

(4) if several persons are appointed as heirs, without any indication as to the manner in which the estate is to be divided between them, such persons take in equal shares unless they are described in any of the following ways:

(*a*) if the testator says: 'I give my estate to my statutory heirs', each of the persons who would take the estate in the event of the testator's intestacy is entitled to his statutory portion (476, 477);

(*b*) if the testator says: 'I give my estate to my kindred', or 'to my nearest kindred', each of the persons among the kindred who would take the estate in the event of the testator's intestacy is entitled to his statutory portion;

(*c*) if the testator says: 'I give my estate to my children', the issue of any deceased child takes in substitution of such child and the division among the children and the issue of deceased children is *per stirpes*:

605   (5) if some persons appointed as heirs are given aliquot shares of the estate, while there is no indication as to the shares to be taken by the others, such others divide the balance in accordance with rule (4); if the aliquot shares given by the will exhaust the whole estate, such aliquot shares abate rateably, on the footing

that each of the heirs, to whom no definite share has been appointed, takes a share equal to the smallest aliquot share expressly given by the will [1];

(6) if any particular share is given to several persons together, rules (1) to (5) are, as between such persons, applied, *mutatis mutandis*; a share given to several persons in this manner is called ' a joint share in the inheritance' (*gemeinschaftlicher Erbteil*)—BGB 2066, 2067, 2088–2093.

cc.   Right of survivorship [2] between co-heirs.

492. The right of survivorship appears in two forms:

(1) survivorship among co-heirs generally;

(2) survivorship as to joint shares.

If a testamentary disposition becomes inoperative, as regards any particular heir, under the rules stated above (485), the following rules are applied in the absence of a contrary indication in the testator's will, and in the absence of a substitutional heir (493) able and willing to take the vacant share:

(1) where, in the case of the whole estate being given to the heirs appointed by the will, the disposition in favour of one of them becomes inoperative, the others divide his share in the proportions in which they are entitled to the inheritance; if in such a case a share in a 'joint share'—491 rule (6)—becomes vacant, the persons entitled to the remaining part of the joint share become entitled in the first place; if no such persons are available the other heirs take the whole of the 'joint share';

(2) if the heirs appointed by the will only take part of the estate (the other part being intended to go to the statutory heirs) a vacant whole share goes to the statutory heirs; but a vacant share in a 'joint share' goes to the persons entitled to the other part of such 'joint share'; where no such person is available, the whole joint share goes to the statutory heirs;

(3) any share in the estate accruing to any heir by virtue of the right of survivorship is, as regards the 'hotchpot liability' (478), and as regards the

606

---

[1]   Illustration: The testator says: I appoint as my heirs my wife and my three children, A, B, and C; and I direct that one half of my estate is to go to my son A, and that each of my children B and C is to take one quarter.   In the result the widow takes $\frac{1}{5}$, A takes $\frac{2}{5}$, and each of the two other children take $\frac{1}{5}$.

[2]   The expression ' survivorship' is for the sake of brevity used as an equivalent for the German *Anwachsungsrecht* (*jus accrescendi*), which means the right of the surviving or continuing heirs to a share lapsed by the death of another heir, or by some other circumstance causing the testamentary disposition in favour of such heir to become inoperative.

liability for legacies and testamentary burdens (497, 501), deemed a separate share—BGB 2094, 2095, 2099.

dd.   Appointment of substitutional heirs.

(1) Mode of appointment.

493. A substitutional heir (*Ersatzerbe*) is an heir appointed to take the place of another heir in the event of the right of inheritance being lost or forfeited by reason of any circumstance rendering the disposition in his favour inoperative (485)—BGB 2096.

A person appointed as heir, in the event of the primarily appointed heir being 'unable' to become heir, is, in the absence of an indication to the contrary, deemed to be appointed substitutional heir for all purposes; the same presumption is applied, if the eventuality mentioned in the will is the 'unwillingness' of the primarily appointed heir—BGB 2097.

(2) Presumption as to reversionary heirs.

A person appointed as 'reversionary heir' (494) is, in the absence of any indication to the contrary, also deemed to be appointed as substitutional heir to the prior interest of the 'limited heir' [1] —BGB 2102 (1).

(3) Presumption as to issue of a deceased child.

The issue of a deceased descendant of the testator, are presumed to be substituted as heirs for such descendant, in so far as they would have taken his place in the event of the testator's intestacy—BGB 2069.

(4) Appointment of co-heirs mutually.

607   If the persons appointed as co-heirs are mutually appointed as substitutional heirs for each other the vacant share of one of them goes to the other co-heirs rateably in proportion to their original shares, but where a share in a joint share is vacant, such share goes to the persons entitled to the remaining part of the joint share—BGB 2098.

---

1   Illustration: A testator gives his estate to his wife for life, appointing his sons *B* and *C* as reversionary heirs; the widow disclaims the inheritance, *B* and *C* take it immediately as substituted heirs.

ee. Appointment of reversionary heirs.

(1) *General rules.*

494. The appointment of reversionary heirs (*Nacherben*) [1] takes the place of the Roman *substitutio fideicommissaria*, but with considerable modifications.

The rules which enable a testator to create successive interests in any part of his estate in favour of persons who may be unborn or unascertained at the date of his death, bring the German law on this subject into close resemblance to English law, and differentiate it from French law, which, as is well known, prohibits ' substitutions' in the great majority of cases.

German law, like English law, does not allow the unlimited creation of successive interests, but the effect of a disregard of the English rule against perpetuities is much more serious than the effect of a disregard of the corresponding German rule.

Under English law a disposition disregarding the rule is void, even if under the particular circumstances of the case the property to which it refers would have become finally vested within the proper period; under German law, on the other hand, a gift is operative, if, as a matter of fact, the final vesting takes place within the period allowed by law. [2]

Under German law a testamentary disposition appointing a reversionary heir is operative:

(*a*) if it is limited to take effect on the happening of any event affecting the limited heir (*e. g.* his death) or the reversionary heir (*e. g.* his attaining a particular age) and if the person to be affected by the decisive event is living at the time of the testator's death;

(*b*) if it is limited to take effect in the event of the birth of a brother or

608

---

[1] The expression *Nacherbe* was formerly used by many writers to indicate a ' substitutional' heir, and it is used in that sense by the Saxon Code. Modern textbooks use the expression exclusively in the sense given to it by the BGB.

[2] Illustration: An English testator gives his estate to *A* for life with remainder to such children of *A* as attain the age of 25. On the testator's death *A* has three children aged respectively 24, 23, and 22, who all subsequently attain the age of 25. The gift to *A*'s children is void, notwithstanding the fact that all the children of *A* attain the age of 25 long before the expiration of 21 years from *A*'s death—*In re* Mervin (1891) 3 Ch. 197. Under German law the gift would have been invalid only as to such children of *A* as would not have attained the age of 25 within 30 years after the testator's death.

sister of any limited heir and in favour of such brother or sister [1] ;

(*c*) in any case if the reversionary share becomes vested in the ultimate reversionary heir within 30 years from the testator's death—BGB 2109.

A reversionary right of inheritance may be made subject to a condition; that is to say the right of the reversionary heir may depend on the fulfilment of a condition precedent (*e. g.* his assumption of the testator's name) or the non-occurrence of a condition subsequent by which the limited heir's interest is to be forfeited (*e. g.* by his discontinuance of the use of the testator's name). As to the rules of interpretation applicable to certain kinds of conditional testamentary gifts, see 500.

(2) *Mode of appointment.*

A reversionary heir may of course be appointed as such by express words, but in the absence of any express direction, or of any evidence contained in the will of a contrary intention, the following intentions as to the appointment of limited heirs and reversionary heirs are presumed:

(1) if it is doubtful whether any person is appointed as reversionary heir, or as substitutional heir, such person is deemed to be appointed as substitutional heir [2] —BGB 2102 (2);

609   (2) if the estate or a share therein is given to two persons successively, or to a named person, with a direction to transfer it to another named person at a given date, or on the happening of a given event, the person named as beneficiary in the first place is deemed to have been appointed limited heir, and the person named as beneficiary in the second place is deemed to have been appointed as reversionary heir—BGB 2100, 2103;

(3) if the estate or a share therein is given by description to any natural person, who, on the testator's death, is not yet living or deemed to be living, or to a corporate body who on the testator's death is not as yet in existence, such natural person or corporate body is presumed to have been appointed reversionary heir [3] —BGB 2101; as to the destination of the intermediate interest, see below

---

1   A gift to *A* for life, remainder to his brothers and sisters for life in the order of their respective ages with an ultimate gift in favour of the youngest member of the class is therefore valid.

2   As mentioned above (493) a person appointed as reversionary heir is deemed to have been appointed as substitutional heir at the same time.

3   If it is shown from other indications in the will that this was not the testator's intention the disposition in favour of the unborn person or non-existent corporation becomes inoperative.

rule (5);

(4) if the estate or a share therein is given so as to be held until a given date, or until the happening of a given event, and no direction is given as to the subsequent destination of the property, the persons who would have been the testator's statutory heirs if he had died at such date, or on the happening of such an event, are the reversionary heirs—BGB 2104.   If the testator has made a gift over to his 'statutory heirs' or his 'kindred', those persons take who would be included in the expression used by the testator—see 491 rule (4)—if he had died at the decisive date, or on the happening of the decisive event—BGB 2066, 2067;

(5) if a reversionary heir is appointed but the intermediate interest is undisposed of the statutory heirs take as limited heirs—BGB 2105;

(6) if the estate or a share therein is given to two persons successively without any indication as to the time of the vesting of the reversionary interest, the person taking a limited interest takes for life—BGB 2106 (1);

(7) if a natural person or corporate body takes the estate or a share therein by virtue of the presumption referred to sub (3), the interest of the limited heirs ceases on the coming into existence of such natural person or of such corporation— BGB 2106 (2).[1]

(3) *Legal nature of limited and of reversionary interest.*

The appointment of a reversionary heir answers the same purposes as the   610
creation of successive legal or equitable interests by an English will or settlement, but in its legal aspect has an entirely different character.   The splitting up of the right of ownership into a number of particular estates and interests, as it exists in English law, is quite unknown to German law.   The limited heir while his interest is in existence is entitled to the whole interest in the estate or in the share therein given to him by the testator; the right of the reversionary heir during such time is purely in the nature of a personal claim, which, however, immediately on the termination of the limited interest becomes transformed into a right of inheritance.

The personal claim of a reversionary heir who is in existence or deemed to be in existence at the time of the testator's death, accrues on such death; the personal claim of a reversionary heir who neither is, nor is deemed to be in existence

---

[1]   Gifts of conditional reversionary rights of inheritance are subject to the same rules of interpretation as conditional legacies (500).

at the time of such death, accrues on his coming into existence; the personal claim to a reversionary interest, given subject to a condition precedent, accrues on the fulfilment of the condition and, in the absence of an indication to the contrary, is forfeited by the death of the reversionary heir before such fulfilment. In any other case the claim of a reversionary heir, who dies before it becomes transformed into a right of inheritance, forms part of his estate.

If the reversionary heir disclaims his right, which he may do as soon as the right accrues, the limited heir, in the absence of a contrary direction, takes an absolute indefeasible interest—BGB 2074, 2108, 2139, 2142.

The appointment of a reversionary heir must be distinguished from a disposition, under which the estate, or a share therein, is given to an heir subject to a right of usufruct in favour of another during his life.   A limited heir is owner of the estate, or of his share therein, whereas a usufructuary, though entitled to claim delivery of possession of the objects subject to his right, has merely a *jus in re aliena*.

b.   Legacies and Testamentary Burdens.

aa.   Definition.

611   **495.** A gift, made by will, which confers on the beneficiary any pecuniary advantage (*Vermögensvorteil*) and does not comprise the whole of the testator's residuary estate, or an aliquot part thereof, is a legacy (*Vermächtniss*) within the meaning of German law—BGB 1939.   The right to a legacy given unconditionally, and without any stipulations as to time, accrues on the testator's death; the right to a legacy given subject to a condition precedent, [1] or to a stipulation as to time, accrues on the fulfilment of the condition, or at the stipulated time. [2]

The legatee (*Vermächtnissnehmer*), as such, has no right of ownership over any object bequeathed to him; his right is in the nature of a personal claim against the person charged by the testator with the burden of the legacy.   The burden of a legacy may be imposed on the heirs generally or on any particular heir or on a person entitled to another legacy—BGB 2147, 2174, 2176, 2177.

The person charged with a legacy may have to deliver a thing, or transfer a

---

[1]   The right to a legacy given to a person who is not living or deemed to be living at the time of the testator's death, or to a person who is to be ascertained on an event which is to happen after the testator's death, accrues on the birth of the legatee or the happening of the event—BGB 2178.

[2]   If the date precedes the testator's death the legacy accrues on the date of the death.

right to the legatee, or do some other act for his benefit (*e. g.* grant him a loan). If the performance of the act directed by the testator is either in its nature impossible, or prohibited by law at the date of accrual, or of immoral character, the bequest is inoperative—BGB 138, 2171.   If it is merely impossible under the special circumstances, the general rule relating to obligatory duties of which the performance is impossible (158) applies.

bb.   *Benefit of legacies.*

496. The following rules apply on this subject:

(1) the benefit of a legacy may be given to any person including one of the   612 heirs; the gift of such a benefit is deemed a legacy, even if the heir to whom it is given is himself charged with the whole or part of its burden [1]—BGB 2150;

(2) if the testator directs that a particular object forming part of his estate is not to go to his testamentary heirs, the statutory heirs become entitled as legatees—BGB 2149;

(3) if a legacy is given to several persons, the same rules are applied as to the ascertainment of the shares and as to the right of survivorship, as in the case of the appointment of several persons as heirs (491, 492)—BGB 2157-2159;

(4) if a legacy is given to the testator's 'statutory heirs', or to his 'kindred', or to his 'children', the beneficiaries are ascertained in the same way as in the case of a corresponding appointment of heirs—491 rule (4);

(5) subject to the provisions of rule (7), a legacy lapses if the legatee dies before the date of accrual, or if he disclaims, or if the testamentary disposition by which the legacy was given was inoperative *ab initio* or was rendered inoperative by some subsequent act or event (484, 485)—BGB 2077-2080, 2160, 2180, 2345, 2352;

(6) if a legacy becomes inoperative as regards a particular legatee, the substitutional legatee (if any) appointed by the testator takes the place of the original legatee, in the same way as a substitutional heir takes the place of the

---

[1] This modification of the Roman law as to *praelegatum* is of practical importance; where the burden is imposed on the heirs generally, it gives the heir to whom the legacy is given an advantage over his co-heirs, but even in a case where there is only one heir who is charged with all the legacies, he derives an advantage from having a legacy given to him.   If a testator leaves his estate, worth £ 20, 000, to his heir A, and gives a legacy of £ 15, 000 to A, and another legacy of £ 15, 000 to B, A and B are each reduced to £ 10, 000. Under Roman law the legacy to A would have been deemed part of the inheritance, and B would have taken the whole £ 15, 000, being the only legatee.

primarily appointed heir—BGB 2190;

(7) where a legacy is given to any descendant of the testator who predeceases him leaving issue, the issue of the deceased legatee take the legacy by substitution, in the same way as the issue of a deceased heir take the inheritance under the same circumstances—493 sub (3)—BGB 2069.

cc. Burden of legacies.

613   **497.** The burden of the legacies or of any particular legacy may be imposed on the heirs generally, or on any particular heir, or on one or more legatees, in such manner and in such proportions as the testator may direct.

The following rules apply in the absence of special directions by the testator to the contrary:

(1) the legacies not specifically charged on any particular persons or person must be borne by the heirs generally;

(2) where any legacy has to be borne by the heirs generally the burden is divided between them *pro rata* of their respective shares in the estate;

(3) where any legacy has to be borne by several legatees, the burden is divided between them *pro rata* of the value of their legacies;

(4) a legatee is not required to perform any obligation imposed upon him before he is himself entitled to claim the benefit of his legacy;

(5) where any heir or legatee charged with any legacy cannot or does not in fact accept the benefit conferred upon him, the burden otherwise to be borne by him is charged on the person benefiting in his place.

The rule of Roman law, which exempted an heir from the liability for legacies imposed upon him, in so far as they prevented him from retaining at least one-quarter of his share in the testator's estate for his own benefit (*Quarta Falcidia*) , has not been adopted by the BGB, but an heir can limit his personal liability for legacies in the same way as he can limit his liability for debts (532) , and a legatee may refuse to perform the obligation imposed upon him in so far as the cost of such performance exceeds the value of the benefit conferred upon him—BGB 2147, 2148, 2161, 2186–2188.

dd.   General, demonstrative, and specific legacies.

(1) General statement.

498. The sub-division of legacies into general, specific, and demonstrative legacies which is familiar to English lawyers, is unknown in Germany, but it fits well into the German rules and offers a convenient framework for the classification   614 of the kinds of legacies allowed by German law.

The bequest of an object described generically which the legatee is entitled to claim without reference to the question whether it forms part of the testator's estate or not (e. g. £ 1, 000 payable in cash, £ 1, 000 Consols, a sewing machine, three dozen bottles of 1887 port wine), is in the following observations classed as a 'general legacy'.

The expression 'specific legacy' is used for the bequest of any object described specifically which, according to the testator's intention, the legatee is not entitled to claim, unless it forms part of his estate (e. g. 'my 100 shares in the Union Bank', 'my sewing machine', 'the three dozen bottles of 1887 port wine in my wine-cellar').

The expression 'demonstrative legacy' is used for the bequest of an object described specifically which the testator wishes the legatee to receive without regard to the fact whether it forms part of his estate or not, it being his intention that such specific object should be procured by the person charged with the legacy in the event of its not forming part of his estate.

(2) Rules as to general legacies.

Where an object generically described is bequeathed to a legatee, he is entitled to receive an object answering the descriptions of a quality suitable to his position in life.   The person charged with the burden of such a legacy is under the same liability as regards title and freedom from defects as the vendor of a movable thing (187).   A legatee to whom a defective object is delivered, may require its replacement by an object free from defects; if the defects have been fraudulently concealed, he may, instead of claiming delivery of an object free from defects, claim damages from the person charged with the legacy for the non-performance of his obligation—BGB 2155 (1), 2182, 2183.

(3) Rules as to specific legacies.

The following rules apply in the absence of any indication to the contrary:

615   (*a*) any bequest of an object described specifically is presumed to be given with the intention that the legatee should have no claim in the event of the object so described not forming part of the testator's estate [1]—BGB 2169 (1);

(*b*) if the testator has bequeathed a specific object, of which he is in possession at the time of his death, without being its owner, he is presumed to have bequeathed the right to possession, unless such right offers no legal advantage to the legatee [2]—BGB 2169 (2);

(*c*) if the bequeathed object is destroyed or removed after the date of the bequest, the testator's claim for compensation (if any) for such destruction or removal is presumed to be substituted for the bequeathed object—BGB 2169 (3);

(*d*) if any claim specifically bequeathed by the testator is satisfied before his death, the legatee is presumed to be entitled to the object delivered in satisfaction of the claim; where the satisfied claim was a claim for the payment of any money, the legatee is entitled to the sum of money received by the testator, whether the estate comprises cash to the like amount or not—BGB 2173;

(*e*) the bequest of a specific thing is presumed to comprise the accessories of such thing, as well as all claims for compensation in respect of any damage done to such thing after the date of the bequest—BGB 2164 [3];

(*f*) the bequeathed object is presumed to be given subject to all incumbrances affecting it at the time of the testator's death [4], [5] —BGB 2165 (1).

---

[1]   If the testator's heirs have a claim to the delivery of the specifically bequeathed object, the legatee is entitled to the assignment of such claim; on the other hand, the legatee has no claim in respect of an object specifically bequeathed which, though forming part of the testator's estate, has to be delivered to another under an agreement for sale made by the testator and binding on the heirs—BGB 2169 (3) (4).

[2]   This rule is applied even in a case in which the testator erroneously assumes that he is the owner—RGZ 4, 261.   Expressed in English conveyancer's language, the rule is that the bequest of a specific object gives the legatee a claim to all the testator's estate and interest in such object.

[3]   As to fruits and profits, see BGB 2184; as to the right of the person charged with the legacy to be compensated for outlay, see BGB 2185.

[4]   If a charge to which the bequeathed object is subject was vested in the testator at the time of his death (377), it must be decided from the surrounding circumstances, whether the benefit of such charge goes to the legatee, or remains vested in the heir—BGB 2165 (2).   As to the legatee's duty to indemnify the heir against his personal liability in respect of any debt charged on the bequeathed object, see BGB 2166, 2167; as to the legatee's liability to discharge the proportionate part of a collective land charge—378 sub (3)—charged on the bequeathed object and other objects, see BGB 2168.

[5]   The German law in this respect is similar to the English law as established by Locke King's Act.

(4) *Rules as to demonstrative legacies.*

The person charged with a demonstrative legacy (see above sub (1)) must,   616
if the object bequeathed does not form part of the estate, procure it for the
legatee [1] ; if the cost of the bequeathed object would be out of proportion to its
value, a sum representing such value must be paid to the legatee—BGB 2169
(1), 2170.

ee. Discretionary and alternative legacies. (Powers of appointment.)

499. A testamentary disposition is generally invalid, if its effect is dependent
upon the determination of any person other than the testator—484; but this
general rule is subject to the following exceptional provisions which apply in the
absence of any indication to the contrary:

(1) the testator may give a legacy to several persons alternatively, power
being given to the person charged with the legacy, or to some other person to
select the legatee; if the donee of the power is unable to exercise it, the legatees
are in the position of joint creditors (183); if the bequeathed object is delivered
to one of the alternative legatees, the others are not entitled to claim any part of
its value—BGB 2151;

(2) the testator may give a legacy to several persons collectively, power being
given to the person charged with the legacy or some other person to apportion the
bequeathed objects among the legatees; if the donee of the power is unable to
exercise it, the several legatees take in equal shares [2] —BGB 2153;

(3) the testator may give several specified objects alternatively to one person,   617
power being given to the person charged with the legacy, or to some other person
to select one of the specified objects; if the donee of the power, in a case where
he is not the person charged with the legacy, is unable to exercise the power
of selection, such power is transferred to the person charged with the legacy—

---

[1]   As regards title and quality the obligations are the same as in the case of the sale of a generically
defined object (187).

[2]   This power of appointment is exactly analogous to a special power of appointment contained in an
English will or settlement; where such a power is given there is generally a clause providing for the division
of the property in default of appointment among all the members of the class in equal shares either
unconditionally or conditionally upon attaining full age or marrying; in the absence of such a clause the
property would not, according to English law, go to the objects of the power, but revert to the testator's estate
or to the settlor.   In German law, a gift to the class in equal shares is presumed in every case in default of
appointment.

BGB 2154;

(4) the testator may determine the purpose for which a legacy is intended, leaving the means to be used for the satisfaction of such purpose to the discretion of the person charged with the legacy or of some other person; he must, however, himself determine who is to receive the legacy [1]; the person on whom the discretionary power is conferred comes under the general rules as to discretionary mode of performance—144 sub (2)—BGB 2156;

(5) the testator may leave the date for the satisfaction of a legacy to the discretion of the person charged therewith; in such a case the date of the death of such person is the latest date for the satisfaction of the legacy—BGB 2181.

ff.   Conditional and reversionary legacies.

(1) General statement.

500. The testator may direct a legacy to become vested at a date subsequent to his death, or on the fulfilment of a condition precedent, or to become divested on the fulfilment of a condition subsequent; a legacy may also be given to a person who is neither living, nor deemed to be living at the time of the testator's death, or to several persons in succession.

A legacy made subject to a condition precedent, or to a stipulation as to time, is forfeited if the condition or the stipulation as to time is not fulfilled within a specified period, which is fixed by the same rules—*mutatis mutandis*—as the rules determining the period within which a reversionary right of inheritance must become vested—494 sub (1).   Such a legacy lapses if it does not become vested in possession within the period allowed by the rules—BGB 2162, 2163.

618

(2) Conditional legacies.

The following rules are, in the absence of any indication to the contrary contained in the testator's will, applied as to the effect of certain kinds of conditional legacies:

(a) a legacy subject to a condition precedent is forfeited by the death of the legatee before the fulfilment of the condition—BGB 2074;

(b) a legacy given on condition that the legatee shall abstain from, or

---

[1]   Where a legacy is given ' to the poor' this is interpreted as a legacy to the public poor relief fund of the commune in the district of which the testator had his last domicil, the authority administering the fund being bound to distribute such legacy among poor persons—BGB 2072.

continue a certain course of action, dependent entirely on his own free choice during an indefinite period of time (*e. g.* during his own life), is deemed to be a legacy subject to a condition subsequent [1]—BGB 2075;

(*c*) a condition imposed for the benefit of a third party is deemed to be fulfilled if such third party refuses to concur in some act required for the fulfilment of the condition—BGB 2076. [2]

(3) *Reversionary legacies.*

The following rules apply as to reversionary legacies:

(*a*) where a legacy is given to two legatees successively, the person to whom such legacy is given in the first instance is entitled to receive the bequeathed object, but subject to the burden of handing it over to the reversionary legatee at the time, or in the event prescribed by the testator;

(*b*) where no direction is given as to the date of transfer, the date of the first legatee's death is deemed to be intended;

(*c*) where a legacy is given to any descendant of the testator subject to a gift over, the testator being ignorant of the fact that the first legatee has any issue, the right of the reversionary legatee is forfeited if the first legatee leaves any issue on his death, unless a contrary intention is shown—BGB 2191;

619

(*d*) a reversionary legatee is presumed to be appointed as substitutional legatee, in the event of the first legatee forfeiting or disclaiming his right—BGB 2191.

gg.   Testamentary burdens.

501. A person entitled to the benefit of a testamentary burden obtains no enforceable right; but the performance of the obligation imposed on the person charged with the burden may be enforced by the heirs jointly, or by one of the co-heirs, or by any other person who would be benefited if the person charged with the burden had to forfeit his benefit under the testator's will—BGB 1940, 2194.

Subject to the modification necessitated by the difference in the legal position of the respective beneficiaries and the special rules stated below, the rules as to

---

[1]   A legacy to *A* subject to his passing the bar examination before a given date comes under rule (*a*); a legacy to *A* on condition that he shall continue to reside in the city of Paderborn comes under rule (*b*).

[2]   Illustration: *A* gives *B* a legacy of £ 1, 000 on condition that *B* takes *A*'s son into partnership; *A*'s son refuses to go into partnership with *B*; the condition is deemed fulfilled.

legacies—496–499—apply, *mutatis mutandis*, to testamentary burdens—BGB 2192.

The special rules provide as follows:

(1) where the purpose of a testamentary burden is defined by the testator he may leave the selection of the beneficiaries, as well as the selection of the means to be employed for the satisfaction of the purpose, to the discretion of the person charged with the burden, or to any third person [1]—BGB 2193;

(2) in any case in which the performance of the obligation imposed on a person charged with a testamentary burden is impossible, owing to any circumstances for which such person is responsible, and also in any case in which the person entitled to demand such performance has obtained a judgment, but has been unable to enforce it, the person charged with the burden must surrender the benefit derived from the non-performance of his obligation in accordance with the rules as to unjustified benefits—298—BGB 2196;

(3) in any case not coming within rule (2) a person taking a benefit under a will subject to a burden, is entitled to retain such benefit, notwithstanding the fact that the performance of the obligation imposed upon him is impossible, unless it appears from the tenor of the will that the testator would not have conferred the benefit except in return for the performance of the obligation—BGB 2195. [2]

c.   Appointment of Executors.

502. A testator may by his will appoint one or more executors, or leave it to the discretion of some other person, [3] or of the Competent Probate Court, to make such an appointment.   He may also appoint or provide for the appointment of any substitutional executors, to take the place of executors who are unable or unwilling to accept the office, or who, having accepted the office, vacate it at any subsequent time.   An executor may also be empowered by the testator to appoint one or more co-executors, and to appoint one or more successors to himself [4]—BGB 2197–2201.

---

[1]   Cf. 499 rule (4).

[2]   A person who receives a testamentary gift subject to a burden is in a more favourable position than a person who receives a similar gift by act *inter vivos*, see 204.

[3]   A person who under the will has such a power of appointment may be required by any beneficiary to exercise it within a specified period; if he fails to comply with such requisition he forfeits the power—BGB 2198 (2).

[4]   As to the nature of an executor's office, see 526, 527.

d.   Miscellaneous Rules of Interpretation.

503. Most of the rules given above, as to the effect of the several kinds of testamentary dispositions, are merely rules of interpretation; they give directions, thought to embody the testator's probable intentions, and are applicable only in so far as there are no indications of a contrary intention.   For the sake of completeness some further miscellaneous rules must be added which, in the absence of any indication to the contrary contained in a testator's will, are applicable to all kinds of testamentary dispositions:

(1) *Testamentary gifts to the issue of a named person.* [1]

Such gifts do not go to any issue who are not living or deemed to be living on the accrual of the gift—BGB 2070.

(2) *Testamentary gifts to classes of persons.*

A gift to any class [2] of persons, or to persons in the testator's domestic service   621 or employed in his professional business and described by their relation to the testator, goes to the persons who, at the date of accrual, form such class or stand in such relation to the testator—BGB 2071.

(3) *Effect of ambiguous description.*

If any beneficiary is designated by a description or name which applies equally to several persons, so that it is impossible to ascertain which of such persons is intended, the gift is divided among all such persons in equal shares [3] —BGB 2073.

(4) *Testamentary gifts by joint will of spouses.*

Where two spouses by their joint will (482) appoint the surviving spouse as heir of the predeceasing spouse, and declare that after the death of the survivor the estate is to go to any third parties (*e. g.* the issue of the marriage), such third parties are deemed to be appointed as heirs to the whole estate of the survivor,

---

[1]   As to testamentary gifts to the testator's 'statutory heirs', or to his 'kindred', or to his 'next of kin', or to his 'children', see 491 rule (4).

[2]   As to gifts to 'the poor', see p. 574 note 1.

[3]   In the case of a testamentary gift to a charitable institution by a description applicable to several institutions of the same class, a similar rule is applicable under English law.   *Re* Alchin's Trusts L. R. 14 Eq. 230.

whether acquired under the joint will or otherwise. [1]

Where any object bequeathed to a legatee by a joint will of two spouses is to be delivered on the death of the surviving spouse, the legatee's right is not deemed to accrue before such surviving spouse's death; the legacy therefore lapses if the legatee predeceases the surviving spouse [2]—BGB 2269.

(5) *Presumption as to equalization of shares.*

If a testator gives to his issue, or to some of them, the portions which they would have received under the statutory rules in the event of his intestacy, any advances made to such issue must be brought into hotchpot, as in the case of intestate succession (478)—BGB 2052.

---

1   Under German common law the third party was deemed to be reversionary heir in respect of the estate of the predeceasing spouse and substituted heir in respect of the estate of the survivor.

2   The same rule of interpretation is applied to dispositions of a corresponding nature contained in a contract of inheritance—BGB 2280.

CHAPTER IV
CONTRACTUAL RIGHT OF INHERITANCE

1.   GENERAL RULES

504. UNDER English law a contract, by which a person covenants that he will   622
make a testamentary disposition in favour of the covenantee must be satisfied out
of the covenantor's estate in the same way as if such a testamentary disposition
had actually been made.

Under German law a covenant to make or to abstain from making any specified
testamentary disposition is entirely inoperative—BGB 2302.   On the other hand,
an agreement *inter vivos* by which one of the parties, by direct disposition,
confers a right of inheritance or a legacy on the other party, if complying with the
requirements mentioned below, is binding on the estate in the same way as a
valid testamentary disposition.   Such an agreement is called a contract of
inheritance (*Erbvertrag*).   The party who by agreement confers any such right
of inheritance or any legacy on another will in the following observations be
referred to as the 'contractor'.

A contract of inheritance may contain dispositions made by each of the
parties in favour of the other, [1] and in the absence of any contrary indication such
dispositions are deemed mutually interdependent—482—BGB 2298.

In a contract of inheritance such dispositions as confer rights of inheritance
or legacies, or impose burdens in the nature of testamentary burdens (501),
can only be revoked in the manner stated below (508); all other dispositions
contained in such a contract are freely revocable, but, if remaining unrevoked
on the contractor's death, they are treated like testamentary dispositions—BGB
2299.

A contract of inheritance must be distinguished from a contractual renunciation
of a right of inheritance (479).

---

1   Reciprocal dispositions of such a nature are frequently contained in a marriage contract (416).

623   The promise of a gift, to be carried out on the death of the promisor in the event of his predeceasing the promisee is invalid, unless made in the form of a contract of inheritance, but a gift completed by delivery which is to be returned in the event of the donor surviving the donee comes under the ordinary rules as to gifts—199—BGB 2301. [1]

2. Capacity of Parties to Contract of Inheritance

505. A contractor who is neither the spouse nor the intended spouse of the other party must be of unrestricted capacity; a spouse or intended spouse who is of restricted capacity, may contract with the assent of his statutory agent, which, in any case in which the statutory agent is a guardian, must be supplemented by the leave of the Guardianship Court—BGB 2275.

3. Form of Contract

506. A contract of inheritance, other than a contract between spouses or intended spouses, is made by declaration before a judge or public notary, both parties being present in person at the same time. In other respects the formalities are the same as those in the case of a publicly declared testamentary disposition—487 sub (2). Where a contract of inheritance is made between spouses or intended spouses it is sufficient to observe the formalities of a marriage contract—416. The document recording a contract of inheritance must, in the absence of a contrary direction by the parties, be placed in official custody; but where the contract includes stipulations to take effect during the life of the contractors (as in the case of an ordinary marriage contract) [2] such a contrary direction is presumed—BGB 2274–2277.

4. Tenor and Effect of Contract of Inheritance

507. The effect of contractual dispositions operative on the death of a contractor is governed by the same rules as the effect of the corresponding testamentary dispositions, and the circumstances or events which render a testamentary disposition

---

[1]   A gift of the last-mentioned description corresponds to the *donatio mortis causa* of English law.

[2]   In so far as a marriage contract—as is frequently the case—contains any provision as to the destination or the fortune of either spouse after death, it has the nature of a contract of inheritance.

inoperative or voidable—484, 485—have the same effect on the corresponding   624
contractual dispositions [1]—BGB 2278, 2279 (1).

A contract of inheritance does not in any way interfere with the power of
either contractor to dispose of any part of his property by act *inter vivos*—BGB
2286.   A contractual heir or legatee is, however, entitled to claim compensation
in the events and in the manner mentioned below:

(1) if the contractor has made any gift (199) with intent to injure a contractual
heir, the latter may at any time within three years from the date of accrual of his
contractual right, claim the return of the gift from the donee under the rules as to
'unjustified benefits (298)';

(2) if the contractor, with intent to injure a contractual legatee, has destroyed
or removed or damaged any object specifically bequeathed to such legatee, the
legatee may, in so far as the heirs are unable to replace the bequeathed object,
claim compensation in money;

(3) if the contractor, with intent to injure a contractual legatee, has sold or
charged any object specifically bequeathed to such legatee, the heirs are bound to
repurchase the object, or to obtain the discharge of the incumbrance; where this
is impossible, or possible only at an exorbitant expense, the heirs must compensate
the legatee in money.   If the bequeathed object has been given away, or charged
by way of gift, a legatee who cannot obtain compensation from the heirs has a
claim against the donee similar to the claim which may arise against a donee
under rule (1)—BGB 2287, 2288.

5.   REVOCATION OF CONTRACT

a.   By Mutual Consent.

508. A contract of inheritance may be revoked by mutual consent in the
following manner:

(1) a contractual disposition conferring a right of inheritance may during the   625

---

[1]   The events in which a testamentary disposition in favour of a spouse or intended spouse becomes
inoperative—485 sub (1) rule (c)—cause the forfeiture of a benefit conferred by a contract of inheritance
made between spouses or intended spouses, even where such benefit is conferred on any third party
(*e.g.* any issue of the marriage or intended marriage)—BGB 2279 (2).   In the case of a voidable
disposition the contractor has the right of avoidance as well as the parties entitled to the right of avoidance
under the general rules—see 484; (for further particulars refer to BGB 2281–2285).

lifetime of both parties be revoked by a contract made in accordance with the same rules as to capacity and form as are applicable to the formation of the contract; such a disposition contained in a contract between two spouses may also be revoked by a joint will of the spouses (482);

(2) a contractual legacy, or the contractual imposition of a burden in the nature of a testamentary burden, may be revoked by the contractor with the assent of the other party to the contract, which assent must be expressed by declaration before a judge or public notary, and is irrevocable—BGB 2290–2292.

b.   One-sided Rescission.

509.   A contractor may rescind a contractual disposition in any of the following events:

(1) if the right of rescission was reserved by the contract;

(2) if the beneficiary was guilty of an act entitling the contractor to deprive him of his compulsory portion (516), or which would have entitled the contractor to deprive him of his portion, had he been one of his issue [1];

(3) if the disposition was made in consideration of an obligation undertaken by the beneficiary (*e. g.* the obligation to pay an annuity to the contractor), and such obligation has ceased to be operative.

The rescission is effected:

(1) in the lifetime of the beneficiary, by personal declaration made by the contractor before a judge or public notary in the presence of the beneficiary;

(2) after the death of the beneficiary by testamentary disposition—BGB 2293–2297.

---

1   The expression beneficiary is here used to indicate the party who can enforce the performance of the obligation incurred by the contract for the benefit of the party intended to be benefited thereby.

CHAPTER V
COMPULSORY RIGHT OF INHERITANCE (*LEGITIM*)

1. INTRODUCTORY OBSERVATIONS

510. THE rules of Roman law as to compulsory rights of inheritance, in their 626 later developments, had a double character. There was a 'formal' right and a 'material' right of inheritance. Under the effect of the formal right a will, in which the testator passed over one of his heirs (*heredes sui*), neither appointing him as heir nor disinheriting him, was void altogether; the praetor on the same ground gave *possessio contra tabulas* to any of the testator's children passed over by him who, by reason of emancipation or otherwise, had ceased to be in the position of *heredes sui*. By the effect of the material right a person entitled to a compulsory portion of the testator's estate was enabled to contest the validity of the will by the *querela inofficiosi testamenti* if the testator failed to give him such portion, or to deprive him of it by express direction on satisfactory grounds. Justinian's legislation put the *actio ad supplendam legitimam* into the place of the *querela inofficiosi testamenti* in any case in which the material right of a compulsory heir was disregarded; the will in such a case was upheld, but the compulsory heir was entitled to claim his portion out of the estate in priority to any legatee, and concurrently with the other heirs; the formal right of inheritance remained in existence in a somewhat modified form. The final result of the Roman development, in its practical aspects, was the testator's complete freedom as regards the appointment of testamentary heirs; the statutory heirs were entitled to be mentioned in the will and to receive their *portio legitima* out of the estate, but they were no longer entitled to be appointed as heirs.

Germanic law proceeded on the opposite principle; the right to take the estate belonged to the natural heirs, and it was only gradually and through the influence of the clergy that a person was allowed to take a certain portion of his estate away from the heir as the 'dead man's part'. In England complete freedom of testamentary disposition was evolved from this by slow stages; in Scotland the 627

Germanic view still prevails, and the same view is taken in the countries governed by the Code Napoléon, where a certain portion of the testator's estate (*réserve*) is always reserved for the natural heirs, who take such portion as heirs while only the remaining portion (*quotité disponible*) may be dealt with by testamentary disposition.

The modern German law has entirely discarded the right of any person to be appointed as heir of another person; under its provisions the right of the testamentary heirs to take possession of the estate cannot be defeated on the ground that the persons entitled to compulsory portions, or some of them, are not included among them; a person entitled to a compulsory portion, unless deprived of the same on a lawful ground, is entitled to receive the value of such portion from the heirs, but he has no direct right over the estate. His claim is a money claim against the testator's heirs, which accrues on the date of the testator's death and is capable of assignment and transmissible on death—BGB 2317.

2. PERSONS ENTITLED TO COMPULSORY PORTIONS

511. The following classes of persons are on principle entitled to compulsory portions (*der Pflichtteilsberechtigte*):

(1) the testator's issue, [1] and, in default of issue, each of his parents;

(2) his spouse.

The compulsory portion is equal to one-half of the statutory portion—BGB 2303.

3. CIRCUMSTANCES UNDER WHICH CLAIM ARISES

512. The following rules apply on this subject:

(1) a person entitled to a compulsory portion will, in the further course of this treatise, be described as 'a compulsory heir'; a compulsory heir who does not receive any benefit under the testator's will has a claim for the value of his

628

---

[1] Such of the issue, as would have been excluded by any ancestor, in the event of the testator having died intestate, are also excluded from the compulsory portion, in so far as such ancestor is entitled to a compulsory portion or has accepted some benefit conferred upon him by the testator's will in lieu of the compulsory portion. If, however, the ancestor has been lawfully deprived of his compulsory portion, and has not received any benefit under the will, the issue are entitled to such compulsory portion. If all the issue have been lawfully deprived, and have not received any benefit the testator's parents take in their place—BGB 2309.

compulsory portion being one-half of his statutory portion, but subject to adjustment under the rules stated below—513, 514;

(2) a compulsory heir who under the testator's will receives a share in the estate which is less than his compulsory portion, has a claim for the deficiency;

(3) a compulsory heir who receives a share in the estate which under the testator's will is subject to any restriction, or gift over, or charged with any legacy or testamentary burden, is entitled to the following rights:

(a) if the share does not exceed the compulsory portion the compulsory heir takes it free from any restriction or charge, and has, moreover, a claim for any difference between the value of the share and the value of the compulsory portion;

(b) if the share exceeds the compulsory portion, the person to whom it is given may, at his option, take it subject to the restriction or charge, or disclaim it; in the latter event a claim arises for the value of his whole compulsory portion;

(4) if the testator has given a legacy to any compulsory heir he may, at his option, either disclaim the legacy [1] and claim his compulsory portion, or take the legacy and, moreover, claim any difference between its value and the value of his compulsory portion.   In the computation of the value of the legacy, any restriction or charge to which it is subject must be disregarded—BGB 2303, 2305, 2306, 2307.

4. COMPUTATION OF COMPULSORY PORTIONS

a. General Rules.

513. On the computation of the value of the compulsory portion, the shares becoming vacant by reason of disclaimer (522), lawful deprivation (516), or declaration of unworthiness (480), are taken into consideration, but a share falling vacant by reason of the renunciation of one of the statutory heirs during the testator's lifetime (479) is left out of account [2] —BGB 2310.

Illustration: A testator being a widower leaves him surviving four children,

---

1   If a share or legacy has been disclaimed on the ground of being subject to a restriction or charge, such disclaimer may be avoided within the period within which the disclaimer of a right of inheritance or legacy may be avoided under the general rules (523), if, at the date of the disclaimer, the restriction or charge had in fact ceased to be operative, and this fact was unknown to the disclaiming party—BGB 2308.

2   The reason for this difference in the treatment of shares becoming vacant by renunciation lies in the fact that such renunciations are generally made in consideration of a payment by the testator, which in effect reduces his estate.

A, *B*, *C*, and *D*.   By his will he appoints *A* sole heir; *B* is deprived of his compulsory portion on a lawful ground; *C* has renounced his right during the testator's lifetime.   *D* is passed over.   The estate is worth £ 9, 000; *C* is left out of account; *D*'s compulsory portion is therefore calculated as if the testator had only left three sons, and consequently amounts to £ 1, 500 being one-half of one-third of £ 9, 000.

Elaborate rules are laid down as to the mode of valuing the estate for the purpose of the computation of the compulsory portion—BGB 2311–2314.

b.   Equalization of Shares.

514. Advances made in the testator's lifetime to any compulsory heir are taken into account in the manner shown by the following rules:

(1) where the party concerned is a descendant of the testator, the following method is applied; in the first place the statutory portion is ascertained, the rules as to hotchpot liability (478) being taken into consideration; the compulsory portion is equal to one-half of the value of the statutory portion so ascertained, but if the advances were expressly made in part satisfaction of the compulsory portion, half the amount of the value of the advances must be deducted from half the amount of the value of the statutory portion [1] ;

(2) where the party concerned is a parent or the surviving spouse of the testator, and the advance was made towards satisfaction of his compulsory portion, the value of the advance is added to the value of the estate and the statutory portion is calculated on that basis; the amount of the compulsory portion is then found by deducting the value of the advance from one-half of the value of the statutory portion; if the advance was not made towards the satisfaction of the compulsory portion the advance is not taken into consideration;

(3) advances made to any descendant in whose place any remoter issue become entitled to a compulsory portion, are brought into account in the same way as if they had been made to such remoter issue—BGB 2315, 2316.

Illustration: A testator who leaves a widow and three sons, *A*, *B*, and *C*,

630

---

[1]   By the application of the rules as to hotchpot liability one-half of the advances is taken into account, in any event; if the advances were expressly made in part satisfaction of the compulsory portion, the deduction of another half from the half value of the statutory portion has the effect of reducing the compulsory portion to the extent of the whole of the advances.

and whose estate is valued at £24, 000—gives nine-tenths thereof to his son A, and the remaining tenth to B. A and B have each received an advance of £5, 000, which would have had to be brought into hotchpot under the rule as to hotchpot liability (478) if the testator had died intestate; the advances were not made towards satisfaction of the compulsory portion of A and B; C has received an advance of £2, 000 towards satisfaction of his compulsory portion.   The widow is entitled to a compulsory portion amounting to $\frac{1}{2}$ of $\frac{1}{4}$ of £24, 000, i. e. £3, 000.   On the division of the remaining £21, 000 between the issue, the advances amounting in the aggregate to £12, 000 must in the first place be added, making £33, 000. B's statutory portion would be $\frac{33000}{3} - 5$, 000 = £6, 000; his compulsory portion is therefore £3, 000; under the will he receives $\frac{21000}{10} = £2$, 100; the balance of £900 must be paid by A. C's statutory portion would be $\frac{33000}{3} - 2$, 000 = £9, 000; his compulsory portion is therefore £4, 500, less $\frac{1}{2}$ of the advance of £2, 000, leaving £3, 500, which must be paid by A. The estate is thus divided as follows:

The widow receives · · · · · · · · · · ·			3, 000
A receives $\frac{9}{10}$ ths of £21, 000	= 18, 900		
less £ 900 due to B and			
£3, 500 due to C · · · ·		4, 400	
			14, 500
B receives under the will $\frac{1}{10}$ th			
of £21, 000 · · · · · ·		2, 100	
From A as shown above · ·		900	
			3, 000
C receives from A as shown above · · · ·			3, 500
			£ 24, 000

c. Augmentation of Compulsory Portion (Effect of Gifts made by Testator in his Lifetime).

515. A compulsory heir may claim as 'augmentation of the compulsory portion' (*Ergänzung des Pflichtteils*) the amount by which such portion would have been increased if the value of any gift made by the deceased in his lifetime has been added to the value of the estate.   Such a claim may be made whether the deceased left a will or died intestate.

Gifts made to any person other than the spouse of the deceased are left out of account if they were made more than ten years before the date of the testator's death; gifts made to the spouse of the deceased are left out of account, if the marriage between the donee and the deceased was dissolved more than ten years before the date of the death of the deceased.

Gifts made in compliance with a moral duty, or the requirements of social propriety, are not taken into consideration in any case.   Gifts made to the person claiming augmentation, or to any of his issue, must be brought into hotchpot. The claim must be satisfied by the testamentary heirs, but a testamentary heir who is himself entitled to a compulsory portion, is not required to make any payment in satisfaction of such a claim which would reduce the value of his remaining share in the testator's estate to a smaller amount than the amount of the value of his compulsory portion.   In so far as the heirs are not liable, or in so far as the person claiming the augmentation of his compulsory portion is himself the only testamentary heir, a claim may be asserted against the donee in accordance with the rules as to 'unjustified benefits' (298)—BGB 2325–2330.

Illustration: A person dies intestate leaving a son A his only statutory heir, and having, one year before his death, given £ 10, 000 to a stranger S.   The value of the estate is £ 5, 000.   A is entitled to a compulsory portion, calculated as if the value of the estate was £ 15, 000; he is therefore short of £ 2, 500, which S has to pay.

5.   Circumstances Justifying Deprivation [1]

a.   Deprivation in Ordinary Cases.

516. A testator may, by express testamentary disposition to that effect, deprive any issue, or a parent, or his spouse, of his right to a compulsory portion on the grounds mentioned below.   The ground of deprivation must be mentioned, and its existence at the date of such testamentary disposition must be proved by any party disputing the claim of the deprived party to his compulsory portion.   If the testator condones the offence constituting the ground of deprivation, he

---

[1]   A person declared 'unworthy to inherit' (480), not being entitled to a statutory portion, is as a matter of course not entitled to a compulsory portion, whether deprived of such portion by the testator or not.

thereby revokes the disposition depriving the offender of his compulsory portion.

The right of deprivation is available against: 632

(1) any of the testator's descendants who: (*a*) makes any attempt against the life of the testator, or of his spouse, or of any of his issue; (*b*) is guilty of wilful ill-treatment of the testator or of his spouse [1]; (*c*) is guilty of a serious criminal offence against the testator or his spouse; (*d*) wilfully fails in his duty as to the testator's maintenance (430, 431); (*e*) leads a dishonourable or immoral life against the testator's wish [2];

(2) a parent who is guilty of one of the offences mentioned sub (1) (*a*) (*c*) and (*d*);

(3) a spouse who is guilty of any matrimonial offence which would entitle the testator to claim a divorce—BGB 2333–2337.

b.   Exheredatio bona mente.

517. As mentioned above—512 rule (3) a compulsory portion is not as a general rule satisfied by any disposition subject to any restriction or gift over; a testator may, however, in any case in which a descendant has by extravagant habits or insolvency endangered his future income to a material extent, protect such descendant against himself in any of the following ways:

(1) by giving him a life interest in his share or legacy, and appointing his statutory heirs as reversionary heirs or legatees;

(2) by directing that his share or legacy shall during his life be under the management of an executor with the effect that he is entitled to the net income but has no power of disposition *inter vivos* over the corpus. [3]

If the descendant permanently amends his ways before the testator's death the restriction becomes inoperative—BGB 2338.

---

[1]   Ill-treatment of the spouse is a ground of deprivation only in so far as he is an ancestor of the person guilty of such ill-treatment.

[2]   If the person in question permanently amends his ways before the testator's death the ground of deprivation ceases to be operative—BGB 2336 (4).

[3]   In neither case can the income be seized by a judgment creditor so as to deprive the person entitled to it of his own maintenance in accordance with his station of life, or of his power to comply with his statutory duties as to the maintenance of others—CPO 863.   It follows that the income cannot be validly assigned (176).   The right to income in any such case is in the nature of a 'protected life interest' under English law, or of an 'alimentary life interest' under Scotch law.   See re Fitzgerald (1904) 1 Ch. 573.

6. Appropriation of Burden of Compulsory Portions

633   **518.** The heirs are liable for the payment of compulsory portions in the same way as they are liable for the discharge of legacies or testamentary burdens not specifically charged on any legatees (497) ; an heir who is himself entitled to a compulsory portion, and has paid part of the claim of a co-heir may, after the division of the estate, claim repayment, in so far as he has retained less than his own compulsory portion.   The deficiency must be borne by the other heirs—BGB 2059 (1) , 2319.

As between the heirs and legatees, and as between the co-heirs *inter se*, the burden of the compulsory portions is, in the absence of a contrary indication in the testator's will—BGB 2324—regulated by the following rules:

(1) the heirs may reduce the legacies [1] in such manner that in the result the legatees contribute *pro rata* of the benefits taken by them to the payment of the compulsory portions [2] —BGB 2318 (1) ;

(2) any person who takes a statutory portion in the place of a compulsory heir, must, as between himself and the other heirs, bear the burden of the compulsory portion payable to such compulsory heir; if the compulsory heir accepts a legacy in lieu of his compulsory portion, the person who takes a statutory portion in his place has to bear the burden of such legacy.   A person to whom the testator bequeaths the share of one of his statutory heirs, is in the same position with reference to this rule as a person who takes a statutory portion under the law of intestate succession—BGB 2320;

Illustration: A testator, who dies a widower, leaving issue two sons *A* and *B*, by his will declares that *B* is not to take any share in his estate.   The result is that the persons who would have been the testator's statutory heirs, if *B* had predeceased the testator, take the statutory portion to which *B*, but for the testator's direction, would have been entitled.   On the testator's death *B* has

634   issue one son *C*; *C* consequently takes *B*'s place; and, as between himself and *A*, has to pay *B*'s compulsory portion; if the will had given *B* a legacy and *B* had accepted the legacy in lieu of his compulsory portion, *C* would—as between

---

1   A similar reduction may be made in respect of testamentary burdens.

2   A legatee who is himself entitled to a compulsory portion must, however, receive at least his compulsory portion.   On the other hand a co-heir is not required to pay his share of the legacies and burdens, in so far as such payment would leave him less than his compulsor portion—BGB 2318 (2) (3).

himself and *A*—have had to bear the burden of the legacy;

(3) if a compulsory heir disclaims a legacy given to him by the testator in lieu of his compulsory portion, the person who would have had to bear the burden of such legacy, if it had been accepted, is liable for the compulsory portion of the disclaiming legatee, to the extent of the saving effected by his being released from the burden of the legacy—BGB 2321;

(4) if any share of the testator's estate, or any legacy, charged with a legacy, [1] is disclaimed by any compulsory heir, the person who takes the benefit rendered vacant by such disclaimer, and who consequently has to bear the burden of the legacy charged thereon and to pay the compulsory portion due to the disclaiming heir, may reduce the legacy in such manner, that, in the result, he retains an amount sufficient for the payment of the compulsory portion—BGB 2322.

---

[1]   The same rule is applied if the share or legacy is charged with a testamentary burden.

CHAPTER VI
THE ADMINISTRATION OF THE ESTATE

1. FUNCTIONS OF COMPETENT PROBATE COURT

a. Precautionary Steps.

635 **519.** THE Competent Probate Court—468 sub (7)—is entitled, *ex officio*, to take such steps for the preservation of the estate of a deceased person as it may deem advisable in any case in which this seems necessary, or in which the identity of the heirs is not established, or in which it is unknown whether the inheritance has been accepted. The steps may include the appointment of a curator of the estate (*Nachlasspfleger*), and an order for the lodgment in Court of any property belonging to the estate.

A curator of the estate must be appointed on the application of any person who wishes to assert a right against the estate by judicial proceedings.

If the heir or one of the co-heirs is a *nasciturus* deemed to be living under the rule stated above—472, the expectant mother is entitled to maintenance out of the share of such *nasciturus* in the estate, down to the time of her confinement, and may for that purpose obtain the appointment of a curator of the estate [1]—BGB 1960, 1961, 1963.

If no heir can be found within a period appearing reasonable under the circumstances, the Competent Probate Court, after having previously complied with the regulations as to the public citation of claimants, must issue a declaration to the effect that there is no heir other than the treasury authority of the State entitled under the circumstances (473). Such a declaration creates the presumption that the authority mentioned therein is the sole statutory heir of the deceased—BGB 1964–1966.

---

[1] The curator of the estate is in the same position as any other curator—454—except that the Competent Probate Court takes the place of the Guardianship Court—BGB 1962.

b.   Opening and Publication of Wills, and
Contracts of Inheritance.

520. As mentioned above, all publicly declared wills must be placed in official custody, whereas holograph wills and contracts of inheritance may be kept in private custody—see 487, 506.   Any person who has in his custody any testamentary disposition or contract of inheritance, is bound immediately on the death of the testator or contractor to deliver such document to the Competent Probate Court.   The Competent Probate Court, on receiving notice of the death of a testator or contractor, whose will or contract of inheritance is in its custody, must fix a date for the opening and publication of such will or contract, and must cite the statutory heirs and all beneficiaries, in so far as this is practicable, for such date.   The will or contract is then opened, [1] and either read aloud (published) or produced to the parties.   Minutes of the proceedings (*Eröffnungsprotokoll*) are taken down and preserved with the records of the Court.

If the will or contract was placed in the custody of any Court other than the Competent Probate Court, such Court opens the will and forwards it with a certified copy of the minutes of the proceedings to the Competent Probate Court, retaining with its own records a certified copy of the will.

The Competent Probate Court has to communicate to each beneficiary who is not present at the opening such part of the contents of the will or contract as affect him.   On the opening of a joint will or contract of inheritance, the dispositions of the surviving testator or contractor are not published, except in so far as it is impossible to sever such dispositions from the dispositions of the predeceasing testator or contractor.

Every will and every contract of inheritance originally placed into official custody is retained by the Competent Probate Court, and any person who can show that he has a legally recognized interest in the contents of a will or contract is entitled to inspect, and to obtain an authenticated copy of, or extract from, the same; in the case of a joint will or contract the right to inspect and to obtain copies is available in respect of the published dispositions exclusively—BGB 2259–2264, 2273, 2300.

636

---

[1]   A direction given by the testator or curator prohibiting the opening of his will or contract of inheritance is invalid—BGB 2263, 2300.

c.   Certificate of Inheritance.

637   **521.** The authenticated copy of a will or contract of inheritance, together with the minutes of the proceedings on the opening or publication thereof, are frequently accepted as *prima facie* evidence of the rights of the parties deriving title thereunder [1] ; in a case of total or partial intestacy other evidence is of course required.   The only evidence which effectually protects a third party acting in reliance thereon is a 'Certificate of Inheritance' (*Erbschein*) issued by the Competent Probate Court, specifying the names of the statutory or testamentary heirs of the deceased, and the shares in which they are respectively entitled.   Such a certificate may either be issued to all the co-heirs jointly, or to each of them as to his share. [2]

If the rights of the heirs are restricted by the appointment of one or more executors, [3] or made subject to the rights of reversionary heirs, the fact must be mentioned in the certificate.

The certificate creates a presumption in favour of the rights shown thereby, and as to freedom from any restrictions not specified therein.   A third party acting on the presumption established by the certificate is fully protected, unless it can be proved that he knew either that the certificate was incorrect, or that the Competent Probate Court had issued an order for the return of the certificate on the ground of its being incorrect.

The Competent Probate Court may on the application of the true heirs or of its own motion order the return of a certificate of inheritance if satisfied that the same is incorrect.   If the certificate is not returned forthwith the Competent Probate Court may order its cancellation (*Kraftloserklärung*).   Such an order has to be publicly advertised in the manner prescribed for public citations, and becomes operative after the lapse of one month from the date of the last

638   advertisement.   Where any estate not coming under the jurisdiction of a Competent German Probate Court comprises objects situate within the German Empire, a

---

1   The Land Registries accept this evidence as to a will only in cases where the will is a publicly declared will—GBO 36.

2   As to the steps to be taken for obtaining a certificate and as to the evidence to be supplied to the Court, see BGB 2354–2360.

3   An executor may also obtain a certificate as to his appointment.   Such a certificate has the same effect and is subject to the same rule as a certificate of inheritance—BGB 2368.   The right is of importance, where executors are appointed in the place of the original executors.

certificate of inheritance may be issued relating to such objects—BGB 2353, 2357, 2361–2369. [1]

2.   ACCEPTANCE AND DISCLAIMER OF INHERITANCE AND LEGACIES

a.   As to Inheritance.

aa.   General statement. [2]

522. The following rules apply on this subject:

(1) the acceptance of a right of inheritance may be express, implied, or tacit; tacit acceptance is deemed to have taken place if no formal disclaimer is made by a publicly certified declaration [3] before the Competent Probate Court within the prescribed period.   The period is six weeks [4] reckoned from the date at which the heir becomes aware of the death of the deceased, and of the ground on which his right arises.   In the case of a right of inheritance arising under a will the period does not begin to run before the publication of the will (520)—BGB 1943–1946;

(2) if any heir dies before the lapse of the prescribed period, without having accepted or disclaimed his right of inheritance, each heir of such heir may, while he is entitled to disclaim his share in such deceased heir's estate, disclaim his interest in such deceased heir's right of inheritance—BGB 1952;

(3) if the estate goes to more than one heir the acceptance or disclaimer of each co-heir refers to his own share only, but a partial or conditional acceptance or disclaimer or an acceptance or disclaimer made subject to any stipulation as to time is inoperative BGB 1947, 1950;

(4) a statutory heir may disclaim a testamentary gift of his statutory portion,   639 and accept the statutory portion accruing to him in consequence of the failure of

---

1   As to the mode of establishing the title to the estate of a person declared to be dead, see BGB 2370.

2   The treasury authority who is the statutory heir if no other heirs are in existence, or if all disclaim or forfeit their rights, has no power to disclaim—BGB 1942 (2).

3   The declaration is preserved by the Court and is open to the inspection of any interested party— BGB 1953 (3).

4   The period is extended to six months in any case in which the person whose estate is administered died domiciled outside the German Empire, and also as regards any individual heir who is outside the German Empire at the commencement of the period—BGB 1944 (3).

such testamentary gift. [1]   A person, to whom a share is given by contract as well as by will, may disclaim his contractual right and accept his testamentary right, and *vice versa*—BGB 1948;

(5) a person entitled on different grounds [2] to several distinct shares in the estate of a deceased, is entitled to disclaim any of such shares and to accept the others—BGB 1951 (1);

(6) a person entitled on the same ground to several distinct shares in the estate of a deceased, who has accepted or disclaimed one of such shares, is deemed to have accepted or disclaimed the other shares including those which have accrued subsequently to the date of such acceptance or disclaimer [3]; but a testator who gives several distinct shares to the same heir, may authorize such heir to accept one and to disclaim the others—BGB 1951 (2) (3);

(7) the fact that any right of inheritance was disclaimed, must be notified by the Competent Probate Court to the party or parties becoming entitled to the vacant share—BGB 1953 (3).

bb. Avoidance of acceptance or disclaimer.

523. The acceptance of a right of inheritance is inoperative, if the acceptor was under a mistake as to the ground of accrual. [4]   Apart from this the declaration of acceptance or disclaimer, and even the omission to disclaim within the prescribed period, may be avoided on the grounds on which any other declaration may be avoided (mistake, fraudulent misrepresentation, unlawful threats—99, 109, 110).   The avoidance is inoperative unless declared by certified act before the Competent Probate Court within a specified period of time.

The avoidance of an acceptance has the effect of a disclaimer, and the

640

---

1   Having regard to the fact that such a person would have to bear the legacies and burdens charged on the testamentary gift, it is difficult to see what advantage he would derive from such a proceeding.

2   There are only three distinct grounds of succession, namely, the testamentary, the contractual, and the statutory right of succession; a person entitled under several wills of the same testator, or under several contracts made by the same contractor, is deemed to be entitled on one ground only—BGB 1951 (2).

3   Illustration: A person takes one share immediately on a testator's death, and another as reversionary heir in the event of his brother's death without issue; his acceptance or disclaimer of the immediate right is deemed to be an acceptance or disclaimer of the contingent reversionary right.

4   In such a case the time for disclaiming runs from the date at which he becomes aware of the true ground of accrual.

avoidance of a disclaimer has the effect of an acceptance [1]—BGB 1949, 1954–1956, 1957 (1).

cc.   *Position of heirs before acceptance.*

524. As mentioned above (472) the estate becomes vested in the heirs on the death of the testator, subject to being divested as to the whole or any share therein by the effect of a disclaimer.   The mere fact that an heir transacts any business on behalf of the estate, does not deprive him of the right of disclaiming his share; if he subsequently disclaims he is, as between himself and the persons in whom the estate becomes ultimately vested, in the position of a person performing voluntary services (301).

The following rules protect third parties dealing with any heirs who subsequently disclaim their shares:

(1) a sale or mortgage of any object forming part of the estate is valid, notwithstanding the subsequent disclaimer on the part of the heirs by whom such sale or mortgage was effected or of some of them, if such sale or mortgage could not have been postponed without detriment to the estate;

(2) any notice relating to the estate communicated to the original heirs, remains valid notwithstanding the subsequent disclaimer on the part of such original heirs or of some of them—BGB 1958, 1959.

b.   As to Legacies.

525. The following rules apply on this subject:

(1) a legacy is accepted or disclaimed by a declaration communicated to the person charged with the burden of such legacy;
                                                                        641

(2) a partial or conditional acceptance or disclaimer of a legacy, or an acceptance or disclaimer made subject to any stipulation as to time is inoperative;

(3) where an object is given to several legatees in undivided shares each legatee may accept or disclaim his share;

(4) if a legatee dies before having accepted or disclaimed, the right to accept or disclaim accrues to his heirs; a legacy, disclaimed by the original legatee or his heirs, goes to the person or persons who would have taken it if the

---

[1]   Where a disclaimer is avoided, the party who became entitled by reason of such disclaimer must be informed by the Court; the act of avoidance must be open to the inspection of any interested party—BGB 1957 (2).

legatee had predeceased the testator or contractor—BGB 2180.

3.   RIGHTS AND DUTIES OF EXECUTOR

a.   Nature of Office.

526. The powers and duties of an executor may, as mentioned above—468 sub (4), include some which, under English terminology, would be described as powers and duties of a trustee under a will.

A person whose capacity is restricted, or whose property is under an executor's management, is disqualified for the office.   There are no other grounds of disqualification.

While a guardian's office cannot be refused except on certain specified grounds, an executor can accept or refuse the office as he pleases.   The acceptance of the office must be declared before the Competent Probate Court, which Court may fix a period of time for acceptance; if the acceptance is not effected within such period, the person concerned is deemed to have disclaimed the office.   The executor's powers come into operation on the acceptance of the office.

An executor can be dismissed from the office by the Competent Probate Court on the ground of misconduct, and can retire from the office at his discretion.   If his capacity ceases to be unrestricted the office is vacated *ipso facto*.

642   While an English executor or trustee, in the absence of an express direction to the contrary, is not entitled to remuneration, a German executor, who acts as trustee, is presumed to be entitled to reasonable remuneration—BGB 2202, 2221, 2225, 2227.

b.   Functions of Executors.

(1) *Ordinary functions.*

527. An executor's ordinary functions are:

(*a*) the discharge of the liabilities of the estate—532 (including compulsory portions, legacies and testamentary burdens);

(*b*) the distribution of the residuary estate among the co-heirs.

In an ordinary case an executor has power, while these duties require performance, to take possession of the estate, and to give a valid discharge for debts, and dispose of any objects forming part thereof; while these powers of the executor are in operation the heirs, though entitled to the legal interest in the estate, have no power of disposition over any object forming part thereof.

An executor is not entitled to make any gratuitous dispositions except for the purpose for which a guardian may make gratuitous dispositions (463).   He may incur obligations binding on the estate, in so far as this is necessary in due course of management, and the heirs are bound at his request to concur in any acts required for that purpose. [1]

The testator may restrict any of the ordinary powers of an executor or make them exercisable as to particular objects only; he may, for instance, appoint an executor merely for the purpose of managing the property given to a particular heir or legatee—BGB 2203–2206, 2208, 2211, 2223.

Where several executors are appointed their powers must, in the absence of any contrary directions, be exercised by all of them jointly; in any case of difference of opinion, the Court must be appealed to; protective measures may be taken by each executor singly.   On the vacation of the office by one of several executors his powers, in the absence of a contrary direction, become vested in the continuing executors—BGB 2224.

(2) *Functions as to settled shares or property.*

In an ordinary case a German executor is *functus officio* after having discharged the liabilities of the estate, and distributed the residuary estate among the heirs; his powers of disposition then come to an end, and the heirs, as legal owners of the objects forming the testator's estate, obtain full powers of disposition over the same.   The testator may, however, direct the executor's powers to be continued for a prescribed period as to the whole estate, or as to any particular share or object.   During the period prescribed by the testator the executor retains his disposing powers, and the legal owners of the estate or of the share or object to which the direction refers remain under the original restrictions.   For all practical purposes the executor is then in the same position as a trustee of settled property under an English will; the fact that under German law the legal interest is vested in the beneficiary, and that under English law it is vested in the trustee, is only of theoretical importance.

643

The period of time during which the executor's powers may be continued is fixed by a rule similar to that regulating the period within which reversionary

---

[1]   The power to incur liabilities may be extended by the testator so as to make it unnecessary for third parties to inquire whether any particular act is necessary in due course of management—BGB 2207.

interests must vest absolutely (494).   A disposition extending the executor's powers over a longer period is not invalid, but, after the lapse of the period allowed by law, the powers of disposition pass from the executors to the legal owners of the property—BGB 2209, 2210, 2214.

A person who takes a share in a testator's estate, subject to an executor's powers of management during his lifetime, is in a position similar to that of a person who takes a life interest in a settled fund vested in trustees under English law.   Gifts of such nature are resorted to by German testators for the purpose of protecting extravagant heirs against themselves, or for safeguarding the interest of reversionary heirs. [1]

(3) *Executor's statutory duties.*

The following rules as to the duties of an executor cannot be modified by any testamentary directions:

644   (*a*) an executor must, immediately on accepting his office, deliver to the heirs a statement setting out, to the best of his knowledge, the particulars of the estate and its liabilities.   At the request of the heirs the statement must be drawn up by a competent official or by a notary;

(*b*) an executor must use proper diligence in the management of the estate and follow the testator's directions, except in so far as the Competent Probate Court gives leave to disregard them; such leave can only be granted in a case in which obedience to the testator's directions would endanger the safety of any part of the estate; the beneficiaries must, in so far as this is practicable, be heard before leave can be granted;

(*c*) as between the executor and the heirs, certain of the rules [2] applicable as between principals and mandataries (231, 232) are applied, *mutatis mutandis*;

(*d*) an executor is liable for any damage caused to the heirs by his wilful or negligent default—BGB 2215, 2216, 2218, 2219, 2220.

---

[1]   The appointment of an executor with power of management during the heir's lifetime, or during a shorter period, is a restriction which, within the prescribed limits, may be objected to by a person entitled to a compulsory portion; see 512 rule (3), 517.

[2]   The rules prohibiting the delegation of powers and imposing the duty to give information and to surrender any benefits arising from the management of the estate are the most important among those referred to in text.

4. RIGHTS OF HEIRS IN RESPECT OF ESTATE

a. Claims of True Heir against Possessor of Estate.

528. A person who takes possession of the estate, or of any part thereof, by virtue of an alleged right of inheritance, to which in fact he is not entitled, [1] is subject to the liabilities and entitled to the rights appearing from the following rules [2] :

(1) he is bound to deliver to the true heirs [3] the objects of which he has taken possession by virtue of his alleged right, or which he has acquired in exchange for any such object, and all fruits and profits derived from any such object; in so far as delivery is impossible, his obligation to compensate the true heirs is determined by the rules as to unjustified benefits (298)—BGB 2018–2021;

645

(2) as from the commencement of judicial proceedings on the part of the true heirs, his liabilities are determined by the same rules as those regulating the liabilities of the possessor of a thing after the commencement of an action for its recovery brought by the true owner (343, 344)—BGB 2023;

(3) if on taking possession he was aware, or, but for his gross negligence, would have been aware, of the paramount claim of the true heirs, he is, from the date of the commencement of such possession, in the same position as if judicial proceedings on the part of the true heirs had been commenced at that date; if the knowledge of such paramount right was acquired, or ought to have been acquired, at any subsequent time the increase in the stringency of the liabilities begins at such time; if he is in *mora solvendi* (252) in respect of his obligation to surrender possession, he becomes subject to the increased liabilities resulting from such *mora solvendi* (253)—BGB 2024 [4] ;

(4) as between himself and an heir whose claim is not barred by prescription, he cannot plead that he has by long possession acquired the ownership of any

---

1   Such a person is called 'possessor of the inheritance' (*Erbschaftsbesitzer*).

2   A person purchasing the estate or any share therein from the possessor is in the same position in relation to the heirs as the original possessor—BGB 2030.

3   If the action is brought by any heir as to his share, the possessor must hand over the objects in his possession to all the heirs jointly or lodge them with a public authority for their joint account.

4   As to the liabilities of a possessor who acquires any object belonging to an estate by means of an unlawful act, see BGB 2025.

thing forming part of the estate—334 [1]—BGB 2026;

(5) he is bound to give all information required by the heir as to the objects composing the estate and their whereabouts [2]—BGB 2027;

(6) he may postpone the delivery of the objects which the true heirs are entitled to claim until repayment of any necessary outlay incurred by him on behalf of the estate, including outlay incurred in the discharge of incumbrances or liabilities of the estate (532)—BGB 2022 (1). [3]

b. Mutual Rights of Co-heirs as to the Estate.

aa. Rights in respect of undivided estate.

646

529. As long as the estate remains undivided, there is a community of ownership between the co-heirs of the type known as *Gemeinschaft zur gesamten Hand* (304), as to which the following rules apply by virtue of BGB 2032:

(1) a co-heir is not entitled to sell his undivided share in any of the objects forming part of the estate, but he may by public act (97) sell and assign his share in the estate as a whole; the other co-heirs in such a case have a statutory right of pre-emption—198, exercisable within two months from the date of the receipt of the notice of the sale; the assignee of a share acquires all the rights and becomes subject to all the liabilities of his predecessor in title, and the assignor is released from such liabilities [4]—BGB 2033–2037;

(2) the objects comprised in the estate are under the joint management of all the co-heirs, each of whom is bound to concur in, and entitled to take, any steps necessary for the preservation of any object; the rules as to the power of a majority, and as to the contributions in respect of outlay, applicable to community of ownership by undivided shares—see 304, rules (2) and (3)—apply,

---

1   An heir may either bring an action claiming his share of the inheritance as a whole, or sue as one of the joint owners of the particular object forming part of the estate; the liabilities of the possessor are governed by the same rules in either case—BGB 2029.

2   The same duty is imposed on any person who without claiming to be heir has taken possession of any object belonging to the estate.   Every member of the household of the deceased is bound to give similar information and may in certain events be put to his oath—BGB 2027 (2), 2028.

3   If a person judicially declared, or otherwise assumed to be dead, was in fact living at the date as from which his death was declared or assumed, the rights of such person against the persons who on such declaration or assumption took possession of his property are regulated by the same rules as the rights exercisable by the true heir against the 'possessor of the inheritance'—BGB 2031.

4   In certain specified events the assignor remains liable; see BGB 2036.

mutatis mutandis; no valid disposition can be made and no valid discharge given, in respect of any object comprised in the estate without the concurrence of all the co-heirs [1] —BGB 2038 (1) , 2039, 2040 (1) ;

(3) the fruits (77) of any object belonging to the estate are not divisible before partition if the partition takes place within a year after the death of the deceased; if the partition takes place at a later time, a division of the net profits may be demanded at the end of each year by each of the co-heirs—BGB 2038 (2) ;

(4) the estate, as between the co-heirs, is deemed to comprise all objects   647
acquired in substitution for any object, or by virtue of any right, comprised therein—BGB 2041;

(5) each of the co-heirs may require any performance due to the estate to be made for the benefit of all the co-heirs jointly, or to be satisfied by lodgment with a public authority (164) , or delivery to a judicially appointed Receiver, for the joint account of the co-heirs; the debtor cannot discharge his obligation by any other mode of performance—BGB 2039.

bb.   Right to claim partition.

530. The right of a co-heir to claim the partition of the estate (*Auseinandersetzung*) is suspended in any of the following events:

(1) if the birth of an expected co-heir has not as yet taken place, or if any question is pending as to the legitimacy of any co-heir, or if an incorporated foundation, appointed as heir by the testator, has not as yet received the required official confirmation (57) ;

(2) if the right to claim partition of the whole estate or of any particular object comprised in it has been excluded by testamentary disposition, either entirely [2] or during a specified period, or been made exercisable after the lapse of a specified period after notice;

(3) if one of the co-heirs requests a postponement of the partition pending

---

[1]   A debtor cannot satisfy his debt to the estate by setting off a debt owing to him by one of the co-heirs—BGB 2040 (2).

[2]   After the lapse of a period, of which the length is determined by a rule similar to that fixing the maximum time for the vesting of a reversionary right—494 sub (1)—the exclusion of the right to partition ceases to be operative—BGB 2044 (2).   It does not at any time operate against a judgment creditor, or the trustee in bankruptcy of one of the co-heirs, either of whom is entitled to claim the partition of the estate notwithstanding the fact that the right to claim partition is suspended as between the co-heirs—BGB 751, 2044 (1) ; KO 16 (2).

the time fixed by public citation for the presentation of creditors' claims issued, or about to be issued, under the rules mentioned below (537)—BGB 2042–2046.

cc.   Procedure on partition.

531. Where an executor has been appointed the partition of the estate has to be carried out by him, but he is bound to take the opinion of the co-heirs on his scheme of division before carrying the same into effect—BGB 2204.

648

The testator may also without appointing an executor leave the mode of division to the discretion of a third party, [1] or give other directions as to the manner in which it is to be carried out.   If no executor is appointed, and no special directions are given, the co-heirs must carry out the partition in accordance with the following rules:

(1) the estate cannot be divided among the co-heirs before all its liabilities (532) have been discharged; any money required for the purpose of discharging liabilities may be raised by the realization of a sufficient part of the estate;

(2) in so far as any particular co-heir is chargeable with any particular liabilities, he must allow such liabilities to be discharged out of the property apportioned to him on the division of the estate;

(3) a sufficient part of the estate must be reserved for the discharge of any liabilities which have not matured, or which are in dispute;

(4) documents relating to the personal affairs of the deceased, or to the whole estate, remain in the joint custody of the co-heirs;

(5) the residue remaining after the discharge of all the liabilities is divided among the co-heirs *pro rata* of their respective shares, but subject to the rules as to equalization of shares referred to above—478, 503 sub (5) [2] —BGB 2046, 2047.

---

[1]   The decision of such third party is not binding on the heirs, if it is obviously inequitable; in such a case the decision is left to the Court—BGB 2048.

[2]   The directions as to the mode of partition given by the testator, may include directions as to particular objects to be taken over by particular heirs in part satisfaction of their respective shares.   Where one of the heirs is to take over a farm (*Landgut*) and no indication is given as to the mode of valuation, the valuation is to be based on the yearly net income—BGB 2049.

5. LIABILITIES OF HEIRS

a. General Rules.

532. The heirs are on principle personally liable to an unlimited extent for the discharge of the liabilities of the estate in the same way as they were under 649 Roman law, but means are provided by which they can limit such liability to the value of the estate. The rules on the subject are more favourable to the heirs than the rules of Roman law relating to the *beneficium inventarii*.

The liabilities of the estate (*Nachlassverbindlichkeiten*) comprise in the first place such of the testator's liabilities as are not extinguished by his death, and in the second place all liabilities to which the heirs as such become subject, *viz.* funeral expenses, compulsory portions, legacies, and testamentary burdens [1] —BGB 1967–1969, 2058.

Under English law a legatee cannot—except under exceptional circumstances— enforce his rights by action against the personal representatives of the deceased, his only remedy being an action for the judicial administration of the estate. Under German law, on the other hand, a legatee, as well as a person entitled to a compulsory portion, has the same remedies as a creditor, though in a case of insolvency his claims rank after the creditors' claims.

The expression ' creditor of the estate ' (*Nachlassgläubiger*) is applied to any person who is entitled to claim a compulsory portion or a legacy, or to enforce a testamentary burden, as well as to a creditor in the strict sense of the word.

b. Methods Applicable for Limiting Heirs' Liability.

aa. General statement.

533. An heir is entitled to the privilege of limiting his liability to the value of the estate, or to the value of the benefit received by him, unless such privilege has been forfeited by certain acts or omissions described below (534).

An heir who has not forfeited the privilege can limit his liability and that of 650

---

[1] A peculiar liability also arises as regards such of the members of the family of the deceased as belong to his household at the time of his death; these persons, in the absence of a contrary testamentary disposition, are during the first thirty days after the death of the deceased entitled to be maintained in the same manner as they were maintained by the deceased, and to use the dwelling-place of the deceased and the household articles contained therein. This right is called *Recht des dreissigsten*—BGB 1969.

his co-heirs to the extent mentioned above by doing any of the following acts:

(1) by filing an inventory of the estate with the Competent Probate Court (534)[1];

(2) by having the estate wound up by an administrator appointed by the Competent Probate Court (*Nachlassverwaltung*) (535) ;

(3) by having the estate wound up in bankruptcy (536).

Where the value of the estate is too small for administration or bankruptcy proceedings, an heir, who has not forfeited the privilege, can limit his liability as regards any particular judgment creditor by surrendering to him all benefits received out of the estate to the extent of the value of such creditor's claim.   A person entitled to a compulsory portion, or to a legacy or to the enforcement of a testamentary burden, has no claim in such a case, unless he can show that his claim would be satisfied if the estate were to be wound up in bankruptcy—BGB 1975, 1976, 1982, 1988 (2) , 1990–1992, 2013, 2063 (1) ; KO 107.

bb.   Forfeiture of privilege of limitation of liability.

534. The privilege of limitation of liability is forfeited by any heir who does not comply in the prescribed manner with an order of the Court, obtained on the application of a creditor of the estate, to take and file in the prescribed manner a statement of the assets and liabilities of the estate (called the inventory) within a specified time[2] (called the ' inventory period' , *Inventarfrist*).

The following rules apply as regards the right to obtain an order to file and make an inventory, and the effects of such an order:

(1) the right of a creditor of the estate to obtain the order cannot be exercised, and the order, if obtained, is inoperative while the estate is under the management of an administrator, or is being administered in bankruptcy, or after the termination of bankruptcy proceedings by the distribution of the estate or the payment of a composition; the applicant must produce *prima facie* evidence of his claim, but the order remains valid, even if the claim proves to be unfounded— BGB 1994, 2000;

(2) if the heir whom the order concerns dies before the lapse of the inventory period, the period is extended as to each heir of such heir to the end of

---

1   Such an inventory creates a presumption as between the heirs and the creditors of the estate as to the estate not comprising any objects other than those set out therein—BGB 2009.

2   As to the length of the period, see BGB 1995–1997.

the period during which he may disclaim his right of inheritance (522)—BGB
1998;

(3) if the heir, whom the order concerns, is under parental power or under
guardianship, a notification of the order must be sent to the Guardianship Court—
BGB 1999;

(4) if the heir, whom the order concerns, has already voluntarily taken and
filed an inventory in the prescribed manner it is a sufficient compliance with the
order to request the Court to refer to such inventory—BGB 1993, 2004;

(5) if the heir, whom the order concerns, makes an application to the Court
for an order directing a public official or notary to take and file an inventory, such
application is deemed a sufficient compliance with the order—BGB 2003;

(6) the taking and filing of an inventory by one of several co-heirs enures to
the benefit of the others excepting such of them as have previously forfeited their
privilege of limitation of liability [1]—BGB 2063 (1) ;

(7) the heir, whom the order concerns, forfeits his privilege of limitation of
liability in any of the following events:

(a) if he does not make and file the inventory, or otherwise comply with the
order, within the inventory period or within such extended time as may under the
special circumstances be allowed—BGB 1994 (1), 1995–1997;

(b) if he wilfully brings about the incompleteness of the statement of assets
or if, with intent to injure the creditors, he causes any non-existing liability to be
included in the statement of liabilities—BGB 2005 (1) [2] ;

(c) if he refuses to give, or wilfully delays, any information required by any   652
public official ordered to take the inventory by the Court (see rule (5) above)—
BGB 2005 (1) ;

(d) the forfeiture of the privilege of limitation of liability operates as between
the heir whom the order concerns and the creditors of the estate, but does not

---

[1]   As to persons taking several shares in the same estate by separate titles, see BGB 2007; as to the
cases in which the husband of a wife entitled as heiress must concur in the making of an inventory, see BGB
2008.

[2]   If the incompleteness of the inventory is not intentional the heir may be ordered to complete his
statement within a specified further time—BGB 2005 (2).   Any creditor of the estate may require the heir,
whom the order concerns, to make a sworn statement as to the accuracy and completeness of the inventory as
originally filed, or subsequently amended; if the heir refuses to make such sworn statement, he forfeits the
privilege of limitation of liability as regards the claim of the creditor by whom the application is made—BGB
2006.

prevent him from claiming limited liability as between himself and his co-heirs— BGB 2063 (2).

cc. *Appointment of an administrator.*

535. In so far as the privilege of limitation of liability under the rules mentioned above—534, is not forfeited, the heirs may on their joint application, at any time before the partition of the estate, obtain an order from the Competent Probate Court for the administration of the estate by an administrator [1]—BGB 1981 (1), 2013, 2062.

The effects of such an order are determined by the following rules:

(1) the heirs' liability becomes restricted to the value of the estate—BGB 1975;

(2) the powers of management and disposition over the estate pass from the heirs to the administrator—BGB 1984 (1) [2];

(3) no action can be brought and no judgment enforced against the heirs in respect of the liabilities of the estate, and all proceedings must be taken against the administrator; the heirs' judgment creditors cannot enforce their rights against the estate in any way—BGB 1984 [3];

(4) the rights and liabilities of the heirs, in respect of their management prior to the date of the order, are determined as follows: in respect of the period preceding the acceptance of the inheritance the rules as to voluntary services (301) apply; in respect of the period from the date of such acceptance down to the date of the order the rules as to mandate (232) apply; the heirs are entitled to be reimbursed out of the estate for all outlay incurred in the discharge of the liabilities of the estate, in so far as they can prove that under the circumstances they were entitled to assume the solvency of the estate [4]—BGB 1978, 1979;

653

---

1 The Court may decline to make the appointment or may rescind the appointment if the assets are insufficient for the payment of costs—BGB 1982, 1988 (2); in either case the heir may, as mentioned above, limit his liability by surrendering the estate to the judgment creditors.

2 The order must be publicly advertised; any third party dealing with the heirs is protected if ignorant of the order; if such dealings take place after the publication of the order such a party must prove his ignorance—BGB 1983, 1984 (1); KO 7, 8.

3 As to the effect of the order on rights of set-off, see BGB 1976, 1977.

4 There is no distinction in this respect between ordinary liabilities on the one hand, and legacies, testamentary burdens, and compulsory portions on the other, but any payments made to legatees, &c. may, subject to certain restrictions, be recovered from the recipients in the event of the estate proving insolvent— KO 222.

(5) the administrator appointed by the Court is not bound to accept the office; if he accepts the office he is entitled to reasonable remuneration; he is in the legal position of a curator and responsible to the heirs as such; he is also responsible to the creditors for any damage arising by reason of any default on his part—BGB 1981 (3), 1985 (2), 1987;

(6) the administrator has to manage the estate, discharge the liabilities, [1] and pay the surplus to the heirs.   Where the claim of any particular creditor is disputed the distribution need not be delayed, if sufficient security is given to the creditor—BGB 1985 (1), 1986 (2).

dd.   Administration in bankruptcy.

536. In any case in which the value of the estate is insufficient for the discharge of the liabilities, excluding legacies and testamentary burdens but including compulsory portions, it is the duty of the heirs or of the administrator to petition for administration in bankruptcy; any heir or administrator who is aware, or, by the application of proper diligence, [2] would have become aware of such insolvency, and fails to comply with such duty, is liable in damages to the creditors—BGB 1980, 1985 (2).

An order for administration in bankruptcy has the same effect as regards the liability of any heir who has not forfeited his privilege of limitation of liability, as an order for administration by an administrator—BGB 1975, 2013. [3]

The following classes of claims provable in the bankruptcy proceedings rank   654 behind other classes; as between themselves they rank in the order in which they are enumerated:

(1) interest on certain specified classes of debts;

(2) fines due from the deceased;

(3) liabilities arising under acts *inter vivos* of a purely voluntary kind;

(4) compulsory portions;

---

1   As to his duty in case of the insolvency of the estate, see 536.

2   The failure to advertise for creditors is as a general rule deemed an omission of proper diligence— BGB 1980 (2).

3   Administration in bankruptcy may be ordered on the petition of any creditor who is not excluded under the rules stated below (537), and of certain other specified classes of persons, as well as on the petition of the heirs or the administrator, but in any case in which the heir has forfeited his privilege of limitation of liability the bankruptcy proceedings have no effect on his personal liability—KO 217–220; BGB 2013.   As to the limitation of liability in a case where administration in bankruptcy is refused or terminated on the ground of the small value of the estate, see 533.

(5) legacies and testamentary burdens—KO 226 (2).

If the bankruptcy is terminated by the distribution of the estate, or by the payment of a composition, the heirs, in so far as they have not forfeited their privilege of limitation of liability, may meet an action brought by a creditor by proving that the estate is exhausted by the distribution, or by the payment of the composition, or by surrendering to the extent of the value of such creditor's claim, in accordance with the rules as to unjustified benefits (298), any surplus which may have remained; but they cannot claim credit for any payment made in satisfaction of any compulsory portion, legacy, or testamentary burden, after the commencement of such creditor's action [1]—BGB 1989, 2000.

ee. Exclusion of creditors.

537. The creditors may be required by public citation (*Aufgebot*) to present their claims within a specified period, and any creditor who, without belonging to one of the excepted privileged classes, [2] does not present his claim within such period, is 'excluded' from the division of the estate, with the result that the heirs in so far as they have not forfeited their privilege of limitation of liability, may meet an action on the part of such a creditor in the same way—*mutatis mutandis*—as they may meet an action brought by a creditor after the termination of bankruptcy proceedings—536—BGB 1973. [3]

c. Special Rules as to Liabilities of Co-heirs.

538. In so far as the co-heirs are personally liable for the liabilities of the estate they are on principle liable jointly and severally.   The assignee of any share, as regards such liability, steps into the shoes of the assignor. [4]

This joint and several liability is modified by the following rules:

(1) before the partition of the estate a co-heir, who has not forfeited the

---

1   Where the administration in bankruptcy is refused or terminated by reason of the small value of the estate, the heirs can limit their liability in the same way as in a case in which the appointment of an administrator is refused on the same ground—p. 608 note 1—BGB 1990, 1991.

2   The privileged classes include any creditor entitled to a secured claim or to any claim arising in respect of a compulsory portion, legacy, or testamentary burden—BGB 1971, 1972.

3   Unsecured creditors who do not present their claims within five years from the death of the deceased are, as a general rule, treated like excluded creditors—BGB 1974.

4   If the assignor is liable in damages for negligence in the management of the estate, or for failure to petition for bankruptcy proceedings, such liability is not discharged by the assignment of his share—BGB 2036, but the purchaser is liable in any event—see BGB 2382 (1).

privilege of the limitation of liability (533), cannot be made personally liable for the debts of the estate; a co-heir, who has forfeited such privilege can be made personally liable for an aliquot part of the debts corresponding to his share in the estate; a creditor of the estate can, before partition, sue the co-heirs jointly and enforce the judgment against the undivided estate—BGB 2059;

(2) after the partition of the estate each of the co-heirs may, as a general rule, be sued in respect of the whole of the liabilities of the estate, but in the case of certain classes of claims a co-heir may be sued only in respect of an aliquot part of the claim proportionate to his share in the estate; these classes of claims are:

(a) claims of 'excluded' creditors or creditors treated as such (537), or of legatees, &c. , who have not presented their claims within the time specified in a public citation;

(b) claims brought forward after the termination of the bankruptcy of the estate by the distribution of the estate or by the payment of a composition [1] —BGB 2060;

(c) claims which have not been sent in within six months after the date of a public notice issued by the co-heir, [2] and of which the co-heir was not aware at the time of the partition—BGB 2061.

656

d.   Dilatory Pleas available in Actions against Heirs.

539. An heir who has not forfeited the privilege of limitation of liability, may postpone the satisfaction of any liability of the estate during a period of three months after the acceptance of the inheritance, but not beyond the date of the taking of an inventory of the estate; an heir who, during the first year after the acceptance of the inheritance, has applied for the issue of a public citation to creditors, may postpone the satisfaction of any liability of the estate until after the termination of the proceedings commenced by such public citation.

Where a 'curator of the estate' has been appointed the periods mentioned above run from the date of his appointment instead of running from the date of the acceptance of the inheritance—BGB 2014–2017.

---

1   A co-heir who is sued either for the whole claim or for his aliquot part may after action brought adopt one of the methods for limiting his liability, unless he has previously forfeited the privilege.

2   Such a notice by a co-heir must be distinguished from the citation issued by the Court; disregard of the citation brings about the 'exclusion' of the creditor; disregard of the notice reduces the liability to an aliquot part of the claim.

6. MUTUAL RIGHTS AND DUTIES OF LIMITED HEIR
AND REVERSIONARY HEIR

a.   General statement.

540. As mentioned above—494 sub (3)—a limited heir is, under the general rule, entitled to take possession of his share in the estate as if he were an absolute heir; but the testator may deprive him of his powers of management and disposition by the appointment of an executor with full powers to continue during the life of the limited heir—BGB 2222.

Even where this precaution is not taken, the reversionary heir is, as a general rule, protected by the rules stated below—541–544.

657   Where the reversionary heir is appointed as heir of so much of the estate as may be left on his coming into possession, the limited heir has free power of disposition, and is released from the ordinary restrictions, but, in the event of his making any gifts out of the estate otherwise than in discharge of a moral duty or in compliance with the rules of social propriety, or of his diminishing the estate with intent to injure the reversionary heir, he is liable in damages—BGB 2137, 2138.

The restrictions and obligations imposed on the limited heir may be modified or excluded by the testamentary dispositions, except in so far as the contrary appears from the rules stated below [1]—BGB 2136.   They resemble to a certain extent the restrictions and obligations imposed upon a usufructuary [2] (360), but it must not be forgotten that a limited heir is the legal owner of the objects comprised in the estate or in his share thereof, whereas a usufructuary is merely entitled to a right over a thing owned by another; in some respects the position of a German limited heir bears a strong resemblance to that of an English legal tenant for life impeachable for waste.

b.   Reversionary Heir's right to Inventory of Estate.

541. The reversionary heir is entitled to demand the taking of an inventory in

---

[1]   A testamentary disposition declaring that the limited heir is to have ' free disposition' (*freie Verfügung*) implies that he is not to be bound by any restrictions or obligations which can be released by the testator—BGB 2137 (2).

[2]   Where the usufruct of a share of the estate is given by a testator the usufructuary is in the position of a legatee, whose legacy is charged on the share of which the usufruct is given.

the prescribed manner at the cost of the estate [1].   He may also, at his own cost, employ experts to examine and report on all immovable and movable things belonging to his share of the estate. [2]   The right to an inventory and the right of examination by experts cannot be modified or excluded by the testator—BGB 2121, 2122, 2136.

Where the reversionary heir has reason to fear that his rights will be materially injured by the management of the limited heir, he is entitled to demand full information from the limited heir as to the state of the property comprised in his share of the estate—BGB 2127, 2136.

658

c.   Right of Reversionary Heir as to Lodgment of Securities, &c.

542. The limited heir is bound to comply with any demand of the reversionary heir requiring him to lodge with a public authority (164) all securities to bearer, and all securities to order indorsed in blank comprised in his share of the estate, or to register all inscribed securities comprised in such share in such manner that they cannot be disposed of without the authorization of the reversionary heir. The limited heir is entitled to retain possession of all coupons and dividend warrants—BGB 2116–2118.

Where it is found that the interests of the reversionary heir are materially endangered by the misconduct or the financial difficulties of the limited heir, security (87) or the appointment of a Receiver may be demanded by the reversionary heir in the same way as in a case where the interests of an owner are endangered by the misconduct or financial difficulties of a usufructuary—360 sub (3)—BGB 2127–2129.

d.   Restrictions on a Limited Heir's Powers of Disposition.

543. The following rules relate to the powers of disposition of the limited heir:

(1) any disposition made by the limited heir relating to any immovable or to any right affecting any immovable [3] comprised in the reversionary heir's share in

---

1   The expression 'the estate' is used for the sake of brevity; if the right of the reversionary heir refers to a share in the estate an inventory of the whole estate may be demanded before partition; after partition the inventory would refer to the share apportioned to the limited heir.

2   The limited heir is entitled to the same right—BGB 2122.

3   The limited heir may give notice to a debtor claiming the repayment of an amount secured by hypothecary charge, land charge, or annuity charge; but the debtor does not obtain a proper discharge, if he

the estate, is inoperative in so far as it interferes with the rights of the latter—BGB 2113 (1);

(2) any gratuitous disposition on the part of the limited heir, or any disposition on his part made for the purpose of performing the promise of a gift, relating to any objects comprised in the reversionary heir's share in the estate is inoperative, except in so far as it is made in compliance with a moral duty or with the rules of social propriety—BGB 2113 (2);

(3) a disposition on the part of a judgment creditor of the limited heir relating to any object comprised in the reversionary heir's share is inoperative in so far as it interferes with the right of the latter—BGB 2115[1];

(4) where a Receiver is appointed under the circumstances mentioned above (542), the limited heir is deprived of all powers of disposition—BGB 2129 (1);

(5) the reversionary heir is bound to give his authorization for any disposition which would be inoperative without such authorization, and which is necessary for the purposes of a proper administration of the estate (e. g. for the purpose of raising money for the discharge of the liabilities of the estate)—BGB 2120;

(6) subject to the rules stated above, the limited heir has full power of disposition over the property comprised in the reversionary heir's share—BGB 2112;

(7) any third party who deals with the limited heir without notice of the restrictions as to his disposing capacity can avail himself of the provisions in favour of persons who in good faith derive title from persons with a defective title (333).[2]   The restrictions arising on the appointment of a Receiver do not become operative as against any debtor who has not received notice of the appointment—BGB 2113 (3), 2129 (2).

e.   Management of Property subject to Right of Reversionary Heir.

544. The property which is in the possession of the limited heir must be managed

---

makes such payment to him without the authorization of the reversionary heir; he may obtain such discharge by lodgment of the sum claimed by the limited heir with a public authority for the joint account of the limited heir and the reversionary heir—BGB 2114.

1   Such a disposition is operative, where it is made in connexion with the enforcement of the claim of one of the creditors of the estate, or of a person entitled to a charge over one of the objects belonging to the estate, in so far as such charge is binding on the reversionary heir as well as on the limited heir—BGB 2115.

2   As regards interests in land it is hardly possible that a third party is without notice of the restrictions, as the Registrar is bound to register the right of the reversionary heir on the registration of the right of the limited heir—GBO 52.

in accordance with the ordinary rules of good management and husbandry, [1] and all money which, according to such rules, has to be invested, must be invested in trustee securities; the limited heir is not required to give a greater degree of diligence than the diligence which he gives to his own affairs (148); he is not responsible for ordinary wear and tear; he is not as a general rule entitled to retain the benefit of fruits (77) raised contrary to the rules of good husbandry.   If he has used any object belonging to the estate, for his own benefit, he must account for its value on the termination of his right; he has power to grant leases, and, on the termination of his right, the rights of the lessees are similar to the rights of a lessee on the sale of the tenement leased to him (215); on the termination of the right of the limited heir, he or his heirs must surrender the property in the state in which it ought to be if it had been managed continuously in accordance with the rules stated above, and to render an account of the management of the estate if required to do so by the reversionary heir—BGB 2119, 2130–2135.

660

f.   Rights of Limited Heir as to Disbursements.

545. The rules on this subject cannot be modified by the testator; they provide as follows:

(1) the ordinary costs of preservation have to be borne by the limited heir;

(2) costs extending beyond the ordinary costs which the limited heir reasonably incurs for the preservation of the property may be defrayed out of corpus; if the limited heir defrays them out of his own means he or his estate is entitled to re-imbursement, when the reversionary heir comes into possession;

(3) any other outlay charged on corpus (*e. g.* legacies, testamentary burdens, &c.) is dealt with in the same way as the outlay mentioned sub (2);

(4) if the limited heir, for the benefit of the property, incurs outlay not provided for by the foregoing rules, he is entitled to re-imbursement in accordance with the rules as to voluntary services (301); he is also entitled to the *jus tollendi*—144 sub (9)—BGB 2124–2126, 2136.

---

1   Where any part of the estate is used for the purpose of producing timber or getting minerals, the reversionary heir or the limited heir may have a scheme drawn up at the cost of the estate fixing the mode in which such purpose is to be carried out, and this scheme may from time to time be modified in accordance with altered circumstances—BGB 2123.

g. Rights and Liabilities of Reversionary Heir on the Termination of the Interest of the Limited Heir.

661   **546.** On the termination of the interest of the 'limited heir' [1] the reversionary heir's share in the estate becomes vested in him, unless he disclaims his right thereto [2]; if he disclaims his share, then in the absence of any contrary direction in the testator's will, it goes to the limited heir or his heirs absolutely; the mother of a 'nasciturus' who is still unborn on the termination of the interest of the limited heir has the same claims as to maintenance during her confinement as the mother of a 'nasciturus' who becomes entitled on the testator's death.

A reversionary heir, by accepting his share in the estate, becomes personally liable in respect of all the outstanding liabilities of the estate, [3] but he may limit his liability by the same methods as another heir.   The inventory taken by or on behalf of the limited heir enures to the benefit of the reversionary heir.   The limited heir on the termination of his right is released from his personal liability in respect of the liabilities of the estate, except in so far as the reversionary heir is exempted from such liability, [4] and except as to any particular liability which must, as between the reversionary heir and the limited heir, be borne by the latter.   The limited heir or his heirs may, however, if he has not forfeited his privilege of limitation of liability, refuse to discharge any liability, in so far as the property which he is or they are still entitled to claim from the estate is insufficient for the purpose—BGB 2139–2146.

---

[1]   The termination must be notified by the limited heir or his heirs to the Competent Probate Court—BGB 2146.

[2]   The right of disclaimer may be exercised at any time after the testator's death—BGB 2142 (1). As long as the limited heir is ignorant of the accrual of the right of the reversionary heir he retains his power of disposition—BGB 2140.

[3]   As to the merger of claims and liabilities, see BGB 2143.

[4]   Such an exemption may exist where legacies and burdens are chargeable exclusively on the interest of the limited heir. A limited heir who has forfeited his privilege of limitation of liability may be liable to a much wider extent than a reversionary heir who is entitled to, and makes use of that privilege.

CHAPTER VII
SALE OF RIGHT OF INHERITANCE

547. As mentioned above (529), a co-heir may sell and assign his share in 662 the estate of the deceased. The whole estate cannot be assigned by the heirs, but an obligatory agreement may be made, by which the heirs jointly agree to deliver or transfer to the purchaser the specific objects forming part of the estate. Such a transaction is called *Erbschaftskauf*, and may refer to objects of which the ownership is for the time being vested in a limited heir as well as to objects vested in possession; the share of a co-heir may also be the subject of such an obligatory agreement.

The following rules apply to an obligatory agreement of the nature described above:

(1) it is inoperative unless made by public act—97—BGB 2371;

(2) the benefit accruing from the lapse of a legacy or testamentary burden or from the satisfaction of the 'hotchpot liability' of any co-heir is, in the absence of an express provision to the contrary, deemed to be included in the sale—BGB 2372;

(3) where the share of any co-heir is sold by such an obligatory agreement, the purchaser is not, in the absence of an agreement to the contrary, entitled to any other share in the estate which, subsequently to such sale, becomes vested in the vendor by virtue of any reversionary right, or by reason of the lapse of a benefit given by the testator to any other heir—BGB 2373;

(4) The vendors are bound to deliver to the purchaser all objects comprised in the estate at the date of the agreement, and to assign all claims for compensation and all obligatory rights to which the estate is entitled at that date; family portraits and family papers are deemed to be excluded unless the contrary has been agreed upon—BGB 2373, 2374;

(5) if the vendors, before the sale, have consumed any object comprised in the estate, or have, at the expense of the estate, gratuitously conferred any benefit 663 on any third party, the purchaser is entitled to compensation unless he made the purchase with knowledge of the facts; he is not entitled to claim compensation in respect of any diminution of the value of the estate due to any other causes—BGB 2375 [1];

(6) each vendor warrants his absolute title to the share sold by him and his freedom from restrictions, as well as the freedom of his share from any legacies or other charges not disclosed to the purchaser; he also warrants that he has not forfeited the privilege of limitation of liability; in other respects the rules as to warranty of title on an ordinary sale—187 sub (1)—are applied—BGB 2376 (1);

(7) there is no warranty as to the quality of the objects comprised in the estate—BGB 2376 (2);

(8) the purchaser, as between himself and the vendors, has to discharge the liabilities of the estate disclosed to him at the time of the sale, and must repay to the vendors, all outlay previously incurred in the discharge of the liabilities for which he is responsible, and all necessary outlay previously incurred for the preservation of the estate prior to the sale; the purchaser must also discharge all taxes and duties payable in respect of the estate, and all outgoings usually charged on corpus [2]—BGB 2378, 2379, 2381;

(9) the purchaser, as between himself and the creditors of the estate, is responsible even in respect of such claims as under rule (8) are chargeable on the vendors; as regards limitation of liability the purchaser steps into the vendor's shoes in every respect—BGB 2382, 2383;

(10) the vendors are bound to give notice of the agreement to the Competent Probate Court; if notice is not given by them or by the purchaser the vendors are liable in damages to the creditors—BGB 2384;

(11) if the purchaser sells the benefit of the agreement to a sub-purchaser the rules relating to the original agreement apply, *mutatis mutandis*, to the new agreement—BGB 2385;

664   (12) the rules relating to an obligatory agreement for the sale of the objects comprised in an estate or in the share of any co-heir apply, *mutatis mutandis*, to an obligatory agreement providing for the gift of the objects comprised in the

---

1   As to merger of claims and liabilities, see BGB 2377.

2   The ordinary outgoings usually charged to income are borne by the purchaser as from the date of the agreement, and he is also entitled to the profits as from that date—BGB 2380.

estate or of a share therein; the person to whom such a gift is promised is not, however, entitled to compensation in respect of any previous diminution in the value of the objects comprised in the agreement, and no warranty of title is implied; if any defect of title has been fraudulently concealed the promisor is liable in damages—BGB 2385 (2).

GENERAL INDEX

Abandoned things:

assumption of possession of, 373. [1]

Abstract promise:

form and effect of, 323.

Acceptance:

of an offer, 98.

of performance, 164.

of goods, 216.

Accession:

loss of ownership by, 400.

Accessories:

definition of, 63.

rule of interpretation as to, 145.

transfer of ownership of, 392.

rights of mortgagee in respect of, 446.

of registered ship, how far affected by right of pledge, 465.

Account stated:

see Mercantile account stated.

Accounts:

duty to furnish, how interpreted, 146.

to be rendered by guardian, 571.

Act-in-the-law:

definition of term, 78.

Act-of-God:

German equivalent of term, 153.

Actio ad supplendam legitimam:

rules of Roman law as to, 626.

Actio negatoria:

modern equivalent of, 410.

Administration of estate of deceased person:

see Estate of a deceased person.

Adoption:

statutory requirements as to, 536.

relationship between adoptor and adopted child, 537.

relationship between adopted child and its kindred, 538.

revocation of, 538.

Adults under guardianship:

rules as to, 557.

Advancement of children:

what constitutes, 546.

Aerial navigation:

right of landowner to object to, how far available, 387.

Affinity:

relation by marriage, how constituted, 530.

Agency:

statutory, 84, 115, 154.

definition of term, 115.

created by act of parties, 116.

1　指书中边码（即原书页码）。——校勘者注

Dipsomania:
effect of, on capacity, 21.
appointment of guardian in case of,
557.

Directorate:
of incorporated society, 39.
of share company, 44.
of co-operative society, 47, 48.
of mutual insurance society, 49.

Distraint, landlord's right of:
see Landlord's right of pledge.

Divorce:
conflict of laws as to, 524, 525.
grounds of, 525, 526.
effect of, 526.

Domestic service:
State legislation as to, 259.

Domicil:
German rules as to, 27.

Donatio sub modo:
German equivalent of, 231.

Drawee and Drawer of bill of exchange:
legal position of, 328.

Drunkenness:
see Dipsomania, Intoxication.

Duress:
effect of, as to declaration of
intention, 110.
effect of, as to marriage, 487.

Earnest money:
effect of payment of, 191.

Emphyteusis:
German equivalent of, 411.

Estate of a deceased person:
vesting of, rule as to, 586.

possession of, 644.
administration of, while undivided,
646.
distribution of, 647, 648.
liabilities of, 649.
limitation of liability in respect of,
how forfeited, 650–652.
administration of, by administrator
or in bankruptcy, 652, 653.
notice to creditors, effect of, 654.

Estoppel:
German equivalent of, 143, 361,
362.

Exceptio plurium concubentium:
when available, 532.

Exchange:
rules as to, 223.

Executors:
nature of office of, distinguished
from that of English executors,
577.
appointment of, how effected, 620.
functions of, 641–644.
see Certificate of Inheritance.

Exheredatio:
in ordinary cases, 631, 632.
bona mente, 632.

Extravagance:
as ground of appointment of a
guardian, 557.

Factories:
liability for accident in, 344.

Factory Acts:
rules of German law carrying out
objects of, 259.

456.

Sale of pledged property:

rules as to exercise of right of, 469–474.

Salvage:

see Maritime salvage.

Security:

right to, how exercised, 76, 77.

Seduction:

right to obtain compensation for, general rules as to, 341, 342.

special damages payable on, under promise to marry, 479, 480.

Self-defence:

rules as to, 74, 75.

Self-help:

general rules as to, 74–76.

as a possessory remedy, 374, 375.

Separate property:

meaning of term in a marriage contract providing for general community of goods, 511.

Separation of goods:

between spouses, circumstances bringing about, 506–508, 516.

effect of, 507, 508.

Servant's character:

employer's duty to furnish, 264.

Services, agreement for:

general rules as to, 258, 259.

payment in kind, how far allowed, 260.

temporary disability of employee, effect of, 261.

employer's duties as to health and morality of employees, 262–264.

Servitude:

deemed to be component part of the dominant tenement, 63.

classification of, 415, 416.

real, personal, meaning of terms, 416.

how created, 416, 417.

effect of quasi-possession, 417.

extinction of, 428–430.

Servitude, personal:

meaning of term, 416.

rules as to usufruct, 422–428.

rules as to restricted, 428.

Servitude, real:

meaning of term, 416, 418.

local transference of, 420.

effect of sub-division of servient or dominant tenement on, 420.

remedies for protection of, 420, 421.

loss by prescription, 421.

Set-off:

general rules as to right of, 180–182.

assignee's rights as to, 196.

Severed products:

ownership of, how acquired, 403.

Share certificate:

rules as to negotiability of, 199.

may be issued to bearer, 200.

Share companies:

rules as to, 43–45.

Shipowners:

liabilities of, 159, 345.

Slander:

see Defamation.

INDEX
TO GERMAN TECHNICAL TERMS [1]

The English equivalent is given exclusively in cases in which the German term does not appear in the place referred to.

---

[1]   It was the author's intention to use the modern German spelling, but in some places in the body of the book the old spelling was inadvertently retained.

[2]   指书中边码（即原书页码）。——校勘者注

aufschiebende, 111.

notwendige, 111.

uneigentliche, 111.

unmögliche, 111.

Befreite Vormundschaft, 558.

Befristetes Rechtsgeschäft, 81.

Belastetes Grundstück, 416.

Bereicherung, ungerechtfertigte, 143.

Bergelohn, 358.

Bergung, 358.

Berufen, 561.

Beschränkte Geschäftsfähigkeit, 20.

Beschränkte persönliche Dienstbarkeiten, 416.

Besitzdiener, Besitzgehilfe, 371.

Bestallung, 565.

Bestandteil, 62.

Besteller, der, 271.

Bestimmungsort, 149.

Beurkundung, 90.

Bewegliche Sachen = movables, 60.

Bildende Künste, 72.

Börsenregister = Bourse Register, 316.

Bösliche Schädigung, 152.

Böswilligkeit, 151.

Bote, 115.

Briefhypothek, Briefgrundschuld, 441.

Buchhypothek, Buchgrundschuld, 441.

Büdnerrecht, 411.

Bürge, 317.

Bürgschaft, 317.

Chikaneverbot, 69.

Creditauftrag, 317.

Darlehen, 255.

Despacheure, 361.

Dienendes Grundstück, 416.

Dienstbarkeiten, 415.

Dienstberechtigte, der, 259.

Dienstleistung, der zur, Verpflichtete, 259.

Dienstvertrag, 258.

Dinglicher Vertrag, 368.

Dingliches Recht, 67.

Draufgabe, 191.

Dreissigsten, Recht des, 649.

Drohung = threats, 110.

Ehe = marriage, 480.

Ehegüterrecht, 495.

Eheliche Lebensgemeinschaft, 492.

Eheliches Güterrecht, 492, 495.

Ehelichkeitserklärung, 533.

Ehescheidung = divorce, 524.

Eheschliessung = celebration of marriage, 480.

Ehevertrag, 496, 497.

Eigenbesitzer, 372.

Eigenhändiges Testament, 599.

Eigentum = ownership, 385.

Eigentum zur gesamten Hand, 387.

Eigentümergrundschuld,

Eigentümerhypothek, 445.

Eingebrachtes Gut, 499.

Eingetragener Verein, 38.

Einigung, 368.

Einrede der Vorausklage, 318.

Eintragungsbewilligung, 380.

Einwilligung, 127.

Elterliche Gewalt, 544.

Empfängnisszeit, 531.

Empfangsbedürftige Willenserklärung, 80.

Empfangstheorie, 87.

BOOK REVIEWS

Book Review 1 [1]

THE PRINCIPLES OF GERMAN CIVIL LAW, by Ernest J. Schuster; pages xlvi, 684, Clarendon Press, 1907.

The rapidly increasing desire for a closer view and wider knowledge of German institutions renders such a book as this specially welcome. Dr. Schuster has carried out his evident aims in a highly practical manner, the result being that for the first time in our own language and with a directness only rendered possible through recent imperial law reform, the outlines of German law are as accessible to us as are those of the common law itself. While, however, the codification which became finally effective in 1900, has done much for the simplification of German jurisprudence—uniformity being now established in many departments where previously there had reigned the infinitely varied differences bequeathed by mediaeval confusion—nevertheless an immense field still lies open to purely state activity (*Landgesetz*). This most important fact is duly appreciated by our author (in his introduction), and he briefly summarizes certain general positions of the Introducing Statute (*Einführungsgesetz*), through which reservations are provided in favor of individual legislation by the States as against the Empire. Later on, too, and as subjects suggest a reference to the matter, many such reservations are noted in greater detail. We could wish, notwithstanding, that the distinctions thus arising had been more sharply emphasized. That there is need for this is seen in the striking recurrence (in sections 56–152 of the *Einführungsgesetz*) of the expression "unberührt bleiben" (there remain untouched); this appears not less than *ninety-two* times in these sections. Noteworthy among the subjects thus excepted from modification by the civil code, is that of the privilege still possessed by reigning families and descendants of houses mediatized after the fall of the old empire to legislate in matters touching their family property and affairs; the faculty in question is known as *Autonomie*, and by its exercise hereditary property and effects (*Stammgüter*) are withdrawn from alienation and preserved within the mystic circle of those possessing Ebenbürtigkeit (equal birth rank). Through this endowment modern representatives of individuals once entitled to membership (*Mitgliedschaft*) in the

1 From *Yale Law Journal*, Vol. 16, 1907, pp. 538–540.

Romano-Germanic Reichstag are, in the department of family law, upon a level with those actually occupying thrones; they are the "*Reichsstandschaft—der hohe Adel*". Their number, in all Germany, however, is very small. At Vienna, in 1815, some twenty-two of these "*standesherrliche*" families were recognized in Prussia, for example, as thus set apart from common men. Prominent names among them are those of *Stollberg*, *Hohenlohe*, *Schönburg*.

While Dr. Schuster briefly sketches, at the outset of his work, preliminary steps leading to the formation of the civil code (*Bürgerliches Gesetzbuch*), he fails to give us any glimpse either of the literature of the subject or of the men whose labors, long ago, laid a foundation for what has been accomplished to-day. Much would be gained by some allusion to the discussions between Thibaut and Savigny. To the impulse given by the former was due that outburst of polemic which signalized the year 1814 and the years following, and whose immediate result while, in a certain sense, negative, successfully brought into a clear light those principles which merely waited the coming of appropriate political conditions to realize the best hopes of their illustrious protagonist. In this connection, too, we miss a reference to the long and picturesque process known as the *Rezeption* of the Roman law, nor have we any indication of the profound influences which sprang from the teaching and writings of *Hugo*, *Eichhorn*, *Wächter*, and other heroes of modern legal progression. While the first code-committee (of 1874) brought forth what was considered a text-book of Roman law institutes rather than a statute for the guidance of practical men and thus incurred much reproach, it is, nevertheless, true (as remarked by Dr. Schuster) that the law of Rome forms the basis of the existing code. The student, therefore, requires some preparatory knowledge of the system hitherto obtaining in Germany—and of which no adequate account is to be found in our own language—before he can fitly approach the statements and analyses of present-day doctrine so carefully and exactly furnished in the book before us. Despite a lack of such aid in our author's pages, it is a pleasure to call attention to his happy employment of the *comparative* method. This feature of the book lends to it a distinct value. From both Roman and English sources are constantly drawn parallels and illustrative references lighting up many a chapter, and imparting great charm to the whole; instances of such treatment are to be found in chapter 4, on "circumstances affecting liability"; in chapter 5, on " discharge of obligations"; in chapter 7, on "transfer of rights and duties"; in the discussion touching "purchase and sale" at page 209; "bailment", at page 297; "the general treatment of torts", at page 334 *seq.* ;

"servitudes" (*Dienstbarkeiten, Reallasten*) , at page 415 *seq.* ; "marriage-law" , at page 489 , where we have an exceptionally valuable tabular comparison with English regulation; and the entire subject of "inheritance" , which forms the closing portion of the work. Excellent, also, is the notice, page 291 *seq.* , concerning "agreements between authors and publishers" .

Prefixed to the introduction are tables showing titles and dates of the recent codes and statutes both German and English commented upon together with English cases cited in the text, and reference-lists of passages cited from the civil and commercial codes, the introducing statute, and the civil procedure act. In the matter of rendering into English the somewhat entangling expressions so characteristic of German legal terminology, our author is, in the main, very fortunate. We should, perhaps, choose *citizenship* as more closely expressing the conception denoted by *Staatsangehörigkeit* than *nationality* given as its equivalent by Dr. Schuster. The difficult term *Rechtsgeschäft* is translated " Act-in-the-law". This expression, naturalized in jurisprudence since the days of Hugo and around which there has arisen a vast literature, is intended to connote the idea of the personal element present in the generation of rights, and thus signifies a declaration of volition through which a right becomes founded, changed, or abolished. Dr. Schuster's characterization, in line with that of *Windscheid*, is "a manifestation of the human will intended to create an effect recognized by law". Of the many definitions to be found in modern treatises probably the clearest is given by Bekker who considers the term as expressing the conception of a juristic actuality whereof will-declaration forms an indispensable element. Dr. Schuster's view of the several departments into which the subject naturally falls— capacity, formation of agreements, interpretation, etc. —is close and sufficient.

In conclusion, we heartily congratulate the author of this valuable work. That it will open new aspects of useful knowledge to many seems well assured. Its appearance is a hopeful sign of the times.

G. E. S.

Book Review 2 [1]

THE PRINCIPLES OF GERMAN CIVIL LAW. By Ernest J. Schuster,
LL. D. (Munich), of Lincoln's Inn, Barrister-at-Law, Oxford: The
Clarendon Press; London and New York: Henry Frowde, 1907,
pp. xlvi, 684.

The author in his preface tells us "this book is intended (1) to assist the
study of English law from a comparative point of view; (2) to give an insight into
the latest and most perfect attempt to systematize the whole of the private law of a
country; (3) to give some practical help to the increasing number of practitioners
who in the course of their daily work have to deal with questions of foreign and
private international law".

The work follows in general the arrangement of the German Civil Code, even
in what Holland calls the "inconvenient inversion of the order of treatment" of
that code (JURISPRUDENCE, 10th Ed., p. 162, Note 1). Full references are
given to the authorities used by the editor, including: a "Table of German Codes
and Statutes", "The Civil Code", "The Commercial Code", etc., and tables of
"English Statutes" and "English Decisions". Dr. Schuster does not, however,
attempt to give us an exegesis of the entire *Bürgerliches Gesetzbuch* and
Handelsgesetzbuch but rather a systematic exposition of the basic principles of law
as illustrated in the German system, with full reference to English statutes and
cases bearing upon the same points. The Introduction gives an historical sketch
of German law, an account of the component parts of German private imperial
law, of the relation of imperial law to state law, and of codes and statutes to
customary law, of the sources of German private law, of the arrangement and
characteristics of the new codes, and of methods of interpretation.

The attitude of the British lawyer and of his American legal cousin toward
comparative law is so aptly expressed in the statement, attributed to a "learned
jurist", that the "comparative jurist is one who knows a little about every system
of law but his own", that it seems no one can write on the subject without at least
referring to this sarcastic definition. The author of the present book quotes this
mouth filling if not soul satisfying description of scholars of his own class, but

---

1   From *Michigan Law Review*, Vol. 6, 1907, pp. 103–104.

turns the definition on the definers by asserting that some of the most honored men in the history of English jurisprudence, including not only writers on English law but also most successful practical lawyers, are known to have a deep and comprehensive knowledge of Roman law or of modern continental law or of both. It seems to the reviewer after a careful perusal of Dr. Schuster's work that the book itself is the author's best defense on this point, for he has succeeded in producing an exceedingly valuable handbook on comparative law, useful to the German or the English student alike, who may desire accurate and usable knowledge of the system other than his own.

The author constantly contrasts the two systems in particular points and occasionally makes extended comparisons of legal institutions in English and German law.   We find, for example, such treatment of the themes of domicil, circumstances affecting liability, special liabilities of particular employments, impossibility of performance, custody of movable things, possession, the effect of impediments to marriage, the position of the wife in the modern law, inheritance, etc., etc.

The work will be as valuable for the practical English lawyer, who needs some point of departure in his excursions into the field of foreign law, as it is interesting to the student of comparative law, for the reference to continental codes and to English legal sources will put the practitioner on the right track in his pursuit of information.   It seems, however, rather a matter of regret that the author has refrained from giving us more bibliographical material, though his reason for this omission—urged in the preface—that such material may be found in the fuller German text books, is possibly sufficient excuse for not unduly increasing the size of his book.

The author's device of inclosing in parentheses the equivalent in the original of English paraphrases of the technical German terms avoids possibly ambiguities that might arise from this source.   The mechanical execution of the book shows the customary high standard of excellence of the press from which it comes, though the form "rocovered", § 345, line 2, has escaped the proofreader.

Dr. Schuster is to be congratulated on having done well a much needed piece of work.   For the use of college and law school classes in modern Roman law, the book will serve as an excellent supplement to the equally well done Institutes of Classical Roman Law issued from the same press some years ago.

J. H. D.

Book Review 3 [1]

THE PRINCIPLES OF GERMAN CIVIL LAW. By Ernest J. Schuster,
LL. D. of Lincoln's Inn, Barrister - at - Law. Oxford: Clarendon
Press, 1907. pp. xlvi, 684.

This work deserves notice not only for its intrinsic usefulness but also for
what its mere publication signifies to the lawyers of all countries where the English
Common Law prevails.

The reasons which will cause it to attract attention in the United States are
fairly traceable to the widespread and deplorable perversion of the ancient and
scientifically defined rule of *stare decisis*.   Notwithstanding the occasional
instances between the times of Coke and Blackstone when the real juridical
function of this great principle was employed to defy logic and solemnly sustain
absurdities it had become in its true sense a bulwark of the Common Law when
the "Commentaries" were written and remains so to-day.

It has likewise always been recognized for its scientific force in the Civil
Law, merely being invoked by a different method.   As the learned Roman
jurisconsults were appealed to for interpretation of the law, so the opinions of
modern Continental jurisconsults are sought through their code commentaries for
utilization by advocates in argument before the courts.

Under the Common Law system no original opinion of commentary has been
deemed acceptable unless uttered amid the insignia of judicial office and supported in principle by the decision of some earlier wearer of the ermine.   During
the period when judges and courts were few it was not possible for the jurisconsults of
the bench to vary much in their interpretation of the law and by reliance upon
decided cases for underlying principles they reached results that were comparatively
uniform.   With the settlement of this country, however, difficulties began to
appear.   Men inadequately trained for judicial duties and of mediocre intelligence
were empowered to announce binding doctrines of jurisprudence bearing the
earmark of inferior minds and the lack of a profound study of the legal bases
involved.   From inability to grasp the true principle, apply it scientifically and
sustain it reasonably arose a widely recognized privilege of citing former decisions

---

1   From *The American Law Register*, Vol. 55, 1907, pp. 384–390.

en bloc and not by way of illustration only. In this originated the vicious diversity of doctrines and the slavish rule of mere case law now prevalent and which make the results of a suit at law as uncertain as the proverbial Chancellor's thumb.

Manifestly this is at variance with the true *stare decisis* rule whether the comparison be made with the early English method or that of the jurisconsults under the Civil Law. In its modern application we are deprived of the only *raison d'etre* which is equally demanded by both those systems, viz: the *rationale* of the doctrine involved in a particular case. Lord Mansfield said in Jones *v.* Randall, Cowp. 37: "The law of England would be a strange science indeed if it were decided upon precedents only. Precedents only serve to illustrate principles, and to give them a fixed authority. "

While this historical departure was not attained in a day, a year, nor in a decade, it has nevertheless been so steadily growing that the profound, logical, doctrinal arguments of earlier years have practically been replaced by mere citations of decisions frequently rendered by men unlearned in the science of jurisprudence and whose utterances would be counted as worthless if unsupported by the judicial office. A widespread appreciation of this fact largely explains the general and special codifications in various States during the past half century. Certainty has been sought in the limitation of precedent to textual interpretation. Concurrently it has led the Bar of the whole country to look with increasing interest toward countries not subject to the English Common Law and with a growing indulgence for codes as a possible specific against the dangers and injustice of *stare decisis* as now applied. Of late years other factors have served to enlarge and fix attention in the same direction. Our phenomenal commercial growth, extraordinary immigration, important international marriages affecting property rights, the recent foreign acquisitions by war and the propensity for travel inherent in our people have obliged the Bar to become better informed as to the private laws of foreign countries. New social, industrial and political problems likewise constantly arouse inquiry as to how other nations have dealt or are now dealing legislatively with them. In this respect it will be recalled that our attention was especially directed to the German Bankruptcy Act, the French Employer's Liability Law and the Swiss Governmental Savings Banks. On the other hand the very concentration upon our own affairs which in former years bound us to the Common Law created a seemingly studied exclusion of other tongues so that but a small part of the profession in this country can boast a knowledge of foreign languages. This has doubtless also been owing to the fact that our own language is fast becoming universal for it is to be noted that even of the English Bar few speak any other save French. As supply follows demand and our broadened relations having created the need only of late years, little has been done in the field of translation. At this time there are English translations of only the following: Civil Code of France; Commercial Code of Germany; the Civil Code of 1889 and the Code of Commerce of 1885 of Spain; and the Civil and Commercial Codes of Japan. As to text books or commentaries there are practically none of importance save Sohm's *Institutes*, beyond what may be termed institutional, such as the works of Grotius, Puffendorf, Savigny and Jhering.

The disadvantage resulting from the field of foreign law being practically inaccessible has within the past few years aroused some activity. The Pennsylvania Bar Association at its meeting in June 1905 appointed a Committee on Comparative Law with instructions to report upon the situation and make recommendations. At the meeting in June 1906 this Committee said in its report:

"It cannot reasonably be doubted that there is a growing inclination to weigh recent extensions of Common Law doctrines and the ever-increasing and sometimes startling Federal and State legislation in the scales of general comparison... A disposition is manifest to test every new legal proposition and every social, political and commercial innovation in the light of experience at home and abroad and by every system of jurisprudence... The Committee is convinced that the American lawyer should have access in English to the great landmarks of jurisprudence and the modern laws of all countries. Fundamental juridic truths constitute the world's institutional law and are confined to no era nor to any one people. "

This was followed by a recommendation that an arrangement be entered into with the University of Pennsylvania to bear the expense of a translation of the Imperial German Civil Code and the Association so ordered. The work it is learned is already half completed and should appear next winter. As projected it will contain a historical introduction and be annotated as to source and interpretation largely on the lines of the admirable translation now being published by the French government through the Committee on Foreign Legislation of the Ministry of Justice.

As a further indication of the general movement mention may be made also of the action of the American Bar Association. At its meeting last August there was appointed a Committee "to suggest a method of co-operation with the several State

Bar Associations, institutions of learning and other interested bodies whereby important legislation of foreign nations affecting the science of jurisprudence can be brought to the attention of American lawyers and become available in the general study of private law".

The degree of general and professional interest is likewise indicated in the growing attention to foreign laws manifested by the law libraries throughout the country.   Harvard University leads with a collection of some ten thousand volumes.   The New York Bar Association, the University of Pennsylvania, the Law Association of Philadelphia, the Northwestern University, and several great institutions of learning and libraries in the West also have large Foreign Law Sections filled with carefully selected works.   The drawback, however, arising from lack of translations, is a serious one which will require time and a more concerted effort of the profession to overcome.   As the movement becomes broader no doubt there will be a response by the publishers both in this country and in England.   The latter seem already more alive to the situation than our own houses.   Last year an English company published "The German Empire" by Dr. Burt E. Howard, containing much of interest to lawyers concerning the courts and procedure, imperial and "particular", which cannot elsewhere be found in English and forming an admirable companion to the work which is before us.

There have also appeared from time to time law magazine articles of interest to students of foreign laws, among which, in this connection, may be mentioned one published in December 1902 and January 1903 in this magazine entitled "The German Civil Code" recounting the growth of German law from the earliest times to 1900 when the Code went into effect.   Finally, we have this work by Dr. Schuster whose wide research, familiarity with his subject and general scholarly attainments are foreshadowed in the preface and fulfilled throughout even to the index.   His declared objects are significant at this period of our legal history:

" (1) to assist the study of English law from a comparative point of view, (2) to give an insight into the latest aad most perfect attempt to systematize the whole of the private law of a country, (3) to give some practical help to the increasing number of practitioners who in the course of their daily work have to deal with questions of foreign and private international law. "

That the English lawyer of to-day is protesting with his American brother against the slavery of case law and the perversion of *stare decisis* is shown by another sentence from his preface:

"Even those who look upon the study of law exclusively as a help to professional success have begun to see that the grasp of legal principles is of greater value than mere knowledge of cases and of isolated rules. "

The importance, the scope and the utility of this work will appear more fully when it is recalled that it does not present a translation of any specific text but is an exposition of the active principles of the whole German law, customary, common, particular and imperial. These terms can be briefly explained. Throughout the territory now embraced within the German Empire customary laws have in various localities resisted all attempt at modification and are recognized as unaffected by legislative action of state or empire. The common law as so termed is understood to be a modified form of the Roman law embodied in Justinian's compilation and "received" in Germany in 1495 under the sanction of the Holy Roman Empire. This was subject to local customary laws and in many regions has been supplemented or displaced by state codes, such as the Bavarian Code of 1756, the Prussian Landrecht of 1794, the Code Napoléon which in 1804 became effective in many provinces, the Badish Landrecht in 1810 and the Saxon Civil Code of 1863. The "particular" laws are those customary or statutory provisions enjoyed by certain cities or localities of various states. The imperial laws are those which have been promulgated since the founding of the Empire in 1871. The force of these respective bodies of laws reaches almost every right and duty in various degrees and the advantage of presenting the subject in the form here adopted is at once apparent. No other way would have enabled the author to indicate the principles actually in force territorially. The further valuable feature is added of constantly recurring English Common Law citations to emphasize differences in principle or illustrate variety of application. It lends a familiarity to the doctrine announced or text cited when its absence would at times confuse, especially in such portions as require the use of German terminology.

These English authorities are also separately tabulated as are all the German Codes and Statutes referred to. These latter number thirty-seven and embrace imperial, state and local substantive law and procedure but their territorial force constantly requires commentaries in connection with the customary, common and particular laws. The whole subject after the Introduction is divided into five books: I, GENERAL RULES OF LAW (Chapters: Persons, —Natural, Corporate, Associate, —Rights, Acts-in-the-law, Prescription), II, LAW OF OBLIGATIONS (Chapters: Nature, Creation, Interpretation, Circumstances, Discharge, Remedial Rights, Transfer, Joint Liabilities and Rights, Transfer of Property, Temporary

Use of Property, Work and Services, Partnership, Aleatory Agreements, Suretyship, Abstract Agreements, Offers of Reward, Unlawful Acts, Obligations imposed by Circumstances), III, LAW OF THINGS (Chapters: General Survey, Possession and Registration, Ownership, Rights of User, Real Rights as Security), IV, FAMILY LAW (Chapters: Husband and Wife, Parent and Child, Guardian and Ward), V, LAW OF INHERITANCE (Chapters: General Survey, Statutory, Testamentary, Contractual, Compulsory (legitim), Administration, Sale of Right of Inheritance).

The usual difficulties in translating technical terms have been encountered by the author but the reader's embarrassment is reduced to a minimum by the happy choice of broad and unmistakable English equivalents where possible, the use of Latin expressions in certain instances and the retention of German words only where they have special designatory force serving to fix the idea more clearly and where an attempt to translate would be cumbersome and confusing. With practical foresight Dr. Schuster has even added an Index to German Technical Terms, so that the student need labor under no uncertainty as to the full scope of any word retained in the original.

While it is impossible in this review to consider the work from the standpoint of conflict of laws or to specially mention the several principles which are without even analogy in our law it is not too much to say that the treatise is comprehensive, practical and scientific to a degree unparallelled save in Blackstone's Commentaries. As the student takes the latter in hand to learn the bases of the English Common Law so can he peruse this work with the assurance of receiving just as broad a knowledge of the principles of the Germanic law. Heretofore there has been no such presentation of the subject. Even in Germany there is no one work so concise, clear, comprehensive and practical; and the only other attempt, that of Professor Ernest Lehr in his " *Traité Elementaire de Droit Civil Germanique* " enlarged from his lectures at the University of Lausanne and published in 1891, while indeed valuable for its historical treatment, really, for the American lawyer, clears away little of the inherent confusion which marks the most intricate system of law known to the civilized world. This task has, however, been accomplished by Dr. Schuster.

W. W. S.

Book Review 4 [1]

THE PRINCIPLES OF GERMAN CIVIL LAW. By Ernest J. Schuster, LL. D (Munich), of Lincoln's Inn, Barrister-at-law. Oxford, at the Clarendon Press: Stephens & Sons, Ltd. , London.

This is a very important work for the student of comparative jurisprudence. It is, we believe, the first attempt to put in a form accessible to English readers the results of that great undertaking by which the German Empire was provided from the year 1900 with a complete code or rather series of codes of civil law—the Civil Code, the Commercial Code and the Code of Civil Procedure. Though in the work before us comparisons are chiefly made with English law, the new Civil Code is specially interesting to Roman-Dutch lawyers from the connection between German and Roman law. The Code of Germany is built upon foundations borrowed from Roman law with additions contributed from Germanic sources. But—what makes it of practical importance to those who see the necessity of making certain reforms in our Roman-Dutch law—it contains provisions of an entirely modern and original character. In the words of Mr. Schuster, "its object was to maintain (as far as this was compatible with the necessities of unification) the connection of the present with the past, but without neglecting the change in the conditions of life brought about by modern social and economical developments". The writer has adopted in his exposition of the German law an arrangement designed to assist English readers. We do not know whether this arrangement is beyond criticism. For example, the first book, dealing with general rules of law in relation to persons, things and rights, and the creation, transfer and extinction of rights, must tend to overlap the third book, which is on the law of things, and the fourth, which is on family law. The second book—on the law of obligations—shows a classification very familiar to students of Roman-Dutch law. Obligations are regarded as being created not only by contracts, but by unlawful acts; and therefore the subject of torts is included under obligations, this book thus necessarily filling up a large portion of the volume. Inheritance, which in our text-books of Roman-Dutch law is generally included in some larger division, is here treated as a separate subject, and provides matter for the fifth and final book

---

1   From *South African Law Journal*, Vol. 24, 1907, pp. 224–225.

of the volume.

We hope in a later number of this JOURNAL to make some comparison between modern German law and the Roman-Dutch law as followed in South Africa. At present, however, we must content ourselves with this brief notice of an exceptionally interesting work. [1]

---

[1]　本篇书评未署名作者。——校勘者注

拉丁语、德语、法语词语表

a mensa et toro　[拉] 夫妻分居，保留夫妻关系但不共寝食

a vinculo matrimonii　[拉] 解除婚姻关系

ab initio　[拉] 自始

ab intestato　[拉] 无遗嘱继承的，未立遗嘱的

Ablösungssumme　[德] 销除金额

Absender　[德]（货物的）托运人

abstrakter Vertrag　[德] 抽象的契约（指不要因契约、无因契约）

Abtretung　[德]（债权的）让与

Abzahlungsgeschäft　[德] 分期付款买卖

actio　[拉] 诉讼

actio ad supplendam　[拉] 追加诉讼

actio ad supplendam legitimam　[拉] 补足法定继承份额之讼（对被继承
人的财产主张法定份额的人提起的诉讼，要求遗嘱受益人补足其法定
继承份额。）

actio contraria　[拉] 反诉

actio directa　[拉] 直接诉讼

actio negatoria　[拉] 排除妨害所有权的诉讼，请求否认的诉讼

ad idem　[拉] 意思的一致，对同一点

ad infinitum　[拉] 无穷，无限，无止境地，永远，到无限之远

Aktiengegellschaft　[德] 股份公司

Allgemeine Gütergemeinschaft　[德] 普通的共同财产制

Allgemeines Berggesetz　[德] 普通矿业法

alluvio　[拉] 淤积地

Altenteil　[德] 终老财产

alveus derelictus　[拉]（因河水改变水道而形成的）干涸河床

an Erfüllungsstatt（亦作 an Erfüllungs Statt）　[德] 代替清偿的。例如
Leistung an Erfüllungs Statt, Hingabe an Erfüllungs Statt 代物清偿。

Aneignung　[德] 先占

Anerberecht　[德] 一子继承制。关于德国一子继承制的简要说明，参见
[德] 雷纳·弗兰克、托比亚斯·海尔姆斯：《德国继承法》（第6版），

王葆蒔、林佳业译，中国政法大学出版社 2015 年版，第 4 页脚注 3。

anfechtbar　　［德］可撤销的

Anfechtbarkeit　　［德］可撤销性

Anfechtungsgegner　　［德］撤销相对人

Anfechtungsgesetz　　［德］撤销法

animus donandi　　［拉］赠与的意思

Anspruch　　［德］请求权

antichresis　　［拉］用益质权（亦译典质收益简约。质权人与出质人达成协议，以质物的孳息清偿债权利息，甚至以多余的孳息折抵债权本金。）

Anwachsung　　［德］应继分的增加

Anwachsungsrecht　　［德］增加应继分的权利

Anweisung　　［德］指示证券

Anweisungempfänger　　［德］指示证券领取人

Arglist　　［德］恶意

arglistig　　［德］恶意的

arglistige Täuschung　　［德］恶意欺诈

arrha（arrae）　　［拉］定金

Aufgebot　　［德］公示催告

Aufgebotsverfahren　　［德］公示催告程序

Aufhebung der ehelichen Gemeinschaft　　［德］夫妻共同财产制的废止

Auflage　　［德］负担

auflösende Bedingung　　［德］解除条件

Aufrechnung　　［德］抵销

aufschiebende Bedingung　　［德］延缓条件，停止条件

Aufsichstrat　　［德］监事会

Auftrag　　［德］委任

Auseinandersetzung　　［德］清算，共同财产的分割，遗产之分割

Ausführungsgesetz　　［德］施行细则

Ausgleichungspflicht　　［德］补偿义务

Äusserungstheorie　　［德］表示主义（意思表示在做出时生效）

Ausstattung　　［德］（商品或服务的）装潢，包装

Ausstattung　　［德］婚嫁立业资金，婚嫁立业财产

Aussteuer　　［德］嫁妆

avulsio　　［拉］冲刷地

Badisches Landrecht　　巴登邦法

Bankdepotgesetz　［德］银行保管库法

bedingtes Rechtsgeschäft　［德］附条件的法律行为

Bedingung　［德］条件

Befrachter　［德］（海运货物的）托运人

befreite Vormundschaft　［德］监护中的义务免除（亦译"经免除的监护义务"或"监护义务的免除"）。参见《德国民法典》第1852条以下。

befristes Rechtsgeschäft　［德］附期限的法律行为

Beistand　［德］辅佐人

belastetes Grundstück　［德］被设定负担的土地（指供役地）

beneficium competentiae　［拉］减少偿还债务额以使债务人能够维持生活之恩典

beneficium excussionis　［拉］先诉抗辩之恩典（基于该恩典，被诉的债务担保人得对债权人提出抗辩，请求对主债务人清偿债务；仅在主债务人不能清偿时，担保人始负清偿责任。）

beneficium inventarii　［拉］财产目录之恩典（亦译"限定承认继承之恩典"，基于该恩典，继承人得将被继承人的财产，作成财产目录，从而仅以该财产目录所确定的财产，对债务负清偿责任。）

Bergelohn　［德］（海上救助）救助费

Bergung und Hülfeleistung　［德］（海上）救助和（海上）援助

berufen　［德］援用（法律）

beschränkte perönliche Dienstbarkeiten　［德］限制的人役权

Besitzdiener　［德］占有辅助人

Besitzgehilfe　［德］占有辅助人

Bestallung　［德］委任书

Bestimmungsort　［德］到达地，目的地

Bildende Künste　［德］造型艺术

bonos mores　［拉］善良风俗

böslich　［德］恶意的

bösliche Schädigung　［德］恶意侵害，恶意危害，恶意损害

böswillig　［德］恶意的

Böswilligkeit　［德］恶意

Bote　［德］使者，传达人

Briefgrundchuld　［德］证券式土地债务

Briefhypothek　［德］证券式抵押权

Buchgrundschuld　［德］登记式土地债务

Buchhypothek　［德］登记式抵押权

Büdnerrecht　［德］小农的权利

Bürge　［德］保证人

Bürgerliches Recht　［德］民法

Bürgschaft　［德］保证

causa　［拉］原因，法律上的原因

civiliter　［拉］民事上的

civiliter mortuus　［拉］民事死亡，法律上的死亡，剥夺权利能力

Codex Maximilianeus Bavaricus Civilis　［德］巴伐利亚马克西米利安民法典。法典以马克西米利安三世·约瑟夫的名字命名，自 1756 年起施行于巴伐利亚公国，至 1900 年 1 月 1 日《德国民法典》施行而失效。另请参见［德］弗朗茨·维亚阿克:《近代私法史——以德意志的发展为观察重点》，陈爱娥、黄建辉译，五南图书出版股份有限公司 2004 年印行，第 311—312 页。

codicil　［拉］遗嘱附书

commixtio　［拉］混合

Commodatum　［拉］使用借贷

communauté légale　［法］法定共同制

communauté réduite aux acquêts　［法］所得共同制

communio　［拉］共有

communio incidens　［拉］意外共有（指非基于共有人意思而发生的共有，例如因共同继承而对遗产的共有。）

condictio　［拉］请求给付之诉

condictio indebiti　［拉］错债索回之诉（因错误而为清偿者，得请求返还所为给付；所称错误，例如清偿标的物属于他人所有，基于不存在或无效之债务而为给付者。）

confusio　［拉］混同

consortium omnis vitae　［拉］包括一切事务的共同体（指夫妻关系中的一切事务均为婚姻共同体的内容）

constitutum possessorium　［拉］占有改定（占有移转协议）

consumitur annulus usu　［拉］因使用而缓慢消耗

contra bonos mores　［拉］违反善良风俗

corporal　［拉］有体的

Creditauftrag　［德］信用委任

cura　［拉］监督，保护，监护，管理

curator absentis　［拉］失踪人的财产管理人

curator ventris　［拉］胎儿保佐人（夫死亡时留有遗腹子时，为胎儿指定的保佐人，由保佐人代表胎儿参与遗产继承并保管分配给胎儿的遗产。)

Darlehen　［德］消费借贷

del credere commission　［拉］保证佣金，保证手续费，商事代理人附带保证的手续费

depositum　［拉］寄托，寄托物

depositum irregulare　［拉］不规则寄托（亦称消费寄托或计额寄托）

derAngewiesene　［德］（指示证券的）被指示人

derAnweisende　［德］（指示证券的）指示人

der Auftraggeber　［德］受任人

der Beauftragte　［德］委任人

der Besteler　［德］定作人

der Dienstberechtigte　［德］雇用人

der Unternehmer　［德］承揽人

der Versichert　［德］被保险人

der zur Dienstleistung Verpflichtete　［德］受雇人

deutsches Privatrecht　［德］德国私法

dienendes Grundstück　［德］供役地，承役地

Dienstbarkeiten　［德］役权

Dienstvertrag　［德］雇佣契约

dies certus an, certus quando　［拉］确定到来，且何时到来亦确定的期限（以日历上的日期为期限）

dies certus an, incertus quando　［拉］事确定，而时不确定的期限（例如以某人死亡为期限）

dies incertus an, certus quando　［拉］事不确定，而时确定的期限（例如以某人满法定婚姻时结婚为期限）

dies incertus an, incertus quando　［拉］事不确定，时亦不确定的期限（例如以某人结婚为期限）

dies interpellat pro homine　［拉］期限代人催告。债务定有清偿期者，如清偿期届至时债务人不为给付，即成立债务人给付迟延，无须债权人催告。另请参见郑玉波著、陈荣隆修订：《民法债编总论》，三民书局 2002 年印行，第 359 页。

diligentia quam suis　［拉］处理自己事务之注意

dinglicher Vertrag　［德］物权契约

dingliches Recht　［德］物权

Dipsomania   ［拉］酒狂，嗜酒狂

Dispacheur   ［法］海损理算人，海损鉴定人，海损清算人

donatio   ［拉］赠与

donatio sub modo   ［拉］附负担的赠与

dos   ［拉］嫁妆，嫁奁

Draufgabe   ［德］定金

Ehegüterrecht   ［德］夫妻财产制

eheliche Lebensgemeinschaft   ［德］婚姻之共同生活，婚姻生活共同体

eheliches Güterrecht   ［德］夫妻财产制

Ehelichkeitserklärung   ［德］婚生宣告

Ehevertrag   ［德］夫妻财产契约

Eigenbesitzer   ［德］自主占有

eigenhändiges Testament   ［德］自书遗嘱

Eigentum zur gesamten Hand   ［德］共同共有

Eigentümergrundschuld   ［德］所有人土地债务

Eigentümerhypotkek   ［德］所有人抵押权

eine der Gattung nach bestimmte Sache   ［德］种类物

Einführungsgesetz   ［德］（法典）施行法

eingebrachtes Gut   ［德］归入的财产

eingetragener Verein   ［德］登记的社团

Einigung   ［德］合意

Einrede der Vorausklage   ［德］先诉抗辩权

einseitig   ［德］单方的

Eintragungsbewilligung   ［德］登记同意书

Einwilligung   ［德］允许（事前同意）

Eisenbahnverkehrsordnung   ［德］铁路运送法，铁路交通法

Eisernviehvertrag   ［德］以土地连同附属于土地的动物为租赁物的用
    益租赁契约（土地承租人依估价受领附属动物，契约终止时，依该
    估价负返还义务。）

elterliche Gewalt   ［德］亲权

Empfänger   ［德］受货人，受领人

Empfängnisszeit   ［德］受胎期间

empfangsbedürftige Willenserklärung   ［德］需受领的意思表示

Empfangstheorie   ［德］到达主义，受领主义（意思表示在到达相对
    人时生效）

emphyteusis   ［拉］永久租借权，永租权，永佃权

emptoris est periculum　［拉］买受人负担风险（已出卖之物，虽未交付，其风险，仍由买受人承担。）

en bloc　［法］作为整体，整个，全部

en nullité　［法］无效

Erbbaurecht　［德］地上权

Erbfall　［德］继承之开始

Erbpacht　［德］永佃

Erbschaft　［德］遗产

Erbschaftsbesitzer　［德］遗产占有人

Erbschaftskauf　［德］遗产买卖

Erbschein　［德］继承证书

erbunwürdig　［德］丧失继承权的

Erbvertrag　［德］继承契约

Erbverzicht　［德］继承之放弃

Erfüllungshalber　［德］为清偿的。例如 Leistung erfüllungshalber 为清偿之给付（亦称间接给付）。

Erfüllungsinteresse　［德］履行利益

Erfüllungsort　［德］履行地

Ergänzung des Pflichtteils　［德］特留份之补足

Erklärungstheorie　［德］表示主义（意思表示的解释，以表意人所表示的意思为准据。）

Eröffnungsprotokoll　［德］遗嘱开视程序之记录

Errichtungsprotokoll　［德］遗嘱订立程序之记录

Errungenschaftsgemeinschaft　［德］所得共同制

Ersatzerbe　［德］预备继承人

Ersitung　［德］取得时效

Ersitzung　［德］取得时效

Erwerbs- und Wirtschaftsgenossenschaft　［德］营利和经济性合作社

ex contractu　［拉］由于契约，契约上的

ex delicto　［拉］由于侵权行为，由于不法行为，由于过失行为

ex officio　［拉］依职权

exceptio　［拉］抗辩

exceptio non adimpleti contractus　［拉］契约未履行的抗辩，契约应同时履行的抗辩

exceptio plurium concumbentium　［拉］在父权诉讼中情人不止一个的答辩

exheredatio　　［拉］剥夺继承权

exheredatio bona mente　　［拉］善意的特留份限制（参见《德国民法典》第 2338 条）

extra commercium　　［拉］非商业（指捐作公用而不构成私人所有权的财产）

Fahrlässigkeit　　［德］过失

Fahrnissgemeinschaft　　［德］动产共同制

Faustpfand　　［德］质物

fehlerhafter Besitz　　［德］瑕疵占有

Feldesstreckung　　［德］采矿范围

Fensterrecht und Lichtrecht　　［德］窗户权和采光权

Fiskus　　［德］国库，公库

Fixgeschäft　　［德］定期行为

fortgesezte Gütergemeinschaft　　［德］延续的共同财产制

forum　　［拉］法院，法庭，裁判所，诉讼的地方，法院的管辖

forum administrationis　　［拉］继承案件管辖法院

Frachtbrief　　［德］托运单，运单

Frachtführer　　［德］承运人，运送人

freies Vermögen　　［德］自由财产

Freizeichen　　［德］自由标记（可自由使用的标记）

functus officio　　［拉］完成任务，卸任，辞职

fundo utilis　　［拉］为土地之便益

Fürsorgerziehungsgesetz　　［德］感化教育法

gegen die guten Sitten　　［德］违背善良风俗

gegenseitige Verträge　　［德］双务契约

Gegenvormund　　［德］监护监督人（亦译监督监护人）

Gehülfen　　［德］帮助，协助

Geisteskrankheit　　［德］精神病，精神错乱

Geistesschwäche　　［德］精神耗弱

Gelegenheitsgesellschaft　　［德］临时合伙

Gemeindevorsteher　　［德］镇长，乡长

Gemeindewaisenrath　　［德］地方孤儿保护委员会

Gemeinschaft　　［德］共有关系；共同关系；共同体

Gemeinschaft des beweglichen Vermögen und der Errungenschaft　　［德］动产及所得共同制

Gemeinschaft nach Bruchteilen　　［德］按份共有

Gemeinschaft zur gesamten Hand　［德］共同共有

gemeinschaftlicher Erbteil　［德］共同应继份

gemeinschaftliches Testament　［德］共同遗嘱

Genehmigung　［德］追认（事后同意）

genera　［拉］不特定物

Genossenschaft　［德］合作社

gerichtliche oder notarielle Beurkundung　［德］法院文书或公正文书

Gesamtgläubiger　［德］连带债权人

Gesamtgrundschuld　［德］总括土地债务，共同土地债务

Gesamtgut　［德］共同财产

Gesamtgutverbindlichkeiten　［德］共同财产之债务

Gesamthänder　［德］共同共有人（亦译公同共有人）

Gesamthypothek　［德］总括抵押权，共同抵押权

Gesamtschuldner　［德］连带债务人

Gesamtschuldverhälniss　［德］连带之债

geschäftsfähig　［德］有行为能力的

Geschäftsfähigkeit　［德］行为能力

Geschäftsführer　［德］（无因管理）管理人

Geschäftsführer　［德］事务执行人

Geschäftsführung ohne Auftrag　［德］无因管理

Geschäftsherr　［德］（无因管理）本人

geschäftsunfähig　［德］无行为能力的

Gesetz　［德］法律

Gesetz betreffend die Abzahlungsgechäfte　［德］分期付款买卖法

Gesetzüber das Verlagsrecht　［德］出版权法

Gesetz über freiwillige Gerichtsbarkeit　［德］非讼事件法（亦译非讼事
件程序法）

gesetzliche Erben　［德］法定继承人

gesetzlicher Erbteil　［德］法定应继份

gesetzlicher Vertreter　［德］法定代理人

gesetzliches Güterrecht　［德］法定财产制

Gewährfrist　［德］担保期间

Gewährleistung　［德］担保

Gewerbeordnung　［德］营利事业法，行业法

gewerbsmässig　［德］职业性的，职业上的

Gläubiger　［德］债权人

Gläubiger-Verzug　　［德］债权人迟延

grobe Fahrlässigkeit　　［德］重过失，重大过失

grosse Haverei　　［德］共同海损（相对于 kleine Haverei，单独海损）

Grundakten　　［德］土地卷宗

Grundbuchsblatt　　［德］土地登记簿簿页

Grunddienstbarkeit　　［德］地役权

Grundschuld　　［德］土地债务

Grundstück des Berechtigten　　［德］权利人的土地（指地役权人的土地）

Grundstückpfandrechte　　［德］土地担保物权

Gründungsfonds　　［德］法人创立基金

Güterrechtsregister　　［德］夫妻财产制登记簿

Gütertreunug　　［德］分别财产制

Haftpflichtgesetz　　［德］责任法

Hammerschlagrecht　　［德］土地所有权人为将木板等动产添附于自己土地上建筑物而进入邻地的权利

Handausgabe　　［德］（书籍的）简明版

Handelsgeschäft　　［德］商行为

Handelsmäkler　　［德］商事居间人

Handlungsagent　　［德］商事代理人，代理商

Handlungsfähigkeit　　［德］行为上之能力

Handlungsvollmacht　　［德］代办权（代办商的代理权），商事代理权

Handschlag　　［德］握手

Hauptmängel　　［德］主要瑕疵

Hauptsache　　［德］主物

Häuslerrecht　　［德］（农村）雇工的权利

Hemmung　　［德］（时效）中止，停止

heredes sui　　［拉］继承人的诉讼

herrschendes Grundstück　　［德］需役地

Hinterlegung　　［德］提存

höhere Gewalt　　［德］不可抗力

Hülfslohn　　［德］（海上援助）援助费

hypotheca　　［拉］抵押权

Hypothek　　［德］抵押权

impedit servitutem medium praedium quod non servit（Dig. 8. 3. 7. 1）.　　［拉］位于两宗土地之间而无地役权负担的土地，阻碍两宗土地间设定

地役权（不相互毗邻的两宗土地，无需设定地役权）。

Imperial Gazette ［德］帝国日报

in der Geschäftsfähigkeit beschränkt ［德］限制行为能力的

in der Seitenlinie verwandt ［德］旁系血亲的

in esse ［拉］实际存在的，确实存在的，实在的

in extenso ［拉］全文，全部，详尽

in flagranti delicto ［拉］在犯罪当场，现行

in gerader Linie verwandt ［德］直系血亲的

in pari delicto ［拉］与有过失

in pari delicto potior est conditio defendentis（possidentis） ［拉］双方过失相等时，被告（或占有人）的地位占优

in personam ［拉］对人（诉讼）

in re ［拉］关于……案，关于……。常被简写为"re"，用于文书的开头，表明文书系关于何种事项或事由。

indebitum ［拉］不应支付，没有负债，非债（尽管实际上已成立债务）

injure grave ［法］严重侮辱，严重伤害。依法国法，严重侮辱构成离婚的正当理由。

insula in flumine nata ［拉］（由河水夹带的泥沙淤积而形成的）沙洲或冲积地

inter absentes ［拉］非对话的；在缺席人之列

inter alia ［拉］除其他事项外，除其他外；尤其，特别是

inter praesentes ［拉］对话的；出席者之间，在场人之间

inter se ［拉］彼此之间，相互

inter vivos ［拉］在生存者之间，在生者之间

intra vires ［拉］权限之内，在正当的权限之内

Inventar ［德］财产目录

Inventarfrist ［德］遗产目录编制期间

ipso facto ［拉］由于行为或事实本身，依事实，当然

jura ［拉］法律，权利

jura in rem ［拉］对世权，绝对权

jure naturae aequum est neminem cum alterius detrimento et injuria fieri locupletiorem（Dig. 50. 17. 206）. ［拉］任何人不得因他人受不利益而使自己非正当地获得利益。

jus accrescendi ［拉］增加应继分的权利

jus in re aliena ［拉］他物权

jus suum deminuit, alterius auxit, hoc est servitutem aedibus suis imposuit
（Dig. 39. 1. 5. 9）.   ［拉］役权使自己减少，而使他人权利增加；
易言之，土地所有人于自己土地上为他人设定役权后，不得再为妨
害该他人于供役地上之权利的行为。

jus tollendi   ［拉］废除权，拆除权

Justizministerialblatt   ［德］法务部公报

Kauf auf Probe   ［德］试验买卖

Kauf nach Probe   ［德］样品买卖

Kaufmann   ［德］商人，销售商

kaufmännischer Verpflichtungsschein   ［德］商人负债字据

Kommanditgesellschaft   ［德］有限合伙

Kommanditgegellschaft auf Aktien   ［德］股份有限合伙

Kommanditist   ［德］（有限合伙中仅以确定的数额对合伙债务负责
的）合伙人

Kommissionär   ［德］行纪人

Konnossement   ［德］（海运的）提单，载货证券

Kontokorrent   ［德］交付计算

Kontokorrent-Vertrag   ［德］交付计算契约

korrespective Verfügungen   ［德］共同处分

Kraftloserklärung   ［德］无效之宣告

La recherche de la paternité est interdite.   ［法］非婚生子女不得请求
其父认领。参见李浩培、吴传颐、孙鸣岗译：《拿破仑法典（法国民
法典）》，商务印书馆 1997 年版，第 340 条第 1 句。

Ladeschein   ［德］内河运送提单

laesio enormis   ［拉］重大损失；损失逾半；因价格不公而解约

Lagerhalter   ［德］仓库营业人

Landgut   ［德］农庄，田产

Landrecht   ［德］邦法

lata culpa   ［拉］重大过失

Lata culpa est nimia negligentia, id est non intelligere quod omnes intelligunt
（Dig. 50. 16. 213. 2）.   ［拉］Lata culpa 指重大过失，即未认识到
任何人均能认识到的事项。

laufende Rechnung   ［德］交互计算

legitima   ［拉］合法的规章制度，有法律根据的规则，法律程序

legitimatio per rescriptum principis   ［拉］通过君主的批示而准正

legitimatio per subsequens matrimonium   ［拉］因嗣后结婚而准正

Leibrentenvertrag ［德］终身定期金契约

Leistung ［德］给付

Leistungsort ［德］给付地

letzlwillige Verfügung ［德］终意处分

Lex Anastasiana 阿那斯塔修法。①该法承认，脱离家长控制而获得自主权利之兄弟姐妹的子女为父系亲属，解放的兄弟姐妹与未解放者享有平等的无遗嘱继承权；②该法规定，如果第三人低于其名义价值购得债权或请求权，就不得再向债务人要求获得高于法定利息的价格补偿。

lex fori ［拉］法院地法，诉讼地法，审判地法

lex loci contractus ［拉］契约地法，契约缔结地法

lex loci solutionis ［拉］契约履行地法

Lex Rhodia ［拉］罗得海法（最早的海上习惯法）

lex Rhodia de jactu ［拉］海上弃物法；罗得法（指为了船只的安全或这为了别的货主的安全而把货物抛入海中时，该货主有权要求分担其损失。）

lex situs ［拉］物之所在地法

lis pendens ［拉］未决的诉讼，未决案件；悬案

locatio conductio ［拉］租赁。按：罗马法中，locatio conductio（租赁）分为物的租赁（locatio conductio rei）、雇佣租赁（locatio conductio operarum）和承揽租赁（locatio conductio operis）。三者分别相当于现在通常所说的租赁、雇佣和承揽。

locatio operarum（locatio conductio operarum） ［拉］雇佣租赁

locatio operis（locatio conductio operis） ［拉］承揽租赁

loco parentis ［拉］代表父亲，代替父亲

longi temporis praescriptio ［拉］长期取得时效

Löschungsbewilligung ［德］涂销同意书

lucus a non lucendo ［拉］矛盾的字源说，不合逻辑的推理，不通的话。按：Lucus a non lucendo 中，lucus 是"小树林"，lucendo 是 lucere 的动名词变格，指"发光、明亮"；Lucus a non lucendo 的意思是：小树林之所以叫"小树林"（lucus），正因为它"不明亮"（non lucendo）。在西方，Lucus a non lucendo 常被用来说明某种事物名不副实。

Mäkler ［德］居间人

Mäklervertrag ［德］居间契约

mandatum crediti ［拉］信用委任

Manifestationseid　［德］声明宣誓

Mark　［德］马克（德国采用欧元前的货币单位）

Miete　［德］使用租赁

Mieter　［德］使用租赁承租人

Mietvertrag　［德］使用租赁契约

Mietzeit　［德］使用租赁期间

Minderjährige　［德］未成年人

Minderkaufmann　［德］不完全商人，小商人（相对于 Vollkaufmann，完全商人，大商人）

Minderung　［德］（因买卖标的物瑕疵而）减价

Mitbesitz　［德］共同占有

Mitbürgen　［德］共同保证人

Miteigentum　［德］共有，按份共有

Miterben　［德］共同继承人

mittelbarer Besitz　［德］间接占有

mora　［拉］迟延

mora accipiendi　［拉］受领迟延

mora solvendi　［拉］履行迟延，给付迟延

Mündel　［德］被监护人

mutatis mutandis　［拉］准用，参照适用

Mutung　［德］设定矿业权的申请

Nacherbe　［德］后位继承人

Nachlassgericht　［德］遗产法院

Nachlassgläubiger　［德］遗产债权人

Nachlasspfleger　［德］遗产保佐人

Nachlassverbindlichkeiten　［德］遗产债务

Nachtrag　［德］（遗嘱）补正书，附书，附言

Nachzettel　［德］（遗嘱）补页，附页

Naclassverwaltung　［德］遗产管理

nam ex lege Aquilia guod alius praestitit alium non relcvat cum sit poena （Dig. 9. 2. 11. 2）．［拉］依《阿奎利亚法》，就损害，数人均应负责任者，其中一人之赔偿，并不免除或减轻其他人应负之责任，犹如刑事责任一样。

nasciturus　［拉］胎儿

nautae, caupones, stabularii　［拉］船主，旅店主，车行主

nec vi, nec clam, nec precario　［拉］非暴力，非欺瞒，非勉强

negotiorum gestio ［拉］事务管理，无因管理

nemo pro parte testatus pro parte intestatus decedere potest. ［拉］无论何人，不得就部分遗产为遗嘱，且不得部分遗产有遗嘱，而部分无遗嘱。另请参见史尚宽：《继承法论》，荣泰印书馆股份有限公司 1980 年印本，第 362 页；黄右昌：《罗马法与现代》，中国方正出版社 2006 年版，第 218 页脚注 2。

nicht rechtsfähiger Verein ［德］无权利能力之社团

nichtig ［德］无效的

Niessbrauch ［德］用益权

Niessbraucher ［德］用益权人

notwendige Bedingung ［德］必要条件

novatio ［拉］（债之）更新

Novation ［德］更新，债务更新

Nutzungspfandrecht ［德］用益质权

obligatorisches Recht ［德］债权

Obligationenrecht ［德］债务法

occupatio ［拉］先占

Offenbarungseid ［德］公开宣誓

offene Handelsgesellschaft ［德］商事无限责任合伙

öffentlich beglaubigt ［德］经认证的

öffentliche Urkunde ［德］公式证书，公证书

oligatorischer Vertrag ［德］债务契约

operae illiberales ［拉］自由人所不从事的劳动，体力劳动，低级劳动

operae liberales ［拉］自由人的劳动，非体力劳动（精神性劳动），高级劳动

operae（单数 opera） ［拉］劳动，工作

Pacht ［德］用益租赁

Pachtvertrag ［德］用益租赁契约

Pachtzeit ［德］用益租赁期间

pactum ［拉］契约，合意

pactum reservati dominii ［拉］保留所有权的契约，保留所有权的合意

Pandektenlehrbücher ［德］潘德克顿教科书

pari passu ［拉］以同样的比例，按相同比例

    rank pari passu 享有同等权益

patria potestas   [拉] 父权，家长权

per capita   [拉] 每人，按人数平均计算，按人数的遗产分配

per stirpes   [拉] 依照家系

    succession per stirpes   代位继承

perpetui usus causa   [拉] 永久使用之目的

Persölichkeitsrecht   [德] 人格权

persönlich haftender Gesellschafter   [德] 应负人之责任的合伙人（即
    有限合伙中对合伙债务应负无限责任的合伙人）

persönliche Dienstbarkeit   [德] 人役权

Pfand   [德] 质物

Pfandgläubiger   [德] 质权人

Pfandrecht   [德] 质权

Pfändung   [德] 扣押

Pfleger   [德] 财产保佐人

Pflichtteil   [德] 特留份

Pflichtteilberechtigte   [德] 特留份权利人

pignus   [拉] 质权

Police   [德] 保险单（保单）

    taxirte Police   [德] 定值保险单（保单）

portio   [拉] 部分，一部分

portio legitima   [拉] 特留份

possessio   [拉] 占有

possessio contra tabulas   [拉] 对遗嘱未指明的继承人给予遗产的占有

potestas   [拉] 权力

Potestativbedingung   [德] 随意条件，任意条件

praelegatum   [拉] 先取继承（向某一继承人先行给付其有权继承之
    遗产的全部或一部分）

praescriptio   [拉] 时效

praescriptio acquisitiva   [拉] 取得时效

praescriptio extinctiva   [拉] 消灭时效

prima facie   [拉] 初步的，表面的，初步看来，表面上看来

pro hac vice   [拉] 仅此一次，仅为此场合，仅限于此种情形

pro rata   [拉] 按比例

pro tanto   [拉] 至此为止，至某一程度

prodigus   [拉] 受监护的成年人

profits à prendre   [法] 采取权，土地收益权（指从他人土地中采取

土地产物的权利)

Prokura　［德］经理权，经理人的代理权

proprio motu　［拉］自愿，自己的意愿

publicum ius est quod ad statum rei Romanae spectat, privatum quod ad singulorum utilitatem pertinet.　［拉］公法调整罗马帝国的利益，私法调整个人的利益。

quae facta laedunt pietatem, existimationem, verecundiam nostram et, ut generaliter dixerim, contra bonos mores fiunt (Dig. 28. 7. 15).　［拉］凡对人的诚敬感、名誉感或自尊心会造成不当影响的行为，一般而言，均有背于善良风俗，因而均为不容许实施的行为。

Quarta Falcidia　［拉］法尔其第法四分之一（在任何情况下，遗产的四分之一必须保留给继承人；为此目的，必要时应按比例减少超过四分之三限额的遗赠。此项规则源于公元前 40 年颁布的《关于遗赠的法尔其第法》［Lex Falcidia de legatis］。）

quasi contractus　［拉］准契约

quasi delictum　［拉］准侵权行为

querela inofficiosi testamenti　［拉］补充应继分之诉（遗嘱人严重违反其对近亲属的义务而处分其遗产者，受害的近亲属得提起此种诉讼，请求全部或部分撤销遗嘱，以维护自己的法定继承分。）

quid pro quo　［拉］报偿；交换条件；交换的

quotité disponible　［法］可自由处分的财产部分。参见李浩培、吴传颐、孙鸣岗译：《拿破仑法典（法国民法典）》，商务印书馆 1997 年版，第 919 条、第 920 条、第 925 条、第 926 条。

raison d'etre　［法］存在的理由，存在理由

ratio iuris　［拉］法律理由

ratio legis　［拉］立法理由

re　参见 in re

Reallasten　［德］实物负担

Recht des dreissigsten　［德］三十日抚养费之权利（参见《德国民法典》第 1969 条）

Rechtsanwaltsordnung　［德］律师条例

Rechtsfähigkeit　［德］权利能力

Rechtsgeschäft　［德］法律行为

Rechtshängigkeit　［德］诉讼系属

régime　［法］制度

Reichstag　［德］帝国议会

Rentengüter　　［德］养老金地产，用养老金买的地产

Rentenschuld　　［德］定期土地债务

res extra commercium　［拉］不融通物，非交易物

res fungibiles　　［拉］代替物

res quae pondere numero mensura constant（Dig. 12. 1. 2）.　　［拉］按重
　　量、数量或大小确定的物；代替物

res quae usu consumuntur　　［拉］经使用即消费的物；消费物

réserve　　［法］遗产中特别保留的部分。参见李浩培、吴传颐、孙鸣
　　岗译：《拿破仑法典（法国民法典）》，商务印书馆 1997 年版，第
　　915 条。

Reugeld　　［德］解约金，（解约时的）赔偿金

Rhederei　　［德］航运公司，航运企业

Ristorno　　［意］（海上保险）保险费的退还

Ristornogebühr　　［德］（保险）退费

Sache　　［德］物

Sacheninbegriff　　［德］物之集合体，集合物

Sachleihe　　［德］物之使用借贷

Schadenseratz　　［德］损害赔偿

Schenkung　　［德］赠与

Schenkuny unter Auflage　　［德］附负担的赠与

Schikaneverbot　　［德］权利滥用之禁止

Schlüsselgewalt　　［德］妻之钥匙权

Schuldanerkenntniss　　［德］债务承认

Schuldner　　［德］债务人

Schuldner-Verzug　　［德］债务人迟延

Schuldübernahme　　［德］债务承担

Schuldverhältniss　　［德］债之关系，债务关系

Schuldverschreibungen auf den Inhaber　　［德］无记名债券、无记名
　　证券

Schuldversprechen　　［德］债务约束

Schürfrecht　　［德］钻探权，勘探权

Seblstschuldner　　［德］主债务人（参见《德国民法典》第 773 条）

Seemanngordnung　　［德］海员法

seetriftige Güter　　［德］漂流物

selbständig　　［德］独立的

Selbsthülfe　　［德］自助

Selbstverteidigung ［德］自卫

servitus in faciendo consistere nequit ［拉］役权不能表现为请求作为

si communem amicum ad cenam invitaverimus tuque eius rei curam suscepisses et ego tibi argentum commodaverim（Dig. 13. 6. 18）. ［拉］物之出借，系为双方利益者，例如，我和你邀请我们共同的朋友共聚晚餐，晚餐由你负责安排，我将银杯借用于你，我注意到，一些权威著述认为，［如果银杯灭失，］你仅对故意负有责任。

Sicherheitshypothek ［德］保全性抵押权

Sicherheitsübereignung ［德］担保性让与

singuli ［拉］自然人；各自，每一，个别，单独

Sondergut ［德］特有财产

Sorgfalt ［德］注意

die Sorgfalt eines ordentlichen Kaufmanns 普通商人之注意

specificatio ［拉］加工

Spedilteur ［德］运送承揽人

Staatsangehörigkeit ［德］国籍

Standesbeamter ［德］户政公务员，民事身份登记官

standesmässiger Unterhalt ［德］与身份相当的生计

stare decisi ［拉］判例有拘束力，依照先例

status quo ante ［拉］原状，以前的状态

Statute De Viris Religiosis 宗教人士法（英国爱德华一世于 1297 年颁布。关于《宗教人士法》的简要介绍，参见张秋实:《爱德华一世时期的土地立法》，载《南京大学法律评论》2012 年第 1 期。）

Stiftung ［德］财团

stille Gesellschaft ［德］隐名合伙

Stockwerkseigentum ［德］楼房分层所有权

strandtriftige Güter ［德］（从搁浅遇难船舶等）冲到岸边的财物

Strandunysordnung ［德］搁浅船舶救助法，沉船救援法

subjektiv dinglich ［德］主观的–对物的（参见《德国民法典》第 1110 条）

subjektiv persönlich ［德］主观的–属人的（参见《德国民法典》第 1111 条）

substitutio fideicommissaria ［拉］世袭的替补继承（后位继承）

sui generis ［拉］特殊的，独特的，自成一类的，与众不同的，独自的

superficies ［拉］地上物，地上权

tatsächiche Gewalt   ［德］事实管领力

Teilbesitz   ［德］部分占有

Teilgrundschuldbrief   ［德］部分土地债务证券

Teilhypothekenbrief   ［德］部分抵押权证券

testamentum   ［拉］遗嘱

testamentum militare   ［拉］战时遗嘱

Todeserklärung   ［德］死亡之宣告

traditio   ［拉］交付

traditio brevi manu   ［拉］简易交付

Trunksucht   ［德］酗酒成癖

uberrimae fidei   ［拉］最大善意，出于至诚，绝对信任

ultra vires   ［拉］超过（法定）权限（的），越权的；越权行为

uneigentliche Bedingung   ［德］不真正条件

ungerechfertigte Bereicherung   ［德］不当得利

ungerechfertigte Bereicherung   ［德］无法律原因，无法律上之原因

universitas   ［拉］法人团体

unmittelbarer Besitz   ［德］直接占有

unmögliche Bedingung   ［德］不能条件

Unterbrechung   ［德］（时效）中断

Unterhaltspflicht   ［德］扶养义务

unvollkommene gegenseitige Verträge   ［德］不完全双务契约

unwesentlicher Bestandteil   ［德］非重要成分

Urheberrecht   ［德］作者权

usque ad coelum   ［拉］（土地所有权）上达天空

usque ad inferos   ［拉］（土地所有权）下至地心

usucapio   ［拉］取得时效

usus fructus earum rerum quae usu consumuntur vel minuuntur（Dig. 7. 5）.
　　［拉］以经使用即消费或减少之物设定的用益权。另请参见米健译：
　　《学说汇纂·第 7 卷·用益权》，法律出版社 1999 年版，第 86 页
　　以下。

ut aliquid faciat quis   ［拉］使某人为某种行为

Verbindung   ［德］附合

verbotene Eigenmacht   ［德］被禁止的私力

verbrauchbare Sachen   ［德］消费物

Verfrachter   ［德］（海运）承运人

Verfügung   ［德］处分

Verfügung von Todes wegen　　［德］死因处分

Vergleich　［德］和解

Verjährung　［德］诉讼时效

Verkehrsbedürfniss　［德］交易上之需要

Verleihung　［德］许可，授与

Verlöbniss　［德］婚约

Vermächtniss　［德］遗赠

Vermächtnissnehmer　［德］受遗赠人，遗赠受领人

Vermengung　［德］融合

Vermischung　［德］混合

Vermögensvorteil　［德］财产利益

Vernehmungstheorie　［德］了解主义（意思表示在相对人了解时生效）

Verpfänder　［德］出质人

Verschollene　［德］失踪人，下落不明者

verschwägert　［德］姻亲的

Verschwendung　［德］挥霍浪费

Versicherungsnehmer　［德］投保人，要保人

Versicherungsverein auf Gegenseitigkeit　［德］相互保险社团

Vertrag　［德］契约

vertragsmassiges Güterrecht　［德］（夫妻）约定财产制

vertretbare Sachen　［德］代替物

Vertretung　［德］代理

Verwahrungsvertrag　［德］寄托契约

Verwaltungsgemeinschaft　［德］共同管理关系，管理共同体

Verwandte erster Ordnung　［德］第一顺位血亲

Verwandte zweiter Ordnung　［德］第二顺位血亲

vice versa　［拉］反之亦然

vindicatio　［拉］请求返还所有物的诉讼

vis major　［拉］不可抗力（主要指暴风雨、地震等自然灾害）

Vollkaufmann　［德］完全商人，大商人（相对于 Minderkaufmann，不完全商人，小商人）

Vollmacht　［德］代理权

Voraus　［德］先取遗产

Vorbehaltsgut　［德］保留的财产

Vorerbe　［德］前位继承人

Vorkauf　［德］先买

vorläufiger Vormund　　［德］临时监护人

Vormerkung　［德］预告登记

Vormund　［德］监护人

Vorsatz　［德］故意

vorsäztlich　［德］故意

Vorstand　［德］董事会

vorwiegend　［德］主要的，占优势的

Wandelung　［德］（因买卖标的物瑕疵而）解约

Warenzeichen　［德］商标

Wechsel　［德］票据（指汇票和本票）

Werkvertrag　［德］承揽契约

wesentlicher Bestandteil　　［德］重要成分

wichtiger Grund　　［德］重大事由，重大原因

Widerspruch　［德］异议

Wiederkauf　［德］买回

Willenserklärung　　［德］意思表示

Willenstheorie　　［德］意思主义（意思表示的解释，以表意人真实的
意思为准据）

Wohnsitz　［德］住所

Zeitbestimmung　　［德］期限，期间

Zubehör　［德］从物

Zug um Zug　　［德］不停顿的，连续不断的。例如 Erfüllung Zug um
Zug 同时履行。

Zurückbehaltungsrecht　　［德］留置权

Zustimmung　［德］同意

Zwischenspediteur　　［德］中间运送承揽人

编校絮言

(一)

《德国民法原理》（The Principles of German Civil Law）为英国学者欧内斯特·约瑟夫·舒斯特（Ernest Joseph Schuster，1850—1924）所著，出版于 1907 年。从时间看，与王宠惠先生的英译本《德国民法典》同年出版。事实上，王宠惠先生确与舒斯特曾有一定的学术上的交往。王宠惠先生在其英译本《德国民法典》的翻译前言（Preface）中说，感谢舒斯特博士对英译《德国民法典》提供过建议和无私地允许在英译本中使用《德国民法原理》的一些英文法律术语[1]。王宠惠的英译本《德国民法典》出版后，舒斯特曾为其撰写评论，这篇评论是目前我们看到的关于王宠惠先生英译本《德国民法典》唯一的一篇书评。在书评中，舒斯特盛赞了王宠惠先生的勤奋和天赋。[2]

从《德国民法原理》的扉页中我们可以了解到，舒斯特当时是英国伦敦林肯律师协会（Lincoln's Inn）[3] 的会员、出庭律师（Barrister-at-law），有慕尼黑大学法学博士学位（L. L. D, Munich）。此外，舒斯特既是当时英国比较立法学会（The Society of Comparative Legislation）的委员会成员[4]，也

---

[1]　依此而言，王宠惠英译本《德国民法典》与舒斯特《德国民法原理》虽在同年出版，但后者应该先于前者较早一些时间。此外，舒斯特在《德国民法原理》序言（Preface）末所署时间为 1906 年 11 月，而王宠惠在英译本《德国民法典》翻译前言（Preface）末所署时间为 1907 年 8 月 1 日。

[2]　Ernest Joseph Schuster, "A Chinese Commentary on the German Civil Code", in: *Journal of the Society of Comparative Legislation*, Vol. 8, No. 2, 1907, pp. 247–249. 中文翻译见欧内斯特·J. 舒斯特："一位中国学者对德国民法典的译注"，陈颐译，载《华东政法学院学报》2006 年第 2 期，第 141—143 页。

[3]　亦译"林肯律师学院"或"林肯律师学会"，是英国伦敦四个培养律师并有权授予律师资格的社团。其他三个分别为格雷律师协会（Gray's Inn）、内殿律师协会（Inner Temple）和中殿律师协会（Middle Temple）。

[4]　见《比较立法学会杂志》1909 年第 10 卷第 2 册（1910）第 207—210 页所载该学会的组成人员名单（*Journal of the Society of Comparative Legislation*, Vol. 10, No. 2, 1910, pp. 207–210）。

是该学会学术刊物《比较立法学会杂志》（Journal of the Society of Comparative Legislation）德国法方面的主要撰稿人，《比较立法学会杂志》上有关德国法律的文字多出其笔下[1]。1896 年，即德国议会通过《德国民法典》的那一年，舒斯特受比较立法学会邀请，先后在内殿律师协会和林肯律师协会发表题为 "The German Civil Code" 的演讲[2]。此外，舒斯特所撰关于德国法的文章 *The Liabilities of Bailees according to German Law*[3]，*The New German Statute as to Cheques*[4]，*The History and Present Condition of the German Divorce Law*[5]，*National health insurance in England and Germany*[6] 等是当时英国法律界了解和研究德国法的重要资料。这些都不难说明舒斯特系 19 世纪末 20 世纪初英国一位重要的德国法专家。[7]

　　舒斯特的主要著作，除《德国民法原理》外，还有：*Die Bürgerliche Rechtspflege in England*，Berlin：F. Vahen，1887；*Die Ehefrau in alter und neuer Zeit: Eine sittengeschichtliche Skizze*，Berlin：Puttkammer und Mühlbrecht，1911[8]；*The Effect of War and Moratorium on Commercial Transactions*，London：Steven and Sons，1914[9]。

1　关于这一点，除《比较立法学会杂志》编辑部 1909 年第 10 卷第 2 册（1910）第 211 页（*Journal of the Society of Comparative Legislation*，Vol. 10，No. 2，1910，p. 211）的明确说明外，该杂志上所载有关德国法的文章亦可证之。

2　两次演讲的内容分别刊登于《法律评论季刊》第 12 卷（1896）第 17—35 页（*The Law Quarterly Review*，Vol. 12，1896，pp. 17-35）和《比较立法学会杂志》第 1 卷（1896—1897）第 191—211 页（*Journal of the Society of Comparative Legislation*，Vol. 1，1896-1897，pp. 191-211），文章标题均为 "The German Civil Code"。

3　In：The *Law Quarterly Review*，Vol. 2，1886，pp. 188-212。

4　In：*Journal of the Society of Comparative Legislation*，Vol. 9，No. 1，1908，pp. 79-83。

5　In：*Journal of the Society of Comparative Legislation*，Vol. 10，No. 2，1910，pp. 229-238。

6　In：*Journal of the Society of Comparative Legislation*，Vol. 12，No. 1，1911，pp. 11-32。

7　值得附带提及的是，欧内斯特 · J. 舒斯特的儿子，艾尔弗雷德 · F. 舒斯特（Alfred F. Schuster）也是一位德国法学者，曾将《德国商法典》译成英文，作为父亲，老舒斯特为儿子的法典翻译撰写了一篇导论（*The German Commercial Code*，translated and briefly annotated by Alfred F. Schuster，with an introduction by Ernest. J. Schuster，London：Stevens and Sons，1911）。时人评论说，从整体上看，小舒斯特的《德国商法典》英译本，无论在译文的可信度和言辞的表达，还是在注释的参考价值方面，都较同时期的另一个《德国商法典》英译本（*The commercial code for the German Empire*，translated by Bernard A. Platt，London：Chapman & Hall，1900）好许多。See Edwin M. Borchard，*Guide to the Law and Legal Literature of Germany*，Washington：Government Printing Office，1912，pp. 99-100。

8　该书同时以英文出版：*The Wife in Ancient and Modern Times*，London：Williams & Norgate，1911 年。国外出版人 Kessinger Publishing 曾于 2010 年依旧版重印过该英文版。

9　国外出版人 Gale-Making of Modern Law 曾于 2013 年依旧版重印过该书。

（二）

《德国民法原理》原书依次包括以下部分：①序言，②目录，③书中所引德国法律及其缩略语表，④《德国民法典》及其他重要法律索引表，⑤书中所引英国法律表，⑥书中所引英国判例索引[1]，⑦导论，⑧第一编民法总则，⑨第二编债法，⑩第三编物法，⑪第四编亲属法，⑫第五编继承法，⑬关键词英语索引，⑭德语术语索引。

如仅从书名上看，《德国民法原理》很容易被理解为纯粹阐述德国民法基本理论的书籍，但实际上是一本比较法著作。舒斯特在序言（Preface）开篇即说，写作此书，旨在：①促进法律人以比较的视角研习英国法；②以最近的立法实践（指《德国民法典》的颁布），揭示一国的全部私法可以通过努力而获得完美的体系化；③为从事涉外法律事务的执业者提供实用的帮助。依循这个宗旨，著者在书中，一方面以《德国民法典》五编和编次（总则、债法、物法、亲属法和继承法）为基本框架，以阐述德国民法基本理论原理为主线，另一方面每当涉及基本的法律问题时，都以英国法的规则做比较说明，还时常辅以事例。为此，《比较立法学会杂志》评论说，舒斯特所著《德国民法原理》既有助于英国人了解德国法，也有助于德国人了解英国法[2]。而在我们看来，这样的比较法著作，对于德国和英国以外国家的人了解和研究德国和英国的法律，自然也会有很好的帮助。

德国为民商分立国家，因此谈及德国民法，通常不包括商法。但《德国民法原理》虽以《德国民法典》五编和编次为基本框架，但内容不限于《德国民法典》的范畴，还涵盖了《德国商法典》的大部分内容，甚至涉及其他法律的有关规定。例如：

1. 在第一编第一部分第一章"人"（Persons）中，涉及《商法典》[3]关于普通商事合伙（Offene Handelsgesellschaft，第105—160条）、有限合伙（Kommanditgesellschaft[4]，第161—177条）、股份有限公司（Aktiengesellschaft，第178—319条）、股份有限合伙（Kommanditgesellschaft auf Aktien[5]，第320—

---

[1] 原书在"英国判例索引"后还附有一个勘误表，因在编校时已依其对书中内容做相应修正，故删。

[2] See *Journal of the Society of Comparative Legislation*, Vol. 10, No. 2, 1910, p. 211.

[3] 以下涉及《德国商法典》的内容，均指当时的规定。

[4] 国内多译为两合公司。

[5] 国内多译为股份两合公司。舒斯特在《德国民法原理》中亦译作 a share company en commandite（参见第40页）。

334 条)、隐名合伙（Stille Gesellschaft，第 335—342 条）的规定，以及《合作社法》关于合作社的规定。

2. 在第一编第一部分第三章"权利"（Rights）中，涉及《商法典》关于商号权（第 17—37 条）、《商标法》关于商标权、著作权法关于著作权[1]，以及《专利法》和《实用新型法》关于发明人之权利的规定。

3. 在第一编第二部分第二章"法律行为"（Acts-in-the-law）中，涉及《商法典》第 48—58 条关于经理权和商事代理权、第 346 条关于商事习惯之适用、第 362 条关于沉默拟制为意思表示、第 377 条关于商事买卖之瑕疵通知的规定。

4. 在第二编第一部分第三章"关于债务履行的解释规则"（Rules of Interpretation as to Performance of Obligatory Duties）中，涉及《商法典》第 352 条关于法定利率、第 353 条到期利息、第 358 条和第 359 条关于给付时间等、第 360 条关于种类之债、第 361 条关于度量衡、重量、货币、时间计算和距离的规定。

5. 在第二编第一部分第六章"债权的救济权"（Remedial Obligatory Rights）中，涉及《商法典》第 348 条违约金、第 369—371 条商事留置权，第 376 条定期商事买卖赔偿请求权的规定。

6. 在第二编第一部分第七章"权利和义务的移转"（Transfer of Rights and Duties）中，涉及《商法典》第 362—365 条关于商人指示证券，以及第 179 条、第 183 条和第 222 条关于股份有限公司股份等规定。

7. 在第二编第二部分债法分则（Rules relating to Particular Kinds of Obligations）中，

（1）论述买卖契约时，涉及《商法典》第 373 条和第 374 条关于买受人的迟延受领、第 377 条关于瑕疵通知、第 380 条关于买卖物重量计算的规定。

（2）论述雇佣契约时，涉及《商法典》关于商业辅助人（第 59—83 条）和商事代理人（第 84—89 条）的规定。

（3）论述居间契约时，涉及《商法典》关于商事居间（第 94—104 条）的规定。

1　当时德国关于著作权（Urheberrecht，亦译作者权）的法律有：《关于美术作品著作权的法律》（Gesetz betreffend das Urheberrecht an Werken der bildenden Künste, vom 9. Januar 1876）；《关于保护摄影作品不受未经许可之临摹的法律》（Gesetz betreffend den Schutz der Photographien gegen unbefugte Nachbildung, vom 10. Januar 1876）；《关于外观设计著作权的法律》（Gesetz betreffend das Urheberrecht an Mustern und Modellen, vom 11. Januar 1876）；《关于文学音乐作品著作权的法律》（Gesetz betreffend das Urheberrecht an Werken der Literatur und der Tonkunst, vom 19. June 1901）；《关于出版权的法律》（Gesetz über das Verlagsrecht, vom 19. June 1901）。

（4）论述寄托契约时，涉及《商法典》关于仓库营业（第416—424条）[1]的规定。

（5）论述民事合伙契约时，涉及《商法典》关于商事合伙的相关规定（第110—121条、第131条、第137—141条、第164条、第167—169条）。

（6）论述法定之债时，涉及《商法典》关于海损（第700—739条）、海上救助（第740—753条）等规定。

（7）论述无因契约时，内容不仅涉及《民法典》关于债务约束、债务承认和指示证券，以及《商法典》关于交互计算的规定，而且涉及票据法（《汇票本票法》《支票法》）上的规定。

（8）专就《商法典》中规定的行纪营业（第383—406条）、承揽运送营业[2]（第407—415条）、货运营业（第425—452条）、铁路货物和旅客运送（第453—473条）、海上货物营业（第556—663条）进行说明。

（9）《民法典》未规定保险契约。《商法典》就海上保险设有详细规定（第778—900条、第905条）。[3]就此《德国民法原理》亦有相当的说明。

（10）德国关于出版契约，不在《民法典》或《著作权法》中规定，而以特别法规定于《出版权法》（Gesetz über das Verlagsrecht, vom 19. Juni 1901）中。但舒斯特鉴于出版契约为债法上之契约的性质[4]，就《出版权法》关于出版契约的规定予以详细说明。[5]

因债法部分涉及《民法典》债法编、《商法典》多数条文以及其他单行法，内容广泛，其篇幅约占全书的三分之一。

1　仓库营业在现行《德国商法典》规定于第467—475h条。

2　承揽运送营业（Speditionsgeschäft）亦译运送代理营业。

3　德国当时关于保险契约，除海上保险外，主要仍由各邦的法律调整。《德国保险契约法》颁布于1908年5月30日，依同时颁布的《保险契约法之施行法》第1条规定，自1910年1月1日起施行。

4　关于出版契约性质上为债法上之契约，参见［德］M. 雷炳德：《著作权法》，张恩民译，法律出版社2005年版，第429—430页。

5　著者在《德国民法原理》中述及出版契约，或许系受瑞士民事立法的影响。在瑞士，出版契约规定于《瑞士债务法》第二编第十二章第380—393条。著者曾发表题为"Report on the Swiss Civil Code of 1906"（in: *Journal of the Society of Comparative Legislation*, Vol. 9, No. 2, 1908, pp. 349-354）和"The Swiss Civil Code"（in: *Journal of Comparative Legislation and International Law*, Vol. 5, No. 4, 1923, pp. 216-226）的文章。值得提及的是，奥地利依1916年3月19日法令（Kaiserliche Verordnung vom 19. März 1916; RGBl. Nr. 69/1916）将出版契约规定于《奥地利普通民法典》第1172条和第1173条。此外，我国"民国民法"（目前在我国台湾地区施行的"民法"）亦仿瑞债立法例，于债编第二章设专门一节规定出版契约（第515—527条）；另请参见史尚宽：《债法各论》，荣泰印书馆股份有限公司1981年印本，第340页。

此外，《德国民法原理》对一些重要的法律问题还时常述及罗马法上的民法规则，间或也会提及法国民法的一些规定。

（三）

《德国民法原理》出版后，颇受赞誉和推崇。就此，书中所附四篇书评足资证明。此外还值得提及的是，出版于 1912 年的《德国法律及法律文献指南》说道，《德国民法原理》无疑是以英语写作德国民法的作品中最杰出的一部[1]；德国人撰写并出版于 1915 年的《德意志帝国的政府与政治》称赞舒斯特是一位著名的德国法专家，《德国民法原理》是一部优秀著作[2]。

事实也表明，《德国民法原理》不愧为一本不可多得的关于德国私法的英文著作，对研究德国民法有着重要的参考价值。

1. 前已述及，王宠惠先生在英译《德国民法典》时采用了舒斯特《德国民法原理》书中的一些英文法律术语。诚如王宠惠先生所言，《德国民法原理》书中为翻译德国民法概念而使用的英文法律术语十分准确和恰当。[3]

2. 沃尔特·鲁韦（Walter Loewy）的《德国民法典》英译本出版于1909 年[4]，美国宾夕法尼亚州律师协会特别委员会在为该译本撰写的翻译前言（Preface）中说，由于德国法全然不同于英美法，许多法律规定和法律术语很难找到相应的英文表达，《德国民法典》的翻译困难重重。幸好有《德国民法原理》的出版，翻译上的诸多难题因其对德国民法关键且重要问题上的清晰阐述而得以解决。该特别委员会鉴于《德国民法原理》对当时研习德国法的不可或缺，在其为该《德国民法典》英译本配加的条文注释和章节参阅资料中，多数都指示参阅《德国民法原理》的相关内容。

3. 出版于 1915 年的《瑞士民法典》英译本[5]，在众多条文的注释中亦指示参阅《德国民法原理》。

4. 出版于 1959 年的《外国法律指南：法国法·德国法·瑞士法》在

---

1 Edwin M. Borchard, *Guide to the Law and Legal Literature of Germany*, Washington: Government Printing Office, 1912, p. 72.

2 Fritz-Konrad Krüger, *Government and Politics of the German Empire*, New York: World Book Company, 1915, p. 307.

3 Chung Hui Wang, *The German Civil Code*, translated and annotated with a historical introduction and appendices, London: Stevens and Sons, 1907, "Preface", p. viii.

4 Walter Loewy (translator), *The Civil Code of the German Empire: as enacted on August 18, 1896, with the Introductory Statute enacted on the same date*, Boston: The Boston Book Company, 1909.

5 Robert P. Shick (translator), Charles Wetherill (annotator), *The Swiss Civil Code of December 10, 1907*, Boston: The Boston Book Company, 1915.

述及德国法参考著作时说，《德国民法原理》虽出版时间较早，但对研习德国民法仍非常有用（very useful）。[1]

此外，国外出版人 Nabu Press 在 2010 年和 2014 年、General Books 在 2012 年、Hardpress Publishing 在 2013 年、Gale-Making of Modern Law 在 2013 年、Forgotten Books 在 2015 年都曾依原版重印过该书。依此亦可足见《德国民法原理》问世虽已逾百年而仍有相当的学术价值和研究参考价值。

（四）

关于本书的编校，需要说明的有以下几点：

1. 书中的著者照片，系编校时加入。照片来源于 1910 年出版的英国《比较立法学会杂志》1909 年第 10 卷第 2 册（*Journal of the Society of Comparative Legislation*, Vol. 10, No. 2, 1909）第 212 页之前的插页。

2. 附录的四篇书评，系编校时加入；其来源，各篇书评中已有表明。

3. 附录的"拉丁语、德语、法语词语表"，系编校时加入；词语辑录自《德国民法原理》，除词语外，也包含书中提到的拉丁语罗马法规则。

4. 书中出现的缩略语，部分略有改动。经改动者，情形如下表：

原书缩略语	修改后缩略语
B. G. B.	BGB
Baden A. G.	Baden AG
Bavarian A. G.	Bavarian AG
C. P. O.	CPO
C. S. A.	CSA
E. G.	EG
E. G.（H. G. B）	EG（HGB）
F. G. G.	FGG
G. B. O.	GBO
G. O.	GO
G. V. R.	GVR
H. G. B.	HGB

1　Charles Szladits, *Guide to Foreign Legal Materials*: *French · German · Swiss*, New York: Oceana Publications Inc. , 1959, p. 301.

原书缩略语	修改后缩略语
K. O.	KO
L. P. A.	LPA
P. I. A.	PIA
Prussian A. G.	Prussian AG
Prussian F. G. G.	Prussian FGG
St. G. B.	StGB
W. O.	WO
Z. V. G.	ZVG

5. 原书出版年代较早，因语言的发展变化，书中个别词汇的拼写有所变化，编校时对此均不作改动。为方便读者识别，对可能影响阅读的词汇，列表新旧拼写（限德语词汇）如下：

原书中的词汇拼写	现行拼写
Creditauftrag	Kreditauftrag
Gehüfe	Gehilfe
korrespectiv	korrespektiv
Mäkler	Makler
Rhederei	Reederei
Selbsthüfe	Selbsthilfe
Sicherheitsübereignung	Sicherungsübereignung
taxirt	taxiert

6. 原书中前后拼写不完全一致的词汇，凡不影响文本意思者，一律不作改动。原书中疑有错误，但编校时无法查明证实者，亦保留原样。

7. 能力所限，虽尽心力，仍难免错误，祈请批评指正（amicusveritatis@163. com）。

戴永盛
2019 年 2 月 27 日